FORGOTTEN HEROES
Kenneth N. Jordan, Sr.

Also by the author
HEROES OF OUR TIME
239 Men of the Vietnam War Awarded the **MEDAL OF HONOR** 1964-1972

FORGOTTEN
HEROES

131 Men of the Korean War
Awarded the
MEDAL OF HONOR
1950-1953

Kenneth N. Jordan, Sr.

Schiffer Military/Aviation History
Atglen, PA

Dedication

THE FORGOTTEN HEROES is dedicated to all of the Korean War veterans who so proudly and gallantly served their country. You are all **Heroes.**

Hero: A person admired for courage, nobility or exploits, especially in war. A person admired for qualities or achievements and regarded as an ideal or model.

Acknowledgements

I would like to express my appreciation to all those who helped me with this book. My wife Louise, son Ken Jr., daughter Kathryn, and a special thank thanks to my daughter Diane who spent many hours helping me with the research and typing of this book. To my family and friends for their help and support. To the people at the Euclid and Willoughby, Ohio Libraries. Last, but certainly not least, the 131 Medal of Honor recipients.

Sources

The Senate Committee on Veterans' Affairs. *Medal of Honor Recipients 1863-1978.* Washington, D.C.: U.S. Government Printing Office, 1979.
The New York Times, New York, NY.
The Cleveland Plain Dealer, Cleveland, OH.
The News Herald, Willoughby, OH.

Book Design by Robert Biondi.

Copyright © 1995 by Kenneth N. Jordan, Sr.
Library of Congress Catalog Number: 95-67620.

Printed in the United States of America.
ISBN: 0-88740-807-9

We are interested in hearing from authors with book ideas on related topics.

Published by Schiffer Publishing Ltd.
77 Lower Valley Road
Atglen, PA 19310
Please write for a free catalog.
This book may be purchased from the publisher.
Please include $2.95 postage.
Try your bookstore first.

Contents

Introduction

The Medal of Honor is the highest military award for bravery that can be given to an individual in the United States of America. The President may award, and present in the name of congress, a Medal of Honor to a person who, while a member of the Armed Forces, distinguished himself conspicuously by gallantry and intrepidity at the risk of his life above and beyond the call of duty.

The Korean War began when the North Korean Army attacked South Korea on June 25th, 1950. The war officially ended with the signing of the Korean Armistice Agreement on July 27, 1953.

During that 37 month period more than 54,000 Americans were killed, over 103,000 were wounded and 131 earned the Medal of Honor.

FORGOTTEN HEROES is about those 131 men.

From the first men, Maj. Gen. William F. Dean and Sgt. George Libby, who earned the Medal of Honor on July 20th 1950, to the last man, Sgt. Ambrosio Guillen, who earned the Medal of Honor on July 25th, 1953, you'll read the actual citations for gallantry above and beyond the call of duty of all 131 Medal of Honor recipients. Interspersed are newspaper accounts of many of the battles and official communiques from Tokyo and Korea.

The Korean War is often referred to as "the forgotten war." For the men and women who fought there and for the families and friends of those who died there it will never be forgotten.

†-Indicates posthumous award.

CHAPTER 1

1950

Note: The following are two newspaper articles from June 25th and 26th, 1950, the beginning of the Korean War:

WAR IS DECLARED BY NORTH KOREANS; FIGHTING ON BORDER
• • •
First Drive Seen Curbed
• • •

SEOUL, Korea, Sunday, June 25 - The Russian-sponsored north Korean Communists invaded the American-supported Republic of South Korea today and their radio followed it up by broadcasting a declaration of war.

The attacks started at dawn. The Northern Pyongyang radio broadcast a declaration of war at 11 A.M. (9 P.M. Eastern Daylight Time Saturday).

North Korean forces attacked generally along the border, but chiefly in the eastern and western areas, in heavy rain after mortar and artillery bombardments which started at 4 A.M. (2 P.M. Eastern Daylight Time Saturday). They were reported two and a half miles inside South Korea at some points.

[The State Department in Washington, receiving reports of the Korean fighting, was preparing to hold the Soviet Union responsible for the outbreak. The Associated Press quoted Korean Ambassador John Myun Chang as saying the North Korean attack was an aggressive action that could not have been carried out "without Soviet direction."]

Shortly after noon the Communists' radio at Pyongyang, the northern capital, said that war had been declared effective at 11 A.M..

A report received at 9:30 A.M. indicated that the North Koreans had captured the town of Kaesong, forty miles northwest of Seoul. Kaesong is headquarters of the First Division of the South Korean Army. It lies almost on the frontier.

It was believed here that eight American Methodist missionaries were in Kaesong - Lyman C. Brannon and his wife, Marian E. Bunds, Nellie Dyer, Mary H. Rosser, Bertha A. Smith, Lawrence A. Zellers and Christopher Jensen. Mrs. Zellers is in Seoul.

United States Ambassador John J. Muccio broadcast a statement to the 2,000 Americans in Korea - including a military mission - over the English-language radio station WVTP on the Communist attack.

The North Korean forces were reported three to four kilometers (1.75 to 2.5 miles) inside the frontier in the Ongjin Peninsula on the west coast.

Below Kangnung, on the east coast, the invaders were reported to have landed from twenty small craft and to have cut the coastal highway.

Ambassador Muccio advised Americans to move about as little as possible. He promised to broadcast all new developments. He said "as yet it cannot be determined whether the northern Communists intend to precipitate all-out warfare."

Presumably the attacks mean a test of strength between the Russian-sponsored and the United States-sponsored section of this country, divided on the line of the Thirty-eighth Parallel.

The North Korean attack came but a few days after John Foster Dulles, special State Department adviser, visited President Syngman Rhee of the Southern republic. Mr. Dulles is now in Tokyo with General MacArthur. Defense Secretary Louis Johnson and Gen. Omar N. Bradley, chairman of the United States Joint Chiefs of Staff Committee, returned to Washington yesterday from Tokyo, where they discussed the Korean and other Far Eastern situations.

There have been frequent guerilla-scale clashes between forces of the Russian-sponsored North Koreans and the South Korean forces, but none apparently have been as large as those reported today.

Threats have been made of an invasion of South Korea. One officer said here, on the basis of early reports: "This looks like the real thing." But there had been no intelligence reports of troop movements or concentration of supplies - such as would be needed for a real campaign - on the North Korean side. Also, the rainy season is just starting, and the season is the worst of the year for troop operations.

Military authorities emphasized that their reports were fragmentary and that the picture of the situation was vague.

Other sources said that South Korea's Army included about 93,000 men with an additional 50,000 police and 6,000 or 7,000 Coast Guardsmen. The United States is uncertain about the exact size of the Soviet-trained North Korean forces but they are believed to be slightly larger.

The Soviet Union, with considerable fanfare, announced that all of its occupation forces had left North Korea by the end of 1948. This was considerably earlier than the main body of United States troops left. United States officials, however, have said that Washington would hold the Soviet Union responsible for the actions of the North Korean Government under the Soviet puppet Kim Il Sung, a reasonably young man who came to power using the name of a venerated Korean elder statesman.

Kaesong, reported captured, is the main town close to the parallel separating North and South Korea. Chun Chon, on the railroad in the northeastern section of the United States zone, is smaller but has valuable silk processing and silk textile manufacturing facilities that the United States has helped to develop as part of its campaign to revive South Korea's economy.

These towns, along with Ongjin Peninsula, have been raided before - sometimes being the scenes of heavy fighting that killed 50 or more persons. Serious guerrilla raids began last year and no United States official has attempted to minimize the danger.

U.N. CALLS FOR CEASE FIRE IN KOREA; DEMANDS NORTH WITHDRAW TROOPS; SETBACK FOR INVADERS REPORTED

• • •

Counter-Attack On

• • •

Line Drives North At Foe After Invader Is 15 Miles From Seoul

• • •

SEOUL, Korea, Monday, June 26 - South Korean troops today launched a counter-attack and reportedly drove the invaders from the Communist North backward five miles on a front twenty-five miles north of Seoul.

Defense Stiffens

Twenty-four hours after they had launched their unprovoked attack upon the Republic of Korea, Communists of North Korea were reported to be in retreat in some sectors.

In the center of the line that stretches across the Thirty-eighth Parallel the Communists were being held, although at one point along the Uijongbu road they were only fifteen miles from the capital city of Seoul. [The United Press said the South Koreans were reported to have stopped heavy tank attacks in this area.]

This morning, according to the South Korean Office of Public Information, South Korean troops pushing northward captured Haeju, capital of Hwanghae Province, which is one mile north of the border and sixty-five miles northwest of Seoul, taking ten anti-aircraft pieces and ten trucks.

Some reports asserted that Red troops at Chumunjin, on the east coast seven miles south of the parallel, seemed to be gradually retreating.

[The Associated Press reported that a United States Mustang fighter had been attacked over Seoul by a Russian-made plane, presumably North Korean. Ten persons having lunch at the United States Embassy said the Mustang drove off the Russian craft, but a United States military adviser stated that the Mustang took evasive action and shook off the Russian plane. The Korean police said that six civilians were killed by two bombs dropped by the plane. It was the first aerial attack on Seoul since the Communist invasion began.]

[An aerial engagement between an American fighter plane and a Soviet-built aircraft was reported by the United States Ambassador in Korea to have taken place over Inchon, where American women and children were being placed aboard evacuation ships. The Americans were receiving protection from a "heavy air cover" of United States planes operating from bases in Japan.]

Last night the official news round-up declared that Red forces estimated at 50,000 were continuing to penetrate and had captured Kaesong, Pochon, and southern territories west of the Imjin River, using tanks and armored infantry and help by guerrillas.

At the time, said the statement, one Red division was attacking Ongjin Peninsula and another division, with heavy artillery, was attacking Chunchon.

People's Army units, said the announcement, had launched at widely separated points along the east coast, where they had been joined by guerrillas, and succeeded in cutting the highway to Samchock, South Korea's largest east coast coal mine five miles south of the border, which stretches 125 miles across Korea.

Meanwhile Seoul, which is only thirty-eight miles south of the border, was being menaced by a Communist force of approximately 3,000, which was attacking Moonsan, only sixteen miles to the north.

Four Korean Divisions

Still another division was reported assaulting defense lines on Taeok Mountain, two miles south of the parallel.

Last night's announcement said that four South Korean divisions were already engaging the enemy and that three more were being brought up into closer reserve positions.

There have been no reports of North Korean tanks able to break through for independent action. At Pochon, ten Red tanks were destroyed.

Shin Song Mo, the acting Premier, has asked John Muccio, the United States Ambassador, to appeal to the United States for airplanes and more arms from Okinawa or Japan.

The curfew tonight began at 9 o'clock, instead of at midnight, as is normal. The prisons, which contain many political prisoners, are heavily guarded, and every city corner is being guarded by alert police armed with carbines.

There are now approximately 2,000 Americans in Korea.

The Communist offensive started at dawn yesterday at several points along the Thirty-eighth Parallel. Kaesong, a city forty-five miles north of here, was taken by the Reds at 9:30 A.M. and another column pushed through to Changdan, twenty miles north of Seoul.

Meanwhile a force estimated at one regiment with ten tanks landed on the east coast and fighting was begun in the west, on the Ongjin Peninsula. In the east, the Reds attacked at Chunchon and Kangnung.

All privately owned buses and trucks were commandeered by the military police for emergency use. Army jeeps equipped with loudspeakers toured the streets, telling soldiers: "Join your units immediately."

A Cabinet statement warned the people to disregard alarmist rumors, adding: "The Republican Army is fervently counter-attacking. The word now knows who is the aggressor in this strategic conflict. We will persevere no matter how great the sacrifice and individual losses."

The Communist drive on Seoul was made under fierce artillery fire. The attackers were also supported with tanks.

The South Korean police and Army were both making active preparations within Seoul for any emergency. Traffic has been cut off here. Thus far, Communist air activity has been slight.

One Soviet-made Yak fighter reconnoitered over Seoul and Kimpo Airport yesterday morning.

The reconnaissance was followed by a raid by five Soviet-type fighters that strafed the Kimpo Airport and the Seoul railroad station. A gasoline tank on the airfield was hit and three persons were injured at the railroad station.

[Reports from Tokyo said that a United States C-54 was fired on at the time but whether this was a civil or military plane was not known. Reports said there were no casualties and that damage to the plane was slight.]

The North Korean dawn attack was followed after five hours by a broadcast from the Soviet-controlled Pyongyang radio, which laid the blame for the surprise attack on an offensive supposed to have been made by the South Koreans along the Thirty-eighth Parallel.

"The People's Republican Army," the broadcast said, repulsed South Korean invading forces at the northern border town of Yongyang. The broadcast added: "The People's Republic [North Korea] wished to remind the South Korean puppet regime that unless the puppets immediately suspended their adventurous military actions, the People's Republic will be obliged to resort to decisive counter-measures."

DEAN, WILLIAM F.

Rank and Organization: Major General, U.S. Army, Commanding General of the 24th Infantry Division.
Born: August 1, 1899, Carlyle, Illinois.
Entered Service At: California.
Place and Date: Taejon, Korea, July 20 and 21, 1950.
Citation: Maj. Gen. Dean distinguished himself by conspicuous gallantry and intrepidity at the repeated risk of his life above and beyond the call of duty. In command of a unit suddenly relieved from occupation duties in Japan and as yet untried in combat, faced with a ruthless and determined enemy, highly trained and overwhelmingly superior in numbers, he felt it his duty to take action which to a man of his military experience and knowledge was clearly apt to result in his death. He personally and alone attacked an enemy tank while armed only with a hand-grenade. He also directed the fire of his tanks from an exposed position with neither cover nor concealment while under observed artillery and small-arms fire. When the town of Taejon was finally overrun he refused to insure his own safety by leaving with the leading elements but remained behind organizing his retreating forces, directing stragglers, and was last seen assisting the wounded to a place of safety. These actions indicate that Maj. Gen.

Dean felt it necessary to sustain the courage and resolution of his troops by examples of excessive gallantry committed always at the threatened portions of his front lines. The magnificent response of his unit to this willing and cheerful sacrifice, made with full knowledge of its certain cost, is history. The success of this phase of the campaign is in large measure due to Maj. Gen. Dean's heroic leadership, courageous and loyal devotion to his men, and his complete disregard for personal safety.

†LIBBY, GEORGE D.

Rank and Organization: Sergeant, U.S. Army, Company C, 3d Engineer Combat Battalion, 24th Infantry Division.
Born: Bridgton, Maine.
Entered Service At: Waterbury, Connecticutt.
Place and Date: Near Taejon, Korea, July 20, 1950.
Citation: Sgt. Libby distinguished himself by conspicuous gallantry and intrepidity in action above and beyond the call of duty. While breaking through an enemy encirclement, the vehicle in which he was riding approached an enemy roadblock and encountered devastating fire which disabled the truck, killing or wounding all the passengers except Sgt. Libby. Taking cover in a ditch Sgt. Libby engaged the enemy and despite the heavy fire crossed the road twice to administer aid to his wounded comrades. He then hailed a passing M-5 artillery tractor and helped the wounded aboard. The enemy directed intense small-arms fire at the driver, and Sgt. Libby, realizing that no one else could operate the vehicle, placed himself between the driver and the enemy thereby shielding him while he returned the fire. During this action he received several wounds in the arms and body. Continuing through the town the tractor made frequent stops and Sgt. Libby helped more wounded aboard. Refusing first-aid, he continued to shield the driver and return the fire of the enemy when another roadblock was encountered. Sgt. Libby received additional wounds but held his position until he lost consciousness. Sgt. Libby's sustained, heroic actions enabled his comrades to reach friendly lines. His dauntless courage and gallant self-sacrifice reflect the highest credit upon himself and uphold the esteemed traditions of the U.S. army.

The following is a newspaper account of the preceding battle for which Maj. Gen. Dean and Sgt. Libby were awarded the Medal of Honor; followed by an official communique:

24TH DIVISION ABANDONS TAEJON;
• • •
RETREAT ORDERLY
• • •

TOKYO, Friday, July 21 - Troops of the United States Twenty-forth Division withdrew last night from the key city of Taejon under heavy pressure by superior forces of North Korean tanks and infantry.

The city, which had been stubbornly held since the enemy forced passage of the Kum River, was evacuated under the cover of darkness. A spokesman said the retreat was orderly, the troops withdrawing down the highway leading southeast toward the communications center at Taegu and the port of Pusan.

North Korean troops, following close on the heels of the hard pressed Americans, launched a fresh attack on prepared positions about four miles southeast of the city, to which the defenders had retreated.

The Americans were fighting off these renewed Communist attacks and continued to block the highway leading southward, Gen. MacArthur announced at 1:45 this afternoon.

The communique was issued after front-line reports had stated that one regiment of North Korean infantry, spearheaded by heavy Soviet-made tanks, was driving against the new defense line in the foothills rising from the flat paddy-lands around Taejon. The invaders were reported to be moving up in strength for a mass onslaught before new United States positions could be consolidated.

Paying tribute to the "splendid delaying action against overwhelming odds" conducted by the Twenty-fourth Division, General MacArthur asserted that the North Koreans had reap no great advantage by the capture of Taejon and asserted there was no cause for discouragement. He implied that the newly proved ability of the United States 3.5-inch rocket launchers to knock out the heavily armored Soviet-made tanks possibly more than outweighed the fall of the stubbornly defended city.

Maj. Gen. William F. Dean, commander of the Twenty-fourth Division, fought most of the day in the front line with his men.

[The Associated Press reported from a United States command post in Korea that anxiety was felt Thursday night for Maj. Gen. William F. Dean, commander of the Twenty-fourth Division, under fire in the fighting withdrawal from Taejon. A headquarters staff officer was quoted as saying that he did not know where Gen. Dean was but "that does not mean that he is missing." In Washington the Defense Department said that it had no report that Gen. Dean was missing.]

Yongdok Is Wiped Out

South of Yongdok, Communist columns were halted by a naval artillery barrage. One United States and one British cruiser, firing heavy guns, wiped out the town of Yongdok, a typical small Korean port whose population in the most part already had been evacuated.

Vice Admiral Charles Turner Joy, commanding naval forces in the Far East, announced that the town had been "destroyed" Wednesday night, with huge fires started that were visible twelve hours later.

Shore fire control parties directed the naval gunners, with results described as "terrific." The naval batteries were then turned on the highway, bridges and the coastal railroad south of the town, to prevent the further movement of North Korean tanks toward Pohang, the invaders withdrawing into the gullies and ravines of the sharp hills running down to the sea, from which they usually have been able to infiltrate during darkness.

Taejon was abandoned after Communist tank-led columns pushed down the right flank of the United States positions guarding Taejon's partly encircled defenders. Units of two infantry regiments, which had been fighting in the front of the city, broke through the Communist ring, enabling the other forces to retreat. Communist tanks and infantry entered the city from the north as the United States forces withdrew.

Gen. MacArthur's communique at 9:40 this morning acknowledged the abandonment of the city in what was characterized as a "running tank and infantry battle" in which the North Koreans used heavy concentrations of armor coordinated-with guerrilla harassment of the United States rear.

The present positions, which the communique did not identify but characterized as "more tenable" than the line of foxholes before Taejon, apparently were in the range of arid hills southeast of the city. Here the roads are cut by small tributaries of the Kum River and the country is cut up by ravines and defiles that make tank operations more difficult than hitherto but may favor the Communists' well-developed infiltration tactics.

[The United States stated that shortly before Gen. MacArthur issued his communique, the North Korean Government radio broadcast a Communist Army communique that the city had been "completely captured" at noon Thursday.]

The United States troops withdrew from Taejon after an all day fight in which the invaders threw in wave after wave of tanks and foot soldiers from morning till dark, disregarding heavy losses. Using the new 3.5 inch rocket launchers, the United States ground defenders knocked out eight heavily armored soviet-made tanks, which have been impervious to the wartime bazookas with which the United States troops previously have been armed.

Airmen flying jets and Mustang fighters in difficult weather preceding the typhoon now moving across the Sea of Japan destroyed five more tanks, with other probables.

The withdrawal began shortly after 9 o'clock last night, and was completed after midnight, with the United States rear guard fighting in the streets of the city.

Reports from the front indicated that the Americans had pulled back to position that had been under preparation since the enemy crossed the Kum River over a partially repaired highway bridge and pushed his regrouped armor forward, menacing the front and right flank and making the withdrawal a matter of time.

Other sections of the front were reported comparatively quiet as the enemy concentrated his strength on the drive down the Taejon-Taegu highway. On the east coast, however, Communist columns were reported to have entered the city of Yongdok, about twenty-five miles north of Pohang, scene of Tuesday's amphibious landing by the United States First Cavalry Division.

OFFICIAL COMMUNIQUÉ:
TOKYO, Friday, July 21 (AP)
— The text of General MacArthur's Communique No. 104 issued at 2:25 P.M. Thursday, Tokyo time (12:25 A.M. Thursday, Eastern Daylight Time):

United States Air Force F-80 jet fighters hit hard at North Korea's elusive air strength on July 19, destroying a total of eighteen aircraft and damaging seven.

North Korean air units, which have been in virtual hiding since the first phase of hostilities, took some of the heaviest blows of the war in Air Force attacks on both airborne and grounded aircraft.

A majority of Air Force claims were scored in strikes at a North Korean airfield near Pyongyang where F-80 rocket and machine-gun fire wiped out fourteen fighters and one twin-engine bomber.

The attack was made under good weather conditions and the F-80s were able to rake the field, at zero altitudes. Many ammunition-loaded North Korean aircraft exploded and burned on the ground. Seven other airplanes were strafed and damaged but were not claimed as destroyed.

Three Yak-9 fighters were shot down in the air north of Taejon in an aerial battle with Fifth Air Force F-80s. Our jets also claimed one other Yak as a probable. Excellent coordination by air-ground control radio was largely responsible for the interception. One F-80 was damaged and forced to make an emergency landing in the Taejon area.

Yesterday's losses bring the total for North Korean aircraft destroyed to seventy-eight airplanes of all types, as compared with our losses of thirty-seven, a large number of which have been the result of operational accidents as opposed to combat losses.

Other F-80 jets of the Fifth Air Force continued an active campaign to interdict the North Korean ground forces on the battle front, cutting the invaders off from their supply sources by systematically destroying bridges, rail facilities, roads, vehicles and other means of communication.

The heavy toll taken by fighter and light bomber strikes in the past three weeks was shown in a diminished number of suitable targets for ground attack, Ground and air observers again called attention to a growing North Korean policy of keeping under cover during daylight hours in the hope of escaping air attacks.

Because of the scarcity of ground targets behind the North Korean lines, damage and destruction for the day was low.

Only three tanks were damaged by American fighters, and the totals for other types of vehicles and ground installations were also well below previous figures. Damage to ten trucks, two locomotives, eight railroad cars and nine miscellaneous vehicles were reported by pilots.

A bridge was damaged by F-80s east of Kongju and a marshalling yard in the Chongju area as worked over with rockets. Houses and buildings were destroyed in Kongju, Chonchiwon and Ansong, all in the western sector.

B-26s of the Fifth Air Force hit bridges and highway targets on the West Coast near Taechon in an attack at the western-most railroad and highway communications channel to North Korean lines in the Junaan area.

Far East Air Forces Bomber Command B-29s stepped up their pounding at strategic bridge and railroad targets in the Seoul area. No damage to the B-29s or injury to our personnel was reported.

The loss of an F-80 in action northwest of Yechon on July 18, has now been confirmed. A Fifth Air Force report indicated that the accident resulted from stress on the aircraft caused by a too rapid pull-up after diving on a ground target. The airplane bellied in to a landing in the Techon area.

Troop carrier aircraft flew 93,300 pounds of military cargo and seventy-six passengers to Korea during the day.

—Text of communique No. 105 issued at 2:55 P.M. Thursday, Tokyo time:

General Headquarters today announced that the President has approved a list of fifteen officers for promotion to and in the grade of general officer. Included on this list are two members of G. H. Q. Brig. Gen. John H. Church was promoted to the rank of temporary major general and Brig. Gen. George I. Back to the rank of permanent brigadier general.

General Church arrived in the Far East Command in October 1949, and has since served as chief on the Ryukus Military Government Section, G. H. Q.

He is a native of Pennsylvania and received his appointment as second lieutenant, infantry, in June 1917. He served with the Twenty-fourth Infantry in France during World War I and with the Forty-fifth and Eighty-fourth Divisions during World War II, participating in the Sicilian, Salerno, Anzio and southern France landings.

In addition to other decorations, General Church is the recipient of the Distinguished Service Cross, Legion of Merit, Purple Heart (two clusters), the Silver Star, and Bronze Star medals.

General Back has been on duty with the Far East Command as signal officer, G. H. Q., and chief, civil communications section, S. C. A. P., since March 1947.

He is a native of Iowa and was commissioned as section lieutenant, Signal Corps, in November 1917, rising to the rank of temporary brigadier general in June 1945.

General Back served in the Mediterranean Theater of Operations during World War II and deputy chief signal officer, Allied Force Headquarters and later as chief signal officer of the theater. He holds the Distinguished Service Medal for his services in that theater, and in addition holds the Legion of Merit, Commander, Order of the British Empire; Grande Official, Order of the Crown of Italy, and the Brazilian War Medal.

—Text of communique No. 106 issued at 2:55 P.M. Thursday, Tokyo time:

According to stories told by hundreds of captured North Korean soldiers, life in a Communist Army is not all "Beer and skittles."

The North Koreans do not surrender easily, because they expect to be executed. Once they find they are not going to be shot, they become anxious to expose the tactics the Communists used to enlist their support. The stories reveal a startlingly low state of training and morale in some of the belatedly organized North Korean units.

A clear picture of a recently formed North Korean infantry division, the Fifteenth, has been assembled by United States intelligence agencies. Battle-tested officers and non-commissioned officers from Manchuria and China formed the core of the division which was activated at Kumhwa, in Northwestern Korea. Specialists, the tank crews, mortar and machine gunners and all the other skilled manpower trained in the North Korean Army, provided the skeleton of the division. The veteran, well-trained cadre was brought to division strength in June of this year with drafted men.

Most of the conscripts were young farmers called up in April 1950, for training in an organization call the "Young Men's Democratic Training School." During the first month, the school taught close order drill and the second month was spent in the field but, in many cases, the trainees fired as little as three practice shots. The training program wasn't as limited in political "education", however, as at frequent intervals, the unit political and cultural officer lectured the men on Communist theory.

On June 26 the students of the Young Men's Democratic School were issued arms and ammunition and officially notified that they were members of the Fifteenth North Korean Infantry Division. The next day they joined in the invasion of the Republic of Korea.

The drafted men feared their brutal, battle-hardened leaders, yet they were afraid to desert because that meant sure death by execution if caught. As a result, they endured the hard marches and the lack of food and rest until July 4, when they had their first combat contact with South Korean units near the Han River.

Better trained units had spear-headed the advance and screened the Fifteenth from the United Nations troops until this time. Their first contact with Republic of Korea defenders brought heavy casualties and panic spread through the ranks of this footsore and weary unit. Only the presence of their fanatic leaders kept them at the battle line—even then many deserted or fled to the rear.

Since then, the Fifteenth Division has been kept in the center of the line where they have experienced moderate successes due mainly to the fact that they face no armor or artillery. Also, they are supported on either flank by older, better-trained North Korean divisions able to carry most of the load in rough going.

Those captured describe morale in the division as extremely low. Already they are badly shaken by the attacks of the combined air fleets flying under the banner of the United Nations.

The appearance of Australian and American airplanes overhead was the first indication the North Korean soldiers had that United Nations forces had joined the Republic of Korea in repelling the invasion.

The prisoners feel that the North Korean Army's success so far has been due to overwhelming numerical superiority combined with temporary advantage in the number of tanks. They say that the men probably will carry on as long as they keep winning, but when they start to lose it will be a different story.

—Text of communique No. 107 issued at 6 P.M. Thursday, Tokyo time:

Bad weather was doing something to Fifth Air Force planes Thursday that the North Koreans could not do and that was holding the striking units to a total of twenty combat missions.

Although only twenty missions were flown against enemy targets, the damage assessment was reported satisfactory with numbers of trucks, other vehicles, troops and buildings being brought under attack.

F-80 fighters attacked an oil dump at Kongju, North of Taejon, and set it ablaze. The oil concentration appeared to be of considerable size. This estimate was based on pilots reports of the flames and smoke spurting from the dump.

Pilots further reported that enemy troops were taking cover in various warehouses and it was necessary to shoot up the buildings in order to neutralize the enemy ground forces. One Texas fighter pilot reported that in order to escape detection one group of North Korean Red troops scurried to hide in a small thatch and lumber building. This was of no avail though because the jet pilots destroyed the building with their rockets.

Belated reports from an Air Force F-51 Mustang base in South Korea revealed that in twenty-one sorties Wednesday afternoon they destroyed fifteen trucks, three gun emplacements and various other types of enemy weapons and equipment. These reports indicated that most of the strafing and ground support by the fighters was performed around Taejon in order to keep most of the enemy in that area pinned to the ground.

One Mustang pilot's plane was damaged by ground fire but he returned safely to his base in South Korea.

—Text of communique No. 108 issued at 7:15 P.M. Thursday, Tokyo time:

The United States Army's new 3.5-inch rocket launcher, which made a highly successful entry into the Korean war today, is a modern version of the Army's World War II 2.36-inch rocket launcher, commonly known as the bazooka.

Battle-tested men of the Twenty-fourth Infantry Division, supplied with the new launcher only a short time before, fired it at seven Red tanks that were approaching Taejon this morning. Result: seven enemy tanks destroyed.

How this modern weapon and its ammunition was manufactured in the United States, shipped to Korea and placed in the hands of our fighting men in a few day's time is another example of the determination of American industry and United States Army logisticians that the armed forces of the free nations will be provided with the best of equipment and supplies, wherever they may be and in the shortest possible time.

Actually, experimental work on the new rocket launcher began about the time World War II ended, when Army ordinance and tactical experts realized the need for an anti-tank weapon with greater armor penetration and faster muzzle velocity than was provided by the 2.36-inch rocket.

United States ordinance continued to make improvements on the 2.36-inch launcher, increasing the range and accuracy, but in the meantime developed the larger weapon. The two are similar except that the new weapon is larger and is fired from the shoulder.

The 3.5-inch rocket launcher is two-piece, smooth-bore, electrically operated weapon of the open tube type and has no recoil. Unlike the 2.36-inch launcher, the new weapon has an attached monopod and a bipod of stabilization when firing from the prone position. Despite its larger size, it weighs only a few pounds more than the older version.

Ammunition for the new launcher is approximately 23 inches long and weighs slightly more than eight pounds. The warhead contains a powerful explosive held in the form of a "shaped charge." The action of the "shaped charge" enables the round to penetrate any armored vehicle presently known. Because of new developments included in the round, it is more accurate and has faster flight time than the earlier models of the 2.36-inch rocket launcher.

Sighting of the new weapon is accomplished by means of a reflecting sight which, when the gunner looks through, superimposes a scale on the field sight. This scale enables the gunner to obtain angular leads on targets moving up to a speed of forty miles an hour.

Although primarily designed as a close-in anti-tank weapon, the 3.5-inch rocket launcher can also be used against fortified positions and—up to its maximum range—for area-type fire against troop concentrations and similar ground targets. Its effect in area-type fire is very similar to that of an 81-mm. mortar-round.

Few weapons can equal the new rocket launcher as a close-in anti-tank weapon, although much larger guns may be superior in range and effect.

—Text of the MacArthur communique No. 109 issued at 12:30 A.M. Thursday, Tokyo time:

North Korean activity seemed concentrated in the Taejon area with the possibility of an all-out attack to secure this rail and communications center. A coordinated infantry-tank attack was launched this afternoon, presumably by the Fourth Communist Division, with the aid of infiltrating guerrillas.

However, final reports indicate that the United States Twenty-fourth Infantry Division is still holding firm despite this sharp increase of Red activity.

Other sectors remained relatively quiet with pressure being exerted in the eastern sector as the enemy Fifteenth and Fifth Divisions continued their action in the areas south of Mungyong and north of Yongju.

—Text of General MacArthur's communique No. 110 released at 9:05 A.M. (7:05 P.M. Thursday, Eastern Daylight Time):

From a small airstrip in Korea, eighteen Eighth Army liaison pilots have rolled up the impressive overall average of approximately 3,000 miles daily in acting as "eyes" for their own artillery and the Air Force.

The pilots and forty-five ground crewmen are members of one of the Eighth Army air liaison units. Their duty has covered an average of eighteen out of each twenty-four hours, leaving them little time for anything else except to eat and sleep.

Missions of this group include reconnaissance flights, fire direction for artillery units, coordination flying for fighter and bomber aircraft, and message and medical supply drops to ground troops at the front. Each flight has averaged about an hour and one-half, while each pilot may be called on to go up from four to five times daily.

Meanwhile, ground crewmen work from before dawn until dark in keeping the light airplanes refueled and serviced. Additionally the crewmen make minor repairs, and also act as guards for aircraft equipment and quarters areas.

Maj. Anthony Rozga of Milwaukee, in command, said nearly all the pilots and observers have been fired on. He pointed out that the light aircraft are exposed to enemy fighters, anti-aircraft and fire from the Communist ground forces.

One of the unit's important operations is to direct incoming fighters and bombers onto their targets. This is possible since pilots and observers in the liaison airplanes operating at low altitudes see installations and troop movements not visible from the fighters and bombers.

Currently one of the leading pilots in this respect is First Lieut. John B. Stanton of Exeter, Mo., who flew fourteen "guidance" missions in nine days. His flight report shows that he was jumped by two North Korean fighters but escaped by "hitting the rock" which means getting close to the ground where planes can easily out-maneuver high-speed enemy fighters.

While attempting to set his airplane down on a narrow road to pick up an observer, First Lieut. George Rogers of Summerville, Ga., ran into high tension wires. The airplane turned over in a rice paddy but Lieut. Rogers was not injured. After removing valuable radio instruments and equipment he chopped holes in the gas tank, set fire to the disabled aircraft and hitch-hiked back to the air strip.

While on a flight over enemy territory, First Lieut. James E. Alvator of Red Bank, N.J., suddenly discovered that four enemy fighter airplanes were converging on him. He immediately hit the rock and succeeded in eluding the pursuers.

Front line troops shout their praise for the liaison pilots, who go up—wearing only sidearms—to direct fire from fighter airplanes, bombers and Eighth Army artillery against the enemy.

Pilots of fighter airplanes are also high in their praise for the Army's liaison pilots. Speaking for his fighter group, Col. Stanton Smith Jr. of San Antonio, Tex., said all our fighter pilots swear by these boys.

"They are doing a marvelous job in bringing us in on the targets," he said.

First Lieut. Edward P. Drummond, of 5502 Thompson St., Philadelphia, a fighter pilot, said the Army's liaison pilots "are the best things we have in Korea for sighting targets in bad weather.

"The other day," he added, "I couldn't find a thing in the soup until this boy shot up through a hole in the clouds and said over his radio:

"Come on in, boy, I've got a thousand Commie troops below for you." I went in but I would never have found them if it hadn't been for that liaison pilot."

A Red regiment is reported in the vicinity of Iri and Nonsan. Another Communist force was observed near the bridge as Kangyong and Yusong.

On The East Coast, enemy troops supported by tanks and artillery were reported to have entered Yongdok.

The Far East Naval Forces continued their successful bombardment upon areas along the East Coast.

Carrier planes of the United States Seventh Fleet operated against airfields in North Korea and reported eighteen planes destroyed and two damaged in ninety-two sorties. In addition, they strafed gunboats at Wonsan, chemical plants at Sansong, oil tank cars, destroyed four locomotives and trucks along the East Coast. The strikes also blasted water tanks and nine locomotives near Hangwon.

The Fifth Air Force announced that seventy-six fighter and twelve B-26 bomber sorties were flown with fourteen enemy fighter aircraft and one twin-engine bomber destroyed. Marshaling yards at Kangyond and Chochiwon were strafed and several bridges were destroyed near the two towns. The Air Force also reported that trucks, railroad cards and other vehicles were destroyed.

—Text of General MacArthur's communique No. 111 issued at 9:40 A.M. (7:40 P.M. Thursday, Eastern Daylight Time):

American forces withdrew from Taejon last midnight after a running tank and infantry battle.

Numerically superior North Korean forces supported by heavy concentrations of artillery and armor forced the United States Twenty-fourth Infantry Division to secure more tenable positions approximately four miles southeast of Taejon.

Heavy infiltration tactics by guerrillas who outflanked the American Army units and coordinated infantry-tank assaults forced the withdrawal.

—Text of General MacArthur's communique No. 112 issued at 12:50 P.M. (10:50 P.M. Thursday, Eastern Daylight Time):

The town of Yongdok has been destroyed by naval gunfire, it was announced today by Vice Admiral Charles T. Joy, commander of Naval Forces in the Far East.

Two cruisers, one American and one British, of the force commanded by Rear Admiral J.M. Higgins, bombarded the occupied town during the evening and night of July 19. An artillery liaison officer reported the results as "terrific."

Large fires were started, with smoke still visible from the ships after twelve hours. In razing the town, naval units worked closely with shore fire-control parties.

After completion of the bombardment of Yongdok, naval units continued interdiction fire on a variety of targets, mostly road junctions, at the request of ground observers.

—The text of General MacArthur's communique No. 113 issued at 1:45 P.M. (11:45 P.M. Thursday, Eastern Daylight Time);

After two days of continuous attack by numerically superior North Korean Communist forces the Twenty-fourth Infantry Division has been forced to withdraw its units from defensive positions in and around Taejon and now is blocking the Red advance east of Taejon.

The Twenty-fourth Division, which has fought a splendid delaying action against overwhelming odds since July 5, is making every yard the Red Army gains increasingly more costly. In yesterday's action eight invader tanks were destroyed by 3.5-inch rocket launchers (larger bazookas) in the hands of well-trained, confident troops. This represents the greatest day's kill by ground troops of Red armor thus far recorded.

The realization, by both American and South Korean soldiers, that the great advantage of the North Korean tank has been so drastically reduced is a definite psychological victory for the armies of the United Nations.

While it cannot be denied that the loss of Taejon, temporary capital of the Republic of Korea, will have its psychological repercussions on the Korean people, from the military point of view its loss carries no special significance. Its abandonment, like that of Seoul, which preceded it, allows the military forces to organize terrain more conducive to military defensive operations.

Low rice-paddies ground to the west of the city forms a natural terrain corridor from that direction. With no dominating terrain on this flank, it was foreseen from the outset that Taejon could not be included in the defensive line on which the defending forces could be used to best advantage.

Temporarily outnumbered, the United Nations forces assisting the Republic of Korea are prepared to cede positions with low defensive potential for positions which can be held with forces currently available and which can act as a springboard for General MacArthur's offensives.

South Korean units continue to hold their positions and to patrol aggressively against the enemy. One regiment of the Capital Division counterattacked to retake Yechon, an often out-for town which has exchanged hands several times during the past three days. Another South Korean unit drove to the outskirts of Pungi, ten miles southwest of Tanyang, and is mopping up two Communist battalions in that area.

The initial reverses of the South Korean Army apparently lulled the Communist invader into a false feeling of security. He now realizes that he is operating against a courageous, aggressive, well-trained army that will oppose effectively his every move until he is defeated.

The entire effort has been supported by United Nations air and naval elements who have enjoyed continued success against Communist facilities. This effort has contributed greatly to the slowing down of the Red advance all along the front and the stopping of the advance in many areas.

Elements of what is believed to be the North Korean Fourth Division are on the plains south of Nonsan. At the present time there is no geographical obstacle confronting these elements. It is believed, however, that Air Force interdiction will prevent this envelopment from becoming a serious threat.

On the east coast Communist troop activities have been confined to the vicinity of Yongdok. Naval air strikes and ship bombardments have impeded supply and reinforcement of enemy troops to a minimum. Several east coast towns were left burning from bombardments by American naval vessels. The Air Force continued interdiction and close support missions as reported in previous communiques.

†SEBILLE, LOUIS J.
Rank and Organization: Major, U.S. Air Force, 67th Fighter-Bomber Squadron, 18th Fighter-Bomber Group, 5th Air Force.
Born: November 21, 1915, Harbor Beach, Michigan.
Entered Service At: Chicago, Illinois.
Place and Date: Near Hanchang, Korea, August 5, 1950.
Citation: Maj. Sebille distinguished himself by conspicuous gallantry and intrepidity at the risk of his life above and beyond the call of duty. During an attack on a camouflaged area containing a concentration of enemy troops, artillery, and armored vehicles, Maj. Sebille's F-51 aircraft was severely damaged by antiaircraft fire. Although fully cognizant of the short period he could remain airborne, he deliberately ignored the possibility of survival by abandoning the aircraft or by crash landing, and continued his attack against the enemy forces threatening the security of friendly ground troops. In his determination to inflict maximum damage upon the enemy, Maj. Sebille again exposed himself to the intense fire of the enemy gun batteries and dived on the target to his death. The superior leadership, daring, and selfless devotion to duty which he displayed in the execution of an extremely dangerous mission were an inspiration to both his subordinates and superiors and reflect the highest credit upon himself, the U.S. Air Force, and the armed forces of the United Nations.

OFFICIAL COMMUNIQUÉ:
EIGHTH ARMY HEADQUARTERS, in Korea, Sunday, Aug. 6 (AP)
—Communiqué 21 issued Saturday at 5:20 A.M. Eastern Daylight Time:

The Air Force is dropping leaflets written in Korean to refugees telling them not to cross the river but to take to the hills, that supplies will be dropped to them.

There are two reports of unidentified planes having strafed friendly installations during the night of 4-5 August. One was in Masan, the other was in the South Korean sector.

J. O. C. (Joint Operations Control) this morning reported five tanks on the west bank of the river in the vicinity of Waegwan. Reports stated four were destroyed by air strikes and artillery fire and that the other one was under attack. No subsequent reports on this action were received. There is a build-up of enemy forces along the Naktong River east and southeast of Sangju. At some points in this area the enemy was crossing the river this afternoon.

Air reconnaissance reported this afternoon that the bridge in the vicinity of Hyopchon was being rebuilt. An air strike was called for to disrupt such repair work.

In the Twenty-fifth Division sector the action was limited to friendly artillery firing against enemy artillery emplacements and troop concentrations.

—Communiqué 22, issued at 10:45 P.M. Saturday, Eastern Daylight Time:

During the last twenty-four hours there have been no large attacks. Action in the south and southwest sectors has been limited to artillery and patrol action. Some pressure has been exerted in the South Korean sector but no large attacks have been reported.

In the Twenty-fifth Division area no heavy attacks were reported yesterday or last night. There was some pressure on the Twenty-seventh Infantry. One company from another unit made an attack on a town in its area only to find it unoccupied. When it returned to its division, it was cut off by the enemy. It is fighting its way out and a relieving unit is on its way.

In the Twenty-fourth Division area reports have been received of movements of small enemy units up to the west banks of the Naktong River. No large concentrations have been reported. One enemy company penetrated into the area but is being contained and repulsed. One of the Twenty-fourth Division patrols crossed the river and penetrated 1,5000 yards into enemy territory to a small village. There were no enemy troops there so the patrol tried to bring in the local Communist party head. He resisted and was shot.

In the First Cavalry Division area aggressive patrolling is being conducted. Reports from these patrols are not complete. There is no enemy pressure in this area but there were active enemy patrols.

There were indications of a build-up in enemy strength south-east of Hamchang. Elements of these forces are crossing the Naktong River to face strong resistance from South Korean forces. One unit in the First South Korean Division has twice let a North Korean battalion cross the river, then annihilated it. Units of the Sixth South Korean Division have reported attacks which are being handled by battalions. In the Eighth South Korean Division one regiment has reported two attacks but that it is successfully repulsing them. In the Capitol Division Area one regiment was forced back 3,000 yards but it organized a counter-attack and returned to its former position. A threat which had developed between Amdong and Yangdok has been successfully contained by South Korean forces.

The Third South Korean Division in the Yongdok area is completing consolidation. It reports no heavy pressure.

TOKYO, Sunday, August 6 (AP)—
—Release 205, issued by General MacArthur at 1:50 A.M. Eastern Daylight Time:

United States Air Force fighter pilots have confirmed the sinking of a 10,000-ton North Korean freighter-transport in the harbor at Inchon on the west coast of southern Korea after a strike by B-26 invader light bombers of the Third Bomb Group late Friday.

Four B-26s flying in formation spotted the target and bombs were dropped. One bomb fell flush on the unarmored deck of the transport on the second bomb run.

An F-80 pilot, Capt. Francis B. Clark of Grand Rapids, Mich., while firing rockets at ships in the dock area at Inchon, said:

"I saw a large transport laying on its side when we finished our mission and left the area."

Credited with making the strike was First Lieut. Kenneth J. Appel, of Milwaukee, Wis. He was flown by First Lieut. Billy M. Jones, of Eastland, Texas, with S/Sgt. Austin G. Roberson, of Hope, Ark., riding the light bomber as gunner.

After the bombs were away, clouds obscured the harbor but fighter pilots who observed the mission from a lower altitude advised the B-26s by radio that the lead plane apparently had made the successful strike. Lieutenant Jones piloted the lead ship.

First Lieut. Richard E. Schultz said several small boats were detected around the transport, apparently taking cargo off for delivery to North Korean forces on shore.

The transportation proved to be a last-minute target, as the B-26's were warming up when flight instructions were changed. Before they returned to base they also started fires in storage warehouses and docks along the Inchon waterfront.

This mission was one of several directed against shipping facilities. Maj. William J. O'Donnell of Philadelphia, Friday led a flight of F-80 jets against eight transports loading troops from tenders at Inchon.

"We went in and launched our rockets on the ships, leaving some of them smoking." he said on return to base. He said this was followed by cannon fire against troops with many killed.

Other targets included trucks loaded with Communist troops, locomotives and railroad cars enroute to the battle areas, bridges, artillery pieces and vehicles.

Maj. Majes H. Buckey, of New Paris, Pa., led a flight of F-80 jets above Inchon. He fired rockets against warehouse buildings. "Large oil fires were visible and extended up to about 8,000 feet," he said.

—Release 206 issued by General MacArthur Saturday at 4:45 A.M. Eastern Daylight Time:

B-29 Superforts from Japan dropped approximately 100 tons of high explosive bombs on railroad marshalling yards at Seoul today with good to excellent results.

Bombing was visual with the B-29s flying in formation.

Lead bombardier for one wave of the attack was Capt. Albert R. Panko of Spokane, Wash. He said: "Smoke and fire from the shops and storage buildings in the yard were plainly visible from the hits scored by the first wave of bombers."

Capt. James L. Sefton of East Chicago, Ind., a bombardier in Panko's flight, said: "Our bombs dropped straight across the choke point. Smoke was up to 7,000 feet when we left the target."

The general trackage and rail sidings were heavily laden with box cars, congested and stationary, as a result of the continuing damaging attacks to the Seoul bridges leading southward to the fighting areas. Smoke rose high from the area after the Superforts had passed along and dropped their bombs.

No fighter opposition was encountered during the attack.

—Release 207, issued by General MacArthur Saturday at 9:00 A.M. Eastern Standard Time:

Cruisers and destroyers operating on the east coast of Korea have a new slogan of "bigger fires, no more troops" these days.

For that was the message shore fire-control parties northeast of Yongdok sent to a United States cruiser after the ship had completed a firing mission on troop concentrations at Nomul-Tong. Large numbers of troops and horses were spotted at the South Korean town with the result that the cruiser opened fire, dispersing the troops and starting large fires in the village.

Several hours later observers aboard the cruiser spotted troops in the town fighting fires. The cruiser opened up her fire again, resulting in the message from shore "bigger fires, no more troops."

The firing was conducted in close coordination with fire-control parties ashore. Nomul-Tong is right on the coast line.

—Release 208 issued by General MacArthur Saturday at 10:50 A.M. Eastern Daylight Time:

American and South Korean forces kept the Communist invaders "off balance" with limited counter-attacks and patrol actions throughout the entire defense area tonight. Fire fights were reported in the southern sector with pressure exerted against the Twenty-seventh and Thirty-fifth United States Infantry regiments in the Chinju area. However, the repeated Communist assaults were driven off with heavy losses inflicted upon the Red troops.

The enemy has continued to shuttle troops and material during the daylight hours, thereby providing excellent targets for artillery and aircraft. This indicates that the Reds are desperately striving for a main effort and an all-out attempt to break through the new defense lines.

Firm contact is expected to be established in the central and northern sectors and evidence points to a regrouping and concentration of enemy forces in the southern sector. indications also show that the Communists might shift the main effort of the attack from the central to the southern area to disrupt the Taegu-Pusan lines of communications.

However, the build-up of enemy strength in the central sector does not diminish the concurrent threat of attempted penetrations through the Taegu corridor.

The enemy has made no advances since the United Nations forces withdrew to the more stable defense line and no crossings have been made in force across the Naktong River.

—Release 209 issued by General MacArthur Saturday, 1:15 P.M. Eastern Daylight Time:

Two British cruisers, supported by two British destroyers, bombarded military targets in Inchon for two hours yesterday. British spotters embarked in United States Navy P-2-V Neptunes, described the firing as accurate and gave an evaluation of the results as "excellent."

The flash report on the two hour bombardment indicated that barracks, oil installations, factories, warehouses, gun emplacements, a railway station, an electric light plant and a transformer station bore the brunt of the British fire.

Carrier-based United States Marine fliers provided fighter cover for the ships and for the Navy spotting planes. Neither the ships nor the planes drew enemy fire.

Rear Admiral W. G. Andrewes, R. N., in command of the west coast blockade and support force flies his flag on one of the cruisers.

The United States naval blockade and support force operating on the east coast of Korea continued blasting enemy troop concentrations, supply lines, communications, road junctions and gun emplacements north of Yongdok throughout the day and maintained a steady stream of harassing fire throughout the night.

Taking advantage of improving weather and consequently more effective use of ground and air spotters, naval guns went to work yesterday maintaining a barrage 1,800 yards ahead of the South Korean Army front line with results described by one shore observer as "perfect."

—Release 210 issued by General MacArthur Saturday 11:30 P.M. Eastern Daylight Time:

The situation in Korea remained relatively stable during the past twenty-four hours. No material changes in lines were effected nor were any substantial enemy advances made. A continued build-up of United Nations strength is in progress. Coupled with the increase of strength of United Nations forces is the systematic destruction of the enemy potential due to the constant attacks by the Air Force and Navy and the great battle losses sustained by him in the ground action.

The Twenty-first and Tenth R. O. K. (Republic of Korea) regiments of the Eighth R. O. K. Division were engaged in heavy fire fights north of Uisong throughout the period. Elements of the Tenth Regiment of this division engaged Communist patrols and killed an unknown number of the enemy. An enemy force estimated as a company was engaged by elements of the First R. O. K. Division forward of its general lines. The R. O. K. Army reported over 1,000 of the enemy killed in action during the past twenty-four hours.

Other than north of Uisong ground action was confined principally to patrolling.

The Marine Air Force attacked military targets in the vicinity of Uiryong, Chinju, Chirye and Sinban. While results of operations have not yet been reported, individual pilot reports indicate considerable damage inflicted.

On the west coast our naval surface units bombarded the port of Inchon. Targets under fire included barracks, factories, gun positions, warehouses, oil installations, electric light plant, railway and a transformer station. The spotters reported the firing results as excellent.

The Air Force maintained its relentless attacks against military targets close in to the battle lines and in the rear areas. Nine enemy aircraft were destroyed and nine were damaged at Kimpo airfield.

—Release 211 issued by Gen. Douglas MacArthur Saturday, midnight Eastern Daylight Time:

In spite of low visibility and poor flying weather in southern sectors on Aug. 5, United States Far East Air Forces and Royal Australian Air Force units continued their full-scale ground support and supply interdiction effort in Korea with successful strikes on targets in the west and north.

Particularly heavy concentrations of fighter and bomber assault were launched at objectives in the Seoul-Inchon area, a major focal point for supply and troop movement from north of the Thirty-eighth Parallel to the Naktong River line.

More than 465 sorties were flown by F. E. A. F. and R. A. A. F. aircraft during the day. The mark was slightly under a record total of approximately 550 sorties flown Aug. 4, when clear skies in all local areas permitted maximum utilization of air power in support of United States and South Korean ground troops on the southern fronts.

Fifth Air Force F-80 jet fighters claimed nine LA-7 or Yak fighters destroyed in a strafing attack on Kimpo airfield near Seoul. An additional nine North Korean fighters were listed as probably destroyed and five were damaged.

The strike raised the United States Air Force claim for North Korean aircraft to fifty-eight destroyed, twenty-four damaged and seventeen probably destroyed.

Yesterday's action followed a B-26 light bomber strike at Osan and Kumchon airfields in which a number of North Korean fighters were probably damaged or destroyed in medium altitude bomb drops.

F. E. A. F. B-29s attacked the Seoul marshalling yards for the second time in two days. Direct hits splintered rolling stock and tore up large quantities of trackage in the yards.

Approximately 100 tons of high explosives were dropped using visual sighting. Preliminary reports indicated sufficient damage in the two strikes to cripple the key rail center for a considerable time.

Other B-29s struck at railroad and highway bridges along the rail and road arteries being used to carry Communist war material south to Seoul.

A railroad bridge near Munsan, twenty-three miles northwest of Seoul, was hit and damaged extensively and good results were obtained in an attack on a highway bridge nearby. A second highway bridge, twenty miles north of Seoul, was observed to have lost one span after the bomb drop and a railroad bridge five miles farther north was damaged.

A single 1,000-pound bomb dropped on a railroad train north-west of Munsan set off a large explosion and fires. Smoke clouds rose to 8,000 feet over the burning wreckage.

B-26 light bombers of the Fifth Air Force stepped up the number of night intruder missions aimed at supply and vehicular movements being carried out by the North Koreans under the cover of darkness.

Night intruder missions were flown to Taejon, Suwon, Seoul and Inchon. Several fires and other evidence of destruction were reported by the pilots making bombing and strafing runs on military concentration points in the northwest sector.

In daylight missions, the B-26s damaged a bridge at Chongsan, twenty miles east of Taejon, and two railroad tunnels ten miles west of Yosu. Rail lines were hit and trackage destroyed at several points near Anyang, ten miles south of Seoul, and also on the Seoul-Inchon link.

A majority of Fifth Air Force F-80 and F-51 fighter missions were flown to points from Chongju north and west to Seoul and Inchon. More than 330 fighter sorties hit rail, road and troop targets behind the North Korean lines.

Fighters attacked and damaged a chemical plant at Haeju, seventy-five miles west of Seoul, as well as warehouses and rail targets in the Inchon area.

F-82s flying daylight missions close to the fighting fronts attacked vehicles, gun positions and other ground objectives with excellent results. A 22,000-gallon gasoline supply dump at Kumchon was fired and a road bridge at Andong damaged by the all-weather fighters.

R. A. A. F. Mustangs, also working in close support of ground echelons, destroyed two fuel dumps at Kochang and Hyopchon. The Mustangs also knocked out or damaged numerous vehicles and strafed troop concentrations in the battle zones.

Targets brought under attack and damaged by the Fifth Air Force and R. A. A. F. fighters included forty-nine vehicles of all types, seventeen locomotives, thirty-four boxcars, fourteen artillery pieces and four warehouses.

One F-51 was hit by North Korean ground fire and crashed behind the lines.

Fifth Air Force cargo planes carried approximately fifty-eight tons of urgently needed military supplies and equipment to the American and South Korean forces during the day.

THOMPSON, WILLIAM

Rank and Organization: Private First Class, U.S. Army, Company M, 24th Infantry Regiment, 25th Infantry Division.
Born: New York, New York.
Entered Service At: Bronx, New York.
Place and Date: Near Haman, Korea, August 6, 1950.
Citation: Pfc. Thompson distinguished himself by conspicuous gallantry and intrepidity above and beyond the call of duty in action against the enemy. While his platoon was reorganizing under the cover of darkness, fanatical enemy forces in overwhelming strength launched a surprise attack on the unit. Pfc. Thompson set up his machine gun in the path of the onslaught and swept the enemy with withering fire, pinning them down momentarily thus permitting the remainder of his platoon to withdraw to a more tenable position. Although hit repeatedly by grenade fragments and small-arms fire, he resisted all efforts of his comrades to induce him to withdraw, steadfastly remained at his machine gun and continued to deliver deadly, accurate fire until mortally wounded by an enemy grenade. Pfc. Thompson's dauntless courage and gallant self-sacrifice reflect the highest credit upon himself and uphold the esteemed traditions of military service.

OFFICIAL COMMUNIQUÉ:
EIGHTH ARMY HEADQUARTERS, in Korea, Monday, Aug. 7 (AP)
—Communiqué 23, issued Sunday:

There were only two areas where action of any consequence was reported during the day.

In the Twenty-fourth Division area there were some reported crossings of the Naktong River. All these patrols were being contained and driven back toward the river.

The area southeast of Hamchang continues to show that the enemy is increasing his strength across the Naktong river. There has been no attack reported as yet although reports show that the enemy is moving infantry and vehicles into the area where the Naktong river bends to the east.

—Communiqué 24, issued Monday at 10:30 A.M. (8:30 P.M., Sunday, Eastern Daylight Time):

During the past twenty-four hours the enemy has continued its build-up generally and launched two local offenses. United Nations forces are engaged in minor offensive action.

In the Twenty-fifth Division area the Second Battalion of the Thirty-fifth Regimental Combat Team was attacked and driven from a position. Elements of the First and Second Battalions were committed and regained the positions. Elements of the United States Marine Corps and Twenty-fifth Division attacked to the south-west on the left flank of the Twenty-fifth's sector.

In the Twenty-fourth Division area North Korean forces made crossings in the southern sector and forced one regiment to withdraw. Another regiment counter-attacked and contained the enemy.

In the First Cavalry Division area there was no enemy action except fire from flat trajectory weapons. Patrols of two regiments crossed the Naktong River, penetrating five to ten miles, reporting negligible enemy forces.

In the R.O.K. (Republic of Korea) area, only patrol action was reported on the left flank. On the right central sector of the R.O.K.line elements of the Capital Division were attacked and driven from the position. The unit counter-attacked and retook the position. The enemy force was estimated at two regiments moving south on the right of the Capital Division. At present this North Korean force is unopposed except for mountainous terrain which allows slow progress.

No activity was reported in the Yongdok area.

An enemy move on the left flank of the United States Twenty-fourth Division is considered the primary threat at present, especially if the enemy is backing that section with a division or more. The other enemy move to the east of the Capital Division is the second threat.

TOKYO, Monday, Aug. 7 (AP)
—Release 212, issued by General MacArthur at 3:50 P.M., Sunday (1:50 A.M., Sunday, Eastern Daylight Time):

Aboard a United States Navy Aircraft Carrier, in Korean waters—Marine fliers of a carrier-borne air group had an old-fashioned Saturday house-cleaning in the Suwon-Inchon-Seoul area yesterday.

Complete demolition of a large tank and truck assembly plant at Inchon and the setting in flames of a fuel-laden tanker by a trio of Leatherneck fighter pilots highlighted a day whose tally in five strikes included three freight trains fired, a railroad bridge at Seoul blasted, an oil refinery and chemical plant at Inchon left blazing, four other factories rocketed and strafed, a railroad tunnel and rolling stock hidden inside blown up, two locomotives destroyed and, after bombardment ammunition was exhausted, over two hundred box cars were machine-gunned.

In addition to these Saturday clean-up chores, the marines flew cover for United States Navy P-2-V Neptunes spotting naval gunfire for the United Nations surface fleet bombardment of Inchon, major seaport and industrial city west of Seoul. Smoke from blazing targets towered five hundred feet and was visible fifty miles at sea.

The big event of the day was amassed by Maj. Kenneth L. Reusser of Santa Ana, Calif., son of Rev. and Mrs. Fred C. Reusser of Portland, Ore. Major Reusser, a one-time University of Georgia football and wrestling star, is entitled to wear the Navy Cross and the Distinguished Flying Cross for action at Guadalcanal and Okinawa. After flying cover for the Navy P-2-V spotters, Reusser dropped down to give some personal attention. He flew roof-high to investigate a large double-winged factory whose 300-foot expanse escaped damage in the bombardment.

Through the windows he saw it was a tank and truck assembly and repair center. Leading his flight back to the carrier to report and rearm, he was given permission to return to Inchon. The enemy, not anticipating a revisit, had failed to empty the plant of its movable rolling stock, and six large tanks, significantly bearing United States Army identification markings, and a score of trucks were in the courtyard.

Three Napalm bombs and a burst of rockets effected the total destruction of the tanks, trucks, factory and contents. Leaving the area at an altitude of fifty feet, Reusser saw that what had appeared from the greater height to be a pier extension was in reality a tanker cleverly camouflaged. His rockets and bombs expended, Reusser raked the hull of the vessel with his 20-mm guns and the tanker disintegrated with a blast that tossed the Navy Corsair almost out of control, denting the wings and fuselage with debris.

Participating in the attacks were Capt. Charles D. Garber, U. S. M. C., of Tacoma Park, Md., and Orange, Calif., and First Lieut. Robert Minnick, U. S. M. C., of Baltimore, Md.

—Release 213, issued by General MacArthur at 5:00 P.M., Sunday (3:00 A.M., Eastern Daylight Time):

Task Force 77 doubled the size of its jet-propelled punch when two 27,000-ton Essex-class carriers went into action in close support of the ground forces in the Southwest sector of South Korea yesterday. The one United States Navy carrier on duty with the Seventh Fleet was recently joined by a sister ship flying the flag of Rear Admiral E. C. Ewen.

The air groups of the two carriers, consisting of Panther jet fighters, Skyraider attack bombers and Corsair fighters, blasted a wide variety of targets in Chinju and in the area west and south of that town.

The span of one bridge was knocked out, hits were made on another with four 500-pound bombs and on a third bridge by three 500-pound bombs. Camouflaged targets in a village near Chinju were hit, starting large fires. Troop concentrations in Sechon were strafed and camouflaged stores near Kuryong were set afire.

Chinju itself was hit by bombs and rockets, causing an undetermined amount of damage. An automotive shop in Kuryong and a large building in a village to the south of that town were destroyed.

A power plant one mile south of Iri was blown up by rocket fire and a factory two miles northwest of Mangyong was damaged.

Trucks and buildings west of Kwangju were strafed, as was an administration building north of Kusan. Fifteen to twenty junks in the Yangsan River and along the west coast were strafed. One junk and one sampan west of Kumje were sunk. Returning pilots reported considerable small boat traffic in this general area.

In the attack on one of the bridges light anti-aircraft fire was encountered, according to a pilot. In a second run on the bridge the anti-aircraft fire was encountered, according to a pilot. In a second run on the bridge the anti-aircraft positions were strafed, resulting in several large explosions.

Task Force 77 is part of the Seventh Fleet, under the over-all command of Vice Admiral Arthur D. Struble.

—Release 214, issued by General MacArthur at 12:20 A.M. Monday (10:20 A.M. Sunday, Eastern Daylight Time):

The Communist forces continued aggressive small-unit attacks and infiltration tactics over the entire front. These, coupled with an initial river crossing five miles southwest of Changnyong and the build-up in the south and center sectors, are further indications that enemy forces still are attempting to sever the Taegu-Pusan lines of communication. The possibility of penetration from the north still exists.

The river crossing five miles southwest of Changnyong was made in the west bend of the river. The estimated strength of this crossing force was about one battalion and are now being engaged by friendly troops.

The fighting in the Chinju area was described as "probing" on the part of the enemy. Enemy troops attempting to infiltrate friendly lines were repulsed. The battle line was still located eleven miles east and seventeen miles southeast of Chinju.

Enemy pressure south of Andong was reported as heavy. Fighting continued heavy at Yongdok and positions remained unchanged.

—Release 215 issued at 1:55 P.M., Monday (11:55 P.M., Sunday, Eastern Daylight Time):

Jumping off at 6:30 A.M. (4:30 P.M., Sunday, Eastern Daylight Time) United States and South Korean forces launched an offensive today on the extreme south of the line. Marine elements of the force are meeting the enemy for the first time. At noon the offensive, heavily supported by air, was reported "progressing on schedule" west of Chungan.

In the center of the western portion of the line, the Red invader succeeded in putting a force across the Naktong River south of Pugong. This force was quickly contained by elements of the United States Thirty-fourth and Nineteenth Regimental Combat Teams. Further north, the R.O.K. (Republic of Korea) Seventeenth Regiment wiped out a pocket of 100 enemy who had slipped across the river.

In the northern sector R.O.K. troops were engaged in heavy patrolling actions throughout the day. Elements of the Capital Division, surrounded by the enemy in the early afternoon, were relieved by the success of a counter-attack later in the day which restored the line to its former position. The R.O.K. Eighth Division repulsed two probing attacks with heavy losses to the Communists.

On another portion of the line, the R.O.K. First Division successfully defended against an enemy thrust. Attacks against the R.O.K. Sixth Division in the vicinity of Yanggi-Dong were followed by a successful counter-attack. The R.O.K. Third Division continued to consolidate its position north of Yongdok.

Fighter aircraft of the Fifth Air Force reported destroying six aircraft on the ground at Pyongyang, a freighter in Yosu harbor, seven trucks and two warehouses. R. A. A. F. Mustangs also reported destroying and damaging a number of trucks and buildings. B-26's bombed a key railroad bridge at Chochinwon to further hamper the enemy's supply system.

†HANDRICH, MELVIN O.

Rank and Organization: Master Sergeant, U.S. Army, Company C, 5th Infantry Regiment.
Born: January 26, 1919, Manawa, Wisconsin.
Entered Service At: Manawa, Wisconsin.
Place and Date: Near Sobuk San Mountain, Korea, August 25 and 26, 1950.
Citation: M/Sgt. Handrich, Company C, distinguished himself by conspicuous gallantry and intrepidity above and beyond the call of duty in action against the enemy. His company was engaged in repulsing an estimated 150 enemy soldiers who were threatening to overrun its position. Near midnight on August 25th, a hostile group over 100 strong attempted to infiltrate the company perimeter. M/Sgt. Handrich, despite the heavy enemy fire, voluntarily left the comparative safety of the defensive area and moved to a forward position where he could direct mortar and artillery fire upon the advancing enemy. He remained at this post for 8 hours directing fire against the enemy who often approached to within 50 feet of his position. Again, on the morning of August 26th, another strong hostile force made an attempt to overrun the company's position. With complete disregard for his safety, M/Sgt. Handrich rose to his feet and from this exposed position fired his rifle and directed mortar and artillery fire on the attackers. At the peak of this action he observed elements of his company preparing to withdraw. He perilously made his way across fire-swept terrain to the defense area where, by example and forceful leadership, he reorganized the men to continue the fight. During the action M/Sgt. Handrich was severely wounded. Refusing to take cover or be evacuated, he returned to his forward position and continued to direct the company's fire. Later a determined enemy attack overran M/Sgt. Handrich's position and he was mortally wounded. When the position was retaken, over 70 enemy dead were counted in the area he had so intrepidly defended. M/Sgt. Handrich's sustained personal bravery, consummate courage, and gallant self-sacrifice reflect untold glory upon himself and the heroic traditions of the military service.

OFFICIAL COMMUNIQUÉ:
TOKYO, Aug. 26 (AP)
—Release 316, issued at 3:45 P.M. Saturday (1:45 A.M. Saturday, Eastern Daylight Time):

Vice Admiral Charles T. Joy, commander of United Nations Naval Forces, today released the following summary of Republic of Korea Navy and Marine activity for the week:

On Aug. 18, following shore bombardment by a Canadian destroyer and under cover of R.O.K. Navy guns, R.O.K. Marines landed and captured the island of Tokchok on the west coast of Korea against light resistance. On Aug. 20 R.O.K. Marines, again under cover of a Canadian destroyer and R.O.K. Navy guns, landed and captured the island of Yongchung against light opposition.

As reported previously, R.O.K. Marines under cover of R.O.K. Navy guns landed and captured Tongyong on the south coast of Korea Aug. 18.

On Aug. 20 an R.O.K. Navy patrol vessel sighted and sank a 100-ton North Korean motor boat loaded with troops off Usuyong. Usuyong is south of Mokpo. The same R.O.K. ship heavily damaged a second motor boat and shelled enemy positions at Usuyong. The following day the same R.O.K. ship captured a motor boat with North Korean liaison personnel aboard.

On Aug. 21 R.O.K. marines landed and captured the island of Soijak. Opposition was light.

A R.O.K. Navy ship covering the landing sank three enemy sailboats carrying reinforcements to the island.

On Aug. 24 a R.O.K. Navy patrol vessel operating near Sorok island (a small island north of Kogum island off the south coast) sank a 50-ton motor boat and five sail boats. Turning toward shore, the R.O.K. ship bombarded and destroyed the enemy headquarters and a supply dump. Fifteen North Korean troops were killed and the rest went into hiding. The R.O.K. ship sustained no damage.

The seizure of the three islands off the west coast of Korea was conducted by the R.O.K. marine units as a means of cutting down further possible water routes for enemy forces to use in supplying their force fighting in the south.

R.O.K. Navy and Marine units on the west coast have been operating under the directions of Rear Admiral W. G. Andrews, Royal Navy.

—Release 317, issued at 3:55 P.M. (1:55 A.M., Saturday, Eastern Daylight Time):

Along the front lines south of Uisong the enemy is exerting heavy pressure on R.O.K. (Republic of Korea) Army units defending that sector. As a result of enemy attacks Aug. 25, R.O.K. forces along the main Uisong-Sinnyong road were forced to withdraw approximately one mile to positions in the vicinity of Chongno, but later counterattacked and regained their earlier positions. Enemy attacks continue in this sector, but R.O.K. defenders are holding their positions.

In the sector northeast of Waegwan, R.O.K. units, supported by American forces, yesterday made gains up to 1,500 yards in the vicinity of Yuhak ridge. Elsewhere in this sector the front remained fairly quiet.

R.O.K. forces in the Pohand sector yesterday met heavy and organized resistance in their attack to the north. Along the east coast R.O.K. units made slight gains near Hunghae, but farther west, in the vicinity of Yonggi, the enemy forced a minor withdrawal of friendly forces.

American forces holding the southern sector of the front continue to receive light probing attacks by the enemy. A sharp midnight attack along the Sobuk ridge was repulsed without loss of ground and with unknown enemy casualties. A later attack on the same area, at 6:15 A.M., was also repelled. At other points in this sector enemy concentrations were dispersed by our artillery fire.

Throughout the central front, our forces continue aggressive patrolling and artillery attacks on enemy supply, artillery positions and troop concentrations. Enemy activity in this sector has been confined to small-scale patrol action.

Elements of the East Coast Naval Patrol furnished gunfire support of ground operations. Targets north of Pohang were bombarded, including a command post, artillery positions, tanks and seven troops concentrations. Other naval units continued patrol and blockade operations on the east, south and west coasts, and naval aircraft rendered close support of ground troops in the battle area.

—Release 318, issued by Gen. Douglas MacArthur at 9:10 P.M. (7:10 A.M., Saturday, Eastern Daylight Time):

United States Air Force B-26 light bombers heavily damaged railroad bridges in the Seoul area and B-29 Superforts struck at key railroad yards in Central and Northern Korea today.

Today's pattern of bombing and fighter attacks was designed to further hamper the Communists' movement of badly needed supplies and reserve forces.

The B-29s unleashed sixty tons of bombs on the key marshalling yards and railroad junction at Kilchu, fifteen miles north of Songjin on the east coast north of the Thirty-eighth Parallel.

Kilchu is the junction point of main rail lines from the northwestern and northeastern portions of Korea. These main lines join at Kilchu and lead down the east coast of Wonsan.

The bombing was carried out under clear visibility and bombardiers reported excellent results on the strike.

Other aircraft of the F.E.A.F. (Far East Air Forces) Bomber Command continued smashing at North Korean bridges and communication lines in the central Korean area. Bombardiers reported some flak coming up from the area surrounding the more important bridges, perhaps indicating Communist concern over the constant pounding the B-29s are giving to their rail and highway lines. Despite the flak the B-29 crews reported good results on the bridges.

Fifth Air Force fighters went more than 300 miles into North Korean territory today in a series of armed reconnaissance flights to hammer at airfields and rail traffic. Both F-80s and F-51s took part.

The F-51s were still flying late today, with night missions also scheduled.

F-80s made fighter sweeps to half a dozen North Korean airfields. Returning pilots reported they had seen dummy airplanes and planes shot up on previous missions. No live planes took to the air to oppose the United Nations fighters.

In the Pyongyang area F-80 pilots checked over the deserted airfield and then found a large factory in a nearby small town. "We rocketed it," said Lieut. Irvin W. May, of 4611 Davenport Street, Washington, D.C.

A pontoon bridge on the west side of Seoul was hit today by 1,000 pound bombs in a B-26 flight led by Lieut. Col. Robert B. Jarrell, of Waxahachie, Tex. "We made eight direct hits on the bridge and put it out of commission," said Colonel Jarrell.

He credited First Lieut. Frank Bullias, a bombardier, of Danville, Ill., with having made the strikes.

Another pontoon bridge also near Seoul was hit by B-26s in a flight led by Capt. James H. Morrow, of Sweetwater, Tex. "We damaged the approach on the north side of the bridge," said Captain Morrow.

Rail supply lines from Poksong to Kumchon were strafed and bombed by B-26's today. Capt. Luther L. Hampton of 2912 Bellaire Boulevard, Houston, Tex., bombed a train near Sangjin. He said he had hit the locomotive and six box cars with considerable damage inflicted.

Enemy supplies moving by rail from Kumchon to Kwanni were seriously damaged by additional B-26s according to two crewmen, Capt. Jayne A. Yooman of Austin, Tex., and Lieut. Donald J. Forns of 6504 Park Lane, Mariemont, Ohio.

In an earlier B-26 mission behind the battle line a locomotive and two box cars were eliminated by Lieut. Melvin R. Stahl of Adel, Iowa, and his crewmen. Lieutenant Stahl said Staff Sgt. Oscar M. Byrd, gunner, of Muscatine, Iowa, and First Lieut. Charles A. Bowers, navigator, of Brooklyn, N.Y., had spotted the train. "Our first bomb hit the middle of the train," said Stahl, and the others hit the train's tail and the engine."

First Lieut.. John W. Jackson of South Gate, Calif., led four F-80 jets to a Communist airdrome south of the Thirty-eighth Parallel in an early morning mission and reported no aircraft and no activity seen. Flying southward, his flight strafed railroad tracks and buildings, with good results.

Two airstrips at Onjong above the Thirty-eighth Parallel were targets for another flight of F-80s, but no Communist planes were seen. "We strafed buildings and barracks on both strips," said Capt. James E. Anderson, Chatom, Ala., leader of the flight.

F-51 pilots reported good rocket and strafing missions between the Thirty-eighth and Fortieth Parallels, along the east coast of Korea. First Lieut. Charles D. Hauver of Poughkeepsie, N.Y., improvised his gun sight when it burned out by using adhesive tape, and got a solid hit on a truck after passing one of the vacated North Korean airfields.

First Lieut. Ray I. Carter of 38 Layer Street, Buffalo, N.Y., detected camouflaged buildings on the east coast at the Thirty-eighth Parallel.

"We hit it with rockets and the buildings collapsed," said Lieutenant Carter.

In the same area First Lieut. James L. Glessner Jr. of Julesburg, Colo., strafed a building. "Parts of it blew fifty feet into the air," he said.

KOUMA, ERNEST R.

Rank and Organization: Master Sergeant (then Sfc.), U.S. Army, Company A, 72d Tank Battalion.
Born: November 23, 1919, Dwight, Nebraska.
Entered Service At: Dwight, Nebraska
Place and Date: Vicinity of Agok, Korea, August 31 and September 1, 1950.
Citation: M/Sgt. Kouma, a tank commander in Company A, distinguished himself by conspicuous gallantry and intrepidity at the risk of his life above and beyond the call of duty in action against the enemy. His unit was engaged in supporting infantry elements on the Naktong River front. Near midnight on August 31, a hostile force estimated at 500 crossed the river and launched a fierce attack against the infantry positions, inflicting heavy casualties. A withdrawal was ordered and his armored unit was given the mission of covering the movement until a secondary position could be established. The enemy assault overran two tanks, destroyed one and forced another to withdraw. Suddenly M/Sgt. Kouma discovered that his tank was the only obstacle in the path of the hostile onslaught. Holding his ground, he gave fire orders to his crew and remained in position throughout the night, fighting off repeated enemy attacks. During one fierce assault, the enemy surrounded his tank and he leaped from the armored turret, exposing himself to a hail of hostile fire, manned the .50 caliber machine gun mounted on the rear deck, and delivered pointblank fire into the fanatical foe. His machine gun emptied, he fire his pistol and threw grenades to keep the enemy from his tank. After more than 9 hours of constant combat and close-in fighting, he withdrew his vehicle to friendly lines. During the withdrawal through 8 miles of hostile territory, M/Sgt. Kouma continued to inflict casualties upon the enemy and exhausted his ammunition in destroying 3 hostile machine gun positions. During this action, M/Sgt. Kouma killed an estimated 250 enemy soldiers. His magnificent stand allowed the infantry sufficient time to reestablish defensive positions. Rejoining his company, although suffering intensely from his wounds, he attempted to resupply his tank and return to the battle area. While being evacuated for medical treatment, his courage was again displayed when he requested to return to the front. M/Sgt. Kouma's superb leadership, heroism, and intense devotion to duty reflect the highest credit upon himself and uphold the esteemed traditions of the U.S. Army.

†OUELLETTE, JOSEPH R.
Rank and Organization: Private First Class, U.S. Army, Company H, 9th Infantry Regiment, 2d Infantry Division.
Born: Lowell, Massachusetts.
Entered Service At: Lowell, Massachusetts.
Place and Date: Near Yongsan, Korea, August 31 to September 3, 1950.
Citation: Pfc. Ouellette distinguished himself by conspicuous gallantry and intrepidity above and beyond the call of duty in action against the enemy in the Makioug-Chang River salient. When an enemy assault cut off and surrounded his unit, he voluntarily made a reconnaissance of a nearby hill under intense enemy fire to locate friendly troop positions and obtain information of the enemy's strength and location. Finding that friendly troops were not on the hill, he worked his way back to his unit under heavy fire. Later, when an airdrop of water was made outside the perimeter, he again braved enemy fire in an attempt to retrieve water for his unit. Finding the dropped cans broken and devoid of water, he returned to his unit. His heroic attempt greatly increased his comrades' morale. When ammunition and grenades ran low, Pfc. Ouellette again slipped out of the perimeter to collect these from the enemy dead. After collecting grenades he was attacked by an enemy soldier. He killed this enemy in hand-to-hand combat, gathered up the ammunition, and returned to his unit. When the enemy attacked on September 3, they assaulted his position with grenades. On 6 occasions Pfc. Ouellette leaped from his foxhole to escape exploding grenades. In doing so, he had to face enemy small-arms fire. He continued his resistance, despite a severe wound, until he lost his life. The extraordinary heroism and intrepidity displayed by Pfc. Ouellette reflect the highest credit upon himself and are in keeping with the esteemed traditions of the military service.

†WATKINS, TRAVIS E.
Rank and Organization: Master Sergeant, U.S. Army, Company H, 9th Infantry Regiment, 2d Infantry Division.
Born: Waldo, Arkansas.
Entered Service At: Texas
Place and Date: Near Yongsan, Korea, August 31 to September 3, 1950.
Citation: M/Sgt. Watkins distinguished himself by conspicuous gallantry and intrepidity above and beyond the call of duty in action against the enemy. When an overwhelming enemy force broke through and isolated 30 men of his unit, he took command, established a perimeter defense and directed action which repelled continuous, fanatical enemy assaults. With his group completely surrounded and cut off, he moved from foxhole to foxhole exposing himself to enemy fire, giving instructions and offering encouragement to his men. Later when the need for ammunition and grenades became critical he shot 2 enemy soldiers 50 yards outside the perimeter and went out alone for their ammunition and weapons. As he picked up their weapons he was attacked by 3 others and wounded. Returning their fire he killed all three and gathering up the weapons of the 5 enemy dead returned to his amazed comrades. During a later assault, 6 enemy soldiers gained a narrow passage and began to throw grenades into the perimeter making it untenable. Realizing the desperate situation and disregarding his wound he rose from his foxhole to engage them with rifle fire. Although immediately hit by a burst from an enemy machine gun he continued to fire until he had killed the grenade throwers. With this threat eliminated he collapsed and despite being paralyzed from the waist down, encouraged his men to hold on. He refused all food, saving it for his comrades, and when it became apparent that help would not arrive in time to hold the position ordered his men to escape to friendly lines. Refusing evacuation as his hopeless condition would burden his comrades, he remained in his position and cheerfully wished them luck. Through his aggressive

leadership and intrepid actions, this small force destroyed nearly 500 of the enemy before abandoning their position. M/Sgt. Watkins' sustained personal bravery and noble self-sacrifice reflect the highest glory upon himself and is in keeping with the esteemed traditions of the U.S. Army.

†HENRY, FREDERICK F.

Rank and Organization: First Lieutenant, U.S. Army, Company F, 28th Infantry Regiment.
Born: Vian, Oklahoma.
Entered Service At: Clinton, Oklahoma.
Place and Date: Vicinity of Am-Dong, Korea, September 1, 1950.
Citation: 1st Lt. Henry, Company F, distinguished himself by conspicuous gallantry and intrepidity above and beyond the call of duty in action against the enemy. His platoon was holding a strategic ridge near the town when they were attacked by a superior enemy force, supported by heavy mortar and artillery fire. Seeing his platoon disorganized by this fanatical assault, he left his foxhole and moving along the line ordered his men to stay in place and keep firing. Encouraged by this heroic action the platoon reformed a defensive line and rained devastating fire on the enemy, checking its advance. Enemy fire had knocked out all communications and 1st Lt. Henry was unable to determine whether or not the main line of resistance was altered to this heavy attack. On his own initiative, although severely wounded, he decided to hold his position as long as possible and ordered the wounded evacuated and their weapons and ammunition brought to him. Establishing a 1-man defensive position, he ordered the platoon's withdrawal and despite his wound and with complete disregard for himself remained behind to cover the movement. When last seen his was singlehandedly firing all available weapons so effectively that he caused an estimated 50 enemy casualties. His ammunition was soon expended and his position was overrun, but his intrepid action saved the platoon and halted the enemy's advance until the main line of resistance was prepared to throw back the attack. 1st Lt. Henry's outstanding gallantry and noble self-sacrifice above and beyond the call of duty reflect the highest honor on him and are in keeping with the esteemed traditions of the U.S. Army.

†SMITH, DAVID M.

Rank and Organization: Private First Class, U.S. Army, Company E, 9th Infantry Regiment, 2d Infantry Division.
Born: November 10, 1926, Livingston, Kentucky.
Entered Service At: Livingston, Kentucky.
Place and Date: Near Yongsan, Korea, September 1, 1950.
Citation: Pfc. Smith distinguished himself by conspicuous gallantry and outstanding courage above and beyond the call of duty against the enemy. Pfc. Smith was a gunner in the mortar section of Company E, emplaced in rugged mountainous terrain and under attack by a numerically superior hostile force. Bitter fighting ensued and the enemy overran forward elements, infiltrated the perimeter, and rendered friendly positions untenable. The mortar section was ordered to withdraw, but the enemy had encircled and closed in on the position. Observing a grenade lobbed at his emplacement, Pfc. Smith shouted a warning to his comrades and, fully aware of the odds against him, flung himself upon it and smothered the explosion with his body. Although mortally wounded in this display of valor, his intrepid act saved 5 men from death or serious injury. Pfc. Smith's inspirational conduct and supreme sacrifice reflect lasting glory on himself and are in keeping with the noble traditions of the infantry of the U.S. Army.

†STORY, LUTHER H.
Rank and Organization: Private First Class, U.S. Army, Company A, 9th Infantry Regiment, 2d Infantry Division.
Born: July 20, 1931, Buena Vista, Georgia.
Entered Service At: Georgia.
Place and Date: Near Agok, Korea, September 1, 1950.
Citation: Pfc. Story distinguished himself by conspicuous gallantry and intrepidity above and beyond the call of duty in action against the enemy. A savage daylight attack by elements of 3 enemy divisions penetrated the thinly held lines of the 9th Infantry. Company A beat off several banzai attacks but was bypassed and in danger of being cut off and surrounded. Pfc. Story, a weapons squad leader, was heavily engaged in stopping the early attacks and had just moved his squad to a position overlooking the Naktong River when he observed a large group of the enemy crossing the river to attack Company A. Seizing a machine gun from his wounded gunner he placed deadly fire on the hostile column killing or wounding an estimated 100 enemy soldiers. Facing certain encirclement the company commander ordered a withdrawal. During the move Pfc. Story noticed the approach of an enemy truck loaded with troops and towing an ammunition trailer. Alerting his comrades to take cover he fearlessly stood in the middle of the road, throwing grenades into the truck. Out of grenades he crawled to his squad, gathered up additional grenades and again attacked the vehicle. During the withdrawal the company was attacked by such superior numbers that it was forced to deploy in a rice-field. Pfc. Story was wounded in this action, but, disregarding his wounds, rallied the men about him and repelled the attack. Realizing that his wounds would hamper his comrades he refused to retire to the next position but remained to cover the company's withdrawal. When last seen he was firing every weapon available and fighting off another hostile assault. Pfc. Story's extraordinary heroism, aggressive leadership, and supreme devotion to duty reflect the highest credit upon himself and were in keeping with the esteemed traditions of the military service.

†TURNER, CHARLES W.
Rank and Organization: Sergeant First Class, U.S. Army, 2d Reconnaissance Company, 2d Infantry Division.
Born: Boston, Massachusetts.
Entered Service At: Massachusetts.
Place and Date: Near Yongsan, Korea, September 1, 1950.
Citation: Sfc. Turner distinguished himself by conspicuous gallantry and intrepidity above and beyond the call of duty in action against the enemy. A large enemy force launched a mortar and automatic weapons supported assault against his platoon. Sfc. Turner, a section leader, quickly organized his unit for defense and then observed that the attack was directed at the tank section 100 yards away. Leaving his secured section he dashed through a hail of fire to the threatened position and, mounting a tank, manned the exposed turret machine gun. Disregarding the intense enemy fire he calmly held his position delivering deadly accurate fire and pointing out targets for the tank's 75mm. gun. His action resulted in the destruction of 7 enemy machine gun nests. Although severely wounded he remained at the gun shouting encouragement to his comrades. During the action the tank received over 50 direct hits; the periscope and antenna were shot away and 3 rounds hit the machine gun mount. Despite this fire he remained at his post until a burst of enemy fire cost him his life. This intrepid and heroic performance enabled the platoon to withdraw and later launch an attack which routed the enemy. Sfc. Turner's valor and example reflect the highest credit upon himself and are in keeping with the esteemed traditions of the U.S. Army.

Note: The following is a newspaper account and official communique of the preceding battles for which Sgt. Kouma, Pfc. Ouellette, Sgt. Watkins, Lt. Henry, Pfc. Smith, Pfc. Story and Pfc. Brown were awarded the Medal of Honor:

FOE LAUNCHES ALL-OUT PUSH FOR PUSAN

• • •

SOME GAINS MADE

• • •

U.S. Speeds Troops to Area to Save Pusan — Invaders Retreat North of Pohang

• • •

TOKYO, Friday, Sept. 1 — The North Korean invaders launched a general assault today on a fifty mile front against positions held by the United States Second and Twenty-fifth Infantry Divisions along the Naktong River line and the South coast approaches to the vital landing port of Pusan.

An Eighth Army communiqué said attacks had been launched all the way from Tuksong, twelve miles southwest of the key city of Taegu, to the south coast area where the defenders stood forty-five miles west of Pusan.

[Late news agency dispatches from the front quoted a Second Division spokesman as having said that some North Korean units had made a five-mile penetration in the area held by the United States Second Infantry Division.]

The full-fledged enemy assault against the United States position in the center and south was launched as pressure against the weary South Korean defenders around Pohang on the east coast eased. In that area, the North Koreans were reported to be withdrawing after their second failure to win the town and the advanced airstrip. Elsewhere along the defense perimeter there was only minor activity.

There were some indications that the North Koreans, after a long lull on the central and southern sections of the front, finally had launched what was considered here as their desperate drive to capture Taegu and Pusan before new Allied reinforcements could turn the tide against them and that they were committing their best reserves to battle.

[United States officers on the battlefront said they believed the Communist onslaught would be crushed by nightfall, The Associated Press reported. Brig. Gen. George Barth of Washington, D.C., was quoted as saying after an inspection of the front Friday morning: "They couldn't have hit us at a better time. We were really ready for them." The officers added they were confident the attack was the last big offensive the Communists could muster on the front closest to Pusan.]

The heaviest pressure of the new Communist drive was against the United States Fifth Combat Team and the Twenty-fifth Infantry Division between the Nam River and the South Coast, but the push against the United States Second Infantry Division at a point where its defense positions joined with those of the Twenty-fifth, also was heavy.

The Eighth Army said two United States regiments were fighting off the lesser attacks on river positions farther north but did not identify their sectors. These attacks were believed to be from the bridgehead across the river the enemy had maintained since last week in the vicinity of Hyonpung and northward at Tuksong.

The communiqué said the enemy had made two crossings on the Naktong west of Changnyong "in force," in the area defended by the Second Division.

As the attack developed United States intelligence sources estimated it as a strong two-pronged drive. The southern arm of the pincers had the mission of seizing Haman and Masan. The northern thrust across the Naktong seemed aimed primarily at the Changnyong-Yongsan road, the main lateral communications line behind the United States Naktong River defenses. The latter push was a more distant threat to the vital road and railroad supply artery between Pusan and Taegu.

The general assault was supported by the heaviest gunfire of the war from tanks, mortars and artillery pieces along the front and at the Naktong River crossing and in the south the North Koreans were committing their reserves of Russian-made armor.

The attack apparently was a coordinated assault launched against the Second Division at 2:40 o'clock in the morning and two hours later against the Twenty-fifth Division.

In the Second Division's zone the enemy had seized high ground east of the river near Pugong astride the Changnyong road but there was no confirmation of reports that the Communists had made a major break-through. [A United Press report said some Communist troops had reached Chogong, four miles south of Changnyong.]

The enemy force, said to be at regimental strength, was faced by United States troops forming a defense line west of the Changnyong-Yonsan road.

An Eighth Army communiqué said penetrations of 2,000 yards had been made against the Twenty-fifth Division forces but that the North Koreans in this salient broke under attack by reserves hurried up to the scene.

"All regiments are heavily engaged and holding their positions," the communiqué said.

By early morning the North Koreans had pushed 1,000 to 1,500 yards across the river with tank concentrations in the rear and they were reported to be digging in their newly won positions. The Eighth Army communiqué said a United States battalion was being moved up to block the advance.

The official announcement estimated the Communist attack was being pushed by three divisions. It said that apparently they were the North Korean Sixth and Seventh between the Nam and the coast and the Fourth Division to the north. Two other divisions were reported to be in reserve—the heaviest concentration of force the invaders had used in this phase of the war.

The North Koreans were following their familiar technique of punching first here and then there along the thinly held 140-mile front striving for a break-through.

Forcing their way between United States defense posts and artillery positions, the North Koreans scored a penetration of about two miles within a few hours of their jump-off. Reports from the front said fighting was in progress in the streets of Haman.

[Counter-attacking troops of the United States Twenty-fifth Division fought their way back through Haman Friday afternoon, The Associated Press reported.]

The attack on the southern front began under bright moonlight and was spearheaded by heavy Russian-made tanks the Communists had kept hidden from the continuous Allied air strikes.

The invaders took heavy losses as they pushed through the United States lines, artillery firing on their columns at pointblank ranges. But once the line had been penetrated the North Koreans fanned out to attack the defenders from the flanks and the rear. Some United States positions thus were reported to be virtually surrounded.

Twenty-fifth Division and Fifth Regimental Combat team veterans were holding their lines doggedly. But as the Communists launched their heavy offensive some enemy groups swept through gaps between the defenders' strong points, despite artillery, mortar and machine-gun fire.

The enemy attack was launched after a heavy barrage of artillery and mortar fire on United States defense redoubts protected by barbed-wire entanglements and some areas by small mine fields. Some sources said the invaders' gunfire was the heaviest of the Korean war as they lavishly expended not only their newly reinforced divisions but their dwindling supplies of munitions.

Against the United States positions, which are a series of protected points with fields of fire between them, the invaders were using a classic pattern of attack not often seen in the fighting over the rough Korean terrain—a barrage falling on and behind the United States posts, a rush of armor through gaps, then waves of infantry following through the holes plugged by the tanks to fan out behind if they could and envelop the front-line defenders.

In the Pohang area the North Koreans were reported to have withdrawn about a mile and the South Koreans were said to have advanced to a point about 500 yards south of the area from which the Communists had launched their latest abortive attempt to capture Pohang.

To the west, where the enemy had captured the town of Kigye—now also a mass of ruins—and had been driving on Pohang from the northwest, little action was reported. The communiqué said only that the enemy maintained "close" contact with the Republican Capital division, which was under fire yesterday from artillery and mortars.

Earlier reports said the South Koreans were holding their positions in the Kigye area. The South Koreans occupy high ground over-looking the town from the south, with the enemy on the ridges to the north side of the trails through the mountains to the north.

Other reports said United Nations forces had withdrawn up to 2,000 yards down the critical Uisong-Sinnyong road and in the area to the west following heavy enemy attacks around Hwasan and Chidong.

On the Uisong highway, the enemy had slipped a force, estimated at a battalion, around the defenders' lines and set up a road block a few miles north of Sinnyong—a penetration of about 5,000 yards. The official spokesman said this road block was well on the way to liquidation yesterday.

OFFICIAL COMMUNIQUÉ:

TOKYO, Saturday, Sept. 2 (AP)
—United States Eighth Army communiqué 67 issued at 8:45 P.M. Friday (6:45 A.M. Friday, Eastern Daylight Time):

Elements of two enemy divisions continued the attack today on the Twenty-fifth Division, driving one penetration to take Haman.

Although some enemy forces have succeeded in getting behind the United States lines, the attack had generally been contained except on the extreme right flanks of the division. By midday the assault had cost the Communists 3,000 dead and three tanks destroyed by ground action.

The right and central elements of the Second Division has contained the attacking Communists by this afternoon as heavy fighting continued throughout the day.

An enemy group infiltrated United States lines and surrounded a regimental command post which fought its way out with the aid of friendly armor.

In the left sector of the division, heavy fighting was reported as far east as Songin, four miles east of the Naktong River. Three tanks were destroyed in this area. The enemy has been using rafts, barges and fords to get men and equipment across the river.

—United States Eighth Army communiqué 68 issued at 10:50 A.M., Saturday (8:50 P.M., Friday, Eastern Daylight Time):

The major weight of the enemy's general offensive on the United Nations western front yesterday was astride the Naktong River east of its junction with the Nam. Greatest penetrations were made in the area just north of the junction.

After repelling an attack last night at 2320 (11:20 P.M.), one platoon of the Twenty-fifth Division was overrun this morning at 0500 hours. Prior to these attacks, the regiment had restored positions lost earlier.

The major penetration made yesterday in the Twenty-fifth Division sector was against the center where the enemy occupied Haman. A United States battalion counter-attacked last night and at last report had restored some of the original positions west of Haman. The northern regiment was penetrated to a depth of 4,000 to 5,000 yards but regained part of the positions lost.

The southern regiment of the Second Division received the heaviest enemy blows yesterday, being forced back to the high ground at Yongsan. This unit was also hit by Communist forces which had penetrated the Twenty-fifth Division and turned north across the Naktong River. The northern regiments against lighter attacks held well, though part of the sector was penetrated up to 7,500 yards.

—Release 360, issued at 3:40 P.M., Friday (1:40 A.M., Friday, Eastern Daylight Time):

An enemy attack, which appears to be an all-out effort, started at midnight along the entire front of the United States Twenty-fifth Division sector. This attack was preceded by heavy artillery, mortar and flat trajectory fire.

Heavy attacks were launched south of Yuchon, where an enemy penetration was repulsed and the position restored, in the vicinity of Haman, where the enemy penetrated approximately 2,000 yards, and also in the vicinity of Masan, near the junction of the Nam and Naktong Rivers, where three river crossings were made, with a penetration of approximately 2,500 yards.

Heavy fighting continues along the entire front but latest reports indicate that the United States Twenty-fifth Division is holding against heavy enemy pressure with the situation remaining fluid. Several small infiltrations behind the lines are being contained and mopped up.

In the United States Second Division sector, two attempted river crossings by the enemy in the area southwest of Sinam were repulsed.

An enemy attack in the vicinity of Tugong succeeded in penetrating approximately 1,500 yards. Another penetration in the vicinity of An was contained and repulsed. Elements of the division are now engaged in mopping up small enemy penetrations.

In the United States First Cavalry Division sector, elements of the division, supported by artillery fire, dispersed a heavy enemy concentration in the vicinity of Tuksong at 3:30 A.M.. A later attack in the same general area was repulsed. Elements of the United States First Cavalry Division are now mopping up small enemy groups which had infiltrated behind the lines.

In the sector south of Uihung, R.O.K. (Republic of Korea) forces attacked and seized hills in the vicinity of Hwagson and Unsan. Otherwise the sector remains relatively quiet.

No significant changes have occurred in the Kigye and Pohang sector since the 1,500-yard advance of the R.O.K. Third Division north and east of Pohang, which was reported earlier.

—Release 361 issued at 4:05 P.M., Friday (2:05 A.M. Friday, Eastern Daylight Time):

A Republic of Korea Navy ship patrolling in the vicinity of Chindo sank six small craft, killing approximately 150 enemy troops, in the period Aug. 28-30.

Three R.O.K. (Republic of Korea) Navy vessels bombarded military targets at Usuyong Aug. 30. A R.O.K. Navy ship patrolling Chinhae Bay Aug. 30 destroyed three motor boats and five sailing craft in latitude approximately 35 degrees north and longitude 128 degrees 30 minutes east.

Guns of United States Navy ships, standing off Pohang, and carrier-based United States Marine flyers yesterday contributed to the advance of United Nations ground forces in the Pohang area.

A pocket of North Korean troops holding up the advance of a tank column several miles east of Kigye was wiped out with napalm, permitting the column to advance half a mile. The Marines followed through by strafing, rocketing and bombing scores of enemy troops falling back under the United Nations' advance.

The entire Marine Air Force yesterday was concentrated in the Pohang area, extending several miles west and north of Tosong with troops, transport and artillery as the prime targets. More than fifteen separate troop concentrations were attacked. One ridge north of Tosong reportedly holding 1,000 troops was heavily bombed and strafed. An airborne air controller reported excellent coverage of the entire area.

United States Navy guns, making use of aerial spotting, blasted twenty-four separate targets yesterday, principally troop concentrations, in the Pohang area. Eight-inch guns of a Navy cruiser and bombs from marine Corsairs teamed up on one target. Results of the day's firing were described by an air spotter as extremely effective.

—Release 362, issued at 9:10 P.M., Friday (7:10 A.M., Friday, Eastern Daylight Time):

All types of United States Air Force planes supported the United Nations ground troops today, the fighters flying close support in the southwest battle area and bombers ranging through Korea to sever means of transporting supplies and reinforcements sorely needed by the Communists.

Early reports from fliers indicate heavy damage to bridges, rail lines, airfields, troop concentrations and vehicles carrying supplies.

B-29 Superforts continued their interdiction of North Korean rail and road communications, already crippled.

On the west coast, where bad weather prevailed, B-26 medium bombers again covered the coast from Seoul on the north to Haenan on the southwest tip of Korea. They struck marshalling yards, bridges, rolling stock and troops.

One B-26 crew spent two hours in a single attack on enemy ground firing positions in the Chinju area. Air controllers spotted the heavy firing. The enemy position was finally silenced, First Lieut. Roger W. Little of Red Bud, Ill., said.

Capt. John Gassler of Boston spotted a train of ten box cars a few miles west of Seoul. He destroyed the locomotive and one box car, setting fire to two others and damaging the rest.

"We got the most out of our nine bombs and 1,000 rounds of .50-caliber ammunition," he said. In the Masan area F-80's strafed troops and artillery pieces, also rocketing supply dumps at that strategic point.

The F-51 Mustangs operated in full force in close support of United Nations troops in the southwest area, and were still at it at sundown. Air controllers sent one flight to a supply dump, which was blown up. They also got an artillery piece and trucks, but the exact positions were not revealed.

With the weather closing down in the southwest area late today, three tanks were strafed and rocketed near Waegwan by F-80 jets.

"We destroyed one tank and damaged the other two," said First Lieut. Thomas W. Queen of San Diego, Calif.

Other F-80's went above the Thirty-eighth Parallel, strafing ten box cars and six passenger cars on a train near the west coast. The same flight damaged six box cars at Masan.

Five hundred-pound bombs were dropped on a bridge near Seoul by F-82's.

—Release 363, issued at 1:15 A.M., Saturday (11:15 A.M. Friday, Eastern Daylight Time):

On the western front, elements of United Nations forces were poised for an all-out fight to restore its positions in the vicinity of the junction of the Naktong and Nam rivers, where enemy forces have driven to Songjin. At last report the enemy was being contained in its drive four miles east of the river junction.

With the exception of Haman in the southern sector, which at last report was held by an estimated enemy group of 300, there was no significant enemy action on other fronts. In the northeast the R.O.K. (Republic of Korea) Third and Capital divisions have been slowed by enemy resistance.

—Release 364, issued by Gen. Douglas MacArthur at 11:10 A.M., Saturday (9:10 P.M., Friday Eastern Daylight Time):

Carrier-based United States Navy airplanes of Task Force 77 swung into action yesterday afternoon in close air support of United Nations ground forces on the western front.

Troop concentrations, transport, supplies and artillery in an around Chogye, Kaepo, Haman and Tuksong were the special targets for the Navy's precision flyers.

Numbers of rafts and small craft on the Naktong River were strafed.

Task Force 77 pilots were blasting strategic targets in North Korea yesterday when Vice Admiral C. T. Joy, commander United Nations naval forces, ordered the Seventh Fleet to give all-out close air support of the ground forces until further notice.

On receipt of the order, the Skyraiders, Corsairs and Panther jets were immediately diverted to the battlefront.

Admiral Joy's order to Vice Admiral Arthur D. Struble, commander of the Seventh Fleet, said a maximum effort would be made until further notice. The orders went out from Navy headquarters at 12:30 P.M. Friday. At 1:15 the first strike of four airplanes was over the battle area.

During strikes Friday morning in the north, the Navy airplanes heavily hit railroad yards at Pyongyang, Seoul, Sariwon, Sinanju, Chunghwa, Munsan and Sunan. Four direct hits were scored on a railroad bridge at Pyongyang. A span of a railroad bridge at Sariwon was dropped. One highway bridge was knocked out at the south end of the Seoul railroad yards. Eight boxcars loaded with ammunition near the Seoul yards were blown up.

The tally for Task Force 77 pilots for the day included: thirty-two railroad cars destroyed and twenty-four damaged; fifteen trucks destroyed and forty-seven damaged; one warehouse destroyed and fifteen damaged, and four barracks buildings damaged.

Task Force 77, a part of the Seventh Fleet, is under the command of Rear Admiral E. C. Ewen, U.S.N.

†BROWN, MELVIN L.

Rank and Organization: Private First Class, U.S. Army, Company D, 8th Engineer Combat Battalion.
Born: Mahaffey, Pennsylvania.
Entered Service At: Erie, Pennsylvania.
Place and Date: Near Kasan, Korea, September 4, 1950.
Citation: Pfc. Brown, Company D, distinguished himself by conspicuous gallantry and intrepidity above and beyond the call of duty in action against the enemy. While his platoon was securing Hill 755 (the Walled City), the enemy, using heavy automatic weapons and small-arms, counterattacked. Taking a position on a 50-foot-high wall he delivered heavy fire on the enemy. His ammunition was soon expended and although wounded, he remained at his post and threw his few grenades into the attackers causing many casualties. When his supply of grenades was exhausted his comrades from nearby foxholes tossed others to him and he left his position, braving a hail of fire, to retrieve and throw them at the enemy. The attackers continued to assault his position and Pfc. Brown, weaponless, drew his entrenching tool from his pack and calmly waited until they one-by-one peered over the wall, delivering each a crushing blow upon the head. Knocking 10 or 12 enemy from the wall, his daring action so inspired his platoon that they repelled the attack and held their position. Pfc. Brown's extraordinary heroism, gallantry, and intrepidity reflect the highest credit upon himself and was in keeping with the honored traditions of the military service. Pfc. Brown was reported missing in action and officially killed in action September 5, 1950.

†KAUFMAN, LOREN R.

Rank and Organization: Sergeant First Class, U.S. Army, Company G, 9th Infantry Regiment.
Born: July 27, 1923, The Dalles, Oregon.
Entered Service At: The Dalles, Oregon.
Place and Date: Near Yongsan, Korea, September 5, 1950.
Citation: Sfc. Kaufman distinguished himself by conspicuous gallantry and intrepidity above and beyond the call of duty in action against the enemy. On the night of September 4th the company was in a defensive position on 2 adjoining hills. His platoon was occupying a strongpoint 2 miles away protecting the battalion flank. Early on September 5th the company was attacked by an enemy battalion and his platoon was ordered to reinforce the company. As his unit moved along a ridge it encountered a hostile encircling force. Sfc. Kaufman, running forward, bayoneted the enemy's lead scout and engaged the column in a rifle and grenade assault. His quick vicious attack so surprised the enemy that they retreated in confusion. When his platoon joined the company he discovered that the enemy had taken commanding ground and pinned the company down in a draw. Without hesitation, Sfc. Kaufman charged

the enemy lines firing his rifle and throwing grenades. During the action, he bayoneted 2 enemy and seizing an unmanned machine gun, delivered deadly fire on the defenders. Following this encounter the company regrouped and resumed the attack. Leading the assault he reached the ridge, destroyed a hostile machine gun position, and routed the remaining enemy. Pursuing the hostile troops he bayoneted 2 more and then rushed a mortar position shooting the gunners. Remnants of the enemy fled to a village and Sfc. Kaufman led a patrol into the town, dispersed them, and burned the buildings. The dauntless courage and resolute intrepid leadership of Sfc. Kaufman were directly responsible for the success of his company in regaining its positions, reflecting great credit upon himself and upholding the esteemed traditions of the military service.

OFFICIAL COMMUNIQUÉ:
TOKYO, Tuesday, Sept. 5 (AP)
—Eighth Army communiqué 74, issued today at 10:50 A.M. (8:50 P.M. Monday, Eastern Daylight Time):

The enemy continued his push through the R.O.K. (Republic of Korea) Capital Division south of Kigye toward Kyongju yesterday and last night. Regrouping friendly forces have been unable to stop the advance as the Communists crossed the Pohang-Yongchon road in force.

Angang changed hands twice yesterday with its present situation unconfirmed. At dawn the Third Division defending Pohang was under heavy infantry and tank attack. The Eighth Division is attempting to restore its right flank which was forced back 1,000 yards yesterday.

An enemy attack in the First Cavalry Division sector northeast of Waegwan, made at 4:30 A.M. today, has made no advance, according to last reports. Late yesterday a unit of the division succeeded in entering the walled town but supporting elements were attacked during the night and driven back.

United States forces attacking west of Yongsan in the Second Division sector advanced more than 3,000 yards yesterday against light to medium resistance. The enemy abandoned supplies, equipment and arms in withdrawing. Units in the north of the sector reported little activity. All elements of the division are in contact.

An enemy attack against the right regiment of the Twenty-fifth Division at 6:30 A.M. succeeded in displacing one company. Reserve units are counter-attacking to restore positions.

—Release 375, issued at 12:10 P.M. Monday (10:10 P.M. Sunday, eastern Daylight Time):

The Navy summary follows carrier-based planes of Task Force 77 responded yesterday to an emergency call for close air support of United Nations ground forces.

Scheduled operations then in progress were halted and Navy Corsair fighter-bombers and Skyraider bombers rushed to the scene of battle west of Masan.

Troop concentrations, tanks, artillery and transport were the targets for the precision Navy pilots. Two tanks were definitely destroyed and a number of troop concentrations in the southern sector were heavily bombed and strafed.

Pilots returning to their carrier bases attacked targets of opportunity in Kwangju, destroyed sixteen warehouses, one factory and seven boxcars. Damage was done to the Kwangju railroad yards with fires visible for thirty miles.

Task Force 77, a part of the Seventh fleet, is under the command of Rear Admiral E. C. Ewen. United States Navy ships, standing off the east and south coasts, continued delivering the direct gunfire support to ground forces north of Pohang and in the Chinhae Bay areas.

The eight-inch guns of a Navy heavy cruiser silenced one artillery battery. Its fire was concentrated on troops, supplies, artillery and road junctions between Paedun and Chindong.

Making use of aerial spotting, five troop concentrations in the southern sector were hit with excellent results.

A British destroyer on the west coast inspected a junk overloaded with North Korean refugees. Asked where they were bound, they answered: "Anywhere but North Korea."

—Release 376, covering aerial operations and issued at 1:25 P.M. Monday (10:25 P.M. Sunday, Eastern Daylight Time):

Far East Air Forces fighters and bombers and Royal Australian Air Force fighters yesterday scoured North Korean front-line positions in nearly 500 combat sorties.

It was the third day of the all-out effort in support of United Nations ground troops and the heaviest tactical air assault in the sixty-nine consecutive days of the Air Force's activity in Korea.

Additional reconnaissance, service and cargo flights by U.S.A.F. aircraft, raised the number of sorties flown to over 600, the highest daily total reached thus far.

A majority of the combat sorties struck targets within or close behind the battle lines. F-80 and F-51 fighters and B-26 light bombers, B-29's medium bombers, R.A.A.F. Mustangs and Marine F-4-U's hammered at tactical targets in all areas of the front, destroying large quantities of Communist material and inflicting many casualties.

B-29's of the F.E.A.F. Bomber Command bombed tactical objectives in nine towns west of the Naktong or on the lines of approach to the northern sector which were in active use by the North Korean forces as staging areas or supply distribution centers.

Marshalling yards, barracks, storage depots and other military targets chosen after careful reconnaissance were hit with 480 tons of bombs.

Results were excellent in all cases. Military installations were left burning and numerous secondary explosions caused by fuel or ammunition depot destruction were observed. The towns attacked were Chechon, Andong, Uisong, Sangju, Chongju, Koreyong, Yongdong, Hyopchon and Samga.

—Release 377, timed at 3:55 P.M. Monday (1:55 A.M. Monday, Eastern Daylight Time):

Small-scale enemy attacks in the vicinity of Kogan, beginning at 7:00 A.M., Sept. 4, were repulsed by elements of the United States Twenty-fifth Infantry Division without loss of ground. Mopping-up action against by-passed, infiltrated enemy pockets of considerable size continues throughout the division sector.

Marine units, operating with the United States Second Infantry Division, have advanced approximately two miles west of Yongsan against heavy resistance. Three enemy tanks were destroyed and large amounts of enemy material were captured during the drive. Elements of the United States Second Infantry Division, operating along the central front, made small gains in organizing and strengthening their positions.

The United States First Cavalry Division continued to defend the Waegwan sector against heavy enemy pressure. One enemy attack across the Naktong River north of Waegwan was repulsed by a counter-attack after enemy forces had seized a hill in that sector. The counter-attack by friendly forces drove the enemy from the high ground and out defensive positions were consolidated. Other elements of the division were forced by heavy enemy attacks to withdraw to positions in the vicinity of Tabu, where a counter-attack is in progress to restore original positions.

R.O.K. (Republic of Korea) Army forces along the northern front continued their defense of the line against repeated enemy attacks. There were local gains and losses registered by our forces, with no material change in defense positions. A heavy attack against elements of the R.O.K. First Division forced slight withdrawals in the area north of Sinnyong, but a later counter-attack restored most of the lost ground. Elements of the R.O.K. Sixth Division repulsed two attacks Sept. 3 with no change in positions.

Units of the R.O.K. Capital Division were forced by heavy attacks yesterday to withdraw southward in the Kigye area. Enemy elements infiltrated into the area north of Angang where they were engaged by United States forces supporting the R.O.K. Army in that sector.

Two attacks Sept. 3 against the R.O.K. Third Division in the area north of Pohang were repulsed. Early today the enemy launched another attack which also was repulsed.

—Release 378, Air, timed at 8:10 P.M. Monday (5:10 A.M. Monday, Eastern Daylight Time):

United States Air Force B-26 light bombers and F-82 night fighters were taking over at dusk tonight after F-80 jets and F-51 Mustangs had hammered the North Korean ground troops incessantly since dawn.

Generally fair weather enabled the day fighters to put in perhaps what will prove to be the busiest of their seventy days in the Korean conflict. They used forward Korean airstrips to replenish their bombs, bullets, rockets and fuel for repeated blows at front-line enemy troops.

Meanwhile, B-29 Superforts of the R.E.A.F. Bomber Command operating in small formations and even individually attacked a series of railway bridges north of the Thirty-eight Parallel to further disrupt Communist logistic channels. Weather was spotty in some sectors and some of the Superforts attacked targets of opportunity rather than their primary target because the latter was obscured by clouds.

Neither fighters nor flak opposed the B-29's which bombed with "generally good to excellent results" according to a preliminary analysis this afternoon.

A flight of F-80 jets led by Lieut. Col. Ben I. Mayo of Fort Smith, Ark., scattered a North Korean troops concentration on a mountainside twenty miles northwest of Taegu at the request of the forward air controller. "That sure beats climbing the mountain to get at them," the controller said. Reporting excellent results, according to First Lieut. Kenneth J. Wilkes of Moscow, Idaho, a pilot in the flight.

The jets worked along the northern battle line in close support, hitting tanks, artillery positions, troop concentrations and railroad rolling stock. In the Pohang area they destroyed ten gasoline tanks concealed under stacks of straw. One flight strafed an airfield near Sinmak, seventy-five miles northwest of Seoul and also the entrance to a railroad tunnel near by.

Marine F-4-U's reported knocking out an artillery emplacement six miles east of Kumwi with napalm [jellied gasoline bombs]. They left the area blazing, they reported.

B-26 crews today fired more than 31,000 rounds of .50-caliber ammunition and 150 high-explosive and fragmentation bombs against North Korean targets. A delayed report told of one B-26 piloted by Capt. James H. Morrow of Sweetwater, Tex., destroying what appeared to be an ammunition train in an attack on a railroad bridge across the Imjin River at Munsan, twenty-two miles northwest of Seoul, before dawn this morning.

"I couldn't see anything on the bridge but my first bomb caused a violent secondary explosion as it hit one of the approaches," Captain Morrow said. He then made several strafing attacks and dropped two more high-explosive bombs on the bridge, resulting in more explosions and fires.

Captain Morrow said that twenty-five minutes after the first bomb was dropped smaller explosions were observed on the bridge. The glare from the burning target was visible from his plane when he was about forty miles south of the target area.

"I still don't know what I hit," the Texan said, "but it sure made a big bang,"

—Release 379, timed at 1:50 A.M. today and issued at 2:15 A.M. (12:15 P.M., Monday, Eastern Daylight Time):

In the United States Twenty-fifth Division sector, United Nations forces continued to eliminate an enemy force that had infiltrated their lines during the day. Units of the Twenty-fifth Division reported receiving enemy high-velocity and mortar fire in this area.

Elements of the United States Second Division, with United States Marines, continued to advance in their sector against light enemy resistance. In this area, enemy groups, accompanied by armor, were reported withdrawing to the west.

Friendly forces in the United States First Cavalry Division sector are reported meeting strong enemy resistance in the walled village of Kasan, approximately fifteen miles northeast of Waegwan. A moderate enemy penetration reported northeast of Waegwan last night is being engaged by friendly forces. Another enemy force is reported about sixteen miles southwest of Taegu, moving toward that city.

Elsewhere on the northern front there has been no significant enemy activity.

—Release 380, timed by Gen. Douglas MacArthur's headquarters at 8:45 A.M. (6:45 P.M., Eastern Daylight Time, Monday):

United States fighter planes took off from Korean airfields around 6:30 A.M. today for another day-long smash at Communist troops along the battle lines. The F-80 jet Shooting Stars were in the air first, followed by F-51 Mustangs.

Weather in Korea today will be clear, according to early morning predictions, with some broken clouds. Visibility will be good.

Night intruder missions were flown by B-26 light bombers and F-82 twin Mustang all-weather fighters. Enemy troops at a small town northeast of Chinju were attacked by one flight of B-26's with napalm and fragmentation bombs, routing them. Capt. Elbert M. Stringer of Moberly, Mo., said he saw eight large fires as his plane left the area.

Some of the B-26s and F-82s struck at rail and road bridges close behind the lines. One railroad bridge at Kumchon was heavily damaged, according to Lieut. Col. Leland A. Walker of Salt Lake City, Utah.

F-82s flew armed reconnaissance missions above the battle line during the night. The returning pilots reported intercepting supplies and reinforcements being moved by the enemy to the southeast area of Korea.

Some F-80 jets and marine Corsairs flew late yesterday afternoon until well after dark. They operated chiefly in the Kigye and Andong areas.

F-80 pilot, First Lieut. Emory E. Hodges of Leaksville, N.C. reported he saw Communist troops retreating about six miles southwest of Kigye.

"We saw them going the opposite direction from the battle areas, making tracks in a dry creek bed," he said. "We strafed them and fired rockets. We made our passes before they finally replied with token fire, but jets in out flight weren't hit."

One F-51 Mustang group from Japan that rearmed and reloaded in Korea flew 110 sorties yesterday, with practically all in close proximity to the fighting United Nations troops. Reports on late flights showed damage included many troops killed, artillery and gun emplacements silenced and vehicles heavily damaged.

H-5 helicopters and L-5 light planes of M.A.T.S. [Military Air Transport Service] air rescue service flew more than thirty missions in close support of United Nations troops on all fronts yesterday.

Twenty-five critically wounded ground troops were safely removed from the fighting zone to hospitals in the rear area. Rescue craft dropped into the front lines with deliveries of whole blood five times and carried in medical personnel and supplies in three missions.

†CRAIG, GORDON M.

Rank and Organization: Corporal, U.S. Army, 16th Reconnaissance Company, 1st Cavalry Division.
Born: August 3, 1929, Brockton, Massachusetts.
Entered Service At: Brockton, Massachusetts.
Place and Date: Near Kasan, Korea, September 10, 1950.
Citation: Cpl. Craig, 16th Reconnaissance Company, distinguished himself by conspicuous gallantry and intrepidity above and beyond the call of duty in action against the enemy. During the attack on a strategic enemy-held hill his company's advance was subjected to intense hostile grenade, mortar and small-arms fire. Cpl. Craig and 4 comrades moved forward to eliminate an enemy machine gun nest that was hampering the company's advance. At that instant an enemy machine-gunner hurled a grenade at the advancing men. Without hesitating or attempting to seek cover for himself, Cpl. Craig threw himself on the grenade and smothered its burst with his body. His intrepid and selfless act, in which he unhesitatingly gave his life for his comrades, inspired them to attack with such ferocity that they annihilated the enemy machine gun crew, enabling the company to continue its attack. Cpl. Craig's noble self-sacrifice reflects the highest credit upon himself and upholds the esteemed traditions of the military service.

OFFICIAL COMMUNIQUÉ:

UNITED STATES EIGHTH ARMY HEADQUARTERS, Korea, Monday, Sept. 11 (U.P.)
—Eighth Army communiqué 84, issued this forenoon:

Regiments of the R.O.K. (Republic of Korea) Eighth Division made general advances of 2,000 yards yesterday across the northern part of the Yongehon-Ryongju road and now hold positions northeast of the road.

In the attack friendly forces captured one tank, one self-propelled gun, four anti-tank guns, one howitzer and seven trucks. There was no change and little activity in the Pohang-Anang sector.

A regiment of the R.O.K. First Division repulsed numerous small attacks in the area southeast of the Walled Town.

Enemy pressure continued against the First Cavalry Division during the past twenty-four hours with most activity concentrated in the Walled Town area where several separate attacks were repulsed. During the night other cavalry elements were forced back 300 yards in the sector east of Waegwan. The road north of Taegu was under heavy artillery fire last night.

An attack against the Second Division before dawn this morning was contained and no ground was lost. Elements of the division were under scattered artillery and mortar fire during the night. Yesterday there was little activity.

Enemy activity against the Twenty-fifth Division during the past twenty-four hours was confined to a small attack against the right-flank unit which was repulsed with no loss of ground.

TOKYO, Monday, Sept. 11 (AP)
—Release 410, issued at 2:10 P.M., Sunday (12:10 A.M. Sunday, Eastern Daylight Time):

Clearing weather Saturday afternoon permitted United States Air Force aircraft to renew their pounding of Communist forces throughout the immediate battle areas. Bomber Command B-29 Superfortresses, meanwhile, continued both the strategic bombing of military-industrial targets in North Korea and the interdiction program against enemy lines of communications.

One hundred eighty-seven of the daily total of 397 sorties were flown in close support of ground operations. Joined by Royal Australian Air Force Mustangs and five United States Marine Corps F-4U Aircraft, Fifth Air Force F-80 jet fighter bombers, F-51 fighters and F-82 all-weather fighters bombed, rocketed and strafed troop positions and tactical targets all along the battle lines. Working under the direct control of Air Force forward controllers, three tanks, eleven trucks, ten other vehicles, six box cars and two road bridges were damaged.

Thirty-seven buildings housing North Korean troops were set afire, resulting in an unknown number of casualties.

Interdiction operations to the rear of enemy positions by F-80 jet fighters seeking out military targets caused unobserved damage in thirty-nine separate areas. Farther north, five buildings at Pyongyang airfield were set afire and six box cars in rail yards in that city damaged by strafing.

Attacking rail yards at Suwon, Seoul, Inchon, Sangju and Osan, B-26 light bombers reported excellent results. At Osan, explosions in a warehouse in the marshaling yards destroyed the building. Trackage in all rail yards was extensively damaged with the choke-point at Osan suffering considerable damage.

Striking at bridges, tunnels and trackage near the West Coast, the light bombers destroyed a small railroad bridge two miles north of Suwon, knocked out a span of a double railroad bridge three miles south of Munsan and damaged a tunnel one mile to the south of that city.

Secondary expositions followed the bombing of a tunnel near Nonsan, indicating either an ammunition dump or a train hiding from the bomber attacks. Another tunnel, fifteen miles northwest of Wonju was damaged and a railroad bridge was destroyed by direct hits.

Night intruder missions were continued against Communist communication lines and vehicular traffic by fourteen B-26 bombers and two F-4U aircraft. They dropped general purpose, fragmentary and napalm bombs on targets near Seoul, Kaesong, Chongju, Inchon, Suwon, Pyongtaek, Chunchon, and Pohang. Damage was observed in this Kaesong marshaling yards where explosions and fire were seen following the bomb run. Explosions were noted along rail lines as well.

F.E.A.F. Bomber Command B-29 Superfortresses heavily attacked the Chosen Nitrogen Explosive plant at Haeju with excellent results. Large secondary explosions followed the visual bombing. Other Superfortresses struck at railroad bridges and tracks, cutting the tracks in nine places between Pyongyang and Sariwon, and in four places between Sariwon and Kaesong.

A highway bridge at Sinanju was hit, destroying three spans. Direct hits on a railroad bridge twenty miles east of Pyongyang knocked out one span. Nine other railroad bridges were damaged by the bombers.

Transport aircraft delivered a total of forty-five tons of cargo and 318 passengers to Korea during the day.

One Royal Australian Air Force Mustang was lost during ground support operations.

—Release 411, issued at 3:50 P.M., Sunday (2:50 A.M., Sunday, Eastern Daylight Time):

Action along the United Nations front was confined largely to small scale and probing attacks by the Reds with some counter-attacks by United Nations ground forces. One attack supported by tanks was broken up in the Second Division sector when artillery dispersed the attacking infantry and the tanks were forced to withdraw. An all-day-long attack against other elements of the division was repulsed.

In the First Cavalry Division sector two small scale enemy attacks supported by artillery and mortar fire failed to gain.

Elements of the R.O.K. (Republic of Korea) Second Corps defended against a heavy day-long attack without loss of ground while other elements of the corps advanced north and captured over 300 small arms in the area north of Yongchon. In the East sector heavy enemy attacks forced elements of United Nations forces to make limited withdrawals to new positions where the attack was contained.

R.O.K. Marines operating in the Tongyong area repulsed an attack without loss of ground.

United Nations forces inflicted 1,377 casualties on the enemy and captured 200 prisoners during the period.

—Release 412, issued 7:15 P.M., Sunday (6:15 A.M., Sunday, Eastern Daylight Time):

United States Air Force B-29 Superforts and F-80 jet Shooting Stars were active today, taking advantage of good flying weather to support United Nations ground troops fighting Communists on four fronts along the Korean battle line.

More than forty B-29s bombed North Korean targets visually. One element struck railroad bridges and marshaling yards in the North and Central sectors of Korea while other Superforts in formation hit a chemical plant at Sunchon (Junson), about thirty miles north of Pyongyang.

The fifty-acre plant produces ammonia and sulphurous acid and chemical fertilizer, all of them necessary to the manufacture of munitions. The factory buildings are constructed of unusually heavy concrete and steel sections. Pre-strike photos indicated that this plant was being converted to production of war materials since the elimination of the primary chemical plant at Konan by B-29 strikes in a three-pronged attack on July 30, Aug. 1, and 3.

Air crews reported good results in the B-29 strikes today. Some flak was reported in the central area of Korea but no enemy fighters were encountered.

The F-80 jets ranged both below and above the Thirty-eighth Parallel today with about 125 sorties reported thus far. About 70 percent of the flights were in support of the ground troops in the battle areas.

The remaining F-80 flights went to the Pyongyang area above the Thirty-eighth. The jets made sweeps on airfields and attacked railroad equipment and convoys southward from Pyongyang in the direction of the battle areas. Returning pilots reported good weather and excellent results.

Today's F-80 effort was an increase of about 50 percent over the last few days, due to good weather, according to Col. James P. Lyle, Denton, Tex., who sent the jets off at first light this morning from a base in Japan. "The interrogation reports show the men hit their targets right on the nose," he said.

Some of the F-80s today set two warehouses containing military stores on fire, damaged a medium tank and smacked several trucks loaded with troops, all in a concentrated area northwest of Pohang. One flight of jets made ten direct hits on a building believed to be an enemy command post at Chinbo, twenty miles west and inland from Yongdok. They also strafed a convoy on the road in that area.

Capt. Edward R. Johnston, Reynolds, Ill., said he hit a railroad tunnel, a bridge, and troops five miles east of Angang. "We routed the troops from under the bridge right where the air controllers said they were," said Captain Johnston, flying an F-80. "There were at least fifteen casualties." His flight also knocked out two field pieces three miles north of the town.

Three camouflaged tanks and enemy troops on the road north of Taegu were attacked by F-80s led by First Lieut. Donald L. Leogering, Minneapolis, Minn. "We got at least three direct hits on two of the tanks and scattered the troops with some killed," he said.

B-26 light bombers and F-51 Mustangs were landing late today and reports were fragmentary. One tank was destroyed and another damaged by F-51s but there were no details.

F-82 twin Mustangs returned today from night intruder missions with pilots reporting the center span of a bridge of the Naktong River knocked out and a ferry damaged by 500-pound bombs.

—Release 413, issued at 3:10 A.M., Monday (2:10 P.M., Sunday Eastern Daylight Time):

In the extreme northeast sector of the United Nations perimeter elements of the R.O.K. (Republic of Korea) Third Division were reported advancing against light enemy resistance.

In the R.O.K. Sixth Division sector enemy action was limited to patrol action during the day. Other units of the R.O.K. Second Corps reported minor enemy attacks but these were repulsed without any loss of ground. United Nations forces in the Yongchon area continued to advance against disorganized enemy resistance.

An enemy attack in the United States First Cavalry Division sector yesterday afternoon was contained. There has been no change in the lines in this area.

Continued enemy patrols were reported by the United States Second Division yesterday afternoon. Counter patrol action by friendly forces accounted for thirty-five killed. Other units of the Second Division continued to eliminate enemy infiltration groups in their rear.

In the United States Twenty-fifth Division sector there was no significant enemy activity.

—Release 414, issued by Gen. Douglas MacArthur at 8:45 A.M., Monday (7:45 P.M., Sunday, Eastern Daylight Time):

The United States Air Force increased its total sorties of all types to about 500 yesterday, with excellent results reported. More than 500 sorties were flown by the Fifth Air Force in support of the United Nations ground troops with the largest percentage of this figure credited to the battle areas.

With good weather forecast again today, F-80 jets and F-51 propeller-driven Mustangs took off at 6:00 A.M. for specific targets in Korea.

The close support sorties yesterday accounted for damage to many tanks, trucks, supply dumps, gun emplacements, military buildings, and boxcars. Some of the Fifth Air Force planes also went above the Thirty-eighth Parallel and damaged boxcars, railroad tracks, and bridges, and other installations and equipment the Communists need badly.

The F.E.A.F. Bomber Command's B-29 Superforts visually bombed North Korean rail bridges, marshaling yards and a chemical plant at Sunchon yesterday. Crews reported the fifty-acre chemical plant, located thirty miles north of Pyongyang, was severely damaged. The plant was important to the Communists' munition industry.

Weather last night permitted some Fifth Air Force planes to further harass and cripple the enemy. All-weather F-82 Twin Mustangs attacked convoys on roads in the Taejon, Pohang, and Waegwan areas. The pilots reported plenty of traffic in that area and a dozen or more vehicles destroyed, with others damaged.

Two Marine F-4U Corsairs were sent to the Yongsan area by air controllers last night where troops were located in small villages, with Untied Nations forces only half a mile away. The troops positions were strafed for twenty minutes. Results were unobserved because of darkness.

Late reports on B-26 light bomber flights that landed early last night showed that the Invaders had worked over supply lines from Seoul to the battle zone, and had flown some missions in direct support of ground forces. Railroad tracks and rolling stock in the Seoul area were attacked with 1,000-pound bombs and strafing attacks.

One flight of four B-26s led by Lieut. Col. Abraham Shook of Clovis, N.M., was directed by air controllers to enemy troop concentrations five miles west of Pohang. "We covered the area with fragmentation bombs and 4,000 rounds of caliber .50 ammunition," Shook said. "The controller said we did the job. I could see several fires as we left."

†LOPEZ, BALDOMERO
Rank and Organization: First Lieutenant, U.S. Marine Corps, Company A, 1st Battalion, 5th Marines, 1st Marine Division (Rein).
Born: August 23, 1925, Tampa, Florida.
Entered Service At: Tampa, Florida.
Place and Date: During Inchon invasion in Korea, September 15, 1950.
Citation: For conspicuous gallantry and intrepidity at the risk of his life above and beyond the call of duty as a rifle platoon commander of Company A, in action against enemy aggressor forces. With his platoon, 1st Lt. Lopez was engaged in the reduction of immediate enemy beach defenses after landing with the assault waves. Exposing himself to hostile fire, he moved forward alongside a bunker and prepared to throw a hand-grenade into the next pillbox whose fire was pinning down that sector of the beach. Taken under fire by an enemy automatic

weapon and hit in the right shoulder and chest as he lifted his arm to throw, he fell backward and dropped the deadly missile. After a moment, he turned and dragged his body forward in an effort to retrieve the grenade and throw it. In critical condition from pain and loss of blood, and unable to grasp the hand-grenade firmly enough to hurl it, he chose to sacrifice himself rather than endanger the lives of his men and, with a sweeping motion of his wounded right arm, cradled the grenade under him and absorbed the full impact of the explosion. His exceptional courage, fortitude, and devotion to duty reflect the highest credit upon 1st Lt. Lopez and the U.S. Naval Service. He gallantly gave his life for his country.

Note: The following is a newspaper account of the preceding battle for which Lt. Lopez was awarded the Medal of Honor:

U.N. FORCES ATTACK IN SOUTH TO PIN DOWN REDS AS ALLIES PUSH SWIFTLY AHEAD TOWARD SEOUL
• • •
Tanks Rushed to Front and Allied Planes Pound Highways
• • •
Fifteen Marines Injured, None Is Killed in Inchon Action
• • •

TOKYO, Saturday, Sept. 16 — While United Nations troops pushed ahead quickly after yesterday's landing by United States marines at Inchon, seaport for the captured Korean Republican capital of Seoul, United Nations forces along the 120-mile Allied perimeter in the south struck offensively today to pin down North Korean divisions and stop them from making any move northward.

Front-line reports that were not, however, confirmed at Gen. Douglas MacArthur's headquarters said that one strike was made from Waegwan northwest, in the direction of Seoul, and the second on the front of the United States Second Division, along the Naktong.

This morning there was no word available of their progress, but observers here believed that the attacks, in the region where the enemy previously had been intensifying his pressure, were holding actions to pin down the North Korean troops rather than attempts to break through and join up with the new beachhead.

From Taegu to Seoul is a distance of about 170 air miles, and along the perimeter the Allied forces heretofore had only a scanty army reserve that could be thrown in for such a blow.

South Korean national police, now part of the Republican armed forces, said that "friendly" troops this morning had reached the town of Kimpo and its airfield—largest and best in Korea. This is about twelve air miles from Wolmi Island, where marines crashed ashore in a massive amphibious landing far behind enemy lines with air, navy and infantry support.

The field, which had been heavily hit by Allied planes, was not yet usable, they said, but was securely held either by United States troops or Korean advance guards.

Other troops, according to the South Korean report, had moved through Inchon, where the marine drive across the causeway from Wolmi, plus two beachhead landings yesterday evening, had controlled the dock area last night. Allied troops were reported to have reached Yongdungpo, a suburb of Seoul, on the south bank of the Han River.

Yongdungpo, about four miles from the center of the capital, is the site of important railroad yards where now ruined bridges cross the Han. There is no word, however, that Allied forces had yet penetrated north of the river.

The Chief of Staff of the Korean Army, in a radio broadcast, asserted optimistically that Seoul was in Allied hands, a statement that was not confirmed by General MacArthur's headquarters.

Air observers spotted a large Communist convoy moving in the vicinity of Kaesong, just south of the Thirty-eighth Parallel, on the road from the North Korean capital at Pyongyang. The trucks were headed southward, and it was indicated that the enemy might be attempting to move up to the Inchon area some of the three divisions he is believed to have held out of the battleline as uncommitted reserve, taking the risk of Allied air attack in daylight hours to get men through to the menaced sector.

It was learned at Pusan, meanwhile, that the South Korean Government, which had left only a small contingent at the temporary capital at Taegu, was rushing preparations to return to Seoul as soon as possible.

At the same time, front line reports, also unconfirmed officially, said that the general Allied drive along the perimeter in the south was at least to prevent Communist forces there from pulling out to reinforce the apparently lightly defended Inchon-Seoul area. Tanks were rushed up to the front and Allied planes, flying through cloudy weather, came down to hit the Communist front and the highways behind, over which troops would have to move northward toward Inchon.

The attacks were reported to have been launched shortly after dawn this morning, with heavy fighting following in most sectors of the front.

An Eighth Army communiqué at 11:10 o'clock this morning, however, made no mention of the morning's activities but reported offensive action by North Koreans except in the eastern sector around Angang, where Korean Republicans scored advances of up to 2,000 yards. The Eighth Army said that the Second Division had lost some ground and that the Twenty-fifth was attacking to regain positions it had lost early yesterday.

Along the front north of Taegu, nearest to the Inchon beachhead many miles away, an attack was launched at 9:00 A.M. by the United States First Cavalry Division, the South Korean First Division and the British brigade of two battalions of the Argyll and Sutherland Highlanders and the Middlesex Regiment.

It was preceded by a violent ten-minute bombardment in which some artillery weapons new to Korea played a part. But in this area low-lying clouds shed intermittent rains that hampered air support.

The main thrust was toward Waegwan, at the crossing of the Naktong on the highway that leads to Taejon and Seoul, down which United States troops retreated after the fall of the capital.

United States and South Korean troops that had been many weeks in the line faced four enemy divisions—estimated at 24,000 men—and front-line reports indicated that the success of the drive depends on the strength of the fresh reserves that the United Nations might be able to throw into the battle.

The attack was under Maj. Gen. Frank W. Milburn, former commander of the United States Seventh Army and deputy commander of the United States Army in Europe. The force under his command—the cavalry, British and the Korean republicans—has now been constituted as the First Corps, second of two new corps organizations formed in Korea.

Wading in mudflats and carrying scaling ladders to climb cliffs and embankments, the marines landed last night on the tiny island of Wolmi, a quarter mile from the main dock area at Inchon and linked with the city by a long concrete causeway. Last evening, as the thirty-foot tide receded, they pushed ashore two beachheads on the mainland and drove inland toward Seoul, twenty-two air miles away, and the Kimpo airfield.

Allied planes soared overhead or swooped down low to hit Communist gun positions to clear the way for the advancing troops, and a fleet of United States and British cruisers and destroyers hovered off-shore to offer gunfire support.

Reports said that thousands of United States infantry were aboard convoy ships or landing to back the first punch delivered by the marines.

One front-line report said that the infantrymen were landing behind the Marines with the morning's tide at 7:45 o'clock. These, like the men of the First Marine Division, were fresh troops. This beachhead attack was made without pulling out forces from the United Nations defense perimeter in the south.

Other reports indicated that the Communists had at least some tanks in the area. One was knocked out as it fired across the causeway yesterday on the Marines on Wolmi Island who were clearing out the remaining pockets with flamethrowers.

Navy and Marine planes fanned out over the roads ahead of the advancing troops to block off enemy attempts to reinforce the Inchon area. Fighters of the Far East Air Forces took off again at 6:00 o'clock this morning in broken clouds as B-26 light bombers returned after night missions. The Air Force announced that 400 sorties were flown yesterday, about half in support of the landing operation.

The landing was the second big amphibious operation of the Korean war. Last July troops of the United States First Cavalry Division went ashore without opposition at Pohang on the east coast. But these troops moved out to hold a section of the hard-pressed United Nations perimeter.

The landing was made under direct observation of General MacArthur, who cruised the beachheads in a naval launch after the marines went ashore. The Tenth Corps, a new unit designation under which the landing force was identified, was under command of his Chief of Staff, Maj. Gen. Edward N. Almond.

The landing came after a convoy of 260 ships, keeping strict radio silence, had cruised around the southern tip of Korea and deep into the Yellow Sea to reach its objective off Inchon. It was preceded by the heaviest bombardment by air and naval guns since the war began.

Forty-eight hours before the landing, cruisers and destroyers under Rear Admiral John M. Higgins, commanding the bombardment force, had moved onshore through tricky, reef-strewn channels to fire pointblank on Communist shore batteries of three-inch guns and lighter seventy-five's from Wolmi to the mouth of the Han River.

Planes followed them from carriers of Rear Admiral John M. Hoskins, raining bombs on the Communist defenses. The final barrage ended only a few seconds before the first waves of marines went ashore at Wolmi Island.

Reports said that the landing was one of the most difficult that the marines—men of the First Division, veterans of Guadalcanal and the Pacific—had yet made. The men waded ashore through deep sticky mud and tidal flats that had been sown with mines, only some of which had been exploded by the naval gunfire. They had cliffs and embankments to scale on Wolmi Island and smaller So Wolmi Do, a tiny island that joins it at low tide and whose lighthouse is one of the beacons at the entrance to Inchon Harbor.

But the preliminary bombardment had knocked out every gun emplacement. Less than half an hour after the first wave had hit the beaches about an hour after dawn, the marines had hoisted the American flag at the highest point on Wolmi.

Tanks and half-tracks lumbered behind the green-clad marine infantrymen as they hit the beachhead, and these took up positions to fire along the causeway to Inchon's docks and sweep any enemy counter-attack from that direction. None was forthcoming. Resistance, according to reports from Korea, was "negligible", and marine casualties were unofficially reported as fifteen hurt or wounded and none killed in the initial landing.

Then the blow at Wolmi was followed by a pause that lasted most of the day. It was not until near sundown that the mainland landing was made as the marines from Wolmi moved over the breakwater to the Inchon docks to thrust inland.

Most recent reports gave no account of enemy resistance, and it was in doubt what the Communist "People's Army" might have been able to throw against the Allied action.

The landing at Inchon was preceded by two diversionary blows, one at Kunsan, 100 miles to the south along the west coast, and another on the east at Pohang. The move at Kunsan was a feint in which the infantry had been instructed to make sure that attention was called to their presence offshore in the hope that Communist troops would be held away from the landing beachhead at Inchon.

Available reports did not make clear whether the landing actually was effected, but either by infantry, planes or gunfire, bridges were knocked out, installations on the small airfield were fired and some bridges were blown in the bluff that an attack from the sea was imminent. Off the east coast the largest United States war vessel, the battleship Missouri, aboard which the Japanese surrender was signed in 1945, played a part in the ruse.

Allied successes were reported at the eastern end of the perimeter south of the South Korean commando landing. The Eighth Army said South Korean troops had occupied Angang, hotly contested crossroads village where the Communists had dug defense positions. This represented an advance of 1,500 to 2,000 yards, crossing the Angang-Pohang road east of the village.

Intelligence officers said that near Angang one enemy regiment "ceased resistance," pulling out so fast that the attacking troops lost contact with it. To the east the enemy was fighting harder along the road and railway leading to Pohang, dropping artillery and mortar fire on the South Korean lines.

One South Korean patrol that crossed the flooded Hyongsang River was forced to withdraw under heavy artillery and small-arms fire yesterday afternoon. The headquarters communiqué said eight North Korean artillery positions had been knocked out during the day's fighting on the eastern front, with Allied air attacks causing heavy casualties among the invaders' ground forces.

One 122-mm. howitzer and three truckloads of ammunition and many small arms were captured, the communiqué said.

According to an official announcement the North Koreans suffered 2,683 casualties during the twenty-four hours ended at 10:00 A.M. yesterday and 166 prisoners had been captured along the whole perimeter.

†MONEGAN, WALTER C., JR.

Rank and Organization: Private First Class, U.S. Marine Corps, Company F, 2d Battalion, 1st Marines, 1st Marine Division (Rein).
Born: December 25, 1930, Melrose, Massachusetts.
Entered Service At: Seattle, Washington.
Place and Date: Near Sosa-ri, Korea, September 17 and 20, 1950.
Citation: For conspicuous gallantry and intrepidity at the risk of his life above and beyond the call of duty while serving as a rocket gunner, attached to Company F, in action against enemy aggressor forces. Dug in on a hill overlooking the main Seoul highway when 6 enemy tanks threatened to break through the battalion position during a predawn attack on September 17th, Pfc. Monegan promptly moved forward with his bazooka, under heavy hostile automatic weapons fire and engaged the lead tank at a range of less than 50 yards. After scoring a direct hit and killing the sole surviving tank-man with his carbine as he came through the escape hatch, he boldly fired 2 more rounds of ammunition at the oncoming tanks, disorganizing the attack and enabling our tank crews to continue blasting their 90-mm. guns. With his own and adjacent company's position threatened by annihilation when an overwhelming enemy tank-infantry force bypassed the area and proceeded toward the battalion command post during the early morning of September 20, he seized his rocket launcher and, in total darkness, charged down the slope of the hill where the tanks had broken through. Quick to act when an illuminating shell lit the area, he scored a direct hit on one of the tanks as hostile fire and automatic-weapons fire raked the area at close range. Again exposing himself, he fired another round to destroy a second tank and, as the rear tank turned to retreat, stood upright to fire and was fatally struck down by hostile machine gun fire when another illuminating shell silhouetted him against the sky. Pfc. Monegan's daring initiative, gallant fighting spirit and courageous devotion to duty were contributing factors in the success of his company in repelling the enemy, and his self-sacrificing efforts throughout, sustain and enhance the highest traditions of the U.S. Naval Service. He gallantly gave his life for his country.

†COLLIER, JOHN W.

Rank and Organization: Corporal, U.S. Army, Company C, 27th Infantry Regiment.
Born: April 3, 1929, Worthington, Kentucky.
Entered Service At: Worthington, Kentucky.
Place and Date: Near Chindong-ni, Korea, September 19, 1950.
Citation: Cpl. Collier, Company C, distinguished himself by conspicuous gallantry and intrepidity above and beyond the call of duty in action against the enemy. While engaged in an assault on a strategic ridge strongly defended by a fanatical enemy, the leading elements of his company encountered intense automatic weapons and grenade fire. Cpl. Collier and 3 comrades volunteered and moved forward to neutralize an enemy machine gun position which was hampering the company's advance, but they were twice repulsed. On the third attempt, Cpl. Collier, despite heavy enemy fire and grenade barrages, moved to an exposed position ahead of his comrades, assaulted and destroyed the machine gun nest, killing at least 4 enemy soldiers. As he returned down the rocky, fire-swept hill and joined his squad, an enemy grenade landed in their midst. Shouting a warning to his comrades, he selflessly and unhesitatingly, threw himself upon the grenade and smothered its explosion with his body. This intrepid action saved his comrades from death or injury. Cpl. Collier's supreme personal bravery, consummate gallantry and noble self-sacrifice reflect untold glory upon himself and uphold the honored traditions of the military service.

†JECELIN, WILLIAM R.

Rank and Organization: Sergeant, U.S. Army, Company C, 35th Infantry Regiment, 25th Infantry Division.
Born: Baltimore, Maryland.
Entered Service At: Baltimore, Maryland.
Place and Date: Near Saga, Korea, September 19, 1950.
Citation: Sgt. Jecelin, Company C, distinguished himself by conspicuous gallantry and intrepidity above and beyond the call of duty in action against the enemy. His company was ordered to secure a prominent, saw-toothed ridge from a well-entrenched and heavily armed enemy. Unable to capture the objective in the first attempt, a frontal and flanking assault was launched. He led his platoon through heavy enemy fire and bursting shells, across rice-fields and rocky terrain, in a direct frontal attack on the ridge in order to draw fire away from the flanks. The unit advanced to the base of the cliff, where intense, accurate hostile fire stopped the attack. Realizing that an assault was the only solution, Sgt. Jecelin rose from his position firing his rifle and throwing grenades as he called on his men to follow him. Despite the intense enemy fire this attack carried to the crest of the ridge where the men were forced to take cover. Again he rallied his men and stormed the enemy strong-point. With fixed bayonets they charged into the face of antitank fire and engaged the enemy in hand-to-hand combat. After clubbing and slashing this force into submission the platoon was forced to take cover from direct frontal fire of a self-propelled gun. Refusing to be stopped he leaped to his feet and through sheer personal courage and fierce determination led his men in a new attack. At this instant a well-camouflaged enemy soldier threw a grenade at the remaining members of the platoon. He immediately lunged and covered the grenade with his body, absorbing the full force of the explosion to save those around him. This incredible courage and willingness to sacrifice himself for his comrades so imbued them with fury that they completely eliminated the enemy force. Sgt. Jecelin's heroic leadership and outstanding gallantry reflect the highest credit upon himself and uphold the esteemed traditions of the military service.

COMMISKEY, HENRY A., SR.
Rank and Organization: First Lieutenant (then 2d Lt.), U.S. Marine Corps, Company C, 1st Battalion, 1st Marines, 1st Marine Division.
Born: January 10, 1927, Hattiesburg, Mississippi.
Entered Service At: Hattiesburg, Mississipp.
Place and Date: Near Yongdungp'o, Korea, September 20, 1950.
Citation: For conspicuous gallantry and intrepidity at the risk of his life above and beyond the call of duty while serving as a platoon leader in Company C, in action against enemy aggressor forces. Directed to attack hostile forces well dug in on Hill 85, Lt. Commiskey spearheaded the assault, charging up the steep slopes on the run. Coolly disregarding the heavy machine gun and small-arms fire, he plunged on well forward of the rest of his platoon and was the first man to reach the crest of the objective. Armed only with a pistol, he jumped into a hostile machine gun emplacement occupied by 5 enemy troops and quickly disposed of 4 of the soldiers with his automatic pistol. Grappling with the 5th, Lt. Commiskey knocked him to the ground and held him until he could obtain a weapon from another member of his platoon and killed the last of the enemy gun-crew. Continuing his bold assault, he moved to the next emplacement, killed 2 more of the enemy and then led his platoon toward the rear nose of the hill to route the remainder of the hostile troops and destroy them as they fled from their positions. His valiant leadership and courageous fighting spirit served to inspire the men of his company to heroic endeavor in seizing the objective and reflect the highest credit upon 1st Lt. Commiskey and the U.S. Naval Service.

OFFICIAL COMMUNIQUÉ:
TOKYO, Thursday, Sept. 21 (AP)
—United States Eighth Army communiqué 100, issued at 8:30 P.M. Wednesday (7:30 A.M. Wednesday, Eastern Daylight Time):

The port of Pohang on the right flank of the United Nations line fell to the R.O.K. (Republic of Korea) Third Division this morning with no organized enemy resistance remaining at noon. On the northwest corner of the line the R.O.K. First Division continued its advance to sever supply routes from Kunwi leading south to the Taegu area. Right flank elements of the division were less than five miles from Kunwi while the left flank extended almost to Tabu.

The river crossing force of the United States Twenty-Fourth Division advanced five miles north today reaching high ground two miles northwest of Waegwan. Another unit attacked to a point three miles north of the city.

In the Second Division sector United States forces captured a hill five miles west of Yongsan against heavy enemy resistance and continued southwest for a four-mile advance. In late afternoon they were near the Naktong opposite Yongsan. Further north other elements of the division continued a build-up of their bridgehead. The bridgehead east of Chogye is now 3,000 yards deep and the one five miles south is approximately 1,000 yards deep.

The center of the Twenty-fifth Division was held back today by strong enemy defenses southwest of Haman. In the northern zone an advance of 8,000 yards put elements in that area near Chungan. On the southern flank United States troops using flame-throwers gained up to 1,500 yards against stubborn enemy pockets.

—United States Eighth Army communiqué 101, issued at 11:10 A.M. Thursday (10:10 P.M. Wednesday, Eastern Daylight Time):

United States forces advancing northwest toward Kumchon are now in control of the road from Taegu into Waegwan, with harassing fire the only interference. Two regiments of the Twenty-fourth Division fought yesterday to positions opposite each other just north of Waegwan. During the night the units on the east bank of the Naktong River began crossing to the west.

R.O.K. (Republic of Korea) First Division troops are encircling enemy forces south of Tabu which are engaged with the First Cavalry Division. R.O.K. troops have cut the road north from the town and United States troops are advancing from the south.

An element of the Second Division advanced 1,000 yards yesterday against the enemy bridgehead in the Hyonpung area. Another divisional unit reached the Naktong River opposite Yongsan late in the afternoon and put patrols across during the night.

The R.O.K. Third Division advanced 2,000 yards after taking Pohang yesterday morning while other R.O.K. units made similar advances all along the northern front against spotty enemy resistance.

—Release 468, issued by General MacArthur's headquarters at 12:15 P.M., Wednesday (11:15 P.M., Tuesday, Eastern Daylight Time):

A near-record number of sorties, 670, were flown Tuesday by United States Far East Air Forces planes. Of the total, the United States Fifth Air Force, Royal Australian and United States Marine fliers flew 500. The R.A.A.F. Mustangs and the Marines, under operational control of the Fifth Air Force, flew twenty-four and twelve of the sorties respectively.

Yesterday's operations were closely coordinated with those of the ground forces to insure maximum support to the attacking United Nations forces.

Communist casualties due to aerial strikes mounted as light bombers and fighters attacked large groups of fleeing troops. A force, estimated at 700, was bombed and strafed just forward of the Second Infantry Division front. Air Force forward controllers reported excellent results. Another group, approximately 1,500 strong, was brought under attack near Waegwan. Becoming confused by the aerial attack, they made easy targets for the B-26 light bombers and F-80 jet fighters.

Supply areas, ammunition dumps, tanks, trucks, rail cars, gun positions and enemy-occupied buildings were attacked with excellent results throughout the immediate battle line. To the rear of these lines light bombers and fighters flew interdiction and night intruder sorties both north and south of the Thirty-seventh Parallel.

The B-26s hit targets in Kumchon, Yongdon, Yoju, Waegwan, Taejon, Sariwon, Chochiwon, Andong, and Tanyang. Trains, rail lines, troop positions, and bridges were bombed with excellent results.

Fifth Air Force claims totaled thirty-five gun positions, a radio station, a power plant, fifteen enemy-occupied buildings, an ammunition dump, two bridges, twelve tanks, four locomotives, twenty-six box cars, one supply area, twenty-two trucks, and thirteen other vehicles either destroyed or damaged.

F.E.A.F. Bomber Command Superfortresses attacked North Korean military-industrial and communications targets in force. A railroad bridge had two spans knocked out by direct hits ten miles north of Kaeson. Rail lines were cut at fifteen separate points between Pyongyang and Sariwon, Suchon and Wonsan, Sariwon and Kumchon, and on the line between Andong and Chechon.

An isolated industrial target at Namchonjom was hit with excellent results and a near-by troop installation attacked with unknown results. At Kan a military storage area was bombed. Secondary explosions followed the bombardment and fires were burning long after the attacking planes had passed over the targets. At Hungnam, the Chosen nitrogen plant was bombed by radar.

With Kimpo airfield secured by United Nations forces a steady airlift of equipment and supplies for units operating in the north was started yesterday afternoon. The newly activated F.E.A.F. Combat Cargo Command delivered a total of 215 tons of cargo and personnel into the recaptured airfield by nightfall.

An additional ninety-seven tons of cargo were airlifted to other Korean bases by troop carrier aircraft.

—Release 469, issued at 3:15 P.M., Wednesday (2:15 A.M., Wednesday, Eastern Daylight Time):

Advance elements of the United States First Marine Division crossed the Han River this morning in the area west of Seoul. R.O.K. (Republic of Korea) marines operating with the United Nations forces in the Inchon-Seoul area have killed an estimated 450 Reds and have captured 927 prisoners since landing at Inchon.

Waegwan was entered yesterday by elements of the United States Twenty-fourth Division while other divisional units continued advances northward in the Naktong bridgehead area against moderate resistance.

Elements of the United States First Cavalry Division continued their advances in the Waegwan area against heavy resistance.

Units of the R.O.K. First Division have entered the Walled City area against stiff opposition. Other divisional elements continued their attack north and northwest in the area north of Taegu.

British units operating with the United States First Corps repulsed an enemy attack yesterday without loss of ground.

Another crossing of the Naktong River was made this morning by elements of the United States Second Division. Units in the original bridgehead continued the build-up in the area.

Units of the United States Twenty-fifth Division continued to advance against moderate opposition in the area west of Haman.

Elements of the R.O.K. Sixth Division reduced a pocket containing an estimated enemy battalion, inflicting heavy losses. The division continued its advance to the north in the Yongchon area.

The R.O.K. Eighth Division advanced several miles against light opposition.

Units of the R.O.K. Capital Division captured the high ground overlooking Kigye against moderate resistance.

Pohang was re-entered this morning by elements of the R.O.K. Division, Other units repulsed an enemy attack and continued their advances north of the Yongsan River.

United Nations forces inflicted 1,980 casualties on the enemy and captured 2,306 prisoners during the period.

—Release 470, issued at 9:00 P.M. Wednesday (8:00 A.M. Wednesday, Eastern Daylight Time):

Sixty B-29 Superforts split up into small formations today, some even flying singly, in an all day assault on thirty-seven separate targets ranging from an important military barracks area at Pyongyang to small sections of a key highway near Sinanju.

The unusual Superfort assignment, which produced excellent results, featured today's United States Air Force support of the United Nations offensive launched several days ago. Fighters again flew in full force from early morning until late evening. Most of the sorties were along the battle line, with excellent attacks by F-80s and F-51s against retreating enemy forces in the Waegwan area.

Some fighters went farther north on interdiction missions, but generally they stayed in the Pusan perimeter area where they could do the most good under careful coaching by ground and air spotters. Light bombers, B-26s were also out in force today in attacks on troops and vehicles from the battle line northward.

B-29s began their take-off from F.E.A.F. Bomber Command bases at dawn with the first flight striking the large North Korean troop training and barracks area in the northern part of the city of Pyongyang. A second flight struck at the troops barracks and replacement staging area located about seven miles east of Pyongyang. Later today a second wave of B-29s bombed the same objective. Moderate flak was reported in the Pyongyang area by the B-29 crews but no enemy fighters were seen.

Five B-29s bombed the rail center and marshaling yards at Sariwon while a smaller flight flew over the important rail line from Pyongyang north to Sinanju, pinpointing a series of bombs along the railroad tracks.

Four B-29s bombed rail and highway bridges north of the Thirty-eighth Parallel while about twelve other Superfortresses roamed far over the western area of North Korea to bomb sections of important roadways and highways in that area.

The big sixty-plane fleet that bombed over Korea today reported that in nearly all cases the bombing was accomplished with excellent results, almost no ground fire opposition, and carried out in clear weather. No enemy fighters were reported by any of the planes.

One B-29 experienced mechanical difficulty while en route to Korea and its aircraft commander made an emergency landing at an unnamed air base in Japan. All crew members were safe.

Troops, gun emplacements and buildings containing supplies and Communists were smashed all along the battle line today. F-51 pilots reported good results in the Pohang and Waegwan areas. On some missions F-51s and F-80s took turns at striking the vulnerable targets.

Reconnaissance aircraft reported many enemy vehicles moving on the highways in a northern direction from Waegwan. Others were reported heading from the north to Chungju. They also saw some troops surrendering.

Many F-80 jets concentrated their firepower on enemy troops near Waegwan, often emptying machine guns into enemy foxholes along the front line.

How closely the ground controllers are coordinating the air strikes is shown by the following reports of two pilots.

First Lieut. W. Sexton Jr., 725 Seventh St., Santa Monica, Calif.: "The controller told us to hit troops in a village near Waegwan. In the middle of our run, he told us to pull up as the troops had begun to surrender."

Capt. Robert A. Walsh of 1701 Marin Ave., Berkeley, Calif.: "The controller radioed our flight of four F-80s to attack a little town near Waegwan. He said that troops there had started to surrender, but renewed the fight when a previous flight had been called off. We expended all of our ammunition, including fifteen rockets, and there were five fires burning when we left."

Other flight leaders reporting good results in the Waegwan area included First Lieut. Leonard A. Levine Jr. of Osseo, Wis.; First Lieut. Norvin C. Evans Jr. of Louisville, Ky., and First Lieut. Robert T. Olsen of Riverside, Calif.

One F-80 flight reported catching eighty to 100 enemy troops on a road. The four planes emptied their guns and fired all of their rockets, and pilots estimated that they hit a third of the troops.

Japan-based F-80s also struck in the vicinity of Sinban, thirty-five miles southwest of Taegu and near Hyopchin. First Lieut. Jack D. Loney of Mentone, Calif., reported the destruction of a gun position there. The ground controller told him that his flight "did a very good job" in twelve strafing runs in the same area, according to First Lieut. Richard D. Moore of 33-51 Eighty-fourth Street, Jackson Heights, Queens, N.Y.

Late reports on night intruder missions flown last night reveal B-26 light bombers had excellent results in attacks against troop and vehicle convoys on highways from Taejon north to a point about sixty miles east of Seoul. Flares were dropped to illuminate the targets.

After the lead plane in a group of three dropped several flares, Lieut. Charles R. Prettyman, Star City, Ind., pilot of one of the other two planes, said: "The visibility the flares gave us was excellent and we damaged the convoy." A low-hanging ground haze prevented accurate evaluation of the damage done. This attack took place eight miles north of Kongju.

Dropping flares, Lieut. John H. Mykiez, Edna, Pa., hit a convoy at a river crossing seventeen miles north of Taejon. "Several vehicles were burning when we left," he said.

—Release 471, issued at 8:40 A.M., Thursday (7:40 P.M., Wednesday, Eastern Daylight Time);

United States Air Force's aggressive support of ground fighting in Korea continued yesterday with more than 560 sorties of all types flown from one end of the peninsula to the other. More than 300 were close-support sorties.

While B-29 Superforts of the F.E.A.F. Bomber Command were ranging all over Korea in small flights, with sixty-three planes attacking thirty-seven separate targets, fighters and light bombers moved in a continuous stream along the Pusan perimeter battle line, bombing and strafing retreating enemy troops.

Hundreds of Communist troops were killed by the aerial assaults with unaccountable damage to tanks, trucks, military buildings, gun emplacements and supply targets.

Fighters again led the parade of United States Air Force planes to Korea this morning. F-80 jets took off from their Japanese base at 5:40 A.M., and first flights of F-51 Mustangs were in the air shortly before 7:00 A.M.

Air activity late yesterday found F-51s operating with good results along the northern battle line. Two Communist tanks were scratched from the list at Tabu. A tunnel was heavily damaged southwest of Tuksong. Main targets were troop concentrations in the hills and they were routed.

F-80 jets concentrated almost entirely in the Waegwan area, where United Nations troops made major advances. Coordination by air controllers flying T-6s proved effective against retreating troops.

Day and early evening missions by B-26 light bombers yesterday accounted for enemy troops killed along the Naktong River line. In addition to general-purpose bombs, napalm and rockets, the Invaders poured 79,500 rounds of .50-caliber ammunition into enemy troops and supplies. Controllers estimated dead troops in the hundreds.

—Communiqué 8 of the United Nations Command, issued at 12:14 A.M. Thursday (11:24 A.M. Wednesday, Eastern Daylight Time):

1. Our converging columns are now at the gateways of Seoul. The Marine Division is moving steadily southeast astride the Han River and on the south bank has reached the outskirts of Yongdungpo, advancing against stiffening resistance.

2. Infantry elements on the south are approaching that section of the main north and south highway between Anyang and Seoul. Enemy casualties continue to be high and the prisoner-of-war count increases hourly. Our casualties are relatively light.

Supplies are coming ashore at 4,000 tons daily and troops off-loading continues. Kimpo airfield is now in full operation. All operations continue on planned schedule.

†OBREGON, EUGENE ARNOLD

Rank and Organization: Private First Class, U.S. Marine Corps, Company G, 3d Battalion, 5th Marines, 1st Marine Division (Rein).
Born: November 12, 1930, Los Angeles, California.
Entered Service At: Los Angeles, California.
Place and Date: Seoul, Korea, September 26, 1950.
Citation: For conspicuous gallantry and intrepidity at the risk of his life above and beyond the call of duty while serving with Company G, in action against enemy aggressor forces. While serving as an ammunition carrier of a machine gun squad in a marine rifle company which was temporarily pinned down by hostile fire, Pfc. Obregon observed a fellow marine fall wounded in the line of fire. Armed only with a pistol, he unhesitatingly dashed from his covered position to the side of the casualty. Firing his pistol with one hand as he ran, he grasped his comrade by the arm with his other hand and, despite the great peril to himself, dragged him to the side of the road. Still under enemy fire, he was bandaging the man's wounds when hostile troops of approximately platoon strength began advancing toward his position. Quickly seizing the wounded marine's carbine, he placed his own body as a shield in front of him and lay there firing accurately and effectively into the hostile group until he himself was fatally wounded by enemy machine gun fire. By his courageous fighting spirit,

fortitude, and loyal devotion to duty, Pfc. Obregon enabled his fellow marines to rescue the wounded man and aided essentially in repelling the attack, thereby sustaining and enhancing the highest traditions of the U.S. Naval Service. He gallantly gave his life for his country.

OFFICIAL COMMUNIQUÉ:
TOKYO, Sept. 26 (AP)
—Tenth Corps communiqué 5 issued at 2:45 P.M. Tuesday (12:45 A.M. Tuesday, Eastern Standard Time):

Three months to the day after the North Koreans launched their surprise attack south of the Thirty-eighth Parallel the combat troops of the Tenth Corps recaptured the capital city of Seoul. In a short period of ten days United States Marine and infantry units augmented by South Korean troops landed on the beaches of Inchon and rapidly thrust their way inland to this important communications center and severed the vital junction on the supply line of the enemy.

The liberation of Seoul was accomplished by a coordinated attack of Tenth Corps troops. The attack started at 0630 hours with an amphibious crossing of the Han River south of Seoul by elements of the United States Seventh Infantry Division coordinated with an attack by the First Marine Division to the west and north from positions along the outskirts of the city north of the Han River.

Heavy enemy resistance consisting mainly of intense small arms fire from well prepared positions along the streets and in the buildings slowed the advance of Marine units but steady progress was made during the day and the high ground west and north of the city was secured.

The Seventh Division crossed the Han River in force against moderate resistance and drove forward to capture the 700-foot hill mass called South Mountain, which overlooks the entire city and commands the east exits.

By 1400 hours 25 September the military defenses of Seoul were broken and the South Korean troops of the Capital City Regiment began mopping up strong groups of the defeated defenders. Reports at the end of this period indicate that the enemy is fleeing the city to the northeast.

The coordination of air, tank, artillery and infantry fire power made possible the seizure of the enemy's defenses in Seoul with minimum casualties.

—Tenth Corps communiqué 6 issued at 5:15 A.M. Wednesday (3:15 P.M. Tuesday, Eastern Standard Time):

Elements of the Seventh Infantry Division of the Tenth Corps made the first contact with elements of the First Cavalry Division, Eighth Army, in a surprise development about four miles south of Suwon shortly after 1100 hours, 26 September.

Activity in this area during the last twenty-four hours had consisted of aggressive patrolling and engagements with small groups of enemy infantry and tanks.

In the Seoul area the enemy launched three counter-attacks during this period in a desperate attempt to stop the steady drive of Tenth Corps troops to clear out the last remaining enemy strong groups in the northern part of the city.

Two night attacks were repulsed by the First Marine Division and elements of the division advanced approximately 2,000 yards in bitter house-to-house fighting. A strong counter-attack was repulsed by the Seventh Division on Hill 233 and the attacking force was destroyed.

The R.O.K. (Republic of Korea) Seventeenth Regiment advanced rapidly to the east of Seoul, north of the Han River and occupied positions on a ridge line eight miles east of the center of the city.

During this period an estimated 650 prisoners of war were captured and 1,700 enemy casualties were reported.

—Eighth Army communiqué 112, issued Tuesday:

Troops of the Twenty-fourth Division were nearing Yongdong this afternoon, two months to the day after United Nations forces abandoned the town and withdrew to the south.

Elements of the division were definitely within five miles of Yongdong and later unconfirmed reports had them on the outskirts of town.

Yongdong is about twenty-five miles from Kumchon, which the Twenty-fourth Division took yesterday.

Reconnaissance elements of the First Cavalry Division reached the Taegu-Seoul route today, entering Chochiwon, twenty-five miles north of Taejon.

A regiment of the Second Division took Kochang, capturing prisoners, guns and tons of ammunition. Other elements of the division were actively engaged in clearing enemy pockets from the areas northeast and southeast of Hyopchon.

A task force of the Twenty-fifth Division moved northwest today, advancing fifteen miles.

Another element of the division crossed the Nam River and occupied Ulryong.

—Eighth Army Communiqué 113 issued at 10:00 A.M. Wednesday (8:00 P.M. Tuesday, Eastern Standard Time):

Forward elements of the First Cavalry Division made contact with the Seventh Division 6,000 yards northwest of Osan last night at 2345. The advance was made against no enemy opposition.

The Twenty-fourth Division, continuing up the main Taegu-Seoul route, was midway between Yongdong and Taejon at dark yesterday.

After capturing Kochang, troops of the Second Division continued southwest and advanced seven miles. Other elements of the division were still engaged in clearing enemy troops between Hyopchon and the Naktong River.

A task force of the Twenty-fifth Division was advancing northwest from Chinju yesterday and at last report had gained fifteen miles against increasing resistance. Most of the division was engaged in reorganizing and clearing small pockets of the enemy in the Uiryong and Chinju areas.

On the northern front R.O.K. (Republic of Korea) forces continued their unopposed advance. On the coast the Third Division moved twenty-six miles during the last twenty-four hours, reaching Toksin. Elements of the Capital Division gained twelve miles to Togye, twenty-four miles northwest of Yongdok.

The Second Division continued northwest between Namchang and Yechon while the Eighth Division had elements seven miles south and southwest of Yongju.

—Release 496 issued by Gen. Douglas MacArthur at 9:50 A.M. Tuesday (7:50 P.M. Monday, Eastern Standard Time):

Aboard U.S.S. Valley Forge off Korea—Combining close air support for Army ground forces with repeated assaults on vital supply lines and installations in Korea Monday, fighters and dive bombers of the U.S.S. Valley Forge delivered shattering blows on Communist troops, trains, and supply dumps.

Under a warm sun, Skyraiders of this flagship commenced the day's air assaults by destroying a train in a tunnel northeast of Haeju, rail tracks north of the tunnel, and by strafing troop trenches, and buildings containing troops or military stores throughout the Haeju area. Two shiny new switch engines also received 500-pounders from the Navy airmen.

In a dive-bomber flight led by Lieut. Robert C. Logan of San Francisco, the Navy carrier planes went to the aid of Army ground forces after a call for help from ground artillery control on a ridge in the heart of Seoul, enemy partially held capital of South Korea. As the dive bombers passed over the city, they received their call from below. They went into action. Enemy troops and artillery were located on one side of the ridge while on the other American soldiers were bearing the brunt of heavy five from over the hill.

The Skyraiders had to first place a 500-pounder on the right side of the small ridge. They did and received the green flag from the Army. They demolished the ridge resistance. Lieutenant Logan returned to the ship after the successful raid to find his Oak Leaf rank of Lieutenant Commander awaiting him, the end of a perfect day for the Valley Forge flier.

Bogging down the enemy forces still more, the Navy planes smashed their 20-mm. cannon fire into a supply dump twelve miles east of Seoul. When the supply dump exploded, sending a roar around the Korean countryside, 5,000 gallons of gasoline went up in a tall mushroom of smoke. Last night, two more brand new switch engines in the railroad marshaling yards at Yangyong lay in ruins making a total of five additions to the ship's box-score board.

Shortly after lunch yesterday, fast jet Panthers were launched from the Valley Forge flight deck in a Navy air strike which left another enemy locomotive well strafed, an oil dump west of Mashu exploded into flames, an 18-car train riddled with 20-mm. cannon fire along with another train at Seuchon, and a 4-passenger-car train near Sinanju raked over by the jet cannons.

—Release 498 issued by Gen. Douglas MacArthur at 4:00 P.M. Tuesday (2:00 A.M. Tuesday, Eastern Standard Time):

Military operations:
Hard fighting United States Marines and elements of the United States Seventh Infantry Division and R.O.K. (Republic of Korea) Army have completed the envelopment and seizure of Seoul, forcing the enemy garrison to flee to the north.

A task force of the United States First Cavalry Division drove twenty miles from Poun yesterday afternoon and entered Chongju. Advance elements of the force raced another ten miles and reached Chochiwon this morning. Chochiwon is approximately fifty-three air miles from Suwon.

Elements of the R.O.K. First Division recorded advances of about ten miles seizing Sonsan and Kaeryong.

Units of the United States Twenty-fourth Division overcame heavy enemy resistance, captured Kumchon and advanced several miles west toward Yongdong.

United States Second Division elements drove to within six miles of Kochang after gaining up to twelve miles yesterday.

Enemy forces in the Sachon area, dispersed by elements of the United States Twenty-fifth Division, fled in confusion, abandoning their arms.

Another unit of the division crossed the Nam River and entered Ulryong this morning. A task force of the division advanced about ten miles northwest of captured Chinju.

Motorized elements of the R.O.K. Sixth Division entered Hamchang after advancing approximately fifteen miles yesterday.

The R.O.K. Eighth Division consolidated its hold on Andong and continued to drive north.

After registering sizable gains, elements of the R.O.K. Capital Division seized Chongsong.

A unit of the R.O.K. Third Division secured Yongdok while other elements reduced enemy pockets throughout the sector.

†CHRISTIANSON, STANLEY R.

Rank and Organization: Private First Class, U.S. Marine Corps, Company E, 2d Battalion, 1st Marines, 1st Marine Division.
Born: January 24, 1925, Mindoro, Wisconsin.
Entered Service At: Mindoro, Wisconsin.
Place and Date: Seoul, Korea, September 29, 1950.
Citation: For conspicuous gallantry and intrepidity at the risk of his life above and beyond the call of duty while serving with Company E, in action against enemy aggressor forces at Hill 132, in the early morning hours. Manning one of the several listening posts covering approaches to the platoon area when the enemy commenced the attack, Pfc. Christianson quickly sent another marine to alert the rest of the platoon. Without orders, he remained in his position and, with full knowledge that he would have slight chance of escape, fired relentlessly at oncoming hostile troops attacking furiously with rifles, automatic weapons, and incendiary grenades. Accounting for 7 enemy dead in the immediate vicinity before his position was overrun and he himself fatally struck down, Pfc. Christianson, by his superb courage, valiant fighting spirit, and devotion to duty, was responsible for allowing the rest of the platoon time to man positions, build up a stronger defense on that flank, and repel the attack with 41 of the enemy destroyed, many more wounded and three taken prisoner. His self-sacrificing actions in the face of overwhelming odds sustain and enhance the finest traditions of the U.S. Naval Service. Pfc. Christianson gallantly gave his life for his country.

OFFICIAL COMMUNIQUÉ:

TOKYO, Saturday, Sept. 30 (AP)
—Release 508, issued at 2:45 P.M. Friday (12:45 A.M. Friday, Eastern Standard Time):

A disorganized and retreating North Korean Army was pounded yesterday in aerial operations that saw the greatest number of sorties dispatched by the United States Far East Air Forces so far in the Korean conflict, a total of 792.

Some aircraft of the Fifth Air Force, Royal Australian Air Force, United States Marine Corps and the R.O.K. Air Force returned to bases with their rockets and bombs still on their shackles due to lack of suitable targets, although excellent flying weather prevailed. The increasingly rapid-break-up of major ground units is held responsible for the disappearance of sizable targets on the ground.

Flying in close support of the advancing Eighth Army, F-51 fighters and F-80 jet fighter-bombers bombed, rocketed and strafed stubborn Communist pockets of resistance in both the First and Ninth Corps areas. Successful attacks eliminated several of these hampering pockets and Air Force forward controllers advised that over 750 enemy troops were killed. Large amounts of war material also were destroyed in these strikes.

B-26 light bombers joined the F-51s and F-80s in both day and night attacks on military targets in and near Sariwon, Chorwan, Pyonggang, Kangnung, Pyongyang, Sinmak, Wonsan, Yongdok, Samchok, Wonju, Yangyang, and Chaeryong. Warehouses, enemy occupied buildings, vehicles, tunnels, bridges, railroad rollingstock, gun emplacements, fuel storage areas, and small vessels were successfully attacked. Sweeps over airfields at Sinmak, Pyongyang, Yonggang, Konan, and Wonsan were once again unproductive, with no evidence of enemy activity noted.

So rapid has been the advance of United Nations ground forces in Korea that now all flights south of about the 37-1/2 Parallel are being controlled by Air Force tactical controllers in T-6 aircraft and jeeps accompanying the forward moving Eighth Army.

Fifth Air Force claims for Thursday totaled thirty-four tanks, 200 vehicles, nine locomotives, forty-six rail cars, nineteen artillery pieces, three supply dumps, sixty-two enemy occupied buildings, fourteen heavy weapon emplacements, three fuel storage areas, a tunnel, three warehouses, a radio station, four barges, and three small boats destroyed or damaged.

Bomber Command B-29s continued the interdiction program, but with an entirely new mission. Previously these attacks were designed to prevent resupply and reinforcement of the Communist armies in the field. With the disintegration of these armies, efforts are now being directed to hamper the fleeing forces in their northward movement to beyond the Thirty-eighth Parallel.

Formations of Superfortresses bombed secondary marshaling yards at Tanchon, Munchen, Sinanju, Yongnam, Songjin, and Chori with excellent results. Other formations and individual B-29s ranged along the rail lines from Hamhung to Chorwon and Pyongyang to the south of the Thirty-eighth Parallel. Sixteen cuts were made in rail lines; two highway bridges at Yonghung each had one span knocked out, as did a railroad bridge near Songjin. Another highway bridge in the vicinity of Yonghung was damaged by direct hits.

Combat Cargo Command aircraft lifted a total of 680 tons of cargo and 464 passengers into Korea during Thursday's operations.

—Release 509, issued by General MacArthur's headquarters at 3:50 P.M. Friday (1:50 A.M. Friday, Eastern Standard Time):

Elements of the United States First Marine Division, the United States Seventh Infantry Division, R.O.K. Army and R.O.K. Marine units continued mopping up in the Seoul area. Units in the area south of Suwon conducted aggressive patrol actions. Many prisoners, in groups up to 100, were taken throughout the Seoul area yesterday.

The United States First Cavalry Division consolidated positions throughout its sector in order to block enemy escape routes from the south.

Elements of the R.O.K. First Division joined First Cavalry Division units in Chochiwon, while other units mopped up in the vicinity of Oksan.

The city of Taejon was recaptured yesterday at 6:00 P.M. by elements of the United States Twenty-fourth Division after overcoming stubborn enemy resistance. Other divisional units continued to block enemy escape routes.

British troops in the Songju area continued to block enemy escape routes to the north.

A unit of the United States Second Division drove approximately forty miles yesterday and seized the important communications city of Chonju. Other elements of the division cleared enemy pockets in the vicinity of Samga and Koryong.

In the largest advance of the day, elements of the United States Twenty-fifth Division raced forty-five miles, seized Namwon, liberated eighty United States prisoners of war and were last reported near Tamyang, some twenty miles southwest of Namwon. Another unit of the division, advancing west from the Uiryong bridge, had reached the area north of Chinju.

Elements of the R.O.K. Sixth Division dispersed an enemy force and secured Mungyong while another unit, in an enveloping movement, raced some forty miles and occupied Chungju, eighteen miles northwest of Mungyong.

R.O.K. Eighth Division units advancing northwest from Yongju seized Tanyang against moderate resistance.

Leading elements of the R.O.K. Capital Division took Yongwol after advancing thirty miles from Chumyang. Many prisoners were taken during the advance.

An enemy force attempting to slow down the northward drive of the R.O.K. Third Division was dispersed and leading elements of the division were last reported twelve miles north of Utchin and still advancing.

A total of 1,645 prisoners was captured by United Nation forces during the period. In addition to the United States and Republic of Korea, units of the following countries are actively participating in the United Nations effort against the North Koreans: Australia, Canada, France, the Netherlands, New Zealand, Philippine Islands, Sweden, and United Kingdom.

—*United States Eighth Army communiqué 117, issued at 7:30 P.M. Friday (5:30 A.M. Friday, Eastern Standard Time):*

Motorized elements of the United Nations forces continued their rapid progress today in the southwest and northwest zones of advance.

Air observation reported that friendly forces had advanced as far west as Iri and Nonsan and as far north as Imokchong and Kumjin. Other moves were made to strengthen the link-up along the Taejon-Seoul axis. There was little enemy action reported.

—*United States Tenth Corps communiqué 9, issued at 3:15 A.M. Saturday (1:15 P.M. Friday, Eastern Standard Time):*

Enemy activity in the Tenth Corps zone during this period (in twenty-four hours of Sept. 29) was confined to four small counter-attacks.

Two of these counter-attacks were launched against the First Marine Division north of Seoul, and two attacks were made against the Seventh R.O.K. (Republic of Korea) Regiment east of Seoul. All were repulsed.

The 187th Airborne Regiment continued to mop up scattered groups of enemy infantry on the Kimpo Peninsula.

In the Seventh Division zone, east of Seoul, twenty-two enemy troops with officers surrendered, bearing safe-conduct passes. Stragglers from the Second and Third North Korean Divisions were identified in the Seventh Division zone during this period.

†YOUNG, ROBERT H.

Rank and Organization: Private First Class, U.S. Army, Company E, 8th Cavalry Regiment, 1st Cavalry Division.
Born: March 4, 1924, Oroville, California.
Entered Service At: Vallejo, California.
Place and Date: North of Kaesong, Korea, October 9, 1950.
Citation: Pfc. Young distinguished himself by conspicuous gallantry and intrepidity above and beyond the call of duty in action against the enemy. His company, spearheading a battalion drive deep in enemy territory, suddenly came under a devastating barrage of enemy mortar and automatic weapons crossfire which inflicted heavy casualties among his comrades and wounded him in the face and shoulder. Refusing to be evacuated, Pfc. Young remained in position and continued to fire at the enemy until wounded a second time. As he awaited first-aid near the company command post the enemy attempted an enveloping movement. Disregarding medical treatment he took an exposed position and firing with deadly accuracy killed 5 of the enemy. During this action he was again hit by hostile fire which knocked him to the ground and destroyed his helmet. Later when supporting tanks moved forward, Pfc. Young, his wounds still unattended, directed tank fire which destroyed 3 enemy gun positions and enabled the company to advance. Wounded again by an enemy mortar burst, and while aiding several of his injured comrades, he demanded that all others be evacuated first. Throughout the course of this action the leadership and combative instinct displayed by Pfc. Young exerted a profound influence on the conduct of the company. His aggressive example effected the whole course of the action and was responsible for its success. Pfc. Young's dauntless courage and intrepidity reflect the highest credit upon himself and uphold the esteemed traditions of the U.S. Army.

OFFICIAL COMMUNIQUÉ:
TOKYO, Oct. 9 (AP)
—Release 537 issued at 3:05 P.M. Monday (1:05 A.M. Monday, Eastern Standard Time):

Aircraft of the United States Far East Air Forces pounded North Korea Sunday as bombers and fighters concentrated their attacks on military targets between the Thirty-eighth and Fortieth Parallels.

In their 104th consecutive day of combat operations, F.E.A.F. planes, seeking to isolate Communist defensive forces from their sources of supplies, destroyed bridges, main highway junctions, and tunnels, as well as hammering numerous small marshaling yards beyond the enemy defensive perimeter.

Thirty-nine Bomber Command Superfortresses, carrying 500 and 1,000 pound bombs, individually and in small elements, attacked seventy-five separate targets from the west coast to the east coast. Fifteen rail bridges, seven highway bridges, thirty secondary marshaling yards, twenty-one sections of rail lines, and a major rail tunnel were bombed, with generally excellent results.

A span was knocked out of a rail bridge at Tondae, one span destroyed in another at Songjin, and two others in the vicinity of Wangsang lost a span each by direct hits. A highway bridge was partially destroyed at Namsi. At Pukchong an important rail tunnel was closed with direct hits on both entrances.

Secondary explosions followed a successful attack by the Superfortresses on a secondary marshaling yard just southeast of Chongju. The yard was undergoing extensive repairs at the time of the attack. Several warehouses were destroyed in the Hamhung marshaling yards when a large force of B-29s attacked the area.

Trackage was destroyed at widely scattered points throughout the areas under attack.

Fifth Air Force light bombers and fighters struck at targets in the same general area hit by the B-29s. F-80 jet fighter-bombers and F-51 fighters hammered vehicles and supply areas in and around Pyongyang, Hungnam, and Suan.

At Chaeryong, enemy-occupied buildings were destroyed by repeated rocketing and strafing attacks, while warehouses in Haeju were left burning. Small-scale vehicular traffic at Chunghwa, Yongju, Sukchon, Chigyong, and Kowon was successfully attacked. A large supply area was left burning at Kumhwa.

Flying 141 close support sorties of the day's total of 576, F-80s and F-51s ranged along the east coast, hammering targets in front of the advancing R.O.K. forces. Quantities of enemy material were destroyed in repeated attacks on fuel dumps, vehicles, gun emplacements, warehouses, supply carts, bridges, troop movements, and railroad rolling stock.

B-26 light bombers, in both day and night operations, struck at military targets in twenty different cities and towns, cutting rail lines, damaging Yonghung, Sukchon, and Hungnam with excellent results. A small convoy just north of Pyongyang containing approximately twenty-five vehicles was brought under attack and at least twelve of the trucks destroyed.

Anti-aircraft fire continued to be active and an F-51 and F-80 were lost behind enemy lines when hit be flak.

Fifth Air Force claims Sunday totaled 108 vehicles, seven locomotives, fifty-six rail cars, four gun emplacements, sixteen supply areas including fuel dumps, forty military buildings, fourteen warehouses, six oil tanks, three ammunition storage areas, and sixteen supply carts destroyed or damaged.

Combat cargo command aircraft lifted a total of ninety-nine tons of cargo and 674 passengers into Korea Sunday.

—Release 538, issued by Gen. Douglas MacArthur's headquarters at 3:25 P.M. Monday (1:35 A.M. Monday, Eastern Standard Time):

During the past twenty-four hours the prisoners of war count continued to mount, with a total of 4,531 Reds being captured during the period. This raises the total of prisoners taken to date to more than 55,000.

Yesterday, United Nations activity consisted largely of continued advances in the eastern sector and mopping up and consolidation throughout the remainder of liberated Korea.

Elements of the R.O.K. (Republic of Korea) Third Division drove to within ten miles of Wonsan against moderate resistance.

Other R.O.K. forces captured Hoeyang and continued to advance to the northwest. In the Hwachon and Chongong areas United nations forces continued to attack against increasing resistance.

†COURSEN, SAMUEL S.
Rank and Organization: First Lieutenant, U.S. Army, Company C, 5th Cavalry Regiment, 1st Cavalry Division.
Born: August 4, 1926, Madison, New Jersey.
Entered Service At: Madison, New Jersey.
Place and Date: Near Kaesong, Korea, October 12, 1950.
Citation: 1st Lt. Coursen distinguished himself by conspicuous gallantry and intrepidity above and beyond the call of duty in action against the enemy. While Company C was attacking Hill 174 under heavy enemy small-arms fire, his platoon received enemy fire from close range. The platoon returned the fire and continued to advance. During this phase one of his men moved into a well camouflaged emplacement, which was thought to be unoccupied, and was wounded by the enemy who were hidden within the emplacement. Seeing the soldier in difficulty he rushed to the man's aid and, without regard for his personal safety, engaged the enemy in hand-to-hand combat in an effort to protect his wounded comrade until he himself was killed. When his body was recovered after the battle 7 enemy dead were found in the emplacement. As the result of 1st Lt. Coursen's violent struggle several of the enemies' heads had been crushed with his rifle. His aggressive and intrepid actions saved the life of the wounded man, eliminated the main position of the enemy roadblock, and greatly inspired the men in his command. 1st Lt. Coursen's extraordinary heroism and intrepidity reflect the highest credit on himself and are in keeping with the honored traditions of the military service.

OFFICIAL COMMUNIQUÉ:
TOKYO, Friday, Oct. 13 (AP)
—Release 546, issued by General MacArthur's headquarters at 1:10 P.M., Thursday (11:10 P.M., Wednesday, Eastern Standard Time):

Aircraft of the United States Far East Air Forces, extending their interdiction operations northward to the Forty-first Parallel, pounded North Korean rail nets and other lines of communication Wednesday as bombers and fighters continued to isolate the battle area from supply sources.

Twenty-four F.E.A.F. Bomber Command Superforts attacked seventy separate targets, including fifteen highway bridges, twenty-three rail bridges, and four secondary marshaling yards. Many cuts were made in rail lines and highway junctions throughout the target areas.

Large fires and secondary explosions followed an attack by the B-29s on a small marshaling yard at Talli. At Sandpo, fires in the marshaling yards sent black smoke 5,000 feet into the air. North of Sinhung a rail bridge was damaged by direct hits and one span was knocked out of a rail bridge at Tanchon. One span each of two highway bridges in the Tanchon vicinity were destroyed, as were the approaches to a highway bridge near Taptong.

Attacking rail lines between Songjin and Hamhung, Pyongyang and Sinanju and to Sonchon, the medium bombers made at least thirty cuts in rails and paralleling highways.

Fifth Air Force B-26 light bombers, F-80 jet fighter-bombers, and F-51 fighters hammered close support and interdiction targets throughout North Korea. In both day and night operations the light bombers attacked military targets in and near Kowon, Pyongyang, Sinanju, Chonghon, Hungnam, Songchon, and Sariwon. Rail lines and moving targets were successfully attacked.

Fighters operating in the R.O.K. (Republic of Korea) and First Cavalry Division sectors attacked vehicles, troops, gun emplacements, supply areas, carts, and troop concentrations. Six vehicles were destroyed and an unknown number of Communist troops killed in an attack on a small convoy near Munchon, while at Imong six artillery pieces were destroyed or damaged in an attack by F-80 jets.

Striking at interdiction targets at Hukkyori, Kowon, Yonghung, Hypohung, and Paup, fires were started in several supply areas and warehouses. Counter air sweeps against the airfields at Sentokoju, Konan, and Konko by the F-80's revealed no activity.

Destroyed or damaged in Wednesday's attacks by Fifth Air Force planes were forty-nine vehicles, thirty-two boxcars, twenty enemy occupied buildings, two small river boats, one small marshaling yard, seven artillery pieces, and three supply areas. Rail lines were cut in several places.

Combat Cargo Command aircraft continued the flow of essential material into Korea, lifting a total of 847 tons of cargo, including 1,131 passengers, Wednesday.

—Release 547, issued by General MacArthur's headquarters at 3:50 P.M., Thursday (1:50 A.M., Thursday, Eastern Standard Time):

The United States First Cavalry Division continued its attack in the area north of Kaesong. Elements of the division repelled two enemy attacks and registered gains up to four miles.

Elements of the R.O.K. (Republic of Korea) First Division advanced north from the vicinity of Sindong against mortar, small arms, and automatic weapons fire. Gains of up to five miles were reported.

A two-pronged attack by the R.O.K. Capital Division mopped up in captured Wonsan and secured the Wonsan airfield. The division reported the capture of 521 prisoners in the area.

The R.O.K. Third Division advanced through Wonsan yesterday against a stubborn enemy supported by heavy mortar and artillery fire. The division reached the northern outskirts after heavy street fighting. Elements of the division continued their attack north of Wonsan.

—Release 548, issued by General MacArthur's headquarters at 11:20 A.M., Friday (9:20 P.M., Thursday, Eastern Standard Time):

Firing at the rate of 15,000 pounds a minute, the United States Navy's mighty battleship Missouri yesterday poured out in less than one hour more than 800,000 pounds of death and destruction on enemy military targets in the city of Chongjin, just thirty-five miles south of the Manchurian border and about 100 miles from the important Russian port of Vladivostok.

The Missouri spearheaded the largest East coast naval movement since the start of the Korean hostilities when thirty-seven ships, including destroyers, cruisers, and aircraft carriers, worked over Communist installations from the industrial city of Songjin practically to the very edge of the Manchurian border. This was the farthest north that Navy ships have struck in force since June 25.

Among the ships participating in this major naval movement were the aircraft carriers Philippine Sea and Valley Forge, the heavy cruisers Helena, Toledo, and Rochester as well as the light cruiser Worcester.

The first sortie of the day from the Valley Forge brought the destruction of one enemy corvette and the bombardment and silencing of four shore battery positions near Sindo. During the twenty-four hour period ending at noon yesterday, Navy planes of Task Force 77 flew a total of 193 sorties.

Meanwhile, on the West coast, British carrier-based Furies and Fireflies blasted troop concentrations, mortar positions, and supply lines in the Changyon and Cho areas.

†WILSON, RICHARD G.

Rank and Organization: Private First Class, U.S. Army, Company I, Medical Company, 187th Airborne Infantry Regiment.
Born: August 19, 1931, Marion, Illinois.
Entered Service At: Cape Girardeau, Missouri.
Place and Date: Opari, Korea, October 21, 1950.
Citation: Pfc. Wilson distinguished himself by conspicuous gallantry and intrepidity above and beyond the call of duty in action against the enemy. As medical aid man attached to Company I, he accompanied the main unit in a reconnaissance in force through the hilly country near Opari. The main body of the company was passing through a narrow valley flanked on three sides by high hills when the enemy laid down a barrage of mortar, automatic-weapons, and small-arms fire. The company suffered a large number of casualties from the intense hostile fire while fighting its way out of the ambush. Pfc. Wilson proceeded at once to move among the wounded and administered aid to them oblivious of the danger to himself, constantly exposing himself to hostile fire. The company commander ordered a withdrawal as the enemy threatened to encircle and isolate the company. As his unit withdrew, Pfc. Wilson assisted wounded men to safety and assured himself that none were left behind. After the company had pulled back he learned that a comrade previously thought dead had been seen to be moving and attempting to crawl to safety. Despite the protests of his comrades, unarmed and facing the merciless enemy, Pfc. Wilson returned to the dangerous position in search of his comrade. Two days later a patrol found him lying beside the man he returned to aid. He had been shot several times while trying to shield and administer aid to the wounded man. Pfc. Wilson's superb personal bravery, consummate courage, and willing self-sacrifice for his comrades reflect untold glory upon himself and uphold the esteemed traditions of the military service.

OFFICIAL COMMUNIQUÉ:

TOKYO, Sunday, Oct. 22 (AP)
—Release 575, issued by General MacArthur's headquarters at 3:30 P.M., Saturday (1:30 A.M., Saturday, Eastern Standard Time):

United Nations forces continue to capture large numbers of North Korean troops. During the last twenty-four hours approximately 7,000 enemy troops have been captured, to raise the grand total of prisoners of war to more than 82,000.

A successful air drop was made by the 187th Airborne R.C.T. (Regimental Combat Team) in the Sukchon-Sunchon area against little or no enemy opposition. Latest reports indicate all units securing their assigned areas. To the southeast, elements of the Sixth R.O.K. (Republic of Korea) Division and the Eighth R.O.K. Division were advancing west of Songchon toward Sunchon.

In the Pyongyang sector all elements of the United Nations forces continued to mop up the scattered enemy remnants prior to pushing north to join with the Sunchon forces. Just south of Pyongyang the Twenty-seventh British Commonwealth Infantry Brigade was mopping up bypassed enemy groups along the route of advance.

In the Wonsan sector the Third R.O.K. Division continued to clean out and secure the area.

In the Hamhung-Hungnam area the R.O.K. Capitol Division is extending its perimeter, with elements in the vicinity of Yongsan, Tokhung, Majon, and Hongwon.

In the areas south of the Thirty-eighth Parallel, United Nations forces continued to ferret out enemy personnel and equipment.

—Release 576, issued by General MacArthur's headquarters at 11:05 A.M. Sunday (9:05 P.M. Saturday, Eastern Standard Time):

Floating and moored mines on both coasts of Korea continued to claim the major share of Navy attention yesterday.

Although hampered by foul weather, there was no let-up in naval air and surface efforts to reduce the menace.

A United States Navy PBM Martin Mariner machine gunned and destroyed one mine off the east coast in the vicinity of the Thirty-ninth Parallel. Three other mines were destroyed by ships off Wonsan.

Carrier-based United States Marine aircraft provided protective air cover for the fleet of minesweepers operating off the east coast, while United States and British Commonwealth fleet units along with the French sloop La Grandiere stood by to render naval gunfire support as necessary.

Minesweeping operations on the west coast were being performed under cover of British Commonwealth naval air and surface units under the command of Rear Admiral W.G. Andrewes, R.N.

Sea Furies and Fireflies operating from the British carrier Theseus on Friday blasted military targets in the Chongju and Sonchon areas. Heavily hit were industrial buildings, train sheds, and warehouses. Pilots returning to their carrier base reported that good targets were hard to find.

—Tenth Corp communiqué 14, issued at 1:00 A.M., Sunday, (11:00 A.M., Saturday, Eastern Standard Time):

Maj. Gen. Edward M. Almond, Commanding General, Tenth Corps, has assumed command of all United Nations and Republic of Korea forces in the Wonsan-Hamhung area on the east flank of the fast moving United Nations advance toward the northern border of Korea.

Advances of Republic of Korea ground units under Tenth Corps operational control were supported by close support aviation of the First Marine Air Wing.

The honor of being the United Nations unit furthermost north in Korea went to the First Infantry Regiment of the R.O.K. Capital Division.

The Tenth Corps commander, during a visit to Hamhung today (Saturday) coordinated plans with forward ground unit leaders for rapid follow-up of the enemy in the corps zone of action. At the time the most advanced units were moving north from Poson-Bong, Ossang, and Puchang.

VAN WINKLE, ARCHIE

Rank and Organization: Staff Sergeant, U.S. Marine Corps Reserve, Company B, 1st Battalion, 7th Marines, 1st Marine Division (Rein).
Born: March 17, 1925, Juneau, Alaska.
Entered Service At: Arlington, Washington.
Place and Date: Vicinity of Sudong, Korea, November 2, 1950.
Citation: For conspicuous gallantry and intrepidity at the risk of his life above and beyond the call of duty while serving as a platoon sergeant in Company B, in action against enemy aggressor forces. Immediately rallying the men in his area after a fanatical and numerically superior enemy force penetrated the center of the line under cover of darkness and pinned down the platoon with a devastating barrage of automatic weapons and grenade fire, S/Sgt. Van Winkle boldly spearheaded a determined attack through withering fire against hostile frontal positions and, though he and all the others that charged with him were wounded, succeeded in enabling his platoon to gain the fire superiority and the opportunity to reorganize. Realizing that the left flank squad was isolated from the rest of the unit, he rushed through 40 yards of fierce enemy fire to reunite his troops despite an elbow wound that rendered one of his arms totally useless. Severely wounded a second time when a direct hit in the chest from a hostile

hand-grenade caused serious and painful wounds, he staunchly refused evacuation and continued to shout orders and words of encouragement to his depleted and battered platoon. Finally carried from his position unconscious from shock and from loss of blood, S/Sgt. Van Winkle served to inspire all who observed him to heroic efforts in successfully repulsing the enemy attack. His superb leadership, valiant fighting spirit, and unfaltering devotion to duty in the face of heavy odds reflect the highest credit upon himself and the U.S. Naval Service.

OFFICIAL COMMUNIQUÉ:

TOKYO, Nov. 2 (AP)
—Release 606, issued by General MacArthur's headquarters at 2:30 P.M., Thursday (12:30 A.M., Thursday, Eastern Standard Time):

United States Far East Air Forces planes encountered Communist aircraft in the air and attacked them also on the ground yesterday in Korea for the first time in weeks as support of battling United Nations ground forces continued.

F.E.A.F. Bomber Command B-29s returned to action for the first time in five days to further assist friendly troops driving toward the border. They bombed rail and highway communications, and rail centers, still being used by the Communists for supply purposes. The Superfort attacks were made from coast to coast near the border.

Engagements with enemy aircraft centered at Sinuiju on the border of northwestern Korea, where three Yak-type planes were shot down by F-51 fighters and a B-26 light bomber. Enemy planes on the ground at an airfield near Sinuiju were under attack by F-80 jets, with nine destroyed and eight damaged. In addition, one jet-type enemy plane was reported damaged and one probably hit by F-51s in an air battle near Sonchon.

One F-80 jet was lost in the strike against enemy planes on the ground at Sinuiju, where flak was reported. Yesterday's sorties totaled 504 with ninety-six being in close support of Eighth Army and other ground units making progress against stiff Communist opposition in far northern Korea. Fifth Air Force fighters and light bombers destroyed or damaged fifty-six vehicles, sixty-five supply carts, three tanks, two railroad tunnels, eighteen supply buildings, seven gun positions, and two fuel dumps in addition to killing more than 100 Communist troops. The planes supported United Nations forces as they drove past Sonchon, Kusong, and other northwestern cities. They also were active in Unsan, Yongpo, Taepyong, Kanggye, and Huichon areas.

A long railroad tunnel north of Huichon was heavily bombed yesterday by B-26 light Invaders, with openings and tracks at both ends damaged. Other B-26s in the Huichon area attacked troop concentrations and eliminated half a dozen vehicles.

Superfort bombing was visual and excellent results reported on all targets which included principal rail and highway lines leading from Songjin on the cost to the north and to the east, the transfer point and marshaling yards at Kanggye, and communications between Kilchu and Chongjin, and Kilchu to Hapsu in the northeast.

The rail line running north to south between Kanggye and Koindong was cut in several places. Bridges and tunnels in both the northwest and northeast were under attack by B-29s. The marshaling yard at Chongjin was damaged heavily, as was the warehouse area at Nanam, where explosions were detected after the bombs hit in the target area.

Leaflet drops were made on a number of Communist-held Korean cities.

F.E.A.F. Combat Cargo Command airlifted 1,493 tons into Korea from Japan, including 946 passengers, and also made an important parachute airdrop to advanced Republic of Korea troops fighting northwest of Huichon. The airdrop consisted of rations, ammunition, and gasoline.

—*Release 607, issued by General MacArthur's headquarters at 4:05 P.M., Thursday (2:05 A.M., Thursday, Eastern Standard Time):*

In the past week over 5,000 more enemy troops have been reported as captured by United Nations forces. Reports from the battle areas indicate the grand total of prisoners of war captured is now approximately 135,000.

The enemy continued to exert heavy pressure in the Unsan sector throughout last night and this morning.

An initial enemy attack yesterday, supported by automatic weapons and mortar fire, made a slight gain against elements of the United States First Cavalry Division west of Unsan. A tank-infantry counter-attack stabilized the division lines. The enemy continued to attack steadily all last night. The attacks were held without loss of ground.

A heavy attack forced elements of the R.O.K. (Republic of Korea) First Division to withdraw to new positions in the area north of Yongpo where the line was stabilized and the intensity of the attack decreased.

Forward elements of the United States Twenty-fourth Division reached the vicinity of Igu against moderate resistance. Another division unit neared Chongko against light resistance.

In the area east of Unsan, elements of the R.O.K. Seventh and Eighth Divisions withdrew to new positions, defending against heavy enemy attacks. Enemy pressure weakened and the positions were stabilized.

Leading elements of the United States Seventh Division contacted the enemy several miles northwest of Pungsan.

†PHILLIPS, LEE H.

Rank and Organization: Corporal, U.S. Marine Corps, Company E, 2d Battalion, 7th Marines, 1st Marine Division (Rein).
Born: February 3, 1930, Stockbridge, Georgia.
Entered Service At: Ben Hill, Georgia.
Place and Date: Korea, November 4, 1950.
Citation: For conspicuous gallantry and intrepidity at the risk of his life above and beyond the call of duty while serving as a squad leader of Company E, in action against enemy aggressor forces. Assuming the point position in the attack against a strongly defended and well-entrenched numerically superior enemy force occupying a vital hill position which had been unsuccessfully assaulted on 5 separate occasions by units of the Marine Corps and other friendly forces, Cpl. Phillips fearlessly led his men in a bayonet charge up the precipitous slope under a deadly hail of hostile mortar, small-arms, and machine gun fire. Quickly rallying his squad when it was pinned down by a heavy and accurate mortar barrage, he continued to lead his men through the bombarded area and, although only 5 members were left in the casualty ridden unit, gained the military crest of the hill where he was immediately subjected to an enemy counterattack. Although greatly outnumbered by an estimated enemy squad, Cpl. Phillips boldly engaged the hostile force with hand-grenades and rifle fire and, exhorting his gallant group of marines to follow him, stormed forward to completely overwhelm the enemy. With only 3 men now left in his squad, he proceeded to spearhead an assault on the last remaining strong-point which was defended by 4 of the enemy on a rocky and almost inaccessible portion of the hill position. Using one hand to climb up the extremely hazardous precipice, he hurled grenades with the other and, with 2 remaining comrades, succeeded in annihilating the pocket of resistance and consolidating the position. Immediately subjected to a sharp counterattack by an estimated enemy squad, he skillfully directed the fire of his men and employed his own weapon with deadly effectiveness to repulse the numerically superior

hostile force. By his valiant leadership, indomitable fighting spirit and resolute determination in the face of heavy odds, Cpl. Phillips served to inspire all who observed him and was directly responsible for the destruction of the enemy stronghold. His great personal valor reflects the highest credit upon himself and enhances and sustains the finest traditions of the U.S. Naval Service. Cpl. Phillips was killed in action November 27, 1950.

†POYNTER, JAMES I.

Rank and Organization: Sergeant, U.S. Marine Corps Reserve, Company A, 1st Battalion, 7th Marines, 1st Marine Division (Rein).
Born: December 1, 1916, Bloomington, Illinois.
Entered Service At: Downey, California.
Place and Date: Near Sudong, Korea, November 4, 1950.
Citation: For conspicuous gallantry and intrepidity at the risk of his life above and beyond the call of duty while serving as a squad leader in a rifle platoon of Company A, in action against enemy aggressor forces during the defense of Hill 532, south of Sudong, Korea. When a vastly outnumbering, well-concealed hostile force launched a sudden, vicious counterattack against his platoon's hasty defensive position, Sgt. Poynter displayed superb skill and courage in leading his squad and directing its fire against the onrushing enemy. With his ranks critically depleted by casualties and he himself critically wounded as the onslaught gained momentum and the hostile force surrounded his position, he seized his bayonet and engaged in bitter hand-to-hand combat as the breakthrough continued. Observing 3 machine guns closing in at a distance of 25 yards, he dashed from his position and, grasping hand-grenades from fallen marines as he ran, charged the emplacements in rapid succession, killing the crews of 2 and putting the other out of action before he fell, mortally wounded. By his self-sacrificing and valiant conduct, Sgt. Poynter inspired the remaining members of his squad to heroic endeavor in bearing down upon and repelling the disorganized enemy, thereby enabling the platoon to move out of the trap to a more favorable tactical position. His indomitable fighting spirit, fortitude, and great personal valor maintained in the face of overwhelming odds sustain and enhance the finest traditions of the U.S. Naval Service. He gallantly gave his life for his country.

OFFICIAL COMMUNIQUÉ:
TOKYO, Saturday, Nov. 4 (AP)
—Release 608 issued by General MacArthur's headquarters at 3:20 P.M. Friday (1:20 A.M., Friday, Eastern Standard Time):

The United States Far East Air Forces stepped up their serial offensive to 560 sorties as they engaged enemy aircraft for the second consecutive day in aerial combat. Pounding a reinforced Communist Army in North Korea for the 129th successive day, large amounts of war material were destroyed in attacks along the battle line and supply routes north of the combat zone.

A formation of four Yak-type aircraft engaged a like number of Fifth Air Force F-51 fighters in the northwest sector between Sonchon and Namsi. The F-51s quickly shot down two of the Yaks and the remainder broke off the engagement and fled to the west.

Enemy tanks were located near Unsan and at least seven were destroyed and another damaged. Hitting large troop concentrations in the same area, F-80 jet fighter-bombers, F-51 fighters and B-26 light bombers inflicted more than 400 casualties on the Reds, destroyed or damaged thirty-four fortified buildings, sixty-eight vehicles, many gun positions, and left many fires burning in troop and supply areas.

South of Huichon additional tank formations were brought under rocketing, and strafing attacks. Four were destroyed at Kujang, two near Sinhung, and another at Noha. Coast support and armed reconnaissance sorties cost the enemy at least 100 casualties in the Kilchu area, another fifty near Mupyong, while undetermined casualties resulted from liberal strafing attacks on troop positions at Kusong, Songchang, and Chongjon.

In a concerted effort to knockout supplies intended for Communist forces, Fifth Air Force planes attacked supply buildings, carts, and dumps in many separate areas. The largest single number of supply carts were destroyed between Yonbong and Chond, where a total of twenty were knocked out by a flight of F-80s.

Bomber Command Superfortresses struck at key interdiction targets beyond the present battle line with good to excellent results. Secondary explosions followed an attack by a small formation of the B-29s on a military staging area just southeast of Namag, a combination rail and highway bridge in the vicinity of Suwon suffered direct hits and a marshaling yard to the south of that town was attacked with good results.

A rail and highway complex at Chuuronjang, on the East Coast, was bombed, with a span being knocked out of each bridge. A rail bridge in the vicinity of Unsong in the central sector of North Korea was probably damaged by direct hits and a highway cut was made near that village. Three bridges in the Kanggye area were bombed with unobserved results.

Combat Cargo Command aircraft continued their airlifting of essential cargo into the battle areas. Another airfield was placed in operation yesterday. This one is at Honpo and cargo planes immediately put it to use, delivering 129 tons of cargo there. Totals for Thursday's cargo operations were 1,110 tons of cargo, 875 passengers, and 139 medical evacuees carried in 238 sorties.

—Release 609, issued by General MacArthur's headquarters at 4:05 P.M., Friday (2:05 A.M., Friday, Eastern Standard Time):

Heavy fighting raged all day yesterday in the Unsan sector as the enemy threw repeated attacks at United Nations forces.

An attempted encirclement of a unit of the United States First Cavalry Division was unsuccessful as the unit fought its way clear. Other elements of the division are attacking north in the Unsan area to contact a divisional unit which has been temporarily cut off by a heavy enemy attack supported by mortars, artillery, and rockets.

The enemy attacked southeast of Unsan with increasing intensity against elements of the R.O.K. (Republic of Korea) First Division and made limited gains. These attacks were contained with little loss of ground.

Reconnaissance elements of the United States Twenty-fourth Division advanced to the vicinity of Namsi and engaged an enemy force, killing 150. The remainder of the enemy withdrew toward the west. Other divisional elements engaged the enemy near Igu.

Elements of the R.O.K. Seventh and Eighth Divisions continued to organize and strengthen new defensive positions.

On the east coast, elements of the R.O.K. Capital Division patrolled in the Kilchu area to maintain contact with the enemy. Another unit of the division repulsed an enemy attack near Pungsan.

An enemy attack against elements of the United States Seventh Division north of Pungsan was repulsed and the Americans advanced to the north.

Patrols from the United States First Marine Division engaged enemy forces south of Majon.

United Nations units in rear areas reported the capture of several hundred prisoners and the dispersal of some enemy bands.

—Release 610, issued by General MacArthur's headquarters at 10:40 A.M., Saturday (8:40 P.M., Friday, Eastern Standard Time):

Vice Admiral C. Turner Joy, commander, United Nations Naval Forces, announced today the completion of minesweeping operations in the inner harbor at Wonsan.

Admiral Joy added: "Of course, you can never be positive you have cleared all of them."

Ships of the invasion fleet, commanded by Rear Admiral James H. Boyle, stood in to the harbor this morning and went alongside the dock, climaxing almost a month of intensive effort to clear what has been described as the most intensive minefield in history.

Elsewhere on the east coast, as on the west coast, minesweeping operations continued without let up. A United States Navy PBM Martin Mariner destroyed two mines in the harbor at Chinnampo.

Unloading of the Seventh United States Infantry Division and R.O.K. (Republic of Korea) Army personnel at Iwon from an amphibious fleet, commanded by Rear Admiral L. A. Thackrey, continued at a rapid rate. Admiral Thackrey flies his flag on the amphibious command ship U.S.S. Eldorado.

From Kojo on to the north of Songjin United States Navy ships of the east coast support force stood by to render direct naval gunfire support of the ground forces as necessary.

United States Marine Corsair pilots flying from the escort carriers U.S.S. Badoeng Strait and U.S.S. Sicily were out in close and general support of elements of the Seventh United States Infantry Division.

The Marine pilots spearheaded the advance of ground forces in the Pungsan area by clearing a ridge of enemy troops. Eleven heavily laden oxcarts proceeding south on a road out of Kapsan were destroyed. Two large oil storage tanks and adjacent structures were set afire in a refinery area southwest of Chongjing. Two anti-aircraft gun positions near Koogu were knocked out. A number of trucks were destroyed or damaged.

—Release 611, issued by General MacArthur's headquarters at 12:35 P.M., Saturday (10:35 P.M. Friday, Eastern Standard Time):

Mounting a total of 583 sorties, with T-6 control aircraft flying a record number of sixty-four of these, the United States Far East Air Forces continued to give maximum aerial support to embattled United Nations ground forces Friday as they fought a reinforced Communist army in North Korea.

Activities of the Fifth Air Force fighters were directed toward both close support and isolation of the battlefield as they attacked heavy supply concentrations to the rear of the lines. The enemy lost considerable artillery, supplies, and vehicles during yesterday's fighter-bomber attacks.

In the First Corps area of operations F-80 jets and F-51s attacked military targets near Unsan, destroying eight flak positions and damaging another, rocketed and strafed five supply buildings, four trucks, and numerous troop positions. At least 160 casualties were observed during the attacks. At Ipsok and near-by Ipsokha just south of Unsan, eight fortified buildings were destroyed and another four left ablaze. A fuel dump was destroyed, two gun positions successfully attacked, and troop and supply areas heavily attacked with undetermined results.

Hammering the Communists in the R.O.K. (Republic of Korea) sector, Fifth Air Force fighters destroyed six trucks, damaging three more, knocked out two artillery pieces and set several supply buildings afire. At Hagu, southeast of Unsan, many troops were strafed as well as supplies with unknown results. The biggest single success of the day by armed reconnaissance flights was eighteen vehicles destroyed and another sixteen damaged in a sweep from Fungyang to Chosan, near the northern border. Ten rail cars were destroyed and ten others damaged in an attack on rail lines near Kuchang.

At Chungok four large camouflaged objects were destroyed and another damaged. Between Hoedok and Changsong seven vehicles and three flak positions were destroyed. Artillery at Kujang was attacked, with three self propelled weapons and two anti-aircraft guns being destroyed. Another four artillery pieces were damaged just south of Taegwan and a tank destroyed near Huichon. Five vehicles and two supply dumps in the vicinity were attacked successfully. Large amounts of supplies were destroyed at Pyorha when eleven supply dumps were rocketed and strafed and twelve barracks were burned to the ground at Sakchu.

Marine aircraft, operating from Wonsan airfield under the operational control of the Fifth Air Force, gave close support to United Nations elements near the northeast coast.

Combat Cargo Command aircraft kept the steady flow of essential cargo and personnel at a high level by flying a total of 1,319 tons of supplies and 475 passengers into Korea. Two hundred and fourteen medical air evacuees were carried out on return trips. A routine resupply drop was made to troops in the vicinity of Pungsan where 30 tons of ammunition and rations were parachuted in.

Bomber Command Superfortresses, hammering at supply lines, dropped a span from both a rail bridge and highway bridge at Kanggye and cut the rail lines out of that city. Excellent results were obtained on a strike at the marshaling yards at Chongjing.

At the end of yesterday's operations known enemy losses stood at 160 vehicles, two tanks, three self-propelled guns, twenty-six artillery and anti-aircraft weapons, one locomotive, thirty-one rail cars, seventeen supply dumps, one fuel storage area, twenty-seven fortified buildings, ten supply buildings, and twenty-five supply carts destroyed or damaged.

†RED CLOUD, MITCHELL, JR.

Rank and Organization: Corporal, U.S. Army, Company E, 19th Infantry Regiment, 24th Infantry Division.
Born: July 2, 1924, Hatfield, Wisconsin.
Entered Service At: Merrilan, Wisconsin.
Place and Date: Near Chonghyon, Korea, November 5, 1950.
Citation: Cpl. Red Cloud, Company E, distinguished himself by conspicuous gallantry and intrepidity above and beyond the call of duty in action against the enemy. From his position on the point of a ridge, immediately in front of the company command post, he was the first to detect the approach of the Chinese Communist forces and give alarm as the enemy charged from a brush-covered area less than 100 feet from him. Springing up he delivered devastating pointblank automatic rifle fire into the advancing enemy. His accurate and intense fire checked this assault and gained time for the company to consolidate its defense. With utter fearlessness he maintained his firing position until severely wounded by enemy fire. Refusing assistance he pulled himself to his feet and wrapping his arm around a tree continued his deadly fire again, until he was fatally wounded. This heroic act stopped the enemy from overrunning his company's position and gained time for reorganization and evacuation of wounded. Cpl. Red Cloud's dauntless courage and gallant self-sacrifice reflects the highest credit upon himself and upholds the esteemed traditions of the U.S. Army.

OFFICIAL COMMUNIQUÉ:
TOKYO, Monday, Nov. 6 (AP)
—United States Tenth Corps communiqué 15, issued Monday morning, covering the twenty-four hour period ended midnight, Nov. 3:

The Tenth Corps attacked to the north against stubborn enemy resistance. Elements of the First Marine Division encountered strong resistance in the area south of Chosin (Changjin) reservoir. Elements of the Army Seventh Division advanced against enemy forces north of Pangsan. In the northeast, the R.O.K. Capital Division surrounded an enemy force in the vicinity of Kilchu. United Nations forces countered enemy harassing attacks in the vicinity of Wonsan.

—Release 615, issued by General MacArthur's headquarters at 1:30 P.M., Sunday (11:30 P.M., Saturday, Eastern Standard Time):

With a Carrier Task Group off Korea—Marine Corsairs from the escort carrier, Task Group 96, flew under heavy coastal weather today to support R.O.K. (Republic of Korea) troops in their advance against strengthening North Korean positions in the mountains of northeast Korea from Pungsan to Kilchu. Some of the flights encountered heavy snowfall over the higher ridges.

Morning flights from the Sicily worked with ground controllers of the R.O.K. Capital Division to knock out two enemy tanks, two trucks, a jeep, a building housing Red troops, and to hit the regimental command position itself in Kilchu.

Succeeding flights from the U.S.S. Badoeng Strait and from First Marine Air Wing units ashore pounded enemy artillery, mortars, and troop positions on the surrounding ridges and gutted several buildings in a factory area on the outskirts of the city.

All flights were directed to specific targets by the ground controllers in the front lines.

Maj. Arnold Lund of Flagstaff, Ariz., reported a fierce artillery duel between the R.O.K. troops, who were south of Kilchu, and the North Koreans who held the city and flanking ridges.

One Red-held ridge appeared to be holding up against incessant R.O.K. attacks and Lund's flight was directed to pummel it with napalm (jellied gasoline) and bombs. Other Marine flights reported for duty with the controller and the streams of rockets, bombs, napalm, and 20mm. shells, from all directions, drove the Reds from one protecting slope to another. Still the artillery duel continued, and air strikes were directed against the enemy gun positions.

Capt. Warren Nichols of Beaumont, Tex., dived down in a napalming attack on a concentration of Red troops. His second squadron, led by T/Sgt. Leo Ihli of Pierre, S.D., followed with 500-pound bombs to tear up the area not covered with the flaming napalm bombs.

"The Reds were shooting at us and the R.O.K.'s were shooting at them. There were bullets flying all over the place," Nichols related.

"After we had chased the Reds across the valley a few times, the R.O.K.'s began to move forward, standing up. They just picked up the panels marking their front lines and started walking up the ridge."

The ground coordinators called for rockets and strafing on the enemy in front of the advancing R.O.K.'s. The 5-inch rockets and 20-mm. shells ripped up the ground in front of the panels as they moved up the hill. Enthusiastic South Korean troops stood up on boulders to get a better look at the show, the pilots reported.

When the Marines left the area the panels were on top of the ridge and the ground coordinator was profuse in his thanks. His troops had been trying to seize the ridge for two days.

Other support flights from the jeep carrier task group hit trenches and heavy gun emplacements on ridges near Pungsan, and a reconnaissance flight up the coastline knocked out an artillery piece and three carts loaded with ammunition, and damaged a tank in a village ten miles north of Changjin. The flight met intense and quite accurate anti-aircraft fire over the airfields near that city, but fortunately none of the planes was hit.

—Release 616, issued by General MacArthur's headquarters, at 5:15 P.M. Sunday (3:15 A.M. Sunday, Eastern Standard Time):

The enemy continued their heavy drive toward Kunu again yesterday. Three attacks by an estimated 3,000 troops within ten hours were launched in the Won area. The third of these attacks was supported by tanks, artillery, and automatic weapons with the main effort a few miles southeast of Won. All were repulsed by determined counter-attacks and defensive fires by the United nations forces. At least four enemy tanks were destroyed in this area during the afternoon by friendly air. Latest reports indicate that the town of Won was in enemy hands.

Elements of the United States Twenty-fourth Division repulsed an enemy attack northwest of Kisong.

A combat patrol of the United States Second Division engaged an estimated 200 enemy in the vicinity of Tokehon resulting in twenty enemy killed.

Elements of the First United States Marine Division were reported to be receiving small arms and mortar fire during their attack in the vicinity of Sudong. An enemy counter-attack was repulsed and latest reports state that the Marines were continuing their advance northward. Other divisional elements continued to eliminate enemy in their area.

The Tenth Philippines Brigade Combat Team reported the capture of 165 prisoners of war during the period.

—Release 617 issued by General MacArthur's headquarters at 12:15 P.M. Monday (10:15 P.M. Monday, Eastern Standard Time):

United States Marine Corsair pilots operating from the escort carriers U.S.S. Sicily and U.S.S. Badoeng Strait were out in force yesterday in close and general support of United States Seventh Infantry elements in the Pungsan and Kapsan area.

Red troop concentrations impeding the advance of United States ground forces were severely mauled by the Marine fliers with bombs, rockets, napalm, and 20-mm. cannon fire.

Destroyed by the hard-hitting Corsairs were two command posts, four military buildings, one fuel dump, several trucks, and several gun emplacements.

Just before dusk last evening a lookout aboard the heavy cruiser U.S.S. Rochester sighted a floating mine in the harbor entrance channel at Wonsan. Bluejackets armed with rifles were immediately dispatched by boat to sink or detonate the drifting menace.

When rifle fire failed to do the job the Rochester got under way for the danger area and destroyed the mine with a few bursts.

†REEM, ROBERT DALE

Rank and Organization: Second Lieutenant, U.S. Marine Corps, Company H, 3d Battalion, 7th Marines, 1st Marine Division (Rein).
Born: October 20, 1925, Lancaster, Pennsylvania.
Entered Service At: Elizabethtown, Pennsylvania.
Place and Date: Vicinity of Chinhung-ni, Korea, November 6, 1950.
Citation: For conspicuous gallantry and intrepidity at the risk of his life above and beyond the call of duty as a platoon commander in Company H, in action against enemy aggressor forces. Grimly determined to dislodge a group of heavy enemy infantry units occupying well-concealed and strongly fortified positions on commanding ground overlooking unprotected terrain. 2d Lt. Reem moved slowly forward up the side of the ridge with his platoon in the face of a veritable hail of shattering hostile machine gun, grenade, and rifle fire. Three times repulsed by a resolute enemy force in achieving his objective, and pinned down by the continuing fury of hostile fire, he rallied and regrouped the heroic men in his depleted and disorganized platoon in preparation for a fourth attack. Issuing last minute orders to his noncommissioned officers when an enemy grenade landed in a depression of the rocky ground in which the group was standing, 2d Lt. Reem unhesitatingly chose to sacrifice himself and, springing upon the deadly missile, absorbed the full impact of the explosion in his body, thus protecting others from serious injury and possible death. Stouthearted and indomitable, he readily yielded his own chance of survival that his subordinate leaders might live to carry on the fight against a fanatic enemy. His superb courage, cool decisiveness, and valiant spirit of self-sacrifice in the face of certain death reflect the highest credit upon 2d Lt. Reem and the U.S. Naval Service. He gallantly gave his life for his country.

OFFICIAL COMMUNIQUÉ:
UNITED STATES EIGHTH ARMY HEADQUARTERS, Korea, Nov. 6 (AP)
—Release issued at 6:00 P.M., Monday (4:00 A.M., Eastern Standard Time):

The enemy attack which was launched this morning at 5:10 against elements of the Twenty-fourth Division (Nineteenth Regiment), drove 1,200 yards into friendly positions before it was repelled at 7:00 A.M. This action took place six miles north of Anju.

Another enemy attack made at 5:30 A.M., two miles east of the above action, was countered by friendly forces and repelled. At 11:30 A.M. there was no enemy contact in the area.

An enemy battalion attacked elements of the R.O.K. Seventh Division (Fifth Regiment) at 11:10 A.M., five miles east of Kunu. The attack was contained with no loss of ground. There were several attacks and counter-attacks in this area today, but at 2:00 P.M., there had been no change in positions.

TOKYO, Tuesday, Nov. 7 (AP)
—Release 619, timed at 4:00 P.M., Monday (2:00 A.M. Eastern Standard Time):

Enemy attacks against United Nations positions in the area south of Yongbyon decreased in intensity yesterday.

Last night an attack against elements of the United States Twenty-fourth Division was repulsed without loss of ground. Some of the enemy that had infiltrated during the fight were eliminated by American patrols.

The Twenty-seventh British Commonwealth Brigade repulsed an enemy probing attack in the Pakchon area.

Units of the United States First Cavalry Division patrolling in the Kuna area captured forty-two of the enemy, destroyed two self-propelled guns, and several truck loads of arms and ammunition. Other divisional elements repelled two enemy probing attacks.

The R.O.K. (Republic of Korea) First Division patrolled the Chongchon River sector to maintain contact with the enemy. Elements of the R.O.K. Sixth Division repulsed an enemy attack in the Kuna area without loss of ground. All units of the R.O.K. Second Corps continued to improve positions throughout the sector.

On the east coast, elements of the R.O.K. Capital Division advanced about six miles east of Kilchu after having repelled an enemy counter-attack and cleared road blocks along the route.

Elements of the United States First Marine Division continued their advance north toward Koto.

Operations against enemy groups in liberated areas were continued by United Nations units.

—Release 620, (Navy summary) issued today at 11:00 A.M. (9:00 P.M., Monday, Eastern Standard Time):

Vice Admiral Turner Joy, commander, United Nations Naval Forces, has ordered Task Force 77 of the Seventh Fleet to provide a continuing maximum air effort in North Korea.

Arriving off the far northern east coast of Korea yesterday (Monday), Task Force 77 immediately went to work on communications lines, supply areas, and troop concentrations.

Task Force 77 is commanded by Rear Admiral E. C. Ewen, who flies his flag on the U.S.S. Philippine Sea. The Seventh Fleet is commanded by Vice Admiral Arthur D. Struble, who flies his flag on the U.S.S. Missouri.

Elsewhere along the East coast yesterday three floating mines were destroyed or otherwise disposed of by the heavy cruiser U.S.S. Rochester, the destroyer U.S.S. Lind, and the oiler U.S.S. Cimarron.

United States Navy ships of the East coast support force were deployed along the coast to render direct naval gunfire support as necessary.

Minesweeping operations on the West coast continued without let up with British Commonwealth ships providing protective fire cover for the operations.

Unloading operations from the amphibious fleets at Wonsan and Iwon continue on schedule.

†MITCHELL, FRANK N.

Rank and Organization: First Lieutenant, U.S. Marine Corps, Company A, 1st Battalion, 7th Marines, 1st Marine Division (Rein).
Born: August 18, 1921, Indian Gap, Texas.
Entered Service At: Roaring Springs, Texas.
Place and Date: Near Hansan-ni, Korea, November 26, 1950.
Citation: For conspicuous gallantry and intrepidity at the risk of his life above and beyond the call of duty as leader of a rifle platoon of Company A, in action against enemy aggressor forces. Leading his platoon in point position during a patrol by his company through a thickly wooded and snow covered area in the vicinity of Hansan-ni, 1st Lt. Mitchell acted immediately when the enemy suddenly opened fire at pointblank range, pinning down his forward elements and inflicting numerous casualties in his ranks. Boldly dashing to the front under blistering fire from automatic weapons and small-arms, he seized an automatic rifle from one of the wounded men and effectively trained it against the attackers and, when his ammunition was expended, picked up and hurled grenades with deadly accuracy, at the same time directing and encouraging in driving the outnumbering enemy from his position. Maneuvering to set up a defense when the enemy furiously counterattacked to the front and left flank, 1st Lt. Mitchell, despite wounds sustained early in the action, reorganized his platoon under the devastating fire, and spearheaded a fierce hand-to-hand struggle to repulse the onslaught. Asking for volunteers to assist in searching for and evacuating the wounded, he personally led a party of litter bearers through the hostile line in growing darkness and, although suffering intense pain from multiple wounds, stormed ahead and waged a single-handed battle against the enemy, successfully covering the withdrawal of his men before he was fatally struck down by a burst of small-arms fire. Stouthearted and indomitable in the face of tremendous odds, 1st Lt. Mitchell, by his fortitude, great personal valor and extraordinary heroism, saved the lives of several marines and inflicted heavy casualties among the aggressors. His unyielding courage throughout reflects the highest credit upon himself and the U.S. Naval Service. He gallantly gave his life for his country.

PITTMAN, JOHN A.

Rank and Organization: Sergeant, U.S. Army, Company C, 23d Infantry Regiment, 2d Infantry Division.
Born: October 15, 1928, Carrolton, Mississippi.
Entered Service At: Carrolton, Mississippi.
Place and Date: Near Kujangdong, Korea, November 26, 1950.
Citation: Sgt. Pittman, distinguished himself by conspicuous gallantry and intrepidity above and beyond the call of duty in action against the enemy. He volunteered to lead his squad in a counterattack to regain commanding terrain lost in an earlier engagement. Moving aggressively forward in the face of intense artillery, mortar, and small-arms fire he was wounded by mortar fragments. Disregarding his wounds he continued to lead and direct his men in a bold advance against the hostile standpoint. During this daring action, an enemy grenade was thrown in the midst of his squad endangering the lives of his comrades. Without hesitation, Sgt. Pittman threw himself on the grenade and absorbed its burst with his body. When a medical aid-man reached him, his first request was to be informed as to how many of his men

were hurt. This intrepid and selfless act saved several of his men from death or serious injury and was an inspiration to the entire command. Sgt. Pittman's extraordinary heroism reflects the highest credit upon himself and is in keeping with the esteemed traditions of the military service.

OFFICIAL COMMUNIQUÉ:
TOKYO, Nov. 24, (AP)
—Release 674 issued at 11:30 A.M. (9:30 A.M., Saturday, Eastern Standard Time):

The eight-inch guns of the United States Navy heavy cruiser St. Paul and the flying artillery of carrier-based United States Marine Corsairs teamed up yesterday in close support of the R.O.K. (Republic of Korea) Capital division in its advance north of Chongjin.

The St. Paul, screened by the destroyer U.S.S. Sperry, bombarded troop concentrations, tanks, supplies, and communications lines. The heavy cruiser flies the flag of Rear Admiral R. H. Hillenkoetter.

Marine pilots operating from the escort carrier Badoeng Strait concentrated their main effort on military targets in the vicinity of Todong, three to five miles north of Chongjin.

One troop column numbering about 300 men was repeatedly rocketed and strafed. Heavy casualties were inflicted. Another troop concentration north of Todong was heavily bombed and strafed.

A roadblock and fortified hill position commanding the avenue of advance was knocked out. Two large storage buildings were destroyed.

The U.S.S. Badoeng Strait flies the flag of Rear Admiral Richard W. Ruble.

The heavy cruiser U.S.S. Rochester continued firing night illumination missions in the Wonsan area.

A floating mine off Kyongsong was destroyed by the destroyer U.S.S. Sperry. British Commonwealth fleet units continued with patrol and blockade operations on the west coast. Minesweeping operations continued on both coasts.

—Release 675 issued at 2:45 P.M. (12:45 A.M. Eastern Standard Time):

United States Far East Air Forces fighters and bombers launched heavy attacks against the Communists Saturday in the second day of the general offensive. Escape routes, supply points, and Red troop concentrations were pounded from the battle lines to the international border.

Bomber Command Superfortresses knocked out sixteen supply points in fire-bomb attacks. Striking along three main supply routes, the B-29s dropped incendiaries on targets of opportunity from Kanggye to near Huichon, Changtienhoku to Kusong, and from Puckchin to the Yalu River. Heavy smoke and fires followed the attacks. One formation of Superfortresses hit the rail bridge at Manpojin and the highway bridge at Changtienhoku with 4,000-pound general purpose bombs.

Fifth Air Force B-26 light bombers of the Third Bomb Group and the 452nd Bomb Wing neared a record number of night intruder sorties as the period came to a close at midnight Saturday. Throughout the previous night and into the day the B-26s had bombed, napalmed, rocketed and strafed thirteen different areas. At dusk large formations of the light bombers were reported over many targets along the battle lines and deep into North Korea.

F-80 jets and F-51 fighters provided aerial cover for ground forces, hitting the Communist in forces from one end of the battle line to the other, and ranging into rear areas destroying lines of communications. In both the First and Ninth Corps areas the fighters rocketed and strafed the enemy throughout the day with excellent results.

Two groups of Communists fled northward after heavy attacks by fighters. An estimated 2,000 enemy troops facing R.O.K. (Republic of Korea) elements in the vicinity of Kujang were routed by the fighters and another group of 500 northeast of Yongbyon suffered many casualties before they broke and ran.

An enemy cavalry unit attempted to attack R.O.K. forces east of Taechon but was repulsed by an air strike that killed at least fifty of the horsemen. Following this attack the fighters destroyed one tank, one self-propelled gun, and two trucks in the same vicinity.

Combat Cargo Command totals for yesterday were 885 tons of cargo, 547 passengers, and 235 medical evacuees.

—Release 676, issued at 4:25 P.M. (2:25 A.M., Eastern Standard Time) today:

United Nations forces continued to advance along the entire front yesterday. The enemy launched several counter-attacks in an effort to slow the drive.

After an advance of about six miles, elements of the United States Twenty-fourth Division entered Chongju against light opposition.

Elements of the R.O.K. (Republic of Korea) First Division repelled an enemy counter-attack near Taechon, but a subsequent counter-attack forced the R.O.K. troops to make a limited withdrawal. The R.O.K. Army unit counter-attacked vigorously and the enemy withdrew toward Taechon. Divisional units continued their advance against moderate resistance.

Enemy resistance stiffened in the face of the attack by elements of the United States Twenty-fifth Division in the Yongpo sector. The enemy used intense mortar fire in an effort to stem the advance.

The United States Second Division registered gains of several miles against small arms, automatic weapons and mortar fire in the Sinhung area.

Elements of the R.O.K. Second Corps continued to advance in the face of moderate enemy resistance in the area north of Tokchon. An enemy counter-attack forced elements of the R.O.K. Eighth Division to make a limited withdrawal.

United States Army troops destroyed an enemy road block near Tongyang and dispersed enemy bands operating in the area.

A tank infantry patrol from the United States First Marine Division dispersed an enemy force near Yudan. The enemy withdrew northwest after the action.

Elements of the United States Seventh Division advanced approximately eight miles northwest of Samsu, encountering light enemy resistance. A combat patrol from the division dispersed an enemy force southwest of Hyesanjin.

Elements of the R.O.K. Third Division advanced about six miles northeast of Hapsu against light resistance.

The R.O.K. Capital Division reached the vicinity of Chongjin after bypassing Nanam yesterday. Strong patrols were sent into Nanam by the R.O.K. units. The enemy continued to offer light resistance in the Chongjin sector.

The United States Tenth Corps reports 616 enemy killed and 230 captured during the last several days.

In the Chongju-Pakchon area the enemy refused to make an appearance.

In the Taechon-Pakchon area, no enemy forces were encountered until 3:15 A.M. Nov. 25, when a hostile battalion launched a counter-attack two and one-half miles east of Taechon. This attack was repulsed but at 7:30 the same morning the enemy renewed his attack and gained 1,500 yards. A successful friendly counter-attack compelled the enemy to withdraw to the high ground three miles east of Taechon. Friendly air strikes accelerated his retirement. At last reports the hostile forces were still withdrawing.

Friendly patrols reported that an enemy force, possibly regimental size, was in the area three miles south-southwest of Taechon. The battalion attack could have been part of the larger unit.

†DESIDERIO, REGINALD B.

Rank and Organization: Captain, U.S. Army, Commanding Officer of Company E, 27th Infantry Regiment, 25th Infantry Division.
Born: September 12, 1918, Clairton, Pennsylvania.
Entered Service At: Gilroy, California.
Place and Date: Near Ipsok, Korea, November 27, 1950.
Citation: Capt. Desiderio distinguished himself by conspicuous gallantry and intrepidity at the repeated risk of his life above and beyond the call of duty. His company was given the mission of defending the command post of a task force against an enemy breakthrough. After personal reconnaissance during darkness and intense enemy fire, he placed his men in defensive positions to repel an attack. Early in the action he was wounded, but refused evacuation and despite enemy fire continued to move among his men checking their positions and making sure that each element was prepared to receive the next attack. Again wounded, he continued to direct his men. By his inspiring leadership he encouraged them to hold their position. In the subsequent fighting when the fanatical enemy succeeded in penetrating the position, he personally charged them with his carbine rifle and grenades, inflicting many casualties until he himself was mortally wounded. His men, spurred on by his intrepid example, repelled this final attack. Capt. Desiderio's heroic leadership, courageous and loyal devotion to duty, and his complete disregard for personal safety reflect the highest honor on him and are in keeping with the esteemed traditions of the U.S. Army.

†FAITH, DON C., JR.

Rank and Organization: Lieutenant Colonel, U.S. Army, commanding officer, 1st Battalion, 32d Infantry Regiment, 7th Infantry Division.
Born: August 26, 1918, Washington, Indiana.
Entered Service At: Washington, Indiana.
Place and Date: Vicinity of Hagaru-ri, Northern Korea, November 27 to December 1, 1950.
Citation: Lt. Col. Faith, commanding officer 1st Battalion, distinguished himself by conspicuous gallantry and intrepidity in action above and beyond the call of duty in the area of the Chosin Reservoir. When the enemy launched a fanatical attack against his battalion, Lt. Col. Faith unhesitatingly exposed himself to heavy enemy fire as he moved about directing the action. When the enemy penetrated the positions, Lt. Col. Faith personally led counterattacks to restore the position. During an attack by his battalion to effect a junction with another U.S. unit, Lt.Col. Faith reconnoitered the route for, and personally directed, the first elements of his command across the ice-covered reservoir and then directed the movement of his vehicles which were loaded with wounded, until all of his command had passed through the enemy fire. Having completed this he crossed the reservoir himself. Assuming command of the unit his force had joined he was given the mission of attacking to join friendly elements to the south. Lt. Col. Faith, although physically exhausted in the bitter cold, organized and launched an attack which was soon stopped by enemy fire. He ran forward under enemy small-arms and automatic-weapons fire, got his men on their feet and personally led the fire attack as it blasted its way through the enemy ring. As they came to a hairpin curve, enemy fire from a roadblock again pinned the column down. Lt. Col. Faith organized a group of men and directed their attack on the enemy positions on the right flank. He then placed himself at the head of another group of men and in the face of direct enemy fire led an attack on the enemy roadblock, firing his pistol and throwing grenades. When he had reached a position approximately 30 yards from the roadblock he was mortally wounded, but continued to direct the attack until the roadblock was overrun. Throughout the 5 days of action Lt. Col. Faith gave no thought to his safety and did not spare himself. His presence each time in the position

of greatest danger was an inspiration to his men. Also, the damage he personally inflicted firing from his position at the head of his men was of material assistance on several occasions. Lt. Col. Faith's outstanding gallantry and noble self-sacrifice above and beyond the call of duty reflects the highest honor on him and are in keeping with the highest traditions of the U.S. Army.

KENNEMORE, ROBERT S.

Rank and Organization: Staff Sergeant, U.S. Marine Corps, Company E, 2d Battalion, 7th Marines, 1st Marine Division (Rein).
Born: June 21, 1920, Greenville, South Carolina.
Entered Service At: Greenville, South Carolina.
Place and Date: North of Yudam-ni, Korea, November 27 and 28, 1950.
Citation: For conspicuous gallantry and intrepidity at the risk of his life above and beyond the call of duty as leader of a machine gun section in Company E, in action against enemy aggressor forces. With the Company's defensive perimeter overrun by a numerically superior hostile force during a savage night attack north of Yudam-ni and his platoon commander seriously wounded, S/Sgt. Kennemore unhesitatingly assumed command, quickly reorganized the unit and directed the men in consolidating the position. When an enemy grenade landed in the midst of a machine gun squad, he bravely place his foot on the missile and, in the face of almost certain death, personally absorbed the full force of the explosion to prevent injury to his fellow marines. By his indomitable courage, outstanding leadership and selfless efforts in behalf of his comrades, S/Sgt. Kennemore was greatly instrumental in driving the enemy from the area and upheld the highest traditions of the U.S. Naval Service.

CAFFERATA, HECTOR A., JR.

Rank and Organization: Private, U.S. Marine Corps Reserve, Company F, 2d Battalion, 7th Marines, 1st Marine Division (Rein).
Born: November 4, 1929, New York, New York.
Entered Service At: Dover, New Jersey.
Place and Date: Korea, November 28, 1950.
Citation: For conspicuous gallantry and intrepidity at the risk of his life above and beyond the call of duty while serving as a rifleman with Company F, in action against enemy aggressor forces. When all the other members of his fire team became casualties, creating a gap in the lines, during the initial phase of a vicious attack launched by a fanatical enemy of regimental strength against his company's hill position, Pvt. Cafferata waged a lone battle with grenades and rifle fire as the attack gained momentum and the enemy threatened penetration through the gap and endangered the integrity of the entire defensive perimeter. Making a target of himself under the devastating fire from automatic weapons, rifles, grenades, and mortars, he maneuvered up and down the line and delivered accurate and effective fire against the onrushing force, killing 15, wounding many more, and forcing the others to withdraw so that reinforcements could move up and consolidate the position. Again fighting desperately against a renewed onslaught later that same morning when a hostile grenade landed in a shallow entrenchment occupied by wounded marines, Pvt. Cafferata rushed into the gully under heavy fire, seized the deadly missile in his right hand and hurled it free of his comrades before it detonated, severing part of one finger and wounding him in the right hand and arm. Courageously ignoring the intense pain, he staunchly fought on until he was struck by a sniper's bullet and forced to submit to evacuation for medical treatment. Stouthearted and indomitable, Pvt. Cafferata, by his fortitude, great personal valor, and dauntless perseverance in the

face of almost certain death, saved the lives of several of his fellow marines and contributed essentially to the success achieved by his company in maintaining its defensive position against tremendous odds. His extraordinary heroism throughout was in keeping with the highest tradition of the U.S. Naval Service.

OFFICIAL COMMUNIQUÉ:
TOKYO, Wednesday, Nov. 29 (AP)
—Release 681 issued by Gen. Douglas MacArthur's headquarters at 4:10 P.M. (2:10 A.M., Eastern Standard Time):

Enemy attacks against United Nations forces in the western sector of Korea mounted in intensity yesterday.

Increasing enemy pressure forced elements of the R.O.K. (Republic of Korea) First Division to make further withdrawals in the Taechon area. Friendly counter-attacks restored some of the lost ground.

Elements of the United States Army Twenty-fifth Division readjusted positions in the face of heavy enemy attacks.

Two heavy enemy attacks against units of the United States Army Second Division were repulsed yesterday.

Heavy enemy pressure forced units of the R.O.K. Second Corps to make additional withdrawals in the Tokchon area.

Advanced elements of the United States First Marine Division contained an enemy attack in the area northwest of Yudam.

The United States Army Seventh Division and the R.O.K. Third Division continued aggressive patrol action throughout yesterday.

An enemy counter-attack against elements of the R.O.K. Capital Division forced a limited withdrawal in the Chongjin sector. A subsequent attack by the R.O.K. Capital Division restored the lost ground. (This report covers the twenty-four-hour period up to 2:00 A.M. Nov. 28) On Nov. 27 the enemy continued heavy pressure along almost the entire western front.

Although enemy pressure during the period was lightest on the extreme left flank of friendly forces, there were attacks in that area also.

Repeated night attacks and deep penetrations by very large enemy forces forced friendly withdrawals in the Uhyon-Tokchon area and in the vicinity of Maengsan. The outcome of this action has not yet been decided.

In the Chongju-Pakchon area a squadron of horse cavalry was observed four miles northwest of Naechongjong. Taken under friendly artillery fire and subjected to an air strike, it suffered about 250 casualties. Artillery also took an undetermined number of enemy under fire seven miles southwest of Taechon.

In the Taechon-Pakchon area, hostile force infiltrated friendly positions five miles east of Taechon. At first contained, it continued to build up and increase its penetration. Two miles south of Taechon, the enemy succeeded in crossing the Chonbang River and penetrating our positions.

An enemy force of foot troops, combined with horse cavalry, launched a three-pronged attack which up to 3:30 P.M. yesterday afternoon had advanced to a point eight miles southeast of Taechon.

In the Unsan-Yongbyon area, strong enemy attacks and considerable infiltration characterized the events yesterday. There was an attack five miles southwest of Unsan; also, four miles southeast of that place, which continued from 4:00 A.M. yesterday and was still strong at noon yesterday. Heavy pressure developed eleven miles northeast of Yongbyon and four and one-half miles northwest of Kujang.

In the Kujang area, strong night attacks occurred Nov. 26-27 northeast of Kujang (area about four miles northeast) which were still continuing yesterday afternoon.

In the Chondong-Pukchang area heavy pressure developed the night of Nov. 25-26 and troop concentrations of one or two battalion size were observed four miles north of Kokchon and one mile north. The tempo of the counter-offensive increased in the Maengsan area.

In the Chongjin-Kilchu area, opposition stiffened late Nov. 26 and a strong counter-attack supported by two tanks and twelve artillery pieces was launched the night of Nov. 26-27.

—Release 682 (Navy) issued by Gen. Douglas MacArthur's headquarters at 10:35 A.M. (8:35 P.M. Tuesday, Eastern Standard Time):

The eight-inch guns of the heavy cruiser St. Paul and the flying artillery of carrier-based Marine Corsairs went to work in close support of the R.O.K. (Republic of Korea) Capital Division, advancing north of Chongjin yesterday.

While the St. Paul provided a steady stream of harassing, interdiction and call-fire support bombardment, the Marine fliers pounded troop concentrations, supplies and vehicular transport. The mauling of one troop concentration enabled friendly forces to move forward immediately.

Skyraiders, Corsairs and Panther jets of fast carrier Task Force 77 roared across North Korea yesterday to blast targets on the western half of the peninsula in a belt extending fifteen miles south of the border.

Rail and highway bridges and troop concentrations were the primary targets of the precision-flying Navy pilots.

One railroad bridge and one highway bridge were destroyed; one railroad and two highway bridges were damaged.

Approximately 200 troops near Kanggye were bombed and strafed with heavy casualties. Another concentration of about 100 troops south of Kanggye was heavily hit. Three other troop concentrations were attacked. More than thirty-five carts carrying supplies for the troops were destroyed.

The Navy fliers also destroyed eight warehouses and an ammunition dump.

A United States PBM Martin Mariner yesterday destroyed three mines near Chinnampo. The United States destroyer Norris exploded a mine on the east coast.

†BAUGH, WILLIAM B.

Rank and Organization: Private First Class, U.S. Marine Corps, Company G, 3d Battalion, 1st Marines, 1st Marine Division (Rein).
Born: July 7, 1930, McKinney, Kentucky.
Entered Service At: Harrison, Ohio.
Place and Date: Along the road from Koto-ri to Hagaru-ri, Korea, November 29, 1950.
Citation: For conspicuous gallantry and intrepidity at the risk of his life above and beyond the call of duty while serving as a member of an antitank assault squad attached to Company G, during a nighttime enemy attack against a motorized column. Acting instantly when a hostile grenade landed in his truck as he and his squad prepared to alight and assist in the repulse of an enemy force delivering intense automatic weapons and grenade fire from deeply entrenched and well-concealed roadside positions, Pfc. Baugh quickly shouted a warning to the other men in the vehicle and, mindful of his personal safety, hurled himself upon the deadly missile, thereby saving his comrades from injury or possible death. Sustaining severe wounds from which he died a short time afterward, Pfc. Baugh, by his superb courage and valiant spirit of self-sacrifice, upheld the highest traditions of the U.S. Naval Service. He gallantly gave his life for his country.

MYERS, REGINALD R.
Rank and Organization: Major, U.S. Marine Corps, 3d Battalion, 1st Marines, 1st Marine Division (Rein).
Born: November 26, 1919, Boise, Idaho.
Entered Service At: Boise, Idaho.
Place and Date: Near Hagaru-ri, Korea, November 29, 1950.
Citation: For conspicuous gallantry and intrepidity at the risk of his life above and beyond the call of duty as the executive officer of the 3d Battalion, in action against enemy aggressor forces. Assuming command of a composite unit of Army and Marine service and headquarters elements totaling approximately 250 men, during a critical stage in the vital defense of the strategically important military base at Hagaru-ri, Maj. Myers immediately initiated a determined and aggressive counterattack against a well-entrenched and cleverly concealed enemy force numbering an estimated 4,000. Severely handicapped by a lack of trained personnel and experienced leaders in his valiant efforts to regain maximum ground prior to daylight, he persisted in constantly exposing himself to intense, accurate, and sustained hostile fire in order to direct and supervise the employment of his men and to encourage and spur them on in pressing the attack. Inexorably moving forward up the steep, snow-covered slope with his depleted group in the face of apparently insurmountable odds, he concurrently directed artillery and mortar fire with superb skill and although losing 170 of his men during 14 hours of raging combat in subzero temperatures, continued to reorganize his unit and spearhead the attack which resulted in 600 enemy killed and 500 wounded. By his exceptional and valorous leadership throughout, Maj. Myers contributed directly to the success of his unit in restoring the perimeter. His resolute spirit of self-sacrifice and unfaltering devotion to duty enhance and sustain the highest traditions of the U.S. Naval Service.

OFFICIAL COMMUNIQUÉ:
TOKYO, Thursday, Nov. 30 (AP)
—Release 683, issued by Gen. Douglas MacArthur's headquarters at 2:40 P.M. Wednesday (12:40 A.M. Wednesday, Eastern Standard Time):

The United States Far East Air Force maintained the momentum of its intensified tactical support of United Nations forces Tuesday. Fifth Air Force fighters and bombers in heavy coordinated aerial assaults hammered the Communists in at least ninety different areas with the major effort centered along the battle line.

F-80 jets, F-51s and B-26s pounded Red troops in all sectors, inflicting heavy casualties. Near Naeyang at least 100 enemy troops were killed and another 100 killed at Yongsansong. Attacks against the Reds in the First Corps and the corps' zones of action took an undetermined toll of the enemy. Vehicles, fortified buildings, supply areas and artillery positions were destroyed in bombing and rocketing attacks.

B-26 light bombers, operating night and day, hit supply routes to the rear with excellent results. A fifteen-car train was destroyed southwest of Kanggye. A train of twenty cars was heavily damaged at Kuryonsong near Sinuiju and another train of approximately twenty cars was strafed with undetermined results at Pihyon.

A flight of F-80 jets made direct hits on the two bridges at Manpojin with 1,000-pound bombs, knocking out at least one span on a highway bridge.

Fifth Air Force known destruction totaled 154 fortified buildings, five artillery emplacements, seven supply areas, three rail tunnels destroyed or damaged, and more than 300 enemy troops killed.

Bomber Command Superfortresses attacked twenty-one targets in northwest Korea, including supply storage areas, communication centers and rail lines. Supply areas at Mupyong, Kanggye, Huichon, Taechon, Huchang, and Kuchang were left ablaze from incendiary attacks. Rail lines were cut at six separate points and a rail bridge in the vicinity of Kuchang suffered direct hits.

Combat Cargo aircraft carried 1,024 tons of cargo, including ammunition and winter clothing, in addition to 593 passengers and 674 medical evacuees yesterday.

—Release 684, issued by Gen. Douglas MacArthur's headquarters at 4:30 P.M. Wednesday (2:30 A.M. Wednesday, Eastern Standard Time):

Strong enemy attacks continued against United Nations forces operating in the western sector of Korea yesterday.

Fierce fighting was reported throughout the area. Hand-to-hand combat was reported in the Wawon area, where elements of the Turkish Brigade, using bayonets, killed approximately 200 enemy.

Elements of the R.O.K. (Republic of Korea) First Division continued to resist the enemy pressure throughout the day as other elements withdrew to positions farther to the southeast. The town of Yongsan changed hands twice during the day's action.

Elements of the United States Twenty-fifth Division continued to readjust and consolidate positions after breaking off from the enemy engagement of the preceding day. A successful planned withdrawal to new positions was accomplished during the period.

Elements of the United States Second Division disengaged with the enemy and withdrew to favorable positions as other elements of the division fought a delaying action to coordinate defensive positions farther south.

Some advances were made in the eastern sector of Korea during yesterday's action as elements of the R.O.K. Capital Division repulsed an enemy counter-attack and continued to advance to the northwest. Elements of the United States First Marine Division repulsed two heavy enemy attacks in the Yudam area early yesterday morning with no loss of ground. Increasing enemy pressure was reported throughout the period.

Elements of the United States Seventh Division were reported as receiving a heavy enemy counter-attack supported by tanks. Other elements of the division engaged in reducing enemy road blocks.

As the tempo of the communist offensive increased on Nov. 28, friendly forces were forced to withdraw to new positions. As of 6:00 P.M. Nov. 28, withdrawals to a designated line were progressing satisfactorily.

On Nov. 27 about 400 enemy were in the area eight miles north-northwest of Naechongjong, where they were brought under friendly artillery fire.

During the night of Nov. 27-28, a considerable force of enemy troops executed a series of frontal and flanking attacks starting from about ten miles north-northeast of Naechongjong, eventually compelling a friendly regiment to withdraw.

In the Taechon area on Nov. 27, an enemy regiment was driven from high ground about three miles southeast of the town by counter-attacking R.O.K. forces. Later a series of enemy counter-attacks developed into an assault on the right flank of the defending R.O.K.s forcing a withdrawal.

On the morning of Nov. 28 the Communists breached R.O.K. defenses two miles northwest of Yongsan, followed by a penetration of the right flank of the friendly unit. Another enemy force pushed in from west of Yongsan and by 10:00 A.M. on Nov. 28, had closed on Yongsan, where the friendly unit, although virtually encircled, continued to give battle.

In the Yongbyon area, attacking enemy were subjected to heavy United Nations air attacks on Nov. 27 but continued to press forward. By the morning of Nov. 28, considerable penetration had been achieved by the enemy. But the results of this action have not been reported.

Heavy enemy pressure continued Nov. 27 against friendly forces disposed north and northeast of Kujang, on the north bank of the Chongchon River. This continuing attack forced the friendly units to withdraw gradually across the river, with the enemy continuing to maintain close contact.

At the close of the period, friendly forces were withdrawing under pressure in the general area of Kyongdong, with the withdrawal progressing in good order.

Near Sunchon, friendly reserves moving forward encountered road blocks and ambushes, but by 6:00 P.M. on Nov. 28, were reported to have gained contact with the troops they had been sent to reinforce, five miles southwest of Pukchang.

Four enemy regiments were thrown into the Pukchang area and by Nov. 28 had driven out defending R.O.K. forces. By 9:30 A.M. Nov. 28 an estimated enemy regiment was in Pukchang, with another regiment a mile west of Taepyong, south of Pukchang. However, at last report, two friendly regiments were believed to be holding the high ground three miles southwest of Pukchang. There is a possibility that friendly forces are still holding out at Maengsan, a town nine miles northeast of Pukchang, which was surrounded by the enemy at noon on Nov. 27.

In the Chosin (Changjin) Reservoir area two enemy forces of about three regiments each attacked friendly forces on Nov. 28, while other enemy groups cut friendly supply lines between Hagaru and Yudam. There were some minor actions all up and down the Hagaru-Hamhung highway. Considerable enemy movements were reported east of the reservoir, and one large enemy group, supported by tanks, attacked friendly positions in the area.

—Release 685 (Navy summary), issued by Gen. Douglas MacArthur's headquarters at 9:50 A.M. (7:50 P.M. Wednesday, Eastern Standard Time):

During the day yesterday and throughout the preceding night the heavy cruiser St. Paul, flying the flag of Rear Admiral Roscoe H. Hillenkoetter, continued to provide pin-point bombardment support of the R.O.K. Capital Division advancing north of Chongjin.

Gun crews of the heavy cruiser trained their eight-inch guns on troop concentrations, gun emplacements and interdiction targets ten miles north of the key industrial city.

Minesweeping operations continue on both coasts despite bitter cold and generally unfavorable weather conditions.

United states Navy P2V Neptunes and PBM Mariners and Royal Air Force Sunderlands were out on regular armed reconnaissance and anti-mine patrols.

British Commonwealth fleet units continue intensive patrol and blockade operations on the west coast to thwart any enemy attempts at water resupply.

Units of the Seventh Fleet continue to patrol Formosa Strait.

†PAGE, JOHN U. D.

Rank and Organization: Lieutenant Colonel, U.S. Army, X Corps Artillery, while attached to the 52d Transportation Truck Battalion.
Born: February 8, 1904, Malahi Island, Luzon, Philippine Islands.
Entered Service At: St Paul, Minnesota.
Place and Date: Near Chosin Reservoir, Korea, November 29 to December 10, 1950.
Citation: Lt. Col. Page, a member of X Corps Artillery, distinguished himself by conspicuous gallantry and intrepidity in action above and beyond the call of duty in a series of exploits. On November 29th, Lt. Col. Page left X Corps Headquarters at Hamhung with the mission of establishing traffic control on the main supply route to 1st Marine Division positions and those of some Army elements on the Chosin Reservoir plateau. Having completed his mission Lt. Col. Page was free to return to the safety of Hamhung but chose to remain on the plateau to aid an isolated signal station, thus being cut off from elements of the marine division. After rescuing his jeep driver by breaking up an ambush near a destroyed bridge, Lt. Col. Page reached the lines of a surrounded marine garrison at Koto-ri. He then voluntarily developed and trained a reserve force of assorted army troops trapped with the marines. By exemplary leadership and tireless devotion he made an effective tactical unit available. In order that casualties might be evacuated, an airstrip was improvised on frozen ground partly

outside of the Koto-ri defensive perimeter which was continually under enemy attack. During 2 such attacks, Lt. Col. Page exposed himself on the airstrip to direct fire on the enemy, and twice mounted the rear deck of a tank, manning the machine gun on the turret to drive the enemy back into a no man's land. On December 3rd, while being flown low over enemy lines in a light observation plane, Lt. Col. Page dropped hand-grenades on Chinese positions and sprayed foxholes with automatic fire from his carbine. After 10 days of constant fighting the marine and army units in the vicinity of the Chosin Reservoir had succeeded in gathering at the edge of the plateau and Lt. Col. Page was flown to Hamhung to arrange for artillery support of the beleaguered troops attempting to break out. Again Lt. Col. Page refused an opportunity to remain in safety and returned to give every assistance to his comrades. As the column slowly moved south Lt. Col. Page joined the rear guard. When it neared the entrance to a narrow pass it came under frequent attacks on both flanks. Mounting an abandoned tank, Lt. Col. Page manned the machine gun, braved heavy return fire, and covered the passing vehicles until the danger diminished. Later when another attack threatened his section of the convoy, then in the middle of the pass, Lt. Col. Page took a machine gun to the hillside and delivered effective counter-fire, remaining exposed while men and vehicles passed through the ambush. On the night of December 10th, the convoy reached the bottom of the pass but was halted by a strong enemy force at the front and on both flanks. Deadly small-arms fire poured into the column. Realizing the danger to the column as it lay motionless, Lt. Col. Page fought his way to the head of the column and plunged forward into the heart of the hostile position. His intrepid action so surprised the enemy that their ranks became disordered and suffered heavy casualties. Heedless of his safety, as he had been throughout the preceding 10 days, Lt. Col. Page remained forward, fiercely engaging the enemy single-handed until mortally wounded. By his valiant and aggressive spirit Lt. Col. Page enabled friendly forces to stand off the enemy. His outstanding courage, unswerving devotion to duty, and supreme self-sacrifice reflect great credit upon Lt. Col. Page and are in keeping with the highest traditions of the military service.

SITTER, CARL L.

Rank and Organization: Captain, U.S. Marine Corps, Company G, 3d Battalion, 1st Marines, 1st Marine Division (Rein).
Born: December 2, 1921, Syracuse, Missouri.
Entered Service At: Pueblo, Colorado.
Place and Date: Hagaru-ri, Korea, November 29 and 30, 1950.
Citation: For conspicuous gallantry and intrepidity at the risk of his life above and beyond the call of duty as commanding officer of Company G, in action against enemy aggressor forces. Ordered to breakthrough enemy-infested territory to reinforce his battalion the morning of November 29th, Capt. Sitter continuously exposed himself to enemy fire as he led his company forward and, despite 25 percent casualties suffered in the furious action, succeeded in driving through to his objective. Assuming the responsibility of attempting to seize and occupy a strategic area occupied by a hostile force of regiment strength deeply entrenched on a snow-covered hill commanding the entire valley southeast of the town, as well as the line of friendly troops withdrawing to the south, he reorganized his depleted units the following morning and boldly led them up the steep, frozen hillside, under blistering fire, encouraging and redeploying his troops as casualties occurred and directing forward platoons as they continued the drive to the top of the ridge. During the night when a vastly outnumbering enemy launched a sudden, vicious counterattack, setting the hill ablaze with mortar, machine gun, and automatic-weapons fire and taking a heavy toll in troops, Capt. Sitter visited each foxhole and gun position, coolly deploying and integrating reinforcing units consisting of service per-

sonnel unfamiliar with infantry tactics into a coordinated combat team and instilling in every man the will and determination to hold his position at all costs. With the enemy penetrating his lines in repeated counterattacks which often required hand-to-hand combat, and, on one occasion infiltrating to the command post with hand-grenades, he fought gallantly with his men in repulsing and killing the fanatic attackers in each encounter. Painfully wounded in the face, arms, and chest by bursting grenades, he staunchly refused to be evacuated and continued to fight on until a successful defense of the area was assured with a loss of the enemy of more than 50 percent dead, wounded and captured. His valiant leadership, superb tactics, and great personal valor throughout 36 hours of bitter combat reflect the highest credit upon Capt. Sitter and the U.S. Naval Service.

OFFICIAL COMMUNIQUÉ:
TOKYO, Nov. 30 (AP)
—Release 686, issued by Gen. Douglas MacArthur's at 2:30 P.M. Thursday (12:30 A.M. Thursday, Eastern Standard Time):

The United States Far East Air Forces mounted another heavy air effort Wednesday as fighters and bombers took a toll of attacking Chinese and North Korean Communists.

Fifth Air Force fighters, joined by the South African Air Force, Royal Australian Air Force, and United States Marines, attacked the enemy in day-long strikes all along the battle line. Bombs, napalm, rockets and machine-gun fire poured into massed Reds at more than ninety points. A sweep against enemy positions at Pukchang cost the enemy nearly 100 troops, eighty fortified buildings, and a gun emplacement. Fighters killed another 300 Communists in the vicinity of Ansang and inflicted many casualties in other areas. The heaviest losses suffered by the Reds from air attacks were in the R.O.K. (Republic of Korea) area, where more than 700 were killed.

B-26 light bombers struck at eighteen supply centers in north intruder sorties.

Included in the targets were supply areas at Sonchon, Sakchu, Unsan, Kuryong, and Chonchon. Fires followed the strikes at most points. An undetermined number of vehicles was destroyed in strafing attacks.

Fifth Air Force attacks cost the enemy at least three tanks, thirty-six vehicles, three supply areas, 280 supply or fortified buildings, eleven artillery pieces, seven carts, and more than 1,200 Communist troops.

Bomber Command Superfortresses continued their assaults on key supply routes, storage areas, and bridges yesterday. One formation struck at the highway bridge at Changtienhokou.

Demolition bombs blanketed the approaches and bridge on the Korean side of the international border. Supply areas at Pukchin, Tongchong, Kanggye, Sakchu, Sonchon, Huichon, and Kwaksan were heavily damaged in firebomb attacks. Rail lines between Sakchu and Sinon, Pyorha and Kanggye and Huichon were severed by direct hits.

The Combat Cargo Command resupplied United Nations forces in the Chosin (Changjin) Reservoir area by air drop Wednesday. Nearly 110 tons of ammunition and supplies were parachuted by C-119's on both the east and west sides of the reservoir. An additional 740 tons of cargo were carried by the Combat Cargo Command in routine operations.

—Release 687 issued by Gen. Douglas MacArthur's headquarters at 4:05 P.M., Thursday (2:05 A.M. Thursday, Eastern Standard Time):

In the northeastern sector of Korea the R.O.K. (Republic of Korea) Capital division continued to advance against moderate enemy resistance.

In the Chosin (Changjin) Reservoir area the enemy continued to press the United States First Marine Division with an almost fanatical determination but paid dearly for his efforts. More than 1,000 enemy were reported killed by the Marines in the past twenty-four hours. The Marines remained heavily engaged in the vicinity of Yudam and successfully repulsed all of the enemy's attacks to dislodge them.

In the United States Eighth Army sector the enemy continued heavy pressure from a point between Chongju and Pakchon on the west across the entire army front.

A vigorous counter-attack by elements of the United States First Cavalry Division succeeded in eliminating a slight enemy penetration in its sector. Other elements of the division engaged in a sharp encounter with an enemy regiment in Sumso and inflicted approximately 600 enemy casualties.

The Turkish Brigade, heavily engaged in hand to hand fighting in the Wawon area, was reinforced by elements of the United States Second Infantry Division.

(Report on forward areas for period of twenty-four hours ended at 2:00 A.M. Nov. 30):

Throughout Nov. 28-29 the enemy continued heavy pressure in nearly all sectors against United Nations forces.

This pressure continued while some friendly units were withdrawing across the Chongchon River near Won.

Early on Nov. 29 the enemy launched a powerful attack crossing the river at several points near Pugwan and Kunu and infiltrated between friendly units.

Continued strong attacks resulting in penetrations were made in the Kunu-Kaechon area throughout Nov. 29. Very heavy fighting in this area continued to the end of the period.

As the attack developed toward Sunchon, five enemy tanks, which have not been observed in any number during the last few days, were sighted.

Enemy activity in the eastern part of North Korea also increased and there was considerable action in the vicinity of Sachang, which is approximately thirty-five miles northwest of Hamhung.

In the Chosin (Changjin) Reservoir area, the tempo of enemy aggressiveness increased, and friendly forces in the general area of Yudam were under sharp attack. Fighting was heavy near Hagaru, where the enemy sustained very heavy losses with only minor gains.

On the east shore of the reservoir in the general vicinity of Sinhung, fighting resulted in heavy enemy losses. Here also enemy tanks were seen.

On the east coast enemy resistance north of Chongjin lessened. Before withdrawing from Chongjin, the enemy mined buildings, roads, and beaches in the town and in the immediate vicinity.

DAVIS, RAYMOND G.

Rank and Organization: Lieutenant Colonel, U.S. Marine Corps, commanding officer, 1st Battalion, 7th Marines, 1st Marine Division (Rein).
Born: January 13, 1915, Fitzgerald, Georgia.
Entered Service At: Atlanta, Georgia.
Place and Date: Vicinity of Hagaru-ri, Korea, December 1 to 4, 1950.
Citation: For conspicuous gallantry and intrepidity at the risk of his life above and beyond the call of duty as commanding officer of the 1st Battalion, in action against enemy aggressor forces. Although keenly aware that the operation involved breaking through a surrounding enemy and advancing 8 miles along primitive icy trails in the bitter cold with every passage disputed by a savage and determined foe, Lt. Col. Davis boldly led his battalion into the attack in a daring attempt to relieve a beleaguered rifle company and to seize, hold, and defend a vital mountain pass controlling the only route available for 2 marine regiments in danger of being cut off by numerically superior hostile forces during their re-deployment to the port of Hungnam. When the battalion immediately encountered strong opposition from entrenched enemy forces commanding high ground in the path of the advance, he promptly spearheaded his unit in a fierce attack up the steep, ice-covered slopes in the face of withering fire and, personally leading the assault groups in a hand-to-hand encounter, drove the hostile troops from their positions, rested his men, and reconnoitered the area under enemy fire to deter-

mine the best route for continuing the mission. Always in the thick of the fighting, Lt. Col. Davis led his battalion over three successive ridges in the deep snow in continuous attacks against the enemy and, constantly inspiring and encouraging his men throughout the night, brought his unit to a point within 1,500 yards of the surrounded rifle company by daybreak. Although knocked to the ground when a shell fragment struck his helmet and 2 bullets pierced his clothing, he arose and fought his way forward at the head of his men until he reached the isolated marines. On the following morning, he bravely led his battalion in securing the vital mountain pass from a strongly entrenched and numerically superior hostile force, carrying all his wounded with him, including 22 litter cases and numerous ambulatory patients. Despite repeated savage and heavy assaults by the enemy, he stubbornly held the vital terrain until the 2 regiments of the division had deployed through the pass and, on the morning of December 4th, led his battalion into Hagaru-ri intact. By his superb leadership, outstanding courage, and brilliant tactical ability, Lt. Col. Davis was directly instrumental in saving the beleaguered rifle company from complete annihilation and enabled the 2 marine regiments to escape possible destruction. His valiant devotion to duty and unyielding fighting spirit in the face of almost insurmountable odds enhance and sustain the highest traditions of the U.S. Naval Service.

†WINDRICH, WILLIAM G.

Rank and Organization: Staff Sergeant, U.S. Marine Corps, Company I, 3d Battalion, 5th Marines, 1st Marine Division (Rein).
Born: May 14, 1921, Chicago, Illinois.
Entered Service At: Hammond, Indiana.
Place and Date: Vicinity of Yudam-ni, Korea, December 1, 1950.
Citation: For conspicuous gallantry and intrepidity at the risk of his life above and beyond the call of duty as a platoon sergeant of Company I, in action against enemy aggressor forces the night of December 1, 1950. Promptly organizing a squad of men when the enemy launched a sudden, vicious counterattack against the forward elements of his company's position, rendering it untenable, S/Sgt. Windrich, armed with a carbine, spearheaded the assault to the top of the knoll immediately confronting the overwhelming forces and, under shattering automatic-weapons, mortar, and grenade fire, directed effective fire to hold back the attackers and cover the withdrawal of our troops to commanding ground. With 7 of his men struck down during the furious action and he himself wounded in the head by a bursting grenade, he made his way to his company's position and, organizing a small group of volunteers, returned with them to evacuate the wounded and dying from the frozen hillside, staunchly refusing medical attention himself. Immediately redeploying the remainder of his troops, S/Sgt. Windrich placed them on the left flank of the defensive sector before the enemy again attacked in force. Wounded in the leg during the bitter fight that followed, he bravely fought on with his men, shouting words of encouragement and directing their fire until the attack was repelled. Refusing evacuation although he was unable to stand, he still continued to direct his platoon in setting up defensive positions until weakened by the bitter cold, excessive loss of blood, and severe pain, he lapsed into unconsciousness and died. His valiant leadership, fortitude, and courageous fighting spirit against tremendous odds served to inspire others to heroic endeavor in holding the objective and reflect the highest credit upon S/Sgt. Windrich and the U.S. Naval Service. He gallantly gave his life for his country.

OFFICIAL COMMUNIQUÉ:
TOKYO, Saturday, Dec. 2 (AP)
—Release 688, issued b General MacArthur's headquarters at 1:25 P.M., Friday (11:25 P.M., Thursday, Eastern Standard Time):

Carrier-based United States Navy and Marine pilots yesterday flew a total of 200 sorties, mostly in close support of ground forces across the entire breadth of North Korea.

United States Navy Skyraiders, F9F Panther jets and Corsairs blasted military targets in the vicinity of Anju, Huichon, Kanggye, Chason, and the Changjin Reservoir.

Five hundred enemy troops crossing the Chongchon River near Anju were heavily attacked with bombs, rockets, and napalm. Heavy casualties were inflicted. Two other troop concentrations near Anju were badly mauled.

On the road between Huichon and Kanggye five troop concentrations were attacked. One ammunition dump was destroyed, twelve trucks were destroyed, ten damaged; four warehouses destroyed, three damaged; one tank was damaged, one bridge was destroyed, three buildings were destroyed, three were damaged. Three trains were bombed and rocketed. Near the Changjin Reservoir napalm was used to good advantage in routing enemy troop concentrations holding ridges cutting off elements of the First Marine Division. Troop concentrations along ridges in the vicinity of the reservoir were napalmed with good results according to the air controller. A number of pill boxes and gun emplacements were knocked out.

In the vicinity of Chasong one warehouse was destroyed and three buses were hit. The marshaling yards were heavily bombed and rocketed.

Marine Corsair pilots operating from the escort carrier U.S.S. Badoeng Strait bombed, rocketed and strafed sixteen different troop concentrations south of the Changjin Reservoir with good results. Northeast of the reservoir, ground controllers estimate the Marine fliers killed about 200 enemy troops, part of a larger number surrounding a Marine platoon.

While carrier-based Navy and Marine fliers were taking a heavy toll of the enemy in widespread air attacks, the 8-inch guns of the heavy cruiser St. Paul continued to pave the way for the advance of the R.O.K. Capital Division north of Chongjin.

The St. Paul provided round-the-clock pinpoint bombardment support of R.O.K. forces in the Pugodong area.

—Release 689 issued by General MacArthur's headquarters at 1:25 P.M., Friday (11:25 P.M., Thursday, Eastern Standard Time):

Unleashing the heaviest aerial assault since early September, the United States Far East Air Forces hammered Chinese Communists throughout Korea Thursday. Nearly 700 sorties were mounted, 500 of them by combat planes controlled by the Fifth Air Force.

B-26 light bombers continued round-the-clock operations in close support of ground troops and striking at supply lines to the rear. Troop positions from Yongbyon to Yongsan were bombed, napalmed, and rocketed by the light bombers with excellent results.

A large fuel storage area near Hwasan exploded under the rockets of one formation. Heavy enemy troop concentrations beyond Anju were hit with napalm. Rocketing attacks inflicted heavy casualties on Reds near Kunu.

Night intruder B-26s pounded vehicular traffic at Tonchang, Kwaksan, Huichon, and Pusangcham. Darkness precluded an accurate estimate of the damage inflicted. A sizable convoy was attacked late last night between Yangsi and Charyongwan. Results of the attack are as yet unreported.

F-80 jets and F-51s concentrating on close support of embattled United Nations forces in the northwest sector, inflicted at least 1,300 casualties on the Communists. Near Kunru the fighters trapped a large body of Red troops in the open and killed an estimated 450 of them. A cavalry unit was attacked as it attempted to ford a small river south of Yongbyon and 100 of the horsemen killed. Another cavalry unit lost 100 troops at Kachang to Maj. Gen. Earle E. Partridge's Fifth Air Force attack. Southwest of Kujang the jets inflicted 300 casualties on a group of Communists and seventy-five more were killed at Kwachon.

Armed reconnaissance F-80 jets sweeping the Yalu River, damaged a recently constructed pontoon bridge near Manpojin in a rocketing attack and knocked out eight artillery pieces at Inhung. Seven supply dumps were left ablaze in Chongnyong.

Marine Aircraft, controlled operationally by the Fifth Air Force, struck heavily at Communist forces in the Chosin (Changjin) Reservoir area. More than 100 close support sorties were flown in the area with unreported results.

In addition to the 1,300 troop casualties, known destruction or damage inflicted by Fifth Air Force planes yesterday totaled one tank, fifty-one vehicles, 275 supply or fortified buildings, seventeen supply areas, thirteen artillery emplacements, five fuel dumps, ninety-two horses, and fifteen rail cars.

Bomber Command B-29s attacked a highway bridge crossing the Yalu River near Changtienhokou, destroying at least one span. Supply areas at Kanggye, Sinchang, and Imsang were successfully attacked and rail and highway cuts made along supply routes leading from the international border to rear areas.

The Combat Cargo Command airdropped more than ninety-two tons of ammunition and supplies to Tenth Corps units in the Changjin Reservoir area. In addition, the transports airlifted more than 500 tons of cargo, including 386 passengers and 637 medical evacuees.

—*Release 690, issued by General MacArthur's headquarters at 3:55 P.M., Friday (1:55 A.M., Friday, Eastern Standard Time):*

Diminishing enemy pressure characterized the activity on the United States Eighth Army front.

A strong enemy force attacked elements of the Twenty-ninth Infantry Brigade, United Kingdom, in the vicinity of Sibyon. The fighting continued on into the early afternoon when the enemy suddenly broke off the engagement after suffering numerous casualties.

Elements of the United states Army 187th Airborne Regimental Combat Team attacked and at last report were still engaged with a strong enemy force in the vicinity of Sachang.

In the United States Army Twenty-fourth Division sector, elements conducted a highly successful rear-guard action in covering the withdrawal of United Nations forces to the south side of the Chongchon River. The bridges across the Chongchon River in the vicinity of Anju and Sananju were destroyed after the withdrawal.

Elements of the United States Army Second Division, in conjunction with the Twenty-seventh British Brigade, attacked an enemy group in the vicinity of Yongwon and by late yesterday afternoon cleared a path to facilitate the withdrawal of the division. One enemy gun was destroyed. In the vicinity of Kunu, other elements of the division attacked enemy troops and guns west of the town, killing an estimated 150 enemy and destroying two gun positions. Approximately 200 casualties were inflicted as a result of an attack on enemy troops northeast of Kunu.

In the northeastern sector, the R.O.K. (Republic of Korea) Capital Division continued to make small gains against moderate enemy resistance.

Pressure against the United States First Marine Division continued. Strongest attacks were from the north against the marines in the vicinity of Yudam.

—*Release 691, issued by General MacArthur's headquarters at 11:10 A.M., Saturday (9:10 P.M. Friday, Eastern Standard Time):*

United States Navy and Marine carrier-based aircraft roared across the entire breadth of North Korea in close support of the ground forces yesterday.

The flying Marines, operating from the escort carrier U.S.S. Badoeng Strait, concentrated their entire effort in support of ground forces in the Changjin (Chosin) Reservoir area.

Rocket, bomb, and napalm attacks were effective against enemy troop concentrations around almost the entire perimeter of the reservoir, particularly at Yudam. As a result of the highly successful air attacks, isolated elements were enabled to rejoin.

United States Navy Skyraiders, Panther jets, and Corsairs of fast Carrier Task Force 77 added their striking power to that of the Marine Corsairs in the Changjin Reservoir area, neutralizing a number of troop concentrations.

The Navy planes worked their way across the entire Korean peninsula, blasting troop concentrations en route. Enemy troops at Kunu and Tokchon were heavily hit with bombs, napalm, rockets, and 20-mm cannon fire.

United States Navy fire support ships, deployed along the east coast, continued to render interdiction, harassing and call-fire support of the ground forces.

Cruiser-based helicopters assisted in the evacuation of wounded troops.

BARBER, WILLIAM E.

Rank and Organization: Captain, U.S. Marine Corps, commanding officer, Company F, 2d Battalion, 7th Marines, 1st Marine Division (Rein).
Born: November 30, 1919, Dehart, Kentucky.
Entered Service At: West Liberty, Kentucky.
Place and Date: Chosin Reservoir area, Korea, November 28 to December 2, 1950.
Citation: For conspicuous gallantry and intrepidity at the risk of his life above and beyond the call of duty as commanding officer of Company F, in action against enemy aggressor forces. Assigned to defend a 3-mile mountain pass along the division's main supply line and commanding the only route of the approach in the march from Yudam-ni to Hagaru-ri, Capt. Barber took position with his battle-weary troops and, before nightfall, had dug in and set up a defense along the frozen, snow-covered hillside. When a force of estimated regimental strength savagely attacked during the night, inflicting heavy casualties and finally surrounding his position following a bitterly fought 7-hour conflict, Capt. Barber, after repulsing the enemy, gave assurance that he could hold if supplied by airdrops and requested permission to stand fast when orders were received by radio to fight his way back to a relieving force after 2 reinforcing units had been driven back under fierce resistance in their attempts to reach the isolated troops. Aware that leaving the position would sever contact with the 8,000 marines trapped at Yudam-ni and jeopardize their chances of joining the 3,000 more awaiting their arrival at Hagaru-ri for the continued drive to the sea, he chose to risk loss of his command rather than sacrifice more men if the enemy seized control and forced a renewed battle to regain the position, or abandon his many wounded who were unable to walk. Although severely wounded in the leg in the early morning of the 29th, Capt. Barber continued to maintain personal control, often moving up and down the lines on a stretcher to direct the defense and consistently encouraging and inspiring his men to supreme efforts despite the staggering opposition. Waging a desperate battle throughout 5 days and 6 nights of repeated onslaughts launched by the fanatical aggressors, he and his heroic command accounted for approximately 1,000 enemy dead in this epic stand in sub-zero weather, and when the company was relieved, only 82 of his original 220 men were able to walk away from the position they so valiantly defended against insuperable odds. His profound faith and courage, great personal valor, and unwavering fortitude were decisive factors in the successful withdrawal of the division from the death trap in the Chosin Reservoir sector and reflect the highest credit upon Capt. Barber, his intrepid officers and men, and the U.S. Naval Service.

†JOHNSON, JAMES E.

Rank and Organization: Sergeant, U.S. Marine Corps, Company J, 3d Battalion, 7th Marines, 1st Marine Division (Rein).
Born: January 1, 1926, Pocatello, Idaho.
Entered Service At: Washington, D.C.
Place and Date: Yudam-ni, Korea, December 2, 1950.
Citation: For conspicuous gallantry and intrepidity at the risk of his life above and beyond the call of duty while serving as a squad leader in a provisional rifle platoon composed of artillery men attached to Company J, in action against enemy aggressor forces. Vastly outnumbered by a well-entrenched and cleverly concealed enemy force wearing the uniforms of friendly troops and attacking his platoon's open and unconcealed positions, Sgt. Johnson unhesitatingly took charge of his platoon in the absence of the leader and, exhibiting great personal valor in the face of heavy barrage of hostile fire, coolly proceeded to move among his men, shouting words of encouragement and inspiration and skillfully directing their fire. Ordered to displace his platoon during the fire fight, he immediately placed himself in an extremely hazardous position from which he could provide covering fire for his men. Fully aware that his voluntary action meant either certain death or capture to himself, he courageously continued to provide effective cover for his men and was last observed in a wounded condition single-handedly engaging enemy troops in close hand-grenade and hand-to-hand fighting. By his valiant and inspiring leadership, Sgt. Johnson was directly responsible for the successful completion of the platoon's displacement and the saving of many lives. His dauntless fighting spirit and unfaltering devotion to duty in the face of terrific odds reflect the highest credit upon himself and the U.S. Naval Service. (Sgt. Johnson was declared missing in action on December 2, 1950, and killed in action as of November 2, 1953).

OFFICIAL COMMUNIQUÉ:
TOKYO, Sunday, Dec. 3 (AP)
—Release 692, issued by General MacArthur's headquarters at 3:00 P.M., Saturday (Saturday, 1:00 A.M., Eastern Standard Time):

Heavy close support of embattled United Nations ground forces marked the 158th consecutive day of combat operations by the United States Far East Air Forces Friday. A total of 727 sorties were flown yesterday, with more than 500 of these operating under the control of the Fifth Air Force.

In the Kunu area, fighters maintained a constant aerial umbrella over rear-guard friendly forces delaying the advance of the Chinese Communists. Continuous air strikes by F-80 jets knocked out several roadblocks, two artillery pieces, and killed an estimated 500 Communists. The United States Eighth Army reported that "very active air support" enabled one regiment and a battalion to escape encirclement by the Reds and that these units were able to rejoin the main body of United Nations forces.

Fifth Air Force F-80s and F-51s inflicted an additional 2,000 casualties on the enemy in large scale close support strikes all along the battle line. Near Sinanju, thirty-five Reds were killed in a sweep by fighters, two tanks were damaged and an ammunition dump was destroyed.

Military targets in Yongbyon suffered heavy damage in a strike that destroyed or damaged fifty-five supply buildings and cost the Communist 175 troops. In and near Won, F-80s rocketed and strafed ridges honeycombed with enemy troops. Air controllers overhead, in T-6 aircraft, reported at least 350 Communist troops were killed, an ammunition dump destroyed, and ten vehicles fired at Taechon, Kaechon, Pyongwon, Kujang, and Yongsan.

B-26 light bombers pounded enemy troops, supplies, and fortified buildings in eleven areas along and to the rear of the battle line. An ammunition train was brought under a fragmentation bomb, napalm, rocket, and machine gun attack in Kunu. More than a fourth of the cars exploded under the concentrated attack.

Near Songchon a formation of B-26s destroyed the greater part of a large body of horse cavalry. The horsemen neither took cover nor dismounted. Military supplies were set afire at Pukchang, Tokchon, Kasan, Yongbyon, and Kujong.

Bomber Command Superfortresses continued the interdiction of enemy supply routes and attacks on military storage areas. They made five cuts in rail lines and cratered highways with 500-pound general purpose bombs. Storage areas at Kwaksan, Namsi, Tokchon, Huichon, Singhung, Sonchon, and Kusong were saturated with incendiary bombs.

Six MiG jet aircraft made a series of determined attacks on a formation of B-29s east of Sinuiju. At least one MiG was damaged in the engagement, with no damage being sustained by any of the Superfortresses.

Nearly 100 tons of ammunition and supplies were dropped to United Nations forces in the Chosen (Changjin) Reservoir area by planes of the Combat Cargo Command. In addition, 879 tons of cargo, 770 passengers, and 1,059 medical evacuees were airlifted during Friday's operations.

—Release 693, issued by General MacArthur's headquarters at 5:05 P.M., Saturday (3:05 A.M., Saturday, Eastern Standard Time):

United Nations forces continued to consolidate and organize defensive positions south of the Chongchon River.

Elements of the United States First Cavalry Division reported 300 prisoners captured during yesterday's operations.

An enemy roadblock in the Kunu area was overcome and elements of the United States Second Division were successful in withdrawing to new defensive positions.

R.O.K. (Republic of Korea) Second Division units engaged an enemy force in the Pechon area.

In the Wonsan area elements of the United States Third Division cleared several enemy roadblocks west of Majo.

Pressure against the United States First Marine Division in the Yudam area continued. The Marines killed 830 of the enemy and captured fifty-three during yesterday's fighting. Units in the Chosen (Changjin) reservoir sector continued to consolidate positions.

In the area north of Chongjin enemy resistance was described as moderate to strong, supported by artillery.

In the United States First Corps sector there was no report of contact along the front, but there were indications of enemy activity in front of the outpost line of resistance. It was reported that small enemy forces were located a few miles south, southwest, and southeast of Anju.

In the United States Ninth Corps sector in the vicinity of Anju-Sunchon, the enemy activity consisted of the establishment of road blocks, one reported north of Sunchon and another north-northwest of the same town. While these hampered the withdrawal of friendly units they were not completely effective.

An air strike on hostile positions south of Kunu was very successful in damage inflicted on the enemy.

Another strike at enemy troops and gun positions on a ridge a few miles northwest of Sunchon materially assisted in reducing a roadblock in the area. An estimated 150 enemy were killed and two gun positions destroyed during the attack. Other strikes in the area northeast of Kunu resulted in a minimum of 200 enemy killed. Airplanes also attacked an undetermined number of enemy north of Sinanju and a large number of hostile troops with armored vehicles in the Kunu area. Air observations on Dec. 1 included a large number of refugees moving south from Sinanju and the Chongchon River area and an estimated 1,000 enemy troops changing from uniforms to white clothing southeast of Kunu.

The enemy action in the Sunchon-Songchon area was mostly of probing nature. An estimated 400 enemy were taken under artillery fire in an area southeast of Sunchon. Artillery pieces and an undetermined number of enemy northeast and southwest of Sinchang were reported.

Air observations indicated a small group of hostile troops and horses north of Sunchon, a regiment of unidentified troops, eleven miles north of Sunchon.

In the Tenth Corps sector in the vicinity of Sachang, an enemy force estimated to be a regiment supported by mortars, automatic weapons, and possibly pack artillery continuously harassed friendly troops. No definitely aggressive action has been noted here for the last two or three days. However, a friendly supply convoy was reported ambushed four miles farther east by an estimated fifty Chinese Communists.

In the Changjin Reservoir area enemy pressure was maintained during the night and continued on Dec. 1 in the vicinity of Yudam. The enemy made repeated attacks from the north. In these attacks the enemy suffered very heavy casualties.

At Hagaru, the enemy launched a determined attack by elements of two unidentified regiments supported by automatic weapons and artillery. The enemy's main effort was from the east and south with a secondary effort from the west. Fighting ranged from moderate to heavy and enemy casualties were reported high.

In the vicinity of Koto, the enemy renewed his probing attacks generally from the southwest and were described as light. Aggressive enemy patrolling continued in this area and light small arms fire was maintained during the afternoon.

In the Chongjin-Kilchu area the enemy resistance was described as moderate to strong supported by artillery and two to four tanks or self-propelled guns. P.O.W.'s taken in the area state that the enemy are withdrawing in small groups with instructions to assemble at Munsan.

—*Release 694, issued by General MacArthur's headquarters at 10:55 A.M., Sunday (8:55 P.M., Saturday, Eastern Standard Time):*

Carrier based United States Navy and Marine pilots continued to take a tremendous toll of enemy troops yesterday in air strikes in close and general support of the ground forces.

A column of about 400 enemy troops and two smaller groups numbering about fifty each near Soksa were heavily bombed and strafed with severe casualties.

At Yops, Navy fliers caught another concentration of about 500 troops. Bombs, napalm, and 20-mm. cannon fire killed many and dispersed the remainder.

In the vicinity of the Chosin (Chanjin) Reservoir Skyraiders, Corsairs, and Panther jets of the fast Carrier Task Force 77 badly mauled six different troop concentrations, destroyed seven buildings housing troops, knocked out two gun positions, and destroyed two warehouses.

At Chungan the Navy fliers destroyed six military buildings. At Hagaru they destroyed three warehouses and damaged seven. At Hwangin they destroyed a camouflaged locomotive.

Adding to the total damage caused by carrier-based aircraft, Marine Corsairs attacking in the Changjin Reservoir area neutralized five troop concentrations, destroyed seventeen buildings and damaged five, destroyed three warehouses and damaged four.

The town of Sinhung, overrun with large numbers of enemy troops was 60 percent destroyed with napalm and bombs by the flying Leathernecks. Sinhung is southeast of the Changjin Reservoir.

United States Navy ships deployed along the east coast continued to provide round-the-clock call fire support of the ground forces.

HUDNER, THOMAS JEROME, JR.

Rank and Organization: Lieutenant (jg.), U.S. Navy, pilot in Fighter Squadron 32, attached to U.S.S. Leyte.
Born: August 31, 1924, Fall River, Massachusetts.
Entered Service At: Fall River, Massachusetts.
Place and Date: Chosin Reservoir area of Korea, December 4, 1950.
Citation: For conspicuous gallantry and intrepidity at the risk of his life above and beyond the call of duty as a pilot in Fighter Squadron 32, while attempting to rescue a squadron mate whose plane, struck by antiaircraft fire and trailing smoke, was forced down behind enemy lines. Quickly maneuvering to circle the downed pilot and protect him from enemy troops infesting the area, Lt. (jg.) Hudner risked his life to save the injured flier who was trapped alive in the burning wreckage. Fully aware of the extreme danger in landing on the rough mountainous terrain, and the scant hope of escape or survival in sub-zero temperature, he put his plane down skillfully in a deliberate wheels-up landing in the presence of enemy troops. With his bare hands, he packed the fuselage with snow to keep the flames away from the pilot and struggled to pull him free. Unsuccessful in this, he returned to his crashed aircraft and radioed other airborne planes, requesting that a helicopter be dispatched with an axe and fire extinguisher. He than remained on the spot despite the continuing danger from enemy action and, with the assistance of the rescue pilot, renewed a desperate but unavailing battle against time, cold, and flames. Lt (jg.) Hudner's exceptionally valiant action and selfless devotion to a shipmate sustain and enhance the highest traditions of the U.S. Naval Service.

OFFICIAL COMMUNIQUÉ:
TOKYO, Tuesday, Dec. 5 (AP)
—Release 698 (air summary), issued by Gen. Douglas MacArthur's headquarters at 2:40 P.M. Monday (12:40 A.M., Monday, Eastern Standard Time):

Although poor weather conditions prevailed throughout the operational area Sunday, planes of the United States Far East Air Forces continued to pound a massing Chinese communist army in Korea.

Fifth Air Force F-80 jets and F-51s struck at Red troops and vehicles in the northwest sector, as B-26 light bombers joined other F-51s and Marine fighters in heavy attacks on the Communists attacking United Nations elements in the Chosin Reservoir area.

Concentrated attacks by F-80s in the Sinanju-Anju arc cost the enemy forty-two supply buildings, one fuel storage area and three vehicles. A troop train was attacked near Anju, the locomotive and fifteen cars heavily damaged by rockets and napalm. Red troops, attempting to flee the train, were strafed with many casualties being inflicted on them. Small convoys throughout the area were attacked with undetermined results. Near Kwaksan, four rail cars were damaged by fighters and seven fortified buildings burned in Udong.

In the Chosin reservoir area, Air Force fighter planes killed an estimated fifty Red troops and burned many supply buildings at Hagaru. Rocketing and strafing attacks by F-51s and F-4Us under the operational control of the Fifth Air Force cost the Communists many troops in Pusong, Sachang, and around the reservoir itself.

B-26s bombed and napalmed enemy troops in Sinha, Changjin, Huksu, and Sojung with excellent results. Military targets northeast of Pyongyang, near Yopa, were set ablaze by napalm attacks.

Preliminary destruction claims by the Fifth Air Force totaled more than 800 enemy troops killed, nineteen vehicles, seventy-five horses, 155 supply or fortified buildings, one tank, and sixteen boxcars destroyed or damaged.

Bomber Command Superfortresses attacked the supply centers of Kunu and Sinanju with incendiary and general purpose bombs with excellent results. Main supply routes leading north and west from Sinanju were cut in many places by direct hits with demolition bombs.

Air drops continued to be the source of supply for United Nations forces fighting the Communists along the Chosin Reservoir. Transports of the Combat Cargo Command parachuted 802 tons of ammunition and supplies into the area yesterday.

Large-scale evacuation of sick and wounded continued, with an estimated 2,400 military personnel evacuated to hospitals. Of that total, 470 were flown from the emergency strip just to the rear of the Chosin battle area. Cargo tonnage during yesterday's operations was 1,447 tons.

—Release 699 issued by Gen. Douglas MacArthur's headquarters at 4:00 P.M., Monday (2:00 A.M., Monday, Eastern Standard Time):

Contact with the enemy was again light yesterday (Sunday) along the western sector of Korea. However, heavy enemy pressure continued in the Chosin (Changjin) Reservoir area.

Several enemy probing attacks in the area south of the Chosin Reservoir were repulsed by elements of the United States First Marine Division. The enemy continued to exert heavy pressure against the marines throughout the sector.

Attacks against elements of United Nations forces in the area northwest of Hamhung forced some United Nations units to make limited withdrawals.

United nations forces in the area to the north and east of Pyongyang consolidated defensive positions and reported only scattered contact with enemy units yesterday.

It is estimated that the Chinese Communist forces opposing the United Nations forces in North Korea now total 268,000. A further breakdown of this figure gives 194,000 Communist troops under the Fourth Field Army on the western side of the Korean peninsula, and another 74,000 on the Eastern front.

These troops form the forward combat echelon. In their rear, stretching back to and across the Yalu River, is the second supporting echelon, which is available for a momentary mass buildup in the direction of projected operations.

The composition of this latter echelon includes upward of 400,000 troops of the Fourth Field Army and the North China Special Army Group, probably 75,000 troops from the Third Field Army, and possibly 75,000 troops from the [word missing] Field Army, which have been reported in the Tumen area or enroute thereto. Thus, a minimum of 550,000 men are available as a huge reservoir in this second supporting echelon.

The remainder of Communist China constitutes other echelon in reserve. Including all categories, the Chinese Communists have about 4,000,000 under arms. Currently, there are other units of the First and Third Field Armies, probably totaling 200,000 additional troops, enroute north to the second or support echelon.

The pressure of these large Communist Chinese forces in Manchuria and North Korea was not the result of a sudden impulse, but must have been preceded by a long period of planning, followed by a considerable time necessary for troop movement, since some of these soldiers came from Central China. Preparations were made long ago. Possibly, the decision to commit them came after it was apparent that the military forces of the North Korean People's Republic had been decisively defeated.

—Release 700, issued today by Gen. Douglas MacArthur's headquarters at 10:55 A.M. (8:55 P.M., Monday, Eastern Standard Time):

The combined all-out effort of carrier-based United States Navy and Marine Corps aircraft yesterday was spent in close support of elements of the First Marine Division and the United States Army Seventh Infantry Division withdrawing in the Chosin (Changjin) reservoir area.

Performing one of the many specialized tasks for which they are specifically trained, the Navy and Marine flyers, flying at treetop level, blasted scores of Chinese Communist troop concentrations around the entire perimeter of the reservoir.

Attacking often within fifty yards of friendly forces, the Navy Skyraiders, Corsairs, and Panther jets and the Marine Corsairs cleared the way for the withdrawing ground forces.

Incidental to the searing attacks on enemy troops, the carrier-based pilots destroyed fifty-two military buildings and damaged forty-four. A frequent tactic of the Communists when air attack is imminent is to drive trucks, tanks, and field pieces into the nearest building.

In addition to the destruction of troops and buildings, the Navy and Marine pilots destroyed four field pieces, five trucks, and one observation post.

Fast carrier Task Force 77 is commanded by Rear Admiral E. C. Ewen. The escort carrier group from which the Marines operate is commanded by Rear Admiral Richard W. Ruble.

United States Navy ships deployed along the east coast provided 'round-the-clock call-fire support of the ground forces.

British Commonwealth fleet units operating along the west coast continued with patrol and blockade operation to thwart any enemy attempts at reinforcement or resupply by water.

Note: The following is a newspaper account of the preceding battles for which S/Sgt. Kennemore, Pvt. Cafferata, Pfc. Baugh, Lt. Col. Faith, Maj. Myers, Lt. Col. Page, Capt. Sitter, Lt. Col. Davis, S/Sgt. Windrich, Capt. Barber, Sgt. Johnson, and Lt. (jg) Hudner were awarded the Medal of Honor:

ENEMY IS CLOSING ON PYONGYANG
• • •
FOE 12 MILES AWAY
• • •
Chinese Communists Continue Drive in Move
To Cut Off Isolated Tenth Corps
• • •

TOKYO, Monday, Dec. 4 - Chinese Communist armies closed in yesterday on Pyongyang, former capital of North Korea, while United Nations troops pulled back generally out of contact with the overwhelming enemy forces.

[According to the United Press, the Eighth Army confirmed that Allied troops were making a general withdrawal from the Pyongyang area, in preparation for evacuation of the city. The First Corps was retreating from its former defense line, about 20 miles north of Pyongyang, while units were withdrawing to "delaying positions" south and west of the city, and Ninth Corps units were leaving positions northeast of pyongyang. The Associated Press said the Eighth Army headquarters, elements of the Ninth Corps, and other United States units began withdrawing from the city.

Sunchon and Sukchon, where a United States parachute drop last October had closed a trap behind the retreating North Koreans abandoning their capital, were yielded to the Chinese, whose advance guards penetrated within 12 to 20 miles of Pyongyang.

The enemy massed in heavy columns on the road, with overcast weather hampering attacks from the air. He was moving south on Pyongyang and east toward Allied bases at Hamhung and Wosan, on the east coast, where the United States Tenth Corps had been isolated from the Eighth Army of Lt. Gen. Walton H. Walker in the west.

[According to The United Press, a high ranking officer at Gen. Douglas MacArthur's headquarters said that units of the South Korean Capital Division had been withdrawn from the area above Chongjin in northeast Korea after some elements had been within less than 30 air miles of the Russian Siberian border. The United States heavy cruiser St. Paul, operating close off shore, has been accompanying this division.]

Meanwhile, in the far northeastern sector, two encircled regiments of the United States First Marine Division fought their way back through a force estimated at two Chinese divisions to Hagaru-ri, at the southern end of the big Changjin (Chosin) Reservoir. They had cut their way back in five days of retreat fighting from Yudam-ni, on the reservoir's west shore, to join other Marines and troops of the Seventh Infantry Division holding Hagaru-ri.

Force Isolated at Hagaru-ri

But at Hagaru-ri they were still isolated from the east coast bases by strong roadblocks that the Communists had built up along the winding mountain road to Hamhung, forty miles away. Marine and Navy fighters flying close support missions through overcast skies and snow flurries reported strong enemy concentrations all around the reservoir as well as on the escape route to the south.

Maj. Gen. Earle E. Partridge, commander of the Fifth Air Force, ordered B-26 light bombers to give maximum support to the Marine and Navy fliers in the attempt to blast the way out by air for the surrounded troops.

The Far East Air Force Combat Cargo Command had evacuated more than 1,200 wounded and trapped Marines and Seventh Infantry soldiers from Hagaru-ri since noon Friday. Unarmed planes used a 3,000-foot airstrip, hurriedly hacked out of what had been a "primitive cow pasture," an announcement said.

Along the whole Korean front, official and unofficial reports gave this general picture:

In the west, the battered Eighth Army was continuing its withdrawal before it could be encircled by the enemy, "trading space for time," as one military spokesman said. Columns of trucks and swarms of refugees were pouring south from Pyongyang, where demolition squads were blowing up equipment that could not be moved.

In the center the enemy appeared concentrating for a new swing around the endangered right flank of the Eighth Army, which was left in the air when the South Korean Republican Second Corps collapsed as the enemy, in strength of more than 200,000 men, threw back Gen. MacArthur's "general assault" north of the Chongchon River.

Enemy artillery was active south of Communist-held Songchon, and intelligence reports indicated an enemy build-up in this area. Almost due east of Pyongyang, enemy troops were moving on the Sokchu-Kangdong road. Headquarters said there "probably" had been a link-up between the Chinese Communists and the North Korean irregulars - soldiers who had been cut off in earlier United Nations advances.

In the east, large numbers of the enemy were moving from Yangdok toward the east coast base at Wonsan. One column of 2,000 was sighted and hit from the air. Enemy troops were reported southeast of Huksu, twenty miles from the east coast base of Hamhung.

[According to The Associated Press, pilots said that Marine and Air Force planes had returned to Huksu Sunday and had "wiped it off the map" in a four-hour attack.]

Along the western front there was little major combat yesterday, with the enemy still moving up after Gen. MacArthur's retreat. United Nations forces had fallen back to a line running ruffly from Chongsan, on the west coast, south to Sukchon and Sunchon and west of Songchon on the right. The situation, headquarters reported, was "relatively" quiet in the west.

The United States First Cavalry Regiment and the British Twenty-seventh Brigade fought up to late Saturday afternoon with an out-numbering enemy force near Hadan, twenty miles northeast of Pyongyang. The Chinese were thrown back after Allied planes had killed 500 in an air strike, and total enemy casualties here were estimated at 700.

Navy pilots yesterday reported striking an enemy company in the little town of Yopa, just west of Hadan, scattering them with fire bombs. The pilots said that United Nations forces had reoccupied the burning town. But later reports said that thousands of Chinese soldiers were swarming over the hills nearby. Some estimates ran as high as 25,000 of the enemy in that region.

Front-line reports said that there was minor contact between the troops of the United States Twenty-fifth Division and South Korean forces covering the retreat south of Sukchon and the Twenty-fourth Division at Sungdong.

Far to the south, where United Nations forces were still fighting guerrillas left behind by retreating North Koreans last fall, elements of the Republican Fifth Division cleared the city of Chunchon, fifty miles northeast of Seoul. This city had been seized by the Communists after they had concentrated in the hills.

CHAPTER 2

1951

†**EDWARDS, JUNIOR D.**
Rank and Organization: Sergeant First Class, U.S. Army, Company E, 23d Infantry Regiment, 2d Infantry Division.
Born: October 7, 1926, Indianola, Iowa.
Entered Service At: Indianola, Iowa.
Place and Date: Near Changbong-ni, Korea, January 2, 1951.
Citation: Sfc. Edwards, Company E, distinguished himself by conspicuous gallantry and intrepidity above and beyond the call of duty in action against the enemy. When his platoon, while assisting in the defense of a strategic hill, was forced out of its position and came under vicious raking fire from an enemy machine gun set up on adjacent high ground, Sfc. Edwards individually charged the hostile emplacement, throwing grenades as he advanced. The enemy withdrew but returned to deliver devastating fire when he had expended his ammunition. Securing a fresh supply of grenades, he again charged the emplacement, neutralized the weapon and killed the crew, but was forced back by hostile small-arms fire. When the enemy emplaced another machine gun and resumed fire, Sfc. Edwards again renewed his supply of grenades, rushed a third time through a vicious hail of fire, silenced this second gun and annihilated its crew. In this third daring assault he was mortally wounded but his indomitable courage and successful action enabled his platoon to regain and hold the vital strong-point. Sfc. Edwards' consummate valor and gallant self-sacrifice reflect the utmost glory upon himself and are in keeping with esteemed traditions of the infantry and military service.

OFFICIAL COMMUNIQUÉ:
TOKYO, Jan. 2 (AP)
—Release 779, issued by Gen. Douglas MacArthur's headquarters at 12:15 P.M. Tuesday (10:15 P.M., Monday, Eastern Standard Time):

United States Far East Air Forces opened the New Year Monday with the heaviest air attacks since the war in Korea began. Incomplete totals for the day already have established a new record of 812 sorties flown by F.E.A.F. airplanes, joined by Royal Australians, South Africans, and land-based Marines. The last previous high total was 802, on Nov. 8.

The tremendous air offensive accounted for at least 2,650 enemy troop casualties as a result of coordinated close-support strikes flown in the battle areas to help neutralize the enemy attacking Eighth Army units. Ground observers who witnessed the effective air onslaught estimated enemy troop casualties at double the figure reported by Air Force pilots.

Air Force fighters and light bombers, flying in clear weather, concentrated more than half of their maximum effort in front line support missions, with attacks made on the enemy as position information was relayed to the pilots and crews by radio from control centers. Strikes were particularly effective in the Korangpo, Kaesong, and Yonchon areas, near where intense ground fighting was reported.

New F-84 Thunderjets of the Twenty-seventh Fighter Escort Group flew the largest number of sorties since being committed to combat, with a record eighty-two individual flights made in close-support and armed reconnaissance. The speedy jets rocked the enemy at Kunu, Yongpyong, Hwachon, Kaesong, Tanchon, Yangmun, Chongong, and a dozen other locations where enemy troops, occupied buildings and equipment were mauled. The F-84 pilots leveled many of the 1,100 troop and supply buildings damaged or destroyed by F.E.A.F. fliers.

F-84s also hit many of the fourteen gun positions, fifteen field pieces, tanks, and other warring equipment being used by the enemy and reported destroyed or damaged. F-84s also damaged a highway bridge, bombed a tunnel, cut rail tracks near Kunu, damaged a rail bridge, and inflicted casualties on an unestimated number of enemy troops at Kaesong. At Chongong an estimated 350 enemy troops were killed or wounded by F-84 Thunderjets.

Other Fifth Air Force planes, F-80 jets, F-51 Mustangs, and B-26 light bombers, inflicted enemy troop casualties and destroyed structures and equipment at Uilchang, Kaesong, Korangpo, Majon, Yangu, Chongong, Sinchon, Yongbyon, Sonchon, Chabong, Sukchon, Chorwon, Hwangju, and Sinanju. The Air Force fighters flew from dawn to darkness, and B-26s operated around the clock—finishing the record day with flare-illuminated intruder sorties last night close to the battle line. The Fifth Air Force divided its efforts about even in support of Eighth Army ground units in the battle areas and attacks on enemy buildups back of the battle line that extends across Korea.

Air Force fighters were joined by South Africans that flew twenty-four sorties in F-51s killing enemy troops and damaging field pieces, a highway bridge, occupied buildings, and other targets in the area surrounding Korangpo and Kaesong. Royal Australians, also flying F-51s left fires raging and buildings leveled at Kumsong and several other locations in North Korea behind the battle line. Land-based marines, in F9F fighter planes, were sent by Fifth Air Force controllers to centers in central Korea back of the line. They destroyed vehicles, supply buildings, oil dumps, and supply carts.

The record offensive included damage to a major barracks area at Myongye, east of Pyongyang, by F.E.A.F. Bomber Command Superforts that dropped about 170 tons of bombs. The B-29s operated in five separate flights, with the two-mile lone target divided into five areas for aiming purposes. Crews reported destruction and damage to most of the 300 one-and two-story wooden barracks in the area. The attack was carried out visually with no opposition from the enemy.

F-86 Sabre jets in day-long combat air patrols over northwest Korea did not encounter enemy aircraft. F.E.A.F. Combat Cargo Command's incomplete figures for yesterday show at least 224 sorties flown in the airlift of cargo and personnel into Korea from Japan.

—Release 780, issued by Gen. Douglas MacArthur's headquarters at 3:55 P.M. Tuesday (1:55 A.M. Tuesday, Eastern Standard Time):

During the night of Dec. 31-Jan. 1, the previous pattern of sporadic small enemy attacks expanded into a series of determined assaults in strength. By 2:00 P.M., Jan. 1, substantial hostile elements had penetrated to a point nine miles northwest of Uijongbu, to six miles south of Tongduchon, and to Kapyong. Along the eastern portion of the front, pressure against the United Nations forces continued unabated.

The vanguard of the Chinese Communist attack in the western and central sector consists of the Thirty-eighth, Thirty-ninth, Fortieth, Forty-second, Sixty-sixth, and fiftieth Chinese Communists Armies (Corps), the leading divisions of which now are exerting heavy pressure in an all-out attack. In addition, a minimum of three North Korean Corps are in the line. The attack is being pressed by the enemy with complete disregard for his losses, which have been extremely heavy.

In the current fighting, prisoners from two divisions of the Thirty-seventh Chinese Communist Army (Corps) indicate the presence of that unit, last identified in the Hungnam perimeter. The presence of these enemy forces which had been employed along the Japan Sea and which consist of at least four Chinese Communist Armies (Corps) and one North Korean Corps, together with other North Korean units identified in the eastern sector, constitutes an additional threat.

Indicative of the political orientation of the North Korean Communist Government and the general character of this war is the following broadcast by Kim Il Sung, the North Korean Prime Minister. The broadcast was delivered as a New Year's greeting for twenty-five minutes over the Pyongyang central broadcasting station Jan. 1, 1951:

"To all brothers and sisters, I, as a representative of the Korean People's Republic, give you a New Year's greeting now. The year 1950 was an epoch-making year when Syngman Rhee and his followers initiated a civil war while we were constructing a democratic country. It surely recorded a leaf in history as a war for the sake of the fatherland. The first half of the year was devoted to the establishment of peace and the latter half to war for the liberation of the fatherland.

"During the period 25 June to 15 August, 1950, the enemy lost 64,000 officers and men, more than 14,000 rifles, and over 10,000 cannons. Surprised by these facts, the Americans mobilized all of their forces in the Pacific area and renewed their attacks which caused our forces to make a temporary retreat. The retreat was accomplished without any serious losses to the main forces of the People's Army.

"The war situation now has changed completely and the enemy has retreated south of the Thirty-eighth Parallel and victory will be in our hands.

"We are not standing alone. From the time war started in our country, the Great Soviet, China, Hungary, Bulgaria, Czechoslovakia, Rumania, and Poland have all given us support and sympathy. When our people's forces retreated, the Chinese people's volunteer corps from our neighboring country came to our assistance. The Americans' greedy intention to throw back the people's forces north of the Yalu River, and to occupy all of Korea, and to invade Asia by using Korea as their base, and to invade the rest of the world, became very clear to us. We will destroy the American imperialistic invaders as the rest of the world expects us to do.

"People's guerrilla forces in the rear of the enemy will annihilate the retreating enemy forces by all possible means. All people will seek revenge on the American imperialistic invaders and Rhee's followers by completely annihilating them."

Enemy forces continued to press their attack against United Nations forces in the Yonchon area and made some gains throughout the day.

Friendly forces maintained contact at points along the main battle line while other United Nations units executed an orderly withdrawal to previously prepared positions.

Some United Nations units in the eastern sector maintained contact with the enemy against increasingly heavy opposition while others withdrew to new defensive positions.

Close air support continued to be effective in dispersing enemy groups and destroying gun and mortar positions throughout the main battle area.

DODD, CARL H.
Rank and Organization: First Lieutenant (then 2d Lt.), U.S. Army, Company E, 5th Infantry Regiment, 24th Infantry Division.
Born: April 21, 1925, Evarts, Kentucky.
Entered Service At: Kenvir, Kentucky.
Place and Date: Near Subuk, Korea, January 30 and 31, 1951.
Citation: Lt. Dodd, Company E, distinguished himself by conspicuous gallantry and intrepidity above and beyond the call of duty in action against the enemy. 1st Lt. Dodd, given the responsibility of spearheading an attack to capture Hill 256, a key terrain feature defended by a well-armed, crafty foe who had withstood several previous assaults, led his platoon forward over hazardous terrain under hostile small-arms, mortar, and artillery fire from well-camouflaged enemy emplacements which reached such intensity that his men faltered. With utter

disregard for his safety, 1st Lt. Dodd moved among his men, reorganized and encouraged them, and then singlehandedly charged the first hostile machine gun nest, killing or wounding all its occupants. Inspired by his incredible courage, his platoon responded magnificently and, fixing bayonets and throwing grenades, closed on the enemy and wiped out every hostile position as it moved relentlessly onward to its initial objective. Securing the first series of enemy positions, 1st Lt. Dodd again reorganized his platoon and led them across a narrow ridge and on to Hill 256. Firing his rifle and throwing grenades, he advanced at the head of his platoon despite the intense, concentrated hostile fire which was brought to bear on their narrow avenue of approach. When his platoon was still 200 yards from their objective he moved ahead and with his last grenade destroyed an enemy mortar killing its crew. Darkness then halted the advance but at daybreak 1st Lt. Dodd, again boldly advancing ahead of his unit, led the platoon through a dense fog against the remaining hostile positions. With bayonet and grenades he continued to set the pace without regard for the danger to his life, until he and his troops had eliminated the last of the defenders and had secured the final objective. First Lt. Dodd's superb leadership and extraordinary heroism inspired his men to overcome this strong enemy defense reflecting the highest credit upon himself and upholding the esteemed traditions of the military service.

†McGOVERN, ROBERT M.

Rank and Organization: First Lieutenant, U.S. Army, Company A, 5th Cavalry Regiment, 1st Cavalry Division.
Born: Washington, D.C.
Entered Service At: Washington, D.C.
Place and Date: Near Kamyangjan-ni, Korea, January 30, 1951.
Citation: 1st Lt. McGovern, a member of Company A, distinguished himself by conspicuous gallantry and intrepidity above and beyond the call of duty in action against an armed enemy of the United Nations. As 1st Lt. McGovern led his platoon up a slope to engage hostile troops emplaced in bunker-type pillboxes with connecting trenches, the unit came under heavy machine gun and rifle fire from the crest of the hill, approximately 75 yards distant. Despite a wound sustained in this initial burst of withering fire, 1st Lt. McGovern, assured the men of his ability to continue on and urged them forward. Forging up the rocky incline, he fearlessly led the platoon to within several yards of its objective when the ruthless foe threw and rolled a vicious barrage of hand-grenades on the group and halted the advance. Enemy fire increased in volume and intensity and 1st Lt. McGovern, realizing that casualties were rapidly increasing and the morale of his men badly shaken, hurled back several grenades before they exploded. Then, disregarding his painful wound and weakened condition, he charged a machine gun emplacement which was raking his position with flanking fire. When he was within 10 yards of the position a burst of fire ripped the carbine from his hands, but, undaunted, he continued his lone-man assault and, firing his pistol and throwing grenades, killed 7 hostile soldiers before falling mortally wounded in front of the gun he had silenced. 1st Lt. McGovern's incredible display of valor imbued his men with indomitable resolution to avenge his death. Fixing bayonets and throwing grenades, they charged with such ferocity that hostile positions were overrun and the enemy routed from the hill. The inspirational leadership, unflinching courage, and intrepid actions of 1st Lt. McGovern reflect utmost glory on himself and the honored traditions of the military service.

OFFICIAL COMMUNIQUÉ:
—TOKYO, Thursday, Feb. 1 (AP) —Far East Air Forces summary of Jan. 30, operations, issued at 1:00 P.M., Wednesday (11:00 P.M., Tuesday, Eastern Standard Time):

Far East Air Forces planes and R.A.A.F., S.A.A.F., and land based Marine planes, under Fifth Air Force operational control, mounted over 810 effective sorties Tuesday. A total of 570 were flown by Fifth Air Force, 130 being in close support of United Nations ground forces.

Fighter-bombers and light bombers destroyed or damaged an estimated 950 buildings used by the enemy for shelter or to store supplies. These buildings were mainly hit in the area

stretching east from Seoul toward Chunchon and along the supply route from Seoul to Pyongyang.

Pilots conservatively estimated about seventy-five casualties inflicted on the enemy, fifty of

them in a single strike near Kunpojang, northwest of Suwon. About fifty-five enemy vehicles were destroyed or damaged.

A highway bridge was claimed destroyed near Sariwon, a railroad bridge was damaged near Kojin on the east coast, and a bridge was damaged near Sindang in the west central section. More than thirty enemy boxcars were damaged or destroyed, fifteen near Sariwon, ten near Hwangju, and five near Sinmak.

Seventeen Japan-based B-29 Superforts of F.E.A.F. Bomber Command hit Pyongyang military targets with about 135 tons of bombs under weather conditions that made radar aiming necessary. Results were unobserved. Some flak was experienced but none of the Superforts were damaged. No enemy fighter planes were intercepted.

The 315th Air Division (Combat Cargo) flew more than 220 sorties, airdropping or landing almost 650 tons of supplies. Highlighting the operation was the delivery of more than 200 tons onto the frozen airstrip at Suwon for United Nations forces fighting a few miles to the north. Led by twenty-five C-54 Skymasters, the transports flew a total of thirty-four sorties into the newly recaptured airfield.

A Third Rescue Squadron helicopter picked up a downed United States pilot behind enemy lines and airlifted him to safety.

—Far East Air Forces release issued at 4:15 P.M., Wednesday (2:15 A.M., Wednesday, Eastern Standard Time):

By noon today Okinawa-based Far East Air Forces B-29s of the 307th and Nineteenth Bomb Groups had dropped approximately 160 tons of explosives on three enemy targets in Korea.

Medium bomber crews radioed to Brig. Gen. James E. Briggs' Bomber Command headquarters in Japan that fifteen of them hit Pyongyang, where a heavy overcast made it necessary for radar operators aboard the Superforts to take over the job of finding the targets and releasing the bombs. Because of clouds, results were unobserved. A supply center at Chunchon in Central Korea south of the Thirty-eighth Parallel was hit by a small formation which dropped 500 pounders visually and observed excellent results.

Excellent results also were observed at a "target of opportunity" near Kyodong, about fifty miles southeast of Wonsan.

There was some anti-aircraft fire received over Pyongyang and none over the other targets. No enemy aircraft were observed.

—Fifth Air Force operational summary issued at 5:00 P.M., Wednesday (3:00 A.M. Wednesday, Eastern Standard Time):

Two radio transmitter stations at Pyongyang were destroyed in an attack by a flight of F-80's of the Forty-ninth Fighter Bomber Wing this afternoon, Maj. Gen. Earle E. Partridge said in his 5:00 P.M. summary of air action.

The same flight also claimed destruction of three flak positions at the North Korean capital before they left the area for attacks on Sariwon, where they destroyed or damaged several buildings.

Other flights from the Forty-ninth reported excellent results in close support attacks in the western sector. One group of four planes made the largest claim of troop casualties inflicted, with 100 enemy troops killed or wounded. Other flights concentrated on buildings housing enemy troops in that sector with five flights claiming over 100 destroyed or damaged.

An important highway bridge was observed by the first flight of the Thirty-fifth Fighter Interceptor Wing and set afire with napalm. However, since it was still partially serviceable the second flight was dispatched and completed the job with bombs.

Other flights of fighters from the Thirty-fifth hit close support targets in the western sector with excellent results. One flight dive-bombed the enemy-occupied village of Takchong and then rocketed and strafed the area, reporting several buildings destroyed and large fires started.

Crews on B-26 light bombers of the 452nd Bomb Wing reported a scarcity of targets at Hamhung today. According to Staff Sgt. Clark V. Watson of Hutchinson, Kan., a gunner, "it's hard to find good targets, for we have burned out almost everything."

As navigator of one of the light bombers that attacked Pongung, near Hamhung, Lieut. Frank N. Moyer of Inglewood, Calif., reported, "One of our napalm must have hit a gas or oil dump. It landed and there was a big belch of orange flame and black smoke."

Light bombers of the Third Bomb Wing reported one large and several small fires following attacks on the town of Kisong.

One flight of F-84 Thunderjets of the Twenty-seventh Fighter Escort Wing reported damaging a bridge near Anuidong. Good results were reported in attacks on buildings housing troops and supplies near Uijongbu and in a village near the east-coast.

The Eighth Fighter Bomber Wing F-80 jets reported large fires in villages in the western sector following attacks with rockets, napalm and machine guns. A village was hard hit south of Chorwon.

A flight of four F-80s of the Fifty-first Fighter Interceptor Wing rocketed and strafed a town north of Seoul. Another flight reported twenty buildings destroyed or damaged near Kaesong.

Maj. John H. Walker of Pleasant Ridge, Mich., reported killing or wounding four enemy soldiers in the western sector. "They were with our 50s, they all fell. One of them fell across the sled and went sliding down the road several feet." Major Walker's flight from the Fifty-first were returning home from a successful mission farther to the north.

Several flights of F-51 Mustangs of the Eighteenth Fighter Bomber Wing attacked targets near the east coast in the Wonson area. One flight claimed three vehicles destroyed while other flights claimed as destroyed a 40-mm. gun position, an ammunition supply building and several large fires were started.

—British Commonwealth release 68, issued at 6:00 P.M., Wednesday (4:00 A.M., Wednesday, Eastern Standard Time):

Pilots of the Australian 77 Fighter Squadron flew fifteen sorties on armed reconnaissance and close support missions over Korea today. They damaged a camouflaged tank and started six large fires in towns and villages.

Enemy anti-aircraft fire opened up on them near Pyongyang damaging one aircraft with .50-caliber fire. The pilot made a safe landing at base with a burst tire.

One of the Australian flights was diverted to give direct support to embattled ground forces between Suwon and Seoul. They napalmed, rocketed and strafed ridges under the direction of an air controller who reported excellent results.

—Far East Naval Headquarters summary, issued at 10:45 A.M. Thursday (8:45 P.M., Wednesday, Eastern Standard Time):

Naval gunfire saturation of the area in the vicinity of the Korean east coast town of Kosong by powerful naval bombardment task forces continued from dawn to dusk yesterday in excellent weather and sea conditions.

Led by the battleship Missouri, morning fusillades poured a continuous flow of destruction on to the beaches, rail, highway, and communications facilities feeding into the area.

The huge 16-inch batteries of the Missouri and the main batteries of the cruisers and destroyers lobbed salvo after salvo onto the beaches and beyond. Visibility for spotting and observation planes was excellent.

Occasionally destroyers left the area of firing ships and darted in close to pound the beaches at point-blank range. There was no return fire.

An afternoon of heavy neutralizing fire saw even ships of predominantly non-combatant types near the beach for a crack at the enemy.

Air strikes continued to rake the roads and communications lines leading into the Kansong-Kosong sector during the bombardment.

Throughout the day rocket ships and destroyers went in close to shore and riddled the shore line with rockets and shells. During these assaults the bigger ships raised their barrage to areas farther back from the coast.

No return fire was encountered during the forays of the smaller ships.

—Eighth Army communique 160, issued at 8:00 P.M. Wednesday (6:00 A.M. Wednesday, Eastern Standard Time):

United Nations forces today continued their slow methodical advance all along the western Korean front with little or no enemy contact. Ground forces inflicted a total of 3,742 enemy casualties Jan. 30.

1. United Nations forces advancing under cover of friendly artillery fire engaged an unknown number of enemy north of Suwon. An enemy company dug in on the high ground seven miles northeast of Suwon stubbornly resisted the advance of friendly elements at noon today. The 100-150 enemy occupying Hill No. 311, six miles northwest of Kumyangjang, offered moderate resistance as friendly units continued to advance, causing the enemy to withdraw to the east. Friendly air observed an estimated enemy company well dug in and covered with mats on a ridge eight miles northeast of Suwon at 10:25 this morning. An enemy assembly area twenty miles east of Seoul and a large series of freshly dug fox-holes in the same area northeast along the Han River for two miles was reported observed at 11:30 A.M.

2. No significant enemy activity was reported on the central front. Friendly air attacked an estimated enemy platoon nine miles north-northeast of Yoju at 8:30 A.M.. Air also reported camouflaged entrenchments overlooking a road junction in this same area.

3. Little or no enemy activity was reported on the eastern-central front.

4. Little or no enemy activity was reported on the eastern front.

—Eighth Army communique 161, issued at 10:15 A.M. Thursday (8:15 P.M. Wednesday, Eastern Standard Time):

Light to moderate resistance was encountered by advancing United Nations forces all along the western front. Little or no enemy contact was reported on the central and east central front. Friendly forces were engaged with an estimated two enemy battalions in Kangnung area.

1. On the west flank United Nations forces advanced to positions nine miles west-northwest of Suwon with little or no enemy contact. Light and sporadic enemy resistance was encountered by friendly

forces six miles north-northwest of Suwon. An estimated enemy company attempted to attack friendly elements six miles north of Suwon at 1800 hours (6:00 P.M.). However, friendly artillery fire was placed on the enemy, forcing him to withdraw. Light to moderate resistance by an unknown number of enemy on Hill 449 four miles north-northeast of Suwan was encountered by friendly elements advancing under cover of friendly artillery fire at 1115 hours (11:15 A.M.) yesterday. By 1500 hours (3:00 P.M.) the enemy had been driven from the hill. The newly won friendly positions were subsequently subjected to a heavy volume of small arms, machine-gun, and 120 mm. mortar fire.

An estimated enemy company well dug in six miles northeast of Suwon constituted the core of enemy resistance in this sector. An estimated 200 enemy five miles north-northwest of Kumyangjang attempting a flanking movement of friendly positions at 1400 hours (2:00 P.M.) were engaged by friendly artillery resulting in an estimated 150 enemy killed. An unknown number of enemy four miles north-northwest of Kumyangjang restricted the advance of a friendly patrol as it approached the crest of a hill in this area. After a brief encounter and an exchange of hand grenades, the friendly patrol withdrew and artillery was placed on the enemy with unknown results.

2. An unknown number of enemy 10 miles north-northeast of Yoju were briefly engaged by a friendly patrol. The enemy was dispersed and the friendly patrol continued on its mission. A patrol entering Hoengsong during 31 January reported no enemy contact.

3. No enemy contact was reported as a strong patrol entered Pyongchang. A friendly patrol engaged an estimated 200 to 300 enemy thirteen miles south of Andong, forcing the enemy to withdraw to northeast. The action resulted in twenty-one enemy killed, eleven wounded, capture of four 81-mm. mortars, three 60-mm. mortars, and some small arms.

4. Friendly forces remained in contact with an estimated two enemy battalions in the Kangnung area. Action consisted primarily of sporadic small arms and automatic weapons fire.

LEE, HUBERT L.

Rank and Organization: Master Sergeant, U.S. Army, Company I, 23d Infantry Regiment, 2d Infantry Division.
Born: February 2, 1915, Arburg, Missouri.
Entered Service At: Leland, Mississippi.
Place and Date: Near Ipo-ri, Korea, February 1, 1951.
Citation: M/Sgt. Lee, a member of Company I, distinguished himself by conspicuous gallantry and intrepidity above and beyond the call of duty in action against the enemy. When his platoon was forced from its position by a numerically superior enemy force, and his platoon leader wounded, M/Sgt. Lee assumed command, regrouped the remnants of his unit, and led them in repeated assaults to regain the position. Within 25 yards of his objective he received a leg wound from grenade fragments, but refused assistance and continued the attack. Although forced to withdraw 5 times, each time he regrouped his remaining men and renewed the assault. Moving forward at the head of his small group in the fifth attempt, he was struck by an exploding grenade, knocked to the ground, and seriously wounded in both legs. Still refusing assistance, he advanced by crawling, rising to his knees to fire, and urging his men to follow. While thus directing the final assault he was wounded a third time, by small-arms fire. Persistently continuing to crawl forward, he directed his men in a final and successful attack which regained the vital objective. His intrepid leadership and determination led to the destruction of 83 of the enemy and withdrawal of the remainder, and was a vital factor in stopping the enemy attack. M/Sgt. Lee's indomitable courage, consummate valor, and outstanding leadership reflect the highest credit upon himself and are in keeping with the finest traditions of the infantry and the U.S. Army.

OFFICIAL COMMUNIQUÉ:
—TOKYO, Friday, Feb. 2 (AP) —Fifth Air Force summary of Thursday morning:

Fifth Air Force night intruders working against flare-illuminated enemy troops along the battle lines last night reported unusually good results and though claims of troop casualties are rarely made at night, a B-26 light bomber did claim seventy-five of enemy killed or wounded in one attack.

Flare-dropping aircraft kept the battle lines ablaze with light throughout the night, both for the benefit of the B-26s and F-82s smashing at enemy targets all night and for the ground troops who were able to observe enemy movements.

Vehicular traffic was sighted mainly on the highways running down the western sector of the enemy territory. Close to 400 vehicles were reported seen from Sinuiju moving southward through Sunchon, Sinanju, Pyongyang, Sariwon, Kaesong, and Seoul. The largest group was reported just north of Kaesong with 100 trucks spotted at Sukchon and fifty north of Pyongyang. No trains were reported moving in North Korea. One B-26 reported observing an area of one square mile burning fiercely at Uiju on the Yalu River although no aerial strikes were made at this point.

Flying over 500 sorties Wednesday, fighters and bombers of the fifth Air Force accounted for over 300 enemy troops killed or wounded. In addition, pilots claimed to have destroyed fifteen vehicles and damaged seven more.

Other pilot claims for the day included destruction of 276 supply buildings and damage to 265. Ten gun positions were claimed destroyed, two villages, three bridges, one fuel dump and one power plant were damaged.

In addition, one tank was destroyed and five pack animals were killed.

Striking at an enemy supply dump, pilots of the Fifth Air Force claimed to have destroyed 400 bags of rice and to have damaged 800.

Six B-26s attacked Pongong and claimed to have destroyed ten troop carriers. Another flight of four B-29s hit a village northeast of Kumsong, with many fires resulting.

In close support attacks on troop positions in the western sector good to excellent results were claimed. One flight claimed fifty casualties. Another flight accounted for two gun positions destroyed, over 100 troops were killed or wounded by a flight of F-80s in one strike. Many enemy-occupied buildings were destroyed or damaged.

In a strike on two enemy-held villages east of Seoul, one flight destroyed or damaged 1,200 bags of rice and hit several buildings.

F-86s and F-80s attacked the Kangnung area with good results. F-80s claimed over seventy-five troop casualties and damage to buildings and gun positions in the eastern sector. Fifteen supply buildings were claimed destroyed and nine vehicles destroyed or damaged in attacks near Suan. One fuel dump was damaged at Kaesong. Northeast of Seoul, one tank and five supply buildings were claimed destroyed. Five gun positions were claimed destroyed and twenty troop casualties were inflicted north of Pyongyang. Two power plants were damaged in the same area.

—Fifth Air Force summary issued at 11:30 A.M., Thursday (9:30 P.M. Wednesday, Eastern Standard Time):

Fifth Air Force fighters smashed at the enemy and flew more than 200 sorties by noon today despite bad weather most of the morning. Low ceilings and target-obscuring ground fogs were reported over most of North Korea, Maj. Gen. Earle E. Partridge said in his midday summary of air action.

F-80s of the Eighth Fighter Bomber Wing reported hitting the rail marshaling yards at Chaeryong with good results and claimed to have damaged several barracks buildings in the same area. These Shooting Stars also smashed at enemy-held villages at Changam and Wontong.

Eighteenth Fighter Bomber Wing F-51s blasted villages housing enemy troops and supplies near Wonsan and at Chumunjin and Pigum. F-80s of the Twenty-ninth Fighter Bomber Wing also hit the

Wonsan sector, claiming twelve buildings destroyed and enemy villages attacked in the vicinity of Musan, Hongjong, and Sonchon.

F-84 Thunderjets of the Twenty-seventh Fighter Escort Wing struck the Changjon area, killing three oxen, claiming destruction of an oxcart and damage to five buildings. Near Sangnung these F-84s reported the destruction of twelve buildings.

The Thirty-fifth Fighter Interceptor Wing F-51s Mustangs reported firing a village near Uijongbu on an armed reconnaissance mission. F-80s of the Fifty-first Fighter Interceptors Wing hit Pyongyang, burning at least four buildings.

—Far East Air Forces summary of Jan. 31 operations, issued at 12:30 P.M., Thursday (10:30 P.M., Wednesday, Eastern Standard Time):

Far East Air Forces planes flew 740 sorties through spotty weather Wednesday to continue the hammering of enemy supply concentrations, troops, transportation facilities, and other installations in Korea.

Flare-dropping F.E.A.F. airplanes illuminated vital supply routes and front line sections at night to help locate enemy vehicular targets and to enable United Nations front line troops to detect enemy approaches.

Vital cargoes of ammunition also were airlifted to front line troops.

Fifth Air Force light bombers and fighter-bombers mounted over 500 effective sorties, about 145 of which were in close support of friendly ground troops that are advancing. Included in the Fifth's total were combat sorties of Australian, South African, Republic of Korea, and land-based United States Marine Corps planes.

Pilots claimed approximately 350 enemy troops killed or wounded. As destroyed or damaged they claimed approximately thirty-five vehicles, 625 enemy-used buildings, five highway bridges, fifteen gun positions, one power plant, two tanks, and 1,200 bags of enemy-stockpiled foodstuffs, probably rice. The foodstuff destruction was in two villages in the area north of Wonju.

Air Force pilots claimed the destruction of one of the tanks in the area south of Chunchon and damage to another in the Chosin (Changjin) Reservoir section far north.

Fighter-bomber pilots found enemy gun positions in several areas and destroyed fifteen. Five were destroyed during an attack on a power plant in the Pyongyang area. Damage to the plant was unobserved but pilots claimed twenty troops killed or wounded. Two gun positions were destroyed north of Suwon and three more were eliminated near Yonghung. Five others were destroyed in guerrilla territory.

Four highway bridges were damaged in an arc east of Sanmak and one was damaged near Uijongbu, north of Seoul. A strike near Yangpyong was listed as causing approximately 100 casualties. R.O.K. fliers claimed inflicting about fifty casualties on the enemy in the east coast sector.

Night intruding B-26 light bombers scoured supply routes and sighted some 100 enemy vehicles. They were attacked with results generally unobserved.

Enemy supply build-ups were attacked at Pyongyang and Chunchon by Okinawa-based B-29 Superforts of Far East Air Forces Bomber Command. Fifteen B-29s used radar to bomb enemy supply storage at Pyongyang, while seven found a hole in the overcast to hit similar installations at Chunchon visually and with good results. More than 190 tons of bombs were dropped by the Superforts. There was some flak over Pyongyang but no enemy fighter interception was experienced.

Combat cargo planes of F.E.F.F.'s 315th Air Division rushed supplies, ammunition, and equipment to forward airfields to supplement other supply sources with an airlift of 760 tons of cargo. No air-to-air contact with the enemy was reported.

—Fifth Air Force summary for the month of January, issued at 5:00 P.M., Thursday (3:00 A.M., Eastern Standard Time):

Flying day and night, fighters and light bombers of the Fifth Air Force mounted over 14,000 effective sorties in providing an aerial umbrella over United Nations forces during January.

Enemy troops were particularly hard hit from the air with over 19,000 reported killed or wounded. This figure represents only those casualties actually observed by pilots. In the past, these claims have proved to be much lower than the actual number of casualties inflicted.

As United Nations lines became stabilized, fighters and light bombers concentrated on buildings being used by the enemy for housing troops and supplies. Over 21,000 of these buildings were destroyed or damaged.

To delay the build-up of Communist forces along United Nations lines pilots attacked their lines of communications and supplies constantly. This interdiction program resulted in destruction or damage of over 1,300 vehicles, 411 units of railroad stock, 271 carts, and 761 pack animals pulling enemy troops or supplies. In addition, seventy-seven bridges, both rail and road, were rendered unserviceable by bombs, rockets, and napalm.

Utilizing napalm and new 11.75-inch Tiny Tim rockets introduced for the first time by F-84 Thunderjets, fighters, and light bombers accounted for destruction of eleven enemy tanks and damage to an additional twenty-seven. Also fifty-five gun positions were destroyed or damaged and several fuel dumps set afire.

January was a month of good hunting for F-84 jet fighters of the Fifth Air Force. In air battles during this period Thunderjets shot down six MiGs and one Yak and probably destroyed one Yak and damaged ten MiGs. One Yak fighter was shot down by an F-51 Mustang.

—Eighth Army communique 162, issued at 8:00 P.M., Thursday (6:00 A.M., Thursday, Eastern Standard Time):

The eight-day-old United Nations forces' limited objective attack continued today as friendly elements advanced slowly throughout the past twelve hours. Enemy resistance and contact were reported as long and sporadic. Turkish elements reported receiving small arms fire while Puerto Rican elements received both small arms and mortar fire. Fighting flared in the area ten miles north-northeast of Yoju as French and United States elements engaged in hand-to-hand combat with an enemy force estimated at two regiments. Bad weather hampered close-in air support during the morning hours. Ground forces inflicted a total of 1,580 casualties on Jan. 31. An unknown number of enemy engaged Turkish elements seven miles northwest of Suwon with small arms fire at 12:15 P.M.. Small arms and mortar fire was also received by Puerto Rican elements from Hills 262 and 297, six miles north-northeast of Suwon at 10:05 A.M..

On the Yoju-Wonju front an estimated reinforced enemy regiment employing mortar, small arms, and automatic weapon fire strongly attacked United Nations elements from the east and west in the area ten miles north-northeast of Yoju at 4:50 A.M.. The fighting was still in progress as of noon with the enemy strength estimated at two regiments. Hand-to-hand fighting was reported as United Nations elements clashed with the enemy.

On the eastern central front, tactical air attacked dug-in enemy on ridges and in villages in an area four to eight miles north of Pyongchang at 11:30 A.M..

Little or no enemy contact or activity was reported on the eastern front.

—Eighth Army communique 163, issued at 10:15 A.M., Friday (8:15 P.M., Thursday, Eastern Standard Time):

United Nations forces continued to advance slowly along the western front as fighting flared in the area ten miles north-northeast of Yoju with United States and French elements reported in hand-to-hand combat with an estimated two enemy regiments. Combined friendly air and ground action forced the enemy to break contact.

1. Turkish elements advanced against light enemy resistance and occupied Hill No. 185, eight miles west-northwest of Suwon at 12:30 A.M. yesterday. United States patrols received some small-arms fire from an unknown number of enemy five miles north-northwest of Suwon. Puerto Rican elements drove the enemy off Hill No. 297, five miles northeast of Suwon. The enemy counter-attacked at 1:00 this morning but were dispersed by 1:40. Friendly elements advanced 1,000 to 3,000 yards in the area northeast of Kumyangjang with no enemy contact being reported. Friendly elements patrolled 4,000 yards north and northeast from positions five miles north of Ichon with no report of enemy contact.

2. An estimated reinforced enemy regiment initiated a strong attack against United States and French elements from the north-northeast and west in an area ten miles north-northeast of Yoju at 4:50 A.M., Feb. 1. The enemy attack increased in intensity by 12:00 with an estimated two regiments committed and as of 1:15 P.M. Friendly elements were reported as engaging the enemy in hand-to-hand combat. Friendly reinforcements were moved up and engaged the enemy with heavy fighting continuing until approximately 5:30 P.M.. The enemy was forced to break contact at 5:30 due to combined friendly air and ground action. No appreciable change in position was reported.

3. An estimated two enemy companies were engaged in the vicinity of Pyongchang at 10:30 A.M. on Feb. 1. The enemy was dispersed after an hour-long engagement. Enemy contact was also reported at points three miles southwest, two miles north, and nine miles southwest of Pyongchang during yesterday's action. An estimated enemy platoon was engaged by friendly elements four miles east of Wonju which resulted in six enemy killed and the remainder breaking contact.

4. Contact continued with an estimated two enemy battalions in the area south and east of Kangning.

—Fifth Air Force operational summary, issued Friday forenoon:

Enemy vehicular traffic was widely scattered last night as Fifth Air Force night intruders spotted approximately 300 vehicles from Huchang in the north to Seoul near the battlefront, Maj. Gen. Earle E. Partridge said in his morning summary of air action.

B-26 light bombers and F-82 night fighters reported the main bulk of the enemy traffic on the road from Sinanju south through Pyongyang, Sariwon, Kaesong, and to Seoul. However, other roads were in use as vehicles were spotted running from Huchang through Kanaggye to Huichon. On the east side of the peninsula, the highway from north of the Chosin (Changjin) Reservoir to Hamhung was well traveled. The night intruder planes attacked these vehicles throughout the night but claimed only about twenty of them definitely destroyed or damaged.

Further hampering the Red convoys, the B-26s reported knocking out a highway bridge between Sinmak and Namchonjom.

Rail traffic was reported at a standstill for the fifth consecutive night.

Along the battle line, flare-dropping aircraft worked in close coordination with B-26s as they struck at two targets and enemy-held villages and towns.

Over 250 enemy troops were claimed killed or wounded Thursday by fighters and light bombers of the Fifth Air Force.

In over 400 effective sorties, pilots also claimed destruction of nine vehicles, one supply dump, one tank, three supply carts, seven gun positions, three bridges, two railroad cars, and nine pack animals. In addition, twelve vehicles, one supply dump, one self-propelled gun, two tanks, five gun positions, one bridge, and eight railroad cars were damaged.

Light bombers: One flight of B-26s attacked Changchon and reported the entire town destroyed. Three flights of the Invaders hit Maengsan, destroying twenty-five supply buildings and damaging four. Ninety percent of the town now is reported as destroyed. Six B-26s claimed 150 troop casualties in the western sector.

Fighters: F-80s and F-84s attacking targets in the western sector claimed destruction of twenty-three enemy supply buildings, four supply stacks, nine pack animals, and damage to over fifty supply buildings.

F-80s and F-84s hit targets east of Seoul and destroyed or damaged several enemy-occupied buildings.

Thunderjet fighters attacked targets of opportunity in the eastern and central sectors, accounting for destruction or damage to over thirty-one enemy supply buildings.

Two railroad cars were destroyed and six damaged by F-80s and F-51s in the Chungchon area. Targets of opportunity were hit in the western sector with excellent result. Two strikes on Sukchon resulted in claims of two bridges, one vehicle, and six supply buildings destroyed. Two vehicles were claimed destroyed at Samso and six gun positions were destroyed and seven damaged at Kangpo. Claims were made for destruction of one tank, one supply dump, five supply buildings, and thirty-five enemy troop casualties inflicted in the Singye area.

Armed reconnaissance flights hit targets of opportunity northeast of Pyongyang with good to excellent results.

Twenty troops were claimed killed or wounded and forty supply buildings destroyed or damaged in the western sector.

Two tanks and one vehicle were damaged in the Hamhung area. Near Sunchon, one self-propelled gun was damaged and the crew of four claimed killed or wounded.

Royal Australian Air Force F-51s, under the operational control of the Fifth Air Force, claimed destruction of 150 enemy-occupied buildings in the Seoul area.

F-51 pilots of the South African Air Force claimed to have destroyed seven vehicles at Yul.

ADAMS, STANLEY T.

Rank and Organization: Master Sergeant (then Sfc.), U.S. Army, Company A, 19th Infantry Regiment.
Born: May 9, 1922, DeSoto, Kansas.
Entered Service At: Olathe, Kansas.
Place and Date: Near Sesim-ni, Korea, February 4, 1951.
Citation: M/Sgt. Adams, of Company A, distinguished himself by conspicuous gallantry and intrepidity above and beyond the call of duty in action against the enemy. At approximately 0100 hours, M/Sgt. Adams' platoon, holding an outpost some 200 yards ahead of his company, came under a determined attack by an estimated 250 enemy troops. Intense small-arms, machine gun, and mortar fire from three sides pressed the platoon back against the main line of resistance. Observing approximately 150 hostile troops silhouetted against the skyline advancing against his platoon, M/Sgt. Adams leaped to his feet, urged his men to fix bayonets, and he, with 13 members of his platoon, charged this hostile force with indomitable courage. Within 50 yards of the enemy M/Sgt. Adams was knocked to the ground when pierced in the leg by an enemy bullet. He jumped to his feet and, ignoring his wound, continued on to close with the enemy when he was knocked down four times from the concussion of grenades which had bounced off his body. Shouting orders he charged the enemy positions and engaged them in hand-to-hand combat where man after man fell before his terrific onslaught with bayonet and rifle butt. After nearly an hour of vicious action, M/Sgt. Adams and his comrades routed the fanatical foe, killing over 50 and forcing the remainder to withdraw. Upon receiving orders that his battalion was moving back, he provided cover fire while his

men withdrew. M/Sgt. Adams' superb leadership, incredible courage, and consummate devotion to duty so inspired his comrades that the enemy attack was completely thwarted, saving his battalion from possible disaster. His sustained personal bravery and indomitable fighting spirit against overwhelming odds reflect the utmost glory upon himself and uphold the finest traditions of the infantry and the military service.

OFFICIAL COMMUNIQUÉ:

—TOKYO, Monday, Feb. 5 (AP) —Far East Air Forces summary 225 issued at 12:10 P.M., Sunday (10:10 P.M., Saturday, Eastern Standard Time), covering operations of Saturday:

B-26 Invaders teamed with F-51 Mustangs to mount a massive strike at enemy troop and supply concentrations just south of Seoul Saturday as Far East Air Forces planes flew more than 730 sorties in Korea.

The eighteen light bombers hit the three-mile square area with 500-pound bombs and twenty-four Mustangs followed up with napalm, rockets, and 50-caliber machine-gun strafing.

Fifth Air Force planes flew 490 effective sorties and more than fifty more were flown by Australian, South African, Republic of Korea, and land-based Marine planes under the operational control of the Fifth Air Force.

Close support sorties were stepped up to more than 140 as F.E.A.F. planes attacked enemy troops and positions immediately in front of the advancing United Nations ground forces.

Pilots of light bombers and fighter-bombers claimed as killed or wounded approximately 100 enemy troops and to have damaged or destroyed about forty-five enemy vehicles, thirty-five boxcars, ten gun emplacements, fifteen supply dumps, 590 enemy-occupied buildings, two tunnels, and two bridges.

Alone and unarmed, an RF-80 jet reconnaissance plane was attacked by fifteen enemy MiG jets over Sinuiju airfield in far northwest Korea. The enemy "boxed in" the RF-80 four times, but each time the United States pilot broke away from them by evasive action and finally lost his attackers.

A highway and road bridge were damaged by Air Force fighters on the routes south from Wonsan, while tunnel entrances were damaged near Sibyon and near Chongon.

Fighter-bombers hit the airfield at Kangdong, damaging two gun positions and vehicles. One damaged aircraft was observed in a revetment, possibly having been hit on a previous mission.

Armed reconnaissance hit at the enemy's vehicular movement as fighter-bombers destroyed ten vehicles on the road from the Chosin (Changjin) Reservoir to Hamhung. Planes patrolled western section railroads and hit boxcars at Sinanju, Anju, Sukchon, and Chunghwa. F-80 Shooting Star jets damaged or destroyed about sixty buildings in six small guerrilla-held villages in central Korea. Twenty-two Okinawa-based B-29s of the Nineteenth and 307th Bomb groups visually dropped about 200 tons of bombs on marshaling yards at Hungnam, Tanchon, and Pyonggang, on a railroad bridge nor of Hulchon and on supply and communications centers in Chunchon. Excellent strikes were reported by crew members.

The 315th Air Division (Combat Cargo) flew 167 sorties, airlifting freight and passengers into Korea. Vital combat items and rations were landed at airfields close behind the front line.

—Far East Air Forces headquarters release issued at 4:00 P.M., Sunday (2:00 A.M., Sunday, Eastern Standard Time):

The Communist enemy's rail transportation system in Korea was given another jolt today when twenty-four Far East Air Forces B-29s dropped about 200 tons of bombs on five railroad bridges and a marshaling yard. Crews of the Okinawa-based Superforts of the Nineteenth and 307th Bomb Groups radioed Brig. Gen. James E. Briggs' Bomber Command headquarters in Japan that results ranged from good to excellent. No flak or enemy air interception was encountered and all bombing was visual.

The strikes followed the sixth successive night in which flare-dropping B-26s ranged enemy main supply routes and failed to spot a single locomotive.

Enemy efforts to repair his constantly bombed-out rail facilities were hindered at Nanan, south of Chongjin on the east coast, where bombs blanketed the tracks and switching point in the rail yard after aerial observation had determined that former bomb damage had been partially repaired.

Five railroad bridges were attacked by formations of Superforts today. Three bridges, near Koin, Kunu, and Sunchon, all located on the main rail route from the Manchurian border to Pyongyang, were struck by B-29s shortly before noon. A fourth bridge, twenty-five miles east of Kaesong, was hit by a B-29 flight, which dropped thirty-two tons of bombs. A fifth bridge was bombed near Anyon, ten miles south of the east coast port of Wonsan.

—Fifth Air Force operational summary issued at 5:00 P.M., Sunday (3:00 A.M., Sunday, Eastern Standard Time):

Four F-84 Thunderjets teamed with four F-51 Mustangs this afternoon to attack enemy troops resisting advancing R.O.K. soldiers in the Kangnung sector, claiming approximately 300 enemy killed or wounded.

Earlier in the day, reported Maj. Gen. Earle E. Partridge, two other flights of F-84s from the Twenty-seventh Fighter Escort Wing hit troops in the same area but results were difficult to observe and only fifteen casualties were claimed. Fifty troops were claimed killed or wounded in this sector this morning by F-80s of the Eighth Fighter-Bomber Wing.

Other F-80s from the Eighth reported excellent results in attacks on villages near Chorwon, Jumchon, Chunchon, and Chunchon-ni. The villages were hit with bombs as well as rockets and napalm.

F-51 Mustangs of the South African Air Force, flying under the operational control of the Fifth Air Force, found lucrative targets in vehicles with fifteen claimed destroyed during the day. All of the vehicles were found in the Namchonjom area, most of them near Yongyo. F-84s also claimed two trucks destroyed in this area.

Two railroad tunnels were damaged with rockets fired by F-51s of the Eighteenth Fighter-Bomber Wing at Sonchon. Several villages were rocketed, strafed, and napalmed in the Wonsan area.

Three flights of F-80s destroyed several supply warehouses in the Kunu area with 500-pound bombs.

Four F-80s claimed fifty enemy troops were killed or wounded on the western front.

The Yongdok airfield was strafed with undetermined results.

—Eighth Army communique 167, issued at 10:15 A.M., Sunday (8:15 P.M., Saturday, Eastern Standard Time):

United Nations forces met steadily increasing resistance from the enemy along the western front. The enemy counter-attacked Turkish elements on Hill 431, eight miles northwest of Suwon, and reoccupied the hill. A counter-attack by two enemy companies was also reported in the area six miles north of Suwon. Early this morning a strong enemy attack of undetermined size hit friendly forces twelve miles north of Ichon.

1—Enemy in reinforced battalion strength counter-attacked friendly positions at 5:05 P.M. and reoccupied Hill 431. Turkish elements broke contact and withdrew to permit friendly artillery to take the enemy under fire. Slightly to the east, United States elements forced an estimated three enemy companies to withdraw to the north and northwest with the aid of friendly artillery. Friendly forces drove the enemy from Hill 383, six miles north of Suwon, at 5:30 P.M. but friendly possession of the hill was short lived as an estimated two enemy companies counter-attacked at 9:30 P.M. causing a friendly displacement of 400 yards. Additional United Nations forces moved in to bolster friendly forces engaged with the enemy.

An estimated two enemy companies maintained contact with friendly elements in the vicinity of Hill 319, seven miles east-northeast of Suwon, until 8:00 P.M.. An estimated enemy battalion strongly resisted the advance of friendly elements nine miles north of Kumyangjang at 11:00 A.M. yesterday.

Friendly air attacked this enemy concentration in a close support mission shortly before noon Feb. 3. Contact was terminated at 4:30 P.M., when friendly forces withdrew to defensive positions for the night.

Friendly elements advancing north of Ichon reported light resistance with an increase of enemy mortar fire. At 2:50 A.M. today a strong enemy attack of undetermined size was reported in the vicinity of Hill 636, twelve miles north of Ichon.

2—Light scattered contact was reported by friendly elements at points five miles northwest of Wonju. Small groups of enemy were observed north of Hoengsong.

3—Friendly elements entered Pyongchang during mid-afternoon Feb. 3, with no report of enemy contact. An enemy mine field was located two miles north of Pyongchang by a friendly patrol. The mine field was not defended. Small patrol contact was made with the enemy ten miles northeast of Wonju. An estimated 200 dug in were also observed in this area.

4—R.O.K. elements on the east coast remained in contact with the three enemy battalions reported previously in the Kangnung area.

—Eighth Army communique 168, issued at 8:00 P.M. Sunday (6:00 A.M. Sunday, Eastern Standard Time):

Light to moderate enemy contact was reported by United Nations forces along the western front as the enemy fought aggressively to delay advancing friendly elements. Enemy casualties inflicted by ground action on Feb. 3 were estimated at 6,601.

1—An estimated reinforced enemy company made a well-executed attack against Turkish elements on Hill 109, ten miles northwest of Suwon, at 4:20 A.M.. However, at 6:00 A.M. the tempo of the attack had slowed to sporadic small-arms fire. R.O.K. (Republic of Korea) elements counter-attacked the enemy on Hill 383, six miles north-northwest of Suwon, with whom they had remained in contact during the night of Feb. 3-4 and secured Hill 383 at 6:00 A.M..

An unknown number of enemy stubbornly resisted the advance of friendly elements at points eight miles northwest of Ichon and nine miles north-northeast of Kumyangjang. An estimated enemy regiment attacked United States elements twelve miles north and northeast of Ichon at 2:50 A.M.. This attack continued throughout the morning during which time a minor infiltration occurred. Friendly elements were forced to withdraw approximately 1,500 yards during the attack which terminated at 12:40 P.M..

2—Little or no action was reported on the Yoju-Wonju front as friendly forces patrolled to their front.

3—An estimated enemy platoon was contacted in the area twelve miles north-northeast of Wonju at 3:00 A.M.. An enemy mine field covered by small-arms fire was encountered by a friendly patrol twelve miles north of Wonju at 7:30 P.M..

4—R.O.K. elements on the east coast remained in contact with an estimated three enemy battalions in the Kangnung area.

—Eighth Army communique 169, issued at 10:15 A.M. Monday (8:15 P.M. Sunday, Eastern Standard Time):

Heavy enemy attacks were launched against United States and Turkish elements in areas west-northwest and northwest of Suwon this morning. The attacks were accompanied by bugle calls, whistles, and beating of drums. Elsewhere along the western front enemy resistance stiffened, permitting only limited gains by United Nations forces.

1. A company-sized enemy attack from Hill 102 (twelve miles west-northwest of Suwon), accompanied by bugle calls and whistles, was launched against United States elements at 2:15 A.M.. This attack was contained at 3:00 A.M., but enemy in battalion strength launched another attack at 3:00 A.M. with small arms and mortar fire, with the point of attack approximately 500 yards south of Hill 102. An

enemy attack of undetermined size was launched against Turkish elements in the vicinity of Hill 109 (ten miles west-northwest of Suwon) by 4:00 A.M..

The attacking force was later estimated to be of battalion size. An unknown number of enemy from Hill 431 (eight miles northwest of Suwon) attacked to the east against United States elements at 4:15 A.M.. Enemy bugle calls and beating of drums in a R.O.K. (Republic of Korea) sector developed into several probing attacks with small arms fire being received shortly after midnight. All was reported quiet in this sector at 4:10 A.M.. Strong enemy resistance limited friendly advances in areas north and northeast of Suwon and northeast of Kumyangjang. As a result of yesterday's attack, the enemy occupied Hill 142, thirteen miles northeast of Ichon.

2. During the afternoon on Feb. 4 enemy in unknown strength with automatic weapons engaged United States elements thirteen miles north-northeast of Yoju. Artillery and mortar fire, followed by an air strike, failed to dislodge the enemy.

3. An estimated enemy platoon was engaged by friendly elements two miles northeast of Hoengsong. Friendly fire caused the enemy to withdraw approximately 1,000 yards, at which point they were taken under friendly artillery fire. An estimated enemy battalion three miles west of Pyongchang was taken under artillery fire at midnight with unknown results.

4. R.O.K. elements remained in contact with an estimated three enemy battalions in the Kangnung area on the east coast.

MILLETT, LEWIS L.

Rank and Organization: Captain, U.S. Army, Company E, 27th Infantry Regiment.
Born: December 15, 1920, Mechanic Falls, Maine.
Entered Service At: Mechanic Falls, Maine.
Place and Date: Vicinity of Soam-ni, Korea, February 7, 1951.
Citation: Capt. Millett, Company E, distinguished himself by conspicuous gallantry and intrepidity above and beyond the call of duty in action against the enemy. While personally leading his company in an attack against a strongly held position he noted that the 1st Platoon was pinned down by small-arms, automatic weapons, and anti-tank fire. Capt. Millett ordered the 3d Platoon forward, placed himself at the head of the two platoons, and, with fixed bayonet, led the assault up the fire-swept hill. In the fierce charge Capt. Millett bayoneted 2 enemy soldiers and boldly continued on, throwing grenades, clubbing and bayoneting the enemy, while urging his men forward by shouting encouragement. Despite vicious opposing fire, the whirlwind hand-to-hand assault carried to the crest of the hill. His dauntless leadership and personal courage so inspired his men that they stormed into the hostile position and used their bayonets with such lethal effect that the enemy fled in wild disorder. During this fierce onslaught Capt. Millett was wounded by grenade fragments but refused evacuation until the objective was taken and firmly secured. The superb leadership, conspicuous courage, and consummate devotion to duty demonstrated by Capt. Millett were directly responsible for the successful accomplishment of a hazardous mission and reflect the highest credit upon himself and the heroic traditions of the military service.

OFFICIAL COMMUNIQUÉ:

TOKYO, Thursday, Feb. 8 (AP)
—Far East Air Forces headquarters summary 228, covering Tuesday's operations, issued at 12:15 P.M., Wednesday (10:15 P.M., Tuesday, Eastern Standard Time):

Far East Air Forces Tuesday directed more than 800 sorties against the enemy in Korea on the 226th consecutive day of air operations with a mass attack of twenty-four B-29 Superforts from Okinawa bases hitting marshaling yards, transfer points, and supply warehouses in Kanggye, important railroad and highway center in central-north Korea close to the Yalu River. Approximately 240 tons of bombs were dropped.

Clear weather enabled the crews of the Superforts to see their bombs pattern the target areas. This attack was a continuation of F.E.A.F. Bomber Command's program of destroying all facilities used by the enemy to move supplies and troops from Manchuria to the fighting front.

The Fifth Air Force, meanwhile, kept up its fighter-bomber and light-bomber attacks on the enemy effectively. More than 590 sorties were flown and these included those of Australian, South African, republic of Korea, and land-based Marine planes under the operational control of the Fifth Air Force. The Marines flew more than 100 sorties.

Widespread fighting on the front lines produced enemy troop targets, and Air Force pilots claimed inflicting more than 700 casualties on the Reds across the battle front south of Seoul to near the east coast. A total of more than 210 close-support missions were flown during the day, including those by the Marines. A strike north of Hoengsong not only left approximately 100 enemy troops killed or wounded, but also damaged two enemy tanks and damaged or destroyed eight vehicles.

The bridges were damaged south of Seoul, and at Koesong, Chunchon, and southwest of Koksan.

A minor guerrilla concentration, which has been under constant attack behind friendly lines in southeast Korea, was hit by Marine planes. Troops and supplies were hit with excellent results.

Twenty-two night-intruder B-26 light bombers attacked enemy front line troops last night under the direction of ground controllers after their targets were illuminated by flares dropped from accompanying aircraft. Results were very successful.

—Eighth Army communiqué 174, issued at 8:00 P.M., Wednesday (6:00 A.M., Wednesday, Eastern Standard Time):

United Nations forces today made limited advances of 2,000 to 3,000 yards as task forces Bartlett, Dolvin, and Fisher probed enemy positions south of the Han River. Task forces Bartlett and Dolvin encountered heavy enemy resistance in an area eight to ten miles southwest of Seoul while Task Force Fisher rumbled north to a point seven miles southeast of Seoul and four miles south of the Han River with no report of enemy contact. Estimated enemy casualties for Feb. 6 were reported at 7,117.

1—United States and Turkish elements on the left flank of the United Nations offensive advanced 2,000 to 3,000 yards against little or no resistance. Leading elements of Task Force Bartlett encountered enemy mines four miles west of Anyang at 10:00 A.M.. The task force met heavy enemy resistance at a point five miles west of Anyang and was reported operating in this same area throughout the afternoon. Leading elements of Task Force Dolvin were heavily engaged by an unknown number of enemy a short distance northeast of Anyang at 8:45 A.M..

At 11:00 A.M. an enemy concentration of undetermined strength two miles north of Anyang engaged other elements of task Force Dolvin. The task force reported heavy resistance as it continued to harass the enemy throughout the afternoon. Task Force Fisher encountered an unguarded minefield eleven miles southeast of Seoul at 9:35 A.M.. The minefield was eliminated and the tank force probed to a point seven miles southeast of Seoul and four miles south of the Han River with no report of enemy contact. Patrol clashes with the enemy were reported seven miles west of Anyang, eight miles north-northeast of Ichon, and nine miles north of Ichon.

2—Light enemy contact was reported on the central front as United Nations forces made limited gains of 2,000 to 3,000 yards throughout the day.

3—United Nations forces continued to patrol aggressively on the eastern-central front and made limited advances throughout the day.

4—A delayed report from the eastern front reported an estimated two enemy battalions offering moderate to heavy resistance as R.O.K. (Republic of Korea) elements advanced to positions three miles east of Kangnung and five miles southwest of Kangnung on Feb. 6. Light enemy resistance was reported as R.O.K. elements secured Kusan (five miles southwest of Kangnung) at 6:30 this morning with other elements securing the high ground three miles west of Kangnung at 7:30 A.M..

—*Fifth Air Force communiqué issued at 10:55 A.M., Thursday (2:55 P.M., Wednesday, Eastern Standard Time):*

Thirteen hundred and fifty vehicles were spotted on highways in enemy territory last night by F.E.A.R. (Far East Air Forces) night intruders. Almost all movement was reported north of the Thirty-eighth Parallel. B-26 light bombers and F-82 twin Mustangs attacked well over 100 of the vehicles, claiming twenty-five damaged or destroyed. Fifth Air Force fliers mounted fifty sorties against enemy targets, towns, and troop concentrations along the battle line as well as vehicles.

The largest convoy of more than 200 trucks in a line eight to ten miles long was sighted just south of Sinuiju, with 150 in scattered groups between Kanggye and Kunui and 100 more near Sonchon. The Pyongyang area had the greatest scattered traffic with 400 trucks in small groups sighted. For the tenth successive night no trains were seen moving.

Flying day and night flights, light bombers and fighters flew 445 sorties striking enemy supply lines and troop concentrations. Twenty vehicles with enemy troops and supplies were claimed destroyed.

In the Chongjin area B-26 pilots claimed one railroad bridge and one railroad car destroyed.

F-80s and F-51s struck close-support targets in the western sector with excellent results. Three self-propelled guns, three vehicles, one tank, and several supply buildings were claimed destroyed. About seventy-five troops were killed or wounded in the Sukkyoi area. Flying close support in the eastern sector, F-84s destroyed or damaged 175 enemy-held buildings, starting many fires. One vehicle was claimed destroyed near Hongchon.

Other flights accounted for over 100 troops killed or wounded in the Sukkyo area. F-84s flying armed reconnaissance destroyed or damaged buildings housing enemy troops and supplies and four vehicles were destroyed near Chuchon. About forty enemy troops and supplies and four vehicles were destroyed near Chuchon. About forty enemy troop casualties were claimed by F-51s in the Pyongyang area and about fifty supply buildings damaged or destroyed.

F-51s of the South African Air Force claimed four vehicles destroyed and many fires started in the Wonsan area. Royal Australian Air Force fliers destroyed one tank and two vehicles in the Huchang area. One F-51 was lost on a strafing run in enemy territory and the pilot is presumed lost.

—*Eighth Army communiqué 175, issued at 10:15 A.M. Thursday (8:15 P.M. Wednesday, Eastern Standard Time):*

Task Force Fisher probing enemy positions ten miles south-southeast of Seoul yesterday encountered two mine fields, one of which contained bangalore torpedoes. After eliminating the obstacle the task force proceeded north and encountered an enemy force which employed Russian-type hand grenades and threw bangalore torpedoes. Friendly armor dispersed the enemy to the north. Patrol contact continued in the area ten miles north and northeast of Ichon. Enemy forces stubbornly resisted friendly advances eight and ten miles west-northwest of Hoengsong.

1. Two enemy counter-attacks were launched against United States elements nine miles south-southwest of Seoul by an estimated 50-60 enemy at 1900 hours (7:00 P.M.). However, the counter-attacks were quickly repulsed by friendly artillery fire. At 1920 hours (7:20 P.M.) ten to twelve rounds of self-propelled fire were received from the north. Task Force Dolvin probed enemy positions one mile west, three miles east, and the area immediately north of Anyang, encountering moderate to heavy resistance. The task force broke contact at 1600 hours (4:00 P.M.) and withdrew for the night. Six to eight rounds of high velocity fire were received by the task force from a point three miles north of Anyang.

Task Force Fisher encountered two mine fields and bangalore torpedoes which were equipped with pull-type firing devices with strings attached running to foxholes twenty-five to thirty yards from the road. Mines and bangalore torpedoes were eliminated and the task force proceeded north. Just north of the mine field (ten miles south-southeast of Seoul) an estimated 200 enemy employing Russian-type hand grenades and throwing bangalore torpedoes were encountered. After a sharp fire fight, during which friendly armor employed direct fire, the enemy withdrew to the north and friendly elements returned to friendly lines. Enemy contact continued in the area ten miles north and northeast of Ichon.

2. An estimated three enemy battalions deployed eight miles west-northwest of Hoengsong, held friendly units to slight gains yesterday. An estimated 3,000 enemy were encountered by R.O.K. (Republic of Korea) elements fourteen miles east of Hoengsong.

3. An estimated enemy battalion was engaged by United Nations forces four miles north of Hoengsong while two enemy battalions were engaged with friendly elements in the area ten miles west-northwest of Hoengsong. The enemy launched a heavy attack against friendly elements fourteen miles east of Hoengsong at 0930 hours (7:30 A.M.) yesterday. No further details available. Light enemy resistance was encountered at a point three miles north-northeast of Hoengsong.

4. An estimated enemy battalion well dug in was reported fifteen miles southeast of Ulsong at 1300 hours (1:00 P.M.).

—United Nations naval forces summary of Feb. 7 operations, issued at 11:30 A.M. Thursday (9:30 P.M. Wednesday, Eastern Standard Time):

Naval air and surface attacks on both coasts of Korea continued with sustained intensity yesterday.

A bombardment task force, including the heavy cruiser St. Paul, stood off Inchon and poured a steady stream of harassing, interdiction and call fire into the area and to the southeast. Many of the firing missions were in direct support of advancing friendly ground forces. The St. Paul is commanded by Capt. C.C. Smith.

Troop concentrations, road junctions, warehouses, and gun positions were the principal targets of the naval shelling, which was performed with the benefit of aerial spotting by Marine Corsairs operating from the light carrier Bataan. Spotters described results of the bombardment as excellent.

Combat sorties by Corsairs from the Bataan were concentrated in the same general area of the surface bombardment. Several company-size entrenchments were put to rout. Thirty buildings and one factory were destroyed. Large fires were started on Wolmi Island. One flight of Corsairs knocked out five anti-aircraft batteries at Sariwon. The Bataan is commanded by Capt. E.T. Neale.

The fleet standing off Kangnung on the east coast continued to provide gunfire support for advancing friendly ground forces.

Other fleet units, including the Australian destroyer Warramunga, ranged to the north along the coast and bombarded targets at Nanam and Yongdee-Gap. At Nanam an ammunition dump, several barracks buildings, and a headquarters building were destroyed. Large fires were started at Yongdee-Gap and entrances to two railroad tunnels were partially sealed.

Navy Skyraiders, Corsairs, and Panther jets of Fast Carrier Task Force 77 yesterday concentrated on bridges and rolling stock in northeast Korea, effecting most of their damage in the vicinity of Tanchon.

Two railroad bridges and two highway bridges were destroyed. Damage was done to more than forty-five boxcars and one locomotive. Four barracks buildings and numerous vehicles were destroyed. A number of troop concentrations were attacked with good effect.

The U.S.S. Princeton, flagship of Task Force 77, is commanded by Capt. W.O. Gallery.

The United Nations Fleet operating in Korean waters includes ships from the Republic of Korea, Canada, the Netherlands, Australia, the United Kingdom, Thailand, New Zealand, and the United States.

†LONG, CHARLES R.

Rank and Organization: Sergeant, U.S. Army, Company M, 38th Infantry Regiment, 2d Infantry Division.
Born: December 10, 1923, Kansas City, Missouri.
Entered Service At: Kansas City, Missouri.
Place and Date: Near Hoengsong, Korea, February 12, 1951.
Citation: Sgt. Long, a member of Company M, distinguished himself by conspicuous gallantry and intrepidity above and beyond the call of duty in action against an armed enemy of the United Nations. When Company M, in a defensive position on Hill 300, was viciously attacked by a numerically superior hostile force at approximately 0300 hours and ordered to withdraw, Sgt. Long, a forward observer for the mortar platoon, voluntarily remained at his post to provide cover by directing mortar fire on the enemy. Maintaining radio contact with his platoon, Sgt. Long coolly directed accurate mortar fire on the advancing foe. He continued firing his carbine and throwing hand-grenades until his position was surrounded and he was mortally wounded. Sgt. Long's inspirational, valorous action halted the onslaught, exacted a heavy toll of enemy casualties, and enabled his company to withdraw, reorganize, counterattack, and regain the hill strong-point. His unflinching courage and noble self-sacrifice reflect the highest credit upon himself and are in keeping with the honored traditions of the military service.

OFFICIAL COMMUNIQUÉ:

TOKYO, Feb. 12. (AP)
—Far East Air Forces summary of Feb. 11 operations, issued Monday forenoon (Sunday night, Eastern Standard Time):

Mounting its greatest effort since Jan. 3, Far East Air Forces sent about 880 sorties against the enemy Sunday, as ground forces were fighting their way back into the Kimpo, Yongdungpo, and Inchon areas. Coincidentally, the greatest number of sorties mounted this year —955—was on Jan. 3, when these areas in the Seoul vicinity were being evacuated by United Nations forces under pressure of numerically superior Communist forces.

Approximately 580 sorties were flown by Fifth Air Force planes and Royal Australian Air Force, South African Air Force, R.O.K.s, and land-based United States Marine planes under the operational control of the Fifth. More than 155 sorties were flown in close support of attacking United Nations ground forces.

Some ten strikes involving approximately forty fighter planes were launched at the enemy in a section north of Ichon in the west central portion of the front, where ground forces encountered stubborn opposition. Results were excellent. Fifth Air Force pilots claimed inflicting about 220 casualties on enemy troops. They also claimed damage or destruction to approximately 1,200 enemy supply buildings and 130 enemy motor vehicles. They destroyed four enemy field pieces, three self-propelled guns, and five gun emplacements, the majority of them in the vicinity of Yongdungpo.

Night intruding B-26 Invaders accounted for more than seventy of the vehicles, chiefly on western and north Korean supply routes. By daylight other B-26 light bombers leveled a powerful attack at enemy supply centers at Namchonjom and reported damage or destruction to more than 110 buildings in which the Communists stored war supplies. Large fires were started. It was estimated the supply area was 80 percent wiped out.

Armed reconnaissance planes destroyed or damaged more than forty vehicles in the Chorwon, Kumhwa, and Sariwon areas. They damaged railroad bridges north of Haeju and near Anju and a highway bridge near Hamhung. Another heavy strike destroyed or damaged more than forty railroad cars at Kaesong and burned approximately 100 drums of oil or gasoline. Night reconnaissance reported sighting about 500 vehicles on supply routes in North Korea scattered over the general area. They were placed under attack.

Minor guerrilla concentrations were attacked by eight F-80s and F-51s in the southeastern mountains. Pilots reported approximately 100 killed and about sixty supply buildings destroyed or damaged.

Japan-based B-29 Superforts of the Ninety-eighth Bomb Group hammered marshaling yards and bridges with more than 200 tons of bombs dropped from twenty-two medium bombers. Weight of the attack was delivered on targets in the Pyongyang, Sunan, and Hwangju areas on the western supply routes. A railroad bridge at Hwangju was attacked. Bombs were seen to hit in the marshaling yards of Pyongyang and Sunan and in the supply area at Sunan. Two spans of a highway bridge at Kanggye were knocked in the water. Some meager flak was encountered over targets. There was no enemy air interception.

The 315th Air Division (Combat Cargo) flew a total of about 280 sorties to deliver more than 975 tons of war material to forward elements of United nations forces during the day. More than forty C-119 flying Boxcars airdropped about 220 tons of this total to friendly troops along the front line. The cargo that was landed consisted mainly of ammunition, with more than 95 tons of aviation ammunition being carried for the Fifth Air Force.

—United Nations Naval Forces summary of Feb. 11 operations, issued at 1:35 P.M., Monday (11:35 P.M., Sunday, Eastern Standard Time):

Carrier-based United States Navy and Marine aircraft were out in day and night attacks in close and deep support of the ground forces.

Marine fliers operating from the carrier Bataan concentrated most of their effort in close support of ground forces advancing on the west coast. Several troop concentrations were attacked with good effect and a number of vehicles were destroyed.

Ranging north of the battle line, one flight of Marines partially sealed two tunnels near Sinmak. Dividing their effort between close and deep support, Navy fliers of Fast Carrier Task Force 77 pounded front-line troop concentrations and blasted communication lines north along the east coast. One concentration of 100 troops crossing the ice-covered Chosin (Changjin) Reservoir was all but wiped out in repeated strafing attacks. Task Force 77, a part of the Seventh Fleet, is commanded by Rear Admiral Ralph A. Ofstie.

Big guns of the Navy continued to harass the enemy on both coasts. On the west coast, a powerful United Nations fleet, including the battleship Missouri, stood by to render direct support of the ground forces. On the east coast, a second powerful fleet led by the cruiser Manchester continued with patrol and general support operations.

The United Nations fleet operating in Korean waters includes ships of Australia, Canada, the Netherlands, New Zealand, Thailand, the Republic of Korea, the United Kingdom, and the United States.

—Fifth Air Force summary, issued at 5:00 P.M., Monday (3:00 A.M., Monday, Eastern Standard Time):

Fighters and light bombers of the Fifth Air Force attacked heavily today at the enemy's supply lines, claiming destruction of sixty-two vehicles by 5:00 P.M.. In addition to vehicle destruction, twelve vehicles were damaged, two tanks claimed destroyed, and another two damaged. Over 450 enemy troops were claimed killed or wounded.

A flight of four F-80s of the Forty-ninth Fighter-Bomber Wing were attacked by four MiG-type aircraft near Chongju. Capt. B. Berger of San Antonio, Tex., flight leader, said: "At approximately 12:30 P.M., at 10,000 feet over Chongju, four MiGs made one firing pass at the flight. Two of the MiGs attacked the flight that was attacking a ground target, while the other two came after our flight which was flying top cover. Our flight immediately went down to attack the MiG's who jumped the bombers (F-80 with 1,000-pound bombs)."

"The MiG's made only one firing pass on the bombers and ourselves and took off north. No damage was done to either friendly or enemy aircraft. The MiGs were not aggressive and they were firing while still out of range. The two that jumped Colonel Murphy (Col. John R. Murphy of Fargo, N.D., group commander) were firing at least 10,000 feet from the nearest F-80."

In a close-support attack in the western sector, about fifty troops were claimed killed or wounded. One supply dump, five buildings, and one gun position were claimed destroyed, while ten more buildings were damaged.

F-51s of the Eighteenth Wing, claimed to have destroyed vehicles (number not given) and damaged two in the Chorwon-Kumhwa area. Four more F-51s led by Capt. Red Webster of Alexandria, La., strafed and rocketed a village, claiming fifty enemy troop casualties and destruction of four houses. Captain Webster said: "Judging from the number of troops around buildings, it is a safe bet that they were really packed inside the structure."

F-80 Shooting Stars of the Fifty-first Fighter-Interceptor Wing attacked two villages in the eastern sector, claiming over 100 enemy troops killed or wounded in napalm (fire bomb) attacks on building areas housing troops and supplies. Other attacks in this sector by F-51s of the Thirty-fifth Fighter-Interceptor Wing accounted for claims of about sixty enemy troop casualties in napalm and rocket attacks.

—*Eighth Army communiqué 184, issued at 10:15 P.M., Monday (8:15 A.M., Monday, Eastern Standard Time):*

Elements of three C.C.F. (Chinese Communist Forces) armies in conjunction with two North Korean corps launched a strong counter-attack against two South Korea divisions in an area north and northwest of Hoengsong early this morning. The enemy counterattack gained momentum during the day forcing United Nations elements to withdraw from their positions. At least two enemy division were reported spearheading the enemy drive on Hoengsong. Enemy casualties inflicted on Feb. 11 by ground action were estimated at 4,734.

The two enemy regiments reported as attempting to cross the Han River immediately south of Seoul at 1:30 this morning (11:30 A.M., Sunday, Eastern Standard Time) have now been established as having been a strong patrol of unknown strength. Intense small-arms fire was received by a friendly patrol in this vicinity at 8:00 A.M.. The patrol observed what appeared to be fifteen North Korean dead in this area. In the United States Third Division sector, air observed 200 to 300 enemy moving south toward friendly troops southeast of Seoul on the south bank of the Han River. An enemy platoon attacked elements of the Nineteenth R.O.K. (Republic of Korea) regiment nine miles north-northwest of Ichon at 6:30 A.M.. The enemy was dispersed with artillery fire.

Air observed an estimated 150 enemy in light green uniforms dug in the vicinity of Hajin at 9:30 A.M..

At last reports one R.O.K. regiment was surrounded north of Hoengsong. Although complete ground reports are not available, air observation reported large groups of enemy moving southeast in this battle zone and reported observing numerous enemy roadblocks to the rear of friendly positions early this morning.

R.O.K. patrols engaged an estimated enemy company in the vicinity of the Thirty-eighth Parallel on the east coast. The engagement lasted approximately two hours, at which time friendly forces broke contact.

†SITMAN, WILLIAM S.

Rank and Organization: Sergeant First Class, U.S. Army, Company M, 23d Infantry Regiment, 2d Infantry Division.
Born: Bellwood, Pennsylvania.
Entered Service At: Bellwood, Pennsylvania.
Place and Date: Near Chipyong-ni, Korea, February 14, 1951.
Citation: Sfc. Sitman distinguished himself by conspicuous gallantry and intrepidity above and beyond the call of duty in action against an armed enemy of the United Nations. Sfc. Sitman, a machine gun section leader of Company M, was attached to Company I, under attack by a numerically superior hostile force. During the encounter when an enemy grenade knocked out his machine gun, a squad from Company I, immediately emplaced a light-machine gun and Sfc. Sitman remained to provide security for the crew. In the ensuing action, the enemy lobbed a grenade into the position and Sfc. Sitman, fully aware of the odds against him, selflessly threw himself on it, absorbing the full force of the explosion with his body. Although mortally wounded in this fearless display of valor, his intrepid act saved 5 men from death or serious injury, and enabled them to continue inflicting withering fire on the ruthless foe throughout the attack. Sfc. Sitman's noble self-sacrifice and consummate devotion to duty reflect lasting glory on himself and uphold the honored traditions of the military service.

OFFICIAL COMMUNIQUÉ:
TOKYO, Thursday, Feb. 15 (AP)
—United Nations Naval Forces summary of Feb. 13 operations, issued at 1:00 P.M., Wednesday (11:00 P.M., Tuesday, Eastern Standard Time):

United Nations Naval Forces continued to bombard the enemy on both coasts of Korea and carrier-based United States Navy and Marine pilots flew 222 sorties in close and deep support of the ground forces.

For the second straight day the United States heavy cruiser St. Paul bombarded targets north of the Han River and west of Seoul. A destroyer force on the east coast shelled enemy forces and installations north of Yangyang.

Marine Corsair pilots from the carrier Bataan and Navy Skyraiders, Corsairs, and Panther jets of Fast Carrier Task Force 77 concentrated their main effort in close support of the ground forces, but successfully attacked a large number of widely scattered targets to the north.

A forty-car train about to enter a tunnel near Songjin was all but completely destroyed.

Numerous troop concentrations were hit with estimated heavy casualties. Thirteen tanks were damaged.

Large fires were started in three supply areas. Forty-six buildings and warehouses were destroyed and thirty-nine were damaged. One highway bridge was damaged.

The United Nations Fleet operating in Korean waters includes ships from Australia, Canada, New Zealand, the United Kingdom, the Netherlands, the Republic of Korea, Thailand, and the United States.

—Far East Air Forces release, issued at 4:00 P.M., Wednesday, (2:00 A.M., Wednesday, Eastern Standard Time):

A big Communist military encampment near Tokchon in North Korea was blasted with high explosives and then fire-bombed this noon by Far East Air Forces B-29 Superforts using the saturation technique against the target. Bombing visually, five flights of the Japan-based Ninety-eighth Bomb Group patterned the 480-building barracks area with 500-pounders and a sixth flight followed with fire-bombs and incendiary clusters.

Twenty-two medium bombers took part in the attack, dropping about 220 tons of bombs. Crewmen reported excellent results.

The attack was the second in three days against enemy barracks areas. Monday, Okinawa-based B-29s hit a large encampment near Pyongyang.

No flak was experienced by the Superforts today, but the first three formations over the target area were subjected to a light attack by enemy fighter planes of an unspecified type, their radio report said. Subsequent flights saw enemy fighters but were not attacked.

Aircraft Commanders radioed Brig. Gen. James E. Briggs' headquarters in Japan that all aircraft were returning to their base after the strike.

Buildings under attack were apparently of a standard wooden construction design and located in a valley between snow-covered mountains approximately 60 miles south of the Manchurian border.

Three other Superforts encountered heavy clouds on a mission to the East Coast and used radar techniques to bomb military targets in Hamhung.

—*Eighth Army communiqué 188, issued at 10:00 P.M., Wednesday (8:00 A.M., Wednesday, Eastern Standard Time):*

Action in the Chipyong area subsided at 11:15 A.M.. However, enemy movement continued south of Chipyong. Heavy movement was reported north and northwest of Wonju with friendly air and artillery attacking large enemy columns moving south in the area north and northwest of Wonju. Enemy casualties inflicted by ground action during Feb. 13 were estimated at 2,265. A delayed report for Feb. 12 claimed an additional 1,427 enemy casualties.

1—The enemy attack two miles northeast of Kyongan subsided at 7:05 A.M.. Enemy attacking seven miles north-northeast of Yoju hit two friendly companies from the north, east, and west. An estimated two enemy platoons were taken under tank fire two miles south-southwest of Chipyong during the morning. Enemy attacks in the Chipyong area subsided at 11:15 A.M.. However, enemy movement continued throughout the area with enemy road blocks and troops reported south of friendly positions in the Chipyong defense perimeter.

2—The enemy attacked a friendly mortar platoon five miles west of Wonju at 8:45 A.M.. At 7:15 A.M. an estimated 1,000 enemy attacked the Netherlands force five miles west-northwest of Wonju. Air reported observing an estimated enemy division moving south and southwest of a point six miles west-northwest of Wonju and observed enemy forces crossing creeks six miles northwest and north-northwest of Wonju. Air also observed a large enemy column moving south in this same area during the morning hours. The enemy forces were taken under heavy air and artillery fire with unknown results.

3—The enemy attack which caused a penetration on Feb. 13 fifteen miles north of Pyongchang by an estimated 600 enemy was reported contained at noon Feb. 13. An estimated enemy regiment attacked friendly elements from the west along the main road in the vicinity five miles north-northwest of Pyongchang during the morning of Feb. 14.

4—No report of any significant enemy action on the eastern front.

—*Eighth Army communiqué 189, issued at 10:15 A.M., Thursday (8:15 P.M., Wednesday, Eastern Standard Time):*

Attempted enemy river crossings in the Yongdungpo area were repulsed. Stubborn enemy resistance continues in the Kyongan sector. Enemy pressure continues in the Koksu area. An all-out attack was launched by the enemy against the Chipyong perimeter at 8:30 P.M.. A heavy enemy attack three miles northeast of Wonju at 9:00 P.M. was repulsed.

1—An enemy platoon reportedly crossed the Han River to the south in boats at 7:00 A.M. Feb. 14 at a point seven miles northwest of Yongdungpo. The enemy was forced to withdraw across the river at 10:30 A.M..

An estimated enemy company attempted to cross the Han River one mile northwest of Yongdungpo but was dispersed by Turkish elements at 1:15 P.M.. An enemy battalion engaged friendly elements ten miles southeast of Seoul from 10:00 A.M. to 5:00 P.M., resulting in the dispersal of the enemy force and 200 enemy war prisoners being taken. Some enemy infiltration was reported in the area nine miles south-southeast of Seoul with scattered enemy groups being engaged throughout the day.

1. Stubborn enemy resistance continued in the areas two miles north and northeast of Kyongan as well as in areas four miles and six miles east-southeast and eight miles west-southwest of Koksu with an estimated enemy battalion employing small arms, mortar, and bazooka fire being reported immediately west of Koksu. The enemy maintained a heavy steady pressure against friendly elements in the area five miles south-southeast of Koksu.

2. At 8:30 P.M. the enemy launched an all-out attack against the friendly perimeter at Chipyong. The initial attack was repulsed at 11:30 P.M.. Friendly elements on the eastern side of the perimeter were under attack at 11:30 P.M., with the attack still in progress as of 2:30 A.M. this morning. French elements in the perimeter were reported under attack from the northwest at 12:20 A.M.. An undetermined number of enemy launched a heavy attack against United Nations forces three miles northwest of Wonju at 9:00 P.M.. However, friendly elements launched a counter-attack at 9:30 P.M., inflicting many enemy casualties. Friendly elements restored their lines at 12 midnight.

3. An estimated enemy battalion was reported as moving south in the vicinity six miles west-northwest of Pyongchang at 12:30 P.M.. A large enemy troop concentration was reported by a friendly patrol six miles east of Pyongchang at 4:00 P.M.. The enemy attack five miles north-northeast of the village was still in progress as of 10:45 A.M., Feb. 14. At last report the enemy was being reinforced and continuing the attack to the east.

4. No significant enemy activity reported from the eastern front.

†KYLE, DARWIN K.

Rank and Organization: Second Lieutenant, U.S. Army, Company K, 7th Infantry Regiment, 3d Infantry Division.
Born: June 1, 1918, Jenkins, Kentucky.
Entered Service At: Racine, West Virginia.
Place and Date: Near Kamil-ni, Korea, February 16, 1951.
Citation: 2d Lt. Kyle distinguished himself by conspicuous gallantry and intrepidity above and beyond the call of duty in action against the enemy. When his platoon had been pinned down by intense fire, he completely exposed himself to move among and encourage his men to continue the advance against enemy forces strongly entrenched on Hill 185. Inspired by his courageous leadership, the platoon resumed the advance but was again pinned down when an enemy machine gun opened fire, wounding 6 of the men. 2d Lt. Kyle immediately charged the hostile emplacement alone, engaged the crew in hand-to-hand combat, killing all 3. Continuing on toward the objective, his platoon suddenly received intense automatic-weapons fire from a well-concealed hostile position on its right flank. Again leading his men in a daring bayonet charge against this position, firing his carbine and throwing grenades, 2d Lt. Kyle personally destroyed 4 of the enemy before he was killed from a burst from an enemy submachine gun. The extraordinary heroism and outstanding leadership of 2d Lt. Kyle, and his gallant self-sacrifice, reflect the highest credit upon himself and are in keeping with the esteemed traditions of the military service.

OFFICIAL COMMUNIQUÉ:
TOKYO, Saturday, Feb. 17 (AP)
—Far East Air Forces summary of Feb. 15 operations, issued at 1:15 P.M., Friday (11;15 P.M., Thursday, Eastern Standard Time):

United States Far East Air Forces went over the 1,000 mark in sorties Thursday for the first time since it began combat operations in Korea last June 26. Fifth Air Force also set a new record of over 700 individual flights. F.E.A.F. 315th Air Division (Combat Cargo) flew more than 300 sorties and F.E.A.F. Bomber Command flew twenty-three to send the total Thursday to over 1,025. Previous high sortie figure was 958 flown on Jan. 3.

Included in the Fifth Air Force's total are sorties flown by Australian, South African, Republic of Korea, and land-based United States Marine Corps planes under the Fifth's operational control.

More than 250 of the Fifth Air Force's sorties were in close support of ground troops and many of the armed reconnaissance flights attacked military targets immediately behind the enemy's front lines.

Further behind the lines, railroad and highway bridges were attacked, supply centers were hit, and a toll was taken of enemy vehicular traffic in interdiction of the Communist effort to deploy forces strategically.

Casualties inflicted on the enemy by Fifth Air Force planes were estimated at 350 and were spread across the battle zone, being heaviest in the areas around Chipyong and north of Wonju.

Fifth Air Force pilots on armed reconnaissance missions attacked enemy vehicles on the west-to-east routes between the Sinmak and Kaesong concentration centers and the Chorwon-Hwachon build-up areas north of the central front. The pilots claimed almost 100 enemy vehicles destroyed or damaged.

Twenty-two B-26 light bombers delivered a heavy attack on an enemy supply center at Hwangju, south of Pyongyang, and started about 100 fires, destroying almost fifty enemy supply buildings and three warehouses and damaging six warehouses.

A total of almost 1,100 enemy-occupied buildings were destroyed or damaged throughout Korea during the day. Twelve Red gun emplacements were destroyed or damaged, sixteen pack animals were killed, twelve box cars were destroyed or damaged, and one tunnel and four bridges were damaged.

The bridges were located near Chorwon in central Korea, south of Chorwon, near Chipyong on the battlefront and near Chongju in northwest Korea. The tunnel was damaged near Sariwon in the western section.

At night, Fifth Air Force planes dropped flares to illuminate vital battle areas for night-ranging B-26 traffic but detected only about seventy vehicles moving over supply routes mostly near Wonsan on the east coast. These were brought under attack.

During the early morning Thursday, a B-26 returning from a night mission was attacked over the Pyongyang area by an enemy aircraft with swept-back wings. The B-26 was not damaged.

Nineteen Okinawa-based B-29s of the 307th and Nineteenth Bomb Groups attacked railroad bridges on the northeastern supply route at Songjin and Pachunjang. They attacked a highway and by-pass bridge at Sukchon north of Pyongyang, hit a highway intersection at Chaeryong in the western section, and bombed a railroad bridge at Pyolchang in central Korea. A span of the Pyolchang bridge was reported knocked down. Approximately 160 tons of bombs were dropped.

The 315th Air Division (Combat Cargo) flew more than 300 sorties and airdropped or landed approximately 450 tons of supplies for front-line troops. It carried a total of more than 1,000 tons of all types of cargo to Korean points and transported more than 2,000 passengers.

—Eighth Army communiqué 192, issued at 8:00 P.M., Friday (6:00 A.M., Friday, Eastern Standard Time):

Enemy forces succeeded in infiltrating friendly positions southeast of Wonju and north of Checon. Enemy forces offered stubborn resistance in the Kyongan and Koksu sectors. Enemy casualties inflicted by ground action on Feb. 15 were estimated at 4,955.

The United States Second Division accounted for 47 percent of this enemy casualty total, which included 2,275 killed and wounded and seventy-seven P.O.W.s (prisoners of war).

1—An enemy squad was engaged by R.O.K. (Republic of Korea) forces seven miles northwest of Yongdungpo at 8:10 A.M.. The enemy was dispersed. Enemy resistance increased in the area three miles north of Kyongan during the morning as the enemy on Hill 327 stubbornly resisted the advance of United States forces. A United States patrol reported an estimated enemy battalion on Hill 584, six miles east-southeast of Kyongan and an estimated enemy regiment in the surrounding area.

2—United States forces in the Koksu area continued to engage the enemy throughout the day. French forces in the Chipyong defense perimeter observed an estimated 1,000 enemy at 5:30 A.M. moving downhill south of the perimeter. Artillery fire dispersed this enemy force. Air observed an estimated 1,000 south-southeast of Chipyong carrying approximately fifty wounded on litters at 8:10 A.M..

3—An estimated 1,000 to 2,000 enemy were reported to have penetrated R.O.K. positions nine miles southeast of Wonju at 1:00 A.M. by a United States patrol. Enemy forces who had infiltrated friendly lines seven miles north-northwest of Chechon were engaged in hand to hand combat at 5:25 A.M.. The enemy was dispersed at 6:15. Artillery engaged an estimated 1,000 enemy moving south of a trail eight miles north-northwest of Chechon.

4—No report of any significant enemy action from the eastern front.

—United Nations Naval Forces summary of Feb. 16 operations, issued at 12:00 noon, Saturday (10:00 P.M., Friday, Eastern Standard Time):

Naval air and surface attacks continued on both coasts of Korea yesterday without let-up.

The heavy cruiser St. Paul bombarded villages, road junctions and machine-gun positions north of the Han River and west of Seoul.

Sea Fury and Firefly pilots operating from H.M.S. Theseus destroyed five anti-aircraft positions northwest of Seoul. Also destroyed were a field gun, a barracks, bridge, and a supply dump.

United States Navy Corsair fighter-bombers, Skyraider attack bombers, and Panther jet fighters heavily hit a number of troop concentrations, destroyed or damaged approximately sixty buildings and destroyed a highway bridge.

Aircraft from the Essex-class carriers Valley Forge and Philippine Sea divided their effort between close and deep support of the ground forces.

A force of United States destroyers including the Lind, Borie, and Ozbourn shelled east coastal targets from Chumunjin to Tanchon.

The Canadian destroyer Athabaskan exploded a mine off the west coast and the United States destroyer Ozbourn destroyed another off the east coast.

The United Nation fleet operating in Korean waters includes ships from the Republic of Korea, Thailand, the Netherlands, the United Kingdom, the United States, New Zealand, Canada and Australia.

Units of the Seventh Fleet continue to patrol Formosa Straits.

—Far East Air Forces summary of Feb. 16 operations, issued at 1:00 P.M., Saturday (11:00 P.M., Friday, Eastern Standard Time):

After mounting its greatest air effort of the Korean conflict Thursday—a total of 1,027 sorties—much of it in close support of the active fighting on the ground, Far East Air Forces were hampered by low-hanging clouds Friday. In the 500-plus sorties, two enemy communications on the east coast were crippled and more than 400 supply buildings were either burned out or damaged.

Fifth Air Force planes flew a total of more than 240 sorties including those in close support of friendly ground troops. One strike against an enemy resistance pocket south of the Han River enabled friendly ground forces to overrun the enemy position in a coordinated attack.

Twenty-two B-26 light bombers of the Fifth Air Force's 452nd Bomb Wing struck enemy supply storage north of Seoul, destroying or damaging ninety buildings and damaging a factory. Royal Australian Air Force F-51 Mustangs flying under the operational control of the fifth Air Force damaged a highway bridge and a railroad bridge near Chonjon, an east coast railroad town about fifty miles north of the Thirty-eighth Parallel.

During the night, planes dropping flares illuminated vital sectors of the battlefront. Okinawa-based B-29s of the F.E.A.F. Bomber Command used radar techniques to bomb military targets in Hamhung and Wonsan on the east coast and also attacked a railroad bridge near Haeju in the western sector, knocking down one span. Twenty-four of the medium bombers dropped more than 180 tons of high explosives on the enemy targets. The 315th Air Division (combat cargo) flew more than 230 sorties to deliver war supplies to Korean points and to carry military personnel between Japan and Korea. Almost 400 tons were air-dropped to front-line troops or landed at fields close behind the battle zone.

—Eighth Army communiqué 193, issued at 10:15 A.M., Saturday (8:15 P.M., Friday, Eastern Standard Time):

United Nations forces have secured Koksu and an armored relief column has reached the Chipyong defense perimeter. United Nations patrols have advanced 4,000 yards and other patrols have probed two miles north of defensive positions in the Wonju area. An enemy regiment has attacked United Nations forces ten miles north-northwest of Chechon.

1. R.O.K. (Republic of Korea) forces secured Hill 96, nine miles northwest of Yongdungpo, at 1330 hours (1:30 P.M.) yesterday. Sporadic exchange of small arms and automatic weapons fire with an enemy squad on the southwestern outskirts of Seoul took place from 1900 to 2000 hours. A United States patrol to the south bank of the Han on the southeastern outskirts of Seoul reported no enemy contact. An unknown number of enemy from the east attacked Puerto Rican forces nine miles east of Seoul at 2245 hours. Fighting was still in progress at 0300 hours this morning with no change in ground positions.

An unknown number of enemy stubbornly resisted the advance of British forces prior to yielding Hill 327, four miles north of Kyongan, at 1215 hours. After a series of attacks and counter-attacks the enemy finally conceded Hill 206, three miles north-northeast of Kyongan, late yesterday afternoon. An unidentified aircraft dropped three bombs in the vicinity five miles east of Kyongan at 1945 hours. An estimated enemy battalion on defense lines from Hill 303 to Hill 142, eleven miles north-northwest of Ichon and an estimated enemy battalion ten miles north-northeast of Ichon were observed by United States patrols during the afternoon of Feb. 16. Artillery fire was placed on the enemy.

2—Koksu was secured by United States forces at 1400 hours. No enemy opposition was reported by friendly armored elements, which returned to Koksu from Chipyong at 1500 hours. A friendly relief column of nineteen ambulances with armored elements succeeded in reaching the Chipyong defense perimeter at 1615 hours. Enemy action in the Chipyong area subsided to sporadic small arms, mortar, and artillery fire. No enemy contact was reported as United nations patrols advanced 4,000 yards forward of the defense perimeter.

3—No enemy contact was reported yesterday as friendly elements patrolled aggressively two miles north of positions in the Wonju area. An estimated enemy regiment attacked friendly elements at 2300 hours until 0200 hours this morning ten miles north-northwest of Chechon. As of last reports the attacks were subsiding. An unknown number of enemy launched an attack against United nations forces six miles north-northeast of Chechon at 2340 hours but were repelled by heavy artillery fire. As of 0045 (12:45 A.M., Saturday) there was no evidence that the enemy would attempt to renew his attack.

4—No report of any significant enemy action on the eastern front.

INGMAN, EINAR H., JR.

Rank and Organization: Sergeant (then Cpl.), U.S. Army, Company E, 17th Infantry Regiment, 7th Infantry Division.
Born: October 6, 1929, Milwaukee, Wisconsin.
Entered Service At: Tomahawk, Wisconsin.
Place and Date: Near Maltari, Korea, February 26, 1951.
Citation: Sgt. Ingman, a member of Company E, distinguished himself by conspicuous gallantry and intrepidity above and beyond the call of duty in action against the enemy. The 2 leading squads of the assault platoon of his company, while attacking a strongly fortified ridge held by the enemy, were pinned down by withering fire and both squad leaders and several men were wounded. Cpl. Ingman assumed command, reorganized and combined the 2 squads, then moved from one position to another, designating fields of fire and giving advice and encouragement to the men. Locating an enemy machine gun position that was raking his men with devastating fire he charged it alone, threw a grenade into the position, and killed the remaining crew with rifle fire. Another enemy machine gun opened fire approximately 15 yards away and inflicted additional casualties to the group and stopped the attack. When Cpl. Ingman charged the second position he was hit by grenade fragments and a hail of fire which seriously wounded him about the face and neck and knocked him to the ground. With incredible courage and stamina, he rose instantly and, using only his rifle, killed the entire gun crew before falling unconscious from his wounds. As a result of the singular action by Cpl. Ingman the defense of the enemy was broken, his squad secured its objective, and more than 100 hostile troops abandoned their weapons and fled in disorganized retreat. Cpl. Ingman's indomitable courage, extraordinary heroism, and superb leadership reflect the highest credit on himself and are in keeping with the esteemed traditions of the infantry and the U.S. Army.

OFFICIAL COMMUNIQUÉ:
TOKYO, Tuesday, Feb. 27 (AP)
—Far East Air Forces headquarters release issued at 4:00 P.M., Monday (2:00 A.M., Monday, Eastern Standard Time):

Communist railroad and supply targets in North Korea were hit another blow by Far East Air Forces medium bombers today as the day-by-day campaign to prevent enemy supplies from reaching front line troops was continued by Japan-based B-29 Superforts of the Ninety-eighth Bomb Group.

Two of the Superforts, although faced with heavy weather, found a hole in the clouds above Pyongyang and dropped sixteen tons of high explosives on the railroad bridge. Crewmen reported excellent results.

Four aircraft dropped thirty-two tons of bombs on the railroad bridge at Hwangju, twenty-one miles south of Pyongyang. The bombs were aimed visually. Good results were reported.

Enemy supply centers on the east coast at Hamhung and Wonsan were hit with more than 100 tons of bombs dropped by fourteen B-29s. The Superforts dropped their explosives by radar through heavy clouds and results were unobserved.

Aircraft commanders radioed Brig. Gen. James E. Brigg, Bomber Command headquarters in Japan, that flak was experienced, only there was no damage to the bombers.

—*Eighth Army communiqué 212, issued at 10:15 A.M., Monday (8:15 P.M., Sunday, Eastern Standard Time):*

United Nations forces west of Yangpyong received sporadic mortar fire during the day (Sunday). The enemy continued to deny entry of friendly probing patrols into the area north of the Han River and west of Yangpyong. Patrols in the Yongdu sector met heavy determined enemy resistance. Republic of Korea forces engaged two Chinese Communist Forces battalions six miles west of Hoengsong. United Nations forces advanced 5,000 to 6,000 yards seven miles west-northwest of Pyongchang. No enemy resistance was encountered in ground advances of 4,000 to 7,000 yards ten miles southeast of Hoengsong.

1. United Nations forces west of Yangpyong reported observing two enemy tanks three miles northwest of Seoul at 1300 hours (1:00 P.M.)—uncamouflaged foxholes on ridges and gullies leading to the main ridge of Hill 348, three miles east of Seoul, and an estimated 10,000 to 12,000 enemy positions, a large percentage of which were occupied, in a radius of four miles from an area eight miles east of Seoul at 1020 hours (10:20 A.M.). Air also observed one tank in a house and another tank in the woods nine miles north-northeast of Kyongan. The enemy continued to deny entry of friendly probing patrols into the area north of the Han River and west of Yangpyong as platoon-sized enemy groups engaged friendly patrols during the day, forcing the withdrawal of friendly patrols.

2. An estimated enemy company engaged a friendly patrol with heavy small arms and mortar fire four miles northeast of Yongdu at 1030 hours (10:30 A.M.), forcing the patrol to withdraw. Two other friendly patrols were forced to withdraw in areas two miles west and immediately south of Yongdu as a result of heavy enemy small arms, automatic weapons, and mortar fire. In the vicinity of Yongdu, an estimated thirty rounds of artillery fire was received by friendly tank patrols at 1100 hours (11:00 A.M.).

A patrol probed the area one mile north-northeast of Yongdu and engaged an unknown number of the enemy, resulting in an estimated fifteen enemy killed. The friendly patrol broke contact at 1100 hours. The estimated two enemy battalions, previously reported opposing British forces five miles southeast of Yongdu, were subjected to air attack. Friendly patrols maintained contact with these enemy groups during the day, receiving sporadic small arms fire.

An estimated two Chinese Communist Forces battalions six miles west of Hoengsong were contacted at 1300 hours (1:00 P.M.) by R.O.K. elements. A fire fight ensued until 1800 hours (6:00 P.M.) at which time the enemy withdrew to the west. At 2315 (11:15 P.M.) an estimated two Chinese Communist Forces companies, preceded by a ten-minute attack against R.O.K. forces four miles west of Hoengsong. These engagements continued until 0130 hours (1:30 A.M.) Monday, at which time the enemy disengaged and withdrew to the north. An estimated enemy battalion was engaged by R.O.K. forces three miles west of Hoengsong at 1300 hours (1:00 P.M.). However, at 1350 hours (1:50 P.M.) the enemy broke contact and withdrew. An estimated three Chinese Communist Forces companies were observed in the area eleven miles west of Hoengsong with another four Chinese Communist Forces companies reported in the area six miles west of Hoengsong.

3. United Nations forces advancing in the area ten miles southeast of Hoengsong advanced 4,000 to 7,000 yards with no enemy contact. United States forces advanced 5,000 to 6,000 yards seven miles west-northwest of Pyongchang against light scattered enemy resistance. An estimated 200 enemy with small arms and automatic weapons and some mortar fire resisted the advance of friendly United States elements four miles north of Pyongchang at 1100 hours (11:00 A.M.) and continued to harass friendly operations until the enemy was dispersed to the west by friendly air and artillery at 1320 hours (1:20 P.M.). No enemy contact was reported by United states troops moving up as much as 5,000 yards to an area five miles north-northeast of Pyongchang. No significant enemy contact was reported in the Chongson area.

4. No report of enemy contact in the east coast area.

—Eighth Army communiqué 213, issued at 8:00 P.M. Monday (6:00 A.M. Monday, Eastern Standard Time):

Little or no enemy action has been along the United nations front during the past twelve hours. Enemy forces along the central-eastern front continued to withdraw to the north. Casualties inflicted by United Nations ground action on Feb. 25 were estimated at 1,861.

1. A United States patrol encountered an unknown number of the enemy two miles south of Seoul where the patrol had crossed the river to the north at 11:00 P.M. on Feb. 25. The patrol withdrew under cover of friendly artillery fire and was engaged by enemy small arms and mortar fire at 11:50 P.M. Feb. 25.

Four enemy artillery pieces were observed near the northwestern outskirts of Seoul and taken under friendly artillery fire with unknown results. Air observed new enemy trenches seven miles east of Seoul along the north bank of the Han River. A unknown number of enemy employing small arms and machine guns from the base of a hill in the vicinity three miles west-northwest of Yangpyong were engaged by a United States patrol at 8:15 A.M. with unknown results.

2. United States elements in the area northeast of Chipyong reported no enemy contact as friendly units continued to patrol north of friendly positions. An estimated twelve-man enemy patrol was dispersed to the north in an area five miles east-northeast of Chipyong.

3. An estimated 100 enemy in the vicinity thirteen miles east in this same area were taken under artillery fire at 10:00 A.M. resulting in an estimated 100 casualties. An estimated 700 to 800 enemy troops moving north were observed by tactical air in the vicinity thirteen miles north-northeast of Pyongchang at 9:50 A.M..

An estimated 600 to 700 enemy troops eighteen miles north of Pyongchang in dug-in positions were also reported during the day.

4. No report of any significant enemy activity on the east coast during the period.

—Eighth Army communiqué 214 issued at 10:15 A.M. Tuesday (8:15 P.M. Monday, Eastern Standard Time):

No enemy contact on Kimpo Peninsula. Enemy continued to deny friendly attempts to probe across Han River. Enemy resistance continues in Yongdu area. Air hit 3,000 to 5,000 enemy in Yongdu sector. Enemy artillery fire received from north on Hoengsong. Air reports estimate enemy division dug in general area three miles northeast of Hoengsong. Light to moderate scattered enemy resistance continues in areas southeast of Hoengsong and north of Pyongchang.

1. No enemy contact was reported as patrols screened the south bank of the Han River and the Kimpo Peninsula. Periodic artillery and anti-tank fire, as well as mortar fire was received from the enemy on the north bank of the Han during the day. The enemy on the north side of the Han River continued to deny friendly attempts to probe across the river. Tactical air reported that all ridges facing the river six miles west and northwest of Yangpyong appeared to be heavily occupied. Small enemy groups were engaged seven miles northeast of Yangpyong during the day.

2. The enemy continued to resist probing attempts in the Yongdu area with heavy and small arms, automatic weapons, and mortar fire. Air observation reported excellent results as a result of air strikes on 3,000 to 5,000 entrenched enemy in the Yongdu area during the day. Enemy in undetermined strength on high ground in front of friendly positions four miles southeast of Yongdu continued to resist friendly ground operations. Patrols in the area west of Hoengsong reported observing a total of six enemy companies three to nine miles west of Hoengsong. An estimated enemy battalion was engaged by Republic of Korea forces three miles west of the city with no change in ground positions reported.

3. At 12:15 this morning an estimated three to four gun batteries north of Hoengsong fired thirty rounds of artillery on United States elements east and southeast of Hoengsong. Air observed an estimated enemy division dug in a general area three miles northeast of Hoengsong. Light scattered resis-

tance continued in the area eight to twelve miles east and southeast of Hoengsong. The enemy resisting friendly advances in a general area five miles west and five north and northwest of Pyongchang was reported withdrawing north. Light enemy resistance was reported as friendly elements advanced in the area six miles northeast of Pyongchang. Light contact was reported in areas six miles northwest and nine miles northwest of Chongson.

4. Air reported an estimated 1,400 enemy troops moving southwest in the area seventeen miles northwest of Kangnung.

—Communiqué 807 of General of the Army Douglas MacArthur's headquarters, for period from 6:00 A.M. Monday to 6:00 A.M. Tuesday (4:00 P.M. Sunday to 4:00 P.M. Monday, Eastern Standard Time):

In Central Korea, United nations assault echelons surmounted obstacles of terrain and weather to move forward and register limited gains. During the period action was centered in the area west of Hoengsong, where United Nations forces encountered determined enemy resistance.

North of Pyongchang, Republic of Korea units made substantial gains against North Korean forces.

Elsewhere on the Korean front, armored and infantry patrols maintained surveillance of enemy formations and directed attacks by tactical aircraft and artillery on located enemy troop concentrations.

Aircraft of Task Force 77 continued to contribute to the mounting damage being inflicted upon the communications system in the Wonsan area, while a devastating ship to shore bombardment was maintained along the east coast.

Supporting fire from the cruiser St. Paul and aircraft from the carrier Bataan silenced a number of gun positions in the Seoul area.

The systematic interdiction of enemy supply lines was maintained by B-29 bombers which dropped 150 tons of bombs on enemy bridges and supply centers in North Korea, as aircraft under control of the Far East Air Forces mounted more than 740 sorties.

Fifth Air Force and attached air units flew 450 sorties over Korea, with pilots reporting destruction or damage to 140 vehicles, 740 enemy occupied buildings, fifteen bridges, nine tunnels, seven railroad cars, and ten gun positions.

†BRITTIN, NELSON V.

Rank and Organization: Sergeant First Class, U.S. Army, Company I, 19th Infantry Regiment.
Born: Audubon, New Jersey.
Entered Service At: Audubon, New Jersey.
Place and Date: Vicinity of Yonggong-ni, Korea, March 7, 1951.
Citation: Sfc. Brittin, a member of Company I, distinguished himself by conspicuous gallantry and intrepidity above and beyond the call of duty in action against the enemy. Volunteering to lead his squad up a hill, with meager cover against murderous fire from the enemy, he ordered his squad to give him support and, in the face of withering fire and bursting shells, he tossed a grenade at the nearest enemy position. On returning to his squad, he was knocked down and wounded by an enemy grenade. Refusing medical attention, he replenished his supply of grenades and returned, hurling grenades into hostile positions and shooting the enemy as they fled. When his weapon jammed, he leaped without hesitation into a foxhole and killed the occupants with his bayonet and the butt of his rifle. He continued to wipe out foxholes and, noting that his squad had been pinned down, he rushed to the rear of a machine gun position, threw a grenade into the nest, and ran to its front, where he killed all 3 occupants with his rifle. Less than 100 yards up the hill, his squad again came under vicious fire from another camouflaged, sandbagged, machine gun nest well-flanked by supporting riflemen. Sfc. Brittin again charged this new position in an aggressive endeavor to silence this

remaining obstacle and ran directly into a burst of automatic fire which killed him instantly. In his sustained and driving action, he had killed 20 enemy soldiers and destroyed 4 automatic weapons. The conspicuous courage, consummate valor, and noble self-sacrifice displayed by Sfc. Brittin enabled his inspired company to attain its objective and reflects the highest glory on himself and the heroic traditions of the military service.

HARVEY, RAYMOND

Rank and Organization: Captain, U.S. Army, Company C, 17th Infantry Regiment.
Born: March 1, 1920, Ford City, Pennsylvania.
Entered Service At: Pasadena, California.
Place and Date: Vicinity of Taemi-Dong, Korea, March 9, 1951.
Citation: Capt. Harvey, Company C, distinguished himself by conspicuous gallantry and intrepidity above and beyond the call of duty in action against the enemy. When his company was pinned down by a barrage of automatic-weapons fire from numerous well-entrenched emplacements, imperiling accomplishment of its mission, Capt. Harvey braved a hail of fire and exploding grenades to advance to the first enemy machine gun nest, killing its crew with grenades. Rushing to the edge of the next emplacement, he killed its crew with carbine fire. He then moved the 1st Platoon forward until it was again halted by a curtain of automatic-weapons fire from well-fortified hostile positions. Disregarding the hail of fire, he personally charged and neutralized a third emplacement. Miraculously escaping death from intense cross-fire, Capt. Harvey continued to lead the assault. Spotting an enemy pillbox well camouflaged by logs, he moved close enough to sweep the emplacement with carbine fire and throw grenades through the openings, annihilating its 5 occupants. Though wounded he then turned to order the company forward, and, suffering agonizing pain, he continued to direct the reduction of the remaining hostile positions, refusing evacuation until assured that the mission would be accomplished. Capt. Harvey's valorous and intrepid actions served as an inspiration to his company, reflecting the utmost glory upon himself and upholding the heroic traditions of the military service.

OFFICIAL COMMUNIQUÉ:
TOKYO, Saturday, March 10 (AP)
—United nations naval forces summary of March 8, operations:

Navy bombarding forces shelled five Communist troop areas yesterday (Thursday) on both Korean coasts. Under the command of Rear Admiral Allen E. Smith, a task group led by the light cruiser Manchester pounded troops, buildings, highway and railroad junctions, bridges, and gun emplacements around Songjin on the east coast. Spotting planes from Task Force 77 reported good results.

United States Navy destroyers continued battering the Wonsan area. Gun emplacements and road junctions again came under the destroyers' five-inch-gun fire.

At Chumunjin, south of Wonsan, the United States Navy destroyer Borie hit troop positions in support of ground operations.

Off the west coast, the heavy cruiser St. Paul threw eight-inch projectiles from her main battery at troop concentrations on the north bank of the Han River, northwest of Seoul. A Royal Navy bombarding group led by the British cruiser Kenya continued hitting targets southwest of Chinnampo.

Enemy supply lines again yesterday were bombed by Corsairs and Skyraiders from Fast Carrier Task Force 77. Concentrating on bridges, the Navy pilots bombed twelve during day long flights.

Other Communist targets attacked included twenty-eight railroad cars, five power boats, and fifty vehicles. A bomb from one of the planes silenced two gun emplacements.

In an attack on four tunnels, four bombs were dropped inside tunnel entrances.

Sea Furies and Fireflies struck again at targets in the Jaeju-Sariwon areas yesterday. The British light carrier Theseus directed strikes against railroads, bridges, and supply dumps. Three engines were attacked by the fighters and bombers in the Chinnampo area.

Martin Mariners and Convair Privateers continued regular patrol flights. Minesweeping operations continue off Korea.

—*United Nations naval forces summary of operations for period 6:00 A.M., March 9, to 6:00 A.M., March 10:*

Navy firepower from the sea and from the air struck far behind enemy lines in Korea yesterday (Friday) as air and sea operations continued to interrupt the flow of men and material to enemy lines.

On the northeast coast, the light cruiser Manchester led the firing by mobile naval artillery on the city of Songjin. Highway and railroad key points were subjected to the second straight day's 6 and 5-inch gun bombardment. Railroad crossings used by the enemy in an attempt to repair roads and bridges battered by the naval guns were set afire, one stockpile of them sending an 800-foot column of smoke into the air.

To the south, military targets at Wonsan were taken under surprise fire by Navy destroyers Walke, English, and Wallace L. Lind. Enemy troops, tricked into believing the entire naval gunfire group that had battered Wonsan for days previous had moved northward, came out into the open and were taken under 5-inch naval gunfire by the waiting destroyers with large numbers of casualties resulting.

On the west coast of Korea, the heavy cruiser St. Paul moved in close to the shoreline in the Inchon region in response to a call-fire request and hurled 8-inch salvos into seven troop concentrations north of Kimpo Airfield.

Bridge-dusting operations by naval aircraft flying from the decks of carriers attached to Fast Carrier Task Force 77 continued far behind the enemy lines in general support of the east-west coast interdiction of enemy supply lines.

—*Far East Air Forces summary of March 8 operations:*

On their 256th consecutive day of combat operations in Korea, the United States Far East Air Forces mounted a record 1,016 sorties Thursday as they strafed, rocketed, and bombed the Communists in air-ground support and interdiction assaults to aid United Nations ground forces in making important gains.

Yesterday F-86 Sabre jets sighted approximately sixty MiG-type enemy aircraft in far northwest Korea. The MiGs were seen on three separate occasions in groups of twenty-five, twenty, and fifteen. However, the enemy planes refused combat and scurried back across the Yalu River to Manchuria with the Sabres in pursuit up to the border line.

Fifth Air Force flew about 750 sorties, of which 280 were in direct aerial support of advancing United Nations troops, which crossed the Han River on the western central front.

In an apparent move to overcome the tremendous losses inflicted by friendly aircraft on Red forces and their supply and transportation facilities, the Communists attempted to transport troops by daylight over North Korean roads between Pyongyang and Sinuiju.

The enemy troops were brought under attack by Fifty-first Fighter Interceptor Wing jet fighters. Two F-80 Shooting Star strikes inflicted about fifty casualties on the Communists, while other Fifth Air Force fighter-bombers inflicted approximately 100 casualties in three strikes between Sinanju and Sinuiju.

The majority of close air support sorties of more than 125 were flown by light bombers and fighter-bombers of Fifth Air Force and attached allied units and shore-based United States Marine planes, in front of elements of the Ninth Corps which crossed the Han River.

More than 500 casualties were inflicted upon the Communists, Fifth Air Force claimed. At the same time damage or destruction was claimed to almost 1,000 enemy-held buildings, 160 motor vehicles, thirty-one boxcars, twenty-five gun emplacements, ten supply dumps (including four ammunition dumps and two fuel dumps) during the day's air operations.

Two tanks, one near Kaesong and another near Sariwon, were attacked and damaged. Six bridges and five tunnels were destroyed or damaged.

Four of these bridges and three tunnels were on the enemy's vital transportation artery between Chunchon, important supply center, and Seoul.

Chunchon was hit by twenty-two Superforts of F.E.A.F.'s Bomber Command, which dropped about 220 tons of high explosives on the supply center. Crew members of the B-29s based on Okinawa with the Nineteenth and 307th Bomb Groups, reported the results of the bombings as excellent, adding that towers of smoke rose to 20,000 feet above the target area.

In another interdiction attack, a Superfort successfully downed two spans of a highway bridge near Pyongyang.

Continuing the resupply of front line combat troops, 315th Air Division (Combat Cargo) transports airdropped 485 tons of combat supplies to United Nations forces. Total air tonnage lifted to Korea was 1,086 as the division's aircraft mounted more than 290 sorties.

—Eighth Army communiqué 235, issued at 8:00 P.M., Friday (6:00 A.M., Friday, Eastern Standard Time):

Light to heavy enemy resistance was reported by United Nations forces as United States First Cavalry units advanced 1,000 to 2,000 yards against diminishing enemy resistance. Canadian and Australian forces gained 1,000 to 1,500 yards while R.O.K. (Republic of Korea) Sixth Division elements registered gains of 1,000 to 3,000 yards.

United Nations forces thirteen miles east of Hoengsong reported constant heavy pressure, while United States Second Division elements drove forward 1,500 yards against an estimated two enemy regiments. The United States Seventh Division elements scored gains of 2,000 yards west-northwest of Pangnim. Delayed reports from the area northeast of Amidong told of limited friendly withdrawals as a result of a North Korean attack in that area. Enemy casualties inflicted on March 8 were estimated as 6,522.

1. United Nations forces south and west of Seoul reported no significant enemy activity during the day. However, United States Twenty-fourth Division elements reported receiving about 300 rounds of mortars between the hours of 4:15 P.M., March 8, and 4:00 this morning, six miles north of Yangpyong. United States Twenty-fourth Division elements reported light enemy resistance during the day.

2. In the Yongdu area the enemy resisted the advance of a United States First Cavalry unit during the early morning. However, at 8:20 A.M. the enemy was forced to withdraw to the northeast as cavalry units continued to advance. Enemy forces engaged other elements of the First Cavalry three miles northeast of Yongu and were taken under artillery fire at 8:00 A.M. with good results. Gains of 1,000 to 2,000 yards were registered against diminishing enemy resistance to the east of Yongdu. Canadian and Australian forces gained 1,000 to 1,500 yards by mid-day. R.O.K. Sixth Division elements registered gains of 1,000 to 3,000 yards.

3. No significant action was reported in the area north of Hoengsong as United States Marine elements patrolled aggressively in their sector. United States Second Division elements gained 2,000 yards in the area west-northwest of Pangnim. United States forces thirteen miles east of Hoengsong were under constant and heavy enemy pressure throughout the day.

4. An enemy force estimated at 3,000 attacked R.O.K. Seventh Division elements during the morning of March 8 causing friendly forces to make a limited withdrawal. Air observation reported a considerable number of enemy troops in the area six miles east and seven miles east-northeast of Amidong. Air strikes were placed on these enemy forces during the afternoon of March 8 with good results.

—*Eighth Army communiqué 236, issued at 10:15 A.M. Saturday (8:15 P.M. Friday, Eastern Standard Time):*

United Nations forces continued to advance against light to heavy enemy resistance during March 9. Three enemy counter-attacks were repulsed in the area six miles northwest of Yangpong. Enemy resistance in the Yongdu area was reported to be diminishing as the enemy withdrew to the north under friendly pressure. Heavy enemy resistance from a well-entrenched enemy was reported by United Nations forces east and northeast of Hoengsong. Stiff enemy resistance was reported by United States Second Division elements during the day.

R.O.K. (Republic of Korea) First Division units reported no enemy contact, while United States Third Division units report light contact through patrol action during the day. United States Twenty-fifth Division elements met light to moderate enemy resistance as they advanced 2,000 to 3,000 yards during the day. A platoon-sized enemy counter-attack three miles southeast of Tokso was repulsed by small arms and mortar fire during the afternoon. Enemy resistance on the United States Twenty-fourth Division left flank sector was moderate to heavy as friendly units reoccupied the high ground five miles northwest of Yangpyong which had been vacated to the enemy the night of March 8. Only light opposition was encountered in the center of the sector as friendly units advanced up to 2,000 yards.

On the right flank resistance was moderate to stubborn. However, gains of 2,000 yards were registered. At 18:00 hours (6:00 P.M.) the enemy launched a counter-attack in the area six miles north-northwest of Yangpyong. The attack was repulsed shortly thereafter. At 19:10 hours the enemy made a banal attack which was repulsed at 19:45 hours. A third attack was launched sometime later but was reported repulsed at 20:30 hours. An estimated 150 enemy attacked at a United States Twenty-fourth Division company position at 02:00 hours this morning. The company withdrew to allow friendly artillery fire to be placed on the enemy.

2. United States First Cavalry elements encountered light resistance as advances up to 4,000 yards were reported. The enemy resistance in the division sector decreased during the day as the enemy withdrew to the north under friendly pressure.

The enemy was reported to have abandoned some equipment in this area. British elements continued to attack and reported gains of 2,000 yards with no reported enemy contact. R.O.K. Sixth Division elements reported light enemy resistance on the left of the division sector and moderate resistance was encountered in the right division sector as friendly units advanced up to 2,000 yards. United States Marines reported light enemy contact during the day. An enemy patrol probed Marine positions at 2215 hours (10:15 P.M.) but was dispersed at 2230 hours.

3. United States Second Division reported limited gains as friendly elements encountered heavy resistance from a well-entrenched enemy to their front. An estimated two enemy regiments are opposing friendly units in the area six miles northeast of Hoengsong.

R.O.K. Units reported moderate to heavy enemy resistance in an area eleven to fifteen miles east of Hoengsong. An undetermined number of enemy attacked R.O.K. elements fifteen miles east of Hoengsong at 0200 this morning, forcing friendly elements to withdraw an estimated 500 yards. A counter-attack was launched and as of 0500 hours nearly all the lost ground had been retaken. United States Seventh Division elements made only minor gains as the enemy bitterly opposed the advance of United States elements. The R.O.K. Seventh Division reported an estimated enemy regiment in the area three miles east of Amidong on the morning of March 8.

4. No significant report from any enemy activity had been received from the east coast area.

—*Communiqué 818 by General of the Army MacArthur's headquarters, for the period 6:00 A.M., March 9, to 6:00 A.M., March 10:*

The United Nations offensive continued northward Friday against light to heavy enemy resistance in registering gains of from one to two miles as our ground forces, supported by air attacks and overwhelming artillery fire, moved forward to dislodge the enemy. In the east-central sector between Hoengsong and Pangnim, United States, French, and Republic of Korea units were engaged in heavy fighting with entrenched enemy troops bitterly contesting our advance. In the west-central sector, the enemy was also exerting heavy pressure on United Nations forces north of Yangpyong, but forward movement continued despite vigorous local counter-attacks. The eastern and western sectors of the line were relatively quiet.

Increasing activity by Republic of Korea guerrillas and United Nations sympathizers behind the Communist lines in Korea, coupled with the continuous attacks on supply lines by United Nations air force and Navy units are adding to the enemy's communications problem and making it increasingly difficult for him to maintain his supply system.

Heavy bombardment marked the second day of interdiction fire on Songjin as naval surface units continued destruction of enemy targets in this strategic highway and railroad center far behind the enemy lines. Farther south, Wonsan was harried by United States Navy destroyers as destruction of bridges by aircraft from Task Force 77 continued to deter the movement of men and material to the hostile front. On the east coast, the heavy cruiser St. Paul provided naval gunfire support for the United Nations ground offensive by neutralizing enemy troop concentrations in the area north of Kimpo Airfield.

Despite unfavorable weather, air support of the United Nations ground offensive continued as more than 400 air sorties were mounted over Korea. B-29 bombers dropped approximately 175 tons of bombs on enemy targets in the Ungnam and Pyongyang areas in North Korea.

†DEWERT, RICHARD DAVID

Rank and Organization: Hospital Corpsman, U.S. Navy, attached to a Marine infantry company, 1st Marine Division.
Born: Taunton, Massachusetts.
Entered Service At: Taunton, Massachusetts.
Place and Date: Korea, April 5, 1951.
Citation: For conspicuous gallantry and intrepidity at the risk of his life above and beyond the call of duty while serving as a HC, in action against enemy aggressor forces. When a fire team from the point platoon of his company was pinned down by a deadly barrage of hostile automatic-weapons fire and suffered many casualties, HC Dewert rushed to the assistance of one of the more seriously wounded and, despite a painful leg wound sustained while dragging the stricken marine to safety, steadfastly refused medical treatment for himself and immediately dashed back through the fire-swept area to carry a second wounded man out of the line of fire. Undaunted by the mounting hail of devastating enemy fire, he bravely moved forward a third time and received another serious wound in the shoulder after discovering that a wounded marine had already died. Still persistent in his refusal to submit to first-aid, he resolutely answered the call of a fourth stricken comrade and, while rendering medical assistance, was himself mortally wounded by a burst of enemy fire. His courageous initiative, great personal valor, and heroic spirit of self-sacrifice in the face of overwhelming odds reflect the highest credit upon HC Dewert and enhance the finest traditions of the U.S. Naval Service. He gallantly gave his life for his country.

OFFICIAL COMMUNIQUÉ:
TOKYO, Friday, April 6 (AP)
—Far East Air Forces summary of April 4, operations:

For the second successive day Far East Air Forces on Wednesday turned back a Communist challenge to United Nations air supremacy over Korea, destroying one and damaging two MiG-15 enemy jet aircraft in the area south of Sinuiju. In addition, F.E.A.F. planes struck heavily at enemy supply concentrations, transportation facilities, and troops as almost 900 sorties were flown in support of United Nations ground operations.

Wednesday's air-to-air encounters took place in the same general area of Tuesday's battles in which three enemy jets were destroyed and five damaged.

Victories were scored by F-86 Sabre jets of the Fifth Air Force's Fourth Fighter Interceptor Wing when twelve of the Sabres engaged in two morning encounters with about twenty-four MiGs. One MiG was seen to crash; another made a forced landing and the pilot was seen to run away from the airplane, and a third, struck by machine-gun fire, streaked across the Yalu River to the sanctuary Manchuria.

During the afternoon, three F-80 Shooting Star jets were fired on by four MiGs, but no damage was sustained or claimed.

Other Fifth Air Force planes, including attached Republic of Korea, South African, Australian and shore-based United States Marines, continued their attack on enemy ground installations and forces, flying over 700 sorties.

Cratering of highways leading into the Communist build-up area went into its second day with approximately forty sections of roads pitted with bomb holes to interdict heavy Communist vehicular traffic. One hundred and thirty vehicles, 100 railroad cars, almost fifty supply, ammunition and fuel dumps, and over 800 enemy-held buildings were destroyed or damaged.

More than 400 casualties were inflicted on enemy troops, 300 of these when F-80 Shooting Star jets of the Fifty-first Fighter Interceptor Wing attacked a concentration of Communists south of Pyongyang.

Two tanks were destroyed north of Kaesong. A bridge was rendered unserviceable near Wonsan, another was damaged near Suchon and a tunnel was damaged near Sinmak.

Night-flying B-26 light bombers and Marine F-4Us and F-7Fs observed a continuation of heavy enemy vehicular traffic. A total of approximately 1,600 enemy vehicles were sighted, of which approximately 800 were moving south, the balance east or west. Five hundred of the vehicles sighted were moving on the Sinanju-Sariwon route in Western Korea. More than 450 of the vehicles sighted were attacked.

Three trains were sighted on western rail lines. Two of them were put under attack.

F.E.A.F. Bomber Command B-29 Superforts based on Okinawa flew twelve night sorties and heavily attacked military targets in the Pyongyang area. Lighter attacks were made on targets closer to the battlelines. Bombs were aimed by radar and results generally were unobserved due to darkness.

Three Hundred and Fifteenth Air Division (Combat Cargo) mounted 173 sorties to transport 1,800 military passengers and about 575 tons of cargo. Included in the cargo was twenty-five tons of rice to feed Korean war orphans on Chejudo Island.

—Fifth Air Force Summary for late Thursday:

Enemy armor, vehicles and supplies took a terrific pounding today as Fifth Air Force tactical aircraft smashed at the Communist build-up of military strength.

By late afternoon 100 vehicles, nine supply dumps, and six tanks had been reported destroyed or damaged.

A total of 741 sorties were reported by 6:00 P.M.. Of this number, 122 were in close support of ground forces while 378 were classed as armed reconnaissance flights with pilots seeking targets of opportunity.

One hundred seventy troop casualties were claimed inflicted on the enemy. Attacks were made on fifteen enemy-occupied towns.

Pilots claimed by late afternoon as destroyed: 300 buildings, one locomotive, four railroad cars, sixteen pack animals, four fuel dumps, two railroad bridges, four field pieces, two flak-gun positions, and one gun emplacement.

Claimed damaged were 100 buildings, fourteen railroad cars, one rail bridge, one highway bridge, one tunnel, twelve field pieces, one airfield, and one gun emplacement.

Fighter aircraft of the First Marine Air Wing accounted for one of the tanks destroyed and two damaged in the area north of Sohung. Near Sonchon, one tank was destroyed by F-80s of the Fifty-first Fighter Interceptor Wing. Shooting Stars of the Eighth Fighter Bomber Wing claimed one destroyed and one damaged north of Namchonjom.

One of the tanks was spotted by an F-51 pilot of the Sixty-seventh Tactical Reconnaissance Wing, Capt. Lloyd W. Simpson of Bay Shore, N.Y.. Captain Simpson said: "I knew I couldn't knock the tank out with my machine guns so I called in a flight of F-80s that were in the area and watched them burn it up with Napalm."

Pilots of the Thirty-fifth Fighter Interceptor Wing reported good hunting today for enemy vehicles. One flight claimed ten destroyed in a strike near Sibyon, while near Chorwon another ten vehicles and a supply dump were destroyed. Five trucks were destroyed north of Singye.

Maj. Duncan P. Daries of Yuba City, Calif., led one flight of F-51s of the Thirty-fifth Wing in an attack near Sohung that claimed eight enemy-occupied buildings and three vehicles destroyed and fifty troops killed or wounded.

Major Daries said: "The troops seemed quite confused, and were running around in circles. One group of them ran into a bunker, and I put a rocket in there with them."

Near Chorwon, a flight of Mustangs of the Thirty-fifth Wing claimed eight trucks, three fuel dumps and six buildings destroyed.

Describing the attack, Maj. Daniel J. Noble of Westfield, Mass., the flight leader, said: "The trucks were just off the highway, parked in a small group of buildings. They, and the fuel stored in the buildings, were burning when we left."

F-51s of the Eighteenth Fighter Bomber Wing claimed excellent results on vehicles near Sohung and Singye.

One flight destroyed twelve vehicles near Sohung, while another destroyed seven in the same general sector. Another flight claimed as destroyed four vehicles and a building in which fuel was stored.

A flight of F-80s of the Forty-ninth Fighter Bomber Wing were directed to buildings and gun emplacements by a "mosquito controller" along the central sector of the battleline. Lieut. Jacksel M. Broughton of Rochester, N.Y., said: "We destroyed two gun emplacements with rockets and killed a gun crew."

Another flight of Shooting Stars from the same wing reported starting ten fires in a large supply dump west of Pyongyang. Nearby, the same flight did some rocketing and strafing of twelve howitzer emplacements. Capt. Arthur B. Morris of Cordele, Ga., flight leader, reported that one of the howitzers was definitely knocked out and the other eleven at least damaged.

F-86 jets reported sighting MiG-15s twice today, with no contact in either case.

This afternoon six MiGs were sighted by a flight of nineteen F-86s and this morning twelve of the Sabre jets spotted eight MiGs. Both MiG flights were over the Sinuiju area and crossed to the privileged side of the Yalu River when the F-86s turned to attack.

—United Nations Naval Forces summary of April 5 operations:

Naval air and surface attacks in close and deep support of the ground forces continued without let-up Thursday.

Navy airmen of Fast Carrier Task Force 77 took a heavy toll in all target categories, blasting troop concentrations, rolling stock, tanks (five destroyed), ammunition dumps, gun emplacements, bridges (three destroyed), vehicles, and buildings.

Most of the deep support attacks by Navy Skyraiders, Corsairs, and Panther jets were flown in the areas west of Hungnam and Wonsan. One railroad tunnel was sealed and railroad tracks were torn up in numerous places.

Strangulation of the east coast transportation network through naval siege continued.

Forty-eight consecutive days of naval bombardment were completed at Wonsan by a destroyer and frigate force. Some of yesterday's most effective firing was concentrated on truck convoys moving toward the city. The Wonsan siege group includes the U.S.S. Zellars and H.M.S. Alacrity.

Twenty-nine days of continuous naval shelling were completed at Songjin, where rail and road networks and railroad sidings were the principal targets. The Songjin bombardment force includes the heavy cruiser St. Paul and the destroyers U.S.S. Wallace L. Lind and U.S.S. Thompson. A number of small craft were destroyed or damaged by other units patrolling the area.

Two hundred and fifty miles north of the battle line, at Chongjin, a force including the destroyer U.S.S. Massey blasted transportation targets and junk traffic.

At the eastern terminus of the battleline the destroyers U.S.S. Hank and U.S.S. Forrest Royal continued to provide direct naval gunfire in support of the ground forces.

On the west coast of Korea, elements of the blockade and bombardment force, including the Royal Navy Frigate Black Swan, the Netherlands destroyer Evertsen, the Australian destroyer Bataan, and R.O.K. navy units, maintained a tight blockade of the shallow waterways.

The blockade and bombardment force, known as Task Force 95, is under the command of Rear Admiral Allan F. Smith; Carrier Task Force 77, a part of the Seventh Fleet, is commanded by Rear Admiral Ralph A. Ofstie.

U.S. Navy Privateers and Mariners and Royal Air Force Sunderlands carried out regular patrols. Minesweeping operations continue on both coasts of Korea.

—Eighth Army communiqué 289, issued at 10:00 P.M., Thursday (8:00 A.M., Thursday, Eastern Standard Time):

Light to moderate enemy resistance was reported on the western Korean front as a United States task force probed enemy-held territory in the Chail area against light enemy resistance. Heavy enemy small arms fire reported in the area north of Chunchon. Enemy casualties inflicted on April 4 were estimated as approximately 1,530.

1. Light to moderate enemy resistance was encountered by United Nations forces advancing on the western Korean front. A United States task force probed enemy-held territory in the Chail area encountering light resistance enroute and dispersing an estimated enemy company in the Chail area at midday.

2. United Nations forces on the central front advanced, generally against light resistance, but with heavy enemy resistance in the form of small arms fire reported in the area north of Chunchon.

3. Light, scattered enemy resistance was reported on the eastern Korean front as limited advances were made during the day.

4. No significant enemy activity has been reported from R.O.K. (Republic of Korea) forces in the east coast area.

—Eighth Army communiqué 290, issued at 10:15 A.M., Friday (8:15 P.M., Thursday, Eastern Standard Time):

Heavy enemy resistance was reported in the Yongpyong and Yongong areas as a United States task force probed enemy-held territory east of Chail. Stubborn enemy resistance was encountered north-north-west of Chunchon. Light to moderate resistance was encountered on the eastern front.

1. No significant enemy activity was reported by United Nations forces in the area northeast of Munsan during the day. Light resistance was reported in the area south and southeast of Yonchon with some enemy artillery fire being received during the day. Heavy enemy resistance was encountered by United Nations troops in the Yongong area. A United States task force probed enemy held territory eight miles north-northwest of Yongong where it engaged an estimated enemy platoon before returning to friendly lines.

2. Light enemy resistance was encountered in the area northwest of Chunchon while United Nations forces north-northwest of Chunchon encountered stubborn enemy resistance from an estimated enemy battalion. Resistance continued until 1300 hours (1:00 P.M.), when friendly troops secured and held positions.

3. Light to moderate enemy resistance was encountered by United Nations forces in the area north-northeast of Chunchon, as friendly forces made limited advances during the day. Light to moderate enemy resistance was also reported in the area north and northeast of Hangye as friendly forces continued to advance during the day.

4. No significant enemy activity has been reported by R.O.K. (Republic of Korea) forces on the east coast.

—Communiqué 845 by General of the Army MacArthur's Headquarters for the period 6:00 A.M., April 5, to 6:00 A.M., April 6:

Resistance to our ground offensive increased considerably Thursday with action focused on the central sector, where pockets of stubborn hostile opposition precipitated heavy fighting.

North and northeast of Uijongbu, advancing United Nations elements met light to moderate resistance which was reduced with the help of air strikes and artillery fire.

In the central sector, substantial gains were registered against entrenched enemy elements bitterly contesting our advance north of Chunchon.

The eastern and western sectors were relatively quiet with patrol clashes constituting most of the action.

Naval, air and surface attacks in support of our ground forces continued. Persistent bombardment of key transportation centers on the east Korean coast was maintained by surface units as hostile truck convoys moving through Wonsan were effectively shelled.

At the eastern end of the battle line destroyers continued to provide direct naval gunfire support to United Nations ground forces. Carrier-based aircraft attacked hostile targets with excellent results.

United Nations land-based aircraft continued close support of our ground troops and interdicted enemy supply lines.

Last night B-29 bombers dropped high explosives on military targets in the Pyongyang, Anju, and Sinanju areas.

South Korean partisans, operating behind enemy lines, have been instrumental in harassing the Communists and contributing materially to our knowledge of hostile dispositions.

†LITTLETON, HERBERT A.

Rank and Organization: Private First Class, U.S. Marine Corps Reserve, Company C, 1st Battalion, 7th Marines, 1st Marine Division (Rein).
Born: July 1, 1930, Mena, Arkansas.
Entered Service At: Blackhawk, South Dakota.
Place and Date: Chungchon, Korea, April 22, 1951.
Citation: For conspicuous gallantry and intrepidity at the risk of his life above and beyond the call of duty while serving as a radio operator with an artillery forward observation team of Company C, in action against enemy aggressor forces. Standing watch when a well-concealed and numerically superior enemy force launched a violent night attack from nearby positions against his company, Pfc. Littleton quickly alerted the forward observation team and immediately moved into an advantageous position to assist in calling down artillery fire on the hostile force. When an enemy grenade was thrown into his vantage point shortly after the arrival of the remainder of the team, he unhesitatingly hurled himself on the deadly missile, absorbing its full, shattering impact in his body. By his prompt action and heroic spirit of self-sacrifice,

he saved the other members of his team from serious injury or death and enabled them to carry on the vital mission which culminated in the repulse of the hostile attack. His indomitable valor in the face of almost certain death reflects the highest credit upon Pfc. Littleton and the U.S. Naval Service. He gallantly gave his life for his country.

OFFICIAL COMMUNIQUÉ:
TOKYO, Monday, April 23 (AP)
—Far East Air Force summary 302 covering Saturday's operations:

The Far East Air Forces Saturday spread a broad pattern of destruction across Communist lines of communication north, south, and east of Pyongyang in a powerful interdiction of enemy efforts to build up his forces in western and central Korea.

A large percentage of the more than ninety sorties were flown against rail lines, tunnels, trains, bridges, and vehicular traffic. F.E.A.F. planes hit enemy targets for the 300th consecutive day of combat operations in Korea.

As the interdiction of transportation targets was stepped up, F.E.A.F. planes also damaged four enemy airfields and chased from North Korea a small number of MiG-15 enemy jet fighters which ventured south of the Yalu River.

In an arc around Pyongyang, Fifth Air Force fighter-bombers and light bombers smashed the entrances to twelve tunnels, ripped up thirty sections of railroad tracks, damaged three bridges, and destroyed or damaged five locomotives, ninety box cars, ninety vehicles, and four sections of highway.

Bomber command Superforts successfully attacked two important highway bridges across the Chongchon River at Anju on the main western route from Manchuria to Pyongyang.

Meanwhile the Bomber Command for the second successive day leveled a B-25 attack on the east coast enemy airfield at Yonpo, while Fifth Air Force fighter bombers hit airfields at Pyongyang, Pyonggang, and Anak.

Eight or more enemy MiG-15s observed south of the Yalu River were attacked and chased back into their Manchurian sanctuary by F-86 Sabre jets.

Fifth Air Force and attached South African, Republic of Korea, and shore-based United States Marine Corps planes, flew almost 700 sorties. In addition to the damage done to enemy lines of communication, they destroyed or damaged seventy buildings in which the enemy harbored supplies or troops, eleven warehouses, fifty supply storage areas, and thirty pack animals.

They inflicted approximately forty casualties on enemy troops and made successful attacks on ten gun positions, ten bunkers, and one field piece.

Attacks on enemy communications continued into the night with B-26 light bombers and Marine planes attacking enemy vehicles and trains with good results. One locomotive and fifteen box cars were destroyed in an attack north of Pyongyang. One hundred and twenty-five vehicles were reported damaged or destroyed on a broad arc behind enemy front lines.

Over 825 tons of war supplies were moved by air to forward airfields by the 315th Air Division (Combat Cargo). Other transport cargo planes dropped leaflets over enemy lines.

—Navy operations summary covering Sunday:

United nations ships maintained the blockade of Communist North Korea's coasts from the front lines northward almost to the Siberian border on the east coast and from the Han estuary to the far north on the west coast Sunday.

On the eastern extremity of the battle line, blockading vessels headed by the destroyer U.S.S. Perkins shelled enemy troops in the vicinity of Kansong. Large fires and explosions were seen as the result of the shelling.

Republic of Korea Navy ships maintained tight blockade patrols along the coast northward toward Wonsan, driving seven enemy small craft ashore.

On the Yellow Sea, blockade ships continued night and day surveillance to prevent enemy movements by sea. Republic of Korea vessels kept a close check on fishing craft in the area to keep Communist sampans from infiltrating the fishing fleet. Only South Koreans and nationals friendly to the United Nations are permitted to fish off Korea's coasts. In addition to the Republic of Korea vessels, other Allied units including the New Zealand frigate Rotoiti and the British frigate Black Swan maintained alert patrols in the area.

Forces led by the heavy cruiser St. Paul continued the siege of Wonsan through the sixty-sixth consecutive day. Radar-controlled guns interdicted highway and rail junctions and key bridges in and near the city. Other siege ships included the destroyers U.S.S. Parks and R.M.S. Cockade and several frigates.

Farther to the north on the east coast the U.S.S. Bausell and U.S.S. Hoquiam patrolled as far as Chongjin, blasting transportation and enemy junk traffic.

At Songjin the U.S.S. Thompson headed the firing line to carry the naval siege of that strategic rail and highway terminus through the forty-sixth straight day.

In the air, Corsair fighters from the U.S.S. Bataan carried out armed reconnaissance flights all along Korea's west coast. Three sampans were damaged west of Chinnampo and twenty buildings and barracks in the area were destroyed or damaged by the hard-hitting marine fliers.

Operating from the carriers Princeton and Philippine Sea off the east coast, Navy Skyraiders flew missions distributed over a wide area as they gave close support to ground troops and carried out deep interdiction assignments.

—Fifth Air Force evening summary for Sunday:

In the biggest Korea air battle since April 12, outnumbered Sabre jets of the Fourth United States Fighter Interceptor Wing knocked down four enemy jets and damaged four more this afternoon.

Twelve American F-86s were involved in a battle against thirty-six MiG-15s.

Two of the MiG-15s were seen to crash and explode. Pilots were seen bailing out of two others. All of the American jet fighters returned safely to their base.

The dogfight ranged from 30,000 feet "to the deck."

The Sabre jets had just entered the Sinuiju area near the Manchurian border, relieving another flight of twelve F-86s when they encountered the Russian-type planes. The enemy jets were apparently trying to intercept the original flight of fuel-low Sabres.

Today's big air battle over the Yalu River boosted Capt. James W. Jabara of Wichita, Kan., into the role of leading MiG killer in the Korean war. Jabara claims one enemy craft destroyed today, bringing his total to date to four destroyed, one probably destroyed and four damaged.

Other Fourth Wing pilots scoring kills today were Lieut. Col. Glen T. Gaglestone of Alhambra, Calif.; Lieut. William B. Yancey, Highland Falls, N.Y., and Lieut. Richard S. Becker, Fleetwood, Pa.

In other actions Sunday Fifth Air Force fighters and bombers had mounted 625 sorties by 6:00 P.M.. Of that number 139 were in support of ground forces and 226 were armed reconnaissance flights. Airmen claimed 550 enemy troops killed or wounded, and said they destroyed 225 buildings, fifty-five vehicles, four supply dumps, one ammunition dump, one tank, three gun emplacements, three field pieces, twenty-one pack animals, and seventeen anti-aircraft gun positions.

They said they damaged 100 buildings, twenty-two vehicles, one tank, one bridge, one tunnel, and three airfields. Fifteen towns were attacked during the day.

—Eighth Army communiqué 323, issued at 8:00 P.M., Sunday (6:00 A.M., Sunday, Eastern Standard Time):

Moderate enemy resistance was encountered northeast of Yonchon. Light enemy resistance was reported on the central front. Patrol clashes continue in the area northeast of Yanggu.

Estimated enemy casualties on April 21, were approximately 1,365.

1. United Nations forces dispersed an estimated 150 dug-in enemy in the area north-northwest of Yonchon with artillery fire during the morning hours. Elsewhere on the western Korean front, attacking United Nations elements in the area northeast of Yonchon met moderate enemy resistance during the day.

Attacking forces east of Chil-Lin encountered light enemy resistance during the day.

2. United Nations forces on the central Korean front met light enemy resistance as they continued to register substantial gains during the day.

3. Light to moderate enemy resistance was encountered on the eastern Korean front as United Nations patrols continued to clash with enemy forces northeast of Yanggu.

4. No significant enemy activity has been reported by Republic of Korea forces on the east coast.

—Eighth Army Communiqué 324, issued at 10:18 A.M. Monday (8:18 P.M., Eastern Standard Time, Sunday):

Enemy activity increased west and northwest of the Imjin River and in the area north-northwest of Yonchon. Heavy enemy resistance was encountered along the western Korean front as the enemy closes in the front line area. Enemy attacks during the evening and early morning hours are causing United Nations elements to withdraw on the central Korean front. Light to heavy enemy resistance continues in the area northeast and east-northeast of Yanggu.

1. Republic of Korea forces patrolling west and northwest of the Imjin River clashed with elements of an estimated enemy battalion in the area east and east-northeast of Kaesong. Enemy activity increased in the area north-northwest of Yonchon. Heavy enemy resistance was encountered in the area north and north-northeast of Yonchon as air and artillery engaged enemy units moving toward the south. All patrols were heavily engaged by the enemy, with friendly elements receiving artillery and mortar fire.

Heavy enemy resistance was also encountered southeast of Chorwon and south-southwest of Kumhwa as enemy units continued to move southward. An estimated enemy company attacked friendly elements south-southwest of Kumhwa, forcing friendly elements to withdraw from the high ground at 10:00 P.M..

2. On the central Korean front enemy resistance increased during the morning, with the enemy launching an attack against friendly forces west of Hwachon at 9:00 P.M., securing a penetration at 10:15 P.M. and causing a withdrawal of friendly forces in this area.

In the area northwest of Hwachon the enemy launched an attack at 1:20 A.M. today, with friendly elements reporting a heavy engagement in progress. Stiff enemy resistance was also reported in the area north and northeast of Hwachon.

3. Light enemy resistance was reported in the area north and north-northwest of Yanggu. Heavy enemy resistance was reported in the area northeast and east-northeast of Yanggu. Enemy groups moving southward in this area were engaged by artillery and air strikes with excellent results.

4. An estimated enemy battalion was engaged by Republic of Korea forces northeast of Inje.

—General Headquarters communiqué 862 covering Sunday's operations:

Hostile resistance to our advance increased considerably Sunday with strong hostile counter-attacks reported in several sectors. In the western sector, sharp patrol clashes and determined enemy attacks west and north of Uijongbu precipitated heavy fighting. In the west central sector, our forces registered limited advances against heavy opposition and counter-attacks. In the east-central sector, advancing troops encountered moderate resistance while farther east hostile activity was generally increasing.

United Nations jet fighters destroyed four enemy MiG-15 jets and damaged four yesterday over northwest Korea without losses to friendly aircraft, while tactical aircraft inflicted heavy casualties on enemy ground troops in persistent low-level attacks. Bombers ranged over the enemy's rear areas, cratering airfields and destroying and damaging motor vehicles attempting to bring supplies into the combat zone.

Naval air and surface units maintained the blockade of both coasts yesterday with east coast transportation centers again the target for our cruisers and destroyers. Continuing effective close support of ground units, surface units shelled hostile troops and supplies on the eastern end of the battle line. On the west coast, carrier-based aircraft blasted supply points and troop concentrations in the vicinity of Chinnampo.

WILSON, HAROLD E.

Rank and Organization: Technical Sergeant, U.S. Marine Corps Reserve, Company G, 3d Battalion, 1st Marines, 1st Marine Division (Rein).
Born: December 5, 1921, Birmingham, Alabama.
Entered Service At: Birmingham, Alabama.
Place and Date: Korea, April 23 and 24, 1951.
Citation: For conspicuous gallantry and intrepidity at the risk of his life above and beyond the call of duty while serving as platoon sergeant of a rifle platoon attached to Company G, in action against enemy aggressor forces on April 23rd and 24th, 1951. When the company outpost was overrun by the enemy while his platoon, firing from hastily constructed foxholes, was engaged in resisting the brunt of a fierce mortar, machine gun, grenade, and small-arms attack launched by hostile forces from high ground under cover of darkness, T/Sgt. Wilson braved intense fire to assist the survivors back into the line and to direct the treatment of casualties. Although twice wounded by gunfire, in the right arm and the left leg, he refused medical aid for himself and continued to move about among his men, shouting words of encouragement. After receiving further wounds in the head and shoulder as the attack increased in intensity, he again insisted on remaining with his unit. Unable to use either arm to fire, and with mounting casualties among our forces, he resupplied his men with rifles and ammunition taken from the wounded. Personally reporting to his company commander on several occasions, he requested and received additional assistance when the enemy attack became even more fierce and, after placing the reinforcements in strategic positions in the line, directed effective fire until blown off his feet by the bursting of a hostile mortar round in his face. Dazed and suffering from concussion, he still refused medical aid and, despite weakness from loss of blood, moved from foxhole to foxhole, directing fire, resupplying ammunition, rendering first aid, and encouraging his men. By his heroic actions in the face of almost certain death, when the unit's ability to hold the disadvantageous position was doubtful, he instilled confidence in his troops, inspiring them to rally repeatedly and turn back the furious assaults. At dawn, after the final attack had been repulsed, he personally accounted for each man in his platoon before walking unassisted 1/2 mile to the aid station where he submitted to treatment. His outstanding courage, initiative, and skilled leadership in the face of overwhelming odds were contributing factors in the success of his company's mission and reflect the highest credit upon T/Sgt. Wilson and the U.S. Naval Service.

OFFICIAL COMMUNIQUÉ:
TOKYO, Tuesday, April 24 (AP)
—Summary of Naval operations Monday:

Skyraiders and Corsairs operating from the carriers U.S.S. Princeton, U.S.S. Philippine Sea, and U.S.S. Bataan flew continuous sorties Monday in close support of the United Nations ground forces fighting in the area of the increased Communist activity.

The Marine and Navy fliers reported killing more than 350 enemy troops among the hordes charging on the battle line. The carrier-based planes also doubled efforts on enemy transportation targets.

At sea the Naval blockade of North Korea continued as Task Force 95 ships carried out their round-the-clock patrols and mine sweeping operations in the Yellow Sea and the Sea of Japan.

Republic of Korea vessels nosed into bays and inlets along both east and west coasts to observe enemy activity ashore. On the eastern end of the battle line, Republic of Korea units and the destroyer U.S.S. Perkins stood by to render artillery support to ground forces.

North of the battle line, siege ships led by the heavy cruiser U.S.S. St. Paul kept up the night and day bombardment of Wonsan. The mighty warship was supported during the day by the destroyer U.S.S. Parks, the frigate U.S.S. Burlington, and several others.

Farther north at Songjin, United Nations Naval units spearheaded by the destroyers U.S.S. Bausell and H.M.S. Cockade battered bridge junctions and bypass routes to discourage enemy movements of supplies southward through that vital transportation center.

Other United Nations ships maintained anti-junk patrols northward to Chongjin, fifty miles south of the Tumen River border of Siberia.

—Far East Air Force operational summary for Sunday:

Continued heavy attacks on enemy-held airfields in Korea and another decisive air victory over enemy MiG-15 jet fighters were features of the Far East Air Forces effort in Korea yesterday (Sunday).

F.E.A.F. planes flew almost 900 sorties. There was stepped-up destruction of enemy ground troops as fighter bombers hit enemy concentrations in front of front line troops.

Eleven B-29 Superforts from bases in Japan and Okinawa ranged the waist of the Korean Peninsula, hitting airfields at Sinmak, Sariwon, and Anak in the west, and Hamhung and Honpo in the east. It was the seventh successive day on which bomber command medium bombers struck at runways from which the enemy might mount air opposition against United Nations planes and ground forces in Korea.

Meantime Fifth Air Force planes put four enemy airfields under attack, fighter bombers hitting those at Sunan, Yongyu, and Pyongyang, while light bombers attacked the field at Ongjinni, all in western Korea.

An estimated thirty-six enemy MiG-15s late yesterday afternoon crossed the Yalu River from Manchuria and attempted to attack twelve F-86 Sabre jets which had been patrolling the south bank. The MiGs in turn were intercepted by twelve fresh Sabres and a battle ensued in which four MiGs were shot down, four damaged. The surviving MiGs fled north across the Yalu. There were no losses among the Sabre jets.

Fifth Air Force and attached Republic of Korea, South African, and shore-based United States Marine Corps planes mounted 680 sorties, stepped up attacks on enemy ground forces in advance of ground troops, and reported inflicting approximately 680 casualties. F-80 Shooting Star jets of the Forty-ninth Fighter Interceptor Group claimed 100 killed. Fighter interceptor group F-80s claimed 200 on the Eastern front.

More than twenty gun positions were attacked successfully. One tank was destroyed, one damaged.

Heavy attacks were continued on supply and transportation targets. Six hundred enemy supply buildings and twenty supply dumps were destroyed or damaged. Transportation destruction and damage included one train, one locomotive, sixty box cars, two boats, forty pack animals, one railroad bridge, three tunnels, three marshaling yards, sections of railroad trackage, sections of highway, and 200 motor vehicles.

Moderately light vehicular traffic was sighted during the night. One hundred vehicles and two trains were attacked.

B-26s and Marine planes continued into the night the attacks on enemy air potential, hitting airfields at Sunan, Sariwon, Yongyu, and Pyongyang. The 315th Air Division (Combat Cargo) flew 200 sorties and airlifted 760 tons of war supplies to forward bases in Korea in support of United Nations forces.

—Eighth Army Communiqué 325, issued at 8:00 P.M., Monday (6:00 A.M., Monday, Eastern Standard Time):

Enemy forces attacked United Nations forces in Korangpo area, south of Kumhwa and north of Inje. Enemy makes penetration on central front, causing withdrawal of friendly elements. United Nations forces withdrawing in good order. Air and artillery take heavy toll of enemy casualties on western front as enemy attempts to cross Imjin River. Enemy casualties inflicted 22 April approximately 2,065.

1. An estimated enemy regiment attempting to cross Imjin River in Korangpo area was hit heavily by air and artillery during early morning hours with United Nations forces holding their positions. United Nations forces in the Yonchon area reported being under attack at 5:20 A.M.. An estimated enemy regiment attacked United Nations forces in the area south-southwest of Kumhwa at 4:30 A.M., causing slight penetration. United Nations forces on western Korea front were reported withdrawing in good order to new defensive positions.

2. United Nations forces on central front were attacked by strong enemy forces with the enemy successfully infiltrating friendly positions, forcing friendly units to withdraw during early morning hours. Attacks on United Nations forces north and west of Hwachon were contained.

3. United Nations forces in Hwachon Reservoir area reported no enemy contact but observed large enemy groups to front of friendly positions. Forces in the Inje area also were hit by attacking forces with enemy successfully infiltrating positions in Inje area.

4. No report of any significant enemy activity has been received from Republic of Korea forces on eastern coast.

—Eighth Army Communiqué 326, issued at 10:15 A.M., Tuesday (8:15 P.M., Eastern Standard Time, Monday):

Enemy crosses Imjin River in Korangpo area. United Nations forces on western front attacked by strong enemy forces causing friendly displacement. Contact with enemy broken in area south of Chorwon. Enemy forces exploit break-through in area south of Kumhwa. Enemy attacks in Hwachon area repulsed. Enemy exerts strong pressure in Yanggu and Inje area, causing friendly displacement in Inje area.

1. Enemy forces crossed the Imjin River in the Korangpo area and engaged friendly United Nations forces east of the river with small arms, automatic weapons, and hand grenades. Enemy action was reported decreasing at 4:00 P.M., and as of 10:00 P.M., only light contact was reported. An estimated enemy regiment was reported in the area west of Munsan on the west bank of the Imjin. An estimated two enemy battalions engaged United Nations forces along the south bank (or east bank) of the Imjin east of Korangpo, causing friendly forces to withdraw to new defensive positions.

United Nations forces in the Yonchon area were also under attack and withdrew during the day to new defensive positions. United Nations forces north and northeast of Yonchon were attacked by an estimated enemy division, forcing friendly elements to displace to the rear during the day. In the area south and south-southeast of Chorwon an estimated enemy division launched a strong attack against United Nations forces, securing penetrations and causing United Nations forces to withdraw to more favorable defensive positions.

2. In the area south of Kumhwa on the central Korean front, strong enemy forces exploited their initial breakthrough and continued to move south in spite of numerous friendly air strikes. The enemy force involved in this exploitation was estimated as an enemy division with cavalry elements in the area east-northwest of Yongong. Friendly units to the rear of this area have adjusted positions to meet the enemy threat with friendly air and artillery engaging this enemy force throughout the day. Enemy attacks in the Hwachon area were repulsed by United Nations forces during the day.

3. In the Yanggu area the enemy exerted heavy pressure with company and battalion-size attacks against United Nations forces. Enemy attacks were repulsed although some enemy infiltrations occurred. In the Inje area, enemy in reinforced battalion strength caused United Nations forces to displace with the situation remaining fluid in this area. Strong enemy attacks were also reported by United Nations forces northeast of Inje.

4. No significant enemy activity has been reported from the east coast area.

—General Headquarters communiqué 363 for the period from 6:00 A.M., April 23, to 6:00 A.M., April 24:

Heavy fighting was general yesterday along the entire front as United Nations forces inflicted heavy casualties on attacking enemy formations. In the western sector, our units adjusted positions under steady pressure. Enemy attacks were contained in the east-central sector although heavy enemy pressure was exerted in this area. The eastern sector remained relatively quiet.

Furnishing continuous close support to ground forces fighting off hostile attacks, naval carrier-based aircraft inflicted heavy casualties on enemy troop concentrations and continued destruction of supplies coming into the combat area.

At sea, the naval blockade of North Korea was maintained as our surface units intensified efforts to prevent use of the east coast supply lines.

Land-based United Nations aircraft mounted over 1,000 sorties yesterday to help our ground units slow hostile attacks. Ranging over the battle area, fighter-bombers inflicted heavy casualties on attacking enemy units, while medium bombers struck hostile troop concentrations along the battle line during the night. Air resupply operations continued.

†GOODBLOOD, CLAIR

Rank and Organization: Corporal, U.S. Army, Company D, 7th Infantry Regiment.
Born: September 18, 1929, Fort Kent, Maine.
Entered Service At: Burnham, Maine.
Place and Date: Near Popsu-dong, Korea, April 24 and 25, 1951.
Citation: Cpl. Goodblood, a member of Company D, distinguished himself by conspicuous gallantry and intrepidity at the risk of his life above and beyond the call of duty in action against an armed enemy of the United Nations. Cpl. Goodblood, a machine-gunner, was attached to Company B in defensive positions on thickly wooded key terrain under attack by a ruthless foe. In bitter fighting which ensued, the numerically superior enemy infiltrated the perimeter, rendering the friendly position untenable. Upon orders to move back, Cpl. Goodblood voluntarily remained to cover the withdrawal and, constantly vulnerable to heavy fire, inflicted withering destruction on the assaulting force. Seeing a grenade lobbed at his position, he shoved his assistant to the ground and flinging himself upon the soldier attempted to shield him. Despite his valorous act both men were wounded. Rejecting aid for himself, he ordered the ammunition bearer to evacuate the injured man for medical treatment. He fear-

lessly maintained his 1-man defense, sweeping the onrushing assailants with fire until an enemy banzai charge carried the hill and silenced his gun. When friendly elements regained the commanding ground, Cpl. Goodblood's body was found lying beside his gun and approximately 100 hostile dead lay in the wake of his field of fire. Through his unflinching courage and willing self-sacrifice the onslaught was retarded, enabling his unit to withdraw, regroup, and resecure the strongpoint. Cpl. Goodblood's inspirational conduct and devotion to duty reflects lasting glory on himself and is in keeping with the noble traditions of the military service.

MIYAMURA, HIROSHI H.

Rank and Organization: Corporal, U.S. Army, Company H, 7th Infantry Regiment, 3rd Infantry Division.
Born: Gallup, New Mexico.
Entered Service At: Gallup, New Mexico.
Place and Date: Near Taejon-ni, Korea, April 24 and 25, 1951.
Citation: Cpl. Miyamura, a member of Company H, distinguished himself by conspicuous gallantry and intrepidity above and beyond the call of duty in action against the enemy. On the night of April 24th, Company H was occupying a defensive position when the enemy fanatically attacked threatening to overrun the position. Cpl. Miyamura, a machine gun squad leader, aware of the imminent danger to his men unhesitatingly jumped from his shelter wielding his bayonet in close hand-to-hand combat killing approximately 10 of the enemy. Returning to his position, he administered first-aid to the wounded and directed their evacuation. As another savage assault hit the line, he manned his machine gun and delivered withering fire until his ammunition was expended. He ordered the squad to withdraw while he stayed behind to render the gun inoperative. He then bayoneted his way through infiltrated enemy soldiers to a second gun emplacement and assisted in its operation. When the intensity of the attack necessitated the withdrawal of the company, Cpl. Miyamura ordered his men to fall back while he remained to cover their movement. He killed more than 50 of the enemy before his ammunition was depleted and he was severely wounded. He maintained his magnificent stand despite his painful wounds, continuing to repel the attack until his position was overrun. When last seen he was fighting ferociously against an overwhelming number of enemy soldiers. Cpl. Miyamura's indomitable heroism and consummate devotion to duty reflect the utmost glory on himself and uphold the illustrious traditions of the military service.

†ESSEBAGGER, JOHN, JR.

Rank and Organization: Corporal, U.S. Army, Company A, 7th Infantry Regiment, 3d Infantry Division.
Born: October 29, 1928, Holland, Michigan.
Entered Service At: Holland, Michigan.
Place and Date: Near Popsudong, Korea, April 25, 1951.
Citation: Cpl. Essebagger, a member of Company A, distinguished himself by conspicuous gallantry and intrepidity above and beyond the call of duty in action against the enemy. Committed to effect a delaying action to cover the 3d Battalion's withdrawal through Company A, Cpl. Essebagger, a member of one of two squads maintaining defensive positions in key terrain and defending the company's right flank, had participated in repulsing numerous attacks. In a frenzied banzai charge the numerically superior enemy seriously threatened the security of the planned route of withdrawal and isolation of the small force. Badly shaken, the

grossly outnumbered detachment started to fall back and Cpl. Essebagger, realizing the impending danger, voluntarily remained to provide security for the withdrawal. Gallantly maintaining a 1-man stand, Cpl. Essebagger raked the menacing hoards with crippling fire and, with the foe closing on the position, left the comparative safety of his shelter and advanced in the face of overwhelming odds, firing his weapon and hurling grenades to disconcert the enemy and afford time for displacement of friendly elements to more tenable positions. Scorning the withering fire and bursting shells, Cpl. Essebagger continued to move forward, inflicting destruction upon the fanatical foe until he was mortally wounded. Cpl. Essebagger's intrepid action and supreme sacrifice exacted a heavy toll in enemy dead and wounded, stemmed the onslaught, and enabled the retiring squads to reach safety. His valorous conduct and devotion to duty reflect lasting glory upon himself and was in keeping with the noblest traditions of the infantry and the U.S. Army.

†GILLILAND, CHARLES L.

Rank and Organization: Corporal (then Pfc.), U.S. Army, Company I, 7th Infantry Regiment, 3d Infantry Division.
Born: May 24, 1933, Mountain Home, Arkansas.
Entered Service At: Yellville (Marion County), Arkansas.
Place and Date: Near Tongmang-ni, Korea, April 25, 1951.
Citation: Cpl. Gilliland, a member of Company I, distinguished himself by conspicuous gallantry and intrepidity above and beyond the call of duty in action against the enemy. A numerically superior hostile force launched a coordinated assault against his company's perimeter, the brunt of which was directed up a narrow passage covered by his automatic rifle. His assistant was killed by enemy fire but Cpl. Gilliland, facing the full force of the assault, poured a steady fire into the foe which stemmed the onslaught. When 2 enemy soldiers escaped his raking fire and infiltrated the sector, he leaped from his foxhole, overtook and killed them both with his pistol. Sustaining a serious head wound in this daring exploit, he refused medical attention and returned to his emplacement to continue his defense of the vital narrow passage. His unit was ordered back to new defensive positions but Cpl. Gilliland volunteered to remain to cover the withdrawal and hold the enemy at bay. His heroic actions and indomitable devotion to duty prevented the enemy from completely overrunning his company's position. Cpl. Gilliland's incredible valor and supreme sacrifice reflect lasting glory upon himself and are in keeping with the honored traditions of the military service.

OFFICIAL COMMUNIQUÉ:
TOKYO, Thursday, April 26 (AP)
—Far East Air Forces summary of April 24 operations:

Heavy casualties were inflicted on enemy troops Tuesday as Far East Air Forces flew continuous low-level assaults in support of United Nations ground forces withstanding determined Communist thrusts. Pilot claims of 1,200 enemy killed or wounded were termed "conservative" by intelligence evaluators, who pointed out that in some 100 instances no specific claims were made by pilots who had strafed, bombed, rocketed or napalmed enemy concentrations.

More than 1,100 sorties were flown by F.E.A.F. and attached R.O.K., South African, and shore-based United States Marine planes.

In addition to the continuous day and night support of ground forces, F.E.A.F. planes struck heavily at enemy-held airfields, shot down an enemy plane in air-to-air combat, disrupted enemy supply routes, and heavily damaged enemy supplies.

The enemy plane destroyed was one of twenty MiG-15 jet fighters which ventured across the Yalu River into northwest Korea where twenty-four F-86s were on patrol. About six planes on each side were involved in the actual fighting and the stricken MiG was seen to spiral slowly to the ground and crash. There was no damage to the friendly planes involved.

Another encounter took place during the night when a B-26 was attacked by an unidentified enemy aircraft over enemy-held territory in western Korea. There was no damage to the B-26.

Enemy-held airfields at Sinmak, Anak, and Pyongyang were attacked by medium bombers, fighter bombers, and light bombers with good results. The attacks marked the fourteenth day in the last fifteen on which F.E.A.F. planes have cratered enemy airfields in Korea to prevent their possible use.

Mounting approximately 825 sorties, Fifth Air Force planes in addition to furnishing close support to front-line troops, destroyed or damaged 900 enemy-hold buildings, twenty-five supply dumps, 140 motor vehicles, six gun positions, one tank, four locomotives, seventy-five boxcars, and four railroad bridges.

Two of the bridges, on the western supply route, were rendered unserviceable.

Meantime a seven-plane flight of Okinawa-based B-29 Superforts heavily damaged a key railroad bridge near Sinanju. Four other Superforts successfully attacked an enemy barracks area near Hungnam on the east coast.

Last night the air attack on front line enemy troops continued by the light of flares. B-29s assisted the lighter Fifth Air Force planes in the assaults.

Ranging farther behind the lines B-26s and Marine night fliers last night observed approximately 1,100 vehicles and five trains on the move. They were heavily attacked with good results.

Air resupply of United Nations forces in Korea was continued by the 315th Air Division (Combat Cargo). Its planes flew 270 sorties to deliver 900 tons of war supplies to forward airbases.

—Fifth Air Force summary of Wednesday evening:

Fighters and bombers of the Fifth Air Force today claimed nearly 1,500 enemy troops killed or wounded as they lashed at Chinese and North Korean Reds driving down the Uijongbu corridor and across the Thirty-eighth Parallel in Central Korea.

Flying 764 sorties by late afternoon, Allied planes smashed at the enemy's flow of supplies and hit targets in direct support of retreating ground forces. In addition to the bag of enemy troops, pilots claimed they destroyed or damaged 550 buildings, thirty-three vehicles, three supply dumps, one fuel dump, one ammunition dump, six enemy tanks, thirty-one rail cars, five gun positions, and eight antiaircraft guns.

F-80s attacked rail cars in the marshaling yards at Kanggye. Maj. Charles B. Morfit of South River, N.J., leader of the flight said: "We didn't stick around for the smoke to settle to see what we did to that marshaling yard, for everyone in the flight was in a hurry to get back and reload so we could hit them again."

Lieut. Archie B. Caldwell of San Bernardino, Calif., led a flight of Shooting Stars in an attack on enemy troops near Kaesong.

"We worked them over with napalm and our machine guns," Caldwell said.

—Far East Naval Headquarters summary of April 25 operations:

2. On the central Korean front, the enemy continued to pour troops through the gap in friendly lines. An estimated enemy division was deployed at attacking United Nations forces in the breakthrough area throughout the day. Slight withdrawals to more advantageous positions were made by United Nations forces under heavy attack from the enemy. The intensity of the attack was reported slowing at 0130 hours this morning. In the Hwachon area strong enemy forces continued to advance as United Nations

forces organized new defensive positions. Enemy contact was maintained throughout the day and heavy enemy casualties were reported inflicted by artillery and aircraft.

3. At the eastern tip of the Hwachon Reservoir United Nations forces repulsed company-size attacks. To the east, enemy elements of company and battalion size continued to attack. However, friendly forces retained command of the situation. The enemy situation in the Inje area remains obscure as United Nations units continued to adjust positions.

4. No significant enemy activity has been reported on the east coast.

United States Navy and Marine carrier-based planes flew over 100 close air support sorties yesterday assisting front line United Nations ground forces in their battle to halt the heavy Communist offensive.

Fast Carrier Task Force 77 launched Skyraiders, Corsairs, and Panther jets from the U.S.S. Philippine Sea and U.S.S. Princeton off the east coast of Korea. The Navy planes concentrated on enemy troops, machine-gun positions, and an enemy tank.

South of Chorwon, a Communist troop-occupied village was two-thirds destroyed by bombs and napalm from the carrier aircraft. Strikes to the north near Hungnam blasted and burned a large fuel dump. In the same area, a by-pass railroad was destroyed.

Marine-piloted Corsairs from the light carrier Bataan killed an estimated 450 enemy soldiers in day-long close air support sorties. Hazy weather in the western sector prevented estimates of Communist casualties in other strikes at troops and buildings.

A total of forty-four enemy-occupied buildings were destroyed during the Marine attacks.

At Hanchon, the Bataan's pilots destroyed or damaged twenty-three large sampans.

Destroyers and frigates from Task Force 95 continued bombardment of east coast rail and road centers. Wonsan and Songjin received another 'round-the-clock pounding from the United Nations mobile artillery.

The destroyer U.S.S. Perkins operated in the Kansong area on the east coast, hitting Communist front-line troops with over 1,000 rounds of ammunition.

Other units of Task Force 95 continued the blockade of both coasts of Korea, as minesweeping operations also continued.

Navy and Royal Air Force patrol bombers made routine flights.

—*Eighth Army Communiqué 328, issued at 11:00 A.M., Wednesday (9:00 P.M., Tuesday, Eastern Standard Time):*

An enemy division continued its attack in the Korangpo area. United Nations forces made slight withdrawals on the western front under heavy enemy pressure. An enemy division continued to exploit its break-through on the central front. United Nations forces engaging this enemy reported the intensity of attack slowing at 0130 hours this morning. United Nations forces repulsed the enemy in the Yanggu area. The enemy situation in the Inje area remained obscure as United Nations forces readjusted positions.

1. Along the Imjin River line an estimated enemy division continued to exert heavy pressure against friendly forces throughout the day (Tuesday). An estimated enemy battalion which had succeeded in penetrating United Nations lines was engaged by a tank task force, forcing the enemy to withdraw to the north. As of 1800 hours (6:00 P.M.) the enemy was being contained and friendly units were holding their positions. The enemy in regimental strength succeeded in penetrating United Nations forces in the area south-southwest of Yonchon made a slight withdrawal to occupy more favorable defensive positions. United Nations forces north-northeast of Yongpyong were forced to make a slight withdrawal under heavy enemy pressure at 0700 hours. Enemy forces continued to build up regimental strength with the enemy launching another attack at 2015 hours, forcing a further displacement of 3,500 yards. Enemy attacks in the area north and west-northwest of Yongong were contained by United Nations forces.

—Eighth Army Communiqué 329, issued at 8:00 P.M., Wednesday (6:00 A.M., Wednesday, Eastern Standard Time):

Heavy enemy pressure continued along the western front as United Nations forces made limited withdrawals during the day. A task force reached surrounded United Nations elements in the area east-southeast of Korangpo. United Nations forces on the central front attacked to contain an enemy penetration. A task force entered Inje with no report of enemy contact. Enemy casualties inflicted by ground action on April 24 were estimated as approximately 4,500.

1. The enemy continued to exert heavy pressure against United Nations forces east of the Imjin River throughout the day. A tank infantry task force has successfully reached United Nations elements surrounded in the area east-southeast of Korangpo. However, no report of extrication of the surrounded forces has as yet been received. The majority of United Nations forces along the western Korean front reported heavy enemy pressure during the night and morning hours causing United Nations forces to make a limited withdrawal along the western front.

2. The intensity of the Chinese attack on the central front was reported decreasing as a United Nations tank infantry task force attacked north and northeast of Kapyong, engaging enemy of company-sized strength. Meanwhile, United Nations elements south-southwest of Hwachon were attacking northwest to contain the enemy penetration.

3. On the eastern Korean front United Nations forces east-northeast of Yanggu repulsed enemy attacks and remained in command of the situation. A tank infantry force entered Inje at 2:20 P.M., reporting no enemy contact.

4. No significant activity has been reported by R.O.K. (Republic of Korea) forces on the east coast.

—Eighth Army Communiqué 330, issued at 10:15 A.M., Thursday (8:15 P.M., Wednesday, Eastern Standard Time):

Enemy continues to reinforce attacking troops in area east of Imjin River. Tank elements linked up with surrounded United Nations elements southeast of Korangpo. No reports of extrication. Heavy enemy pressure continues along western front as United Nations forces make limited withdrawals. Intensity of enemy attack decreases on central front. Enemy continues to attack in Yanggu and Inje areas.

1. Initial heavy enemy pressure against United Nations forces northeast of Munsan was reported lessening during afternoon hours. However, friendly forces reported a build-up and enemy reinforcements arriving in the area south-southeast of Korangpo at 1530 (4:30 P.M.). At 1200 hours elements of a friendly tank battalion were successful in breaking through and linking up with surrounded United Nations forces in the area southeast of Korangpo. No report of extrications has as yet been received. Heavy enemy pressure continued against United Nations forces in the area east-northeast of Munsan as limited withdrawals were being made during the day. United Nations forces in the area south of Yonchon displaced to new defensive positions under heavy enemy pressure.

The enemy continued to attack United Nations forces in the Yongong area, causing friendly forces to break contact and withdraw. Withdrawing elements encountered an enemy road block defended by an estimated two enemy battalions but were able to withdraw around this enemy by taking an alternate route. As of 2300 hours United Nations forces were heavily engaged in the area east of Changpo.

2. On the central Korean front enemy attacks against friendly elements became noticeably lighter and less determined during the day. This sector was reportedly relatively quiet at 2000 hours. In the area south of Hwachon light enemy contact was reported by all elements in the sector with light to moderate enemy attacks being repulsed.

3. Company-sized enemy units continued to attack United Nations forces in the Yanggu area, with all enemy attacks being repulsed. Battalion-sized attacks continued in the area east-northeast of Yanggu with an enemy build-up reported in that area.

An unknown number of enemy attacked United Nations forces at 0225 this morning in the area east-northeast of Yanggu, but no further details are available at this time. In the Inje area the enemy continued his attack against United Nations forces, causing friendly forces to make limited withdrawals and readjust positions. To the east an enemy regiment was reported in contact with friendly forces.

4. Little or no enemy contact has been reported on the east coast.

—General Headquarters communiqué 865, covering the twenty-four hours to 6:00 A.M., Thursday:

Intensity of enemy pressure on United Nations lines decreased Wednesday although heavy fighting continued in the western and east-central sectors as our units executed planned withdrawals to new defensive positions. In the west-central sector, positions were adjusted according to plan as our forces inflicted heavy casualties on the enemy at all points of contact. Activity in the eastern sector was limited to patrol encounters.

Naval air and surface units continued to assist front line ground forces in Korea yesterday as carrier-based aircraft concentrated on enemy personnel and weapons in low level attacks along the front. Ranging behind enemy lines, fuel dumps and supplies were destroyed near Chorwon. Bombardment of East Coast rail and road centers continued as Wonsan and Songjin were again shelled. Blockade operations of the entire peninsula continued.

Furnishing continuous support to our ground units, land-based United Nations aircraft again mounted over 1,000 sorties against attacking hostile troops. Heavy casualties were inflicted as our low-level attack planes delivered napalm, rockets, and bombs on enemy personnel and material. Bombers disrupted communications lines and attacks continued into the night as flares were dropped to illuminate the battlefield. Combat Cargo aircraft continued to supply forward units.

†DUKE, RAY E.

Rank and Organization: Sergeant First Class, U.S. Army, Company C, 21st Infantry Regiment, 24th Infantry Division.
Born: May 9, 1923, Whitwell, Tennessee.
Entered Service At: Whitwell (Marion County), Tennessee.
Place and Date: Near Mugok, Korea, April 26, 1951.
Citation: Sfc. Duke, a member of Company C, distinguished himself by conspicuous gallantry and intrepidity above and beyond the call of duty in action against the enemy. Upon learning that several of his men were isolated and heavily engaged in an area yielded by his platoon when ordered to withdraw, he led a small force in a daring assault which recovered the position and the beleaguered men. Another enemy attack in strength resulted in numerous casualties but Sfc. Duke, although wounded by mortar fragments, calmly moved along his platoon line to coordinate fields of fire and to urge his men to hold firm in the bitter encounter. Wounded a second time he received first-aid and returned to his position. When the enemy again attacked shortly after dawn, despite his wounds, Sfc. Duke repeatedly braved withering fire to insure maximum defense of each position. Threatened with annihilation and with mounting casualties, the platoon was again ordered to withdraw when Sfc. Duke was wounded a third time in both legs and was unable to walk. Realizing that he was impeding the progress of 2 comrades who were carrying him from the hill, he urged them to leave him and seek safety. He was last seen pouring devastating fire into the ranks of the onrushing assailants. The consummate courage, superb leadership, and heroic actions of Sfc. Duke, displayed during intensive actions against overwhelming odds, reflect the highest credit upon himself, the infantry and the U.S. Army.

OFFICIAL COMMUNIQUÉ:
TOKYO, Friday, April 27 (AP)
—Far East Air Forces summary of April 25 operations:

Communist troops coming into the open in their attack on United Nations ground forces Wednesday again were targets for Far East Air Forces light bombers and fighter-bombers.

Casualties inflicted on the enemy by low-level air attacks were conservatively estimated at 1,500, bringing to over 5,000 the number of Reds killed or wounded by F.E.A.F. planes in the first four days and nights of the enemy offensive.

F.E.A.F. warplanes yesterday flew approximately 1,150 sorties, the greatest number mounted in a single, twenty-four hour period since March 23 and the second greatest effort of the Korean war.

As close support missions took a heavy toll of Communist front-line troops, Bomber Command Superforts from Okinawa and Japan bases again attacked enemy airstrips in western Korea, thirteen of the B-29s cratering runways at the Yongyu and Sariwon fields with approximately 110 tons of high explosives. It was the tenth consecutive day of Superfort neutralization of enemy air potential. F-80 Shooting Star jets attacked enemy airfields at Anak and Pyongyang.

F.E.A.F.'s F-86 Sabre jet Yalu River patrol had a brief brush with enemy MiG-15s which ventured into North Korea from their Manchurian sanctuary. There was firing but no damage was claimed or sustained by the Sabre jets.

Fifth Air Force and attached R.O.K., South African, and shore-based United States Marine Corps planes flew approximately 880 sorties, putting the greater weight of the effort in close support of the ground forces. Good flying weather assisted pilots in directing heavy strafing, rocketing, bombing, and napalming attacks against enemy troops. Claims of 1,500 casualties did not include some thirty-five strikes in which no assessment of enemy slain was made.

Shore-based Marine pilots, under the operational control of the Fifth Air Force, reported inflicting 500 casualties of which 400 were scored in two strikes.

Shooting Star jets told of 100 casualties in each of two strikes, and Thunderjet pilots reported killing or wounding 100 of the enemy by strafing in the western section of the front.

In addition to inflicting heavy losses of enemy troops, Fifth Air Force planes hit enemy combat equipment, transportation targets, and supply storage with good results.

Four enemy tanks were destroyed and one was damaged. Fifteen gun positions were successfully attacked. Nine tunnels, six highway bridges, thirty-five boxcars, ninety motor vehicles, and one locomotive were damaged or destroyed, the pattern of attack covering highways and railroads converging on Pyongyang.

In the enemy's build-up area behind the battlefronts, 1,000 enemy-held buildings, twenty-five supply dumps, and 300 barrels of petrol products were burned.

Attacks on the enemy continued into the night with B-29s joining B-26 and Marine planes in strikes near the front-lines, while other B-26s and Marines ranged rear areas. Flare-dropping planes illuminated many of the targets.

Approximately 3,400 enemy vehicles and two trains were sighted moving over enemy supply routes with the heaviest movement along the network of highways from Sinuiju to Sinanju to Pyongyang to Sariwon. Successful attacks were made on many of them.

Airfields at Wonsan and Pyongyang were attacked during the night.

Six hundred tons of war supplies were flown to forward United Nations airbases by 230 transport-cargo planes of the 315th Air Division (Combat Cargo). Wounded United Nations personnel were flown out of forward airbases to rear hospitals for speedy medical attention.

omb strikes on two of the three railroad bridges across the Han River near Seoul, July 3, 1950. (U.S. Air Force)

en of the 24th Infantry Regiment move up to the firing line in Korea, July 18, 1950. (U.S. Army)

Infantry men scout along a highway as M-4 tanks wait around the bend, August 13, 1950. (U.S. Army)

Marines west of Yongsan during the battle of Naktong Bulge, September 4, 1950. (U.S. Marine Corps)

Marines lead a patrol in "Mop-up" of Wolmi Island, September 15, 1950. (U.S. Marine Corps)

The first wave of LCVPs head for the beaches at Inchon, September 15, 1950. (U.S. Marine Corps)

1/Lt. Baldomero Lopez climbs out of an LCVP on Red Beach, Inchon, September 15, 1950. Lt. Lopez was later awarded the Medal of Honor. (U.S. Marine Corps)

Marines in the battle for Seoul, September 27, 1950. (U.S. Marine Corps)

Soldiers of the 9th Infantry Division on an M-26 Pershing tank near the Naktong Peimeter, September 1950. (U.S. Army)

1st Division marines fighting house-to-house in Seoul, September 1950. (U.S. Army)

Marines help a wounded comrade on the outskirst of Seoul, September 1950. (U.S. Marine Corps)

7th Division infantry wait as a Sherman tank clears a barricade during the fighting in Seoul, September 1950. (U.S. Army)

Marines overlooking the Han River Valley near Seoul, four days after the Inchon landing, September 1950. (U.S. Navy)

Marines of the 5th and 7th Regiments during their withdrawal from the Chosin Reservoir, December 1950. (U.S. Marine Corps)

The USS Begor loading the last United Nations landing craft as the harbor at Hungnam is destroyed. (U.S. Navy)

The broken bridge just below Funchlin Pass, between Koto-Ri and Chinhung-Ni, December 1950. (National Archives)

arines wait for a roadblock to be cleared between Yudam-Ni and Hagaru-Ri, December 1, 1950. (U.S. Marine Corps)

arines of the 1st Division occupy rugged terrain along the MSR (Main Supply Route), early December 1950. (U.S. Marine orps)

Marines south of Koto-Ri about to descend through Funchilin Pass, December 10, 1950. (U.S. Marine Corps)

Marines in defensive positions during withdrawal from the Chosin Reservoir, December 1950. (U.S. Marine Corps)

arine Corsairs have just struck Chinese positions in the Chosin Reservoir area, December 1950. (U.S. Marine Corps)

he 1st Marine Division pulls out of the Chosin Reservoir. (U.S. Marine Corps)

Infantrymen take cover from Chinese mortar fire as they fight their way to the Han River, February 13, 1951. (U.S. Army)

Infantrymen of the 24th Infantry Division move up an enemy-held hill in the central sector, March 19, 1951. (U.S. Army)

Infantrymen of the 3rd Division moving toward Uijongbu, March 23 1951. (U.S. Army)

Infantry of the 25th Division in central Korea, late March 1951. (U.S. Army)

Marines take cover behind a tank while it fires on communist troops ahead, Hongchon area, May 22, 1951. (U.S. Marine Corps)

Cavalry troops move across rice paddies to Hill 513, north of Tokchong, June 1, 1951. (U.S. Army)

Marines of the 1st Division relax by a hut after destroying an enemy sniper's nest, September 24, 1951. (U.S. Marine Corps)

Medics of the 2nd Division administer first aid to wounded soldiers, February 1952. (U.S. Army)

Soldiers of the 179th Infantry Regiment, 45th Division on Heartbreak Ridge, October 1952. (Courtesy Jim Kaltenbach)

45th Division soldier checking on a patrol on Heartbreak Ridge, October 1952. (Courtesy Jim Kaltenbach)

—Fifth Air Force summary of late Thursday;

Fifth Air Force tactical aircraft mounted more than 100 sorties in front line close support of United Nations troops and claimed at least 450 enemy troops killed or wounded by 6:00 P.M. today, despite heavy smoke and haze in the battle area. Lieut. Gen. Earle E. Partridge said in his evening summary of air activity.

Many additional enemy troops were believed to have been killed or wounded in the front line strikes but poor visibility limited pilot observation of strikes in most instances.

By 6:00 P.M. today, south Korean, land based Marine, South African, Australian, and Fifth Air Force pilots had mounted more than 600 effective sorties against enemy targets. A large portion of these strikes hit targets of opportunity just north of the battle line.

In addition to the troop casualties, pilots reported they destroyed or damaged 300 enemy occupied buildings, eighteen enemy held towns, twenty-nine vehicles, six supply dumps, a fuel dump, one ammunition dump, eleven rail cars, two railroad bridges, two road bridges, two anti-aircraft gun positions, three enemy airfields, and a MiG-15 jet.

F-4Us and F-7Fs of the First Marine Air Wing, working in close support in the western sector, claimed to have killed or wounded more than 100 enemy troops and destroyed six supply vehicles.

—United Nations Naval Forces summary of April 26 operations:

Navy and Marine pilots swarmed over enemy front-line troop concentrations yesterday, napalming, bombing, and strafing despite poor visibility.

Skyraiders and Corsairs from Fast Carrier Task Force 77 scored over 750 casualties with the results of numerous other attacks unknown due to hazy weather.

Controllers reported excellent coverage in the west-central battle sector.

North of Seoul the Navy strikes bombed 500 Communist troops on a ridge, with controllers reporting heavy enemy casualties. Communist-occupied villages, trucks, and other troop assembly areas were bombed and napalmed.

Flying from the light carrier U.S.S. Bataan, Marine Corsairs scorched enemy forward positions with napalm in the western sector yesterday.

The Marine close-air-support specialists chalked up many Chinese casualties in day-long strikes.

The Navy's mobile seaborne artillery blasted North Korean troops on the eastern end of the battle front yesterday.

The destroyer Perkins lobbed 5-inch shells into enemy positions from midnight until daylight yesterday morning.

The destroyers U.S.S. Parks and H.M.S. Comus carried the naval bombardment of Wonsan into its sixtieth day, shelling the Kalma Peninsula airstrip, gun positions, and rail and road junctions.

The airstrip and hangars were battered by naval gunfire after an unidentified plane was observed in the area.

The siege of Songjin continued, marking the fiftieth day of shellfire on that seaport. H.M.S. Cockade and the U.S.S. Bausell hit bridges, tunnels, warehouses, and highways in that area.

Interdiction of enemy supply routes at the northern seaport of Chongjin continued, with the U.S.S. Thompson and U.S.S. Hoquiam shelling rail and road junctions.

—Eighth Army communiqué 331, issued at 8:00 P.M., Thursday (5:00 A.M., Thursday, Eastern Standard Time):

United Nations forces south of Munsan repulsed all attacks during the day. Heavy enemy pressure continues in the area southeast of Korangpo and along the Yonchon-Uijongbu route. Enemy continues to attack in the Inje area. United Nations forces fight stiff delaying action as they withdraw to new defensive position. Enemy casualties inflicted on 24 April estimated as approximately 7,155 by ground action.

1. United Nations forces south of Munsan held firmly throughout the day repulsing all enemy attacks in their sector. In the area southeast of Korangpo the situation remained obscure as the enemy continued to exert heavy pressure toward the Yonchon-Uijongbu artery. Two enemy penetrations in the area south of Yongong were contained by United Nations forces during the day. As of last reports United Nations forces on the western Korean front were fighting a stiff delaying action as they withdrew to new defensive positions.

2. On the central Korean front, United Nations forces attacked enemy forces attempting to exploit their initial penetration with a task force driving 3,000 to 4,000 yards northeast into enemy-held territory. Task force reported moderate to intense small arms and automatic weapons fire enroute and during its return. As of last reports United Nations forces were fighting a stiff delaying action as they withdrew to new defensive positions.

3. Little or no enemy contact was reported by United Nations forces in the area south of Hwachon during the day. However, at 2:45 P.M. elements were reported engaged with an estimated enemy battalion south of the western tip of the reservoir. The enemy continued his company to battalion sized attack in the Yanggu area with no appreciable gain. Heavy enemy pressure continued in the Inje area and in the area east of Inje.

4. Little or no enemy contact has been reported by R.O.K. (Republic of Korea) forces on the east coast.

—Eighth Army communiqué 332, issued at 10:15 A.M., Friday (8:15 P.M., Thursday, Eastern Standard Time):

Elements of an estimated five enemy divisions continued to exert pressure on United Nations forces in the south and southeast of Korangpo. Heavy enemy pressure is continuing along the Seoul-Uijongbu corridor. An enemy force surrounded a United Nations force north of Uijongbu. A tank force extricated surrounded United Nations elements. The enemy attacked in the area north-northeast of Uijongbu. Hand-to-hand combat flared in the area west of Kapyong. Enemy pressure continued on the eastern front.

1. United Nations forces in the area south of Munsan counter-attacked at daylight yesterday and by noon the majority of friendly positions had been restored. Enemy attacks throughout the day were contained with many enemy casualties resulting from air and artillery action. The fighting continued until late afternoon at which time the United Nations forces broke contact and withdrew to prearranged positions. An estimated enemy division driving southeast from Korangpo toward the Uijongbu-Seoul axis was engaged by air and artillery throughout the day. Enemy forces north of Uijongbu succeeded in surrounding friendly elements during the night. However, by 0730, friendly tank elements had counterattacked and succeeded in extricating the surrounded force. United Nations forces continued to fight a stubborn delaying action as they withdrew to new defensive positions. At 2150 hours an enemy unit on horses and a large concentration of enemy were reported in the area north-northeast of Uijongbu. At 2200 hours the enemy (believed to be the same group) launched an attack against United Nations forces in this area securing a slight penetration. However, the attack was reported contained as of 2240 hours.

2. United Nations forces in the area west of Kapyong were engaged with an estimated enemy battalion at 1830 hours in a heavy firefight and hand-to-hand combat as friendly elements strongly defended their positions. As of 0200 this morning the action was still in progress. Enemy action on the central Korean front was reported decreasing as United Nations forces continued to stubbornly defend their positions.

3. On the eastern front the enemy continued to exert pressure by launching attacks of company to battalion size. However, United Nations forces were successful in containing or repulsing all attacks

during the day. In the Inje area determined enemy attacks caused some friendly elements to withdraw to more favorable terrain positions.

4. R.O.K. (Republic of Korea) forces on the east coast reported no enemy contact as of 1800 hours yesterday.

—*General Headquarters communiqué 866, covering the twenty-four hours ended at 6:00 A.M., April 27:*

Operations proceeded according to plan Thursday as United Nations ground forces continued withdrawals to new defensive positions. Disengagements were generally successful although fighting was severe in the west and west-central sectors where heavy casualties were inflicted on the enemy. Probing attacks in the east-central sector were contained as units adjusted positions. The eastern sector remained relatively quiet.

Carrier-based aircraft struck front-line troop concentrations yesterday in persistent low-level attacks despite ground haze. Heavy casualties were inflicted and enemy vehicles and supply points in the combat area were destroyed and damaged. At sea, surface units continued interdiction of enemy supply routes in the Wonsan-Songjin-Chongjin arc.

Fighter bombers continued incessant attacks on hostile ground troops and land-based United Nations aircraft again mounted approximately 1,000 sorties. Bombers continued cratering of airfields in North Korea and interdiction of enemy supply lines. In the air-to-air combat, four enemy jet aircraft were intercepted sixty miles south of the Yalu River by three friendly jet fighters. One MiG-15 was damaged as the hostile aircraft fled northward without damaging the friendly interceptors.

†MOYER, DONALD R.

Rank and Organization: Sergeant First Class, U.S. Army, Company E, 35th Infantry Regiment.
Born: April 15, 1930, Pontiac, Michigan.
Entered Service At: Keego Harbor, Oakland, Michigan.
Place and Date: Near Seoul, Korea, May 20, 1951.
Citation: Sfc. Moyer, assistant platoon leader of Company E, distinguished himself by conspicuous gallantry and intrepidity at the risk of his life above and beyond the call of duty in action against an armed enemy of the United Nations. Sfc. Moyer's platoon was committed to attack and secure commanding terrain stubbornly defended by a numerically superior hostile force emplaced in well-fortified positions. Advancing up the rocky hill, the leading elements came under intense automatic-weapons, small-arms, and grenade fire, wounding the platoon leader and the platoon sergeant. Sfc. Moyer, realizing the success of the mission was imperiled, rushed to the head of the faltering column, assumed command and urged the men forward. Inspired by Sfc. Moyer's unflinching courage, the troops responded magnificently, but as they reached the final approaches to the rugged crest of the hill, enemy fire increased in volume and intensity and the fanatical foe showered the platoon with grenades. Undaunted, the valiant group forged ahead, and as they neared the top of the hill, the enemy hurled a grenade into their midst. Sfc. Moyer, fully aware of the odds against him, unhesitatingly threw himself on the grenade, absorbing the full blast of the explosion with his body. Although mortally wounded in this fearless display of valor, Sfc. Moyer's intrepid act saved several of his comrades from death or serious injury, and his inspirational leadership and consummate devotion to duty contributed significantly to the subsequent seizure of the enemy stronghold and reflect lasting glory on himself and the noble traditions of the military service.

OFFICIAL COMMUNIQUÉ:
TOKYO, Monday, May 21 (AP)
—Naval operations summary covering Sunday:

Continuing the all-out effort to stop the Communist offensive in Korea, United Nations naval forces yesterday pounded front line enemy troops from the air and blasted east and west coast supply centers from the sea.

Fast Carrier Task Force 77 launched Navy fighters and bombers for 'round-the-clock attacks on enemy forces and installations. In a few cases where controllers were able to assess damage, they reported navy pilots had caused at least 700 enemy casualties during close air support strikes across the front lines.

In other attacks on Red infantrymen, the Navy planes were credited by controllers with 80 to 100 percent coverage.

During the past four days, the Skyraiders, Corsairs, and Panthers have accounted for at least 1,750 confirmed enemy killed or wounded. Over 826 sorties were flown in that period by Task Force 77 pilots from the carriers Boxer, Philippine Sea, and Princeton.

The Navy pilots hit Communist supply lines yesterday, knocking out supply dumps, bridges, and buildings. Since Thursday the Navy aerial bombardment has destroyed or damaged 336 buildings housing troops or supplies, over ten ammo and supply dumps, over 100 vehicles, sixty-eight railroad cars, seventeen bridges, and three trains.

Navy bombardment forces struck in five places along both coasts yesterday, as the shelling of Communist ports was intensified.

The battleship New Jersey, flagship of Vice Admiral Harold M. Martin, commander, Seventh Fleet, fired over fifty-six tons of steel and high explosives at bridges and highways north of Kansong early yesterday morning. This is the first bombardment by the newest and biggest addition to the United Nations naval forces off Korea. The New Jersey last fired her 16-inch guns at hostile forces on Aug. 8, 1945, while shelling Wake Island.

Communists at Wonsan were again raked by United States naval gunfire from four destroyers. The bombarding group scored direct hits on a truck convoy north of the city yesterday morning. The destroyers Bass, Duncan, Craig, and Tucker shelled bridges, road, marshaling yards, and enemy gun emplacements of Kalma Peninsula.

In the pre-dawn firing the ships teamed up with Air Force night intruders in attacks on Communist attempts to run supplies southward through the blockade.

Destroyers and frigates patrolled and bombarded railroads and rolling stock between Songjin and Chongjin to the north. The destroyer Stickell spotted a train five miles south of Chuuronjang. After a heavy bombardment, the Stickell reported large fires and explosions in the area.

The frigate Burlington caught several North Korean small craft with main and secondary battery fire before dawn yesterday off Songjin. H.M.S. Black Swan, operating in the same area, picked off an enemy anti-aircraft gun emplacement north of the city.

To the south, on the east coast, the destroyer U.S.S. Isbell fired day-long bombardment at enemy troops and repair crews north and south of Yangyang. Over 200 rounds were poured out by the destroyer, with many hits observed.

The British cruiser Ceylon continued naval gunfire on the west coast near Ullyul. Aerial observers reported that anti-aircraft batteries in the area were well plastered by the cruiser's 6-inch shells.

—Far East Air Forces summary of May 20 operations:

Enemy jet fighters unsuccessfully challenged Allied air power over Korea and the entire weight of the B-29 Superfort effort shifted from interdiction to close aerial support of United Nations ground forces to stem the Communist offensive as Far East Air Forces aircraft mounted more than 1,140 sorties yesterday.

Three Communist MiG-type jets were shot down, one probably destroyed and five damaged in a twenty minute air battle with F-86 Sabre jets of the Fourth Fighter Interceptor Wing south of Sinuiju in far northwest Korea.

Approximately fifty Russian-made Communist jets and twenty-eight F-86s participated in the engagement.

The dogfight started when fourteen F-86 fighters sighted a large formation of MiGs. The enemy jets accepted the air challenge and the rest of the Sabre jets swooped into the fray which ranged from altitudes of 35,000 to 5,000 feet.

It was the first encounter with the MiGs since May 12 when sixteen of the enemy jets were engaged by twelve F-86s with one MiG being damaged.

Capt. James Jabara, 101 North Broadway, Wichita, Kan., shot down two of the MiGs, becoming the first jet ace in aviation history. His victories yesterday bring to six his record for the Korean war.

During the last four days, B-26 light bombers of Fifth Air Force and Superforts of F.E.A.F.'s Bomber Command have dropped 3,000 500-pound proximity-fused air-bursting bombs in night operations against Communist troops in front of friendly ground forces.

The bombs were aimed by a newly employed radar technique which permits night bombing with an accuracy comparable to visual daylight bombing.

Last night Superforts from the Nineteenth, Ninety-eighth, and 307th Bomb Groups, along with Fifth Air Force B-26 Invaders, dropped about 1,000 of the 500-pound air-bursting missiles with pinpoint bombing of Communist front-line forces.

Fifth Air Force mounted about 850 sorties as its fighters, fighter-bombers, and light bombers ranged over North Korean areas and along the Communist battle zone, dropping high explosives and napalm and strafing Red troops.

More than 280 close air support sorties were flown by Fifth Air Force aircraft and attached allied units, most of these were flown in support of friendly forces along the central front.

Approximately 500 Communist troop casualties were inflicted by Fifth Air Force planes. Destroyed or damaged were about 850 enemy-held buildings, 100 railroad cars, sixty-five vehicles, fifteen gun positions, nine tunnels, five bridges, five locomotives, two fuel dumps, one railroad station and rail trackage was severed in fourteen places.

During the night eighty-nine sorties were mounted by tactical aircraft and they destroyed or damaged two bridges, fifteen vehicles, and a ferry boat at Tosan, about twenty miles west of Chorwon. A series of secondary explosions were observed when the ferry boat was hit.

Transports of the 315 Air Division (Combat Cargo) airlifted about 1,180 tons of supplies and ammunition as the organization stepped-up its cargo-carrying mission in the support of allied forces in Korea.

The division mounted more than 265 sorties and carried more than 1,000 passengers under the "Operation Relax" program.

—*Eighth Army communiqué 380, issued at 9:00 A.M. Monday (7:00 P.M. Sunday, Eastern Daylight Time):*

Light to moderate enemy resistance was encountered on the western front as United Nations forces struck at the enemy with strong reconnaissance force during the day. Heavy fighting continued in the area south-southeast and east-southeast of Changgong (Chongpyong). Bitter fighting with company or battalion-size enemy units continued in the area east-southeast of Changgong.

Enemy attacks west-southwest of Hangye were repulsed with heavy enemy casualties. Enemy continues to exert determined heavy pressure east and northeast of Pungam. Little or no enemy contact reported on the east coast.

1. Light to moderate enemy resistance from enemy company and battalion-size units was encountered by R.O.K. (Republic of Korea) forces in the area northwest and north-northwest of Seoul as strong reconnaissance elements advanced up to 10,000 yards during the day. Stiff enemy resistance from an estimated enemy battalion was encountered by United States Army elements north of Seoul as friendly elements engaged enemy forces forward of main-line positions. An enemy platoon was engaged in the Uijongbu area at 1040 hours (10:40 A.M.). Advances of 4,500 yards were registered in the area northeast of Seoul as United Nation Army elements engaged company-size enemy units throughout the day. United Nations forces in the area east-northeast of Seoul reported light enemy contact with friendly elements to their front.

2. Heavy enemy resistance from elements of two enemy regiments was reported by R.O.K. forces in the area south-southeast and southeast of Changgong. Heavy enemy contact continued in the area south of Kapyong (east-southeast of Changgong) as enemy in regimental strength continued to attack friendly forces in the area. Action was reported continuing as of 0200 hours this morning. Sharp, bitter fighting was reported in the area east-southeast of Changgong as friendly forces engaged company to battalion-size enemy units during the day. At 0445 hours an estimated 2,000 enemy launched an attack against United States elements west-southwest of Hangye—this engagement continued until 0930 hours at which time the enemy withdrew to the north after having suffered heavy casualties.

3. The enemy made light probing attacks against the western sector of the United States Second Division front while the enemy momentum of the attack on the eastern division front showed signs of decreasing. An estimated 1,000 enemy attacked elements of the United States Second Division westnorthwest of Pungam at 0300 hours with the action continuing until 1730 hours, by which time friendly ground, artillery, and air bombardment had inflicted heavy enemy casualties, forcing the enemy to withdraw. The enemy continued to exert determined heavy pressure against R.O.K. forces in the area east and east-northeast of Pungam, using elements of regimental size. Little or no enemy contact was reported by R.O.K. forces on the east coast.

—General Headquarters communiqué 890, issued at 10:10 A.M. Monday (8:10 P.M. Sunday, Eastern Daylight Time):

The United Nations line in Korea generally held firm Sunday despite several strong enemy attacks on the eastern and east-central front. Limited advances were registered by friendly units in the western and west-central sectors against light to heavy resistance as the enemy continued to suffer severe casualties all along the front.

United Nations aircraft engaged enemy jet fighters in a series of air battles over northwest Korea yesterday. Three enemy MiG-15s were destroyed, one was probably destroyed and five were damaged without loss of friendly aircraft. Tactical aircraft attacked enemy troops during the day and night as destruction of enemy supplies continued. Transport-cargo aircraft airlifted supplies to forward United Nations airbases.

Continuing support of United Nations ground units, carrier-based aircraft, and surface units attacked enemy troop concentrations and bombarded coastal supply centers. Truck convoys and trains attempting to bring hostile supplies southward were hit during the night as blockade operations of the peninsula continued.

RODRIGUEZ, JOSEPH C.

Rank and Organization: Sergeant (then Pfc.), U.S. Army, Company F, 17th Infantry Regiment, 7th Infantry Division.
Born: November 14, 1928, San Bernardino, California.
Entered Service At: California.
Place and Date: Near Munye-ri, Korea, May 21, 1951.
Citation: Sgt. Rodriguez distinguished himself by conspicuous gallantry and intrepidity at the risk of his life above and beyond the call of duty in action against an armed enemy of the United Nations. Sgt. Rodriguez, an assistant squad leader of the 2d Platoon, was participating in an attack against a fanatical hostile force occupying well-fortified positions on rugged commanding terrain, when his squad's advance was halted within approximately 60 yards by a withering barrage of automatic-weapons and small-arms fire from 5 emplacements directly to the front and right and left flanks, together with grenades which the enemy rolled down the hill toward the advancing troops. Fully aware of the odds against him, Sgt. Rodriguez leaped to his feet, dashed 60 yards up the fire-swept slope and, after lobbing grenades into the first foxhole with deadly accuracy, ran around the left flank, silenced an automatic-weapon with two grenades and continued his whirlwind assault to the top of the peak, wiping out two more foxholes and then, reaching the right flank, he tossed grenades into the remaining emplacement, destroying the gun and annihilating its crew. Sgt. Rodriguez' intrepid actions exacted a toll of 15 enemy dead and, as a result of his incredible display of valor, the defense of the opposition was broken, and the enemy routed, and the strategic strong-point secured. His unflinching courage under fire and inspirational devotion to duty reflects the highest credit on himself and upholds the honored traditions of the military service.

OFFICIAL COMMUNIQUÉ:
TOKYO, Tuesday, May 22 (AP)
—Naval operations summary for Monday:

Navy carrier-based planes killed or wounded an estimated 650 enemy soldiers yesterday during close air support flights, bringing the five-day total to 2,400. Launched from fast Carrier Task Force 77, the fighters and bombers continued attacks on front line Communists in the eastern sector.

Northwest of Songsan, Philippine Sea and Boxer pilots scored an estimated 400 casualties and destroyed two heavy artillery pieces and two machine gun emplacements. Five miles to the east, they killed or wounded another hundred Red infantrymen.

The Skyraiders, Panthers, and Corsairs flew armed reconnaissance flights after rain and low clouds slowed the close air support. South of Hagaru, the carrier planes damaged or destroyed four tanks and trailers with rockets and napalm. One of the navy pilots got a direct napalm hit on another tank fifty miles north of Kosong on the east coast.

Although bad weather prevented full-scale afternoon sorties, Task Force 77 pilots destroyed or damaged thirty-seven trucks, forty boxcars, and fifty-one buildings in flights as far north as Kilchu.

The U.S.S. New Jersey led bombardment forces on the east coast, adding her heavy 16-inch gunfire in the siege of Wonsan. Her two-thousand-pound shells silenced enemy shore batteries which fired at United Nations bombarding ships the sixth time in as many days.

With the light cruiser Manchester and destroyers U.S.S. Duncan and U.S.S. Mason, the battleship blasted bridges, railroad marshaling yards, truck areas, and gun emplacements.

The destroyer Isbell yesterday morning completed thirty-six continuous hours of bombarding enemy troop concentrations, road blocks, and bridges near Yangyang at the Thirty-eighth Parallel on the east coast.

Fires and secondary explosions were observed as the Isbell scored many hits. Aerial spotters reported one bridge totally destroyed with fires still burning several hours after the bombardment.

Patrolling north of Kansong in the morning, one destroyer shelled troops and gun emplacements. Poor visibility prevented damage assessment.

Destroyers U.S.S. Tucker, H.M.C.S. Nootka, and frigate Sausalito pounded rail traffic and roads near Songjin. The Tucker cut railroad tracks in thirteen places between Songjin and Tanchon to the south.

To the north, the destroyer Stickell bombarded rail and road junctions near Chongjin during blockade patrols.

—Eighth Army communiqué 381, issued at 7:00 P.M., Monday (5:00 A.M., Monday, Eastern Daylight Time):

United Nations forces made limited advances against enemy forces on the western front with light to moderate enemy resistance being reported.

Reconnaissance elements entered Munsan at 10:00 A.M.. Company-sized enemy units continued to be engaged along the central front as enemy activity showed a slight decrease over the previous period. The United States Second Division repulsed six probing attacks during the night with enemy contact reported as light during the morning hours. Elsewhere on the eastern front, enemy contact was reported light to moderate. Enemy casualties inflicted by the United States Second Division during the period of 16 May to 20 May inclusive were estimated as 37,750.

1. Republic of Korea forces north-northwest of Seoul encountered light enemy resistance as reconnaissance elements entered the town of Munsan at 10:00 A.M. with little or no enemy contact. Untied States Army elements north of Seoul made limited gains throughout the day encountering light enemy resistance. A task force entering Uijongbu during the morning reported no enemy contact. Light to moderate enemy resistance was reported northeast of Seoul as United States elements east-northeast of Seoul reported receiving small arms and automatic weapons fire, and hand grenades from an undetermined number of enemy to their front.

2. United Nations forces west-southwest and southwest of Changgong reported light enemy contact with the exceptions of United States Army elements southwest of Changgong who were unable to advance due to heavy enemy fire from a dug-in enemy to their front. Light to moderate enemy contact was also reported by Republic of Korea forces south, southeast, and east-southeast of Changgong as limited gains were made during the day. An estimated enemy battalion in this area was engaged with artillery fire which resulted in heavy enemy casualties. Enemy activity in the corps sector decreased from the previous period in that the majority of the enemy units engaged were estimated to be of company size.

3. A total of six probing attacks were repulsed during the night by United States Second Division elements. The front became relatively quiet at 7:30 A.M., with light enemy contact reported during the morning hours. Enemy action along the corps front consisted of company to battalion-sized activity during the day. Light enemy contact was reported in the Pungam and Mabaejae area during the morning hours.

4. Light scattered enemy activity was reported in the east coast areas as Republic of Korea forces patrolled and readjusted positions.

—General Headquarters communiqué 891, issued at 9:45 A.M., Tuesday (7:45 P.M., Monday, Eastern Daylight Time):

Enemy forces in the east-central and eastern sectors continued probing United Nations positions yesterday but failed to dislodge friendly units. In the western and west-central sectors, advancing United Nations troops encountered light to moderate resistance as they fought northward.

Led by the U.S.S. New Jersey, naval surface units bombarded east coast transportation lines, hampering enemy efforts to supply forward units. Although weather restricted operations yesterday afternoon, carrier-based aircraft rendered close support to ground units by attacking hostile troop concentrations and gun emplacements all across the front.

Assaults by B-29 bombers continued last night in close support of United Nations ground forces along the central and east-central sectors. Tactical aircraft inflicted casualties on hostile troops as attacks were launched against the enemy's rear lines of supply and communications. Cargo transports airlifted heavy tonnages of supplies to friendly front-line forces in Korea.

†MORELAND, WHITT L.

Rank and Organization: Private First Class, U.S. Marine Corps Reserve, Company C, 1st Battalion, 5th Marines, 1st Marine Division (Rein).
Born: March 7, 1930, Waco, Texas.
Entered Service At: Austin, Texas.
Place and Date: Kwagch'i-Dong, Korea, May 29, 1951.
Citation: For conspicuous gallantry and intrepidity at the risk of his life above and beyond the call of duty while serving as an intelligence scout attached to Company C, in action against enemy aggressor forces. Voluntarily accompanying a rifle platoon in a daring assault against a strongly defended enemy hill position, Pfc. Moreland delivered accurate rifle fire on the hostile emplacement and thereby aided materially in seizing the objective. After the position had been secured, he unhesitatingly led a party forward to neutralize an enemy bunker which he had observed some 400 meters beyond, and boldly moving through a fire-swept area, almost reached the hostile emplacement when the enemy launched a volley of hand-grenades on his group. Quick to act despite the personal danger involved, he kicked several grenades off the ridge line where they exploded harmlessly and, while attempting to kick away another, slipped and fell near the deadly missile. Aware that the sputtering grenade would explode before he could regain his feet and dispose of it, he shouted a warning to his comrades, covered the missile with his body and absorbed the full blast of the explosion and, in saving companions from possible injury or death, was mortally wounded. His heroic initiative and valiant spirit of self-sacrifice in the face of certain death reflects the highest credit upon Pfc. Moreland and the U.S. Naval Service. He gallantly gave his life for his country.

OFFICIAL COMMUNIQUÉ:
TOKYO, Wednesday, May 30 (AP)
—Far East Air Forces operational summary for Monday:

Withdrawing Communist forces were kept under the pressure of constant air attack in Korea Monday by Far East Air Forces warplanes, while four Fifth Air Force Sabre jets engaged eight enemy MiG-15 jet fighters during a patrol mission south of Sinuiju. One of the MiGs was damaged.

F.E.A.F. aircraft yesterday flew more than 975 sorties under fair weather conditions. Supply points and transportation facilities in enemy rear areas were hit during persistent strikes by fighter-bombers and B-26 invaders on Communist-occupied buildings, rolling stock, vehicles, pack animals, rail lines, bridges, and tunnels.

Heavy casualties were also inflicted on disorganized enemy troops. A large tonnage of necessary supplies was airlifted from Japan to the battlefront by 315th Air Division (Combat Cargo) aircraft.

Fifth Air Force and attached R.O.K., South African, and shore-based Marine planes flew 741 sorties, of which more than 170 were in direct close support of the steadily advancing friendly ground forces. B-26 invaders of the 452d Light Bomb Wing damaged a bridge eight miles north of Kumchon and destroyed fifteen railroad cars in the marshaling yards at Sinmak.

Trackage was severed in five places on the key railway between Sinanju and Pyongyang, and along the route to Sariwon by F-51 Mustang fighter-bombers of the Eighteenth Fighter-Bomber Wing. Forty-ninth Fighter-Bomber Wing F-80s destroyed three gun positions and inflicted 150 enemy troop casualties ten miles west and southwest of Chorwon along the central front.

Pilots reported destroying or damaging a total of 745 Communist-held buildings, seventy vehicles, thirty supply carts, forty-five pack animals, eighty-five railroad cars, twenty-five gun positions, twenty supply dumps, three railroad bridges, and two tunnels. Railway tracks were cut in eight places, while more than 850 enemy casualties were inflicted on enemy troops.

During night operations B-26 invaders of the Third Bomb Wing sighted considerable vehicular traffic on roads in enemy rear areas. Of 225 vehicles attacked, approximately eighty were destroyed or damaged. Superforts of the F.E.A.F.'s Bomber Command, flying from Okinawa, struck at two enemy airfields by visually dropping more than 120 tons of bombs to neutralize the two strips, preventing their possible use by the Communist airpower.

The B-29 medium bombers of the Nineteenth and 307th Bomb Groups launched strikes against the newly constructed "downtown" strip at Pyongyang and the recently enlarged Yongyu airfield. Both attacks were reported as successful by bomber crew members. Aircraft commanders said they encountered moderate flak over the target areas, but that no fighter opposition was seen.

The 315th Air Division (Combat Cargo) followed up its resupply of friendly front-line forces by airlifting more than 1,000 tons of material to forward bases in Korea. Approximately 825 passengers were carried by the transports under the rest and recuperation program.

—*Eighth Army communiqué 397, issued Tuesday at 7:00 P.M. (5:00 A.M. Tuesday, Eastern Daylight Time):*

R.O.K. (Republic of Korea) patrols cross the Imjin River. Task Force probes north of Yonchon. Two small groups of enemy surrender to army forces southwest of Hwachon. United Nations forces reach south bank of the Hwachon Reservoir. Friendly forces engaged with enemy regiments southeast of Yanggu. Resistance continues in the area northeast of Inje. R.O.K. forces on east coast continue their advance.

R.O.K. forces again probed across the Imjin River and engaged elements of an estimated three enemy companies during the day. To the east, army forces probing along the Uijongbu-Yongchon road advanced to a point north of Yonchon. Other army elements in the Yongpyong area encountered an unknown number of enemy, as advances of 3,000 to 9,000 yards were registered during the day.

United Nations forces in the area northeast of the Yongong sector advanced 3,000 yards, encountering an estimated 200-250 enemy at 10:45 A.M.. Army forces southwest of Hwachon advanced 1,000 yards against resistance from an estimated eighty enemy. Resistance was overcome as enemy surrendered. In the rear areas northwest of Chonchon, army forces engaged an estimated 100 enemy. The action resulted in the enemy surrendering. Army forces in the Hwachon area sent strong armored patrols north of Hwachon during the day.

United Nations forces engaged an enemy company in the area south of the Hwachon Reservoir, dispersing the enemy and continuing their advance to the south bank of the reservoir. Meanwhile, other United Nations forces were engaged with an estimated enemy regiment in the area southwest of Yanggu. Army elements in the Inje area adjusted their positions, reporting light enemy contact during the day. United States Army forces in the Hyon sector advanced 7,000 yards with little or no enemy contact. A task force operating northeast of Inje reported many small groups harassing friendly elements from positions on commanding terrain.

Little or no enemy contact was reported on the east coast, as R.O.K. forces continued their advances north-northwest of Yangyang.

—Navy operations summary for Tuesday:

United Nations warships and carrier-based aircraft pressed the attack on Communist troops and supply lines yesterday.

Navy close air support strikes caused well over 350 casualties in the eastern sector.

Skyraiders and Corsairs bombed, napalmed, and strafed Red soldiers, gun emplacements and buildings north and northeast of Inje.

North of Kumwha, Navy pilots killed an estimated 100 well entrenched infantrymen.

Prior to noon yesterday, armed reconnaissance flights destroyed over sixty troop-occupied buildings and thirty-three vehicles in central and northeast Korea above the Thirty-eighth Parallel.

Although darkness prevented accurate assessment of enemy casualties, gunfire from the destroyer Isbell got "excellent coverage" during bombardment of an estimated battalion northwest of Kansong Monday night and early yesterday morning.

United States Navy destroyers again teamed up with Air Force night intruders at Wonsan. The destroyer Brinkley Base illuminated a forty-truck convoy with starshells, allowing the Air Force spotter to make a successful bombing run which severely damaged several trucks.

Kalma Peninsula shore batteries, railroad bridges, marshaling yards, and beach defenses were shelled by the U.S.S. Bass, U.S.S. Duncan and U.S.S. Mason.

Patrolling far to the north, the destroyer Stickell sank a 100-ton motor junk and damaged ten sampans near Chingjin.

Later in the day, the Stickell shelled bridges and flat cars near Songjin. Air spotters reported several hits.

The Canadian destroyer Nootka and the United States frigate Burlington also got direct hits on vehicles, gun emplacements and sampans.

—Eighth Army communiqué 398, issued at 9:00 A.M. Wednesday (7:00 P.M. Tuesday, Eastern Daylight Time):

Republic of Korea forces engaged enemy battalion west of Imjin River. Heavy enemy resistance from enemy regiment encountered immediately south of Yonchon. Army forces reached Hantan River in Yongpyong area.

Patrols report battalion to regimental size enemy units to their front in area west-southwest of Hwachon.

Stubborn resistance encountered in the Hwachon area. United Nations forces reach Hwachon reservoir.

Heavy enemy resistance encountered in the Inje area, west and north-northeast of Inje. Republic of Korea forces enter Kansong.

1. Moderate to stubborn enemy resistance was encountered by Republic of Korea forces crossing the Imjin River as friendly forces became engaged with an estimated enemy battalion.

Limited advances were made during the day as friendly forces broke contact at 6:30 P.M..

Army forces in the Yonchon area initially engaged scattered enemy groups of platoon size. However, by 2:00 P.M., friendly elements were in firm contact with elements of an estimated enemy regiment firmly entrenched on the high ground on both sides of the road south of Yonchon.

Action continued until late afternoon when Army forces went into a defensive perimeter for the night.

In the Yongpyong area, Army forces encountered light to no enemy resistance as they advanced to the vicinity of the Hantan River.

2. An estimated 250 enemy were engaged by United Nations forces west-southwest of Hwachon at 10:45 A.M..

This action continued throughout the day with the enemy withdrawing at 8:00 P.M.. Patrols operating in this sector reported enemy groups of battalion to regimental size to their front. In the Hwachon area the enemy continued to stubbornly resist the friendly advance north and east of the city.

An enemy battalion counter-attacking was engaged with artillery with excellent results. An enemy company was engaged in the area south of the Hwachon Reservoir—the enemy was dispersed and friendly forces registered gains of 8,500 yards during the day.

3. Heavy enemy resistance was encountered by friendly forces in the area south-southeast of Yanggu and the attack continued against a well-entrenched enemy.

Air, artillery, and ground fire engaged the enemy throughout the day with friendly forces reporting limited gains.

Enemy resistance in the Inje area and in the area west of Inje stiffened during the day.

Stiffened enemy resistance was encountered by Army forces north and northeast of Inje as friendly gains were limited to 2,000 yards.

4. No significant enemy activity was reported on the east coast as Republic of Korea forces entered Kansong.

—General Headquarters communiqué 899 issued at 10:25 A.M. Wednesday (8:25 P.M. Tuesday, Eastern Daylight Time):

United Nations ground forces continued to advance in Korea yesterday against increasing enemy resistance. In the western sector friendly units made advances up to five miles against light resistance. Strong enemy counter-attacks of United Nations elements in the Hwachon-Inje areas. Along the east coast friendly units continued to advance without opposition.

Carrier aircraft supported advancing United Nations ground forces with attacks on enemy troop positions and gun emplacements in the Kumhwa and Inje areas with excellent results. Surface units shelled enemy shore batteries, rail bridges, marshaling yards, and beach defenses along the east coast from Chongjin to Kansong. United Nations destroyers assisted land-based night bombers in attacks on enemy truck convoys in the Wonsan area.

Land-based aircraft inflicted heavy casualties on withdrawing enemy ground forces and severely damaged supply and transportation facilities in the battle area. Medium bombers attacked the important marshaling yard at Kowon and rail bridges at Kanggye. Resupply of advancing friendly units by Combat Cargo aircraft continued.

HERNANDEZ, RODOLFO P.

Rank and Organization: Corporal, U.S. Army, Company G, 187th Airborne Regimental Combat Team.
Born: April 14, 1931, Colton, California.
Entered Service At: Fowler, California.
Place and Date: Near Wontong-ni, Korea, May 31, 1951.
Citation: Corporal Hernandez, a member of Company G, distinguished himself by conspicuous gallantry and intrepidity above and beyond the call of duty in action against the enemy. His platoon, in defensive positions on Hill 420, came under ruthless attack by a numerically superior and fanatical hostile force, accompanied by heavy artillery, mortar, and machine gun fire which inflicted numerous casualties on the platoon. His comrades were forced to withdraw due to lack of ammunition but Cpl. Hernandez, although wounded in an exchange of hand-grenades, continued to deliver deadly fire into the ranks of the onrushing assailants until a ruptured cartridge rendered his rifle inoperative. Immediately leaving his position, Cpl. Hernandez rushed the enemy armed only with rifle and bayonet. Fearlessly engaging the foe, he killed 6 of the enemy before falling unconscious from grenade, bayonet, and bullet

wounds but his heroic action momentarily halted the enemy advance and enabled his unit to counterattack and retake the lost ground. The indomitable fighting spirit, outstanding courage, and tenacious devotion to duty clearly demonstrated by Cpl. Hernandez reflects the highest credit upon himself, the infantry, and the U.S. Army.

OFFICIAL COMMUNIQUÉ:
TOKYO, Friday, June 1 (AP)
—Far East Air Forces summary, issued at 12:10 P.M. Thursday (10:10 P.M. Wednesday, Eastern Daylight Time):

Air attacks were made on the enemy build-up area around Pyongyang Wednesday as Far East Air Forces fighter-bombers flew through low-hanging clouds and rain to deny Communists badly needed supplies.

B-26 Invader light bombers ranged deeper into the enemy's rear area to strike at other supply points, highways, and storehouses. B-29 Superforts assaulted Red troop concentrations in the battlezone last night.

More than 240 sorties were flown by F.E.A.F. aircraft in spite of the bad weather.

F-80 and F-84 fighter-bombers attacked and destroyed a number of enemy-held buildings just north of the fighting front in the central sector as Fifth Air Force flew 130 sorties. Five camouflaged vehicles, believed to be tanks were destroyed; 100 Communist-occupied buildings and seventy-five vehicles were destroyed or damaged.

Three Bomber Command Superforts assisted by radar dropped 120 500-pound air-bursting bombs on Red troops in the battle zone east of the Hwachon Reservoir, while two other B-29s radar bombed a valuable enemy storage area in western Korea at Kyomipo.

B-26s in pre-dawn attacks, bombed enemy airfields at Pyong, Sinanju, and Ogyo, in western North Korea. The Invader crew which struck at the Ogyo strip reported starting four large fires. Night-flying Marine aircraft, under the operational control of Fifth Air Force, attacked enemy supplies, troops, railroad cars, and vehicular traffic.

The 315th Air Division (Combat Cargo) flew more than 100 sorties to deliver combat supplies to Korean airheads.

—United Nations Naval Forces summary of May 31 operations:

United States Navy planes launched from aircraft carriers U.S.S. Boxer and U.S.S. Bon Homme Richard blasted enemy troops entrenched on a ridge north of Hwachon in the central sector yesterday with excellent results. Controllers credited the carrier pilots with 90 percent coverage of the area.

Bad weather during the initial day of Korean operations for the newly-arrived floating airfield Bon Homme Richard limited the Navy strikes.

Task Force 77 aircraft spotted for naval shore bombardment at Wonsan yesterday. Navy pilots bombed and napalmed eight troop-occupied barracks in the area, leaving several in flames. Other targets destroyed included boxcars, trucks, anti-aircraft batteries, and supply dumps.

Rear Admiral William G. Tomlinson, currently commanding the Fast Carrier Task Force, reported that since May 16, Navy aircraft caused over 4,200 enemy casualties as well as destroying or damaging 475 trucks and vehicles, twenty-one warehouses, 1,250 buildings, fifty-six supply dumps, eighty-four emplacements, and twelve bridges.

Naval shore bombardment of military targets in the Wonsan area continued yesterday as the destroyers Mason and Hawkins raked highways and bridges, and plastered gun positions on Kalma and Modo peninsulas.

The light cruiser Manchester shelled enemy troop concentrations northwest of Kansong with unobserved results. Far to the north, the destroyer Fiske and frigate Burlington bombarded bridges and gun emplacements near Songjin, registering many hits.

Marine-manned Corsairs from the light carrier Bataan roared into action over North Korea yesterday, after heavy fog had hampered operations off the west coast. The fighter-bombers hit warehouses, tunnels, and a power substation during sorties in the Haeju-Chinnampo area.

—Eighth Army communiqué 401, issued at 7:00 P.M., Thursday (5:00 A.M., Thursday, Eastern Daylight Time):

Small enemy groups were encountered as United Nations forces patrolled aggressively on the western front. An enemy battalion suffered heavy casualties northeast of Yonggong on May 30. United Nations forces captured enemy equipment in the area north-northeast and northeast of Yonggong. Enemy attack in Inje area repulsed. R.O.K. (Republic of Korea) patrol discovers supply dump on Yongdae area.

1. United Nations forces on the western Korean front patrolled aggressively throughout the day, encountering small enemy groups forward of main line positions.

2. A delayed report of action occurring between 8:00 A.M. and 6:00 P.M., 30 May accounted for 559 enemy killed, seventy-nine P.O.W.s (prisoners), and captured enemy equipment, including thirteen Russian trucks loaded with tires and ammo and seven A-A (anti-aircraft) guns. Action occurred as friendly forces engaged an enemy battalion northeast of Yonggong. United Nations forces reported engaging small enemy groups in the same general area today with friendly forces discovering a supply dump containing 6,000 C.C.F. (Chinese Communist Forces) fatigue uniforms. United Nations forces on the central front continued to patrol aggressively, with an attack by fifteen enemy in the Hwachon area repulsed which resulted in ten enemy killed.

3. United States forces in the Yanggu area continued their attack, registering gains of 2,000 to 3,000 yards against moderate enemy resistance. Several enemy attacks in the Inje area were repulsed during the morning with the enemy breaking contact at 8:30 A.M.. A R.O.K. patrol in the Yongdae area discovered an enemy supply dump containing enemy blankets and shoes.

—Eighth Army communiqué 402, issued at 9:00 A.M., Friday (7:00 P.M., Thursday, Eastern Daylight Time):

R.O.K. (Republic of Korea) patrols cross Imjin River. Moderate enemy resistance reported in Yonchon area. Heavy enemy resistance encountered north of Yongpyong. Light to moderate enemy resistance encountered northeast of Yongpyong and north of Yonggong. Stubborn enemy resistance reported in the Yanggu area and in the Inje area. An estimated 600 enemy attacked United Nations forces east-southeast of Inje, causing friendly forces to make limited withdrawals.

1. Light enemy contact was reported by R.O.K. patrols west of the Imjin River. Moderate enemy resistance was encountered in the Yonchon area as friendly forces patrolled and adjusted positions. Heavy enemy resistance was encountered by leading army elements which had crossed the Hantan River in the area north of Yongpyong.

2. Light to moderate enemy resistance was reported by United Nations forces in the area northeast of Yongpyong and north of Yonggong. A probing attack by an estimated enemy battalion northeast of Yonggong at 1130 hours (11:30 A.M. Thursday) was dispersed with aid of artillery fire at 1415 hours. No significant enemy contact was reported in the Hwachon area as friendly forces continued to engage small enemy groups during the day.

3. Light enemy resistance was encountered by United Nations forces as they secured the ground north of the Hwachon Reservoir. Stubborn enemy resistance was encountered as friendly forces advanced 2,000 to 3,000 yards in the Yanggu sector. Friendly elements reported receiving a heavy volume of mortar and artillery fire during the day.

Enemy in regimental strength continued to resist stubbornly in the Inje area. A slight penetration northeast of Inje at 530 hours was contained and eliminated at 0715 hours. An estimated 600 enemy continued to engage friendly elements east-southeast of Inje and forced friendly forces to make a limited withdrawal. An estimated 300 enemy launched a determined attack in the area north of Hyon, causing friendly elements to withdraw under heavy enemy pressure. Friendly forces withdrew approximately 1,500 yards to establish a new defensive line. Stubborn enemy resistance continued in the area north-northeast of Inje, continuing to limit the advance of friendly forces in this area.

4. Light enemy contact was reported on the remainder of the eastern front.

—General Headquarters communiqué 901, issued at 10:45 A.M., Friday (8:45 P.M., Thursday, Eastern Daylight Time):

Action in Korea yesterday centered in the east-central sector, where elements of United Nations ground forces repulsed several strong counter-attacks while others made advances up to three miles. In the western sector, friendly patrols encountered light to heavy resistance from enemy units of platoon to regimental size.

Along the west-central front United Nations combat patrols engaged in sharp fights with several scattered enemy groups. In the eastern sector friendly units continued to advance against minor resistance.

Land-based aircraft continued attacks on enemy troop positions and battle areas. In a jet encounter, Sabre jets destroyed two enemy MiG-15 aircraft and damaged one over northwest Korea yesterday. Medium bombers carried out attacks on key railroad bridges in the Chongju and Hulchon areas.

Naval surface units bombarded enemy gun positions, troop concentrations and transportation targets along the east coast in the Songjin-Wonsan-Jansong areas. Carrier-based aircraft assisted surface elements during the bombardment phase and followed with attacks on troop positions and supply facilities in the Hwachon and Chinnampo areas.

†CHARLTON, CORNELIUS H.

Rank and Organization: Sergeant, U.S. Army, Company C, 24th Infantry Regiment, 25th Infantry Division.
Born: July 24, 1929, East Gulf, West Virginia.
Entered Service At: Bronx, New York.
Place and Date: Near Chipo-ri, Korea, June 2, 1951.
Citation: Sgt. Charlton, a member of Company C, distinguished himself by conspicuous gallantry and intrepidity above and beyond the call of duty in action against the enemy. His platoon was attacking heavily defended hostile positions on commanding ground when the leader was wounded and evacuated. Sgt. Charlton assumed command, rallied the men, and spearheaded the assault against the hill. Personally eliminating 2 hostile positions and killing 6 of the enemy with his rifle fire and grenades, he continued up the slope until the unit suffered heavy casualties and became pinned down. Regrouping the men he led them forward only to be again hurled back by a shower of grenades. Despite a severe chest wound, Sgt. Charlton refused medical attention and led a third daring charge which carried to the crest of the ridge. Observing that the remaining emplacement which had retarded the advance was situated on the reverse slope, he charged it alone, was again hit by a grenade but raked the position with a devastating fire which eliminated it and routed the defenders. The wounds received during his daring exploits resulted in his death but his indomitable courage, superb leadership, and gallant self-sacrifice reflects the highest credit upon himself, the infantry, and the military service.

OFFICIAL COMMUNIQUÉ:
TOKYO, Sunday, June 3 (AP)
—Far East Air Forces summary 343, covering operations Friday:

Far East Air Forces continued to throttle enemy supply channels as heavy Communist counter-air operations were smashed for the second consecutive day when Fifth Air Force F-86 Sabre jet pilots and a Bomber Command B-29 Superfort gunner destroyed three MiG-15 jet fighters and damaged two more.

Striking successfully at an important rail bridge on the Sinanju-Sinuiju Railroad, a formation of four B-29s of the Ninety-Eighth Bomb Wing, flying from Japan, were attacked by a swarm of at least twenty-five MiGs.

Escorting Sabre jets, of the Fourth Fighter Interceptor Wing, drove off the enemy, downing two, with no loss to themselves. Two of the B-29s were damaged in the running air battle but landed safely at friendly airfields.

Three MiGs attacked four Sabre jets earlier in the day near Namsidong and two of the Red fighter planes were damaged in the engagement.

Two other formations of Bomber Command Superforts, flying from Japan and Okinawa bases, visually bombed key railroad bridges with excellent results, crew members reporting many direct hits. Over 160 tons of high explosives were dropped on the two bridges. No flak or fighters were encountered.

Over 1,000 sorties were flown in generally good weather during the day by F.E.A.F. aircraft as strongly effective operations throughout enemy territory in Korea were carried out.

Fifth Air Force and attached South African, R.O.K. (Republic of Korea), and Marine shore-based aircraft kept up their persistent attacks on Communist military installations, material storage points, rolling stock, and supply routes. More than 800 sorties were flown in these operations, with more than 200 being in direct support of United Nations ground forces. Three friendly fighters were lost, all to ground fire.

B-26 Invaders of the 452nd Light Bomb Group destroyed four locomotives and damaged two in an attack on the marshaling yards near Pyongyang.

Pilots and gunners of Fifth Air Force aircraft confirmed approximately 550 casualties were inflicted on enemy troops. More than 450 enemy-held buildings, twenty-five pack animals, fifteen gun positions, four warehouses, 120 supply carts, six locomotives, sixty railroad cars, and 130 miscellaneous vehicles were reported destroyed or damaged. A fuel dump was destroyed and a tunnel and an electrical sub-station were seriously damaged.

Tactical aircraft flew eighty sorties during the night. The greatest number of vehicles destroyed during night operations was reported when 110 were permanently put out of action by Fifth Air Force war planes. Heavy damage was inflicted on about forty others. Six towns near Wonsan, known to be enemy supply centers were also heavily attacked during the night.

B-26s and four night-flying B-29 Superforts struck at enemy troop concentrations in the battle zone in a continuation of these highly successful attacks which employ a radar technique to bomb immediately ahead of friendly forces.

Three Hundred Fifteenth Air Division (Combat Cargo) C-119 flying boxcars and C-46 Commandos teamed up to air-drop supplies to ground units, while other combat cargo aircraft delivered 1,056 tons of material from Japan to United Nations forces in Korea during 204 sorties.

—United Nations Naval Forces summary of June 2 operations:

United Nations Naval air operations were intensified yesterday as strikes were launched from the Essex-class carriers U.S.S. Princeton, U.S.S. Boxer, and U.S.S. Bon Homme Richard.

Fast Carrier Task Force 77 Skyraiders, Corsairs and Panthers cut Communist transportation lines during bridge strikes deep in North Korea. Nine bridges were wrecked or heavily damaged prior to noon yesterday. Most of the bridges were in the Communist rail line between Hamhung and Wonsan.

Enemy front-line troops and gun positions were blasted by carrier pilots in the eastern sector. On the east coast between Kosong and Kansong the Navy fliers attacked an estimated 150 troops and artillery positions causing many casualties and much damage. North of Inje, twenty-five Red soldiers were killed and two heavy mortars destroyed. Navy fighter-bombers scored heavy damage during strafing runs on ten gun positions northeast of Inje.

Eight-inch gunfire from the heavy cruiser Los Angeles rained on Communist troop concentrations northeast and east of Kosong early yesterday. The destroyer Rush shelled warehouses, roads, and bridges in the same area. Two battalion-size enemy troop concentrations were taken under fire by the two ships.

Destroyers Kennedy, Fechteler, and Hawkins continued the bombardment of Wonsan now in its fifteenth consecutive week. Accurate gunfire from the Kennedy battered an enemy gun position with eight direct hits. The destroyer then put three out of ten rounds of 5-inch ammo in caves concealing shore batteries on Kalma peninsula.

Displaying similar accuracy, the Hawkins and Fechteler bombarded troops, supply buildings, and harassed roads in the area.

The destroyer Fiske and destroyer-minesweeper Thompson ranged from Songjin north to Chongjin bombarding bridges and other transportation targets. Patrol frigates Burlington and Everett concentrated gunfire on bridges in the Sonjin area.

—Eighth Army communiqué 405, issued at 7:00 P.M., Saturday (5:00 A.M., Saturday, Eastern Daylight Time):

Light enemy resistance reported in Imjin River area as United Nation forces adjust positions and patrol. Light to moderate resistance reported in the Hwachon and Inje areas as United Nations forces continue their attack. Enemy shells Hwachon during early morning. Two enemy concentrations reported north of Inje.

1. United Nations forces in the Imjin River area continued to adjust positions and patrol aggressively throughout the day. Patrols encountered platoon to company-sized enemy forces east as well as west of the Imjin River. An attack by an estimated 150 enemy at 5:435 A.M. was repulsed shortly thereafter.

2. Attacking United Nations forces in Hwachon Reservoir area encountered light to moderate enemy resistance during the day. Advances of 3,000 yards were registered on some sectors of the front. A total of 120 rounds of enemy artillery fire fell in the city of Hwachon between 2:00 A.M. and 3:00 A.M.. Enemy resistance in the Hwachon area was limited to platoon and company-sized engagements.

3. Light to moderate enemy resistance was also reported in the Inje area as United Nations forces continued their attack. Air observation reported two large enemy concentrations in the area which were taken under air attack.

—Eighth Army communiqué 406, issued at 9:00 A.M., Sunday (7:00 P.M., Saturday, Eastern Daylight Time):

United Nations forces encountered heavy enemy resistance north of Imjin River. Small scattered enemy groups were encountered in Yonchon area. Enemy battalion launched series of probing attacks north and northeast of Yonong. Stubborn resistance reported in the area west of Hwachon, and at Hwachon and Yanggu.

1. United Nations forces encountered heavy enemy resistance as they launched attacks west and north of the Imjin River.

Stubborn resistance was reported in the area by numerous company-size enemy elements while light enemy resistance was reported by patrols searching the area west of the Munsan.

Enemy resistance decreased in the Yonchon area as friendly forces continued to engage small scattered enemy groups during the day.

Light enemy resistance was encountered by United Nations forces north of the Hantan River bridge-head in the area north of Yongpyong. Elements of an estimated enemy battalion launched a series of probing attacks against United Nations forces north and north-northwest of Yongong at 2230 hours (10:30 P.M., Saturday) with the enemy withdrawing at 0110 hours this morning.

2. Initially light enemy resistance became stubborn during the day as the enemy reinforces his strength to an estimated 1,000 in the area north-northeast of Yongong.

Friendly elements with the aid of artillery fire succeeded in dispersing the enemy to the north at 1830 hours. At 2100 hours the enemy in battalion strength launched a counter-attack with the action continuing until 0010 hours at which time the action had subsided to sporadic small arms fire.

Enemy in up to battalion-size units continued to offer stubborn delaying action in the area west of Hwachon during the day.

Stubborn delaying action in the Hwachon area limited friendly gains to 1,000 to 3,000 yards during the day.

3. No significant enemy action was reported by United Nations forces in the area north-northeast and northeast of Hwachon.

Enemy resistance in the Yanggu area varied from moderate to heavy as friendly elements continued their attacks registering limited gains during the day.

Enemy resistance in the Inje area continued as moderate with friendly forces making limited gains during the day.

—General Headquarters communiqué 903, covering developments of June 2:

United Nations forces made gains of up to two miles along the central Korean front Saturday despite stubborn resistance from enemy elements defending from well dug-in positions supported by artillery and mortar fire. In the western sector, R.O.K. (Republic of Korea) units engaged several company-sized groups, forcing the enemy to withdraw. Two enemy attacks against friendly elements in the area south-east of Chorwon were repulsed. Along the eastern sector, United Nations elements continued their advances against negligible resistance.

Land-based aircraft rendered close and deep support of ground elements, striking troop concentrations and positions along the front and supply and communications facilities in North Korea.

Carrier aircraft intensified their attacks against communication targets in northeastern Korea, hitting bridges along the Hamhung-Wonsan rail line while other naval aircraft attacked troop positions along the eastern battlefront. Surface units fired on troop concentrations in the Kosong area and enemy gun positions and storage facilities in the vicinity of Wonsan.

WILSON, BENJAMIN F.
Rank and Organization: First Lieutenant (then M/Sgt.), U.S. Army, Company I, 31st Infantry Regiment, 7th Infantry Division.
Born: Vashon, Washington.
Entered Service At: Vashon, Washington.
Place and Date: Near Hwach'on-Myon, Korea, June 5, 1951.
Citation: 1st Lt. Wilson distinguished himself by conspicuous gallantry and intrepidity above and beyond the call of duty in action against the enemy. Company I was committed to attack and secure commanding terrain stubbornly defended by a numerically superior hostile force emplaced in well-fortified positions. When the spearheading element was pinned down by withering hostile fire, he dashed forward and, firing his rifle and throwing grenades, neutral-

ized the position denying the advance and killed 4 enemy soldiers manning sub-machine guns. After the assault platoon moved up, occupied the position, and a base of fire was established, he led a bayonet attack which reduced the objective and killed approximately 27 hostile soldiers. While friendly forces were consolidating the newly won gain, the enemy launched a counterattack and 1st Lt. Wilson, realizing the imminent threat of being overrun, made a determined lone-man charge, killing 7 and wounding 2 of the enemy, and routing the remainder in disorder. After the position was organized, he led an assault carrying to approximately 15 yards of the final objective, when enemy fire halted the advance. He ordered the platoon to withdraw and, although painfully wounded in this action, remained to provide covering fire. During an ensuing counterattack, the commanding officer and 1st Platoon leader became casualties. Unhesitatingly, 1st Lt. Wilson charged the enemy ranks and fought valiantly, killing 3 enemy soldiers with his rifle before it was wrested from his hands, and annihilating 4 others with his entrenching tool. His courageous delaying action enabled his comrades to reorganize and effect an orderly withdrawal. While directing evacuation of the wounded, he suffered a second wound, but elected to remain in the position until assured that all of the men had reached safety. 1st Lt. Wilson's sustained valor and intrepid actions reflect utmost credit upon himself and uphold the honored traditions of the military service.

OFFICIAL COMMUNIQUÉ:
TOKYO, Wednesday, June 6 (AP)
—Far East Air Forces summary 346, issued at 11:15 A.M., Tuesday (9:15 P.M., Eastern Daylight Time, Monday):

Far East Air Forces warplanes yesterday mounted more than 600 sorties in the face of continued poor weather to strike at Communist supply routes, highway and rail traffic, and build-up points in rear areas.

B-29 Superforts of F.E.A.F.'s Bomber Command flew through multi-layer clouds to radar-drop eighty tons of 2,000 pound demolition bombs on an important Communist supply center at Yonghung. The Ninety-eighth Bomb Group Superforts, flying from Japan bases were not attacked by enemy fighters and did not encounter flak as they bombed the material point, midway between Wonsan and Hungnam on the east coast rail line.

More than 380 sorties were flown by Fifth Air Force and attached South African and Marine shore-based aircraft. The Fifth's light bombers and fighter-bombers maintained their attacks on Red build-up centers in the enemy's rear and struck at main transportation arteries with napalm (fire bombs), bombs, and .80 caliber machine guns. Several close-support sorties were flown as weather permitted.

More than 150 Communist-held buildings were damaged or destroyed along with approximately sixty vehicles, twenty oil drums, two fuel dumps, twenty-two railroad cars, two ammo dumps, five gun positions, two supply stacks, and two bridges. One tunnel was believed closed. One F-51 Mustang fighter plane was lost due to enemy ground fire. The pilot was recovered in friendly territory.

During the night, five B-29 Superforts ranged along the battle zone, using radar bombing techniques, to attack enemy troops concentrations with air bursting bombs.

In a pre-dawn attack, B-26 invaders of the Third Bomb Wing, caught and destroyed a train west of Sinmak. Following up the attack, a formation of Marine fighter-bombers destroyed ten oars of the same train and confirmed the initial destruction of it by the B-26s.

B-26s also attacked two airfields at Pyonggang and Onjin and destroyed or damaged approximately twenty vehicles in spite of limited visibility and very low ceilings.

Transports of the 315th Air Division (Combat Cargo) delivered 950 tons of supplies and equipment to United Nations forces in the battle area, flying over 200 sorties.

—Far East Naval Headquarters summary covering Tuesday's operations:

United States and Royal Navy pilots continued interdiction strikes at enemy supply lines and troop concentrations in over 230 sorties flown yesterday. Navy aerial bombardment accounted for an estimated 280 Communist casualties in the central and western sectors.

The H.M.S. Glory's Sea Furies and Fireflies struck hard at Red installations ranging from Chinnampo to north of Kaesong. Royal Navy pilots destroyed or damaged twenty-three troop-occupied buildings, fifteen oxcarts, gun positions, a railroad bridge, and an ammunition dump. The Glory's pilots caused 185 casualties.

U.S.S. Princeton and U.S.S. Bon Homme Richard aircraft launched from Task Force 77 killed seventy-five Communist infantrymen south of Chorwon yesterday. Other strikes battered six bridges in the rail line between Wonsan and Hamhung.

Gun positions in the Kosong area were knocked out by the carrier-based planes. Supply dumps, vehicles, tanks, and a locomotive were among the enemy targets destroyed or damaged.

The United States Navy bombarding group at Wonsan continued shelling enemy gun emplacements, troops, and vehicles. Before dawn, the destroyers illuminated targets for air force night intruder bombing runs.

Blockade and bombarding patrols also continued to the north. The destroyer Fiske concentrated on bridges south of Songjin, scoring several direct hits The destroyer-minesweeper Thompson shelled transportation targets near Nanam and at Songjin. Nine junks, a gun emplacement, and a bridge were hit by the frigate Everett south of Songjin.

—Eighth Army communiqué 411, issued at 7:00 P.M., Tuesday (5:00 A.M., Tuesday, Eastern Daylight Time):

Light to moderate enemy contact reported north of the Imjin River. Enemy resistance decreased in the Yonchon and Yongpyong areas. Heavy enemy resistance continues in the Hwachon area. Light to heavy enemy contact encountered in the Yanggu and Inje sector.

1. Light enemy contact was reported by United Nations troops patrolling west and north of the Imjin River. In the area east of Korangpo other United Nations forces encountered heavy small-arms and automatic-weapons fire as friendly elements crossed to the north bank of the Imjin River. Enemy contact in the Yonchon area decreased as Eighth Army forces registered gains of 2,000 to 3,000 yards.

2. Initial heavy resistance in the area north and northeast of Yongpyong decreased at 10:20 A.M. as enemy forces staged a limited withdrawal allowing friendly forces to advance against light scattered enemy resistance. Light to moderate enemy resistance continued in the area north northwest of Hwachon with action continuing as of 1:00 P.M.. Heavy enemy resistance was also reported in the area north of Hwachon where an estimated enemy regiment limited friendly gains to 500 yards.

3. Eighth Army forces advancing 1,500 yards in the area northeast of Yanggu engaged an undetermined number of enemy during the morning hours. The enemy was dispersed to the north, with friendly forces continuing to receive sporadic small-arms and automatic-weapons fire. Other Eighth Army units north of Inje reported being heavily engaged during the day with the action continuing as of 1:00 P.M.. A well-entrenched enemy regiment was observed in the area north-northeast of Yanggu.

An enemy battalion offered heavy resistance to friendly forces in the area north of Hangye.

4. Two enemy companies were encountered in the area west-southwest of Kansong. An enemy company attacking friendly troops in this area secured a penetration at 11:45 A.M.. However, friendly forces counter-attacked, repulsing the enemy at 12:30 P.M..

—Eighth Army communiqué 412, issued at 9:45 A.M., Wednesday (7:45 P.M., Eastern Daylight Time, Tuesday):

A slight decrease in enemy resistance was reported in the Yonchon and Yongpyong areas as enemy forces staged a limited withdrawal with company sized elements continuing to fight a rear-guard action. Heavy enemy resistance continued in the Hwachon area and west-northwest of Hwachon. Moderate to heavy resistance was encountered in the Inje area with three enemy counter-attacks in the area west-southwest of Kansong.

1. United Nations forces patrolling west and north of the Imjin River encountered platoon to company-size enemy units during the day. Friendly forces in the area east of Korangpo crossed the Imjin River and were engaged by a heavy volume of enemy fire from an estimated two enemy companies causing friendly forces to withdraw.

Meanwhile, in the Yonchon area friendly forces encountered light to moderate resistance and repulsed a counter-attack by an estimated enemy company. Enemy forces were reported to have initiated a limited withdrawal during the evening hours. Enemy resistance in the area north of Yongpyong decreased to light as enemy platoon to company-size units continued to fight a rear guard action while enemy in battalion size staged a limited withdrawal to the north.

2. Eighth Army forces in the area west-northwest of Hwachon encountered light to moderate enemy resistance during the day and reported an estimated two enemy regiments dug in forward of their position. In the Hwachon area another two enemy regiments astride the Hwachon-Kumhwa road continued to offer heavy stubborn resistance during the day, initiating a limited withdrawal to what is believed to be more favorable defensive positions immediately to the north.

3. Light enemy resistance from an undetermined number of enemy was encountered in the Yanggu sector as friendly forces advanced 1,500 yards dispersing the enemy. Heavy enemy resistance was reported in the area north and north-northwest of Inje as Eighth Army forces engaged elements of an estimated enemy regiment with action continuing throughout the day. Friendly forces registered limited advances in this area throughout the period.

4. Enemy units of company size launched a series of three counter-attacks in the area west-south-west of Kansong during the day all of which were repulsed by Eighth Army forces with sporadic enemy fire continuing in the area.

—General Headquarters communiqué 906 issued at 11:15 A.M. Wednesday (9:15 P.M., Eastern Daylight Time, Tuesday):

United Nations ground units supported by artillery fire and air strikes, continued to move forward in Korea yesterday as the enemy fought to halt the advance from well organized defensive positions. In the rugged mountainous terrain on the east-central front United Nations units made only minor gains against increasing enemy resistance.

Carrier-based aircraft inflicted heavy damage on enemy troop concentrations, gun positions, vehicles, and supply dumps in the central sector and along both coasts. Surface elements attacked troops positions, bridges, and supply points along the east coast.

Despite poor weather, land-based fighter aircraft continued support of United Nations ground units by inflicting severe damage on enemy installations in the battle area. Medium bombers attacked enemy supply points along the west coast. Cargo aircraft continued air supply of friendly ground units.

†HANSON, JACK G.

Rank and Organization: Private First Class, U.S. Army, Company F, 31st Infantry Regiment.
Born: September 18, 1930, Escaptawpa, Mississippi.
Entered Service At: Galveston, Texas.
Place and Date: Near Pachi-dong, Korea, June 7, 1951.
Citation: Pfc. Hanson, a machine gunner with the 1st Platoon, Company F, distinguished himself by conspicuous gallantry and intrepidity at the risk of his life above and beyond the call of duty in action against an armed enemy of the United Nations. The company, in defensive positions on two strategic hills separated by a wide saddle, was ruthlessly attacked at approximately 0300 hours, the brunt of which centered on the approach to the divide within range of Pfc. Hanson's machine gun. In the initial phase of the action, 4 riflemen were wounded and evacuated and the numerically superior enemy, advancing under cover of darkness, infiltrated and posed an imminent threat to the security of the command post and weapons platoon. Upon orders to move to key terrain above and to the right of Pfc. Hanson's position, he voluntarily remained to provide protective fire for the withdrawal. Subsequent to the retiring elements fighting a rear-guard action to the new location, it was learned that Pfc. Hanson's assistant gunner and 3 riflemen had been wounded and had crawled to safety, and that he was maintaining a lone-man defense. After the 1st Platoon reorganized, counterattacked, and resecured its original positions at approximately 0530 hours, Pfc. Hanson's body was found lying in front of his emplacement, his machine gun ammunition expended, his empty pistol in his right hand, and a machete with blood on the blade in his left hand, and approximately 22 enemy dead lay in the wake of his action. Pfc. Hanson's consummate valor, inspirational conduct, and willing self-sacrifice enabled the company to contain the enemy and regain the commanding ground, and reflects lasting glory on himself and the noble traditions of the military service.

OFFICIAL COMMUNIQUÉ:
TOKYO, Friday, June 8 (AP)
—Far East Air Forces' summary of June 7 operations:

Bridges and marshaling yards on Western Korea routes were heavily and successfully attacked Wednesday as Far East Air Forces warplanes destroyed facilities for the movement of supplies to the Communist defenses in the Pyonggang-Chorwon-Kumhwa triangle.

F.E.A.F. planes hit their targets in high level and low level attacks and inflicted considerable damage to rolling stock as well as cutting railroad tracks and highways with bomb craters. Fighter-bombers flew in close support of friendly infantry and inflicted over 500 casualties on the enemy.

Approximately 970 sorties were flown by F.E.A.F.

Of these almost 700 were mounted by Fifth Air Force and attached South African and shore-based Marine planes.

B-26 light bombers hit railroad bridges near Chongju, Sunchon, and Pyongyang while fighter-bombers made successful strikes at bridges near Sukchon and Sonchon. Marshaling yards were attacked near Namchonjom, Kumchon, and other places.

Fifth Air Force and attached pilots reported destroying or damaging four locomotives, seventy-five railroad cars, ninety motor vehicles, seven bridges, one ferry boat, and cutting highways or railroads in about fifty places. More than 600 enemy-held buildings were hit, thirty-three pack animals were destroyed, seven gun positions were knocked out, a tank was damaged, and fifteen supply dumps fired.

One enemy MiG-15 detached from a flight of five to make a firing pass at two F-80s in northwest Korea. No damage was reported.

Thirteen Bomber Command Superforts attacked a marshaling yard at Chinnampo on the West coast and supply storage at Hamhung on the East coast. More than 100 tons of bombs were dropped.

Excellent results were observed at Chinnampo where clear skies made visual bombing possible. At Hamhung the target was bombed by radar through a heavy undercast and results were not observed.

Last night Superforts, light bombers, and marine planes teamed up to drop more than 300 air-bursting 500-pound bombs by radar techniques on enemy troops and other military targets in the enemy's defensive area.

Other light bombers and marine aircraft ranged over enemy rear areas attacking heavy vehicular traffic and bombing four enemy airfields. They were aided by flare-dropping aircraft.

The 315th Air Division (Combat Cargo) flew almost 250 sorties to deliver more than 1,100 tons of combat supplies from Japan to Korean airheads.

—United Nations Naval Forces summary of June 7 operations:

United Nations naval bombardment of Communist installations continued yesterday. Royal Navy ships and aircraft operating off the west coast of Korea pounded enemy troops, junks, supply routes, and artillery positions.

Sea Furies and Fireflies launched from H.M.S. Glory sank four junks and damaged others off Hanchon. Sweeping south to Chinampo, British pilots destroyed or damaged four artillery pieces, an anti-aircraft battery, and a tractor.

South of the city, Royal Navy bombs destroyed a supply dump and eight buildings and severely damaged a bridge.

H.M.S. Ceylon and H.M.S. Cossack shelled troops concentrated near Changyon west of Jaeju on the Changsan Peninsula. Air spotters said coverage was excellent with many fires started. Before dark yesterday, an estimated 200 enemy opened fire on the cruiser Ceylon. The British ship returned fire, pouring 130 6-inch shells at the group southwest of Ullyul. Many enemy casualties were suffered as the Red force was dispersed.

Bombardment of Wonsan's highway system and military supply points continued as the siege entered its sixteenth week.

The destroyers Kennedy, Hawkins, and Fechteler hit troops, trucks, supply buildings, and road junctions. Shore batteries on Kalma and Hodo Peninsulas continued to receive naval gunfire.

The destroyer U.S.S. Rupertus and the Colombian frigate Almirate Padilla shelled bridges, warehouses, shore batteries, and highways in the Songjin area.

Rail and highway bridges were fired at by the destroyer-minesweeper Thompson in the same area.

Minesweeping operations continued as the Redstart, Heron, and Waxbill operated between Wonsan and Kosang. With the Wonsan bombardment group were the minesweepers Curlew, Gull, and Mockingbird.

Delayed reports indicated that the U.S.S. New Jersey rained 16-inch shells on troop-occupied villages and buildings northwest of Changjon Wednesday, June 6. Changjon is about ten miles up the east coast from Kosong.

Using aerial spotters, the battlewagon destroyed at least seven buildings and leveled other areas.

—Eighth Army communiqué 415, issued at 7:00 P.M., Thursday (5:00 A.M., Thursday, Eastern Daylight Time):

Slight decrease of enemy resistance was reported on central front with heavy stubborn resistance continuing in Hwachon and Inje areas. Increase in mortar and artillery fire noted during the day. Eighth Army forces continued to attack, registering limited gains during morning hours.

1. Little or no enemy contact was reported in the Munsan-Korangpo areas as Eighth Army forces continued to conduct reconnaissance in areas north and west of Imjin River. Friendly forces patrolling in the area west of Yonchon encountered small groups of enemy during the morning hours. Eighth Army forces in the Yonchon area advanced 1,000 to 2,000 yards against light enemy contact but re-

ported receiving mortar and artillery fire during the advance. Light enemy contact also was reported in the Yongpong sector as friendly elements advanced 2,000 yards during the morning hours. Friendly forces reported receiving heavy artillery at 9:10 A.M.. Light enemy contact was reported in the area north of Yongong while in the area north-northeast of Yongong friendly forces engaged an estimated enemy battalion. Action resulted in 115 killed, twenty prisoners, and considerable enemy equipment captured.

2. Heavy enemy resistance continued in Hwachon area as battalion-sized enemy units clung stubbornly to defensive positions and launched platoon and company-sized counter-attacks against Eighth Army forces.

3. Heavy enemy resistance again was encountered in the area north and north-northwest in Inje, limiting friendly advances during the day.

4. North-northwest of Hangye, Eighth Army forces were engaged with an estimated 600 enemy offering stubborn resistance to friendly forces attempting to secure high ground in that area. Platoon to company-sized enemy units were reported in the area southwest and north-northwest of Kansong.

—Eighth Army communiqué 416, issued at 10:00 A.M., Friday (8:00 P.M., Thursday, Eastern Daylight Time):

Eighth Army forces continued their attack against light to heavy enemy resistance with stubborn enemy resistance continuing in the Yonchon and the Yanggu-Inje areas. Gains of from 1,000 to 4,000 yards were registered against enemy delaying action.

1. Little or no enemy contact was reported by Eighth Army troops patrolling in the area north and west of the Imjin River. Friendly elements in the Yonchon area advanced 1,000 to 2,000 yards against moderate to heavy enemy resistance as well as some enemy artillery fire. Eighth Army forces in the Yongpyong area reported light to moderate enemy resistance as friendly forces made advances of 1,000 to 4,000 yards during the day. Little or no enemy resistance was experienced in the area north of Yongong.

2. Eighth Army forces in the area north-northeast of Yongong engaged an undetermined number of enemy which resulted in 113 enemy killed, twenty prisoners of war, and some enemy equipment being captured.

3. Friendly forces continued their attack in the area north of Hwachon against an estimated enemy battalion, while other Eighth Army forces in the area north-northwest and northwest of Hwachon reported light enemy resistance during the day. Heavy enemy resistance continued in the area northeast of Yanggu and north of Inje as friendly forces continued to attack.

4. Light enemy resistance was reported by Eighth Army forces on the remainder of the eastern front.

—General Headquarters communiqué 908, for the twenty-four hours ended 6:00 A.M., Friday (4:00 P.M., Thursday, Eastern Daylight Time):

United Nations forces registered gains of up to two miles along the western Korean battlefront Thursday despite stubborn resistance from enemy delaying forces fighting from a series of prepared defensive positions supported by artillery and mortar fire. In the eastern sector several enemy counter-attacks were successfully repulsed.

Land-based fighter and light bomber aircraft continued support of United Nations ground elements by striking enemy positions along the battle line and attacking rear area communications and supply targets. Medium and light bombers made night attacks against enemy troop concentrations in central Korea.

Naval surface units continued their bombardment of enemy installations along both coasts of Korea as carrier-based aircraft struck enemy shipping along the west coast and troop concentrations and gun positions in the area south of Chinnampo.

†ABRELL, CHARLES G.

Rank and Organization: Corporal, U.S. Marine Corps, Company E, 2d Battalion, 1st Marines, 1st Marine Division (Rein).
Born: August 12, 1931, Terre Haute, Indiana.
Entered Service At: Terre Haute, Indiana.
Place and Date: Hangnyong, Korea, June 10, 1951.
Citation: For conspicuous gallantry and intrepidity at the risk of his life above and beyond the call of duty while serving as a fire team leader in Company E, in action against enemy aggressor forces. While advancing with his platoon in an attack against well-concealed and heavily fortified enemy hill positions, Cpl. Abrell voluntarily rushed forward through the assaulting squad which was pinned down by a hail of intense and accurate automatic-weapons fire from a hostile bunker situated on commanding ground. Although previously wounded by enemy hand-grenade fragments, he proceeded to carry out a bold, singlehanded attack against the bunker, exhorting his comrades to follow him. Sustaining two additional wounds as he stormed toward the emplacement, he resolutely pulled the pin from a grenade clutched in his hand and hurled himself bodily into the bunker with the live missile still in his grasp. Fatally wounded in the resulting explosion which killed the entire enemy gun crew within the stronghold, Cpl. Abrell, by his valiant spirit of self-sacrifice in the face of certain death, served to inspire all of his comrades and contributed directly to the success of his platoon in obtaining its objective. His superb courage and heroic initiative sustain and enhance the highest traditions of the U.S. Naval Service. He gallantly gave his life for his country.

OFFICIAL COMMUNIQUÉ:
TOKYO, Monday, June 11 (AP)
—Far East Air Forces operation summary for Saturday:

Destruction of enemy means of supplying his defensively deployed troops in the "Iron Triangle" of central Korea was continued relentlessly Saturday by Far East Air Forces warplanes which mounted 850 sorties in variable weather.

F-80 Shooting Star jets successfully attacked a bridge near Sukchon while F-84 Thunderjets struck a supply center in the Sonchon area northeast of Pyongyang.

B-26 light bombers attacked enemy barracks areas at Kyomipo and Chaeryong and a marshaling yard at Sinmak.

Southern bank of the Yalu River was patrolled by F-86 Sabre jets.

Four enemy MiG-15 jet fighters were sighted but they refused combat.

Continued support was given friendly ground forces in their advance toward the enemy's defense positions. Dug-in Communists and their gun positions were struck by both jets and propeller-driven F-51 Mustangs. Nature of the enemy positions caused pilots to report many unobserved results, but machine-gun fire, napalm bombs, rockets, and explosive bombs were seen to hit designated targets repeatedly.

Fifth Air Force and attached South African and shore-based Marine planes reported destroying or damaging 700 enemy-held buildings, eighty motor vehicles, sixty-five railroad cars, one locomotive, and a dozen pack animals.

Eight gun positions were neutralized, six bridges were successfully attacked, and five tunnel entrances were damaged. Supply and fuel dumps were burned out.

One F-51 Mustang was lost to enemy ground fire.

Last night F.E.A.F. planes continued to hit the enemy. Five Bomber Command Superforts from Okinawa attacked enemy troop and supply concentrations in the Kumhwa-Chorwon-Pyonggang triangle with approximately 200 deadly air-bursting 500-pound bombs aimed by radar techniques.

Combat Cargo planes of the 315th Air Division maintained a steady airborne stream of combat supplies from Japan to Korea, landing ammunition, rations, and fuel at advanced airbases and making one airdrop to forward friendly forces.

—Far East Air Forces operational summary for Sunday:

Seventy-two F-84 Thunderjets delivered a massive assault on enemy supply storage, transportation facilities, and gun positions in the Sonchon area northeast of Pyongyang yesterday as Far East Air Forces warplanes mounted 900 sorties in cloudy Korean skies and through frequent rain showers.

Pilots of the Fifth Air Force jets saw their bombs, napalm (fire-bomb) tanks, machine-gun fire, and rockets strike warehouses, enemy-held supply buildings, barracks, box cars, gun positions, and other military targets with destructive effect. The area under attack includes junction points of the western Korea rail and highway routes with those which lead across the isthmus to the east coast. Pilots observed secondary explosions and as they left the area barracks buildings were ablaze.

Meantime, other F.E.A.F. planes were fanning out over western Korea in interdiction attacks from low level, while all-weather Okinawa-based Superforts struck from high altitudes and fighter bombers ranged the battle zone in close support of United Nations infantry.

F-51 Mustangs attacked the road-net leading from Pyongyang to Sibyong at the western gateway to the Communist so-called "Iron Triangle." They destroyed a bridge and cut highways and railroad tracks in thirty places to retard the movement of supplies to enemy troops, defensively deployed.

Fifth Air Force and attached South African and shore-based Marine aircraft flew 620 sorties, of which eighty-five were in close support of ground forces. Many more were flown against targets in the immediate rear of enemy lines.

Pilots also reported destroying or damaging 400 enemy-held buildings, ten dumps of supplies, forty box cars, ninety vehicles, one locomotive, one tank, fifteen gun positions, forty pack animals, and seven ferryboats.

Bomber Command Superforts struck the marshaling yard at Sariwon on the main railroad line south from Pyongyang, a supply center at Haeju, and a rail bridge near Pyongyang. Thirteen medium bombers participated and they aimed their high explosives through a thick undercast by means of radar.

Last night F.E.A.F. put about ninety sorties of bombers, reconnaissance aircraft, and flare-dropping planes into the air. Two B-29s and fourteen B-26s attacked enemy troop concentrations and other military targets with air-bursting bombs aided by radar. The attacks were delivered across the battlefront.

Moderately heavy enemy vehicular traffic was sighted on routes behind enemy lines and was placed under attack. One train was sighted near Kumchon, attacked and heavily damaged.

Eight enemy-held airfields were bombed. They were Pyongyang Downtown, Pyongyang East, Sinanju, Onjong, Sunan, Sariwon, Pyonggang, and Ogyo.

More than 900 tons of a wide variety of supplies were flown into Korea from Japan by 250 sorties of transport-cargo planes of the 315th Air Division (Combat Cargo). The bulk of the tonnage was ammunition, rations, and fuel to forward airbases.

—Summary of Naval operations for Sunday:

Heavy cruisers and destroyers continued plastering Communist east coast highways and railroads yesterday in the Nanam, Songjin, Wonsan, and Kosong-Kansong areas.

U.S.S. Helena, U.S.S. Cunningham, and U.S.S. Bradford shelled road junctions, tunnels, and bridges between Tundong and Nanam, south of Chongjin.

United Nations seaborne marksmen again scored many hits on transportation targets at Sonjin. The Colombian frigate Almirante Padilla pounded a bridge, tunnel entrance, and a locomotive in the tunnel with at least ten bullseyes and many near misses.

U.S.S. Rupertus gun crews accurately shelled two tunnels south of Songjin, registering ten direct hits. Another ten 5-inch shells landed on a bridge in the same area. The destroyer-minesweeper Thompson continued interdiction of bridge approaches and route intersections.

Wonsan vehicular traffic was again bombarded by United States Navy destroyers. Troops and gun emplacements were also hit. U.S.S. Evans sank four sampans and damaged six during daylight hours.

Heavy cruiser Los Angeles shelled troops and command posts midway between Kansong and Kosong at long range yesterday with effective results.

Royal Navy pilots launched from the light carrier H.M.S. Glory continued attacks on west coast supply lines. Ranging from Pyongyang south to Haeju, the Sea Furies and Fireflies accounted for twelve boxcars, ten trucks, nine oxcarts, ten junks, two warehouses, and many buildings destroyed or damaged during yesterday's strikes.

East of Haeju, the British aircraft bombed and rocketed an enemy-occupied village. Large explosions and huge fires were observed as Communist ammunition stores exploded. Clouds of smoke soared 2,000 feet in the air. Many buildings were destroyed in the attack.

Task Force 77 night hecklers struck in central and northeast Korea early yesterday morning. The Skyraider pilots destroyed or damaged a bridge, nine trucks, a tank, and twenty-five railroad cars. Later flights were hampered by bad weather.

—Eighth Army communiqué 421, issued at 8:00 P.M., Sunday (6:00 A.M., Sunday, Eastern Daylight Time):

Eighth Army forces continued their advance toward the vital centers of Chorwon and Kumhwa against decreasing enemy resistance. Moderate to heavy enemy resistance continued in the Yonchon, Hwachon, and Yanggu-Inje areas.

1. Eighth Army forces in the Munsan-Korangpo sector continued to patrol during the day and reported little or no enemy contact. Friendly elements patrolling in the Yonchon area encountered moderate to heavy enemy resistance and reported receiving mortar and light artillery fire. Eighth Army forces in the area south-southwest of Chorwon advanced 2,000 yards against light to moderate enemy resistance from an estimated enemy battalion while farther to the east, advances of 3,000 to 4,000 yards were registered with little or no enemy contact reported.

2. United Nations forces in the area south and southwest of Kumhwa advanced 4,000 yards, reporting little or no enemy contact with friendly forces south-southeast of Kumhwa, advancing 3,000 yards against light enemy contact. (Two lines censored.)

3. In the Hwachon area resistance decreased to light to moderate as Eighth Army forces advanced 2,000 to 3,000 yards against company-sized enemy delaying units. In the area northeast of Hwachon other United Nations forces made limited advances against an enemy battalion which made a limited withdrawal during the afternoon hours. Heavy enemy resistance by elements of an estimated enemy regiment restricted advances in the area northwest of Yanggu. Limited advances of 500 to 1,000 yards were registered by Eighth Army forces in the Yanggu-Inje area against continued heavy enemy resistance.

4. On the remainder of the eastern front, light to moderate resistance was experienced as platoon to battalion-sized enemy units were engaged by United Nations forces.

—General Headquarters communiqué 911, issued at 11:20 A.M., Monday (9:20 P.M., Sunday, Eastern Daylight Time):

On the Korean battlefront yesterday, United Nations ground units continued to advance against enemy forces fighting strong rear guard delaying actions.

In the western and west-central sectors, moderate gains were made against decreasing enemy resistance. Along the east-central front, the forward advance was slowed by enemy forces in well-entrenched defensive positions.

Cruisers and destroyers of United Nations Naval Forces continued bombardment of highways and railroads in the Songjin, Wonsan, and Kansong areas; troop concentrations and gun emplacements were also attacked with excellent results.

On the west coast of Korea, aircraft launched from a British carrier attacked enemy transportation facilities and supply points in the Pyongyang and Haeju areas; near Haeju, large explosions and fires were observed as an enemy ammunition dump was destroyed.

Land-based fighters and light bombers struck heavily at enemy lines of communication and flew close support missions along the battlefront while medium bombers attacked targets of opportunity on the west coast. Combat Cargo aircraft maintained the airlift of supplies to Korean bases.

†BENNETT, EMORY L.

Rank and Organization: Private First Class, U.S. Army, Company B, 15th Infantry Regiment, 3d Infantry Division.
Born: December 20, 1929, New Smyrna Beach, Florida.
Entered Service At: Cocoa, Florida.
Place and Date: Near Sobangsan, Korea, June 24, 1951.
Citation: Pfc. Bennett, a member of Company B, distinguished himself by conspicuous gallantry and intrepidity at the risk of his life above and beyond the call of duty in action against an armed enemy of the United Nations. At approximately 0200 hours, 2 enemy battalions swarmed up the ridge line in a ferocious banzai charge in an attempt to dislodge Pfc. Bennett's company from its defensive positions. Meeting the challenge, the gallant defenders delivered destructive retaliation, but the enemy pressed the assault with fanatical determination and the integrity of the perimeter was imperiled. Fully aware of the odds against him, Pfc. Bennett unhesitatingly left his foxhole, moved through withering fire, stood within full view of the enemy and, employing his automatic rifle, poured crippling fire into the ranks of the onrushing assailants, inflicting numerous casualties. Although wounded, Pfc. Bennett gallantly maintained his 1-man defense and the attack was momentarily halted. During this lull in the battle, the company regrouped for a counterattack, but the numerically superior foe soon infiltrated into the position. Upon orders to move back, Pfc. Bennett voluntarily remained to provide covering fire for the withdrawing elements and, defying the enemy, continued to sweep the charging foe with devastating fire until mortally wounded. His willing self-sacrifice and intrepid actions saved the position from being overrun and enabled the company to effect an orderly withdrawal. Pfc. Bennett's unflinching courage and consummate devotion to duty reflects lasting glory upon himself and the military service.

OFFICIAL COMMUNIQUÉ:
TOKYO, Monday, June 25 (AP)
—Far East Air Forces summary covering Saturday operations:

Far East Air Forces fighters and fighter-bombers intensified their close support strikes Saturday to minimize enemy build-ups of troops and supplies along the front. Airfields were also hit hard as F.E.A.F. planes flew 820 sorties.

Fifth Air Force and attached South African and shore-based Marine aircraft mounted 600 sorties as they continued their interdiction of enemy transportation facilities and equipment as well as attacking enemy targets along the front lines in support of friendly ground forces.

Concentrating on the central and western sectors of the front, fighters and fighter-bombers flew over 100 close-support missions.

Throughout last night, B-26 Invader light bombers hammered at enemy airfields. Using radar, the light bombers attacked Sinanju, Pyong, Anak, Haeju, Sariwon, Hwangju, and Sinmak airfields to continue the neutralization program.

Six Bomber Command B-29 Superforts of the Ninety-eighth Bomb Group, by daylight, attacked enemy airfields at Ogye, Yyong, and Anak in western Korea yesterday with observers reporting hits on the runways in all strikes.

Flak was experienced over the targets and some of the medium bombers sighted unidentified aircraft, but none of them attacked.

A lone B-29 of the Okinawa-based Nineteenth Group hit an ammunition storage dump north of Kaesong. The crew reported seeing secondary explosions after their bombs hit the target.

Combat Cargo airlifted over 600 tons of supplies to the United Nations forces in Korea as planes of the 315th Air Division (Combat Cargo) flew 175 missions yesterday.

In addition to 130 tons of ammunition, twenty-two tons of fresh vegetables were flown to forward airstrips for front-line troops.

—*Far East Air Forces summary of Sunday's operations:*

Far East Air Force warplanes took advantage of good flying weather in Korea yesterday to concentrate on neutralizing enemy airfields as fighter bombers, medium, and light bombers attacked about thirty Communist airfields in the western section of North Korea.

Mounting a total of 850 sorties, F.E.A.F. aircraft also continued their interdiction attacks on enemy supply routes, and close support strikes in front of United Nations ground troops in all sectors of the battlefront.

F-80 Shooting Star jets encountered Communist jet fighters in the Sinanju area after they had strafed an enemy airfield. During the ten minute air battle that raged from 6,000 feet down to 500 feet, pilots of the F-80 Shooting Stars damaged four of the high-speed enemy jets. All F-80s engaged in the fight returned safely.

Fifth Air Force and attached South African and shore-based Marine aircraft flew 690 sorties, striking at enemy front-line troops, supply areas, communication, and transportation facilities.

Pilots reported inflicting more than 300 casualties on enemy troops. They also destroyed or damaged sixty-five vehicles, one locomotive, twenty-five railroad cars, six supply carts, 350 enemy occupied buildings, one supply dump, six ammunition and fuel dumps, nine warehouses, thirteen rail and highway bridges, forty-four pack animals, two tunnels, one railroad station, and thirty enemy gun positions. Highways and rail lines were cut in forty-five places to hamper the movement of enemy supplies and troops.

One F-80 Shooting Star was lost to enemy ground fire in the Sinanju area.

During the night and in pre-dawn attacks, Fifth Air Force planes flew ninety-five sorties.

B-26 Invader light bombers attacked enemy ground troops along the front-lines with air-bursting 500-pound bombs using radar techniques to aim the high explosives. Other B-26's attacked enemy vehicles and trains along the enemy's main supply routes in North Korea.

One B-26 reported being attacked by a twin-engine enemy aircraft early this morning. There was no damage reported by the B-26.

In the flat coastal plains of central North Korea, enemy airfields at Yongyu, Sunan, Sariwon, Ongjin, Haeju, Pyong, and Sariwon South were attacked during the night by B-26s using radar aiming techniques.

Marine F-7F aircraft, working with the aid of flare-dropping C-47s, reported destroying or damaging three enemy tanks.

Bomber Command B-29 Superforts from the Okinawa-based 19th Bomb Group visually bombed the airfields at Sinanju and Hwangju with seventy tons of demolition bombs. Direct hits were scored on the runways at both airfields.

One Superfort also of the 19th Bomb Group bombed the marshaling yard at Hungnam on the east coast of Korea with excellent results.

Combat Cargo transports flew 178 sorties yesterday as they airlifted 875 tons of cargo to resupply United Nations troops.

—Summary of naval operations covering Sunday:

United States and Royal Navy aircraft swarmed over enemy front-line positions and rear areas, Sunday, flying over 260 sorties.

Fast Carrier Task Force 77 sent Skyraiders, Panthers, and Corsairs roaring to the attack. Navy pilots caused heavy enemy casualties during close air support strikes in areas north and east of Chorwon and Kumhwa.

Controllers reported excellent coverage in several positions as the carrier-based fighters and bombers strafed and napalmed large numbers of enemy troops on ridges, in trenches, and in the open. One controller north of Chorwon said that one napalm bomb killed at least ten Communists and injured many more as the Navy airmen swept over an enemy battalion.

U.S.S. Boxer and U.S.S. Princeton pilots plastered Communist gun positions, buildings, and vehicles during the day. They destroyed or damaged seven bridges during strikes at east coastal rail and road networks. Near Yonghung, one quarter of a railroad bridge was destroyed by one 2,000-pound bomb.

H.M.S. Glory launched Sea Furies and Fireflies in both close and deep-support missions. The British aircraft supported front-line troops north of Inje with good coverage reported.

The Royal Navy pilots destroyed or damaged three junks at Chinnampo. Ranging north, they started a large fire, severely damaging a factory in Pyongyang.

At the eastern extremity of the battle line, the heavy cruiser Toledo, destroyers Stormes and Isbell, and frigate Everett supported United Nations Troops with naval gunfire. Eight and 5-inch shells from the mobile seaborne artillery reached far inland to shatter Communist positions and allow United Nations infantrymen to advance south of Kosong.

The destroyers Waller, Bass, and Duncan continued bombarding enemy transport targets at Wonsan. The Waller scored four hits out of five rounds fired at a truck convoy near the city. The three destroyers started several fires in the area hitting gun positions, fuel dumps, and troop centers.

Another United Nations bombarding group was in action Sunday to the north of Songjin. The U.S.S. Stickell, the British frigate Whitesand Bay, and Colombian frigate Almirante Padilla again teamed up to batter bridges, roads, and enemy shore batteries.

The Whitesand Bay shelled a bridge south of the city, registering many hits and causing casualties among the Communist group attempting to repair the bridge. The warships also scored hits on four sampans yesterday.

—Eighth Army communiqué 448, issued at 10:00 A.M., Sunday (8:00 P.M., Saturday, Eastern Daylight Time):

An enemy regiment forced to withdraw in areas northwest of Korangpo. Counter-attack by enemy company repulsed northeast of Chorwon. Enemy battalion attack against United Nations forces northeast of Yanggu. United Nations forces made limited withdrawals, counter-attacked and regained their positions. Enemy attack by two companies repulsed in area north of Inje.

1. Eighth Army forces attacking in the area north and northwest of Korangpo encountered stubborn enemy resistance from an estimated enemy regiment during the morning. However, by early afternoon the enemy broke contact and withdrew to the north. Determined resistance from several enemy groups of platoon to company size were encountered by friendly patrols in areas west, northwest, and north of Yongchong. Enemy groups of undetermined strength were encountered by friendly patrols in the area north and north-northeast of Chorwon. Friendly forces in the area northeast of Chorwon

engaged an undetermined number of the enemy at 9:30 A.M.. An estimated enemy company counter-attacked friendly forces in this area at 6:35 P.M.. The enemy was repulsed at 7:30 P.M..

2. Light enemy contact continued in the Kumhwa sector and in the area east of Kumhwa. No significant enemy activity was reported by United Nations forces in the area north of Hwachon.

3. Light enemy probing attacks were repulsed in the area north-northeast of Yanggu. At 2:15 A.M., June 28, an unknown number of enemy attacked United Nations forces north-northeast of Yanggu. At 2:45 A.M. friendly forces reported being engaged with an estimated enemy battalion. The engagement continued until 5:30 A.M., at which time United Nations forces made a slight withdrawal. At 6:10 A.M. Eighth Army forces counter-attacked and restored their positions against moderate resistance.

At 12:45 A.M. an unknown number of enemy attacked other United Nations forces northeast of Yanggu, with action continuing as of last report. An estimated two enemy companies attacked United Nations forces north of Inje, with the attack repulsed at 2:00 A.M., June 23.

4. Light enemy resistance was reported along the remainder of the eastern front.

—Eighth Army communiqué 449, issued at 8:00 P.M., Sunday (6:00 A.M., Sunday, Eastern Daylight Time):

Light enemy contact on the western front. Two enemy battalions attacked United Nations forces north-east of Chorwon. An enemy regiment contacted east-northeast of Kumhwa. A light probing attack was reported in the area north of Hwachon and northeast of Yanggu. A company-sized attack north of Inje was repulsed.

1. Little or no enemy contact was reported in the area north of Munsan and Korangpo during the day. Light enemy contact was reported by patrols in the area west of Yonghon. A tank patrol probing west of Chorwon encountered a tank trap covered by fire and reported receiving mortar and artillery fire. An estimated two enemy battalions engaged United Nations forces northeast of Chorwon at 2:25 A.M., forcing friendly forces to withdraw.

2. Eighth Army patrol encountered an estimated enemy regiment in the area east- northeast of Kumhwa and withdrew to allow artillery fire to fall on the enemy position. United Nations forces in the area north of Hwachon reported three light probing attacks, all of which were repulsed after brief engagement.

3. Light enemy contact was reported by other Eighth Army patrols in the area northwest of Yanggu. Three probing attacks by an undetermined number of enemy east of Yanggu. All attacks were repulsed. An enemy company attacked friendly forces north of Inje. The attack was repulsed.

4. No significant enemy activity was reported on the remainder of the eastern front.

—Eighth Army communiqué 450, issued at 10:00 A.M., Monday (8:00 P.M., Sunday, Eastern Daylight Time):

Enemy battalion engaged west of Yonchon. Task force west of Chorwon encounters road block defended by enemy. Two enemy battalions counter-attacked United Nations forces northeast of Chorwon causing friendly forces to withdraw. Enemy counter-attack in area east of Kumhwa. Enemy attack north of Inje. Moderate enemy resistance reported in the area west and west-northwest of Kansong.

1. Little or no enemy contact reported in the area north of Munsan and Korangpo. Eighth Army patrols engaged an estimated enemy battalion in the area west of Yonchon during the day. A task force probing west of Chorwon encountered an enemy roadblock covered by enemy fire, causing task force to disengage and withdraw. At 0225 (1:25 A.M.) 24 June, two enemy battalions counter-attacked United Nations forces northeast of Chorwon forcing friendly elements to withdraw from the high ground they had previously secured.

2. Eighth Army forces east of Kumhwa secured the high ground in that area at 1330 hours (1:30 P.M.). Shortly thereafter an estimated enemy battalion counter-attacked forcing friendly forces to with-

draw at 1700 hours. United Nations forces counter-attacked and met heavy enemy resistance, where-upon friendly forces withdrew to the base of the hill and placed artillery fire on the enemy position.

3. No significant enemy activity was reported in the area north of Hwachon. Several light pre-dawn attacks launched against United Nations forces in this area were quickly repulsed. Eighth Army patrols in the area north-northeast of Hwachon engaged an estimated 350 enemy at 1350 hours, withdrawing after a brief fire fight. Light enemy resistance continued in the area northwest of Yanggu and in the area north and northeast of Yanggu. At 2300 hours an unknown number of enemy, supported by a heavy volume of mortar and artillery fire, attacked United Nations forces north of Inje. No further report of action.

4. Light to moderate enemy resistance was reported in the area west of Kansong as friendly forces engaged an estimated two enemy companies. Moderate enemy resistance from an estimated two enemy companies was also reported in the area west-northwest of Kansong.

—General Headquarters communiqué 925, issued at 11:00 A.M., Monday (9:00 P.M., Sunday, Eastern Daylight Time):

United Nations combat patrols continued to probe enemy positions along the Korean front yesterday. In the western and west-central sector, friendly tank-infantry task forces encountered stubborn resis-tance from enemy delaying units. Along the east-central and eastern fronts, friendly units repulsed sev-eral probing attacks and patrolled with light to moderate contact.

Land-based Shooting Star jets damaged four MiG-15 aircraft in an air battle over northwest Korea. Other fighters and light bombers carried out attacks on front-line troop positions, supply points, com-munication lines, and transportation facilities in the battle area. Enemy airfields at Hwangju and Sinanju and a marshaling yard on the east coast were attacked by medium bombers during the period. Combat Cargo aircraft continued aerial resupply operations to bases in Korea.

United Nations naval elements supported friendly ground units with naval gunfire on enemy troop positions in the vicinity of Kosong while blockade and interdiction operations were continued in the Wonsan and Songjin areas.

Carrier-based aircraft attacked gun positions and transportation facilities near Yonghung and troop concentrations along the Chorwon-Kumhwa axis with excellent results.

†KOELSCH, JOHN KELVIN

Rank and Organization: Lieutenant (jg.), U.S. Navy, Navy helicopter rescue unit.
Born: London, England.
Entered Service At: Los Angeles, California.
Place and Date: North Korea, July 3, 1951.
Citation: For conspicuous gallantry and intrepidity at the risk of his life above and beyond the call of duty while serving with a Navy helicopter rescue unit. Although darkness was rapidly approaching when information was received that a marine aviator had been shot down and was trapped by the enemy in mountainous terrain deep in hostile territory, Lt. (jg.) Koelsch voluntarily flew a helicopter to the reported position of the downed airman in an attempt to effect a rescue. With an almost solid overcast concealing everything below the mountain peaks, he descended in his unarmed and vulnerable aircraft without the accompanying fighter escort to an extremely low altitude beneath the cloud level and began a systematic search. Despite the increasingly intense enemy fire, which struck his helicopter on one occasion, he persisted in his mission until he succeeded in locating the downed pilot, who was suffering from serious burns on the arms and legs. While the pilot was being hoisted into the aircraft, it was struck again by an accurate burst of hostile fire and crashed on the side of the moun-tain. Quickly extricating his crewmen and the aviator from the wreckage, Lt. (jg.) Koelsch led

them from the vicinity in an effort to escape from hostile troops, evading the enemy forces for 9 days and rendering such medical attention as possible to his severely burned companion until all were captured. Up to the time of his death while still a captive of the enemy, Lt. (jg.) Koelsch steadfastly refused to aid his captors in any manner and served to inspire his fellow prisoners by his fortitude and consideration for others. His great personal valor and heroic spirit of self-sacrifice throughout, sustain and enhance the finest traditions of the U.S. Naval Service.

OFFICIAL COMMUNIQUÉ:
TOKYO, July 3 (AP)
—Far East Air Forces summary covering Monday's operations:

Far East Air Forces fighters and fighter-bombers flew through rain showers and under low-hanging clouds Monday to make intensive low-level bombing, rocket, and strafing attacks on enemy airfields, while other flights pounded enemy-held buildings, cut rail lines, and attacked bridges throughout central and western North Korea as F.E.A.F. warplanes flew 650 sorties.

F-84 Thunderjets attacked the airfield in Hwangju in a flak-suppression mission with excellent results reported. The enemy airfield at Haeju, south of Chinnampo on the west coast, was hit by F-51 Mustangs. The propeller-driven fighter-bombers cratered the runway with 500-pound bombs, and strafed buildings and supply areas.

F-80 Shooting Star jets attacked rail lines, roads, and enemy-held buildings in central and western North Korea from Sariwon to the Pyongyang area. The main railroad between Chinnampo on the west coast and the North Korean capital of Pyongyang was cut in many places and three bridges were knocked out.

Fifth Air Force and attached South African and shore-based Marine aircraft flew 485 sorties yesterday, of which seventy-five were in close support of United Nations ground forces.

Returning Fifth Air Force pilots reported destroying or damaging eleven gun positions, four pack animals, fourteen supply storage areas, six rail bridges, one ammunition storage dump, 285 enemy-occupied buildings, two fuel storage areas, six highway bridges, and about forty-five vehicles. Rail lines and highways were cut in forty places. Pilots reported inflicting 125 enemy troop casualties during their attacks.

Two friendly aircraft, a Marine F-4U and an F-51 Mustang were lost to enemy ground fire.

B-26 Invader light bombers hit enemy airfields at Hwangju, Sinanju and Ogyo several times during the night with radar-assisted bombing, as night flying aircraft flew over eighty sorties.

Four separate attacks were made on the airstrip at Sinanju, three on Ogyo, and two on Hwangju to prevent the Communists from repairing the damaged runways.

Other B-26s operated along the main supply routes throughout North Korea, attacking vehicles and supply areas, while other light bombers dropped 500-pound air-bursting bombs on front-line enemy troops, supplies and other military targets, aided by radar to aim the high explosives.

Marine F-7Fs, operating behind the battlefront with C-47 fliers dropping transports, attacked vehicles and supply areas.

Bomber Command B-29 Superforts of the Ninety-eighth Bomb Group hammered the military barracks area at Hungnam on the east coast yesterday as they dropped thirty tons of high explosives on the target. Radar aiming was used by the medium bombers. The thick undercast prevented observation of results.

A single B-29 attacked the enemy airfield of Sariwon in western Korea. Radar aiming was used to drop the high explosives on the airstrip.

All of the Superforts returned safely to their base.

Transports of the 315th Air Division (Combat Cargo) continued to airlift supplies to United Nations forces in Korea yesterday as they flew 165 sorties and hauled over 500 tons of cargo.

—Summary of naval operations off Korea July 3:

United Nations naval bombardment ships off the east coast of North Korea fired through fog and rain Tuesday as they kept hammering away at the enemy.

The mighty eight-inch guns of two heavy cruisers, the U.S.S. Toledo and U.S.S. Los Angeles, were trained at Communist targets in the area of the east coast battle line in close support to ground forces.

Concentrating on enemy troop concentrations, gun positions, and supply and ammunition dumps with the larger ships were the destroyers U.S.S. Bradford and U.S.S. Rupertus. More than 150 rounds of eight and five-inch high explosives were directed toward the Reds by the four ships during the day.

At Wonsan, working over buildings of military importance, troop areas, and gun positions, were the destroyers U.S.S. Evans, U.S.S. Blue, and patrol frigate U.S.S. Everett. In the late afternoon the bombardment force was taken under fire by shore batteries and heavy enemy shelling lasted for about an hour and fifteen minutes before the Communists were silenced.

The Canadian destroyer H.M.C.S. Huron was again in the Songjin area and as a result of her day long firing scored seven direct hits on a railroad bridge and three on a highway span.

Patrolling farther north, the destroyer escort U.S.S. Naifeh and patrol frigate U.S.S. Sausalito continued to blast away at rail and highway facilities and buildings believed to be housing troops in the Chongjin area.

Task Force 77 planes from the U.S.S. Boxer and U.S.S. Bon Homme Richard off the east coast were carrier-bound most of Tuesday as weather over their target area would not permit extensive operations.

But on the west coast, with more favorable conditions, Marine pilots from the U.S.S. Sicily put in a busy day flying close air-support missions and hitting troops housing and supply facilities away from the fighting front.

Among successes tallied by the Leathernecks were fourteen barrack-type buildings destroyed and eight badly damaged, all in the Chinnampo area.

—Eighth Army communiqué 466, issued at 10:00 A.M., Tuesday (8:00 P.M., Monday, Eastern Daylight Time):

Stubborn enemy resistance continues in area northeast of Chorwon. United Nations forces northeast of Yanggu interdict enemy area with air and artillery. Enemy mortar and artillery fire increases in Yonchon area and northwest of Yanggu.

1. Light enemy contact reported by Eighth Army patrols in area north of Imjin River. Light to moderate resistance and an increase in enemy mortar and artillery fire reported by United Nations patrols in the area west and northwest of Yonchon. An estimated enemy battalion contacted by friendly patrols in area northeast of Chorwon during the day. Moderate to heavy enemy resistance from estimated two enemy battalions well dug in and supported by automatic weapons, machine guns, and 76-mm. artillery fire was encountered in area northeast of Chorwon during the day.

2. At 11:00 P.M. Monday an estimated three enemy platoons were dispersed by artillery fire while action with a remaining platoon continued as of midnight. An enemy force of battalion size was encountered by patrol elements south-southwest of Kumsong. Long-range artillery fire was reported by Eighth Army forces in areas north of Hwachon. Light enemy contact continued on remainder of front as United Nations forces continued their aggressive patrolling.

3. Light enemy contact with platoon and company-sized enemy units was reported in area northwest of Yanggu.

—*Eighth Army communiqué 467, released at 8:00 P.M., Tuesday (6:00 A.M., Tuesday, Eastern Daylight Time):*

Moderate enemy resistance continued in area northeast of Chorwon while light enemy contact was reported along the remainder of the Korean front.

1. United Nations forces in the area north and north-northwest of Korangpo engaged elements of an estimated enemy battalion with one enemy company dispersed to the north and action continuing with another enemy company as of 3:00 P.M.. Light enemy contact from small enemy groups was reported along the remainder of the western front.

2. Moderate enemy resistance continued in the area northeast of Chorwon as United Nations forces continued to engage dug-in enemy forces. Light contact from small enemy groups was reported along he remainder of the central front.

3. Light enemy contact from squad to platoon-sized enemy units was experienced on the eastern front with friendly forces in the area west-northwest of Kansong engaging two enemy companies during the day.

—*Eighth Army communiqué 468, issued at 10:00 A.M., Wednesday (8:00 P.M., Tuesday, Eastern Daylight Time):*

United Nations forces engaged enemy battalions in area north of Korangpo. Heavy enemy mortar and artillery fire received in area west and northwest of Yonchon. Attacking United Nations forces secured high ground in area south and south-southeast of Pyonggang. Light to moderate enemy resistance continued on the remainder of the Korean front.

1. United Nations forces engaged an estimated enemy battalion in the area north of Korangpo during the day. Heavy enemy artillery and mortar fire was received by friendly patrol elements probing enemy positions in the area west and northwest of Yonchon. An estimated enemy battalion was engaged in the area northwest of Yonchon at 2:35 P.M.. Friendly patrols broke contact at 4:00 P.M.. Attacking United Nations forces in the area south and south-southeast of Pyonggang secured the high ground at 6:30 P.M. against moderate enemy resistance.

2. Patrols in the area south-southwest of Kumsong engaged platoon to company-size enemy units during the day while other patrols in the area north and north-northwest of Hwachon reported light to moderate enemy resistance from platoon to company-size enemy units. Light enemy contact was reported on the remainder of the central front.

3. United Nations forces north of Inje received a platoon-size enemy probing attack at 7:00 P.M.. The attack was repulsed and the enemy withdrew at 8:30 P.M.. Light to moderate enemy resistance was encountered by other United Nations patrols northwest of Kansong from company-size enemy units.

—*Headquarters communiqué 933, issued at 11:10 A.M., Tuesday (9:10 P.M., Monday, Eastern Daylight Time):*

Activity along the United Nations front yesterday (Monday) consisted of friendly patrols ranging forward from front-line positions and engaging numerous enemy groups which offered light to moderate resistance. In the west-central sector United Nations forces repulsed one attack.

Carrier-based aircraft bombed and strafed supply dumps in the Chorwon area and vehicles, railroad and highway bridges in the Wonsan-Songjin area. Elements attacked warehouse areas in the Chinnampo area with good results. Naval surface elements attacked troop concentrations, gun positions, and transportation targets in the Wonsan area while other elements covered United Nations forces in the Kansong-Kosong area.

Land-based fighters and light bombers attacked enemy troop positions, vehicular traffic, storage facilities, and lines of communications. Medium bombers struck enemy barracks areas at Hungnam and the airfield at Sariwon. Combat Cargo transports continued the resupply of United Nations ground forces.

†MENDONCA, LEROY A.

Rank and Organization: Sergeant, U.S. Army, Company B, 7th Infantry Regiment, 3d Infantry Division.
Born: Honolulu, Hawaii.
Entered Service At: Honolulu, Hawaii.
Place and Date: Near Chich-on, Korea, July 4, 1951.
Citation: Sgt. Mendonca distinguished himself by conspicuous gallantry and intrepidity above and beyond the call of duty in action against the enemy. After his platoon, in an exhaustive fight, had captured Hill 586, the newly won positions were assaulted during the night by a numerically superior enemy force. When the 1st Platoon positions were outflanked and under great pressure and the platoon was ordered to withdraw to a secondary line of defense, Sgt. Mendonca voluntarily remained in an exposed position and covered the platoon's withdrawal. Although under murderous enemy fire, he fired his weapon and hurled grenades at the onrushing enemy until his supply of ammunition was exhausted. He fought on, clubbing with his rifle and using his bayonet until he was mortally wounded. After the action it was estimated that Sgt. Mendonca had accounted for 37 enemy casualties. His daring actions stalled the crushing assault, protecting the platoon's withdrawal to secondary positions, and enabling the entire unit to repel the enemy attack and retain possession of the vital hilltop position. Sgt. Mendonca's extraordinary gallantry and exemplary valor are in keeping with the highest traditions of the U.S. Army.

OFFICIAL COMMUNIQUÉ:

TOKYO, Thursday, July 5 (AP)
—Far East Air Forces summary of July 3 operations:
Ninety-nine Far East Air Forces warplanes coordinated Tuesday in high and low level attacks on a key Communist airfields in western Korea and the Downtown Pyongyang strip.

Thirty-two heavily armed F-84 Thunderjets roared over the target area at low level, singling out and assaulting anti-aircraft positions with such good results that six B-29 Superforts experienced only moderate flak as they dropped more than 850 of their 100-pound bombs on the airdrome.

The B-29s were escorted by thirty-three F-86 Sabre jets and no enemy air opposition developed.

Following the medium bomber attack, F-80 Shooting Star jets rocketed and strafed airfield installations.

This attack came on a day in which F.E.A.F. planes flew 675 sorties in variable weather. It continued the intensified airfield neutralization program which has prevented the Communists from mounting any effective air opposition to United Nations ground forces from the fifteen key fields in western Korea they have been repairing and improving since March.

Three other B-29s successfully struck the airfield at Hwangju, due south of Pyongyang.

Fifth Air Force and attached South African and shore-based Marine aircraft mounted approximately 530 sorties of which 130 were in close air support of friendly ground forces. F-80 Shooting Star jet pilots reported damaging approximately 200 enemy vehicles southeast of Sunchon in west central Korea. Other F-80 Shooting Stars achieved considerable destruction of boxcars in a napalm attack on the enemy marshaling yard at Kyomipo south of Pyongyang. F-51 Mustangs inflicted substantial casualties on enemy troops holding field entrenchments in forward western Korea positions.

In addition to the B-29 Pyongyang strike F-80s hit the enemy airfield at Kangdong, northeast of Pyongyang.

F-84 Thunderjets attacked military targets between Pyongyang and Sinanju while Marine planes hit rail and bridge targets and troop areas in east central Korea.

One hundred sorties were flown last night (Tuesday night). Four B-29s and twelve B-26s attacked forward enemy positions with 500-pound air-bursting bombs, aimed by the employment of radar techniques.

Other B-26s attacked western enemy airfields at Ogyo, Anak, and Pyong.

In 130 sorties the 315th Air Division (Combat Cargo) transported approximately 530 tons of combat supplies and equipment from Japan to Korea.

In yesterday's operations an F-82 twin Mustang was destroyed by ground fire. Its crew was rescued. A B-26 light bomber is missing.

—Far East Air Forces summary of July 4 operations:

Regardless of low-hanging clouds and heavy rain showers that sometimes limited visibility to less than two miles, Far East Air Forces warplanes continued to hammer enemy communication lines, bridges, buildings and, airfields Wednesday as F.E.A.F. planes mounted 625 sorties.

United Nations fighters and fighter bombers destroyed or damaged sixteen bridges in yesterday's attacks against Communist supply lines behind the battle front.

Fifth Air Force and attached South African and shore-based Marine aircraft flew over 400 sorties, as F-51 Mustangs hit roads, bridges, and enemy-occupied buildings in west central Korea, while Marine aircraft attacked similar targets in the east. The highways and rail lines from Wonsan to Pyonggang were hit hard by Marine fighter bombers as they cut roads and attacked vehicles to prevent supplies from reaching Communist front-line troops.

Sixteen South African F-51 Mustangs attacked enemy supply buildings in the west central sector with good results. They also cut highways in several places.

Poor visibility prevented many of the pilots from observing results of their attacks, but 100 buildings, three gun positions, ten supply storage areas, sixteen bridges, one locomotive, twenty-two pack animals, and over 100 vehicles were reported destroyed or damaged. Highways and rail lines were cut in twenty places.

Night-flying aircraft flew sixty sorties during the hours of darkness. B-26 Invader light bombers operated along the enemy main supply routes throughout North Korea in spite of poor visibility. Other B-26s, aided by radar, attacked the enemy airfields at Kangdong and Sinanju and hit the Sunan airstrip twice during the night.

Marine F-7Fs and F-4Us operating with C-47 flare-dropping transports, attacked enemy vehicles. One locomotive was reported destroyed in an attack.

Seven Bomber Command B-29 Superforts of the Okinawa-based 307th Bomb Group blasted the marshaling yards in the important Communist supply center of Hungnam on the east coast with fifty tons of high explosives. Bombing was by radar and a thick undercast prevented observation of results.

A single Superfort hit the enemy airlift at Ongjin on the coast west of Waesong, while another B-29 attacked the supply center of Haeju.

The medium bombers encountered no enemy opposition and all aircraft returned to base.

Transports of the 315th Air Division (Combat Cargo) airlifted 480 tons of cargo to United Nations troops in Korea yesterday as they flew 200 sorties.

—United Nations Naval Forces summary of July 4 operations:

United States Navy and Marine carrier-based aircraft continued attacks Wednesday on front-line enemy positions and rear-area supply lines.

Fighters and bombers launched from U.S.S. Bon Homme Richard and U.S.S. Boxer ranged from the eastern sector of the battlefront northward to the Wonsan area. Navy fliers destroyed or damaged over twenty-five military-occupied buildings as well as numerous supply dumps in the Kojo territory on the east coast.

The escort carrier Sicily provided Marine Corsair strikes at the enemy northwest of Kansong across Korea to Chinnampo. Blasting buildings, supplies, and gun positions, the Marines killed over fifty Communist soldiers during day-long attacks.

At the eastern end of the fighting line, the U.S.S. New Jersey opened up with her 16-inch guns yesterday hitting an enemy command post. Task Force 77 pilots attacked enemy infantry positions in the same area between Kansong and Kosong.

Before dawn yesterday, the destroyer Cunningham poured over 130 rounds of 5-inch explosives at enemy patrols and concentrations south of Kosong with deadly effect.

The United Nations siege force at Wonsan continued shelling the transportation complex despite rain and fog in the area. Troops and artillery were hit by destroyers Blue and Evans who teamed up with Air Force night intruders in pre-dawn bombardment.

Bridges, railroads, and highways were pounded by the Canadian destroyer Huron and United States Navy frigate Sausalito far to the north at Chongjin and Chuuronjang. The frigate started large fires and observed secondary explosions when her 3-inch guns registered on enemy targets. Destroyer escort U.S.S. Naifeh hit similar transportation installations in the Songjin area.

—Eighth Army communiqué 469, issued at 8:00 P.M., Wednesday (6:00 A.M., Wednesday, Eastern Daylight Time):

Eighth Army patrols along the Korean front report light enemy contact.

1. Eighth Army patrols in the area north and northwest of Korangpo and west and northwest of Yonchon reported receiving long-range small arms fire from enemy forces of platoon and company size. A sharp decrease in enemy artillery and mortar fire was reported in the Yonchon area. Eighth Army forces southeast of Pyonggang remained in contact with elements of an estimated enemy battalion until approximately 8:00 P.M. at which time the enemy made a limited withdrawal. No significant attacks were reported in this area during the day.

2. An enemy company attacked United Nations forces east-northeast of Kumhwa. The attack was repulsed. Light enemy contact was reported on the remainder of the front as Eighth Army forces continued to patrol.

3. Light enemy contact and a decrease in enemy artillery and mortar fire was reported along the East Korean front.

—Eighth Army communiqué 470, issued at 10:00 A.M., Thursday (8:00 P.M., Wednesday, Eastern Daylight Time):

Patrol enters Kaesong. Enemy counter-attacks in area south and south-southeast of Pyonggang—attacks repulsed. Enemy attacks east-northeast of Kumhwa repulsed. Light enemy contact reported on all the remainder of the Korean front.

1. A platoon-sized friendly patrol entered Kaesong at 1300 hours (1:00 P.M. Wednesday) with no enemy contact. Another patrol immediately west of Kaesong reported receiving small arms fire at 1500 hours and withdrew to friendly lines. Minor enemy contact was reported in the area north of Korangpo. Light enemy contact was reported by patrols in the area west and northwest of Yonchon and in the Chorwon area. Enemy counter-attacks against United Nations forces on the high ground south and southeast of Pyonggang at 0300 hours 4 July were repulsed at 0530 hours. United Nations forces destroyed enemy fortifications in this area during the day with no further significant enemy contact.

2. An estimated two enemy companies northeast of Kumhwa attacked United Nations forces at 1030 hours—the attack was dispersed with the aid of artillery fire.

A series of light probing attacks were reported in the area east and east-northeast of Kumhwa, all of which were repulsed. Light to moderate enemy resistance from company-sized enemy units were reported in the area south and south-southeast of Kumsong. Light enemy contact and a sharp decrease in enemy resistance from company sized units was reported in the area south and southeast of Kumsong. Light enemy contact was reported on the remainder of the central front.

3. Light enemy contact and a sharp decrease in enemy mortar and artillery fire was reported along the eastern front as Eighth Army forces continued their aggressive patrolling.

—General Headquarters communiqué 935, for the twenty-four hours ended 6:00 A.M. Thursday (4:00 P.M., Wednesday, Eastern Daylight Time):

Action on the Korean front yesterday was limited to numerous clashes between United Nations combat patrols and enemy groups from squad to company size. Scattered light contacts were made by friendly tank-infantry patrols in the western sector while at other points along the front friendly elements encountered stubborn resistance from enemy screening forces.

Carrier-based aircraft attacked supply areas, gun positions, build-up areas, and troop positions along the battle line. Bridges, rail lines, and gun positions were bombarded by surface units in the Wonsan complex and the Chongjin-Chuuronjang areas. Enemy troop concentrations in the Kansong-Kosong area were also attacked during the period.

Marshaling yards near the east coast city of Hungnam were the principal targets of land-based medium bombers yesterday. Other targets hit were enemy front-line positions and military installations along the west coast. Fighters and fighter bombers attacked bridges, rail lines, vehicular traffic, and troop concentrations in the battle area. Transport cargo planes continued resupply operations.

†HARTELL, LEE R.

Rank and Organization: First Lieutenant, U.S. Army, Battery A, 15th Field Artillery Battalion, 2d Infantry Division.
Born: Philadelphia, Pennsylvania.
Entered Service At: Danbury, Connecticutt.
Place and Date: Near Kobangsan-ni, Korea, August 27, 1951.
Citation: 1st Lt. Hartell, a member of Battery A, distinguished himself by conspicuous gallantry and intrepidity above and beyond the call of duty in action against an armed enemy of the United Nations. During the darkness of early morning, the enemy launched a ruthless attack against friendly positions on a rugged mountainous ridge. 1st Lt. Hartell, attached to Company B, 9th Infantry Regiment, as forward observer, quickly moved his radio to an exposed vantage on the ridge line to adjust defensive fires. Realizing the tactical advantage of illuminating the area of approach, he called for flares and then directed crippling fire into the onrushing assailants. At this juncture a large force of hostile troops swarmed up the slope in a banzai charge and came within 10 yards of 1st Lt. Hartell's position. 1st Lt. Hartell sustained a severe hand wound in the ensuing encounter, but grasped the microphone with his other hand and maintained his magnificent stand until the front and left flank of the company were protected by a close-in wall of withering fire, causing the fanatical foe to disperse and fall back momentarily. After the numerically superior enemy overran an outpost and was closing on his position, 1st Lt. Hartell, in a final radio call, urged the friendly elements to fire both batteries continuously. Although mortally wounded, 1st Lt. Hartell's intrepid actions contributed significantly to stemming the onslaught and enabled his company to maintain the strategic strongpoint. His consummate valor and unwavering devotion to duty reflect lasting glory on himself and uphold the noble traditions of the military service.

OFFICIAL COMMUNIQUÉ:
TOKYO, Tuesday, Aug. 28 (AP)
—Far East naval summary covering Monday's operations:

Communist highways and rail installations were again battered heavily yesterday by United Nations Navy surface forces on the east and west coasts of Korea.

Task Force 95 warships of Wonsan dueled with heavy Communist artillery, well-concealed in cliff sides yesterday for the third consecutive day. Destroyers Hopewell and Parkes and accompanying L8MR8 (Landing ships medium rocket) poured round after round of effective counter-battery fire at the Red shore batteries.

The Hopewell's main battery scored ten direct hits in the center of a bivouac area early yesterday, causing heavy damage. She blasted ten enemy-occupied buildings, shelled a bridge and vehicles, and got six bullseyes on a troop shelter. The Parkes completely destroyed a gun position and killed the Red soldiers grouped around it. L8MR 325 picked off an ammo dump with her five-inch battery.

During the Communist gunfire Sunday morning, the United Nations destroyers were straddled but suffered no damage or personnel casualties. Firing at ranges from five to seven miles, the shore guns attempted to hit the siege force with about fifty-five large-caliber rounds between 9:25 and 10:40 A.M..

Late Monday afternoon, the U.S.S. Los Angeles arrived in the Kosong-Kansong area from Fast Carrier Task Force 77 to give gunfire support to battling R.O.K. (Republic of Korea) troops. Early last night she opened up on Red infantry concentrations at long range with her big eight-inch guns.

In the same area, Task Force 95 destroyer U.S.S. Wedderburn continued pounding away at entrenched enemy soldiers. The destroyer had fired call-fire missions at nine separate targets before daylight yesterday morning. Delayed reports indicated the Wedderburn exchanged heavy gunfire with shore batteries on the Kojo area, midway between Wonsan and Kosong last Friday afternoon. The Red artillery poured over 100 rounds at the Wedderburn as she zigzagged out of range. However, her main batteries pinpointed at least two of the artillery positions, killing over fifty troops.

On the west coast, British frigates Mounts Bay and Morecambe Bay hit troops and gun positions near Pungdong on the north bank of the Han River.

Task Force 95 escort carrier U.S.S. Sicily launched limited sorties yesterday in the face of very low ceilings over target areas. Marine Corsairs napalmed (fire-bombed) and strafed entrenched enemy soldiers in the Haeju area.

Far to the north on the east coast, other Task Force 95 warships bombarded North Korean supply routes while on blockade patrol.

—Far East Air Forces summary 428, covering Sunday's operations:

Land based warplanes under the operational control of Far East Air Forces flew over 900 sorties yesterday for the second consecutive day, as favorable weather continued in the target area.

Fifth Air Force and attached South African, Australian, and shore-based Marine aircraft flew 720 sorties, with F-80 Shooting Star jets. F-84 Thunderjets and propeller-driven F-51 Mustangs concentrating on disrupting enemy rail networks as they intensified their interdiction of rolling stock, trackage, and bridges.

F-80 Shooting Stars also attacked gun positions protecting a marshaling yard between Anju and Sinanju. The aircraft scored thirteen direct hits on the flak positions with 500-pound bombs, silencing the guns. Near Chaeryong, another flight of F-80s strafed a group of trucks, destroying one and damaging eleven of the camouflaged vehicles.

F-84 Thunderjets reported excellent results as they attacked flak positions at the Pyong airfield before a strike by B-29 Superforts. Others cut rail trackage between Pyongyang and Sariwon. Marine aircraft attacked a large supply area in the eastern sector with bombs and machine-guns, while others cut rail lines and damaged bridges.

F-51 Mustangs hit rail cars and cut trackage between Anju and Kunui, while other of the propeller-driven fighter-bombers attacked enemy front-line positions in close support of United Nations ground troops. F-86 Sabre jets flew sweeps in "MiG Alley" yesterday, but no enemy fighters were encountered by the swept-wing jets.

One T-6 spotter plane was lost to enemy ground fire yesterday. The crew was picked up by a rescue aircraft and returned to friendly lines.

Returning Fifth Air Force pilots reported destroying or damaging 340 enemy occupied buildings, fifty supply carts, two locomotives, ten warehouses, two boats, 160 railroad cars, and 700 vehicles. Rail lines were cut in seventy places and ten bridges were destroyed or damaged. Pilots also reported inflicting 100 casualties on enemy troops and killing forty pack animals during their air strikes.

Sixteen Bomber Command B-29 Superforts of the Japan and Okinawa-based Ninety-eighth Bomb Wing and Nineteenth Bomb Group pounded an enemy airfield and a marshaling yard with 160 tons of high explosives yesterday. Seven of the Nineteenth Group medium bombers visually dropped 1,000 100-pound bombs on the Kunu marshaling yard northeast of Sinanju. Excellent results were reported by the crews, with secondary explosions observed in the target area.

Almost 1,300 100-pound bombs were rained on the enemy airfield at Pyong by nine Superforts of the Ninety-eighth Bomb Wing. Excellent bomb patterns were reported by the crews. The runway was severely damaged by the strike, preventing enemy aircraft from operating from the field. Some flak was encountered over the target, but no enemy fighters attempted to attack the Superforts or their Royal Australian Meteor jet fighter escorts.

Over 100 sorties were flown by Navy B-26 Invader light bombers and Marine F-7Fs and F-4Us. Aided by flare-dropping transports, the night Intruders attacked enemy vehicles on the main supply routes throughout North Korea during the hours of darkness, and reported destroying or damaging 100 in pre-dawn strikes.

An enemy locomotive and ten cars were damaged in a pre-dawn attack by a B-26 of the Third Bomb Wing. The train was between Ariwon and Sinmak when the light bomber smashed it with bombs and machine-guns, severely damaging the locomotive and all ten cars.

B-29 Superforts operated along the battlefront, radar-aiming 500-pound bombs on enemy front-line military targets.

Combat Cargo transports of the 315th Air Division continued to airlift supplies to United Nations forces in Korea as they flew 170 sorties hauling almost 900 tons of supplies. Over 100 tons of fresh vegetables were airlifted to front-line United Nations units, and C-119 transports air-dropped forty tons of supplies and rations to forward troops.

†KRZYZOWSKI, EDWARD C.

Rank and Organization: Captain, U.S. Army, Company B, 9th Infantry Regiment, 2d Infantry Division.
Born: January 16, 1914, Chicago, Illinois.
Entered Service At: Cicero, Illinois.
Place and Date: Near Tondul, Korea, August 31 to September 3, 1951.
Citation: Capt. Krzyzowski distinguished himself by conspicuous gallantry and indomitable courage above and beyond the call of duty in action against the enemy as commanding officer of Company B. Spearheading an assault against strongly defended Hill 700, his company came under vicious crossfire and grenade attack from enemy bunkers. Creeping up the fire-swept hill, he personally eliminated 1 bunker with his grenades and wiped out a second with carbine fire. Forced to retire to more tenable positions for the night, the company, led by Capt Krzyzowski, resumed the attack the following day, gaining several hundred yards and inflicting numerous casualties. Overwhelmed by the numerically superior hostile force, he ordered his men to evacuate the wounded and move back. Providing protective fire for their safe

withdrawal, he was wounded again by grenade fragments, but refused evacuation and continued to direct the defense. On September 3rd, he led his valiant unit in another assault which overran several hostile positions, but again the company was pinned down by murderous fire. Courageously advancing alone to an open knoll to plot mortar concentrations against the hill, he was killed instantly by an enemy sniper's fire. Capt Krzyzowski's consummate fortitude, heroic leadership, and gallant self-sacrifice, so clearly demonstrated through 3 days of bitter combat, reflect the highest credit and lasting glory on himself, the infantry, and the U.S. Army.

†LYELL, WILLIAM F.

Rank and Organization: Corporal, U.S. Army, Company F, 17th Infantry Regiment, 7th Infantry Division.
Born: Hickman County, Tennessee.
Entered Service At: Old Hickory, Tennessee.
Place and Date: Near Chup'a-ri, Korea, August 31, 1951.
Citation: Cpl. Lyell, a member of Company F, distinguished himself by conspicuous gallantry and intrepidity above and beyond the call of duty in action against the enemy. When his platoon leader was killed, Cpl. Lyell assumed command and led his unit in an assault on strongly fortified enemy positions located on commanding terrain. When his platoon came under vicious, raking fire which halted the forward movement, Cpl. Lyell seized a 57mm recoilless rifle and unhesitatingly moved ahead to a suitable firing position from which he delivered deadly accurate fire completely destroying an enemy bunker, killing its occupants. He then returned to his platoon and was resuming the assault when the unit was again subjected to intense hostile fire from 2 other bunkers. Disregarding his personal safety, armed with grenades, he charged forward hurling grenades into 1 of the enemy emplacements, and although painfully wounded in this action he pressed on destroying the bunker and killing 6 of the foe. He then continued his attack against a third enemy position, throwing grenades as he ran forward, annihilating 4 enemy soldiers. He then led his platoon to the north slope of the hill where positions were occupied from which effective fire was delivered against the enemy in support of friendly troops moving up. Fearlessly exposing himself to enemy fire, he continuously moved about directing and encouraging his men until he was mortally wounded by enemy mortar fire. Cpl. Lyell's extraordinary heroism, indomitable courage, and aggressive leadership reflect great credit upon himself and are in keeping with the highest traditions of the military service.

OFFICIAL COMMUNIQUÉ:
TOKYO, Saturday, Sept. 1 (AP)
—United Nations Naval Forces summary of Aug. 31 operations:

Seaborne artillery of ships of the Seventh Fleet combined with airborne artillery of planes from Fast Carrier Task Force 77 yesterday (Friday) to level the full fury of Navy air and sea warfare on enemy troops south of Kosong.

    The big guns of the battleship U.S.S. New Jersey began laying in 16-inch and 5-inch salvoes at 6:45 A.M. and did not cease fire until nearly midnight.

    This was one of the heaviest concentrations of air and sea attack forces to strike at the Communists as fighting increased on the ground.

    The battleship New Jersey, flagship of Vice Admiral Harold M. Martin, U.S.N., Commander Seventh Fleet, expended more than 116,000 pounds of explosives against troop and transport concentrations of the enemy in the Kossong area.

Fighter bombers from the fast carriers Essex and Bon Homme Richard raided pre-designated targets in the same area, then ranged northward along the east Korean coast to blast gun positions ashore in the Wonsan area and railroad bridges and roadbeds just south of Songjin.

The heavy cruiser U.S.S. Helena in company with the destroyers, Wedderburn, Orleck, and Marshall fired tons of high explosives at enemy assembly points, bridges, and supply routes in support of the intense east Korean coast assault. The rocket ship (LSMR) 525 arched more than 500 rockets into enemy positions.

The destroyer John R. Craig's action against enemy factories, ammunition caves, bridges, railways, and highway junctions in the Songjin area marked the northernmost point at which the powerful east coast naval air and surface assault was felt.

Task Force 77 Skyraiders and Corsairs met some of the heaviest anti-aircraft opposition they have yet encountered in the wide-scale operation. Flak thrown up by Red AA guns damaged four Corsair planes flying from the Essex and Bon Homme Richard. All planes landed safely, three setting down on South Korean airfields.

The Task Force 77 scoreboard at the end of the day's assault read as follows: Twenty-six buildings destroyed, twelve damaged; twelve bridges destroyed, eighteen damaged; fifteen supply carts destroyed, nine damaged; eight gun emplacements destroyed, three damaged; eight vehicles destroyed, seventeen damaged. Also counted in the enemy casualties was a sizable supply dump and lumber pile which went up in flames after being rocketed and napalmed by the low-flying planes.

On the west Korean coast, the jeep carrier U.S.S. Sicily maneuvered in Yellow Sea waters to break through heavy frontal weather so her United States Marine Corps "Deathrattler" planes could strike at supply buildings and enemy rolling stock in the Yonan-Chinnampo region. Forty-five enemy storage points south of Chinnampo were taken under attack by the Leatherneck fliers. Fifteen were destroyed, thirty damaged.

—Eighth Army communiqué 561 issued at 10:00 A.M., Saturday (8:00 P.M., Friday, Eastern Daylight Time):

Light enemy contact reported along the western Korean front. Attacking United Nations forces made limited gains in the area south and southeast of Kumsong. Attacking United Nations forces in the area north and northeast of Yanggu and north of Inje encountered light to heavy enemy resistance but reported making limited gains during the day.

1. Patrolling United Nations elements along the western Korean front encountered light resistance from squad to platoon-sized enemy groups during the day. Contacts were reported in the areas west-northwest of Korangpo and west, northwest, and north of Yonchon.

2. Brief patrol contacts were reported in the area south of Pyonggang, northwest of Kumwha, northeast and east-northeast of Kumwha. During the early morning hours three probing attacks by enemy forces in up to company strength were repulsed in the area south and south-southeast of Kumsong. Attacking United Nations forces made limited gains as they encountered light to moderate resistance from company-sized enemy units in the area south-southeast of Kumsong. Stubborn resistance from an estimated enemy battalion was encountered by attacking United Nations forces in the area southeast of Kumsong as attacking elements made limited gains during the day.

3. Attacking R.O.K. (Republic of Korea) forces reported moderate to heavy enemy resistance in the area north of Yanggu from battalion-sized enemy units. R.O.K. forces secured one hill in the area at 1830 hours with action against another hill continuing until 1600 hours at which time R.O.K. forces broke contact and made a slight withdrawal for the night.

Attacking United Nations forces in the area north-northeast of Yanggu encountered light to moderate enemy resistance from company-sized enemy units, securing one hill at 2145 hours with action elsewhere in the sector continuing until 1945 hours, at which time United Nations forces broke contact and consolidated positions for the night. Friendly attacking forces reported receiving a moderate volume of mortar and artillery fire during the day. Attacking United Nations forces in the area north of Inje reported light to moderate enemy resistance and reported encountering intensive anti-personnel mine fields as they secured one hill in the area at 1520 hours. Light enemy contact continued along the remainder of the eastern Korean battlefront.

—General Headquarters communiqué 993, covering Aug. 31 operations:

United Nations ground forces along the central and east-central fronts in Korea yesterday continued to advance against heavy enemy resistance and received several counter-attacks by hostile groups up to battalion size. Friendly elements adjusted positions elsewhere along the front while patrols made only scattered contact with enemy forces of squad and platoon strength.

United Nations warships and carrier-based aircraft combined their tremendous firepower to strike hard at enemy troops in the Kansong area in one of the heaviest sea, naval, and air attacks of the Korean campaign. Naval and Marine aircraft blasted targets in advance of United Nations ground forces south of Kansong and also hit gun positions, railroad bridges, and supply routes on the east coast from Wonsan north to Songjin.

Task Force surface units shelled enemy assembly points, bridges, ammunition dumps, factories, and railway and highway junctions in the intense east Korean coast assault while carriers operating on the west coast launched air strikes against supply storage points and rolling stock in the Yunan-Chinnampo region.

Land-based fighter-bombers continued their attacks against rail lines, vehicles and bridges in North Korea while F-86 Sabre jets flew fighter sweeps to the northeast without encountering the enemy. Light bombers struck enemy vehicular traffic along supply routes leading to the battlefront and medium bombers attacked the marshaling yard at Yangdok and the supply center at Kyomipo. Large quantities of military supplies for United Nations forces in Korea were transported by Combat Cargo aircraft.

CRUMP, JERRY K.

Rank and Organization: Corporal, U.S. Army, Company L, 7th Infantry Regiment, 3d Infantry Division.
Born: February 18, 1933, Charlotte, North Carolina.
Entered Service At: Forest City, North Carolina.
Place and Date: Near Chorwon, Korea, September 6 and 7, 1951.
Citation: Cpl. Crump, a member of Company L, distinguished himself by conspicuous gallantry and intrepidity above and beyond the call of duty in action against the enemy. During the night a numerically superior hostile force launched an assault against his platoon on Hill 284, overrunning friendly positions and swarming into the sector. Cpl. Crump repeatedly exposed himself to deliver effective fire into the ranks of the assailants, inflicting numerous casualties. Observing 2 enemy soldiers endeavoring to capture a friendly machine gun, he charged and killed both with his bayonet, regaining control of the weapon. Returning to his position, now occupied by 4 of his wounded comrades, he continued his accurate fire into enemy troops surrounding his emplacement. When a hostile soldier hurled a grenade into the position, Cpl. Crump immediately flung himself over the missile, absorbing the blast with his body and saving his comrades from death or serious injury. His aggressive actions had so inspired his comrades that a spirited counterattack drove the enemy from the perimeter. Cpl. Crump's heroic devotion to duty, indomitable fighting spirit, and willingness to sacrifice himself to save his comrades reflect the highest credit upon himself, the infantry, and the U.S. Army.

†KANELL, BILLIE G.
Rank and Organization: Private, U.S. Army, Company I, 35th Infantry Regiment, 25th Infantry Division.
Born: June 26, 1931, Poplar Bluff, Missouri.
Entered Service At: Poplar Bluff, Missouri.
Place and Date: Near Pyongyang, Korea, September 7, 1951.
Citation: Pvt. Kanell, a member of Company I, distinguished himself by conspicuous gallantry and outstanding courage above and beyond the call of duty in action against the enemy. A numerically superior hostile force had launched a fanatical assault against friendly positions, supported by mortar and artillery fire, when Pvt. Kanell stood in his emplacement exposed to enemy observation and action and delivered accurate fire into the ranks of the assailants. An enemy grenade was hurled into his emplacement and Pvt. Kanell threw himself upon the grenade, absorbing the blast with his body to protect 2 of his comrades from serious injury or possible death. A few seconds later another grenade was thrown into the emplacement and, although seriously wounded by the first missile, he summoned his waning strength to roll toward the second grenade and used his body as a shield to again protect his comrades. He was mortally wounded as a result of his heroic actions. His indomitable courage, sustained fortitude against overwhelming odds, and gallant self-sacrifice reflect the highest credit upon himself, the infantry, and the U.S. Army.

OFFICIAL COMMUNIQUÉ:
TOKYO, Saturday, Sept. 8 (AP)
—Far East Air Forces summary of Thursday's operations:

Far East Air Forces warplanes destroyed or damaged a record number of enemy vehicles Thursday with night-flying B-26 light bombers and Marine fighters accounting for the majority of the 857 vehicles destroyed or damaged during the period ending at midnight Sept. 6.

F.E.A.F. aircraft flew 770 sorties as clear weather prevailed throughout the target area.

Fifth Air Force and attached South African, Australian, and shore-based Marine planes mounted 580 effective sorties as fighter bombers concentrated on disrupting enemy rail networks and aiding United Nations ground forces in close air support strikes.

B-26 light bombers of the Third and 452nd Bomb Wings plus Marine night fighters of the First Marine Air Wing set a new record for destruction of enemy vehicular traffic as they destroyed the majority of the 857 vehicles destroyed or damaged. The previous record number destroyed or damaged was established on 25 August of this year when 806 vehicles were claimed by F.E.A.F. pilots.

The light bombers and Marines, aided by flare-dropping aircraft, operated along the enemy main supply routes throughout North Korea during the night attacking vehicles with bombs, napalm (jellied gasoline), and machine-guns.

F-80 Shooting Star jets bombed and rocketed rail targets in the Anju area, attacking rolling stock, and destroying a rail bridge.

Others attacked gun positions near Sunchon. A rail bridge in the vicinity of Sinmak was also damaged by the F-80s.

F-84 Thunderjets cut rail lines in ten places between Pyongyang and Hwangju while others of the heavily armed jets attacked enemy gun positions in the Sinanju area with excellent results. Twelve Thunderjets flew escort-missions.

Propeller-driven F-51 Mustangs knocked out five enemy bridges along the enemy's western supply routes.

Enemy troops in the west and east-central sectors of the battle zone were attacked by the fighter bombers as they aided United Nations troops in close air strikes using napalm, rockets, bombs, and machine-guns to inflict casualties on enemy troops.

Marine fighters knocked out two enemy tanks west of the Imjin River with rockets and napalm. Two bridges northeast of Singye were blasted by the Marines and rail lines between Pyongyang and Samdung were cut in ten places.

F-86 Sabre jets and twin-jet Meteor fighters flew sweeps in northwest Korea. No enemy fighters challenged the United Nations fighters.

Enemy Yak-type fighter planes made two attacks on T-6 spotter planes yesterday in the Kumsong area. The Yak made several firing passes but the Mosquito escaped without damage.

Fifth Air Force pilots reported destroying or damaging two Russian-built T-34 tanks, ten gun positions, seventy-five enemy-occupied buildings, four supply storage areas, twelve railroad cars, four trailers, fifteen bridges, and 857 vehicles. Pilots also reported inflicting 150 enemy troop casualties. Rail lines were cut in sixty-five places.

Bomber Command B-29 Superforts of the Okinawa-based 307th Bomb Wing and the Japan-based Ninety-eighth Wing struck enemy rail facilities yesterday to impede the flow of Communist war supplies by rail to front-line enemy troops.

Twelve Superforts of the Ninety-eighth hit the railroad bridge at Sinanju in northwest Korea with 1,000-pound bombs. Visual aiming was used to drop the high explosives on the important rail bridges. Excellent results were reported by the crews.

Nine medium bombers from the 307th pounded the railroad marshaling yard at Chongju with maximum loads of 500-pound bombs. Excellent results were reported as the bombardiers aimed their bombs visually.

Two other Superforts hit the supply center at Wonsan on the east coast while a single B-29 dropped 500-pound bombs on the marshaling yard at Hwangju, south of the North Korean capital of Pyongyang.

Some flak was experienced by the medium bombers but no enemy fighters attacked them, and all aircraft returned safely to their base.

Combat Cargo transports continued the air supply of United Nations forces in Korea as they flew over 160 sorties and airlifted 590 tons of cargo.

Seven C-119 Flying Boxcars air dropped twenty-five tons of supplies and rations to forward United Nations ground units in the east central sector of the battle zone.

During the night, B-29 Superforts teamed with B-26 light bombers to radar-drop 500-pound air-bursting bombs on front-line enemy troop concentrations, supplies, and equipment.

—Eighth Army communiqué 568, issued 10:00 A.M., Saturday (8:00 P.M., Friday, Eastern Daylight Time):

An attack by two enemy companies in the area northwest of Chorwon was repulsed during the morning hours. Enemy battalion launched attack in area south-southeast of Pyonggang. Light enemy contact reported along the remainder of Korea battlefront.

1. United Nations forces engaged platoon to company-sized enemy groups in the area northwest of Korangpo during the day. Light enemy contact was experienced by patrolling United Nations forces in the Yonchon area. United Nations forces in the area northwest of Chorwon were attacked by an estimated enemy company at 2315 hours with the enemy withdrawing at 0550 hours. Two enemy companies preceded by a smokescreen again attacked United Nations forces in this area at 0530 hours. With the aid of reinforcements, United Nations forces caused the enemy to withdraw at 0710 hours.

2. United Nations positions south-southeast of Pyonggang were attacked by an estimated enemy battalion at 0030 hours. The enemy attack was repulsed and action ceased at 0250 hours. The enemy launched another attack at 0550 hours with the attack being repulsed at 0650 hours. Friendly reinforcements continued to engage the enemy until 1100 hours at which time the enemy withdrew. Light contact with squad to platoon-sized enemy units was reported in the Kumhwa area as well as in the area south and southeast of Kumsong.

3. United Nations forces along the eastern Korean front patrolled and reported engaging squad to platoon-sized enemy units during the day.

—*General Headquarters communiqué 1,000, issued at 9:30 A.M., Saturday (7:30 P.M., Friday, Eastern Daylight Time):*

In the west and west-central sectors of the Korean battle front yesterday United Nations ground forces repulsed several counter-attacks by enemy groups up to battalion size, while friendly elements in the east-central sector turned back a number of light probing attacks with the aid of supporting artillery and air strikes. Elsewhere along the battle line, United Nations patrols made only scattered contacts with the enemy as friendly units continued to adjust positions.

Land-based fighter-bombers, in close air support of friendly ground elements, inflicted severe casualties on enemy troop positions and also attacked gun emplacements, bridges, railroad targets, and supply points behind the battle front. Light bombers, flying during the hours of darkness, again struck enemy vehicular traffic while medium bombers blasted front-line troop positions with air-bursting bombs. Combat Cargo air transports continued the aerial resupply of United Nations forces in Korea.

In operations along the east coast of Korea, United Nations carrier-based aircraft attacked supply routes and highway and rail bridges in the Wonsan, Hongwon, Hamhung, Muchon, and Hwachang areas, while on the west coast, naval planes hit troop positions and gun emplacements in advance of friendly ground elements.

Task Force surface units, in continued interdiction strikes against enemy supply routes along the east coast, shelled railroads, rail and highway junctions, and a newly repaired bridge south of Songjin and also pounded troop positions and gun emplacements from the Kosong area north to Wonsan. On the west coast, naval warships blasted enemy troops, pillboxes, and trenchworks in the Haeju-Chinnampo region and attacked dug-in troops along the north bank of the Han River above Inchon.

†MAUSERT, FREDERICK W., III

Rank and Organization: Sergeant, U.S. Marine Corps, Company B, 1st Battalion, 7th Marines, 1st Marine Division (Rein).
Born: May 2, 1930, Cambridge, New York.
Entered Service At: Dresher, Pennsylvania.
Place and Date: Songnap-yong, Korea, September 12, 1951.
Citation: For conspicuous gallantry and intrepidity at the risk of his life above and beyond the call of duty while serving as a squad leader in Company B, in action against enemy aggressor forces. With his company pinned down and suffering heavy casualties under murderous machine gun, rifle, artillery, and mortar fire laid down from heavily fortified, deeply entrenched hostile strongholds on Hill 673, Sgt Mausert unhesitatingly left his covered position and ran through a heavily mined and fire-swept area to bring back 2 critically wounded men to the comparative safety of the lines. Staunchly refusing evacuation despite a painful head wound sustained during this voluntary act, he insisted on remaining with his squad and, with his platoon ordered into the assault moments later, took the point position and led his men in a furious bayonet charge against the first of a literally impregnable series of bunkers. Stunned and knocked to the ground when another bullet struck his helmet, he regained his feet and resumed his drive, personally silencing the machine gun and leading his men in eliminating several other emplacements in the area. Promptly reorganizing his unit for a renewed fight to the final objective on the top of the ridge, Sgt. Mausert boldly left his position when the enemy's fire gained momentum and, making a target of himself, boldly advanced alone into the face of the machine gun, drawing the fire away from his men and enabling them to move into position to assault. Again severely wounded when the enemy's fire found its mark, he still

refused aid and continued spearheading the assault to the top-most machine gun nest and bunkers, the last bulwark of the fanatic aggressors. Leaping into the wall of fire, he destroyed another machine gun before he was mortally wounded by bursting grenades and machine gun fire. Stouthearted and indomitable, Sgt. Mauser, by his fortitude, great personal valor and extraordinary heroism in the face of almost certain death, had inspired his men to sweep on, overrun and finally secure the objective. His unyielding courage throughout reflects the highest credit upon himself and the U.S. Naval Service. He gallantly gave his life for his country.

†RAMER, GEORGE H.

Rank and Organization: Second Lieutenant, U.S. Marine Corps Reserve, Company I, 3d Battalion, 7th Marines, 1st Marine Division (Rein).
Born: March 27, 1927, Meyersdale, Pennsylvania.
Entered Service At: Lewisburg, Pennsylvania.
Place and Date: Korea, September 12, 1951.
Citation: For conspicuous gallantry and intrepidity at the risk of his life above and beyond the call of duty as leader of the 3d Platoon of Company I, in action against enemy aggressor forces. Ordered to attack and seize hostile positions atop a hill, vigorously defended by well-entrenched enemy forces delivering mass small-arms, mortar, and machine gun fire, 2d Lt. Ramer fearlessly led his men up the steep slopes and, although he and the majority of his unit were wounded during the ascent, boldly continued to spearhead the assault. With the terrain becoming more precipitous near the summit and the climb more perilous as the hostile forces added grenades to the devastating hail of fire, he staunchly carried the attack to the top, personally annihilated 1 enemy bunker with grenade and carbine fire and captured the objective with his remaining 8 men. Unable to hold the position against an immediate, overwhelming hostile counterattack, he ordered his group to withdraw and singlehandedly fought the enemy to furnish cover for his men and for the evacuation of 3 fatally wounded marines. Severely wounded a second time, 2d Lt. Ramer refused aid when his men returned to help him and, after ordering them to seek shelter, courageously manned his post until the hostile troops overran his position and he fell mortally wounded. His indomitable fighting spirit, inspiring leadership and unselfish concern for others in the face of death, reflects the highest credit upon 2d Lt. Ramer and the U.S. Naval Service. He gallantly gave his life for his country.

†SUDUT, JEROME A.

Rank and Organization: Second Lieutenant, U.S. Army, Company B, 27th Infantry Regiment, 25th Infantry Division.
Born: Wausau, Wisconsin.
Entered Service At: Wisconsin.
Place and Date: Near Kumhwa, Korea, September 12, 1951.
Citation: 2d Lt. Sudut distinguished himself by conspicuous gallantry and intrepidity above and beyond the call of duty in action against the enemy. His platoon, attacking heavily fortified and strategically located hostile emplacements, had been stopped by intense fire from a large bunker containing several firing posts. Armed with submachine gun, pistol, and grenades, 2d Lt. Sudut charged the emplacement alone through vicious hostile fire, killing 3 of the occupants and dispersing the remainder. Painfully wounded, he returned to reorganize his platoon, refused evacuation and led his men in a renewed attack. The enemy had returned to the bunker by means of connecting trenches from other emplacements and the platoon was again halted by devastating fire. Accompanied by an automatic-rifleman, 2d Lt. Sudut again charged into close-range fire to eliminate the position. When the rifleman was

wounded, 2d Lt. Sudut seized his weapon and continued alone, killing 3 of the 4 remaining occupants. Though mortally wounded and his ammunition exhausted, he jumped into the emplacement and killed the remaining soldier with his trench knife. His singlehanded assaults so inspired his comrades that they continued the attack and drove the enemy from the hill, securing the objective. 2d Lt. Sudut's consummate fighting spirit, outstanding leadership, and gallant self-sacrifice are in keeping with the finest tradition of the infantry and the U.S. Army.

OFFICIAL COMMUNIQUÉ:
TOKYO, Thursday, Sept. 13 (AP)
—United Nations Naval Forces summary of Tuesday's operations:

The relentless search tactics of Task Force 77 continued to exact a heavy toll of enemy supplies, rail lines, and equipment and troop emplacements. Airmen from the two roving airdromes U.S.S. Essex and U.S.S. Boxer ranged over most of central Korea on another day of Operation Strangle in close support strikes and concentrated destruction of railroad cars.

Boxer pilots were the lead-off hitters as Panther jets from that ship spotted and attacked two long trains near Kiohang, northeast of Pyongyang. Next in the line-up were Skyraiders and Corsairs who delivered 100 and 500-pound bombs in the area. Turning northward, the same flight brought an estimated 300 railroad cars under fire. Afternoon sorties returned to add to the mass destruction. Tabulations at the end of the day's operations showed four locomotives knocked out, 150 railroad cars destroyed, and 136 others badly damaged.

A flight of Essex Skyraiders swept north of Wonsan to destroy one railroad bridge, damaged another, and eliminated four railroad cars.

C.T.F. 77 pilots also continued their close support work as they bombed and napalmed the enemy in pinpoint strikes along the front. Total tally for these missions included sixteen enemy troops killed, two mortar positions destroyed, ten supply dumps and six warehouses damaged, twelve bridges shattered, forty-one buildings, eighteen gun emplacements, and a lumber pile all wiped out.

U.S.S. Sicily flights ranged over the area from Yonan to north of Chinnampo, wreaking destruction on troop housing, road and rail bridges, enemy small craft, box cars, and troops. Near Haeju alert pilots spotted and destroyed six troop barracks, damaged a rail bridge, road bridge, and more than ten box cars.

First Marine Air Wing Corsairs concentrated on a small area to slash at red gun positions, troops, and supplies. Jet aircraft methodically knocked out rail lines and roads in several sectors.

Two artillery pieces were destroyed and two damaged in an attack which also scored 75 percent coverage of enemy bunker positions.

Surface units continued their vigilant coverage of both coasts, breaking coastal supply lines, hitting personnel concentrations and supply dumps, and obliterating many gun emplacements. The heavy cruiser U.S.S. Toledo penetrated deep into Wonsan harbor, engaged shore batteries in a forty-five minute duel, and silenced four of the six enemy batteries with 296 rounds from her 5 and 8-inch rifles.

To the north, in the Kalmagak Peninsula area, minesweepers continued their routine operations under the protective wing of the destroyer escort Moore.

The Moore silenced shore batteries which attacked the minesweepers, with the aid of a comforting air cover which air-spotted and strafed the area.

South of Wonsan city the destroyer Parks engaged in similar operations destroying an ammunition dump, scoring seven direct hits on a bivouac area, attacking neighboring rail and highway lines and silencing the threat of several gun emplacements.

Around the Han River section the British frigate Cardigan Bay, Australian frigate H.M.A.S. Murchison, and U.S.S. Banaki harassed enemy troops and inflicted damaging casualties.

—United Nations Naval Forces summary of Wednesday's operations:

Death and destruction rained from the skies and the seas yesterday as the naval sea and air units unleashed their terrific power over most of North Korea. The busy planes of Task Force 77 were well on their way toward equaling their record of Tuesday as over 200 targets consumed the deadly fire of the Essex and Boxer aircraft. Swarming over most of the east coast from Chongjin south to Kosong, they hit nearly everything in sight that could be of use to the enemy, destroying forty-seven buildings, nine bridges, thirty-four boxcars, eight gun positions, four warehouses and a pretentious array of supply dumps, trucks, small houses, vessels, and troop concentrations.

Reds on the west coast were also having a bad time at the hands of Sicily planes that swooped low over Haeju leaving seventy-six buildings either thoroughly air-conditioned or cinderized. Southeast of Haeju in the Han River estuary, the frigate Cardigan Bay practiced her specialty of illuminating the countryside with star shells during the early morning hours so that she and her colleagues could blast troop concentrations and gun emplacements.

The methodical peppering of Wonsan continued during the day. While a spotting plane hovered over the city to direct fire, the destroyers Parks and Craig and destroyer escort Moore hit the juiciest targets with gratifying results.

One shell was all that was needed for a building housing ammunition but the railroad station and marshaling yards required several more. The cruiser Toledo, under fire but unhit, ignored the insult and systematically lobbed her big shells into gun emplacements, railroad junctions, and warehouses after her job at the station was completed. Gunners on the destroyer Craig were satisfied with the large fire started as a result of a direct hit of her heavy guns.

Bright moonlight Tuesday night proved an ally to the ships at Songjin and three trains were observed finding new hiding places. The game ended abruptly yesterday morning as the destroyers Charity and Thompson together with the destroyer escort Naifeh opened up on the three spots with telling effect.

The cocky little destroyer Perkins at Kosong also had a field day eliminating eight small vessels then turning her guns to seven troop positions on the beach.

—Far East Air Forces summary of Tuesday's operations:

Massive destruction of enemy vehicular traffic was continued Tuesday as Far East Air Forces warplanes flew 845 sorties in generally good weather. Approximately 455 enemy motor trucks, trying to substitute for the Communists battered rail communications lines, were destroyed or damaged. The bulk of them were hit in the hours of darkness on western Korean highways by night-flying B-26 light bombers, assisted by flare-dropping aircraft.

For the fourth successive day enemy MiG-15 jets slipped south from their Manchurian sanctuary to challenge United Nations air supremacy. They made three separate attacks on fighter bombers, which were striking ground targets. In the air-to-air fighting that followed, one MiG was probably destroyed by an F-84 Thunderjet and one was damaged by an F-80 Shooting Star jet.

Fifth Air Force and attached planes flew 695 sorties. Of these, 140 were mounted by shore-based Marine aircraft and thirty-six by Australian and South African aircraft under the operational control of Fifth.

Fighter bombers continued their attacks on the enemy's rail lines, ranging western trackage to crater out rails and cross ties in ninety-five places. During these attacks supply buildings and anti-aircraft gun positions were successfully hit.

On central Korean rail lines the fighter bombers found and destroyed a thirty-car train and three locomotives. Boxcars and locomotives were attacked at other localities.

Eighty close air support strikes by F-51 Mustangs and Marine F-4Us hit enemy troops, bunkers, and gun positions along the battle front, with the heaviest close support concentration being in the eastern mountainous section. Nature of the terrain and enemy defensive positions prohibited pilot evaluation of casualties inflicted on the enemy in these strikes, but observation planes reported counting fifty bodies after one strike.

Fifth Air Force and attached pilots reported destroying or damaging 125 enemy-held buildings, ten gun positions, twenty-five supply carts, eight barracks buildings, twenty bridges, and one boat. They reported destroying forty pack animals being used by the enemy to supplement his rail and motor transportation of supplies.

F.E.A.F. Bomber Command Superforts flying from both Japan and Okinawa bases kept hammering at enemy railroad marshaling yards in western Korea, hitting those at Sinanju, Namchonjom, and Masan. The bombardiers aimed quarter-ton bombs visually in clear weather and observed some highly successful hits. The thirteen medium bombers taking part in these operations experienced flak in some places but encountered no enemy air opposition.

Tuesday night three B-29s teamed with nine B-26 light bombers to attack enemy front-line troop and supply concentrations with air-bursting quarter-ton bombs aimed by radar techniques.

Friendly troops battling in the mountains of eastern Korea received sixty-five tons of supplies, parachuted from giant C-119 Flying Boxcars of the 315th Air Division (Combat Cargo). The drops were made without incident. During the day, 315th flew 140 sorties and delivered 545 tons of supplies from Japan to Korea. They transported 1,200 rest-leave personnel.

—Eighth Army communiqué 572, issued 10:00 A.M., Wednesday (9:00 P.M., Tuesday, Eastern Daylight Time):

United Nations forces maintained positions and patrolled reporting light enemy contact along western and west central fronts. Stubborn enemy resistance was encountered by attacking United Nations forces in the area north-northwest and north-northeast of Yanggu. Two enemy companies attack in area northwest of the Punchbowl. Attacking United Nations forces limited gains in area north of Inje. Two enemy battalions offered stubborn resistance in area west of Kansong.

1. Patrolling United Nations forces reported brief engagements with squad to company-size enemy units in the area west and north of Korangpo during the day. No significant enemy contact was encountered by patrolling United Nations forces in the Yonchon area. Other United Nations forces engaged enemy groups of undetermined strength to the area north-northwest of Chorwon during the morning hours. Light contact with enemy units up to platoon strength was reported in the Kumhwa sector.

2. United Nations patrols in the area south and south-southeast of Kumsong engaged several enemy groups in platoon to company strength during the day. Squad to company-size enemy contact was reported in the area southeast of Kumsong. In the area north-northwest of Yanggu, an estimated enemy battalion fiercely resisted attacking United Nations forces from 0100 to 0800 hours, at which time friendly elements withdrew.

3. An estimated enemy battalion employing a heavy volume of small arms, automatic weapons, and hand grenades, engaged friendly attacking elements in the area north-northeast of Yanggu at 0455. Heavy fighting continued in this area as of 2300 hours. Two enemy companies supported by artillery fire launched an attack against United Nations forces northwest of the Punchbowl at 1830 hours. United Nations forces made a slight withdrawal and the action continued as of 2400 hours.

Attacking United Nations forces in the area north of Inje engaged an estimated two enemy battalions and made limited gains against moderate to heavy enemy resistance. The enemy launched a counterattack in the area west of Kansong, employing an estimated two enemy battalions. United Nations elements withdrew approximately 200 yards, resumed the attack and restored their previous position by 0720 hours. United Nations forces continued the attack and were counter-attacked by an enemy battalion at 1900 hours, forcing friendly elements to make a limited withdrawal at 1920 hours. United Nations forces broke contact at 1940 hours.

—Eighth Army communiqué 573, issued at 10:00 A.M., Thursday (9:00 P.M., Wednesday, Eastern Daylight Time):

Light to moderate enemy resistance was reported along the western Korean front as United Nations forces adjusted positions and patrolled. Attacking United Nations forces northeast of Kumhwa inflicted heavy casualties on the enemy. An enemy regiment offered stubborn resistance to attacking United Nations forces northwest of Yanggu. Attacking United Nations forces made limited gains as they overcame stubborn enemy resistance in the area north-northeast of Yanggu and north of Inje. Enemy forces continued to offer stubborn resistance in the area west of Kansong. No significant enemy activity was reported in the Korangpo sector as United Nations forces adjusted positions and patrolled. Platoon to company-sized enemy resistance was reported in the area west-southwest of Yonchon. Light enemy contact was reported by other United Nations forces in the area west and north of Yonchon. Little or no enemy contact was reported in the Chorwon area. Enemy platoons offered light to moderate resistance as United Nations forces mounted limited objective attacks and secured their objective during the day.

1. Attacking United Nations forces east-northeast of Kumhwa engaged an enemy company and inflicted heavy enemy casualties as they secured the high ground in the area. Light to moderate resistance from enemy units in up to company strength was reported by patrolling United Nations forces south and south-southeast of Kumsong. Light attacks by squad and company-sized enemy units were repelled in the area southeast of Kumsong. Attacking United Nations forces in the area north-northwest of Yanggu encountered stubborn resistance from an estimated enemy regiment entrenched on the high ground in the area. Little or no gains were reported for the day.

2. Remnants of an estimated enemy battalion in the area north-northeast of Yonggu fought stubbornly against attacking United Nations forces until 1500 hours (3;00 P.M.) at which time the enemy resistance was overcome and the hill secured. An enemy company launched an attack against United Nations forces northwest of the Punchbowl at 2000 hours (8:00 P.M.)—the attack was repulsed at 2100 hours. Attacking United Nations forces in the area north of Inje overcame stubborn enemy resistance to secure two hills in the area during the day. In the area west of Kansong, two enemy battalions continued to offer stubborn resistance to attacking friendly units.

—General Headquarters communiqué 1,004 for the twenty-four hours ended 6:00 A.M., Wednesday (5:00 P.M., Tuesday, Eastern Daylight Time):

Yesterday (Tuesday) in Korea the most significant ground action took place in the east-central sector of the battlefront where advancing United Nations forces encountered heavy resistance from battalion-size enemy units. In other sectors of the front, friendly elements again adjusted positions while patrols made only minor contacts with small hostile groups as they continued to probe enemy strong points and defensive positions.

United Nations carrier-based aircraft operating over central Korea attacked enemy trains and rail cars in the Kichang area northeast of Pyongyang and also hit troop positions, gun emplacements, supply dumps, storage warehouses, bridges, and rolling stock along the east coast from the ground battle line north of Wonsan. Naval and Marine aircraft flying over the west coast attacked enemy troops, gun positions, supplies, rail lines, roads, bridges, and small craft in the Haeju-Yonan-Chinnampo region. Task force surface elements, continuing interdiction strikes against enemy ground forces and supply lines along the east coast, shelled troop concentrations, gun emplacements, ammunition and supply dumps, shore batteries, rail lines, and bridges from Losong north to Songjin, while on the west coast, naval warships again bombarded enemy troops along the north bank of the Han River estuary.

Land-based fighter-bombers probably destroyed one enemy MiG-15 aircraft and damaged another in the fourth successive day of air-to-air encounters over Korea, while other fighter-bombers napalmed and strafed enemy front-line troops and heavily damaged enemy rail lines and rolling stock.

Light bombers continued the heavy destruction of enemy vehicular traffic and medium bombers hit marshaling yards in western Korea. Combat Cargo aircraft continued the airlift of supplies to forward and rear bases in Korea.

—General Headquarters communiqué 1,005, for the twenty-four hours ended 6:00 A.M., Thursday (5:00 P.M., Wednesday, Eastern Daylight Time):

Action on the Korean front yesterday (Wednesday) was concentrated in the west-central and east-central sectors where advancing United Nations forces continued to encounter moderate to heavy enemy resistance. In other sectors of the front friendly patrols continued to probe enemy positions with minor enemy contact.

United Nations carrier-based aircraft concentrated their attacks on supply buildings, bridges, rail cars, gun positions, boats, and troop positions on the east coast from Chongjin south to Kosong. Big guns of naval surface vessels continued to bombard the Wonsan, Songjin, and Kosong areas, shelling ammunition dumps, railroad stations, marshaling yards, gun emplacements, and railroad trains.

Land-based fighter-planes damaged three enemy MiG-15 aircraft in several encounters over western Korea yesterday. Fighter-bombers continued to attack enemy rail supply routes while light bombers kept up attacks on enemy vehicular traffic throughout the night. Medium bombers hit marshaling yards and supply centers on both sides of the Korean Peninsula. Combat cargo air-transports delivered a large quantity of military supplies to United Nations forces in Korea.

†GOMEZ, EDWARD

Rank and Organization: Private First Class, U.S. Marine Corps Reserve, Company E, 2d Battalion, 1st Marines, 1st Marine Division.
Born: August 10, 1932, Omaha, Nebraska.
Entered Service At: Omaha, Nebraska.
Place and Date: Korea, Hill 749, September 14, 1951.
Citation: For conspicuous gallantry and intrepidity at the risk of his life above and beyond the call of duty while serving as an ammunition bearer in Company E, in action against enemy aggressor forces. Boldly advancing with his squad in support of a group of riflemen assaulting a series of strongly fortified and bitterly defended hostile positions on Hill 749, Pfc. Gomez consistently exposed himself to the withering barrage to keep his machine gun supplied with ammunition during the drive forward to seize the objective. As his squad deployed to meet an imminent counterattack, he voluntarily moved down an abandoned trench to search for a new location for the gun and, when a hostile grenade landed between himself and his weapon, shouted a warning to those around him as he grasped the activated charge in his hand. Determined to save his comrades, he unhesitatingly chose to sacrifice himself and, diving into the ditch with the deadly missile, absorbed the shattering violence of the explosion with his body. By his stouthearted courage, incomparable valor, and decisive spirit of self-sacrifice, Pfc. Gomez inspired the others to heroic efforts in subsequently repelling the outnumbering foe, and his valiant conduct throughout sustained and enhanced the finest traditions of the U.S. Naval Service. He gallantly gave his life for his country.

†WALMSLEY, JOHN S., JR.

Rank and Organization: Captain, U.S. Air Force, 8th Bombardment Squadron, 3d Bomb Group.
Born: January 7, 1920, Baltimore, Maryland.
Entered Service At: Baltimore, Maryland.
Place and Date: Near Yangdok, Korea, September 14, 1951.
Citation: Capt. Walmsley distinguished himself by conspicuous gallantry and intrepidity at the risk of his life above and beyond the call of duty. While flying a B-26 aircraft on a night combat mission with the objective of developing new tactics, Capt. Walmsley sighted an enemy supply train which had been assigned top priority as a target of opportunity. He immediately attacked, producing a strike which disabled the train and, when his ammunition was expended, radioed for friendly aircraft in the area to complete destruction of the target. Employing the searchlight mounted on his aircraft, he guided another B-26 aircraft to the target area, meanwhile constantly exposing himself to enemy fire. Directing an incoming B-26 pilot, he twice boldly aligned himself with the target, his searchlight illuminating the area, in a determined effort to give the attacking aircraft full visibility. As the friendly aircraft prepared for the attack, Capt. Walmsley descended into the valley in a low level run over the target with searchlight blazing, selflessly exposing himself to vicious enemy antiaircraft fire. In his determination to inflict maximum damage on the enemy, he refused to employ evasive tactics and valiantly pressed forward straight through an intense barrage, thus insuring complete destruction of the enemy's vitally needed war cargo. While he courageously pressed his attack Capt. Walmsley's was hit and crashed into the surrounding mountains, exploding upon impact. His heroic initiative and daring aggressiveness in completing this important mission in the face of overwhelming opposition and at the risk of his life, reflects the highest credit upon himself and the U.S. Air Force.

OFFICIAL COMMUNIQUÉ:
TOKYO, Saturday, Sept. 15 (AP)
—Far East Air Forces summary of Thursday's operations:

Enemy troops were napalmed in their foxholes and bunkers and survivors were pinned down with aerial machine-gun fire Thursday as Far East Air Forces warplanes continued effective close air support of United Nations ground forces engaged in limited offensive operations in central Korea.

Taking full advantage of excellent weather, F.E.A.F. and attached aircraft mounted 943 sorties, the greatest number flown in a single twenty-four hour period since June 24, when 962 were mounted.

In addition to close support of the ground forces, F.E.A.F. jet and propellered fighter bombers continued to shred enemy rail lines, while light bombers, flying in hours of darkness, took another heavy toll of Communist supply trucks. During the first thirteen days of September F.E.A.F. pilots successfully attacked 7,400 enemy vehicles, destroying 2,200 and heavily damaging 5,200.

One F-51 Mustang was lost in Northwest Korea when three MiG-15 enemy jet fighters attacked a flight of friendly aircraft bombing rail targets. The MiGs escaped without damage. It was the sixth successive day of air-to-air action in Korea.

F-86 Sabre jets, sweeping northwest Korea in search of the enemy, sighted a total of sixty-four MiGs, but the Communist aircraft stayed out of range of the Sabre jets.

Fifth Air Force and attached units mounted 710 sorties. Of these approximately 135 were flown by shore-based Marine aircraft and approximately forty-five by Australian and South African planes.

F-51s teamed with F-4Us to hit enemy front-line positions with more than seventy sorties. Napalm and machine-gun fire accounted for fifty observed enemy casualties, but terrain and battle smoke prohibited any casualty claims on many strikes where good coverage was achieved.

Pilots saw friendly troops advance and [take] positions they had hit.

Other F-51s ranged enemy supply lines, cratering tracks and attacking gun positions. Near Suan, a camouflaged tank was destroyed and five other camouflaged objects successfully attacked.

F-80 Shooting Star jets worked over western main supply routes. Marshaling yards, bridges, and supply buildings were damaged. Gun positions were knocked out, rail tracks were cratered. Box cars were strafed and napalmed with good results at Kangdong, Chaeryong, and Haeju in western Korea. The train at Haeju appeared to be hauling iron ore, pilots reported.

Hours-of-darkness operations Thursday took a toll of almost 400 enemy vehicles. The bulk of the destruction was achieved by B-26 light bombers aided by flare-dropping aircraft. The B-26s also hit a train east of Pyongyang and observed secondary explosions.

Secondary explosions and fires also were observed after a strike against enemy barracks in the vicinity of Chongju in northwest Korea.

Eleven B-29 Superforts of F.E.A.F. Bomber Command flew from their Japanese base to drop 1,000-pound bombs on the 2,000-foot-long highway bridge across the Taedong River at Pyongyang, a vital choke point in the enemy's main western supply route. Crewmen reported the pattern of their bombs covered the bridge. Just before the B-29s attacked, F-84 Thunderjets swept in low to hit enemy anti-aircraft positions with 500-pound bombs in a flak-suppression mission. The B-29s were escorted to their target by MD-8 Meteor jets. They were not challenged by enemy aircraft.

Two other B-29s attacked east coast targets, one the airfield at Wonsan and the other the marshaling yard at Munpyong.

Cargo-transport planes of the 315th Air Division (Combat Cargo) flew 215 sorties and airlifted 610 tons of airfreight and 1,200 rest-leave personnel. Thirty-six tons of supplies were parachuted to forward friendly troops in the eastern Korean mountains.

At night diminished enemy vehicular traffic was noted despite clear weather and a large number of night sorties. The traffic was put under successful attack. Three B-29s and two B-26s hammered enemy front-line positions with more than 130 quarter-ton air-bursting bombs, which were aimed by accurate radar techniques to disrupt enemy night operations close to friendly front lines.

—United Nations Naval Forces summary of Friday's operations:

The veteran planes from the U.S.S. Essex and the U.S.S. Boxer contributed materially to the success of Operation Strangle yesterday (Friday) as they swarmed over much of North Korea dropping their heavy loads of explosives on hundreds of targets.

Four rear admirals of the United States Navy were on hand to witness the day's activities and the well-practiced fliers really put on a show, destroying sixty railroad cars, forty-one buildings, five barracks housing enemy troops, and four bridges.

Supplementing this total they damaged seventy-one box cars, eleven bridges, and killed seventy-nine troops as they ranged from Wonsan north to Hungnam and west halfway across the peninsula. Near Wonsan 150 troops were observed thoughtlessly grouped together. The ensuing strafing runs netted a large percentage of casualties.

Guests of Rear Admiral John Perry on his flagship Essex were Rear Admirals G.C. Dyer, W.C. Tomlinson, R.E. Libby and J.W. Roper, each commanders of major Pacific Fleet units.

On the west coast, Marine fliers of the carrier Sicily scoured the area from Chinnampo south to Haeju, destroying forty supply buildings plus many railroad cars, hidden supply piles, and troop concentrations.

The naval surface units also saturated Communist-held territory with their heavy ordnance. Near Kosong the destroyer Perkins slugged it out with the Reds on the beach, killing an undetermined number of troops and starting several major fires in the area.

Fires also lit the sky at Wonsan as the destroyer Parks peppered the besieged city's gun emplacements, transportation facilities, and troop positions. Sharing honors at Wonsan, the escort vessel Moore lobbed round after round of heavy ammunition at five troop housing areas.

Songjin helplessly absorbed the deathly 8-inch shells from the heavy cruiser Toledo. Troop concentrations and transportation facilities were the primary targets, but the big guns also accounted for the destruction of a railroad bridge and a by-pass. In company with the Toledo were the Task Force 95, destroyers Craig, Charity, and Thompson, which pin-pointed and registered direct hits on bridges, small ships, supply dumps, and trains.

—Eighth Army communiqué 575, issued at 10:00 A.M., Saturday (9:00 P.M. Friday, Eastern Daylight Time):

Light enemy contact was reported along the western Korean front. Light to moderate enemy resistance was reported along the central Korean front as United Nations patrols engaged squad to company size enemy units. Stubborn enemy resistance continued in the areas north-northwest of Yanggu and west of Kansong as enemy forces up to regimental strength continued to defend their positions.

1. United Nations forces along the western Korean front adjusted positions and patrolled, reporting light enemy contact with squad and platoon-sized enemy units.

2. An enemy platoon employing a heavy volume of fire was forced to withdraw after a one-half hour fire fight in the area south of Pyonggang. An enemy company attacked United Nations forces east-northeast of Kumhwa at 0015 hours but was forced to withdraw by friendly artillery fire. Two enemy platoons probed United Nations positions east-northeast of Kumhwa at 2000 hours and were forced to withdraw at 2150 hours. United Nations forces patrolling the area south of Kumsong engaged an enemy company at 0855 hours with heavy fighting continuing until 1600 hours, at which time the friendly patrol withdrew.

3. An enemy regiment previously reported in the area north-northwest of Yanggu continued to defend its positions with little or no gains reported by attacking United Nations forces. Other attacking United Nations forces in the area north-northeast of Yanggu engaged an estimated enemy battalion from 0700 to 2000 hours, at which time friendly elements withdrew. In the area northwest of the Punchbowl, platoon to company sized enemy units were engaged by United Nations patrol. Attacking United Nations forces in the area northeast of the Punchbowl reported making limited gains, while, attacking forces in the area west of Kansong met stubborn resistance from an estimated enemy regiment.

—General Headquarters communiqué 1,007, for the twenty-four hours ended 6:00 A.M., Saturday (5:00 P.M., Friday, Eastern Daylight Time):

Ground action in Korea yesterday (Friday) remained heavy in the east-central sector where United Nations elements continued to encounter stubborn resistance from enemy units up to regimental strength. Elsewhere along the front, only minor enemy contacts were made.

Carrier-based aircraft in day-long flights damaged bridges and rail rolling stock in the Wonsan and Hungnam areas. Other targets hit included supply buildings, rail cars, supply dumps, and troops concentrations in the Chinnampo and Haeju areas. Guns from naval surface units bombarded troop concentrations, barracks, gun emplacements, transportation facilities, small ships, and supply dumps in the area of Kosong, Wonsan, and Songjin.

Land-based fighter-bombers flew close support missions for ground forces and attacked enemy gun positions, supply buildings, and rail facilities as medium bombers struck the important rail bridge at Huichon and supply areas near Wonsan. Light bombers destroyed enemy vehicular traffic along main supply routes during the night. Combat Cargo transport aircraft continued to airlift supplies to United Nations forces in Korea.

†VITTORI, JOSEPH

Rank and Organization: Corporal, U.S. Marine Corps Reserve, Company F, 2d Battalion, 1st Marines, 1st Marine Division.
Born: August 1, 1929, Beverly, Massachusetts.
Entered Service At: Beverly Massachusetts.
Place and Date: Hill 749, Korea, September 15 and 16, 1951.
Citation: For conspicuous gallantry and intrepidity at the risk of his life above and beyond the call of duty while serving as an automatic-rifleman in Company F, in action against enemy aggressor forces. With a forward platoon suffering heavy casualties and forced to withdraw under a vicious enemy counterattack as his company assaulted strong hostile forces entrenched on Hill 749, Cpl. Vittori boldly rushed through the withdrawing troops with 2 other volunteers from his reserve platoon and plunged directly into the midst of the enemy. Overwhelming them in a fierce hand-to-hand struggle, he enabled his company to consolidate its positions to meet further imminent onslaughts. Quick to respond to an urgent call for a rifleman to defend a heavy machine gun positioned on the extreme point of the northern flank and virtually isolated from the remainder of the unit when the enemy again struck in force during the night, he assumed position under the devastating barrage and, fighting a singlehanded battle, leaped from one flank to the other, covering each foxhole in turn as casualties continued to mount, manning a machine gun when the gunner was struck down and making repeated trips through the heaviest shellfire to replenish ammunition. With the situation becoming extremely critical, reinforcing units to the rear pinned down under the blistering attack and foxholes left practically void by dead and wounded for a distance of 100 yards, Cpl. Vittori continued his valiant stand, refusing to give ground as the enemy penetrated to within a few feet of his position, simulating strength in the line and denying the foe physical occupation of the ground. Mortally wounded by the enemy machine gun and rifle bullets while persisting in his magnificent defense of the sector where approximately 200 enemy dead were found the following morning, Cpl. Vittori, by his fortitude, stouthearted courage, and great personal valor, had kept the point position intact despite the tremendous odds and undoubtedly prevented the entire battalion position from collapsing. His extraordinary heroism throughout the furious night-long battle reflects the highest credit upon himself and the U.S. Naval Service. He gallantly gave his life for his country.

OFFICIAL COMMUNIQUÉ:

TOKYO, Monday, Sept. 17 (AP)
—Far East Air Forces summary of Saturday's operations:

United States Air force fighter-bombers Saturday cratered enemy railroad tracks in fifty places and last night light bombers took a toll of twelve enemy locomotives and 170 box cars. It was the heaviest night blow at Communist locomotives in more than four months.

The fighter-bombers (F-84s, F-80s, and F-51s) attacked three important sections of rail lines in western Korea on a day in which Far East Air Forces and attached planes mounted a total of 615 sorties. The attacks generally were on railroad lines running south from Sinanju, Kunu, and Pyongyang.

Disruption of enemy rail facilities by these constant cratering attacks has forced the Communists to resort to much shutting over relatively short stretches of tracks, with frequent offloading and reloading of supplies. This has imposed a tremendous logistical handicap on the enemy's effort to build up combat material at his front lines for offensive or defensive action.

Trains, unable to reach the protection of the numerous Korean tunnels as a result of these track-cratering attacks, have frequently become easy targets for fighter-bombers and light bombers.

Biggest destruction last night was achieved on the trans-peninsula line between Kunu and Yangdok. Successful attacks were also made in the west between Pyongyang and Sariwon and on the east coast north of Wonsan.

For the second successive day, Far East Air Forces jets (United States F-86 Sabres and Australian MD-8 Meteors) swept northwest Korea without encountering enemy aircraft.

In the interdiction strikes against enemy rail lines F.E.A.F. planes not only cratered tracks but destroyed and damaged box cars, bridges, gun positions, and supply buildings.

Forty close air support sorties by shore-based Marine F-4Us and United States Air Force F-51s were hurled at enemy front-line positions in front of aggressive United Nations ground troops.

The weight of the effort was in the mountainous section of eastern Korea where bitter fighting was in progress for key hill positions. Approximately eighty casualties were observed inflicted on enemy troops, but in many strikes where good coverage of targets was observed, smoke, rain, and the nature of the terrain prohibited definite claims.

During the hours of darkness and in rather bad weather Saturday, B-26 light bombers, aided by Marine F-7s and F-4Us and flare-dropping U.S.A.F. aircraft, destroyed or damaged approximately 105 enemy vehicles as they continued to hammer the enemy's nocturnal highway supply movement.

Fifth Air Force and attached planes flew 410 sorties of which seventy were by shore-based Marine aircraft and thirty by Australian and South African planes. The sorties were mounted in weather bad in the forenoon but improving later. Pilots reported encountering icing and turbulence in clouds at medium altitudes.

F.E.A.F. Bomber Command sent a lone Superfort in a radar strike against the east coast marshaling yard at Kowon. Last night, three B-29s dropped 120 proximity-fused quarter-ton bombs on enemy front-line troops and supply concentrations, particularly in the eastern sector.

Transport-cargo planes of the 315th Air Division flew 200 sorties and delivered 585 tons of combat supplies from Japan to Korea in support of United Nations armed forces. Of this airhaul, sixty-five tons were parachuted from giant C-119 Flying Box Cars to forward United Nations elements battling the enemy in rugged mountain wilderness. Twelve hundred rest-leave personnel were airlifted.

One T-6 observation plane was lost yesterday to enemy ground fire.

—Eighth Army communiqué 577, issued 10:00 A.M., Monday (9:00 P.M. Sunday, Eastern Daylight Time):

Light to moderate enemy resistance encountered along the Korean western front. Attack by elements of an enemy regiment supported by mortar and artillery fire repulsed in the area north-northeast of Kumhwa. Enemy company forced to withdraw in the area south of Kumsong. Stubborn enemy resistance continues in area north-northwest and north of Yanggu. enemy battalion encountered in area northwest of the Punchbowl. Heavy enemy counterattack repulsed in the area northeast of the Punchbowl. Hand-to-hand combat reported in the area west of Kansong.

1. United Nations forces patrolling in the Korangpo area encountered enemy squad and platoon sized units during the day. Other United Nations forces in the area northeast of Korangpo engaged an estimated enemy company and reported receiving a total of 140 rounds of enemy 82-mm. fire during the engagement. An engagement with two enemy platoons was reported in the area northwest of Yonchon. United Nations forces patrolling in the area south-southwest of Pyongyang encountered an undetermined number of enemy and went through to adjust artillery fire on the enemy.

2. Elements of an estimated enemy regiment supported by 500 to 600 rounds of artillery fire attacked United Nations forces in the area north-northeast of Kumhwa at 2300 hours (11:00 P.M.) Sept. 15. The attack was repulsed at 0010 hours 16 Sept., with the enemy sustaining eighty-two counted killed in action.

A well-entrenched enemy company on the high ground south-southeast of Kumsong was forced to withdraw by attacking United Nations forces during the day. Elsewhere on the central front, United Nations patrols briefly engaged enemy platoon-sized units during the day.

3. Enemy forces entrenched in the area north-northwest of Yanggu continued to defend their positions against attacking United Nations forces. Enemy forces in bunkered positions in the area north of Yanggu continued to offer stubborn resistance as United Nations forces continued their attack.

Light to moderate resistance was encountered in the area northwest of the Punchbowl as an esti-mated enemy battalion restricted the advance of other attacking United Nations elements. In the area northeast of the Punchbowl, elements of an enemy battalion launched heavy counterattacks against friendly forces during the night 15-16 Sept.. All attacks were repulsed. Elsewhere in this area an enemy battalion in bunkered positions on the north slope of a hill offered heavy resistance from 1050 to 1800, at which time the enemy was forced to withdraw. Hand-to-hand combat with elements of a reinforced enemy company was reported in the area west of Kansong as its forces continued to attack to secure the high ground in the area.

†PILILAAU, HERBERT K.

Rank and Organization: Private First Class, U.S. Army, Company C, 23rd Infantry Regiment, 2d Infantry Division.
Born: October 10, 1928, Waianae, Oahu, Hawaii.
Entered Service At: Oahu, Hawaii.
Place and Date: Near Pia-ri, Korea, September 17, 1951.
Citation: Pfc. Pililaau, a member of Company C, distinguished himself by conspicuous gal-lantry and intrepidity above and beyond the call of duty in action against the enemy. The enemy sent wave after wave of fanatical troops against his platoon which held a key terrain feature on "Heartbreak Ridge." Valiantly defending its position, the unit repulsed each attack until ammunition became practically exhausted and it was ordered to withdraw to a new position. Voluntarily remaining behind to cover the withdrawal, Pfc. Pililaau fired his auto-matic weapon into the ranks of the assailants, threw all of his hand-grenades and, with ammu-nition exhausted, closed with the foe in hand-to-hand combat, courageously fighting with his trench knife and bare fists until finally overcome and mortally wounded. When the position was subsequently retaken, more than 40 enemy dead were counted in the area he had so valiantly defended. His heroic devotion to duty, indomitable fighting spirit, and gallant self-sacrifice reflects the highest credit upon himself, the infantry, and the U.S. Army.

OFFICIAL COMMUNIQUÉ:
TOKYO, Tuesday, Sept. 18 (AP)
—Far East Air Forces summary, covering Sunday's operations:

Cloudy weather and scattered rain showers in Korea yesterday failed to stop Far East Air Force war-planes from destroying or damaging 300 Communist railroad cars, the largest number since May 2, 1951, when 485 were claimed by F.E.A.F. pilots. Over 640 sorties were flown yesterday, with Fifth Air Force and attached planes mounting 425 of these.

Enemy rail facilities continued to be primary targets for fighter-bombers as F-84 Thunderjets, F-80 Shooting Star jets and propeller-driven F-51 Mustangs cut trackage all along the main western rail net-works from Chongju to Sariwon, and along the trans-peninsular line from Sunchon to Kowon on the east coast.

F-84 Thunderjets attacked rail targets between Pyongyang and Sariwon with pilots reporting sev-eral rail cars destroyed and trackage cut in twenty-seven places. F-80 Shooting Star jets destroyed three of four anti-aircraft gun positions discovered near Pyongyang, while other flights cut rail lines and burned box cars.

Sixty close-support air strikes were flown yesterday by fighter-bombers in support of United Na-tions ground forces, as they battled deeply dug in Red troops in the mountainous terrain of the east-central front. F-51 Mustangs attacked the enemy bunkers and troops with napalm, rockets, and ma-chine-gun fire. No claims of enemy troop casualties were made by the Mustang pilots because of poor visibility and smoke.

There were no enemy fighters encountered by F.E.A.F. aircraft during the day.

Fifth Air Force pilots reported destroying or damaging twenty-five gun positions, 115 enemy-occupied buildings, six bridges, one marshaling yard, twenty-five warehouses, 150 vehicles, three bunkers, and 300 railroad cars. Highways and rail lines were cut in fifty-five places. Almost fifty enemy troop casualties were reported inflicted by air strikes.

All-weather B-29 Superforts of the F.E.A.F. Bomber Command hit several types of targets in North Korea yesterday, the main effort being a supply center, a marshaling yard, and an airfield. Three medium bombers of the Okinawa-based 307th Bomb Wing hit the Communist supply center of Kyomipo, west coast river port, with 1,000-pound bombs, while two others of the same unit attacked supplies at Chinnampo, west of Kyomipo.

Five Superforts of the Japan-based Ninety-eighth Bomb Wing struck the enemy airfield at Wonsan on the east coast of Korea. Visual bombing was used to drop the 1,000-pound bombs on the airstrip and storage area. Two other United States Air Force B-29s attacked the important marshaling yard at Kowon, junction point for the trans-peninsular and east coast rail lines. Crews reported good results on the strike. Some flak but no enemy fighters were encountered by the Superforts.

Combat Cargo transports of the 315th Air Division continued to airlift supplies to United Nations forces in Korea yesterday, as they flew over 190 sorties to bring in 555 tons of supplies and equipment. Over 1,100 United Nations personnel on rest leave were carried to or from Korea.

Last night over 100 sorties were flown by B-26 light bombers, Marine fighters, and other night-flying aircraft. Preliminary reports indicate that four trains and many vehicles were successfully attacked as the night-flyers operated along enemy supply routes throughout North Korea.

Three B-29 Superforts radar-dropped 500-pound air-bursting bombs on enemy front-line troops and supplies during the hours of darkness.

—United Nations Naval Forces summary of Monday's operations:

United Nations Naval Forces continued heavy interdiction of Communist supply lines in North Korea yesterday (Monday). Railroad rolling stock was the prime target for Task Force 77 fliers, with several locomotives and over 110 boxcars destroyed or damaged.

Flying from fast carriers U.S.S. Essex and U.S.S. Boxer, Navy fighters and dive-bombers knocked out or severely damaged five bridges before noon Monday.

A sixty-foot section was dropped from one near Pyong while two spans were wrecked during attacks on another in the same area.

Close air-support strikes assisted battling Eighth Army troops in the eastern sector southwest of Kosong. Controllers reported excellent coverage in several cases, with one task force pilot credited with forty enemy killed.

Task Force 95 surface units again unleashed heavy naval gunfire at Red supply lanes on the east coast from Chongjin south to Kosong.

The Australian destroyer Anzac and destroyer-minesweeper Thompson roamed to the north on blockade and bombardment missions between Songjin and Chongjin. The Australian warship battered rail and road junctions at Chuuronjang and Tunam, while the minesweeper shelled similar targets at Nanam and Kyongsong. The U.S.S. Naifeh continued attacks on other transportation targets at Songjin and near Tanchon.

Red shore guns on Kalma Peninsula in Wonsan Harbor opened up again yesterday noon attempting to sink United Nations small craft check-sweeping the bay. Heavy counter-battery fire from the destroyer U.S.S. Moore screened the minesweeping boats as they speeded out of range.

The Moore and U.S.S. Parks shelled Wonsan rail installations and road intersections before dawn Monday, keeping Communist traffic at a minimum. The Parks also provided star shells to illuminate enemy targets for Air Force night intruder bombing runs.

Direct naval gunfire support was again provided for Eighth Army soldiers by the destroyer Parkins in the Kosong area. Enemy troop concentrations were principal targets for the Task Force 95 warship as she pounded away steadily during night and day firing.

—Eighth Army communiqué 578, issued at 10:00 A.M., Tuesday (9:00 P.M., Monday, Eastern Daylight Time) covering Monday's operations:

Light enemy contact reported along the western and central Korean front as United Nations forces maintained positions and patrolled. Attacking United Nations forces north-northwest and northwest of Yanggu encountered stubborn enemy resistance from elements of an estimated enemy regiment. Enemy counter-attacks repulsed in the area north of Yanggu. Two enemy battalions offered light to moderate resistance to attacking United Nations forces on the Punchbowl. Scattered groups of enemy continue to resist attacking United Nations forces in the area west of Kansong.

1. United Nations forces along the western Korean front maintained positions and patrolled, encountering light resistance from squad to company size enemy units.

2. United Nations units along the central Korean battlefront maintained positions and patrolled, reporting light contact with platoon and company size enemy elements.

3. Elements of an estimated enemy regiment on the high ground north-northwest and northwest of Yanggu continued to defend their positions against attacking United Nations forces. Minor gains were reported by attacking United Nations forces. Enemy counter-attacks in up to battalion strength were repulsed in the area north of Yanggu. Light to moderate resistance from an estimated two enemy battalions in the area northwest of the Punchbowl was reported as attacking United Nations forces reported making limited gains in this area. Scattered groups of enemy on the high ground west of Kansong continued to resist attacking United Nations forces during the day.

—General Headquarters communiqué 1,009, covering Sunday's operations:

United Nations ground forces in Korea continued heavy fighting on the east-central front against well dug-in enemy forces. Several sharp clashes occurred in the west-central sector as scattered enemy resistance appeared in other areas along the front.

Enemy gun positions, troop concentrations, railroads, supply buildings, ammunition dumps, and bridges were primary targets of carrier-based planes of United Nations naval units. Guns from surface vessels of the fleet hit enemy gun emplacements north of Kosong. The shelling of Wonsan continued, with direct hits scored on shore batteries. Songjin was hit hard, while on the west coast the area southwest of Chinnampo and enemy positions in the mouth of the Han River were bombarded.

Land-based warplanes continued methodical destruction of enemy communications, as fighter-bombers and light bombers hit rail targets throughout most of North Korea. Medium bombers attacked an enemy airfield at Wonsan, a supply center at Kyomipo and a marshaling yard at Kowon. Night flying medium bombers truck front-line enemy troop traffic. Combat Cargo planes continued to supply United Nations forces in Korea.

—General Headquarters communiqué 1,010, covering Monday's operations:

Along the battlefront in Korea yesterday (Monday), United Nations ground forces continued to adjust positions and to probe enemy strong points and prepared defenses. Action was heaviest in the east-central sector where advancing friendly elements encountered heavy resistance from well-entrenched hostile groups of company to regimental strength. In the eastern sector, friendly units made limited gains against light to moderate resistance while, in the western and west-central sectors, United Nations patrols made numerous light contacts with small enemy forces which were dispersed with the assistance of supporting mortar and artillery fire.

United Nations carrier-based fighters and dive-bombers, operating over the east coastal area of Korea, attacked enemy troop positions along the battlefront and also hit bridges and railroad rolling stock in heavy interdiction strikes against North Korean supply routes. Task Force surface elements shelled enemy troop concentrations, rail and road junctions, shore batteries, and communications networks from the Kosong region northward to Wonsan, Songjin and Chongjin.

Land-based fighter-bombers attacked enemy front-line troops in close support of United Nations ground units and also struck highways and rail lines in the mounting destruction of enemy supply and communications facilities. During the hours of darkness, light bombers again attacked enemy vehicular traffic while medium bombers, in day and night operations, blasted front-line troop concentrations and the marshaling yard at Hwangju. Combat Cargo aircraft continued to airlift military supplies and equipment to forward and rear bases in Korea.

†DAVENPORT, JACK A.

Rank and Organization: Corporal, U.S. Marine Corps, Company G, 3d Battalion, 5th Marines, 1st Marine Division.
Born: September 7, 1931, Kansas City, Missouri.
Entered Service At: Mission, Kansas.
Place and Date: Vicinity of Songnae-Dong, Korea, September 21, 1951.
Citation: For conspicuous gallantry and intrepidity at the risk of his life above and beyond the call of duty while serving as a squad leader in Company G, in action against enemy aggressor forces. Early in the morning, while expertly directing the defense of his position during a probing attack by hostile forces attempting to infiltrate the area, Cpl. Davenport, acting quickly when an enemy grenade fell into the foxhole which he was occupying with another marine, skillfully located the deadly projectile in the dark and, undeterred by the personal risk involved, heroically threw himself over the live missile, thereby saving his companion from serious injury or possible death. His cool and resourceful leadership were contributing factors in the successful repulse of the enemy attack and his superb courage and admirable spirit of self-sacrifice in the face of almost certain death enhance and sustain the highest traditions of the U.S. Naval Service. Cpl. Davenport gallantly gave his life for his country.

OFFICIAL COMMUNIQUÉ:
TOKYO, Saturday, Sept. 22 (AP)
—Far East Air Forces summary of Thursday's operations:

Far East Air Forces warplanes encountered clear weather yesterday (Thursday) over North Korea as they flew 935 sorties. Fighter and fighter-bombers engaged in air to air battles with Communist MiG-15 jet fighters while others continued their heavy attacks on enemy vehicles and rail facilities to choke off supplies from reaching front-line enemy troops.

F-86 Sabre jets, F-84 Thunderjets, and F-80 Shooting Star jets encountered enemy MiGs in six air battles over northeast Korea. F-86 Sabre jets damaged two of the speedy enemy jets in a twenty-minute fight south of Sinuiju. Another MiG was damaged. There were two other engagements by F-84s and MiGs in which only two firing passes were made with no damage sustained by either side.

An RF-80 photo aircraft was jumped by twelve enemy jets near Anju but escaped undamaged.

A total of three MiGs were damaged in the air battles, with an F-80 reported damaged.

Fifth Air Force flew 740 sorties, of which South African, Australian, and shore-based Marine aircraft mounted 175.

Fighter bombers continued to hammer enemy rail facilities as they cut trackage in 100 places and destroyed or damaged sixteen locomotives and 215 railroad cars in their communication lines. Over

500 enemy vehicles were also destroyed or damaged by F.E.A.F. planes during the period as they attempted to haul supplies to Communist front-line troops.

Other fighter bombers hit rail and highway bridges, gun positions, and tunnels, while over sixty close support air strikes were flown to aid United Nations ground forces along the battlefront.

Returning pilots reported destroying or damaging fifteen gun positions, three warehouses, 580 enemy occupied buildings, thirty-five supply carts, three supply storage areas, five fuel storage dumps, eight tunnels, and fifteen bridges. Sixteen enemy troop casualties were inflicted and forty pack animals killed.

United States Air Force B-29 Superforts of the Okinawa-based Nineteenth Bomb Group attacked the important railroad bridge at Sunchon with 1,000-pound bombs.

Eight of the bomber Command Superforts flew through intense flak to assault the seventeen-span steel bridge. Visual aiming was used and excellent results were reported by the air crew.

Superforts had left the bridge unserviceable after an attack on Sept. 1, but repairs had been completed and the attack yesterday knocked it our again.

Two other Superforts struck the enemy airfield at Wonsan on the east coast. Bombardiers visually dropped their bombs and scored hits on the runway and taxi strips.

No enemy fighters were encountered by the medium bombers or their escorting Meteor jet fighters.

Preliminary reports of night activity indicate that over 100 sorties were flown by B-26 light bombers and Marine night fighters. Moderately heavy vehicular traffic was sighted with pilots reporting 570 destroyed or damaged. Eight locomotives were also reported destroyed or damaged in pre-dawn attacks.

B-26s teamed with B-29s to radar-drop 500-pound air-bursting bombs on enemy front-line troop concentrations, supplies, and equipment during the night.

—Eighth Army communiqué 582, covering Friday's operations:

Four squad to company-size attacks repulsed in area north of Yonchon. United States task forces conducting armored raids along the central Korean front encountered light to heavy enemy resistance from platoon to battalion size enemy groups employing anti-tank fire and mines and a heavy volume of mortar and artillery fire. Stubborn enemy resistance continued in areas northwest and north of Yanggu. Attacking United Nations forces secured high ground in area west of Kansong.

1. United Nations patrols reported light enemy contact in the Korangpo area during the day. Four attacks by squad to company size enemy units were repulsed in the area north of Yonchon during the late evening hours. A tank-infantry patrol in the area west of Chorwon encountered determined resistance from an unknown number of enemy entrenched in bunker-type emplacements.

2. Platoon to battalion-size enemy groups utilizing tank obstacles, anti-tank mines, anti-tank fire, and a heavy volume of mortar and artillery fire offered light to heavy resistance, as United Nations tank forces raided enemy-held territory along the central Korean front. A task force in the area southeast of Pyonggang was engaged by an undetermined number of the enemy. However, the task force secured its objective, forcing the enemy to withdraw. A task force in the area northwest of Kumhwa encountered a heavy volume of mortar and artillery fire. Another task force operating in the area southwest of Kumsong engaged an undetermined number of enemy and reported receiving a heavy volume of mortar and artillery fire. Heavy fighting continued until 1615 hours at which time the task forces withdrew after inflicting heavy enemy casualties. Moderate to heavy enemy resistance was reported in the area south-southeast and southeast of Kumsong as other task force elements engaged company to battalion-size enemy units during the day.

3. Company-size enemy groups in the area northwest of Yanggu continued to stubbornly resist attacking United Nations forces. United Nation patrols in the area north of Yanggu met stubborn resistance from enemy units in up to battalion strength while other United Nation elements in the area

reported receiving harassing and interdictory mortar and artillery fire. Attacking United Nations forces northwest of the "Punchbowl" continued to meet stubborn enemy resistance.

Enemy resistance in the area west of Kansong was overcome and attacking United Nation forces secured the high ground in the area at 1800 hours.

†BURRIS, TONY K.

Rank and Organization: Sergeant First Class, U.S. Army, Company L, 38th Infantry Regiment, 2d Infantry Division.
Born: Blanchard, Oklahoma.
Entered Service At: Blanchard, Oklahoma.
Place and Date: Vicinity of Mungdung-ni, Korea, October 8 and 9, 1951.
Citation: Sfc. Burris, a member of Company L, distinguished himself by conspicuous gallantry and outstanding courage above and beyond the call of duty. On October 8, when his company encountered intense fire from an entrenched hostile force, Sfc. Burris charged forward alone, throwing grenades into the position and destroying approximately 15 of the enemy. On the following day, spearheading a new assault on enemy positions on the next ridge, he was wounded by machine gun fire but continued the assault, reaching the crest of the ridge ahead of his unit and sustaining a second wound. Calling for a 57mm. recoilless rifle team, he deliberately exposed himself to draw hostile fire and reveal the enemy position. The enemy machine gun emplacement was destroyed. The company then moved forward and prepared to assault other positions on the ridge line. Sfc. Burris, refusing evacuation and submitting only to emergency treatment, joined the unit in its renewed attack but fire from hostile emplacements halted the advance. Sfc. Burris rose to his feet, charged forward and destroyed the first emplacement with its heavy machine gun and crew of 6 men. Moving out to the next emplacement, and throwing his last grenade which destroyed this position, he fell mortally wounded by enemy fire. Inspired by his consummate gallantry, his comrades renewed a spirited assault which overran enemy positions and secured Hill 605, a strategic position in the battle for "Heartbreak Ridge." Sfc. Burris' indomitable fighting spirit, outstanding heroism, and gallant self-sacrifice reflects the highest glory upon himself, the infantry, and the U.S. Army.

OFFICIAL COMMUNIQUÉ:
TOKYO, Wednesday, Oct. 10 (AP)
—Far East Air Forces summary 471, covering Monday's operations:

Heaviest casualties since late in June were inflicted on enemy troops by Far East Air Forces warplanes Monday, as F.E.A.F. aircraft mounted 880 sorties. Pilots reported approximately 430 Communists killed or wounded as a result of their close support strikes, the greatest casualty figure in a single day's operations in more than three months.

Meantime, F.E.A.F. kept up the hammering interdiction of enemy supply routes in the methodical campaign of logistical attrition it has been waging against the Communists since early summer.

Fifth Air Force and attached units mounted 645 sorties of which 140 were by shore-based Marine aircraft and fifty by Australian and South African planes.

By day fighter bombers, including United States Air Force F-51s, F-80s, F-84s and Marine F-4Us and F-9Fs, ranged enemy rail routes, particularly in western Korea, cratering tracks, hitting rail cars, and putting bridges under successful attack.

During the hours of darkness in the twenty-four hour period ending midnight Monday, B-26 light bombers, aided by Marine aircraft and flare-dropping and reconnaissance aircraft, continued their attacks on enemy motor vehicles seeking to move supplies to enemy front-line troops. Pilots reported the destruction of 435 of these vehicles. They also attacked bridges, gun positions, and supply buildings. Near Kyomipo, in western Korea, fires and secondary explosions followed their strikes against enemy-held buildings.

Eighth Bomber Command Superforts dropped 1,000-pound bombs at the wooden by-pass rail bridge near Songchon. The high-explosive missiles were aimed visually and good results were observed. The Superforts were escorted by Australian flown MD-8 Meteor jets and there was no enemy air opposition.

Immediately preceding the attack, F-84 Thunderjets, flying at low level, neutralized enemy anti-aircraft positions protecting the target and the big bombers experienced no flak as they made their drops. The Thunderjets also put the marshaling yard at Songchon under bombing attack with good results.

F-86 Sabre jets swept northwest Korea but were not challenged by enemy aircraft.

Eighty close-air support strikes were flown for friendly front-line units with F-4Us hitting in the east and South African F-51s in the west. Bunkers were destroyed, an ammunition dump was blown up, and excellent coverage was achieved with napalm fire bombs on enemy dug-in positions.

Fifth Air Force and attached pilots reported inflicting 430 casualties on enemy troops and destroying twenty-five pack animals. They destroyed or damaged two tanks, fifteen gun positions, seventy supply buildings, forty-five rail cars, and sixteen bridges. Rail trackage was bomb-cratered in sixty-four places. Strafing and bombing knocked out 435 enemy motor trucks.

One F-84 Thunderjet was hit by flak and crashed in enemy territory.

Transport-cargo planes of the 315th Air Division (Combat Cargo) flew 220 sorties and hauled 640 tons of passengers and cargo on the Japan-Korea airlift.

Last night moderate enemy vehicular traffic was sighted and successfully attacked by B-26 light bombers. Twelve B-26s and three B-29s attacked enemy front-line positions with air-bursting quarter-ton bombs, aimed by radar techniques.

—Far East Naval Headquarters released the following summary of operations for Tuesday:

United Nations Navy planes swept over North Korea in intensified attacks yesterday, and Navy cruisers, destroyers, and frigates continued knocking out Communist transportation routes and gun emplacements on both coasts.

Planes from Fast Carrier Task Force 77 continued hitting Communist railroads, cutting tracks in thirty-five places and damaging or destroying three locomotives and seventy-five railroad cars during day-long flights. Strikes unloaded bombs and rockets on enemy military targets from south of Wonsan to northwest of Songjin on the east coast.

Task Force 77 bombarding warships reached inland with their big guns as the Navy cruiser Los Angeles battered Wonsan road and rail targets. During attacks on transportation routes around the city, the cruiser and supporting destroyers silenced enemy shore batteries attempting to slow the siege. Destroyers Swenson, Twining, and Epperson added their five-inch batteries to the rain of shellfire on Wonsan, designed to deny the road and rail center to the enemy.

Task Force 95 escort-carrier U.S.S. Rendova launched her Marine aircraft again over targets in the Haeju area. The Devilcat Squadron based aboard the carrier knocked out two bridges as well as blocking a rail tunnel northwest of Haeju. Southwest of the city, an estimated 200 troops were strafed by the Leatherneck pilots.

Blockading vessels from Task Force 95 continued to shell enemy installations off both coasts. H.M.S. Ceylon battered the Haeju approaches with six-inch gunfire during night and day bombardments. Enemy troop positions on the Tungsan peninsula took a beating, with aerial spotters from the Rendova reporting many hits.

On the east coast, the destroyer Colahan continued her destruction of front-line enemy supply dumps and troop positions. Near Konsong, the destroyer from Task Force 95 was credited with 90 percent destruction of a supply area. In the same area, another supply center was destroyed and fifty enemy troops killed.

Far to the north, other Task Force 95 blockade ships continued bombardment and patrols. Destroyers Erben and Renshaw and destroyer-minesweeper Thompson hit rail and road junctions and bridges between Songjin and Chongjin.

—Eighth Army communiqué 600 covering Monday's operations:

Enemy attacks in area west of Yonchon were repulsed by elements of the First Commonwealth Division. Attacking forces of the United Nations First Cavalry Division continued to encounter stubborn enemy resistance in the area northwest and north-northwest of Yonchon. Light enemy contact was reported by United Nations forces along the central Korean front. Attacking United Nations forces in the area north-northwest and north of Yanggu reported stubborn enemy resistance, but reported securing one hill during the day. Attacking United Nations forces which had secured a foothold on a hill northwest of the "Punchbowl" were forced to withdraw.

United Nations patrols in the Korangpo area reported light enemy contact during the day. Elements of the First Commonwealth Division repulsed an attack by an undetermined number of enemy in the area west of Yonchon during the early morning hours. An estimated enemy battalion preceded by a heavy concentration of artillery fire launched an attack during the early morning hours in the area west of Yonchon. Close combat continued until 5:00 A.M. at which time the attack was contained and the enemy withdrew, leaving 120 counted enemy killed in action.

In the area northwest and north-northwest of Yonchon enemy units of undetermined strength, employing a heavy volume of fire, supported by mortar and artillery, continued to offer stubborn resistance to attacking forces of the United Nations First Cavalry Division. Light enemy probing attacks and light patrol contacts were reported in the Chorwon area by United Nations forces as they maintained positions and patrolled.

United Nations forces along the central Korean battlefront maintained positions and patrolled reporting light enemy probing attacks and patrol contacts with squad to company-sized enemy units during the day.

Attacking United Nations forces in the area north-northwest of Yanggu continued to meet moderate to heavy enemy resistance from an estimated enemy battalion entrenched on the high ground. In the area north of Yanggu, other attacking United Nations forces also encountered stubborn enemy resistance from enemy in battalion strength. United Nations forces secured one hill in the area during the day as the enemy was forced to make a limited withdrawal.

Attacking United Nations forces which had secured a foothold on the high ground northwest of the "Punchbowl" were forced to make a limited withdrawal at 4:20 P.M.. Elsewhere along the eastern Korean front only light enemy patrol contact was reported.

—Eighth Army Communiqué 601, covering Tuesday's action up to noon (10:00 P.M., Monday, Eastern Standard Time):

Attacking forces of the United States First Cavalry Division made limited gains against moderate to heavy resistance in the area north-northwest of Yonchon. Stubborn enemy resistance continued in the area northwest and north of Yanggu.

United Nations forces patrolling in the area west and north of Korangpo reported light enemy contact during the morning hours. United Nations forces of the First Commonwealth Division in the area west of Yonchon reported no significant enemy contact during the morning hours. In the area northwest of Yonchon, light enemy contact was reported while other elements of the United States First Cavalry Division in the area north-northwest of Yonchon reported advancing 2,000 yards and being heavily engaged as of midday.

Elsewhere in this area, friendly forces repulsed several night probing attacks during the night and early morning hours, and repulsed a company-sized enemy attack at 7:30 A.M.. No significant enemy contact was reported in the Chorwon area, and United Nations forces continued to patrol.

Tank-infantry patrols along the west-central Korean front reported light enemy contact. United Nations forces in the area southeast of Kumsong reported a brief firefight with an enemy company during the morning hours.

Attacking United Nations forces in the area north-northwest of Yanggu continued to meet stubborn enemy resistance from an estimated enemy battalion on the high ground in their front, with little or no gains reported. Attacking United Nations forces in the area north of Yanggu met heavy enemy resistance which restricted their gains to 200 to 400 yards during the morning hours.

Light enemy contact was reported along the remainder of the eastern Korean front.

—Eighth Army Communiqué 602, covering Tuesday's operations:

Attacking United Nations troops encountered light to moderate resistance in area north of Korangpo. Stubborn enemy resistance continued in area north-northwest of Yonchon as elements of the United States First Cavalry Division continued their attack. Light contact was reported along the central front as patrolling United Nations forces reported numerous patrol contacts. During the day, attacking United Nations forces in the area north-northwest and north of Yanggu continued to meet stubborn resistance but reported securing one key terrain feature during the day.

1. Squad to company-sized units offered light to moderate resistance to attacking United Nations forces in area north of Korangpo. Light enemy contact was encountered in area west of Yonchon by First Commonwealth Division forces, while elements of the United States Third Division in area north-northwest of Yonchon continued to encounter stubborn enemy resistance during the day. An attack by an estimated enemy company in the area north of Chorwon at 0330 hours was repulsed at 0445 hours.

2. Tank Infantry patrols operating in the area southeast of Pyonggang reported light enemy contact while United Nations forces in the Kumhwa sector reported three brief patrol clashes and a light enemy probing attack during the day. United Nations forces patrolling in the area south and south-southeast of Kumsong reported numerous patrol contacts during the day. Patrol engagements with enemy units of platoon to company size were reported in the area southeast of Kumsong.

3. Enemy forces in company to battalion strength continued to offer stubborn determined resistance in the area north-northwest and north of Yanggu as United Nations forces continued to press their attack. One key terrain feature in the area north-northwest of Yanggu was secured at 1715 hours. Elsewhere along the eastern Korean battlefront little or no significant enemy action was reported.

BURKE, LLOYD L.

Rank and Organization: First Lieutenant, U.S. Army, Company G, 5th Cavalry Regiment, 1st Cavalry Division.
Born: September 29, 1924, Tichnor, Arkansas.
Entered Service At: Stuttgart, Arkansas.
Place and Date: Near Chong-dong, Korea, October 28, 1951.
Citation: 1st Lt. Burke distinguished himself by conspicuous gallantry and outstanding courage above and beyond the call of duty in action against the enemy. Intense enemy fire had pinned down leading elements of his company committed to secure commanding ground when 1st Lt. Burke left the command post to rally and urge the men to follow him toward 3 bunkers impeding the advance. Dashing to an exposed vantage point he threw several grenades at the bunkers, then returning for an M1 rifle and adapter, he made a lone assault, wiping out the position and killing the crew. Closing on the center bunker he lobbed grenades through the opening and, with his pistol, killed 3 of its occupants attempting to surround him.

Ordering his men forward he charged the third emplacement, catching several grenades in midair and hurling them back at the enemy. Inspired by his display of valor his men stormed forward, overran the hostile position, but were again pinned down by increased fire. Securing a light machine gun and 3 boxes of ammunition, 1st Lt. Burke dashed through the impact area to an open knoll, set up his gun and poured a crippling fire into the ranks of the enemy, killing approximately 75. Although wounded, he ordered more ammunition, reloading and destroying 2 mortar emplacements and a machine gun position with his accurate fire. Cradling the weapon in his arms he then led his men forward, killing some 25 more of the retreating enemy and securing the objective. 1st Lt. Burke's heroic action and daring exploits inspired his small force of 35 troops. His unflinching courage and outstanding leadership reflects the highest credit upon himself, the infantry, and the U.S. Army.

OFFICIAL COMMUNIQUÉ:
TOKYO, Monday, Oct. 29 (AP)
—Far East Air Forces summary of Saturday's operations:

The grueling battle for air superiority in northwest Korea entered its seventh consecutive day Saturday with pitched morning engagements in the Sinanju area resulting in destruction or damage to nineteen enemy MiG-15 jets, as Far East Air Forces pilots and aerial gunners outshot the determined and aggressive Communists. There were no friendly losses in the air engagements.

Three enemy jets were destroyed and three probably destroyed by gunners of Okinawa-based United States Air Force Superforts, which were attacked as eight of them bombed the important railroad bypass bridge at Sinanju. Nine other MiGs were damaged by F-84 Thunderjets, two by F-86 Sabre jets and two by Australian pilots flying British-made MD-8 Meteor jets.

The encounters took place within the period of one hour and at one time at least 105 enemy jets were in the air at the same time.

F-80 Shooting Star jets and F-51 Mustangs were attacked shortly after 10:00 o'clock in the Kunu and Sinanju areas by approximately fifty MiGs in two encounters which resulted in no damage to either side.

A few minutes later a patrol of F-86 Sabre jets encountered an estimated 105 MiGs in the vicinity of Sinanju and, although greatly outnumbered, damaged two of the enemy.

As the B-29s went in to their bomb run against the Sinanju bridge they were subjected to a heavy and determined attack despite vigorous protection from their escort of F-84 Thunderjets and MD-8 Meteors. One of the B-29s was damaged but managed to reach a friendly airbase in Korea. Superfort gunners and the escorting fighter pilots destroyed three MiGs, probably destroyed three and damaged four.

About an hour later some thirty F-84 Thunderjets on rail-cratering missions in the same area engaged an estimated fifty MiGs and damaged seven.

No further encounters were reported during the day, but Saturday morning, before dawn, two B-26 light bombers reported ineffective attacks had been made on them by single-engined, propellered enemy night fliers.

Yesterday (Saturday), F.E.A.F. planes mounted a total of 1,000 sorties in good weather. Of these, 810 were flown by Fifth Air Force, shore-based Marines contributed 150 of Fifth's sorties, while Republic of Korea, Australian, and South African pilots flew sixty-five.

In addition to countering enemy air attacks, Fifth Air Force jets kept up the relentless attack on enemy rail and highway transportation routes, cratering tracks in ninety-five places and destroying 255 enemy vehicles. Close air support by fighter bombers inflicted casualties on enemy troops along the battleline, knocked out gun positions, and destroyed bunkers.

Fifth Air Force and attached pilots reported inflicting 150 casualties on enemy troops, knocking out eighteen gun positions, and destroying twenty-five pack animals used by the enemy. They destroyed or damaged 150 enemy-held buildings, three bridges, three warehouses, twenty rail cars, and fifteen supply carts.

F.E.A.F. Bomber Command Superforts hit the by-pass bridge at Sinanju. Others attacked the marshaling yard at Hambusong in eastern Korea, those at Maenjung and Chongju in northwest Korea, and the one at Masan in western Korea. Airfields were attacked at Saamcham and Sinmak. By night, four B-29s hit enemy troop concentrations along the front-lines with lethal, air-bursting, fragmentation bombs.

Transport-cargo planes of the 315th Air Division flew 170 sorties and airlifted 600 tons of war supplies and passengers.

One F-51 Mustang was lost to enemy ground fire Saturday. The pilot was rescued.

Saturday night enemy vehicular traffic continued to increase, with approximately 4,300 trucks sighted by B-26 and Marine aircraft which ranged Communist supply routes. Pilots reported attacks on this traffic were very successful.

—United Nations Naval Forces summary of Sunday's operations:

United Nations Naval Forces continued to pound Red supply routes and frontal positions from the sea and air yesterday (Sunday) as the carriers Essex, Antietam, and Rendova launched air strikes and the heavy cruiser Toledo and smaller warships attacked along the coastline.

The fast carriers in Task Force 77 sent one large flight to scorch Communist installations near Togogae in northeastern Korea. Navy pilots reported several buildings blown to bits as direct hits were scored.

The area was burning and smoke billowed up to 6,000 feet. Other strikes worked over rail installations along the east coast.

Marine Devilcat Squadron Corsairs, flying from the escort carrier Rendova, hit enemy supply buildings near Haeju with effective results. The Marines from the Task Force 95 floating airfield killed an estimated forty-five enemy troops and destroyed or damaged twenty-five buildings, twenty-six junks and sampans, and four gun positions during the day.

After celebrating her fifth birthday Saturday by causing 115 enemy casualties, the heavy cruiser Toledo and escorting destroyer U.S.S. MacKenzie maintained the bombardment of Communist troops, gun emplacements, and supply points in the Kansong-Kosong area.

Despite poor visibility, the cruiser poured 8-inch gunfire on Red infantry positions and shelled bunkers. The destroyer MacKenzie had a big day, firing over 600 rounds from her main batteries north of Kosong. In one area thirty to forty large stacks of supplies were destroyed. Northwest of the town, an ammo dump was pinpointed and over fifty buildings went up in smoke as secondary explosions caused heavy casualties among troops in the area.

The MacKenzie's sharpshooters then turned on another supply center, destroying four more buildings, burning another four, along with ten more stacks of supplies. The destroyer is flagship of Destroyer Division 72.

Farther north on the east coast, Task Force 95 warships continued the siege of Wonsan. The Stormes and Seiverling were on the firing line early in the morning. Saturday, the destroyer Stormes fought it out with an enemy shore battery on Hodopando. While taking evasive action, shortly after noon Saturday, the destroyer poured out over 120 rounds in less than five minutes. Although straddled several times, the Stormes suffered no damage or casualties and silenced the enemy gun position.

The destroyer Cony scored hits on a rail bridge and by-pass south of Songjin, while the destroyer H.M.S. Concord steamed to Chuuonjang to shell bridge approaches. The waterfront area at Chongjin was again worked over early Sunday by the destroyer-minesweeper Carmick.

The destroyer escort Ulvert M. Moore, which suffered damage from shore batteries at Hungnam on Oct. 17, started fires on troop barracks south of the seaport yesterday.

On the west coast, the Canadian destroyer Cayuga battered Red positions on the north shore of Taedong Bay, while H.M.S. Amethyst shelled four troop and gun positions on the north bank of the Han River.

—Eighth Army communiqué 639 issued at 6:00 P.M., Sunday (4:00 A.M., Sunday, Eastern Standard Time):

United Nations forces take hill northwest of Yonchon. United Nations patrols on central front destroy bunkers south of Pyonggang, encounter heavy enemy mortar and artillery fire near Kumsong. Friendly forces secure hill northwest of Yanggu, advance 1,000 to 2,000 yards west of Punchbowl.

1. United Nations forces secured a hill northwest of Yonchon against enemy resistance which had dwindled to almost nothing following yesterday's (Saturday's) two unsuccessful friendly attempts to gain the high ground. Elsewhere along the western Korean battlefront, United Nations forces adjusted positions and patrolled with light to moderate resistance from small enemy groups.

2. United Nations patrols in the vicinity of Kumsong encountered a heavy volume of mortar and artillery fire before returning to their bases. A friendly patrol destroyed six bunkers south of Pyonggang, while other United Nations elements in the area were moderately engaged defending against a probing attack by an enemy unit of unknown strength.

No significant action was reported from the remainder of the central front as United Nations forces consolidated positions and patrolled.

3. United Nations elements secured an additional hill northwest of Yanggu following a successful attack against light to moderate resistance from an enemy company. Friendly forces advancing in the area west of the Punchbowl made gains of from 1,000 to 2,000 yards against moderate enemy resistance. No significant action was reported elsewhere along the eastern front as United Nations units maintained positions and patrolled.

—Eighth Army communiqué 640, covering Sunday's operations:

United Nations forces take two hills northwest of Yonchon, inflict heavy enemy casualties in area. Tank-infantry elements damage eighty bunkers near Kumsong. Two hills taken west of Punchbowl.

1. United Nations forces secured two hill areas northwest of Yonchon against weakening enemy resistance. Friendly forces employed artillery against an enemy unit of company size in the same general area, with an estimated 15 percent enemy casualties resulting from the engagement. Elsewhere along the western Korean battlefront, United Nations units maintained positions and patrolled with light contact and squad to platoon size enemy groups.

2. United Nations tank-infantry elements raiding in vicinity of Kumsong encountered a heavy volume of enemy mortar and artillery fire but succeeded in damaging eighty enemy bunkers and inflicting casualties at more than ninety before returning to their bases. Six additional bunkers were destroyed by friendly forces south of Pyonggang, southeast of Kumsong, an enemy unit withdrew after five hours of heavy fighting. Elsewhere along the central front, United Nations forces maintained positions and patrolled.

3. United Nations elements secured a key hill northwest of Yanggu against stubborn enemy resistance. Friendly forces made limited gains against moderate enemy resistance west of the Punchbowl. No significant action was reported from the remainder of the eastern front, as United Nations forces continued to maintain positions and patrol.

—General Headquarters communiqué 1,051 covering Sunday's operations:

In the east-central sector of the Korean battlefront yesterday (Sunday), advancing United Nations ground forces encountered stubborn resistance from dug-in enemy elements up to battalion strength. Elsewhere along the battle line, friendly forces maintained positions and continued to probe enemy strong points and defenses. Scattered contacts with squad and platoon-sized enemy groups were made by United Nations tank and tank-infantry reconnaissance elements which reported destroying or damaging a number of bunkers and inflicting numerous casualties upon the enemy.

United Nations carrier-based aircraft attacked enemy-occupied buildings near Togogae in northeast Korea while Marine Corsairs, operating over the west coast, destroyed or damaged twenty-five buildings, twenty-six junks and sampans, and four gun positions near Haeju. Task Force surface elements on blockade and escort patrol along the east coast continued the bombardment of enemy troops, supply routes, and communications facilities from the Kosong-Kansong region northward to Chongjin. On the west coast, other naval warships shelled enemy positions on the north shore of Taedong Bay and along the north bank of the Han River.

United Nations land-based light bombers continued to take a heavy toll of enemy motor vehicles as Far East Air Forces in good weather mounted more than 1,000 sorties. Air fighting raged for the eighth successive day as friendly Sabre jets destroyed one MiG-15 enemy jet and damaged another in the skies over northwest Korea. Fighter-bombers cratered enemy rail tracks in 100 places and flew close air-support for friendly front line troops inflicting 150 casualties on the enemy. Medium bombers hit the rail by-pass bridge at Songchon and also struck marshaling yards, airfields, and other military targets in enemy territory. Transport-cargo planes continued the airlift of supplies to United Nations forces in Korea.

†JORDAN, MACK A.
Rank and Organization: Private First Class, U.S. Army, Company K, 21st Infantry Regiment, 24th Infantry Division.
Born: December 8, 1928, Collins, Mississippi.
Entered Service At: Collins, Mississippi.
Place and Date: Near Kumsong, Korea, November 15, 1951.
Citation: Pfc. Jordan, a member of Company K, distinguished himself by conspicuous gallantry and indomitable courage above and beyond the call of duty in action against the enemy. As a squad leader of the 3d Platoon, he was participating in a night attack on key terrain against a fanatical hostile force when the advance was halted by intense small-arms and automatic-weapons fire and a vicious barrage of hand-grenades. Upon orders for the platoon to withdraw and reorganize, Pfc. Jordan voluntarily remained behind to provide covering fire. Crawling toward an enemy machine gun emplacement, he threw 3 hand-grenades and neutralized the gun. He then rushed the position delivering a devastating hail of fire, killing several of the enemy and forcing the remainder to fall back to new positions. He courageously attempted to move forward to silence another machine gun but, before he could leave his position, the ruthless foe hurled explosives down the hill and in the ensuing blast both legs were severed. Despite mortal combat wounds, he continued to deliver deadly fire and held off the assailants until the platoon returned. Pfc. Jordan's unflinching courage and gallant self-sacrifice reflects lasting glory upon himself and upholds the noble traditions of the infantry and the military service.

OFFICIAL COMMUNIQUÉ:
TOKYO, Friday, Nov. 16 (AP)
—Far East Air Force summary of Thursday's operations:
Approaching winter again brought inclement weather conditions to Korea Thursday. Far East Air Forces warplanes, nevertheless, flew 335 sorties in attacks against Communist airfields, supply routes, and front-line positions.

Fifth Air Force pilots flew 100 of these sorties and returning pilots reported the destruction of an enemy warehouse. Supply buildings were fired by the fighter-bomber pilots and twenty-five vehicles were destroyed.

Weather reconnaissance planes maintained a patrol in northwest Korea and reported no contacts with enemy jets.

During the hours of darkness for the period ended midnight Thursday, B-26 light bombers and night-flying Marine fighters ranged enemy supply lines, attacking the majority of vehicles reported destroyed.

Ten of the light bombers attacked the marshaling yards at Sinanju and Pyongyang, dropping their missiles by radar techniques.

United States Air Force B-29 Superfort bombers at night again attacked airfields in northwest Korea, with two medium bombers from the Ninety-eighth Bomb Wing radar-aiming 100-pound explosives at the Taechon and Namsi strips.

An additional two Superforts of the Ninety-eighth Wing struck the Namsi airfield, continuing the program to deny use of these fields to Communist planes.

The supply center and barracks area at Hungnam also came under attack by the all-weather medium bombers as they struck selected military targets north of the battle line.

Three B-29s overnight ranged enemy front-lines, making a series of drops on enemy troop concentrations opposing United Nations forces. Radar techniques were used.

A B-26 light bomber joined forces with the medium bombers also to radar-aim quarter-ton air-bursting bombs on strategically located enemy front-line troops. Other preliminary reports of the night's activities indicated that the B-26 night intruders and night-flying Marine fighters sighted only a few supply vehicles. Fifteen were destroyed.

Five Communist supply trains were brought under attack by the night-flying planes and a locomotive and twelve rail cars were destroyed or damaged as the Fifth Air Force planes flew through rain and fog along rear-area highways and rail lines.

The Japan-Korea airlift operation continued despite bad weather and 315th Air Division transport planes flew 220 sorties, delivering 635 tons of cargo, which included approximately 2,000 passengers and medical evacuees.

—United Nations Naval Forces summary of Thursday's operations:

Despite bad weather along both coasts of Korea yesterday (Thursday), Marine Corsairs were launched from the escort carrier U.S.S. Rendova in the afternoon to kill over thirty-five enemy troops and destroy or damage more than thirty-one Red warehouses and supply-filled buildings.

Rain and very rough seas hampered air operations, but the Marines struck at the supply installations near Ullyul, southwest of Haeju, and south of Chinnampo. West of Songwha, a group of enemy soldiers were caught in the open and an estimated thirty-five were killed.

Elsewhere along the west coast other Task Force 95 warships continued patrols. The Royal Navy frigate H.M.S. Whitesand Bay shelled troops southwest of Chinnampo and moving farther up the coastline, bombarded gun positions in six areas.

The British destroyer Comus patrolled far to the north early in the day, attacking a troop concentration on an island off the tip of the Cholsan Peninsula less than forty miles from the mouth of the Yalu River. H.M.S. Murchison operating in the Han River, continued bombardment of Communist troops on the north bank of the river.

At the eastern extremity of the battleline near Kosong, the destroyer De Haven kept up her attacks on Communist positions with well over 100 main battery rounds fired before dawn. The De Haven reported that her naval gunfire support on Nov. 12 and 13 was lauded by a United Nations east coast corps commander. The ground force commander said that it was "outstanding" and that many enemy were killed in action "due to your excellent illumination and fire support."

Warships from the United Nations blockade and escort force operating between Chongjin and Songjin also encountered rainy weather Thursday. The destroyer Purdy and destroyer-minesweeper Doyle hit rail installations at Songjin during the day. Earlier the destroyer-minesweeper with her sister ship, the U.S.S. Endicott, roamed to the north hitting similar targets at Chongjin, Odejin, and Chuuronjang. The Australian destroyer Tobruk shelled a marshaling yard and other rail targets at Tanchon and near Songjin.

Interdiction by destroyers continued at Wonsan and Hungnam. A delayed report indicated the minesweepers Redstart and Ptarmigan came under heavy enemy shore battery fire Wednesday afternoon. Three Red guns opened up but scored no damage or casualties to the sweepers at Hungman.

—Eighth Army communiqué 675, for the twelve hours to noon Thursday:

No significant activities reported from western and central fronts. United Nations units lose and recapture advance position northwest of Yanggu.

1. No significant action was reported from the western Korean battlefront as United Nations forces maintained positions and patrolled.

2. Only light contact with small enemy groups developed during the period along the central front, where United Nations units adjusted positions and patrolled.

3. Heaviest action of the period occurred northwest of Yanggu, where two enemy platoons attacking at night forced a friendly unit to withdraw from an advance position. United Nations elements quickly regrouped, counter-attacked, retook the position, and pursued the enemy back to his own lines. No significant activity was reported from the remainder of the eastern front, as United Nations forces adjusted positions and patrolled.

—Eighth Army communiqué 676, issued at 10:00 A.M., Friday (8:00 P.M., Thursday, Eastern Standard Time):

No significant activity reported from western front. Only light contact developed along central front. United Nations units lose and recapture advance position northwest of Yanggu.

1. No significant activity was reported during the period from the western Korean battlefront, as United Nations forces maintained positions and patrolled.

2. Friendly units along the central front maintained and adjusted positions and patrolled during the period. United Nations patrols reported only light contact with enemy groups up to platoon in strength.

3. Two enemy platoons, attacking at midnight, forced a friendly unit to withdraw from an advanced position. United Nations elements counter-attacked at dawn, however, recaptured the positions and pursued the enemy to his own lines northwest of Yanggu. United Nations units south of Kosong repulsed a night probing attack by an enemy platoon. Patrol contact again was most frequent in the area northwest of the Punchbowl, where United Nations units fought light to moderate engagements with enemy units up to a platoon in strength located in well-defended bunker and trench positions. A light probing attack by an enemy platoon was repulsed in the same area. Elsewhere along the eastern front, United Nations forces adjusted positions and patrolled.

—General Headquarters communiqué 1,069, covering Thursday's operations:

There was little change in the conduct of ground fighting along the Korean battlefront yesterday (Thursday). United Nations Command units patrolled and maintained and adjusted their positions all along the line. The patrols made only minor enemy contacts. Probing efforts launched by enemy elements up to company size were beaten off by our forces on the western, the east-central, and the eastern fronts.

Enemy-held warehouses, supply buildings, and troop areas were targets for carrier-based aircraft operating in spite of bad weather and choppy seas.

Surface craft trained their big guns on enemy troops, gun positions, marshaling yards, and communications up and down the coasts in the Korean battle zone. Other United Nations Command naval units continued patrols and blockading of North Korean ports.

Poor flying weather hampered day operations of the United Nations Air Forces, but during the night our medium bombers continued attacks on enemy-held airfields in Northwest Korea. Other medium bombers hit enemy troops and selected military targets. Light bombers, also operating under cover of darkness, struck railroad marshaling yards at Pyongyang and Sinanju and enemy front-line troops. The Korean airlift continued to be serviced by our transport cargo planes.

STONE, JAMES L.
Rank and Organization: First Lieutenant, U.S. Army, Company E, 8th Cavalry Regiment, 1st Cavalry Division.
Born: December 27, 1922, Pine Bluff, Arkansas.
Entered Service At: Houston, Texas.
Place and Date: Near Sokkogae, Korea, November 21 and 22, 1951.
Citation: 1st Lt. Stone distinguished himself by conspicuous gallantry and indomitable courage above and beyond the call of duty in action against the enemy. When his platoon, holding a vital outpost position, was attacked by overwhelming Chinese forces, 1st Lt. Stone stood erect and, exposed to the terrific enemy fire, calmly directed his men in the defense. A defensive flamethrower failing to function, he personally moved to its location, further exposing himself, and personally repaired the weapon. Throughout the second attack, 1st Lt. Stone, though painfully wounded, personally carried the only remaining light machine gun from place to place in the position in order to bring fire upon the Chinese advancing from two directions. Throughout he continued to encourage and direct his depleted platoon in its hopeless defense. Although again wounded, he continued the fight with his carbine, still exposing himself as an example to his men. When this final overwhelming assault swept over the platoon's position his voice could still be heard faintly urging his men to carry on, until he lost consciousness. Only because of this officer's driving spirit and heroic action was the platoon emboldened to make its brave but hopeless last ditch stand. Lt. Stone's consummate devotion to duty reflects great credit upon himself and the U.S. Army.

OFFICIAL COMMUNIQUÉ:
TOKYO, Friday, Nov. 23 (AP)
—United Nations Naval Forces summary of Thursday's operations:

Although rain and heavy seas off both coasts of Korea slowed United Nations naval air operations yesterday (Thursday), fast Carrier Task Force 77 succeeded in launching morning flights from U.S.S. Essex and U.S.S. Bon Homme Richard.

Navy carrier-based pilots again struck at North Korean rail lines and northeastern supply points.

Bon Homme Richard Skyraiders and Corsairs flew effective close air support flights Thursday against front-line Communist soldiers. Controllers credited the Navy fliers with 95 percent coverage of the area hit, but were not able to estimate enemy casualties.

Dawn Hecklers from the Bon Homme Richard damaged a rail by-pass and a large warehouse at Hungnam. Moving south the same strike knocked out a rail bridge and heavily damaged three more warehouses.

Later they caught a large truck convoy and burned eleven of the vehicles.

Despite limited air operation, Task Force 77 fliers chalked up six railroad bridges, five large warehouses, three junks, and eleven trucks as destroyed or damaged. Rail tracks were cut in thirty-five places.

Task Force 77 heavy cruiser U.S.S. Los Angeles provided close naval gunfire support to Eighth Army troops along the east end of the battle line south of Kosong. More than 250 8-inch and 5-inch shells were poured on Red positions by the Los Angeles.

During night firing, shore fire control parties reported the cruiser's accurate gunfire dispersed enemy infantrymen, causing many casualties.

In direct close support of front-line United Nations troops, her gunfire reportedly broke up Communist preparations for a company-sized attack.

During thirty-five firing missions, machine-gun positions were silenced and an unestimated number of casualties caused.

Warships from the United Nations blockade and escort force continued to harass Red supply lines along the northeast coast of Korea. The destroyer Prudy shelled warehouses and transportation routes at Songjin while at Wonsan other Task Force 95 surface vessels conducted similar bombardments.

Off the west coast, escort carrier U.S.S. Rendova was forced to cancel flights because of heavy weather.

New Zealand frigate Hawea, steamed close inshore on the North side of Taedong Bay to illuminate and open fire on Red troop positions early in the day.

—Far East Air Forces summary of Thursday's operations:

Far East Air Forces neutralization of enemy airfields was moved northward last night as ten United States Air Force B-29 Superforts attacked the runways and revetments at Uiju, northeast of Sinuiju and south of the Yalu River. MiG-15 enemy jet fighters had been observed using this field.

The attack, culminating a day on which F.E.A.F. planes mounted 465 sorties, was pressed in the face of heavy anti-aircraft fire and a concentration of Communist search-lights. Enemy night fighters approached the Superforts during the attack but did not fire.

For the past month F.E.A.F. Bomber Command Superforts have been hitting the three enemy airfields of Sammcham, Namsi, and Taechon farther to the south, almost nightly, keeping them inoperable in spite of persistent efforts by enemy labor gangs to keep them repaired. Last night's attack was the first of the war by bombers against an enemy airfield on which MiGs were based.

Five medium bombers from an Okinawa base teamed with five more from Japan to first drop quarter-ton air-bursting bombs on the Uiju field. The area was blanketed with tens of thousands of pieces of high-velocity steel fragments designed to damage grounded enemy planes and hold down action by the Communist anti-aircraft batteries. The air-bursting bombs were then followed by full complements of 100-pound demolition missiles designed to crater runways and revetments. Preliminary reports indicated "good results."

In other night air attacks the medium bombers operated in close air support of United Nations front line troops. They also struck the Hungnam supply area and the Chinnampo marshaling yards.

Fifth Air Force planes flew 270 sorties of the F.E.A.F. total, concentrating against enemy front-line positions, as weather conditions curtailed day interdiction strikes. Fifth and attached R.O.K. (Republic of Korea), South African, and shore-based Marine pilots reported successful sorties against enemy troops and bunkers. Pilots reported inflicting 245 casualties on enemy forces and destroying fifteen bunker-type fortifications. Seventy close air support sorties were flown.

In night operations for the period ended midnight Thursday, night intruder light bombers and Marine aircraft ranged Communist rear areas, locating and destroying 225 vehicles, enemy-occupied buildings, and gun positions and successfully attacking supply areas.

The Korean airlift continued in force with supplies and passengers being safely delivered to Korean and Japan airports as 315th Air Division cargo transport planes flew 176 sorties and carried 620 tons of cargo.

Thursday night B-26 light bombers, aided by Marine fighters and flare-dropping planes, experienced bad weather over the enemy's supply lines. They sighted a decreased number of vehicles and, according to preliminary reports, destroyed more than 301 of the supply carriers. Night intruders again unleashed their radar-aimed bomb loads on marshaling yards with two hitting the Sinanju rail center and eight others attacking the Sunchon rail yard.

Thirteen light bombers flew in close air support of United Nations front line forces Thursday night dropping 500-pound anti-personnel missiles on opposing troops.

—Eighth Army communiqué 689, for the twelve hours to noon Thursday:

Heavy enemy attack failed to penetrate United Nations main lines west of Chorwon. Minor enemy probing attacks repulsed southwest of Kumsong and east of Pukhan River.

1. The enemy early in the period continued heavy pressure along the central sector of the Western Korean battle front, hitting in strength at several advance positions west of Chorwon. At one point in the sector, a United Nations unit which had been reported surrounded, fought off an attack by an enemy battalion and retained its advance positions. A second advance position was overrun and driven in by an estimated two enemy battalions attacking through wire and a hail of both enemy and United Nations artillery.

A coordinated attack by elements of an enemy regiment against two other advanced positions in the same sector was repulsed. All enemy attacks were accompanied by a heavy concentration of supporting artillery and mortar fire. By dawn, all action had ceased. No enemy penetrations into main United Nations lines were reported. No significant activity developed along the remainder of the western front as United Nations units adjusted positions and patrolled.

2. Minor probing attacks by enemy units up to two platoons in strength were repulsed southwest of Kumsong and east of the Pukhan River in the major actions reported during the period from the central front. United Nations forces along the remainder of the central front adjusted positions and patrolled.

3. No significant activity developed during the period from the eastern front, as United Nations forces continued to adjust positions and patrol during the period.

—Eighth Army communiqué 690, covering Thursday's operations:

Heavy enemy attacks repulsed west and southwest of Chorwon. United Nations units turned back minor probes southwest of Kumsong and east of the Pukhan River. Patrol contact frequent northwest of Yanggu.

1. Early in the period the enemy continued his heavy pressure against the western front, hitting in strength at several advance positions west and southwest of Chorwon. The enemy attacked in battalion strength at four points and in company strength at another point across a five-mile sector, with all attacks preceded and accompanied by heavy concentration of mortar and artillery fire. At one point, a United Nations unit managed to retain its position after reporting it was surrounded by an enemy battalion. At another point, a friendly position was overrun after two separate assaults by an enemy battalion attacking in waves through a hail of United Nations and its own artillery. United Nations units later reoccupied the position, however, with no enemy contact. Main United Nations lines were not penetrated during the attacks. Light enemy contact reported from the remainder of the western Korean battle front, as United Nations forces adjusted positions and patrolled.

2. A series of probing attacks by enemy units up to a company in strength were repulsed north of Kumhwa, southwest of Kumsong, and east of the Pukhan River. No other significant activity was reported from the remainder of the central front, as United Nations units adjusted positions and patrolled.

3. Patrol contacts were most frequent during the period in the area northwest of Yanggu, where United Nations units encountered light to moderate resistance from enemy groups up to a battalion in strength before returning to their bases. In the area northwest of the Punchbowl an attack by an enemy

company was dispersed with the aid of an air strike. Light patrol contact was reported from the remainder of the eastern front.

—General Headquarters communiqué 1,076, for the twenty-four hours ended 6:00 A.M. Friday (4:00 P.M., Thursday, Eastern Standard Time):

United Nations ground forces in Korea yesterday (Thursday) adjusted positions and patrolled. In the west-central, east-central, and eastern sectors, several probing attacks by enemy forces up to two companies in strength were repulsed by friendly elements. United Nations reconnaissance forces continued to seek out enemy defenses all along the battleline, encountering only scattered resistance from small hostile groups.

Land-based fighter-bombers continued close air support of United Nations front-line infantrymen, while light bombers destroyed a large number of enemy vehicles along supply routes leading to the battlefront. Medium bombers attacked the new enemy airfield at Uiju last night, dropping high explosive bombs on the runways and revetments where enemy MiG-15 jet planes had been spotted by reconnaissance aircraft. Transport-cargo planes continued the air-lift of supplies to United Nations forces in Korea.

Carrier-based aircraft, operating along the east coast, attacked enemy rail lines, supply points, junks, rail bridges, warehouses, and supply trucks from Hungnam to the north and also flew close air support missions for friendly ground elements along the battleline. Task Force warships bombarded enemy troop positions near Kosong and also blasted warehouses and transportation routes at Wonsan and Songjin. On the west coast, United Nations surface vessels shelled troop positions along the north side of Taedong Bay.

†KNIGHT, NOAH O.

Rank and Organization: Private First Class, U.S. Army, Company F, 7th Infantry Regiment, 3d Infantry Division.
Born: October 27, 1929, Chesterfield County, South Carolina.
Entered Service At: Jefferson, South Carolina.
Place and Date: Near Kowang-San, Korea, November 23 and 24, 1951.
Citation: Pfc. Knight, a member of Company F, distinguished himself by conspicuous gallantry and indomitable courage above and beyond the call of duty in action against the enemy. He occupied a key position in the defense perimeter when waves of enemy troops passed through their own artillery and mortar concentrations and charged the company position. Two direct hits from an enemy emplacement demolished his bunker and wounded him. Disregarding personal safety, he moved to a shallow depression for a better firing vantage. Unable to deliver effective fire from his position, he left his shelter, moved through heavy fire in full view of the enemy and, firing into the ranks of the relentless assailants, inflicted numerous casualties, momentarily stemming the attack. Later during another vicious onslaught, he observed an enemy squad infiltrating the position and, counterattacking, killed or wounded the entire group. Expending the last of his ammunition, he discovered 3 enemy soldiers entering the friendly position with demolition charges. Realizing the explosives would enable the enemy to exploit the breach, he fearlessly rushed forward and disabled 2 assailants with the butt of his rifle when the third exploded a demolition charge killing the 3 enemy soldiers and mortally wounding Pfc. Knight. Pfc. Knight's supreme sacrifice and consummate devotion to duty reflects lasting glory upon himself and upholds the noble traditions of the military service.

OFFICIAL COMMUNIQUÉ:
TOKYO, Sunday, Nov. 25 (AP)
—United Nations Naval Forces summary of Saturday's operations:

United Nations warships continued to harass front-line Communist infantrymen with naval gunfire and again hit rear area transportation centers along both coasts of Korea.

Elements of the United Nations blockade and escort force furnished the fire power during Navy attacks. In the Kosong-Kansong area, the destroyers Tingey and Bristol Friday night and before daylight Saturday rained over 675 rounds of 5-inch ammo on enemy troops and artillery positions. The two Task Force 95 warships illuminated with starshells similar targets for United Nations spotters.

Surface vessels off Wonsan dueled late in the afternoon with Red shore batteries on Kalma Peninsula. The destroyer Hyman was raked with shrapnel after being straddled while in close on a firing mission. Personnel casualties were suffered. Communist artillery on Hodo Peninsula and on the mainland also opened up on the bombarding ships but failed to cause any damage or casualties.

The destroyer-minesweeper Endicott fired at bridges north and south of Songjin despite snow in the area. Fast Carrier Task Force 77 also experienced foul weather off the east coast. No combat sorties were flown. On the west coast, Australian Navy pilots were kept on the flight deck of H.M.A.S. Sydney because of heavy seas.

The British frigate Whitesand Bay continued to harass enemy troop concentrations on the north bank of the Han while the Canadian destroyer Cayuga pounded a gun position on the coast southwest of Chinnampo.

Rear Admiral Ralph A. Ofstie, acting commander, Naval Forces, Far East, revealed late in the day that the battleship U.S.S. Wisconsin had arrived in the Far East. The Iowa-class battlewagon arrived at Fleet Activities, Yokosuka, from Pearl Harbor on Nov. 21.

During the latter part of the week Vice Admiral Harold M. Martin, commander, Seventh Fleet, transferred his flag to the Wisconsin, which is commanded by Capt. Thomas Burrowes, U.S.N.. Saturday the Prime Minister of Japan, Shigeru Yoshia, had an informal visit with Admiral Martin and went on a short tour of the Wisconsin.

The Wisconsin was launched on Dec. 7, 1943, and commissioned on April 16, 1944, at the Philadelphia Naval Shipyard. The 45,000-ton warship was decommissioned in July, 1948, and recommissioned on March 3, 1951.

Earlier this year the Wisconsin carried midshipmen on a cruise, visiting during June and July Edinburgh, Scotland; Lisbon, Portugal, and Guantanamo Bay, Cuba.

A 1925 Naval Academy graduate, Captain Burrowes commanded the destroyers U.S.S. O'Brien and U.S.S. Adner Read during World War II and later Destroyer Division 106.

Captain Burrowes is a native of Brooklyn, N.Y. His current residence is in Washington, D.C., where he was assigned, prior to assuming command of the Wisconsin, to the office of the Chief of Naval Operations.

The Wisconsin, third battleship to appear in the Far East since the beginning of the Korean war, is a veteran of the Leyte, Luzon, Iwo Jima, and Okinawa operations during World War II.

—Far East Air Forces summary of Saturday's operations:

Jet-versus-jet air-fighting took place over western and northwestern Korea for the second successive day Saturday as Far East Air Forces warplanes mounted 885 sorties in support of United Nations operations. Four enemy MiG-15 jet fighters were damaged while the United States Air Force F-86 Sabre jets and F-80 Shooting Star jets, which engaged them, sustained neither loss nor damage.

Methodical destruction of enemy railroad tracks continued throughout the day. In hours of darkness many enemy supply vehicles were knocked out. Close-support strikes inflicted substantial casualties on enemy troops. High-level, radar-aimed bombings kept enemy airfields in northwest Korea inoperable.

Fifth Air Force and attached Australian, South African, R.O.K. (Republic of Korea), and shore-based Marine aircraft flew 695 of F.E.A.F's sorties. A combat patrol of F-86 Sabre jets encountered thirty Communist MiG-15 jet fighters over Korea south of Sinuiju during the morning and damaged three of them. Shortly after mid-day four F-80s on a track-cratering mission near Pyongyang were attacked by four MiGs. The slower F-80s turned into the MiGs, damaging one.

The track-cratering program, which has virtually stopped all railroading south of Pyongyang, went ahead. Steel rails were blown from cross ties at 145 places by low-level fighter-bomber attacks. Strikes ranged the lines from Sinanju to Pyongyang, from Kunu to Pyongyang, north of Sariwon, south of Sonsan and on the trans-peninsula route. In these strikes three locomotives were damaged, fourteen rail cars were hit, and thirty-five supply buildings were fired.

One hundred close air support strikes hit enemy combat troops across the battlefront with well-directed machine-gun fire and blazing napalm. Pilots of United States Air Force F-51 Mustangs and shore-based Marine F-4U Corsairs reported inflicting 180 casualties. Ground forces observers, however, reported 200 casualties had been inflicted by air strikes on enemy troops on a single hill in western Korea, where pilots had reported only fifty casualties.

After the strikes, friendly forces advanced and captured the hill. Gun positions and bunkers were knocked out in other places.

B-26 light bombers and shore-based Marine F-4Us and F-7Fs, aided by flare-dropping aircraft, destroyed 270 enemy motor vehicles during the hours of darkness in the twenty-four hour period ended midnight Saturday, continuing the highly successful attrition campaign to deny enemy front-line troops war supplies and rations. Destruction of enemy rail lines has forced the Communists to extend vulnerable vehicular supply routes.

Last night F.E.A.F. Bomber Command B-29 Superforts from Japan and Okinawa bases radar-aimed 100-pound bombs at the enemy's northwestern airfields at Namsi and Taechon to crater runways and neutralize these potential air bases. Three medium bombers took part in the attack, and although they experienced intense flak, all returned safely. Two B-29s attacked the rail by-pass bridge at Songchon, four hit the Hambusong marshaling yard and two attacked the Ongchon marshaling yard on the East Coast.

Four B-29s teamed with fourteen B-26s to drop 270 air-bursting, quarter-ton bombs on enemy troop concentrations along the battle-front, disrupting Communist night activity with many thousands of high-velocity fragments.

Other B-26s ranged enemy highways, observing and attacking moderately heavy traffic. Preliminary reports indicated the destruction of eighty-five vehicles. The B-26s also attacked railroad marshaling yards at Sinanju and Sunchon, using radar techniques.

Transport-cargo planes of the 315th Air Division flew 170 sorties and airlifted 545 tons of war supplies and military personnel in support of the United Nations operations in Korea.

—Eighth Army communiqué 693, for the twelve hours ended noon Saturday:

Enemy continues heavy pressure west of Yonchon. Two advance positions lost and regained south of Kumsong. Several engagements with enemy battalions reported from eastern front.

1. The enemy continued to exert heavy pressure against United Nations positions west of Yonchon. Between midnight and dawn two heavy attacks by an undetermined number of enemy were repulsed at one point, while at another a United Nations unit reported limited advances in a counter-attack to regain a hill position lost in the previous period. No significant action was reported from the remainder of the western Korean battlefront, as United Nations forces continued to adjust positions and patrol.

2. United Nations units withdrew from two advance positions southwest of Kumsong during an attack by elements of an enemy battalion early in the period, counter-attacked and regained the posi-

tions shortly before dawn in the only significant action reported during the period from the central front, as United Nations forces maintained positions and patrolled.

3. Action along the eastern front continued to center in the area northwest of Yanggu where a United Nations unit took a hill and lost it for the second time in an attack by an enemy battalion, and in the area northwest of the Punchbowl where enemy attacks of battalion strength were repulsed at three points. Elsewhere along the eastern front United Nations forces maintained position and patrolled.

—Eighth Army communiqué 694, covering Saturday's operations:

United Nations forces fight heavy engagements for two hill positions west of Yonchon. United Nations units hold for second time northwest of Yanggu. Three enemy battalions attack unsuccessfully northwest of Punchbowl.

1. Heaviest action of the period again centered in the area west of Yonchon where United Nations forces fought stubbornly throughout the day to regain possession of an important hill position yielded to the enemy Nov. 23. United Nations units temporarily resecured the hill at sunset, but lost a portion of it in a subsequent enemy counter-attack. Action was also heavy at an adjacent hill position, which United Nations forces managed to regain, though a portion of it was yielded temporarily. Elsewhere along the western Korean battlefront, United Nations forces maintained positions and patrolled with light contact with enemy groups up to a platoon in strength.

2. Elements of an enemy battalion continued pressure against United Nations advanced positions southwest of Kumsong early in the period. At one point, a United Nations unit withdrew and enemy pursued, forcing a slight penetration into the main lines. Engagements developed at three other points in the same area, but United Nations forces forced the enemy to withdraw from all points of action and resecured all ground lost. Only light contact with small enemy groups developed along the remainder of the central front, as United Nations elements maintained positions and patrolled.

3. Action along the eastern front centered in the area northwest of Yanggu where a United Nations unit took a hill and lost it for the second time in an attack by an enemy battalion, and northwest of the Punchbowl, where night attacks by enemy battalions were repulsed at three points before dawn. Elsewhere along the eastern front, United Nations forces reported light patrol contacts with enemy groups up to two platoons in strength.

—General Headquarters communiqué 1,078, for the twenty-four hours ended 6:00 A.M., Sunday (4:00 P.M., Saturday, Eastern Standard Time):

In the western sector of the Korean battlefront, United Nations forces advanced to secure positions along high ground against heavy mortar and artillery fire. Last night (Saturday night) friendly elements in this sector received a heavy counter-attack by an unknown number of the enemy and one unit was forced off the position, after a nine-hour engagement, during which time United Nations elements received heavy enemy tank fire, the hostile forces broke contact and withdrew.

In the west-central sector, two small enemy probing attacks were repulsed, while along the east-central front, United Nations elements were counter-attacked by a reinforced enemy battalion and were forced to make slight withdrawals, in the eastern sector, friendly units were attacked by an estimated two enemy battalions. The action continued at the close of the period with no ground lost. Elsewhere along the battle line, United Nations forces continued to maintain or adjust positions and patrol, encountering only scattered resistance from small enemy groups.

United Nations jet fighters damaged four enemy MiG-15 aircraft in aerial engagements over northwest Korea. Land-based fighter-bombers cratered enemy rail lines in the Pyongyang-Sinuiju area and also inflicted numerous casualties on enemy troops in close air-support of United Nations ground forces. Light bombers, flying during the hours of darkness, attacked and destroyed approximately 270 enemy supply vehicles, while medium bombers again blasted the enemy airfields at Namsi and Taechon. Light and medium bombers also dropped air-bursting bombs on enemy front-line troop concentrations. Transport-cargo planes continued the airlift of supplies and military personnel in support of United Nations operations in Korea.

Task force surface elements, operating along the east coast, shelled enemy troop and artillery positions in the Kosong-Kansong region and also blasted enemy shore batteries near Wonsan and along the Hodo Peninsula. Despite snow in the area, other naval warships bombarded enemy supply routes and bridges north and south of Songjin. On the west coast, task force destroyers and frigates continued to shell enemy troop concentrations and gun positions along the north bank of the Han River and on the coast southwest of Chinnampo.

CHAPTER 3

1952

ROSSER, RONALD E.
Rank and Organization: Corporal, U.S. Army, Heavy Mortar Company, 38th Infantry Regiment, 2d Infantry Division.
Born: October 24, 1929, Columbus, Ohio.
Entered Service At: Crooksville, Ohio.
Place and Date: Vicinity of Ponggilli, Korea, January 12, 1952.
Citation: Cpl. Rosser distinguished himself by conspicuous gallantry and intrepidity above and beyond the call of duty. While assaulting heavily fortified enemy hill positions, Company L, 37th Infantry Regiment, was stopped by fierce automatic-weapons, small-arms, artillery, and mortar fire. Cpl. Rosser, a forward observer, was with the lead platoon of Company L, when it came under fire from 2 directions. Cpl. Rosser turned his radio over to his assistant and, disregarding the enemy fire, charged the enemy positions armed with only his carbine and a grenade. At the first bunker, he silenced its occupants with a burst from his weapon. Gaining the top of the hill, he killed 2 enemy soldiers, and then went down the trench, killing 5 more as he advanced. He then hurled his grenade into a bunker and shot 2 other soldiers as they emerged. Having exhausted his ammunition, he returned through the enemy fire to obtain more ammunition and grenades and charged the hill once more. Calling on others to follow him, he assaulted 2 more enemy bunkers. Although those who attempted to join him became casualties, Cpl. Rosser once again exhausted his ammunition, obtained a new supply, and returning to the hilltop a third time, hurled grenades into the enemy positions. During this heroic action Cpl. Rosser singlehandedly killed at least 13 of the enemy. After exhausting his ammunition he accompanied the withdrawing platoon, and though himself wounded, made several trips across open terrain, still under enemy fire, to help remove other men injured more serious then himself. This outstanding soldier's courageous and selfless devotion to duty is worthy of emulation by all men. He has contributed magnificently to the high tradition of the military service.

OFFICIAL COMMUNIQUÉ:
TOKYO, Sunday, Jan. 13 (AP)
—Far East Air Forces summary of Korean War operations for the week Jan. 5-11:

Communist transport facilities received further destructive blows during the week ended Jan. 11, as Far East Air Forces warplanes, including those of attached units, flew more than 5,400 sorties in a continuation of Operation Strangle, it was announced by Lieut. Gen. O.P. Weyland, F.E.A.F. commanding general.

Enemy MiG-15 jet fighters were repulsed with heavy losses when they attempted to interfere with these interdiction strikes. Fifth Air Force F-86 Sabre jets and F-80 Shooting Stars shot down twelve MiGs, damaged fourteen, and drove others back to their Manchurian bases. Friendly planes lost during these air-to-air engagements were three F-86 Sabre jets.

Fighter bombers and light bombers of Fifth Air Force, South African, Republic of Korea Air Forces, and shore-based aircraft of the First Marine Air Wing continued relentless bomb, rocket, napalm, and strafing strikes on Communist rail and vehicular supply routes. Fifth and attached units flew 4,150 sorties.

Slashing attacks against the enemy's crumbling rail network accounted for destruction or damage to twenty-two locomotives, 480 rail cars, four tunnels, twenty-six bridges, and rail lines cut and cratered in 600 places. Marshaling yards and installations were badly battered.

B-26 light bombers and Marine fighter-bombers ranged rear areas and main highway networks to seek out vehicular convoys at night. Movement of vehicles during the period was comparatively light as snow and ice covered North Korean highways. With flare-dropping aircraft illuminating the furtive targets, 475 supply-laden trucks were destroyed. This effective night team also made road cuts, and added their destructive weight to the assault on marshaling yards, rolling stock, and enemy airfields.

In close air support sorties, Fifth Air Force tactical planes silenced more than 100 gun positions, damaged another twenty-five, and inflicted 380 troop casualties. In strikes at supply build-ups, fifteen stockpiles of war materials were burned. Nearly 400 buildings housing enemy supplies, equipment, and troops were bombed, strafed, and napalmed.

Friendly losses from enemy ground fire, designed to protect important supply and transport targets, totaled thirteen and included four F-80 Shooting Stars, four F-51 Mustangs, three F-84 Thunderjets, one B-26 light bomber, and one F-4F fighter-bomber of the Marine Air Wing. United Nations ground forces remained free from hostile air attack as F.E.A.F. aircraft retained air superiority over the Korean battlefront. There were no enemy aircraft losses to ground fire for the simple reason that they made no attacks on our ground installations or positions.

Bomber Command B-29 Superforts continued to radar-aim their heavy tonnages of high explosives on enemy targets during the week. Bypass rail bridges at Sunchon, Sinanju, and Songchon, the Kunu marshaling yards and Communist airfields at Sinanju and Hwangju were heavily bombed. The important west coast supply storage area at Chinnampo was hit, and the Superforts gave close air support nightly during the week by dropping 500-pound air-bursting bombs over front-line bunkers and troop concentrations. Ground fire ranging from meager to intense met the medium bomber formations, but all returned safely.

Destruction and damage to MiG aircraft during the period brought the totals for the war to date to 201 destroyed, fifty-one probably destroyed, and 325 damaged, a total of 577. Aircraft of all types destroyed and damaged in the air and on the ground total 336 destroyed, 100 probably destroyed, and 380 damaged, a total of 816. Destruction and damage claims are subject to re-evaluation and subsequent change.

—Far East Air Forces summary of Saturday's operations:

A main railroad route west of the Chongchon River in extreme northwest Korea was among Communist targets effectively attacked Saturday as war planes of Far East Air Forces mounted 935 sorties.

Fifth Air Force F-84 Thunderjets etched a fiery path of destruction along the important enemy supply line between Sonchon and Sinanju during multiple strikes. At Sonchon the Thunderjets caught three supply trains racing for the shelter of a tunnel, destroying two of the locomotives and damaging the other. The mouth of the tunnel was bombed ahead of the fleeing targets and they were trapped in the open.

During attacks in that sector, tracks were cratered in thirty places, forty rail cars destroyed or damaged, a third locomotive destroyed, and two others damaged.

Of the total F.E.A.F. sorties, 685 were flown by Fifth Air Force and attached Royal Australian, South African, Republic of Korea, and land-based Marine pilots.

Between Sinanju and Pyongyang, the F-84 Shooting Stars teamed with F-51 Mustangs and Marine fighter-bombers to score multiple rail cuts between Huichon and Kunu and from Songchon to Pyongyang.

In strikes close behind enemy lines F-51s and Marine F-4Fs destroyed twelve gun emplacements, three field pieces, three mortars, and two anti-aircraft positions. They inflicted about sixty-five casualties on enemy troops.

During the day, approximately 200 Red MiG-15 jet fighters were sighted during patrol sweeps over northwest Korea by F-86 Sabre jets. Some of the observed enemy jets elected to stay within their sanctuary west of the Yalu River. During four brief encounters there were negative claims.

Destruction during the period includes more than 105 troop casualties inflicted, 100 rail cuts, three rail bridges knocked out and six others damaged, three tanks destroyed, and one damaged, 165 supply buildings destroyed or damaged, and seventy rail cars destroyed or damaged.

As around-the-clock attacks on enemy targets continued, medium bombers of the Okinawa-based 307th Bomb Wing on Saturday night dropped ninety tons of 500-pound high explosives on the Sinanju East rail by-pass bridge across the Chongchon River. The Superforts encountered meager flak but no enemy fighters. All returned safely. Five other B-29s flew in close air support of United Nations front-line forces, dropping quarter-ton air-bursting bombs on Communist troop concentrations.

B-29 light bombers and Marine aircraft ranged in the night over enemy supply routes. Pilots reported a light sighting of vehicular traffic, with twenty supply trucks destroyed.

Cargo transports of the F.E.A.F. 315th Air Division flew 155 sorties to airlift 575 tons of supplies and personnel in continued support of United Nations operations.

—United Nations Naval Forces summary of Saturday's operations:

Battleship Wisconsin returned to the fire support area off the east coast terminus of the battle line Friday night to work her secondary 5-inch gun battery on the Reds. Saturday, the super-dreadnought opened with 16-inch salvos and laid approximately 125 tons of the high explosives on Communist front-line installations. An estimated 150 Red troops were killed or wounded in heavy bombardments that destroyed or damaged twenty-six troop shelters, collapsed seven troop and supply caves, and damaged five bunkers.

U.S.S. Essex and Valley Forge Navy attack fliers from Task Force 77 farther north in Japan Sea waters struck the east coast rail and road complex in carrier-borne assaults that destroyed or damaged forty-eight rail cars, nine bridges, and four locomotives.

At Wonsan, destroyers U.S.S. MacKenzie and Gregory fired on Red shore gun positions with concentrated 5-inch gun fire that started fires and caused secondary explosions in the target areas.

Destroyer Halsey Powell at Hungnam landed direct hits on a mobile radar power unit erected on the coastline and on two railroad bridges in the same area.

U.S.S. Porterfield, Doyle, and Edmonds worked with New Zealand patrol frigate Taupo off Songjin's coastline to shell bridges, rail and road junctions, and suspected troop billets.

British destroyer Constance and Canadian destroyer escort Cayuga shelled Red troops and mortar positions on Korea's west coast with unreported final results.

—Eighth Army communiqué 791, for the twelve hours to noon Saturday:

United Nations forces raid enemy positions along western and central front.

1. Several United Nations raiding units were in operation along the western front, as United Nations forces maintained positions and patrolled. Light to moderate engagements with enemy units up to a platoon in strength were reported, with one raiding patrol fighting a moderate action against elements of an enemy platoon from 11:05 P.M. Friday until 2:35 A.M. Saturday northwest of Yonchon, and with

a raiding party west of Chorwon receiving very heavy small-arms and automatic weapons fire from an enemy group of undetermined strength from 8:40 A.M. until 9:30 A.M. Saturday, when United Nations tanks were called in for support.

2. Light contact with enemy units up to a platoon in strength developed along the central front, as United Nations elements maintained positions, patrolled, and raided enemy-held territory.

3. United Nations forces along the eastern front reported light to moderate contact with small enemy groups, as they maintained positions and patrolled.

—Eighth Army communiqué 792, for Saturday's operations:

United Nations forces raid enemy positions along western and central fronts.

1. Several United Nations raiding units, some of them supported by tanks, were in operation along the western front, as United Nations forces maintained positions and patrolled. Light to moderate engagements with enemy units up to a platoon in strength were reported, with one raiding patrol fighting a moderate action against elements of an enemy platoon from 11:05 P.M., Friday, to 2:35 A.M., Saturday, northwest of Yonchon, and with a raiding party west of Chorwon receiving very heavy small-arms and automatic weapons fire from an enemy group of undetermined strength from 8:40 A.M. until 9:30 A.M., when United Nations tanks were called in to fire on enemy bunkers.

2. Light contact with enemy units up to a platoon in strength developed along the central front, as United Nations elements maintained positions, patrolled and raided enemy-held territory with tank and infantry units.

3. United Nations forces along the eastern front reported light to moderate contact with enemy groups up to two squads in strength, as they continued to maintain positions and patrol.

—General Headquarters communiqué 1,127 for Saturday's operations:

There was no significant ground fighting in Korea Saturday. Though United Nations forces patrolled actively, they reported only minor contacts with a few small enemy groups.

In the air war, United Nations fighter-bombers struck at rail lines, bridges, and enemy buildings, while tanks, bunkers, and gun positions were hit in air strikes close to the battle line. During the night, medium bombers attacked the Sinanju East rail by-pass bridge and flew in close support of friendly ground forces as light bombers concentrated on enemy supply vehicles. Cargo-transport aircraft continued their support of United Nations operations.

Surface vessels of the United Nations fleet fired on shore targets at Wonsan, Hungnam, and Songjin, hitting bridges, rail, and road targets. Other friendly warships continued to shell enemy troop concentrations and front-line installations on Korea's east and west coasts. Carrier-based naval aircraft struck the east coast rail and road network, destroying or damaging rail cars, locomotives, and bridges.

†DAVIS, GEORGE ANDREW, JR.
Rank and Organization: Major, U.S. Air Force, CO, 334th Fighter Squadron, 4th Fighter Group, 5th Air Force.
Born: December 1, 1920, Dublin, Texas.
Entered Service At: Lubbock, Texas.
Place and Date: Near Sinuiju-Yalu River, Korea, February 10, 1952.
Citation: Maj. Davis distinguished himself by conspicuous gallantry and intrepidity at the risk of his life above and beyond the call of duty. While leading a flight of 4 F-86 Saberjets on a combat aerial patrol mission near the Manchurian border, Maj. Davis' element leader ran out of oxygen and was forced to retire from the flight with his wingman accompanying him. Maj. Davis and the remaining F-86s continued the mission and sighted a formation of approxi-

mately 12 enemy MiG-15 aircraft speeding southward toward an area where friendly fighter-bombers were conducting low-level operations against the Communists lines of communications. With selfless disregard for the numerical superiority of the enemy, Maj. Davis positioned his 2 aircraft, then dove at the MiG formation. While speeding through the formation from the rear, he singled out a MiG-15 and destroyed it with a concentrated burst of fire. Although he was now under continuous fire from the enemy fighters at his rear, Maj. Davis sustained his attack. He fired at another MiG-15 which, bursting into smoke and flames, went into a vertical dive. Rather than maintain his superior speed and evade the enemy fire being concentrated on him, he elected to reduce his speed and sought out still a third MiG-15. During this latest attack his aircraft sustained a direct hit, went out of control, then crashed into a mountain 30 miles south of the Yalu River. Maj. Davis' bold attack completely disrupted the enemy formation, permitting the friendly fighter-bombers to successfully complete their interdiction mission. Maj. Davis, by his indomitable fighting spirit, heroic aggressiveness, and superb courage in engaging the enemy against formidable odds exemplified valor at its highest.

OFFICIAL COMMUNIQUÉ:
TOKYO, Monday, Feb. 11 (AP)
—Far East Air Forces summary of Saturday's operations:

The Communists' crippled transportation system suffered further fiery attacks Saturday although heavy clouds and snow flurries during a part of the period limited war planes of Far East Air Forces to 530 effective sorties.

Fighter-bombers dipped through the overcast to make repeated strikes on main rail routes in northwest Korea, with tracks cratered in forty-five places. Rail cars were destroyed, a railroad bridge blasted, and enemy-held supply warehouses along the route set afire with bombs, napalm, and strafing attacks.

Fifth Air Force and attached Royal Australian, Republic of Korea, and land-based Marine pilots flew 340 of the total F.E.A.F. sorties.

Along the rail line between Sukchon and Pyongyang, F-84 Thunderjets blasted tracks in more than twenty places. They also knocked out a rail bridge in the Pyongyang area.

F-80 Shooting Stars cratered tracks between Sunchon and Samdong. Other rail cuts were scored between Sunchon and Paup, in the Sinmak area, and from Sariwon to Sinchon.

Marine F-4U Corsairs struck against a Communist supply center southwest of Kosong, with resultant fires and explosions destroying five storage buildings and four supply stacks. In close air support strikes southwest of Ando, the Marines destroyed four field pieces.

Flying protective cover for the fighter-bombers, F-86 Sabre jet pilots probably destroyed one enemy MiG-15 jet fighter and damaged three others during encounters over northwest Korea. One of the MiGs was probably shot down and another damaged during a clash between the Chongchon and Yalu Rivers when eighteen Sabre jets observed over 100 of the enemy fighters and engaged elements of the formation.

At the same time one MiG was hit when nine F-86s observed approximately thirty enemy jets and encountered twelve of them at over 40,000 feet altitude in the Sinanju area. The third Red fighter was damaged when eighteen Sabres observed fifty MiGs between Pyongyang and the Chongchon River and engaged approximately forty of them at 40,000 feet altitude.

Total destruction for the period include seventy supply buildings destroyed or damaged, two locomotives damaged, six gun positions silenced, and ten troop casualties inflicted.

Attacks against enemy targets continued around the clock as medium bombers of the F.E.A.F. Bomber Command on Saturday night hit the rail complex in northwest Korea. Ten Superforts of the Okinawa-based Nineteenth Bomb Group used radar-aiming methods to drop 100 tons of 500-pound high explosives on the Chongju rail bridge, a link in the main route between Manchuria and Sinanju. In the strike, F.E.A.F. Bomber Command unloaded its 100,000th ton of bombs on enemy targets in Korea since the outbreak of the conflict. Three other Superforts during the night flew in close air support of United Nations front line forces, dropping 500-pound air-bursting bombs on enemy troop concentrations immediately behind the battle line.

B-26 light bombers and Marine aircraft mounted ninety sorties Saturday night. Ranging over Red roadways, the war planes destroyed fifty enemy supply vehicles. In other attacks, three locomotives and approximately twenty rail cars were destroyed. B-26s used radar aiming methods to bomb the marshaling yards at Sunchon.

Cargo transports of the F.E.A.F. 315th Air Division flew 175 sorties to airlift 635 tons of supplies and personnel in continued support of United Nations operations.

—United Nations Naval Forces summary of Sunday's operations:

Heavy cruiser U.S.S. Rochester set the pace for other surface bombardment elements off Korea's east coast. Off the battle line at Kansong, Rochester fired 231 rounds of 8-inch and 5-inch shells at twenty-two Red targets in the enemy battle line during pre-dawn harassment and interdicting missions. With daylight, Rochester continued working her guns and damaged twenty-two defense bunkers in Red lines. Eight direct hits demolished one bunker with unestimated enemy casualties. Rochester's gunnery also damaged three gun positions, and damaged the underwater foundation of a newly laid enemy pontoon bridge. Two links in the bridge were destroyed.

Destroyers U.S.S. Shields and U.S.S. Thomas were in company with Rochester to provide naval artillery support to United Nations troops in the line. Shields fired night harassment missions at Red mortar and anti-aircraft gun positions and worked her guns on an 82mm. mortar position, two 76mm. guns, two anti-aircraft gun positions, a truck parking area, and a bridge under repair.

At Songjin, destroyer-minesweeper U.S.S. Endicott knocked the underpinning from a railway bridge previously damaged and on which Red labor parties were attempting repairs. Trackage was left hanging in the air as the cribbing supports beneath it collapsed.

At Hungnam, destroyer Halsey Powell laid suppression fire on Red coastal gun emplacements to provide suppression fire for mine-sweepers clearing offshore waters for heavier ship bombardment.

At Wonsan, destroyer U.S.S. Twining sank three sampans, dispersed troops, destroyed a cave-sheltered command post, damaged railroad tank cars, destroyed a dock, and destroyed or damaged eight buildings. Twining also exploded a mine with .30-caliber fire in the harbor.

In the Yellow Sea operating areas, Navy rocket ship LSMR 401 fired 250 rockets into Red positions in coastal defense dugouts southwest of Haeju. Canadian destroyer escort H.M.C.S. Sioux worked thirty-two rounds of shells into an enemy-held village near Songhwa. Light carrier H.M.S. Glory launched fifty-two sorties of Sea Furies and Fireflies that struck at camouflaged troop and supply positions, supply shelters, and Red defenses from Kumchon west across the Ongjin Peninsula.

Skyraiders and Corsairs from carriers Philippine Sea and Valley Forge bombed anti-aircraft positions, napalmed buildings, destroyed road bridges, and cut Red rail track in the Hungnam-Kowon-Wonsan area. Forty Reds were killed in strafing runs that also saw supply trucks shot up and set afire.

First Marine Air Wing pilots destroyed twenty-nine trucks, eight buildings, a fuel tanker, and damaged thirteen trucks near Yoeyang. Close air support missions destroyed Communist bunker positions facing United Nations troops and killed an unestimated number of enemy defenders.

—Eighth Army communiqué 849, for the twelve hours to noon Sunday:

No significant enemy contact was reported from western and central fronts. Light probe by enemy squad repulsed northwest of the Punchbowl.

1. No significant enemy contact was reported from the western Korean battlefront.

2. No significant enemy contact was reported during the period from the central Korean battle-front.

3. Along the eastern front, a United Nations patrol reported light contact with enemy units up to two squads in strength with most contacts developing west of the Namsi River. Northwest of the Punchbowl, an enemy squad probed United Nations positions at 3:00 A.M. and was dispersed after a fifteen minute fire fight.

—Eighth Army communiqué 850, covering Sunday's operations:

United Nations patrol fights brief engagement with reinforced enemy platoon north of Korangpo. Light probe by enemy squad repulsed northeast of Punchbowl.

1. Except for an action north of Korangpo in which a United Nations patrol at 0430 (4:30 A.M., Feb. 10), engaged a reinforced enemy platoon and directed mortar and artillery fire on the enemy during a brief fire fight, no significant enemy contact was reported during the period from the western Korean battlefront.

2. Except for two brief actions west of the Pukhan River in which United Nations patrols at 0900 and 1140 fought brief, light engagements with enemy squads in bunkers, no significant enemy contact developed along the central front.

3. Along the eastern front United Nations patrols reported light contact with enemy units up to two squads in strength, with most engagements developing just west of the Nam River. Northeast of the Punchbowl an enemy squad probed United Nations positions at 0300 and was dispersed after a fifteen minute fire fight.

—General Headquarters communiqué 1,156, for Sunday's operations:

There was little ground action in Korea as United Nations patrols reported only minor contacts with scattered enemy groups.

Surface vessels of the United Nations Fleet provided gunfire support for friendly ground troops at the eastern terminus of the battleline. Farther north, other United Nations warships hit a rail bridge at Songjin, laid fire on enemy gun positions at Hungnam and damaged or destroyed rail tank cars, a dock, and enemy buildings at Wonsan. Surface elements operating in waters off Korea's west coast hit enemy targets southwest of Haeju and near Songhwa. Carrier-based naval aircraft struck at troops and supply positions from Kumchon west across the Ongjin Peninsula.

Land-based medium bombers attacked the Sinhung railroad bridge, which spans the Chongchon River, and the Hamhung marshaling yards. Fighter-bombers hit rail lines and rolling stock, while light bombers concentrated on enemy vehicle traffic. Several MiG-15 jets were destroyed or damaged in air-to-air clashes with friendly aircraft. Cargo-transport planes continued to support operations in Korea.

†WOMACK, BRYANT E.

Rank and Organization: Private First Class, U.S. Army, Medical Company, 14th Infantry Regiment, 25th Infantry Division.
Born: Mill Springs, North Carolina.
Entered Service At: Mill Springs, North Carolina.
Place and Date: Near Sokso-ri, Korea, March 12, 1952.
Citation: Pfc. Womack distinguished himself by conspicuous gallantry and intrepidity above and beyond the call of duty in action against the enemy. Pfc. Womack was the only medical aid man attached to a night combat patrol when sudden contact with a numerically superior enemy force produced numerous casualties. Pfc. Womack went immediately to their aid, although this necessitated exposing himself to a devastating hail of enemy fire, during which

he was seriously wounded. Refusing medical aid for himself, he continued moving among his comrades to administer aid. While he was aiding one man, he was again struck by enemy mortar fire, this time suffering the loss of his right arm. Although he knew the consequences should immediate aid not be administered, he still refused aid and insisted that all efforts be made for the benefit of others that were wounded. Although unable to perform the task himself, he remained on the scene and directed others in first-aid techniques. The last man to withdraw, he walked until he collapsed from loss of blood, and died a few minutes later while being carried by his comrades. The extraordinary heroism, outstanding courage, and unswerving devotion to his duties displayed by Pfc. Womack reflects the utmost distinction upon himself and uphold the esteemed tradition of the U.S. Army.

OFFICIAL COMMUNIQUÉ:
TOKYO, Thursday, March 13 (AP)
—Far East Air Forces summary of Tuesday's operations:

Supplies which the Communists had slipped through the tight choke applied on their transportation system in northern Korea by continuous interdiction strikes during Operation Strangle, met a fiery reception immediately behind the battle line Tuesday as war planes of Far East Air Forces mounted 1,100 effective sorties.

Fifth Air Force fighter-bombers, operating under protective cover of F-86 Sabre jets, turned a four-mile square supply storage and troop training area near Sinmak, thirty miles northwest of the Panmunjom conference site, into a blazing inferno with bombs and napalm. F-80 Shooting Stars made repeated attacks on the sector, where the Communists had attempted to camouflage the supply stacks with straw roofs, and dropped more than 33,300 gallons of searing napalm onto the targets. They also saturated the stacks with 300,000 pounds of bombs and 45,000 machine-gun bullets. It was believed to be the most intense napalm attack on a single area since the start of the Korean conflict. During the attack at least thirty-two enemy flak positions were destroyed.

While protecting the F-80s and other fighter-bombers on interdiction strikes, the Sabre jets engaged Communist MiG-15s for the second consecutive day. Four of the enemy jets were destroyed, one probably destroyed and five damaged, with an additional probable and another damage claim awaiting evaluation of gun-camera film.

Fifth Air Force and attached Royal Australian, South African, R.O.K. (Republic of Korea), and land-based Marine pilots flew 930 of the total F.E.A.F. sorties.

F-84 Thunderjets ranged over the enemy's main rail routes, cratering tracks in fifty-five places between Huichon and Junu, and damaging twenty-five boxcars. From Namsi to Chongju in extreme northwest Korea, the F-84s scored more than ten rail cuts.

In close air support strikes against Red positions immediately behind the battle line, F-51 Mustangs and Marine Corsairs destroyed forty-five troop and supply bunkers and damaged three others, and knocked out ten gun positions. Supply buildings were destroyed and troop casualties inflicted.

The fighter-bombers ripped rails in ten places on the line between Kyomipo and Namchonjom, and left ten additional craters on the tracks east of Sukchon.

One of the Red MiGs was shot down early yesterday when sixteen F-86s observed fifty enemy jets between Pyongyang and Sinuiju and engaged elements of the formations at between 20,000 and 37,000 feet altitude. At approximately the same time, 175 MiGs were observed by twenty-six F-86s between the Chongchong and Yalu Rivers, with one of the enemy jets probably destroyed and four others damaged in a clash at altitudes from 25,000 to 40,000 feet.

Another MiG destruction was scored over northwest Korea in mid-morning when eight Sabre jets engaged twelve of the enemy jets.

In two afternoon engagements — one ranging from Sinanju to Suiho and the other in the Sinanju area — two MiGs were destroyed, one probably destroyed and two damaged. One of the battles was between nineteen Sabres and elements of a fifty-five MiG formation. The other was between twenty-six F-86s and elements of sixty enemy jets.

Total destruction for the period includes seventy-five enemy-held supply buildings destroyed or damaged, over forty gun positions silenced, rail cuts in 120 places, fifty bunkers destroyed or damaged, three rail bridges damaged, three tunnels blasted, and over fifty-five rail cars destroyed or damaged.

—Far East Air Forces summary of Wednesday's operations:

For the third consecutive day, Far East Air Forces warplanes mounted more than 1,000 sorties to continue heavy interdiction attacks against the Communist transportation system in North Korea and knock enemy jet fighters from the sky. Sorties flown totaled 1,005.

While Communist rail lines were subjected to 125 cuts in three main areas, F-86 Sabre jets downed four enemy MiG-15s in fierce aerial duels over northwest Korea and damaged two others. The air-to-air destruction was made as the Sabres flew protective cover for the deadly fighter-bombers.

Fifth Air Force and attached Royal Australian, South African, Republic of Korea, and land-based Marine pilots flew 780 of the total F.E.A.F. sorties.

F-84 Thunderjets and F-80 Shooting Stars scored sixty-five cuts on the main rail lines from Songchon to Chongju in extreme northwest Korea and from Huichon to Kunu. The Thunderjets, flying on the deck along the Huichon-Kunu line, destroyed a locomotive and five rail cars and made one road cut. Two tunnels were sealed by the F-84s near Huichon and a rail bridge blasted in the same area.

Propeller-driven F-51 Mustangs, some of which were flown by R.A.A.F. pilots, worked over areas close behind enemy lines, destroying ten supply and troop shelters, twenty buildings, five revetments, and closed the mouth of a railroad tunnel. They also destroyed ten boats in the Bay of Chongjin off the east coast.

Other Mustangs, accompanied by Marine fighter-bombers, blasted rails in ten places from Pyongyang to Sariwon; in ten spots from Sariwon to Sinmak, and cratered the rail line east of Sunchon in fifteen locations.

In close air support sorties, Mustangs teamed with Marine aircraft to make strikes by direction of T-6 Mosquitoes. They hit targets from the area northeast of Kaesong all the way to the east coast, silencing five mortar positions, destroying fifteen troop bunkers.

Total destruction against the enemy included thirty-five supply buildings destroyed and thirty-five damaged, fifteen vehicles destroyed, twenty gun positions silenced, five supply dumps set afire, ten rail cards destroyed, and two search-lights rendered inoperative.

In the air-to-air clashes, the enemy jets were knocked down and damaged in an encounter between 25,000 and 40,000 feet altitude near the Yalu River. Twenty Sabre jets clashed with elements of a seventeen-jet enemy formation, which was attempting to break through the protective screen and attack fighter-bombers which were blasting rails.

In three other patrols during the morning and early afternoon, the Sabre jets observed MiGs but did not encounter the enemy aircraft.

Seven B-29s of F.E.A.F. Bomber Command's Okinawa-based 307th Bomb Wing, using radar-aiming methods, at night dropped seventy tons of high explosives on the Pyongyang airfield. Three Superforts flew in close air support of United Nations front-line forces, dropping tons of air-bursting bombs on enemy troops and supplies close behind the battle line. The mission marked the 30,000th tons of bombs dropped by the 307th since the start of the Korean War and rounded out the 13,000th mission of the conflict for F.E.A.F. Bomber Command.

Two medium bombers blasted a steel mill at Kyomipo being used as a storage area, while another Superfort used visual methods in dropping its bombs on a supply area. No enemy flak or fighter opposition was reported by any of the B-29s.

Light bombers and Marine aircraft at night destroyed fifteen enemy vehicles and one locomotive was damaged. Eleven B-26s flew in close air support of United Nations front-line forces.

Cargo transports of F.E.A.F.'s 315th Air Division flew 210 sorties, airlifting 580 tons of personnel and supplies in support of United Nations operations.

—United Nations naval forces summary of Wednesday's operations:

Bombs and rockets from the planes of the aircraft carriers U.S.S. Valley Forge and U.S.S. Antietam, and the cruisers U.S.S. St. Paul and U.S.S. Manchester hit railroad bridges, gun positions, bunkers, warehouses, and cut rails in 146 places on Korea's east coast.

Valley Forge and Antietam aircraft, operating in the Wonsan-Hamhung area, smashed five railroad bridges, five railroad bypasses, and thirty-four buildings housing troops or supplies. Destroyed or damaged were nineteen trucks and thirty small boats.

Marine planes from the carrier U.S.S. Bairoko swarmed south and west of Chinnampo and flattened eighteen buildings housing possible Red supplies and troops. Eleven more buildings were listed as damaged. One warehouse was destroyed and two damaged, one railroad car destroyed and one damaged, five bunkers damaged, three gun positions destroyed and two damaged, and one highway bridge damaged. A railroad bridge west of Haeju was knocked out with one 500-pound bomb.

The light cruiser H.M.S. Belfast and the destroyer Charity pounded gun positions on the west coast southwest of Chinnampo with unobserved results.

In the Kosong-Kanson areas along the east coast the heavy cruiser St. Paul destroyed three bunkers and damaged five and shelled troop shelters, automatic weapons and artillery positions.

The light cruiser Manchester on the east coast battle line fired night harassing and interdiction fire on eighteen targets. During the day with the aid of an air spotter, she hit supply targets and scored direct hits on two camouflaged supply dumps which started fires.

The destroyer U.S.S. Higbee, also at the battle line on the east coast fired night harassing and interdiction fire. During the day she scored direct hits on mortar positions, a 76-mm. gun, bunkers, a bridge, and an observation post. Another hit on a known supply dump caused a secondary explosion. At Hungnam the destroyer Silverstein destroyed a warehouse and hit barracks areas.

First Marine Air Wing pilots raided the Sariwon, Sinmak, and Singosan areas to cut rails in nineteen places, explode ammunition dumps, bomb gun positions, and hit bunkers.

—Eighth Army communiqué 911, for the twelve hours to noon Wednesday:

Groups of fifteen and six enemy attack United Nations positions northeast of the Punchbowl. Enemy units fire on positions of the Twenty-fifth Division and Turkish brigade.

1. No significant enemy contact was reported during the period from the western Korean battlefront.

2. No significant enemy contact was reported during the period from the central front.

3. One group of fifteen enemy and another group of six attacked United Nations positions northeast of the Punchbowl at 12:15 A.M.. The first group withdrew after a thirty-minute fire fight, the second after five minutes of fighting. An enemy group of undetermined strength directed long-range small arms fire on a position of the United States Twenty-fifth Infantry Division for ten minutes ended at 4:55 A.M.. Long-range small arms fire from a second enemy group of undetermined strength fell on a position of the Turkish Brigade for fifteen minutes ended at 5:00 A.M.. In other actions reported from the eastern front, United Nations patrols west of the Mundung Valley fought light engagements with enemy units up to two squads in strength.

—Eighth Army communiqué 912, covering Wednesday's operations:

Twenty-fifth Division repulses coordinated attacks by enemy battalion. Fortieth Division tanks damage twenty bunkers and trenches east-southeast of Kumsong. Enemy probes repulsed northeast of Punchbowl.

1. A United Nations unit west-northwest of Yonchon withdrew from an advanced position at 2315 (11:15 P.M., March 12) following an attack by an estimated fifty to sixty enemy. Also reported from the western Korean battle front were several light patrol engagements with enemy units up to two squads in strength in the area northwest of Yonchon.

2. Tanks of the United States Fortieth Infantry Division firing at targets east-southeast of Kumsong from 0900 to 1000 damaged an estimated twenty bunkers and trenches and one automatic weapons emplacement. Light patrol contacts with small enemy groups developed elsewhere along the central front.

3. Elements of the United States Twenty-fifth Infantry Division repulsed a series of coordinated artillery and mortar-supported attacks by elements of an enemy battalion which began shortly after 2200. Between 2210 and 2230 enemy companies attacked two positions of the Turkish Brigade and an enemy unit of undetermined strength (attacked units) of the United States Thirty-fifth Infantry Regiment. Artillery and mortar fire were directed against the enemy and firing ceased at 2245. One position of the Turkish Brigade was re-attacked at 2235, but the enemy was driven off in a five-minute fight. One group of fifteen enemy and another group of six attacked United Nations position northeast of the Punchbowl at 0015. The first group withdrew after a thirty-minute fire fight, the second after five minutes of fighting. In other actions reported from the eastern front, United Nations patrols fought light to moderate engagements with enemy units up to a platoon in strength with most contacts developing in the area west of the Mundung Valley, while enemy groups of undetermined strength fired briefly on positions of the Turkish Brigade and United States Thirty-fifth Infantry Regiment and on a United Nations position northeast of the Punchbowl during the period.

—General Headquarters communiqué 1,187, for Wednesday's operations:

Principal ground action in Korea occurred along the east-central sector of the front where United Nations forces repulsed several enemy attempts to probe friendly positions. Elsewhere, activity was limited to patrolling, with only scattered minor contacts reported.

Naval air and surface elements hit enemy rail lines, bridges, gun positions, bunkers, and warehouses along Korea's east coast, and gun positions, supply areas, bridges, and bunkers in the west coast area.

Land-based United Nations fighter aircraft clashed again with enemy jet fighters over North Korea, damaging or destroying several enemy planes. Fighter-bombers inflicted troop casualties, silenced gun positions, and blasted enemy bunkers in close support strikes. During the night medium bombers attacked the Pyongyang airfield, a steel mill at Kyomipo and flew support missions for front-line forces. Light bombers concentrated on enemy rail and road traffic. Cargo-transport aircraft continued to provide logistic support for United Nations combat operations.

DEWEY, DUANE E.

Rank and Organization: Corporal, U.S. Marine Corps Reserve, Company E, 2d Battalion, 5th Marines, 1st Marine Division (Rein).
Born: November 16, 1931, Grand Rapids, Michigan.
Entered Service At: Muskegon, Michigan.
Place and Date: Near Panmunjon, Korea, April 16, 1952.
Citation: For conspicuous gallantry and intrepidity at the risk of his life above and beyond the call of duty while serving as a gunner in a machine gun platoon of Company E, in action against enemy aggressor forces. When an enemy grenade landed close to his position while he and his assistant gunner were receiving medical attention for their wounds during a fierce night attack by numerically superior hostile forces, Cpl. Dewey, although suffering intense pain, immediately pulled the corpsman to the ground and, shouting a warning to the other

marines around him, bravely smothered the deadly missile with his body, personally absorbing the full force of the explosion to save his comrades from injury or possible death. His indomitable courage, outstanding initiative, and valiant efforts in behalf of others in the face of almost certain death reflects the highest credit upon Cpl. Dewey and enhance the finest traditions of the U.S. Naval Service.

OFFICIAL COMMUNIQUÉ:
TOKYO, Thursday, April 17 (AP)
—Allied naval summary for Wednesday:

Naval surface elements ranged along the Korean east coast yesterday pouring shells on enemy transportation and supply targets. Marine fliers from the carrier Bairoko hammered bunkers, buildings, and gun positions southwest of Chinnampo on the west coast.

The battleship Iowa and destroyer MacKenzie trained their guns on eighteen targets on the battle line on the east coast, and sent 180 rounds into Red supply areas.

With good visibility over the target area during the morning, the carrier Bairoko's Marine fliers hit hard at enemy positions southwest of Chinnampo. They destroyed or damaged twenty buildings, started many fires, and accounted for nineteen bunkers or gun positions. One tunnel was blocked and rails were slashed in several places.

First Marine Air Wing planes supported United Nations troops on the eastern and central fronts. Marine pilots cut thirty-three Red bunkers and leveled three enemy command posts. During close support sorties, troops were mauled, four mortar positions knocked out, and thirteen buildings left blazing. Other Marine fliers continued pounding North Korea supply routes and cut rails in nine places north and south of Pyongyang.

On the east coast battle line, the cruiser St. Paul and destroyer Hanson used an air spotter for hits on a supply dump and on buildings. Fires and secondary explosions were caused. Area fire was conducted in the Kojo area.

The destroyer Hamner continued the bombardment of the Kojo area with night-harassing and interdiction strikes. Troops, supply areas, and a fueling point were shelled. She continued firing during daylight on gun positions along the battle line and was later joined by the guns of the destroyer Moore. Other ships and planes carried out minesweeping and patrol missions.

—Far East Air Forces operational summary 662, for Tuesday:

Restrictive operational weather failed to provide complete protection for the Communists' battered transportation network in northern Korea Tuesday, and fighter-bombers dipped through the overcast to make destructive strikes, as warplanes of the Far East Air Forces were limited to 255 effective sorties. Fifth Air Force and attached Royal Australian pilots flew ninety-five of the total F.E.A.F. sorties.

F-84 Thunderjets found cloud openings and made a successful bombing and strafing attack on a string of boxcars on a siding near Chinnampo on the west coast of North Korea. Ten of the rail cars were damaged. A supply truck was destroyed near Sunchon.

F-80 Shooting Stars and Australian MK-8 Meteors made strikes on a rail line between Sariwon and Namchonjom, cratering tracks in four places. F-86 Sabre jets flew patrol sweeps over northwest Korea, but made no contact with enemy MiG-15s.

Medium bombers of the F.E.A.F. Bomber Command's Okinawa-based 307th Bomb Wing last night used radar-aiming methods to drop ninety tons of high explosives on the Chongju rail bridge as attacks against the enemy continued around the clock. Crews reported meager flak over the target, but no enemy fighters were encountered. The rail system in the Chongi sector has been repeatedly blasted in recent weeks by fighter-bombers during daylight hours. Two other Superforts last night flew in close air support of United Nations front-line forces, dropping air-bursting bombs on Communist troops and supply concentrations immediately behind the battle line.

B-26 light bombers and Marine aircraft last night mounted ninety sorties and ranged over Communist transportation routes. Pilots reported a moderate sighting of traffic, with approximately forty supply-laden vehicles destroyed. Two locomotives and twelve rail cars also were destroyed. Nine B-26s made radar drops on Red troops and supply positions immediately behind the battle line.

Cargo transports of the F.E.A.F. 315th Air Division yesterday flew 150 sorties to airlift 490 tons of supplies and personnel in continued logistical support of United Nations operation.

—Eighth Army Communiqué 949:

United Nations troops recapture position east of Pukhan River. Enemy units probe twice west of Munsan, twice west of Korangpo.

1. Enemy units of up to platoon strength probed two United Nations positions west of Munsan and two west of Korangpo between 11:00 P.M., Tuesday and 1:25 A.M., Wednesday. Three of the probes were repulsed in fire fights lasting up to fifty minutes. In the fourth action a unit withdrew from a small advance position west of Korangpo after a twenty-five minute attack by an enemy group of undetermined strength supported by 600 rounds of enemy artillery fire. United Nations forces along the eastern sector of the western Korean battle front reported light patrol contacts with enemy units up to two squads in strength.

2. Counterattacking United Nations units at 2:00 A.M., Tuesday, recaptured an advance position east of the Pukhan River from which they previously had withdrawn after an attack by two enemy companies. United Nations forces along the eastern sector of the front reported light patrol contacts with small enemy groups.

3. Light patrol contacts with enemy units up to a platoon in strength developed during the period along the eastern front.

—Eighth Army tactical summary 32:

Four enemy groups, ranging in size from two squads to a unit estimated at 300 enemy in strength, attacked United Nations positions on the far western front late Tuesday night and early Wednesday morning.

The largest group struck a half-hour before midnight west of Korangpo, supporting the attack with mortar and artillery fire. United Nations defensive action forced a cessation of enemy small-arms fire at 12:40 A.M., Wednesday, and in automatic weapons, mortar and artillery fire by 1:20 A.M. Thirty-one enemy were killed in the action.

Seventy-five enemy attacked a small advance position northwest of Korangpo at 11:00 P.M., Tuesday, supported by 600 rounds of artillery and mortar fire. United Nations troops occupying the position withdrew at 11:25 P.M.

An enemy platoon probed west of Munsan at 11:50 P.M., Tuesday, and withdrew after fifty minutes of fighting. Two enemy squads probed in the same area at 1:25 A.M., Wednesday, and were repulsed in a brief fire fight.

In another action west of Munsan early this morning, a United Nations raiding unit crossed the Sachon River and twice assaulted an enemy hill position, receiving heavy enemy small-arms fire each time. The action was over at 3:35 A.M., Wednesday, with United Nations units disengaging after an hour of fighting.

Two enemy units of undetermined strength engaged United Nations positions west of the Mundung Valley at midnight Tuesday and 12:55 A.M., Wednesday. They withdrew from the earlier engagement after a two-hour fight and from the latter after a brief contest.

Light engagements with enemy groups up to a platoon in strength have been reported so far today by United Nations patrols operating along the Eighth Army front, with most contacts developing in the east-central sector.

—General Headquarters communiqué, 1222, for twenty-four hours ended 6:00 A.M., Thursday (4:00 P.M., Wednesday, Eastern Standard Time):

A delayed report indicates the enemy launched two attacks against United Nations ground positions on the western Korean battlefront the night of April 15-16. No ground was lost by friendly forces in the first attack. In the second, United Nations forces withdrew a short distance to the main battle positions. Yesterday, along the front, light patrol contacts were reported.

Carrier-based Navy planes struck southwest of Chinnampo yesterday on the west coast and damaged or destroyed enemy bunkers, buildings, and gun positions. Surface elements patrolled along the east coast, shelling enemy transportation routes and supply targets.

Interdiction attacks were continued yesterday by Air Force planes against enemy rail and supply facilities. Fighter-bombers inflicted troop casualties and multiple rail cuts, knocked out enemy gun positions and troop bunkers, and damaged road and rail bridges. No enemy aircraft were encountered by United Nations planes flying protective missions for the bombers over northwest Korea. Medium bombers last night hit the west rail bypass of the Sinanju bridge complex. Air-bursting bombs were dropped last night on enemy troop and supply concentrations.

†CHAMPAGNE, DAVID B.

Rank and Organization: Corporal, U.S Marine Corps, Company A, 1st Battalion, 7th Marines, 1st Marine Division (Rein).
Born: November 13, 1932, Waterville, Maryland.
Entered Service At: Wakefield, Rhode Island.
Place and Date: Korea, May 28, 1952.
Citation: For conspicuous gallantry and intrepidity at the risk of his life above and beyond the call of duty while serving as a fire team leader of Company A, in action against enemy aggressor forces. Advancing with his platoon in the initial assault of the company against a strongly fortified and heavily defended hill position, Cpl. Champagne skillfully led his fire team through a veritable hail of intense enemy machine gun, small-arms, and grenade fire, overrunning trenches and a series of almost impregnable bunker positions before reaching the crest of the hill and placing his men in defensive positions. Suffering a painful leg wound while assisting in repelling the ensuing hostile counterattack, which was launched under cover of a murderous hail of mortar and artillery fire, he steadfastly refused evacuation and fearlessly continued to control his fire team. When the enemy counterattack increased in intensity, and a hostile grenade landed in the midst of the fire team, Cpl. Champagne unhesitatingly seized the deadly missile and hurled it in the direction of the approaching enemy. As the grenade left his hand, it exploded, blowing off his hand and throwing him out of the trench. Mortally wounded by enemy mortar fire while in this exposed position, Cpl. Champagne, by his valiant leadership, fortitude, and gallant spirit of self-sacrifice in the face of almost certain death, undoubtedly saved the lives of several of his fellow marines. His heroic actions served to inspire all who observed him and reflect the highest credit upon himself and the U.S. Naval Service. He gallantly gave his life for his country.

†KELLY, JOHN D.

Rank and Organization: Private First Class, U.S. Marine Corps, Company C, 1st Battalion, 7th Marines, 1st Marine Division (Rein).
Born: July 8, 1928, Youngstown, Ohio.
Entered Service At: Homestead, Pennsylvania.
Place and Date: Korea, May 28, 1952.
Citation: For conspicuous gallantry and intrepidity at the risk of his life above and beyond the call of duty while serving as a radio operator of Company C, in action against enemy aggressor forces. With his platoon pinned down by a numerically superior enemy force employing intense mortar, artillery, grenade, and small-arms fire, Pfc. Kelly requested permission to leave his radio in the care of another man and to participate in an assault on enemy key positions. Fearlessly charging forward in the face of a murderous hail of machine gun fire and hand-grenades, he initiated a daring attack against a hostile strongpoint and personally neutralized the position, killing 2 of the enemy. Unyielding in the face of heavy odds, he continued forward and singlehandedly assaulted a machine gun bunker. Although painfully wounded, he bravely charged the bunker and destroyed it, killing 3 of the enemy. Courageously continuing his 1-man assault, he again stormed forward in a valiant attempt to wipe out a third bunker and boldly delivered point-blank fire into the aperture of the hostile emplacement. Mortally wounded by enemy fire while carrying out this heroic action, Pfc. Kelly, by his great personal valor and aggressive spirit, inspired his comrades to sweep on, overrun and secure the objective. His extraordinary heroism in the face of almost certain death reflects the highest credit upon himself and enhances the finest tradition of the U.S. Naval Service. He gallantly gave his life for his country.

OFFICIAL COMMUNIQUÉ:
TOKYO, Thursday, May 29 (AP)
—Far East Air Forces summary of Tuesday's operations:

Communist front-line positions were subjected to further destructive air strikes Tuesday as warplanes of Far East Air Forces mounted 755 sorties, despite deteriorating weather.

Fighter-bombers flew sixty effective sorties along the battle line, knocking out bunkers, silencing gun positions, and inflicting enemy troop casualties.

Fifth Air Force and attached Royal Australian, South African, R.O.K., and land-based Marine pilots mounted 555 of the total F.E.A.F. sorties.

F-51 Mustangs teamed with Marine Corsairs and Skyraiders to hit Red battle line positions with high explosive bombs, rockets, napalm, and machine-gun fire in low level attacks. They blasted more than fifty troop and supply bunkers, destroyed twenty-five gun positions and damaged five others, and inflicted seventy troop casualties.

At the tip of the battle line on the east coast, the fighter-bombers sank ten small Communist boats.

Meanwhile, the enemy's battered transportation network suffered additional mutilation. F-80 Shooting Stars and F-51 Mustangs concentrated their firepower on the line between Sinanju and Sukchon, where they ripped rails in twenty places.

Along the same stretch of trackage, Marine Corsairs scored additional cuts.

On the line north of Pyonggang, jet fighter-bombers teamed with Republic of Korea Mustangs to crater tracks in more than ten locations. F-86 Sabre jets, flying protective cover for the rail-slashing fighter-bombers, destroyed one enemy MiG-15 in the only air engagement of the day. The battle ensued when a screening force of twenty-one Sabres intercepted two MiGs about twenty miles south of the Yalu River and over the Yellow Sea. The kill was scored by a jet Ace, Maj. Donald E. Adams of the Fifty-first Fighter Interceptor Wing, to bring his total score of enemy jets to six and one-half. Total destruction during the period includes sixty rail cuts, one road bridge knocked out, and twenty-five buildings destroyed.

B-29 Superforts of F.E.A.F. Bomber Command's Okinawa-based 307th Bomb Wing on Tuesday night struck a vital transportation link in extreme northwest Korea as air attacks against enemy targets continued around the clock. Ten Superforts employed electronic aiming techniques to drop 100 tons of high explosives on the Kogunyong rail bridge by-pass between Namsi and Sonchon, on the main line from Antung into the Sinanju gateway. Crews reported meager flak and no fighter opposition. One B-29 blasted the marshaling yards at Chinampo and another flew in close air support of United Nations front-line forces, dropping high explosives on Red troop and supply concentrations immediately behind the battleline.

—Eighth Army communiqué 991, for Tuesday's operations:

Three United Nations patrols kill thirty enemy in long engagements northwest of Korangpo. Seven enemy probes repulsed on western front.

Three United Nations patrols operating northwest of Korangpo killed thirty enemy in fire fights up to three hours and forty minutes in length with enemy groups of two-squad and platoon strength between 0210 and 1425. A United Nations patrol engaged an enemy platoon at a hill position west of Munsan at 1235. The patrol, with tank and infantry reinforcements, drove the enemy off the position, secured it at 1530 and returned to its base at 1815. United Nations troops at positions east of Panmunjom repulsed three enemy probes between 2215 and 2400 in fire fights up to forty-five minutes in length. Light enemy probes were repulsed at two advanced positions west-northwest of Yonchon and one northwest of Yonchon in fire fights up to thirty minutes in length developing at 0050, 1850, and 2355. United Nations troops at a small advance position west of Chorwon repulsed a light enemy probe in a brief fire fight at 2340. No other significant enemy activity was reported during the period from the western Korean battlefront.

Two enemy squads probing a small advance position northwest of Kumhwa at 2045 were driven off with the aid of mortar fire in a brief fire fight. United Nations patrols along the central front fought light engagements up to ten minutes in length with small enemy groups.

—Eighth Army tactical summary 71, for Wednesday:

United Nations troops raided three enemy hill positions west of Korangpo in the western sector of the Eighth Army front early Wednesday, killing and wounding at least thirty enemy before returning to their base during the morning.

The raiders jumped off at 3:00 A.M. and were on their easternmost objective an hour later on the westernmost hill at 5:55 and on the higher center hill at 6:00.

Heavy enemy artillery fire fell on the United Nations troops during the fire fight and United Nations tank fire aided in forcing the enemy withdrawal. All three raiding groups returned to their bases during the morning. The early report of enemy casualties is incomplete, covering only the action at the western objective.

United Nations tanks firing on central front targets north of Kumhwa between 7:35 and 9:10 A.M. damaged eighty-one bunkers, six weapons emplacements, and twelve communications trenches.

Scattered patrol contacts reported since midnight were brief, light engagements with enemy units up to two squads in strength.

—United Nations Command communiqué 1,264, for Wednesday's activities:

A sharp clash developed in the western sector of the Korean battle front (Wednesday) as a small friendly raid ran into intense enemy small arms, automatic weapons, and mortar fire. In the west central sector, an armored force destroyed and damaged enemy installations. Several small enemy probes were repulsed during the period.

United Nations Command naval surface craft bombarded enemy military positions on the northeast coast of Korea. Shore batteries, anti-aircraft gun positions, and mortar installations were destroyed. Carrier-based aircraft operating on the west coast destroyed storage tanks and a group of warehouses.

Targets truck by land-based aircraft included the Huichon rail bridge complex and the Hamhung marshaling yard. Other planes flew front-line support missions and sought out enemy targets in North Korea.

BLEAK, DAVID B.
Rank and Organization: Sergeant, U.S. Army, Medical Company, 223d Infantry Regiment, 40th Infantry Division.
Born: February 27, 1932, Idaho Falls, Idaho.
Entered Service At: Shelley, Idaho.
Place and Date: Vicinity of Minari-gol, Korea, June 14, 1952.
Citation: Sgt. Bleak, a member of the medical company, distinguished himself by conspicuous gallantry and indomitable courage above and beyond the call of duty in action against the enemy. As a medical aid-man, he volunteered to accompany a reconnaissance patrol committed to engage the enemy and capture a prisoner for interrogation. Forging up the rugged slope of the key terrain, the group was subjected to intense automatic-weapons and small-arms fire and suffered several casualties. After administering to the wounded, he continued to advance with the patrol. Nearing the military crest of the hill, while attempting to cross the fire-swept area to attend the wounded, he came under hostile fire from a small group of the enemy concealed in a trench. Entering the trench he closed with the enemy, killed 2 with his bare hands and a third with his trench knife. Moving from the emplacement, he saw a concussion grenade fall in front of a companion and, quickly shifting his position, shielded the man from the impact of the blast. Later, while ministering to the wounded, he was struck by a hostile bullet but, despite the wound, he undertook to evacuate a wounded comrade. As he moved down the hill with his heavy burden, he was attacked by 2 enemy soldiers with fixed bayonets. Closing with the aggressors, he grabbed them and smacked their heads together, then carried his helpless comrade down the hill to safety. Sgt. Bleak's dauntless courage and intrepid actions reflect utmost credit upon himself and are in keeping with the honored tradition of the military service.

†SPEICHER, CLIFTON T.
Rank and Organization: Corporal, U.S. Army, Company F, 223d Infantry Regiment, 40th Infantry Division.
Born: March 25, 1931, Gray, Pennsylvania.
Entered Service At: Gray, Pennsylvania.
Place and Date: Near Minari-gol, Korea, June 14, 1952.
Citation: Cpl. Speicher distinguished himself by conspicuous gallantry and indomitable courage above and beyond the call of duty in action against the enemy. While participating in an assault to secure a key terrain feature, Cpl. Speicher's squad was pinned down by withering small-arms, mortar, and machine gun fire. Although already wounded he left the comparative safety of his position, and made a daring charge against the machine gun emplacement. Within 10 yards of the goal, he was again wounded by small-arms fire but continued on, entered the bunker, killed 2 hostile soldiers with his rifle, a third with his bayonet, and silenced the machine gun. Inspired by this incredible display of valor, the men quickly moved up and completed the mission. Dazed and shaken, he walked to the foot of the hill where he collapsed and died. Cpl. Speicher's consummate sacrifice and unflinching devotion to duty reflect lasting glory upon himself and uphold the noble traditions of the military service.

OFFICIAL COMMUNIQUÉ:
TOKYO, Sunday, June 15 (AP)
—Far East Air Forces operational summary 730:

Communist battleline positions and transportation routes were subjected to destructive attacks by Far East Air Forces warplanes yesterday as the F.E.A.F., Friday, mounted 980 effective sorties.

Two principal areas in the Communist rail system were blasted by fighter-bombers, which inflicted thirty rail cuts near Hwangju, and another thirty cuts north of Haeju. Other fighter-bombers blasted the Red front-line positions with rockets, bombs, and napalm, inflicting 125 enemy troop casualties during the strikes.

Fifth Air Force and attached Royal Australian, South African, R.O.K., and land-based Marine pilots teamed in making the interdiction and close-air-support attacks. F-80 Shooting Stars and F-84 Thunderjets blasted the rails at Hwangju, also destroying six rail cars in that area. United States Air Force and R.O.K. Mustangs teamed with Marine fighter-bombers to slash the trackage near Haeju.

Shooting Stars, Mustangs, Thunderjets and Marine Fighter-bombers flew close air support for United Nations ground forces, roaring all along the battle front, but concentrating on the eastern sector.

In an area about five miles from Kumsong, the fighter-bombers inflicted 110 enemy troop casualties. They also silenced twenty-five gun positions, blasted nine troop bunkers and exploded an ammunition dump. Other fighter-bombers hit the west end of the enemy's main line of resistance, as well as northeast of Kumhwa and near the "Punchbowl" area.

Total destruction inflicted on the enemy during the period included fifty-five troop casualties, forty-five gun positions silenced, thirty enemy-held buildings destroyed and five damaged, ten rail cars destroyed, two rail bridges damaged, and seventy-five rail and five road cuts.

F-86 Sabre jets, flying protective screen for the fighter-bombers yesterday, did not sight any MiG-15s aloft. However, just before noon, two MiGs attacked two Marine Banshees in the Chinnampo area. The Banshees, flying reconnaissance, turned into the MiGs but no damages were inflicted on the Russian-built jets, nor was any damage suffered by the Marine twin-jet aircraft.

Medium bombers of the F.E.A.F. Bomber Command's Okinawa-based Nineteenth Bomb Group, using electronic techniques, last night dropped high explosives on the rail bridge complex at Huichon. This is the fifth time in one week that the big bombers have hit the important Communist transportation link which connects Kanggye and Kusu. Meager flak was encountered, but no fighters were sighted.

The Superforts also hit the Hamhung marshaling yard and flew close air support for United Nations ground forces along the western sector of the front lines.

B-26 light bombers and shore-based Marine aircraft last night destroyed sixty of a moderate sighting of enemy supply laden vehicles attempting to move southward toward Communist front lines. The enemy traffic was attacked on highways from Pyongyang to Sarimon, from Kangdong and Yangdok to Singye, from Yongpo to Sibyon, and from Wonsan to Pyonggang.

Cargo transports of the F.E.A.F.'s 315th Air Division yesterday airlifted 200 tons of personnel and supplies in continued logistical support of United Nations combat operations.

—Eighth Army communiqué 1,008, for Friday's operations:

United States Forty-fifth Infantry Division troops captured two more positions in a hill mass west of Chorwon and were fighting off a counter-attack by an enemy battalion at the close of the period. Other United nations troops continued raids along the western sector of the front, while tank units blasted enemy fortifications forward of the central sector. Air strikes killed 200 enemy north of Kumsong. Enemy mortars and artillery fired 8,283 rounds on United nations positions from 6:00 P.M. June 12, to 6:00 P.M. June 13.

Western sector: Fighting continued west of Chorwon as troops of the United States Forty-fifth Infantry Division repulsed a counter-attack against an advance position captured in an attack on an enemy hill mass June 12. Action throughout the night was relatively light. Artillery fire dispersed the enemy forming at a hill to the west-northwest at 2:25 A.M..

At dawn, Forty-fifth Division troops attacked to disorganize another enemy group forming on the hill. Sporadic firing continued throughout the day until 3:00 P.M., when Forty-fifth Division elements, supported by tanks, attacked the hill to the west-northwest and another to the north in the hill mass. Both hills were occupied against light resistance by 6:35 P.M. At the close of the period, an enemy battalion was counter-attacking.

Forty-fifth Division troops repulsed a light probe at another advance position in the area in a twenty-five minute fight ending at 2:25 A.M.. A United Nations raiding party killed an estimated 102 enemy in a fifty-five minute action ending at 1:05 A.M. west of Korangpo. Other raiding units were in operation west-northwest and northwest of Yonchon. Patrols fought engagements up to fifty minutes in length with enemy units up to a platoon in strength.

Central sector: United Nations tanks fired on targets southeast of Pyonggang, southwest of Kumsong, and southeast of Kumsong during the period, damaging at least fifty-eight enemy bunkers and additional fortifications. United Nations troops southeast of Kumsong repulsed six probes of enemy groups of from squad to company strength in brief fire fights between 9:10 P.M., June 12, and 2:00 A.M., June 13. Patrols fought engagements up to an hour and forty-five minutes in length with enemy groups up to a platoon in strength. Air strikes killed 200 enemy north of Kumsong.

Eastern sector: United Nations troops in the "Punchbowl" area repulsed three light probes by squad-size enemy groups in brief fire fights between 12:15 A.M., and 3:00 A.M.. Patrols fought engagements up to an hour in length with enemy groups up to two platoons in strength.

—Eighth Army tactical summary 88, for Saturday:

United States Forty-fifth Division troops stood fast west of Chorwon last night as they defended a newly captured hill mass against a counter-attacking enemy battalion. The Thunderbirds had taken one hill in the mass in bitter fighting Thursday, repulsed several counter-attacks, and captured the other two against light resistance Friday afternoon.

A Chinese battalion, supported by tanks, tried to drive a wedge across the hill mass at 11:40 P.M., Friday. The Thunderbirds repulsed the enemy in a sharp clash that was over at 2:25 A.M., Saturday. Light, sporadic firing has continued at the western sector hill mass since the Chinese withdrew.

A United Nations raiding party captured and occupied an enemy position west of the Pukhan River, where Chinese troops had been inching forward, increasingly a threat to United Nations positions in the area. They drove two enemy squads off the position in a two-hour fight ending at dawn Saturday. Moving fifty yards to the east, they fought until 10:22 A.M., and forced an enemy units of undetermined strength to withdraw. The Chinese remained in the area, however.

A United Nations raiding unit operating northwest of Yonchon fought briefly with an enemy platoon at 8:20 P.M., Friday and split into three elements which fought separate engagements up to fifty minutes in length with enemy units up to two platoons in strength. The raiders returned to their base at 3:30 A.M..

An enemy unit of undetermined strength probed a small United Nations advance position west of Korangpo at 2:55 A.M.. The occupying United Nations unit withdrew after a brief fire fight. Patrol contacts reported from the Eighth Army front, since midnight there have been engagements up to an hour in length against enemy units up to a platoon in strength, and were most frequent west of the Pukhan River and on the central sector and northeast of the "Punchbowl" and south of Kosong.

—United Nations Command communiqué 1281, for Saturday's operations:

An estimated enemy battalion attacked United Nations positions on the western front Saturday in an engagement which lasted more than two hours before our forces repulsed the enemy. As a result of the action, heavy enemy casualties were reported. One other smaller enemy attack against a friendly forward position also was repulsed. Elsewhere across the Korean battle front, patrol activities continued with minor contacts being made.

Naval destroyers bombarded coastal supply lines in northeast Korea and also laid heavy fire on enemy targets in the Songjin area. Carrier-based planes hammered at enemy supply lines on both coasts.

Fighter-bombers struck hard at the enemy, knocking out gun positions, inflicting troop casualties, blasting bunkers, destroying buildings, inflicting rail cuts, and attacking rolling stock. Saturday night, medium bombers dropped high explosives on the rail bridge complex at Huichon and on the Hamhung marshaling yard. Other United Nations aircraft flew close support missions for ground troops and destroyed enemy supply-laden vehicles attempting to move toward the front.

†SHUCK, WILLIAM E., JR.

Rank and Organization: Staff Sergeant, U.S. Marine Corps, Company G, 3d Battalion, 7th Marines, 1st Marine Division.
Born: August 16, 1926, Cumberland, Maryland.
Entered Service At: Cumberland, Maryland.
Place and Date: Korea, July 3, 1952.
Citation: For conspicuous gallantry and intrepidity at the risk of his life above and beyond the call of duty while serving as a squad leader of Company G, in action against enemy aggressor forces. When his platoon was subjected to a devastating barrage of enemy small-arms, grenade, artillery, and mortar fire during an assault against strongly fortified hill positions well forward of the main line of resistance, S/Sgt. Shuck, although painfully wounded, refused medical attention and continued to lead his machine gun squad in the attack. Unhesitatingly assuming command of a rifle squad when the leader became a casualty, he skillfully organized the 2 squads into an attacking force and led 2 more daring assaults upon the hostile positions. Wounded a second time, he steadfastly refused evacuation and remained in the foremost position under heavy fire until assured that all dead and wounded were evacuated. Mortally wounded by an enemy sniper bullet while voluntarily assisting in the removal of the last casualty, S/Sgt. Shuck, by his fortitude and great personal valor in the face of overwhelming odds, served to inspire all who observed him. His unyielding courage throughout reflects the highest credit upon himself and the U.S. Naval Service. He gallantly gave his life for his country.

OFFICIAL COMMUNIQUÉ:
TOKYO, Friday, July 4 (AP)
—Far East Air Forces summary of Wednesday's operations:

Despite adverse weather conditions, warplanes of the Far East Air Forces made destructive strikes against enemy positions at the front lines and also hit Communist transportation targets in North Korea, as F.E.A.F., Wednesday, mounted 400 effective sorties.

While clouds obscured most targets for the fourth consecutive day, fighter-bombers found holes in the overcast and blasted Communist gun positions at the front and supply targets in rear areas.

Fifth Air Force and attached R.O.K. and land-based Marine pilots teamed to fly limited interdiction and close air support during the day.

Shooting Stars and Thunderjets teamed with R.O.K. Mustangs to fly armed reconnaissance over enemy supply routes. Fighter-bombers cratered rails in three places about three miles south of Wonsan on the East Coast. On the West Coast, the fighter-bombers destroyed a supply truck north of Chinnampo and also knocked out four gun positions.

Closer to the battle line, fighter-bombers destroyed two rail cars and damaged three others at Pyonggang, and damaged another about twenty miles west of Ando.

For the fourth consecutive day, B-26 light bombers continued to blast the enemy around the clock. Fifty B-26s flew close air support for United Nations ground forces along the battlefront, causing fires and secondary explosions.

The light bombers continued the close air support strikes Wednesday night as forty B-26s hit enemy troop and supply positions along the front. Results were unassessed. Other B-26s attacked a supply area at Haeju, also with unobserved results.

Total destruction inflicted on the enemy during the period included four gun positions silenced, two buildings damaged, two rail cars destroyed and four damaged, and three rail cuts.

F-86 Sabre jets flew weather reconnaissance, but did not sight any MiG-15s.

Medium bombers of F.E.A.F. Bomber Command's Okinawa-based Nineteenth Bomb Group, using electronic techniques, during the night dropped high explosives on the Sangwang rail bridge south of Huichon in north-central Korea. Flak was reported as meager to intense, and enemy night fighters were sighted but did not attack.

Other Superforts of the Okinawa-based 307th Bomb Wing in the night dropped high explosives by electronic aiming methods on the often-hit and much-repaired Huichon rail bridge complex. Meager to moderate flak was encountered and fighters made non-firing passes on several of the bombers.

Other Superforts hit the Yongmi rail bridge immediately northwest of Sinanju, again employing electronic methods to aim their bomb loads through the cloud cover. Flak was meager to moderate and no enemy fighters were sighted. Another 307th Superfort hit the Hungnam chemical plant, which has been used as a storage area. A single B-29 flew close air support for United nations ground forces at the battle line, dropping deep-penetrating bombs on enemy troop and supply concentrations. No opposition was reported over the two latter targets.

Cargo transports of F.E.A.F.'s 315th Air Division airlifted 550 tons of personnel and supplies in continued logistical support of United Nations combat operations.

—United nations Naval Forces summary of Thursday's operations:

Power plants in extreme north-eastern Korea were again the target of Task Force 77 as three carriers launched afternoon strikes against the electrical complexes of Kyosen and Puryong.

At Kyosen, No. 2 penstocks were cut in three places and the south end of the main power house was gutted with a direct hit. Intense suppression fire was laid on gun positions surrounding the plant, but no destruction claims were made on these targets.

At Kyosen No. 3, two direct hits were scored on the power house, the transformer yard received additional damage, and a near-by highway bridge was hit.

The Puryong plant turbine house was damaged, two cuts were made in the penstocks, and several auxiliary buildings were destroyed and damaged.

A fourth carrier was in full operation in the Yellow Sea where flying conditions have been unfavorable for the past week. U.S.S. Bataan launched forty Corsair missions over Red territory north of Chinnampo. The Marine pilots destroyed two rail bridges, fourteen buildings, two bunkers, one gun position, and four jeeps.

U.S.S. Iowa's 16-inch guns shelled Chongjin throughout the afternoon and accounted for widespread damage and destruction in marshaling yards, factories, warehouses, and similar industrial facilities. Haze hung over the target area and detailed assessment was not made.

The cruiser, U.S.S. Helena with destroyer U.S.S. Soley in company worked exclusively against Red bunkers along the east coast near Kosong. Spotting conditions were excellent and good coverage of all areas was reported. At least eleven bunkers were damaged and five destroyed.

The destroyers U.S.S. Van Valkenberg and U.S.S. Parks maintained a watch at Wonsan and fired on rail and industrial targets there. Destroyer escort McCoy Reynolds fired on an important rail bridge near the city.

The destroyer escort U.S.S. Carrier patrolled northward from Hungnam to fire on a strategic rail bridge which the enemy is attempting to repair. Enroute she was attacked by two coastal guns and spent twenty minutes in counter-battery fire. Thirty rounds fell in close proximity to the vessel but she was not hit.

U.S.S. Orleck moved into the Songjin area to relieve U.S.S. Jarvis as gunfire support ship for sweeping operations in the area. During darkness she fired on a rail bridge and on industrial targets in and near that city. U.S.S. Doyle operated against similar targets in the same area.

Only two ships were reported in surface action in the Yellow Sea. H.M.S. Comus fired thirty-two rounds at gun emplacements and U.S.S. PC 703 laid 128 rounds of 3-inch on troop and gun positions in the Haejin approaches.

—Eighth Army tactical summary 107, for Thursday:

Three United Nations raiding parties attacked enemy-held positions northwest of Kumwha and east and south of Panmunjom early Thursday morning. Patrol engagements were fought along the remainder of the Eighth Army front.

A United Nations raiding party attacked hill positions occupied by an unknown number of enemy northwest of Kumwha at 6:40 A.M. The United Nations assault elements were heavily engaged on the objective at 6:50 A.M., and at 7:31 they were reinforced by another United Nations unit. The objective was secured at 7:50 and the raiders remained on the positions until ordered to withdraw at 8:30 A.M..

Another United Nations unit, raiding east of Panmunjom, engaged an enemy unit of undetermined strength in a brief fire fight at 6:24 A.M. before withdrawing and calling in artillery on the enemy positions.

A United Nations patrol killed eleven in a brief clash with an enemy unit two to three squads in strength northwest of Korangpo at 6:15 A.M..

Other patrols fought engagements up to ten minutes in length against enemy units up to a reinforced platoon in strength.

—United Nations Command communiqué 1,300, for the twenty-four hours ended 6:00 A.M., Friday, Korea time:

United Nations Command ground forces conducted a series of raiding parties to disrupt the enemy. Three raiding parties were dispatched in the western sector and succeeded in inflicting casualties on hostile forces. Friendly artillery and air were employed in these actions. In the west-central sector a friendly raid party engaged an unknown number of enemy in a limited objective attack. The objective was secured before the friendly forces were ordered to withdraw. Enemy probes were thrown at United Nations positions in several locales, which resulted in sharp fights. In the western sector, friendly forces withdrew and placed artillery on attacking enemy troops and then reoccupied outpost positions in two different engagements. In three separate probes in another part of the western sector, the enemy was thrown back after fire fights of eighty-five minutes, seventy minutes, and twenty-five minutes.

United Nations Command front line troops received close air support from our fighter-bombers, light bombers, and medium bombers. Other land-based aircraft cratered rails, silenced gun positions, blasted bunkers, and inflicted troop casualties during the day's fight. During the night, medium bombers attacked the Hungnam chemical plant used as a storage area.

Aircraft carriers operating in the Sea of Japan launched planes that attacked enemy installations, including electrical stations, factories, and industrial plants. Surface vessels conducted gun strikes against Chongjin and continued bombardment, patrol, and minesweeping operations.

†KILMER, JOHN E.
Rank and Organization: Hospital Corpsman, U.S. Navy, attached to duty as a medical corpsman with a Marine rifle company in the 1st Marine Division.
Born: August 15, 1930, Highland Park, Illinois.
Entered Service At: Houston, Texas.
Place and Date: Korea, August 13, 1952.
Citation: For conspicuous gallantry and intrepidity at the risk of his life above and beyond the call of duty in action against enemy aggressor forces. With his company engaged in defending a vitally important hill position well forward of the main line of resistance during an assault by large concentrations of hostile troops, HC Kilmer repeatedly braved intense enemy mortar, artillery, and sniper fire to move from one position to another, administering aid to the wounded and expediting their evacuation. Painfully wounded himself when struck by mortar fragments while moving to the aid of a casualty, he persisted in his efforts and inched his way to the side of the stricken marine through a hail of enemy shells falling around him. Undaunted by the devastating hostile fire, he skillfully administered first-aid to his comrade and, as another mounting barrage of enemy fire shattered the immediate area, unhesitatingly shielded the wounded man with his body. Mortally wounded by flying shrapnel while carrying out this heroic action, HC Kilmer, by his great personal valor and gallant spirit of self-sacrifice in saving the life of a comrade, served to inspire all who observed him. His unyielding devotion to duty in the face of heavy odds reflects the highest credit upon himself and enhances the finest traditions of the U.S. Naval Service. He gallantly gave his life for another.

†HAMMOND, LESTER, JR.
Rank and Organization: Corporal, U.S. Army, Company A, 187th Airborne Regimental Combat Team.
Born: March 25, 1931, Wayland, Missouri.
Entered Service At: Quincy, Illinois.
Place and Date: Near Kumwha, Korea, August 14, 1952.
Citation: Cpl. Hammond, a radio operator with Company A, distinguished himself by conspicuous gallantry and outstanding courage above and beyond the call of duty in action against the enemy. Cpl. Hammond was a member of a 6 man reconnaissance patrol which had penetrated approximately 3,500 yards into enemy-held territory. Ambushed and partially surrounded by a large hostile force, the small group opened fire, then quickly withdrew up a narrow ravine in search of protective cover. Despite a wound sustained in the initial exchange of fire and imminent danger of being overrun by a numerically superior foe, he refused to seek shelter and, remaining in an exposed place, called for artillery fire to support a defensive action. Constantly vulnerable to enemy observation and action, he coordinated and directed crippling fire on the assailants, inflicting heavy casualties and repulsing several attempts to overrun friendly positions. Although wounded a second time, he remained steadfast and maintained his stand until mortally wounded. His indomitable fighting spirit set an inspiring example of valor to his comrades and, through his actions, the onslaught was stemmed, enabling a friendly platoon to reach the beleaguered patrol, evacuate the wounded, and effect a safe withdrawal to friendly lines. Cpl. Hammond's unflinching courage and consummate devotion to duty reflect lasting glory on himself and uphold the finest traditions of the military service.

OFFICIAL COMMUNIQUÉ:
TOKYO, Friday, Aug. 15 (AP)
—Far East Air Forces summary 781 for Wednesday's operations:

Fighter-bombers of the Far East Air Forces yesterday hit a number of military targets in the Sariwon and Samdung areas, and then night-flying medium and light bombers returned during darkness to inflict further destruction in the same vicinities.

F-80 Shooting Stars and F-84 Thunderjets of the Fifth Air Force started the fierce United Nations attacks during the day when they struck a marshaling yard north of Samdung. Heavy black smoke obscured most of the area, but at least four supply buildings were left in ruins, eight rail cars were destroyed, and rails were cratered in several places.

In the Sariwon and Yonan areas, Marine fighter-bombers, R.O.K. (Republic of Korea) Mustangs, and Royal Australian twin-jet Meteors leveled thirty supply buildings and started large fires and secondary explosions.

Then, after darkness, twenty-five Superforts of the Far East Air Force Bomber Command's Okinawa-based 307th Bomb Wing returned to west coast targets, attacking a supply center at Anak, just west of Sariwon. The Superfort's high explosives fell on stockpiled war material. One crew member said "The explosions looked like oil wells burning . . . They mushroomed red with a lot of smoke in them and a white glare at the top as if gases were burning off." Crews reported meager flak and no enemy fighter opposition.

Meanwhile, night-flying B-26s and Marine fighter-bombers were returning to the Samdung area farther north, as they continued the round-the-clock strikes. The night intruders dropped high explosives on a supply complex at Samdung near the rail yard blasted by fighter-bombers earlier in the day.

Other fighter-bombers concentrated on flying close air support during the day, attacking dug-in enemy troop and supply concentrations along the front. The war craft were utilized primarily on the western sector, and mostly in support of the Marine forces fighting on "Siberia Hill."

In other activity last night, one 307th B-29 Superfort and B-26 night intruders flew close air support. Other B-26s hit targets of opportunity at Sinchon and Sepo, and patrolled enemy supply routes. Far East Air Forces aircraft flew 905 effective sorties during the period. Of these, 370 were in support of the United Nations army, with 290 being combat missions.

Total destruction inflicted on the Reds during the period includes five bunkers destroyed and five others damaged, forty-five gun positions silenced, 120 enemy-held buildings leveled and fifteen others damaged, eight rail cars destroyed and two damaged, eighty Red troop casualties inflicted, four rail bridges damaged, ten rail and three road cuts.

F-86 Sabre jets patrolled the skies over northwest Korea yesterday, but sighted no airborne enemy MiG-15s. However, propeller-driven F-51 Mustangs observed a flight of six MiGs off the west coast of Korea yesterday, but the MiGs did not attack.

Cargo transports of the Far East Air Force's 315th Air Division yesterday airlifted 565 tons of personnel and supplies as they continued to fly logistical support for United Nations combat operations.

—Far East Naval Headquarters summary for Thursday:

Carrier-based Panther jets, Corsairs, and Skyraiders struck at Communist rolling stock, supply areas, and gun positions in dawn to dusk attacks extending from Chongjin to Wonsan.

Some Task Force 77 planes spotted for bombarding warships while others flew in close support of United Nations infantrymen.

U.S.S. Essex sent jets to Hungnam in the early morning to destroy two buildings and three box cars, and damage a number of these targets. Propeller-driven planes in the same area cut rail lines, damaged a rail bridge and a factory, and knocked down several storage facilities.

Troop concentrations near Pyong were attacked by U.S.S. Bon Homme Richard pilots at dawn. Four buildings in the vicinity also were hit. Later strikes were against gun positions on Hodo Pando near Wonsan and along the eastern front.

The battleship U.S.S. Iowa stood off Kosong to fire both 16-inch and 5-inch shells into Red front-line objectives. One bunker was destroyed, one bunker was damaged, six troop shelters were wiped out, and hundreds of enemy troops were dispersed. The big guns also silenced several enemy artillery strong points.

Cruiser U.S.S. Helena and destroyer U.S.S. Taylor were also near the eastern front. One 76-mm. gun bunker was destroyed and one was damaged. Two other bunkers were destroyed and two were damaged.

Destroyer U.S.S. Van Valkenburgh operated independently against front-line targets with excellent results for the day's shoot. Five bunkers, two machine-guns, and five houses were destroyed and coverage of all target areas was above 80 percent.

Three United States destroyers, Barton, Tingey, and Jarvis, continued destructive attacks at Wonsan. Hundreds of Red casualties were inflicted as the ships fired on troops attempting to extinguish flames set by destroyer shells. Other Reds were killed as they dug new gun emplacements or repaired battered bridges.

Destroyer U.S.S. Soley watched the coast from Hungnam to Chaho, firing on the coastal railroad and on gun emplacements built to protect vulnerable stretches of track. Several construction crews were dispersed with casualties and additional damage was done to the roadbed. One sampan surrendered voluntarily and the twenty-eight civilians embarked were sent in a R.O.K. (Republic of Korea) Navy craft.

At Songjin destroyer U.S.S. Porter engaged three 105-mm. gun batteries at dawn and exchanged fire for several hours. Carrier pilots volunteered assistance but Porter declined the offer and finished off the battle with a long-handed victory.

In the Yellow Sea, both air and surface elements of Rear Admiral H.E. Gingrich's Task Force 95 were busy against the enemy.

H.M.S. Ocean's aircraft knocked down six road and one rail bridges, destroyed four gun positions, destroyed two buildings and damaged several others in the factory area, and wiped out many enemy troop bunkers, shelters, and one transformer station.

In Taedong, west of Haeju, H.M.N.Z.S. Rotoiti and H.M.C.S. Crusader fired on a troop concentration and intercepted one armed junk. H.M.A.S. Condamine and H.M.S. Concord attacked Red guns near Chodo and Haeju.

—Eighth Army tactical summary 149, for Thursday:

Chinese troops early Thursday made their fourth and weakest attempt to retake Bunker Hill, east of Panmunjom, which United States Marines captured from them early Tuesday.

A Chinese unit of undetermined strength—perhaps elements of a battalion which unsuccessfully assaulted the hill late Wednesday—attacked at 2:25 A.M.. The attack, described at the front as "not very aggressive" was repulsed in about four minutes of fighting.

Two enemy platoons attacked and occupied a United Nations advance position just east of the Pukhan River on the east-central sector.

The enemy attacked at 3:35 A.M. and the occupying unit withdrew after ten minutes. United Nations troops at 6:50 A.M. counter-attacked two enemy squads left to defend the hill and withdrew at 11:20 A.M..

Early morning raids and patrol clashes against enemy groups up to two platoons in strength highlighted action along the remainder of the Eighth Army front Thursday.

One United Nations raiding unit killed twelve Chinese in a brief but bitter fight with enemy of unknown strength shortly after midnight north of Korango.

Other United Nations raiders engaged a second enemy group on the forward slopes of a hill west-northwest of Yonchon at 2:18 A.M.. The enemy withdrew to the crest of the hill after fifteen minutes of fighting and detonated bangalore torpedoes as the raiders advanced. Fighting continued to 3:50 A.M. when the raiders withdrew. Twenty-nine Chinese were estimated to have been killed in this action.

A series of patrol clashes stretched over a twenty-hour period at an enemy-held hill position west-northwest of Yonchon.

United Nations patrols twice occupied the hill and twice withdrew from it, fighting engagements up to nearly two hours in length against platoon-size enemy units. United Nations patrol was again advancing at 12:45 P.M., Thursday.

—Eighth Army communiqué 1,070, for Thursday's activities:

United States Marines successfully defended Bunker Hill against a brief early morning attack. United Nations patrols fought a series of actions over a twenty-one hour period at an enemy hill northwest of Yonchon. Other raiding units and patrols estimated killing nearly 100 enemy in sharp clashes in the western and central sectors. A United Nations unit withdrew from an advance position in the east-central sector. Enemy mortars and artillery fired 8,468 rounds during the twenty-four hour period ending at 6:00 P.M., 1,778 fewer than were fired in the preceding twenty-four hours.

Western sector: United States Marines defending Bunker Hill, east of Panmunjom, repulsed an attack by an enemy unit of undetermined strength ended at 2:30 A.M.. Patrol clashes up to three hours and forty minutes in length against enemy units up to a platoon in strength continued at an enemy hill position west-northwest of Yonchon from 4:45 P.M., Aug. 13, through 2:41 P.M., Aug. 14, with United Nations troops occupying the hill twice and the enemy regaining control when the fight broke off.

United Nations units killed twelve enemy in a ten-minute fight shortly after midnight north of Korangpo, and estimated killing twenty-nine more in a two hour and five minute action west-northwest of Chorwon, which broke off at 4:23 A.M.. Two enemy squads probing a United Nations advance position west-northwest of Chorwon at 8:40 P.M. were repulsed in forty-five minutes.

Central sector: A United Nations patrol estimated killing fifty-five enemy in three engagements between 11:30 A.M. and 2:35 P.M., fighting part of the time from a cave. United Nations elements occupying an advance position east of the Pukhan River withdrew at 3:45 A.M. after a ten minute probe by two enemy platoons, counter-attacked at 7:00 A.M., and withdrew again at 11:20 A.M.. Patrols fought engagements up to ten minutes in length with enemy groups up to two platoons in strength.

Eastern sector: United Nations patrols fought engagements up to an hour and thirty minutes in length with enemy groups up to a platoon in strength.

—United Nations Command communiqué 1,342, for the twenty-four hours to 6:00 A.M., Friday, Korea time:

Heaviest ground action in Korea once again was in the western sector. One United Nations Command element there repulsed an attack from an estimated enemy battalion after a fifty-five minute engagement and later beat off another attack from an unknown number of enemy. Other action in the western sector included that of a friendly raiding party which engaged a small number of enemy for ten minutes before withdrawing. A friendly unit on a limited objective mission engaged an unknown number of enemy and withdrew, but returned shortly thereafter to gain the objective. Several short skirmishes occurred in this area throughout the period with the friendly unit finally withdrawing upon order. A western patrol engaged an unknown number of enemy for more than two hours before returning to our lines.

Elsewhere, the enemy launched attacks at our lines in the central and eastern sectors. The probe in the eastern sector was repulsed, but our forces made a limited withdrawal in the face of the enemy attack in the central sector.

Carrier-based aircraft of the United Nations Naval Forces struck at enemy rolling stock, supply areas, and gun positions in day-long attacks extending from Chongjin to Wonsan. Other planes directed fire for bombarding warships or flew close air support for United Nations Command front-line troops.

Gun fire from surface units was effective on the eastern front, while other warships covered the remainder of the east coast.

Our land-based war planes continued to hammer enemy positions at the front and strike enemy troops and supply concentrations in rear areas. Fighter-bombers listed enemy supply routes, gun positions, buildings, troops, and bunkers as their targets for the day's missions. Light bombers in a daylight attack hit an airfield near Pyonggang, and during the night, flew close air support and hit a troop concentration at Yonan.

SIMANEK, ROBERT E.

Rank and Organization: Private First Class, U.S. Marine Corps, Company F, 2d Battalion, 5th Marines, 1st Marine Division (Rein).
Born: April 26, 1930, Detroit, Michigan.
Entered Service At: Detroit, Michigan.
Place and Date: Korea, August 17, 1952.
Citation: For conspicuous gallantry and intrepidity at the risk of his life above and beyond the call of duty while serving with Company F, in action against enemy aggressor forces. While accompanying a patrol en route to occupy a combat outpost forward of friendly lines, Pfc. Simanek exhibited a high degree of courage and a resolute spirit of self-sacrifice in protecting the lives of his fellow marines. With his unit ambushed by an intense concentration of enemy mortar and small-arms fire, and suffering heavy casualties, he was forced to seek cover with the remaining members of the patrol in a nearby trench line. Determined to save his comrades when a hostile grenade was hurled into their midst, he unhesitatingly threw himself on the deadly missile absorbing the shattering violence of the exploding charge in his body and shielding his fellow marines from serious injury or death. Gravely wounded as a result of his heroic action, Pfc. Simanek, by his daring initiative and great personal valor in the face of almost certain death, served to inspire all who observed him and upheld the highest traditions of the U.S. Naval Service.

OFFICIAL COMMUNIQUÉ:
TOKYO, Monday, Aug. 18 (AP)
—United Nations Naval Forces summary of Sunday's operations:

H.M.S. Ocean flew the 600th sorties of her current Yellow Sea patrol during Sunday's operations in western Korea. Rocket projectiles launched from Sea Fury and Firefly aircraft accounted for the major damage reported by British naval pilots.

At the extreme tip of the Ongjin Peninsula, a transformer station was strafed and put out of action as orange flames shot skyward. Another spectacular display was achieved southeast of Haeju when full loads of rockets were dumped into the mouths of two caves hiding coastal guns.

One rail bridge north of Chinnampo was knocked into the riverbed and nine sampans were sunk and four damaged in inshore waters. Other destruction was inflicted on one ferry boat, one command post, six ox carts, and two storage dumps. Damage was charged to one radar station, one village, and several huts and buildings housing Red troops.

The Canadian destroyer Crusader figured in the only surface action in the Yellow Sea when she broke off a bombardment of troop billets in the Haeju approaches to capture an enemy junk which ventured on the scene.

The battleship U.S.S. Iowa screened by destroyer U.S.S. Sproston fired 165 5-inch rounds against the enemy's eastern front during darkness. Most targets were supply points and routes designated by infantry commanders ashore.

At daylight, Iowa destroyed two bunkers, damaged four others, and sliced communication trenches in eight places.

Destroyer U.S.S. Tingey also gave front-line support, silencing two 76-mm. guns, destroying four bunkers, and dispersing traffic along a highway.

The destroyers U.S.S. Barton and U.S.S. Boyd hit warehouses in Wonsan and intercepted traffic on coastal highways.

In far northern Korean waters, H.M.S. Mounts Bay operated near friendly Yangdo Island and illuminated the enemy coast in that vicinity. The destroyers U.S.S. Thompson and U.S.S. McDermott fired on rail bridges near Tanchon and then swept north and south of Songjin to drive sampans from the sea. Two R.O.K. (Republic of Korea) Navy torpedo boats participated in this mission. Red coastal artillery fired a few wild salvos at the patrolling ships but no damage was done.

Near Sinpo, the minesweeper U.S.S. Zeal chased four sampans ashore. Other sweepers and small craft sought shelter from the approaching Typhoon Karen.

—Eighth Army communiqué 1,072, for Saturday's operations:

United States Marines repulsed the seventh enemy attempt since Aug. 12, to recapture "Bunker Hill." Four enemy platoons, supported by heavy mortar and artillery fire, unsuccessfully probed a United Nations advance position east of the Pukhan River. Enemy mortars and artillery fired 8,471 rounds during the twenty-four hour period ending at 6:00 P.M., 1,089 fewer than were fired in the preceding twenty-four hours.

Western sector: An enemy battalion attacked "Bunker Hill" east of Panmunjom, at 12:30 A.M.. Defending United States Marines drove the enemy back at 3:50 A.M.. Enemy of unknown strength fired long-range small arms and automatic weapons at the position at 5:20 A.M., but defensive fire forced them to cease ten minutes later. No other significant enemy contact was reported during the period.

Central sector: Four enemy platoons, supported by 2,150 rounds of mortar and artillery fire, probed a United Nations advance position east of the Pukhan River at 2:05 A.M., were repulsed at 3:35 A.M. and left the area at 4:10 A.M.. An estimated thirty-nine enemy were killed and twenty-five were wounded in action. One United Nations patrol fought briefly at 1:50 P.M. with three enemy entrenched in the same area. Other patrols fought engagements up to ten minutes in length with enemy units up to two squads in strength.

Eastern sector: An enemy platoon probed a United Nations advance position west of the Mundung Valley at 9:40 P.M. and was repulsed in a thirty-five minute exchange of fire. Small enemy groups probing south of Kosong at 3:55 and 9:40 A.M. were repulsed in a seventy minute fire fight. An enemy squad probed northeast of the Punchbowl at 9:00 A.M., and was driven off five minutes later. Patrols fought engagements up to fifteen minutes in length with enemy units up to two squads in strength.

—Eighth Army tactical summary 152, for Sunday:

Attacking United Nations troops closed with the Chinese in hand-to-hand combat early Sunday to re-capture an advance position yielded Tuesday morning east of the Pukhan River.

The United Nations infantrymen engaged a Chinese platoon defending the position at 4:45 A.M.. At 7:10 A.M., they were fighting in hand-to-hand combat and twenty-five minutes later, the Chinese withdrew 400 meters to the east.

A sporadic small arms fire fight continued at the position for most of the morning.

Activity was relatively light elsewhere along the Eighth Army front Sunday.

One United Nations patrol killed seven North Koreans in a ten minute fire fight with a squad west of Kansong. Other patrols fought engagements up to fifty minutes in length with small enemy groups.

—Eighth Army communiqué 1,073, for Sunday's operations:

United Nations troops fought in hand-to-hand combat to recapture a hill position east of the Pukhan River during the morning, but enemy troops attacked and reoccupied it just before noontime. Light probes and patrol contacts developed elsewhere along the army front. Enemy artillery and mortars fired 7,903 rounds during the twenty-four hour period ended at 6:00 P.M., 568 rounds fewer than were fired in the preceding twenty-four hours.

Western sector: Small enemy groups probing United Nations advance positions north of Korangpo and west of Chorwon between 8:10 and 11:20 P.M. were repulsed in brief fire fights. United Nations patrols fought engagements against small enemy groups.

Central sector: United Nations troops attacking to recapture an advance hill position east of the Pukhan River engaged an enemy platoon on the position at 4:40 A.M., closed in hand-to-hand combat at 7:10 A.M., and occupied the position at 7:35 A.M.. The enemy withdrew to the east, counter-attacked at 11:50 A.M., and regained the position in a brief fire fight. United Nations patrols fought engagements up to fifteen minutes in length with small enemy groups.

Eastern sector: United Nations patrols fought engagements up to twenty-five minutes in length with enemy units up to two squads in strength.

—United Nations Command communiqué 1,345, for the twenty-four hours to 6:00 A.M., Monday, Korea time:

Korea ground action was relatively light, with the east-central front the scene of battles for possession of forward positions. United Nations forces there regained ground lost late last week, but later gave up the positions again as the enemy counter-attacked. Forward elements in the eastern sector repulsed an enemy attack. Elsewhere, along the entire front, friendly forces maintained their positions and continued patrol action.

Carrier-based aircraft of United Nations Naval Forces operated in the Yellow Sea against Ongjin Peninsula targets. On the eastern front, surface elements supported United Nations troops and bombarded targets in the Wonsan and Songjin areas. Smaller surface vessels took refuge from the approaching typhoon.

Land-based war planes converged on Pyongyang as fighter-bombers silenced gun positions, leveled enemy-held buildings, inflicted enemy troop casualties, fired fuel storage areas, blasted bunkers, and attacked other supply areas there. Daylight-flying light bombers started fires and set off secondary explosions in a troop and supply complex at Ongjin. A medium bomber flew close air support for United Nations ground forces along the western sector.

For the sixth consecutive day, friendly fighters sighted no enemy fighter planes in the northwest area of Korea, although fighter-bombers reported seeing three enemy aircraft in the Sunchon sector. No contacts were made.

McLAUGHLIN, ALFORD L.

Rank and Organization: Private First Class, U.S. Marine Corps, Company L, 3d Battalion, 5th Marines, 1st Marine Division (Rein).
Born: March 18, 1928, Leeds, Alabama.
Entered Service At: Leeds, Alabama.
Place and Date: Korea, September 4 and 5, 1952.
Citation: For conspicuous gallantry and intrepidity at the risk of his life above and beyond the call of duty while serving as a machine-gunner of Company L, in action against enemy aggressor forces on the night of September 4-5, 1952. Volunteering for his second continuous tour of duty on a strategic outpost far in advance of the main line of resistance, Pfc. McLaughlin, although operating under a barrage of enemy artillery and mortar fire, set up plans for the defense of his position which proved decisive in the successful defense of the outpost. When hostile forces attacked in battalion strength during the night, he maintained a constant flow of devastating fire upon the enemy, alternately employing 2 machine guns, a carbine, and hand-grenades. Although painfully wounded, he bravely fired the machine guns from the hip until his hands became blistered by the extreme heat from the weapons and, placing the guns on the ground to allow them to cool, continued to defend the position with his carbine and grenades. Standing up in full view, he shouted words of encouragement to his comrades above the din of battle and, throughout a series of fanatical attacks, sprayed the surrounding area with deadly fire, accounting for an estimated 150 enemy dead and 50 wounded. By his indomitable courage, superb leadership, and valiant fighting spirit in the face of overwhelming odds, Pfc. McLaughlin served to inspire his fellow marines in their gallant stand against the enemy and was directly instrumental in preventing the vital outpost from falling into the hands of a determined and numerically superior hostile force. His outstanding heroism and unwavering devotion to duty reflect the highest credit upon himself and enhance the finest traditions of the U.S. Naval Service.

†BENFORD, EDWARD C.

Rank and Organization: Hospital Corpsman Third Class, U.S. Navy, attached to a company in the 1st Marine Division.
Born: January 15, 1931, Staten Island, New York.
Entered Service At: Philadelphia, Pennsylvania.
Place and Date: Korea, September 5, 1952.
Citation: For conspicuous gallantry and intrepidity at the risk of his life above and beyond the call of duty while serving in operations against enemy aggressor forces. When his company was subjected to heavy artillery and mortar barrages, followed by a determined assault during the hours of darkness by an enemy force estimated at battalion strength, HC3c. Benford resolutely moved from position to position in the face of intense hostile fire, treating the wounded and lending words of encouragement. Leaving the protection of his sheltered position to treat the wounded when the platoon area in which he was working was attack from both the front and rear, he moved forward to an exposed ridge line where he observed 2 marines in a large crater. As he approached the 2 men to determine their condition, an enemy soldier threw 2 grenades into the crater while 2 other enemy charged the position. Picking up a grenade in each hand, HC3c. Benford leaped out of the crater and hurled himself against the onrushing hostile soldiers, pushing the grenades against their chests and killing both the attackers. Mortally wounded while carrying out this heroic act, HC3c. Benford, by his great personal valor and resolute spirit of self-sacrifice in the face of almost certain death, was directly responsible for saving the lives of his 2 comrades. His exceptional courage reflects the highest credit upon himself and enhances the finest traditions of the U.S. Naval Service. He gallantly gave his life for others.

†GARCIA, FERNANDO LUIS

Rank and Organization: Private First Class, U.S. Marine Corps, Company I, 3d Battalion, 5th Marines, 1st Marine Division.
Born: October 14, 1929, Utuado, Puerto Rico.
Entered Service At: San Juan, Puerto Rico.
Place and Date: Korea, September 5, 1952.
Citation: For conspicuous gallantry and intrepidity at the risk of his life above and beyond the call of duty while serving as a member of Company I, in action against enemy aggressor forces. While participating in the defense of a combat outpost located more than 1 mile forward of the main line of resistance during a savage night attack by a fanatical enemy force employing grenades, mortars, and artillery, Pfc. Garcia, although suffering painful wounds, moved through the intense hail of hostile fire to a supply point to secure more hand-grenades. Quick to act when a hostile grenade landed nearby, endangering the life of another marine, as well as his own, he unhesitatingly chose to sacrifice himself and immediately threw his body on the deadly missile, receiving the full impact of the explosion. His great personal valor and cool decision in the face of almost certain death, sustain and enhance the finest traditions of the U.S. Naval Service. He gallantly gave his life for his country.

OFFICIAL COMMUNIQUÉ:
TOKYO, Saturday, Sept. 6 (AP)
—Far East Naval Forces summary of Thursday's operations:

Planes from carrier H.M.S. Ocean in the Yellow Sea struck at enemy installations in western Korea.

The planes hit targets along the coast and inland from Chinnampo to Haeju. Using rocket projectiles, 500-pound bombs, and 20 mm. shells, the planes destroyed two rail bridges, three road bridges, four vehicles, and six sampans. Two houses, three troop billets, three transformers, gun positions, two storage huts, and bunkers were also destroyed. At least an additional six houses were left burning, a number of ox carts forming a train were damaged, four other storage huts, rail bridges, and troop billets were also strafed and damaged.

In the last seven days of operational weather, over 583 sorties have been launched from the decks of the British light carrier.

H.M.S. Cardigan Bay and U.S.S. Bradford, also on the west coast, carried out practice shooting at troops moving south-west of Haeju, causing some casualties.

There were no air operations from the Sea of Japan. Rear Admiral Herbert E. Regan, U.S.N., of Seattle, Wash., on U.S.S. Bon Homme Richard, assumed command of Task Force 77.

On the east coast, the U.S.S. Bremerton, screened by the destroyer Rupertus, continued support of United Nations troops. Four bunkers were destroyed and an additional four damaged, and a number of cuts in Communist trenches were observed. During the day the Bremerton fired her 12,000th 5-inch round into enemy positions and her 5,000th round of 8-inch.

U.S.S. Tingey, while on patrol from Kosong to Kojo, sank several mines and dispersed troops working on bunkers.

South of Tanchon, destroyer U.S.S. Blue laid shells in a billeting area, dispersing the troops.

—Eighth Army tactical summery 171, for Friday:

Separate enemy groups hit United Nations positions on the western front in an 8,000 meter zone extending eastward from Bunker Hill, east of Panmunjom.

An enemy battalion attacked Bunker Hill at 1 A.M. after a probe by a platoon at 10:30 P.M. Thursday. United Nations troops fought back eight columns of the enemy as they attacked the advance position in a two hour battle. Enemy artillery and mortars rained 2,250 rounds on the positions as

Chinese troops stormed the hill. An estimated 300 enemy were killed in this action, as United Nations small-arms, artillery, mortars, and tank fire cut them down. At some places the enemy was able to come within hand-grenade distance of United Nations positions. Farther to the east, an enemy unit of undetermined strength was beaten back in a twenty-five minute fire fight starting at 1:05 A.M..

Three United Nations advance positions still farther to the east were hit by enemy units of undetermined strength at 1 A.M.. The enemy was driven off in all three actions after two hours of fighting. An estimated 19 enemy were killed at these positions.

Two United Nations advance positions to the west of the Imjin River were probed, one by an enemy unit of undetermined strength at long range at 2:10 A.M., and the other by a reinforced enemy platoon at 1:30 A.M.. A total of ten enemy were estimated killed and 25 wounded in the action at 1:30.

A United Nations advance position west of the Mundung Valley was probed by thirteen enemy in a fifteen minute fire fight starting at 3:10 A.M..

Northwest of Yonchon, a United Nations patrol killed an estimated twenty-five enemy in a forty-five minute fire fight starting at 12:35 A.M..

Elsewhere along the Eighth Army front patrols fought engagements up to fifteen minutes in length with enemy groups up to a squad in strength. Patrol contacts were most frequent in the eastern sector.

—Eighth Army communiqué 1,092, for Friday's activities:

United Nations positions on Bunker Hill were attacked by an enemy battalion at 1 A.M., as six other enemy groups probed along an 8,000-meter front in the western sector. Two other light probes were reported, one in the central sector and one in the east. Enemy artillery and mortars fired 10,525 rounds during the twenty-four hour period ending at 6 P.M., 5,778 more rounds than were fired in the preceding twenty-four hours. More than half the rounds fell in the area east of panmunjom.

Western sector: An enemy battalion attacked Bunker Hill, east of Panmunjom, at 1 A.M. and was driven back with an estimated 300 killed after a two-hour fire fight during which the Chinese threw more than 2,000 rounds of mortar and artillery on United Nations positions. Six other enemy probes were reported farther to the east, all at the same approximate time, as the enemy hit along an 8,000 meter front. A United Nations patrol operating northwest of Yonchon inflicted an estimated twelve casualties on a group of sixty enemy as they fought for fifteen minutes starting at 10:20 P.M.. Other patrols fought brief engagements with enemy groups up to two squads in strength.

Central sector: Two enemy squads probing a United Nations advance position east-southeast of Kumsong at 11:20 P.M. were repulsed in a brief fire fight. Patrols fought engagements up to ten minutes in length with enemy units up to two squads in strength.

Eastern sector: An enemy group thirteen strong probing a United Nations advance position west of the Mundung Valley at 8:10 A.M. was driven back after a brief fire fight. Patrols fought engagements up to fifteen minutes in length with enemy units up to a squad in strength.

—United Nations Command communiqué 1,364 for the twenty-four hours to 6 A.M. Saturday, Korean time:

Ground action in Korea Friday centered around a series of engagements in the western sector. United Nations Command elements in that area repulsed a series of probing attacks and patrols up to battalion strength. An outpost in the east-central sector repulsed an enemy patrol after a fifteen-minute fight. Our patrols reported skirmishes, mostly of a light nature, in several areas of the front.

Carrier based planes attacked enemy supply areas and gun positions. Surface elements of the United Nations Command Fleet took enemy targets of opportunity under fire during the period's operations.

In daytime Air Forces activities friendly fighter-bombers hit a mine ore processing plant at Sinhung, enemy bunkers, guns, buildings, and troops. Light bombers in daylight sorties attacked a supply center and flew close air support missions. Once again there were air to air battles between our fighters and enemy jets. During the night medium bombers hit a supply center at Hamhung and flew close air support missions.

†MARTINEZ, BENITO

Rank and Organization: Corporal, U.S. Army, Company A, 27th Infantry Regiment, 25th Infantry Division.
Born: March 21, 1931, Fort Hancock, Texas.
Entered Service At: Fort Hancock, Texas.
Place and Date: Near Satae-ri, Korea, September 6, 1952.
Citation: Cpl. Martinez, a machine-gunner with Company A, distinguished himself by conspicuous gallantry and outstanding courage above and beyond the call of duty in action against the enemy. While manning a listening post forward of the main line of resistance, his position was attacked by a hostile force of reinforced company strength. In the bitter fighting which ensued, the enemy infiltrated the defensive perimeter and, realizing that encirclement was imminent, Cpl. Martinez elected to remain at his post in an attempt to stem the onslaught. In a daring defense, he raked the attacking troops with crippling fire, inflicting numerous casualties. Although contacted by sound power phone several times, he insisted that no attempt be made to rescue him because of the danger involved. Soon thereafter, the hostile forces rushed the emplacement, forcing him to make a limited withdrawal with only an automatic rifle and pistol to defend himself. After a courageous 6-hour stand and shortly before dawn, he called in for the last time, stating that the enemy was converging on his position. His magnificent stand enabled friendly elements to reorganize, attack, and regain the key terrain. Cpl. Martinez' incredible valor and supreme sacrifice reflect lasting glory upon himself and are in keeping with the honored traditions of the military service.

†PORTER, DONN F.

Rank and Organization: Sergeant, U.S. Army, Company G, 14th Infantry Regiment, 25th Infantry Division.
Born: March 1, 1931, Sewickly, Pennsylvania.
Entered Service At: Baltimore, Maryland.
Place and Date: Near Mundung-ni, Korea, September 7, 1952.
Citation: Sgt. Porter, a member of Company G, distinguished himself by conspicuous gallantry and outstanding courage above and beyond the call of duty in action against the enemy. Advancing under cover of intense mortar and artillery fire, 2 hostile platoons attacked a combat outpost commanded by Sgt. Porter, destroyed communications, and killed 2 of his 3-man crew. Gallantly maintaining his position, he poured deadly accurate fire into the ranks of the enemy, killing 15 and dispersing the remainder. After falling back under a hail of fire, the determined foe reorganized and stormed forward in an attempt to overrun the outpost. Without hesitation, Sgt. Porter jumped from his position with bayonet fixed and, meeting the onslaught in close combat, killed hostile soldiers and routed the attack. While returning to the outpost, he was killed by an artillery burst, but his courageous actions forced the enemy to break off the engagement and thwarted a surprise attack on the main line of resistance. Sgt. Porter's incredible display of valor, gallant self-sacrifice, and consummate devotion to duty reflect the highest credit upon himself and uphold the noble traditions of the military service.

OFFICIAL COMMUNIQUÉ:
TOKYO, Monday, Sept. 8 (AP)
—Far East Naval Forces summary of Saturday's operations:

The Wonsan, Hungnam, and Tanchon areas were pounded in before-dawn-to-dusk assaults by planes from U.S.S. Princeton and U.S.S. Bon Homme Richard.

Morning hecklers led off by knocking down two warehouses on the beach opposite Mayang-do. They also made six rail cuts and damaged one box car. South of Wonsan, other early flying jets poured rockets into a camouflaged supply dump while Skyraiders damaged a warehouse and rail bridge near Sinchang. At noon, Corsairs were in the Hungnam region to hit three sampans, damaged three buildings, and destroy one other.

Eight Skyraiders from Bon Homme Richard joined with Princeton pilots to fly close support for United Nations infantrymen during the afternoon. They claimed nineteen bunkers destroyed and two damaged, four mortar positions destroyed and four damaged, and four automatic weapon positions destroyed and three damaged.

Princeton pilots dived into a valley to destroy a supply dump and railroad terminal. Five rail cars, a bridge, and a coal loading tipple were destroyed after the stored munitions had been fired with napalm.

In later afternoon attacks, Princeton fliers destroyed eight more supply buildings, fifteen rail cars, and a rail bridge.

Flak at some targets was moderate to heavy, but all planes returned safely.

The cruiser U.S.S. Helena and destroyers U.S.S. Wolke and U.S.S. Tingey fired in the front-line and Kojo areas against enemy bunkers, trenches, and guns. Two bunkers were destroyed and four were damaged, four buildings were knocked down, and numerous fires started, and one observation post and one mortar position were hit.

The destroyers U.S.S. Vammen, U.S.S. Lewis, and U.S.S. Cunningham and the frigate U.S.S. Evansville operated in Wonsan Harbor. The ships fired on truck convoys moving in darkness and on box cars in the marshaling yards. Results were unobserved.

The destroyer U.S.S. Evans, destroyer-escort U.S.S. Naifeh, frigate U.S.S. Condamine, and destroyer-minesweeper U.S.S. Armick operated between Sangdo-gap and Songjin. One locomotive was sighted at Pyong and a long complete train was spotted a few miles further north. More than 100 rounds of 5-inch were fired against this target, and damage was claimed from the many hits and near misses.

In the Yellow Sea, the cruiser H.M.S. Belfast and destroyer U.S.S. Radford fired on the enemy coast near Chodo cooperating with Marine aircraft from U.S.S. Sicily, which laid a heavy attack on gun positions in that vicinity.

In the Haeju area, U.S.S. Marsh and U.S.S. PC-702 carried out bombardments of North Korean troop concentrations.

—Far East Air Forces summary of Saturday's operations:

Fighter-bombers of Fifth Air Force on Saturday concentrated their attacks against a sprawling Communist Army headquarters on Korea's east coast, as United States Air Force all-weather medium bombers at night made further attacks against manufacturing and military supply targets in Pyongyang.

F-80 Shooting Stars joined land-based Marine fighter-bombers and Royal Australian Meteor jets to attack the big army headquarters. The fighter-bombers unleashed heavy demolition bombs, rockets and machine-gun fire into the target area.

Reconnaissance pilots reported the fighter-bombers left the area in "blazing ruins." The United Nations ordinance accounted for the destruction of fifty-five buildings in the area, damage to twenty others, and the setting off of ten large fires and three secondary explosions.

During the day, B-26 light bombers attacked a tungsten mine southeast of Yangdok. Although a partial cloud cover prevented complete assessment of destruction, two secondary explosions were observed and three buildings destroyed or damaged.

Medium bombers of F.E.A.F. Bomber Command's Japan-based Ninety-eighth Bomb Wing, using electronic-aiming techniques, at night dropped high explosives on a large manufacturing and supply storage area in northeast Pyongyang. Crews reported only light flak and no enemy fighter attacks. Two Superforts, of the 307th Bomb Wing, flew close air support for United Nations ground forces along the western and central sectors of the battle front. A Nineteenth Bomb Group B-29 attacked a marshaling yard at Chinnampo. None of these bombers was opposed by enemy flak or fighters.

Also during daylight hours, other fighter-bombers battered Communist troop and supply positions along the front. Bunkers were blasted gun positions silenced and several enemy-held buildings fired.

F-86 Sabre jets, flying screen for the fighter-bombers, engaged Russian-built enemy MiG-15s in two air battles during the day. Sabre claims of one MiG destroyed and another damaged are pending official confirmation.

Total destruction inflicted on the Communists during the period included forty bunkers destroyed and ten others damaged, twenty-five gun positions silenced, 130 buildings leveled and forty damaged, fifty-five troop casualties, one rail and four road cuts, five supply dumps destroyed, a transformer station damaged, and two tanks and one warehouse destroyed.

B-26 night intruders Saturday night destroyed fifty Communist supply trucks along main enemy supply routes in North Korea. Other light bombers attacked supplies at Kangdong, and also cratered highway junctions at Suan and southeast of Singosan. B-26s also joined land-based Marine fighter-bombers to provide close air support for United Nations ground forces along the western sector of the front and in other scattered areas.

F.E.A.F. Saturday mounted 825 effective sorties, of which 205 were in support of the United Nations Army. Of these, 140 were combat-type missions. Cargo transports of F.E.A.F.'s 315 Air Division airlifted 445 tons of personnel and supplies in continued logistical support of United Nations combat operations.

—Eighth Army communiqué 1,093, for Saturday's operations:

Enemy activity was on the increase along the Eighth Army front, with heavy enemy probes east of Panmunjom, west of the Pukhan River and east of the Satae Valley in the Twenty-fifth United States Division sector. Enemy mortars and artillery fired 9,595 rounds during the twenty-four hour period ended at 6:00 P.M., 930 rounds fewer than were fired in the previous twenty-four hours.

Western sector: Bunker Hill, east of Panmunjom, was probed twice by enemy groups of undetermined strength and platoon strength at 3:35 A.M. and 8:55 P.M.. The platoon came within hand grenade range of United Nations positions, but was thrown back after fifteen minutes of fighting. Two enemy companies attacked a United Nations advance position south of Panmunjom and were beaten back in a thirty minute fight. The enemy threw 1,000 rounds of artillery and mortar fire at United Nations positions during this engagement. Just to the north-northeast of this position, other United Nations advance positions were attacked by a Chinese company at 7:30 P.M.. The enemy was driven off after one hour and forty-five minutes of fighting in which the opposing forces clashed in hand-to-hand combat. Chinese mortars and artillery fired 3,700 rounds during the battle.

A total of sixty enemy were estimated killed in the two actions. A small United Nations advance position west-northwest of Korangpo was probed by an unknown number of enemy ten minutes after midnight for thirty-five minutes. Another advance position in the same area was attacked by an unknown number of enemy at 7:20 P.M. after a heavy artillery barrage. At 8:20 the United Nations troops were locked in hand-to-hand combat with the enemy. Action continued at the close of the period. Two other United Nations advance positions in the same area were attacked at 7:20 P.M. by enemy of undetermined strength and United Nations troops drove off the attackers in one hour and half. Two small enemy groups probing United Nations advance positions west of Yonchon at 9:40 P.M. and 9:50 P.M. were repulsed in brief fire fights. Patrols fought engagements up to ten minutes in length against enemy groups up to a reinforced platoon in strength.

Central sector: United Nations troops on Capitol Hill west of the Pukhan River were attacked by an enemy company at 7:20 P.M. and fell back slightly. They counter-attacked at 8:50 and by 11:00 P.M. were locked in hand-to-hand combat with the enemy. Action continued at the close of the period. Chinese artillery and mortars fired 10,500 rounds during this action.

An enemy platoon supported by three tanks attacking United Nations advance positions west of Capitol Hill was repulsed to thirty minutes. A Chinese company attacked another United Nations advance position in the same area. The enemy threw in 4,400 rounds of mortar and artillery fire and United Nations troops withdrew slightly. United Nations forces counter-attacked at 9:30 P.M. and the action continues. Patrols fought engagements up to five minutes in length with enemy units up to a platoon in strength.

Eastern sector: Twenty-fifth Division troops at Sandbag Castle, east of the Satae Valley, drove off an attack by an enemy platoon at 12:45 A.M. The enemy, reinforced, threw 1,200 rounds of artillery at the position; and by 7:55, they were engaged in hand-to-hand combat. By 3:05 P.M., the enemy had left, and all action had ceased. Two enemy squads probing a United Nations advance position farther to the east were repulsed in a forty minute fire fight. Patrols fought engagements up to eighteen minutes in length with enemy groups up to a squad in strength.

—Eighth Army tactical summary for Sunday:

A United Nations unit which was surrounded late Saturday night by an enemy battalion on a hill position west-northwest of Korangpo-ri was completely in possession of the position by dawn with the surrounding enemy having retreated to their own lines.

United Nations troops were counter-attacking Capitol Hill in the central sector, where they were forced to withdraw last night under a Communist artillery concentration of 14,000 rounds. They hit Chinese positions several times after midnight and fought their way to within twenty yards of the hill. At last report the battle continued.

United States Twenty-fifth Division troops at positions east and west of the Satae Valley drove back two enemy assaults, the last at 2:30 A.M. as the Chinese continued to probe the Tropic Lightning Division sector.

Slightly to the west, other Twenty-fifth Division positions were probed three times by small enemy groups between seven minutes after midnight and 1:00 A.M.. All probes were beaten back.

Elsewhere along the Eighth Army front patrols fought engagements up to thirty minutes in length with enemy units up to two squads in strength.

—United Nations Command communiqué 1,366, for the twenty-four hours to 6:00 A.M., Monday, Korea time:

The Korean battle front continued active, with fighting reported from most sectors of the front. Seven separate enemy attacks were reported by United Nations Command forces. The largest was a two-company attack in the east-central sector which lasted approximately two hours and a half. Other attacks occurred in the western and central sectors, where action continued at the close of the period.

In addition to these attacks, the enemy made seven unsuccessful probing attempts, six in the east-central sector and one in the western sector.

Land-based war planes of the United Nations Command continued interdiction and close air support missions despite low hanging clouds over some target areas. Fighter-bombers struck hard at enemy gun positions, buildings, troops, and bunkers. Fighters registered good results against enemy jet planes in six air battles. During the night, medium bombers flew close air support for friendly troops in the western and central sectors while light bombers attacked enemy trucks.

Naval surface craft operated in foggy weather along both coasts. Carrier-based planes hit targets from Kojo to Tanchon on the east coast while others directed their efforts at enemy-held bridges in western North Korea.

†KELSO, JACK WILLIAM

Rank and Organization: Private First Class, U.S. Marine Corps, Company I, 3d Battalion, 7th Marines, 1st Marine Division (Rein).
Born: January 23, 1934, Madera, California.
Entered Service At: Caruthers, California.
Place and Date: Korea, October 2, 1952.
Citation: For conspicuous gallantry and intrepidity at the risk of his life above and beyond the call of duty while serving as a rifleman of Company I, in action against enemy aggressor forces. When both the platoon commander and the platoon sergeant became casualties during the defense of a vital outpost against a numerically superior enemy force attacking at night under cover of intense small-arms, grenade, and mortar fire, Pfc. Kelso bravely exposed himself to the hail of enemy fire in a determined effort to reorganize the unit and to repel the onrushing attackers. Forced to seek cover, along with 4 other marines, in a nearby bunker which immediately came under attack, he unhesitatingly picked up an enemy grenade which landed in the shelter, rushed out into the open and hurled it back at the enemy. Although painfully wounded when the grenade exploded as it left his hand, and again forced to seek the protection of the bunker when the hostile fire became more intensified, Pfc. Kelso refused to remain in his position of comparative safety and moved out into the fire-swept area to return the enemy fire, thereby permitting the pinned-down marines in the bunker to escape. Mortally wounded while providing covering fire for his comrades, Pfc. Kelso, by his valiant fighting spirit, aggressive determination, and self-sacrificing efforts in behalf of others, served to inspire all who observed him. His heroic actions sustain and enhance the highest traditions of the U.S. Naval Service. He gallantly gave his life for his country.

OFFICIAL COMMUNIQUÉ:
TOKYO, Friday, Oct. 3 (AP)
—Far East Air Forces summary of Wednesday's operations:

Fifth Air Force fighter-bombers and B-26 light bombers struck heavily Wednesday at enemy troop and supply concentrations and front line positions, from the Haeju peninsula to the Wonsan sector, with additional B-26s continuing the strike into the night.

F-80s, F-51s, F-84s, and Marine landbased aircraft struck scattered troop and supply targets around Haeju, Yangdok, Sinchon, and Wonsan, destroying fifteen buildings and damaging seven. Two bridges were also damaged. Other F-84s left a troop billeting area southwest of Wonsan in flames.

Southeast of Yangdok, F-80s and F-84s leveled buildings of a supply complex. Marine aircraft and Australian Meteor jets, attacking supply areas north of Kumsong, fired storage buildings.

Northwest of Singye, Third Bomb Wing B-26s struck a supply area during the day, with excellent results reported.

Fighter-bomber close support activity ranged all across the front, as T-6 Mosquito spotting aircraft directed the jet and propellered aircraft onto their targets. Concentrating their attacks in the Punchbowl and Kumsong areas and on the western front, the fighter-bombers destroyed forty-five bunkers, ten gun positions, three mortars, and two supply shelters. Secondary explosions in one area indicated hits on fuel or ammunition stores.

B-26 night intruders added to their rolling-stock score by destroying two locomotives and damaging one, between Hongwon and Tong on the east coast. In addition, ten boxcars were destroyed and ten damaged.

B-26s also destroyed fifty Red vehicles along Red supply routes, and inflicted road blocks near Namchonjom and Yongpo. Other light bombers attacked a supply area at Chunghwa and teamed with Marine aircraft in close air support on the west end on the front line and around Kumsong.

One B-29 of the Nineteenth Bomb Group attacked front line positions on the western end on the front Wednesday night, with no enemy opposition.

F-86 Sabre jets, flying screen for the fighter-bombers, were unable to engage wary enemy MiG-15s during the day, although a few were sighted.

Total destruction during the period included eighty-five bunkers knocked out, twenty-five buildings leveled and ten damaged, fifteen rail and five road cuts inflicted, two supply stacks fired, eight searchlights knocked out, two road bridges damaged, and one tunnel sealed.

F.E.A.F. on Wednesday mounted 950 sorties, of which 240 were in support of the United Nations Army. Of these, 190 were combat-type missions. Cargo transports of F.E.A.F.'s 315th Air Division airlifted 400 tons of personnel and supplies in continued logistical support of United Nations forces.

—Far East Naval Forces summary of Thursday's operations:

Marine pilots from the carrier U.S.S. Sicily struck at supply areas, transportation facilities, and gun positions in northwestern Korea.

The planes leveled seven buildings and damaged seven others. A radio transformer was knocked out, along with three gun positions and three command posts. A supply area north of Changyon was bombed and strafed and five supply shelters were destroyed.

In later strikes, the Leathernecks hit several bridges, five vehicle revetments, and one rail target.

On the eastern coast, the destroyer U.S.S. Boyd fired at two trains near Hungnam. Over seventy-two hits were scored on the first train, as secondary explosions erupted and cars burned. Seven hits on the second train also resulted in explosions and

cars being set afire. Air spotters reported the trains had suffered severe damage.

Cruiser U.S.S. Juneau and destroyer U.S.S. Bradford fired at interdiction targets south of Kosang. Several bunkers were damaged and gun positions were fired upon with unobserved results.

Destroyer U.S.S. Jenkins and U.S.S. Taylor, with the aid of shore fire-control parties, laid harassing fire on troops and gun positions near Wonsan. One gun cavern was sealed, and troops near by were dispersed. One train and a sampan were also fired upon, but results were unobserved.

Destroyer U.S.S. Tingey, while operating near Kosong, destroyed one bunker, damaged four, and scored three cuts in trench lines.

Minesweeper U.S.S. Devastator drove eight sampans ashore at Songdo-gap, south of Songjin. Minesweeper U.S.S. Shoveler also destroyed a sampan in that area.

In the west coast surface action, H.M.S. Cossack fired at a gun position in a cave. After firing fourteen rounds, shore spotters reported the cave sealed. H.M.A.S. Anzac fired at troops and gun positions south of Haeju, with unobserved results.

—Eighth Army Tactical Summary 198, for Thursday:

R.O.K. Third Division troops clawed their way to within fifty yards of the crest of Wire Hill, the eastern most of two hill positions east of the Pukhan River seized by the Chinese Monday morning.

The R.O.K. infantrymen attacked the hill Wednesday evening and at 7:25 P.M. were locked in hand-to-hand combat with an enemy company. By 1:40 A.M., Thursday, action had temporarily ceased with the R.O.K.s staying in positions 100 yards from the crest of the objective.

At 5:30 A.M. the R.O.K. troops renewed the attack and by 6:40 the fighting had become intense. The action slackened off again at 7:40, with the R.O.K.s receiving a heavy volume of Chinese artillery and mortar fire.

The fight flared up again at 10:35 A.M., with elements of the Third R.O.K. force fighting their way to within fifty yards of the crest. The Chinese hit these elements with a platoon-size counterattack at 10:45 A.M., but the R.O.K.s held their ground. Action was continuing at 3 P.M..

R.O.K. Sixth Division troops defending a hill east of Kumsong were attacked by two enemy platoons at 5:15 A.M.. The Chinese reinforced to company strength by 5:45, but the attack was repulsed and the enemy was forced to withdraw by 6:25 A.M..

Elsewhere along the Eighth Army front, patrols fought engagements up to forty-five minutes in length with enemy groups up to thirty in strength.

—United Nations Command communiqué 1,391, for the twenty-four hours to 6 A.M. Friday, Korean time:

The central sector of the Korean battle front was once again the scene of heaviest fighting. In one action United Nations Command forces succeeded in regaining a key position after an all-day fight. In the same sector the enemy attacked friendly positions with four platoons, but were repulsed after a ten-hour engagement. A United Nations Command listening post on the western front withdrew after an enemy attack in company strength. Probes directed at our lines in the western and east-central sectors were repulsed.

Carrier-based planes continued interdiction operations in northwest Korea. United Nations Command Fleet surface action included front-line strikes, bombardment at Wonsan, and at other strategic points in enemy-held territory.

Land-based fighter-bombers hit enemy transportation and battle front positions. Fighters made their first claims of the month against enemy fighters. During night operations, medium bombers attacked an enemy replacement depot and bivouac area, while light bombers destroyed an enemy locomotive and supply vehicles.

†WATKINS, LEWIS G.

Rank and Organization: Staff Sergeant, U.S. Marine Corps, Company I, 3d Battalion, 7th Marines, 1st Marine Division.
Born: June 6, 1925, Seneca, South Carolina.
Entered Service At: Seneca, South Carolina.
Place and Date: Korea, October 7, 1952.
Citation: For conspicuous gallantry and intrepidity at the risk of his life above and beyond the call of duty while serving as a guide of a rifle platoon of Company I, in action against enemy aggressor forces during the hours of darkness on the morning of October 7, 1952. With his platoon assigned the mission of retaking an outpost which had been overrun by the enemy earlier in the night, S/Sgt. Watkins skillfully led his unit in the assault up the designated hill. Although painfully wounded when a well-entrenched hostile force at the crest of the hill engaged the platoon with intense small-arms and grenade fire, he gallantly continued to lead his men. Obtaining an automatic rifle from one of the wounded men, he assisted in pinning down an enemy machine gun holding up the assault. When an enemy grenade landed among S/Sgt. Watkins and several other marines while they were moving forward through a trench on the hill crest, he immediately pushed his companions aside, placed himself in a position to shield them and picked up the deadly missile in an attempt to throw it outside the trench. Mortally wounded when the grenade exploded in his hand, S/Sgt. Watkins, by his great personal valor in the face of almost certain death, saved the lives of several of his comrades and contributed materially to the success of the mission. His extraordinary heroism, inspirational leadership, and resolute spirit of self-sacrifice reflect the highest credit upon himself and enhance the finest traditions of the U.S. Naval Service. He gallantly gave his life for his country.

OFFICIAL COMMUNIQUÉ:
TOKYO, Wednesday, Oct. 8 (AP)
Eighth Army tactical summary for Tuesday:

Chinese troops captured seven positions Monday night and Tuesday morning in a sweeping series of attacks along two-thirds of the Eighth Army front. However, Eighth Army troops stood firm at most points, beating back fanatical attacks, which at two places were in regimental strength.

The Chinese struck in strength south of Panmunjom, around "Bunker Hill", northwest of Korangpo, along a nine-mile front in the Yonchon area, west and northwest of Chorwon, east of Kumsong, east and west of the Pukhan River, and west of the Mundung Valley.

The Reds main effort was directed at "White Horse Hill", northwest of Chorwon, and at a neighboring western sector peak to the west-southwest. A Chinese regiment assaulted each hill in a frenzied drive that brought them close enough for hand-to-hand combat and, in some cases, fist fights, but the defenders held firm and the Chinese were thrown back with heavy losses.

The Chinese temporarily occupied a small nose on the eastern slope of "White Horse Hill" during the action, but a hand-to-hand counter-attack restored it at 10:35 P.M..

Reports on the remaining actions were still being evaluated at Eighth Army headquarters late Tuesday afternoon. They indicated that the Chinese had taken a low hill south of Panmunjom in a battalion-size assault late Monday night and repulsed a United Nations dawn counter-attack; captured a small hill position east of "T-Bone Hill", in the Chorwon sector, in a two-platoon attack just before dawn Tuesday; gained a position south of Pyonggang in an evening attack by a reinforced enemy company, heavily supported by artillery, mortar, and machine-gun fire, and held it against a counter-attack at first light; successfully attacked an advance position northwest of "Finger Ridge", and remained in control at 2:00 P.M. against counter-action that began at dawn; won control of a position on "Finger Ridge" at 4:00 A.M. in a fight that resumed as defending troops counter-attacked at 6:40 A.M. and 10:00 A.M.; forced defending troops off an advance position west of the Mundung Valley at 3:10 A.M..

In one of the major efforts, a Chinese battalion, supported by seven tanks, assaulted positions east of Kumsong at 7:45 P.M., Monday. The Communists were forced back at 10:50 P.M., re-attacked at 4:30 A.M., Tuesday, and were driven off by heavy defensive artillery fire.

Eighth Army troops on "Capital Hill" repulsed two attacks—a dusk assault by a reinforced company, and a later attack by two companies. East of the Pukhan River, other Eighth Army troops drove off two attacking Chinese companies in a 3 hour 20 minute fight.

Eighth Army troops in the "Bunker Hill" area, and at frequently contested hills in the Yonchon area, held their posts against attacks in up to two-company strength.

—United Nations Command headquarters communiqué for twenty-four hours ended 6:00 A.M., Wednesday, Korean time:

Heavy ground action in Korea continued yesterday. All sectors were active, with the most intense fighting occurring in the western and central sectors. In the western sector, engagements up to eleven hours in length were reported. Some friendly outposts withdrew in this area under heavy enemy attacks. Some were restored when United Nations Command forces counter-attacked and drove the enemy back. Action continued in this sector at the close of the period.

In the west-central sector the Communists attacked with units up to battalion strength. After effecting a slight penetration in the United Nations lines, the enemy was stopped and our forces restored the lost area and were pursing the enemy at the close of the period. Several probes at outposts were reported in this sector also.

Daylong, see-saw battles raged in the central sector with elements of both sides attacking and counter-attacking for key positions. Several actions in this region centered around outpost positions. Action was continuing in this area early today.

Forward elements in the east-central sector withdrew to other outpost positions after two attacks from an estimated two enemy platoons. Elsewhere in this sector our units repulsed two hostile probes.

On the eastern front, outposts of the United Nations Command reported repulsing three enemy probing attacks. During the day's actions friendly forces inflicted heavy casualties on the aggressive enemy troops.

United Nations Command land-based warplanes continued to strike enemy transportation and front-line targets. Fighter-bombers flew close support against enemy targets, destroying bunkers and gun positions and inflicting enemy troop casualties.

During the night, medium bombers attacked an ore-processing plant at Taeyudong, forty miles south of the Suiho Reservoir. Night intruder bombers continued their assaults on enemy supply vehicles and attacked enemy rail lines and rolling stock.

The heaviest naval action reported was conducted by surface craft of the United Nations Command fleet. South of Kosong, ships directed fire on enemy supply areas and troop concentrations. South of Tanchon they disrupted a railroad complex, while north of Hungnam hostile sampans were targets. On the west coast, ships of the fleet turned their guns on enemy troops ashore.

WEST, ERNEST E.

Rank and Organization: Private First Class, U.S. Army, Company L, 14th Infantry Regiment, 25th Infantry Division.
Born: September 2, 1931, Russell, Kentucky.
Entered Service At: Wurtland, Kentucky.
Place and Date: Near Satae-ri, Korea, October 12, 1952.
Citation: Pfc. West distinguished himself by conspicuous gallantry and intrepidity above and beyond the call of duty in action against the enemy. He voluntarily accompanied a contingent to locate and destroy a reported enemy outpost. Nearing the objective, the patrol was ambushed and suffered numerous casualties. Observing his wounded leader lying in an exposed position, Pfc. West ordered the troops to withdraw, then braved intense fire to reach and assist him. While attempting evacuation, he was attacked by 3 hostile soldiers employing grenades and small-arms fire. Quickly shifting his body to shield the officer, he killed the assailants with his rifle, then carried the helpless man to safety. He was critically wounded and lost an eye in this action, but courageously returned through withering fire and bursting shells to assist the wounded. While evacuating 2 comrades, he closed with and killed 3 more of the foe. Pfc. West's indomitable spirit, consummate valor, and intrepid actions inspired all who observed him and reflect the highest credit on himself and uphold the honored traditions of the military service.

OFFICIAL COMMUNIQUÉ:
TOKYO, Monday, Oct. 13 (AP)
—Far East Air Forces summary of Saturday's operations:

While war planes of Far East Air Forces struck at enemy troops and supply concentrations, transportation facilities, and battle line positions in day and night strikes Saturday, F-86 Sabre jet pilots scored their highest one-day total of the month as they shot down six enemy MiG-15s.

United States Air Force fighter-bombers, flying 350 interdiction and close support sorties during the day, destroyed 100 enemy buildings throughout North Korea and knocked out thirty Communist gun positions and bunkers along the front-lines.

More than eighty enemy MiG-15s were sighted during the day, as F-86 pilots engaged the enemy jets three times between the Yalu and Chongchong Rivers. Five of the Russian-built jet fighters were destroyed in two morning engagements with the sixth destruction coming in the afternoon.

Ten B-29 Superforts of F.E.A.F. Bomber Command hit enemy targets at Hwangju, Taegumi, and Pongchong-ol Saturday night, meeting only meager enemy flak over Hwangju. Five other Superforts in the night struck enemy positions along the battle front.

F.E.A.F. Saturday mounted 925 sorties of which 260 were in support of the United Nations Army. Of these, 195 were combat-type missions. Cargo transports of F.E.A.F.'s 315th Air Division airlifted 565 tons of supplies and personnel in support of United Nations forces.

—Far East Air Forces summary of Sunday's operations:

Far East Air Forces warcraft, in virtual around-the-clock strikes Sunday and early Monday, concentrated their bomb loads and fire power on enemy troop billeting and supply areas, as F.E.A.F. mounted the second-highest twenty-four hour sorties total of the war.

While fighter-bombers in daylight were pounding more than thirty targets, F-86 Sabre jets destroyed four Red MiG-15 fighters and damaged two others, running their two-day score to ten and two.

United States Air Force B-26 night invaders and B-29 Superforts took up the attack after dark, hitting fourteen troop and supply concentrations.

F.E.A.F. flew 1,412 sorties, second to the record of 1,535 flown Aug.. 29, of this year.

F-84 Thunderjets early Sunday hit a large troop billeting area between Namsi-dong and Sonchon, scoring fifty direct bomb hits. North of Oro, F-80 Shooting Stars struck a military headquarters and storage area, leveling buildings and exploding an ammunition dump.

Marine Panther jets attacked an Army headquarters near Pyongyang, and Thunderjets bombed a large rail bridge west of Yangdok. Australian Meteors and R.O.K. F-51's hit a troop concentration north of Yonan, destroying and damaging twenty buildings. Other fighter-bombers, hitting diversified targets, destroyed and damaged buildings and started fires among ammunition and fuel stores.

Fighter-bombers also struck heavily at enemy front-line positions during the day.

Sabre jets, during the morning, destroyed three MiGs and damaged two, and then shot down another in an afternoon encounter.

Twenty-six Superforts of F.E.A.F. Bomber Command struck nine troop concentration and supply areas after midnight on the Haeju Peninsula near Chongdan, southeast of Haeju and west of Panmunjom. The bombs started fires visible fifty miles away. More than 3,000 troops were in the area, being readied for front-line duty, according to reconnaissance photo interpreters. No opposition was met by the Superforts. Two other B-29s hit Red battle line positions.

B-26s last night destroyed 105 supply vehicles moving southward and inflicted four road blocks along supply routes.

Of the 1,412 F.E.A.F. sorties, 420 were in support of the United Nations Army. Of these, 360 were combat-type missions. Cargo transports of F.E.A.F.'s 315th Air Division airlifted 500 tons of supplies and personnel in support of United Nations forces.

—Far East Naval Forces summary of Saturday's operations:

Clearing skies in late afternoon allowed Task Force 77 planes to fly reconnaissance and close support missions. The abbreviated air operations from the U.S.S. Kearsarge and U.S.S. Essex were successful in assisting to strengthen ground positions for battle-line troops. In one sector, two rocket launchers were silenced while bombs, rockets, and strafing fire destroyed nine enemy bunkers, killed nineteen troops, and tore up forty yards of trench along the front-lines.

Panther jets from the Essex struck a power plant near Kyosen and heavy secondary explosions were reported. The jets also destroyed five trucks, one building, and damaged four other buildings.

The heavy cruiser U.S.S. Los Angeles returned to action in Korean waters and fired in support of friendly troops on the battle line. Shore spotters reported 8-inch guns destroyed five small bunkers, two large bunkers, one observation post, and 100 yards of trench.

The destroyer U.S.S. Tingey, operating off Kojo, fired on road embankments, bunkers, bridges, and a guard post. Two direct hits were scored on one bridge and later firing destroyed one house, damaged another, and caused one secondary explosion.

In the Yellow Sea, the British cruiser H.M.S. Newcastle working the Taechong-do area fired at gun mortars and junks, with good results.

—Eighth Army communiqué 1,128 for Saturday's operations:

Fighting continued into the sixth day at White Horse Mountain northwest of Chorwon, with the enemy once again forcing defenders off the crest in a late afternoon assault. Enemy groups up to two reinforced companies in strength were repulsed in attacks against four advance positions of the R.O.K. Third Division east of the Pukhan River. Enemy artillery and mortars fired 21,434 rounds during the twenty-four hour period ended at 6:00 P.M., 12,846 rounds more than were fired in the preceding twenty-four hours.

Western sector: United States Second Infantry Division elements raided enemy positions on T-Bone hill west of Chorwon between 12:30 and 7:55 A.M.. Three other Eighth Army raiding groups conducted shorter raids after midnight west of Yonchon. Small enemy groups probing advance positions west-northwest of Yonchon at 6:25 A.M. and 9:10 P.M. and Bunker Hill, east of Panmunjom, at 10:55 P.M. were driven off in ten and twenty minute fire fights. Patrols in the Yonchon and Chorwon areas fought engagements up to thirty minutes in length with enemy groups up to a platoon in strength.

Central sector: Heavy fighting continued into the sixth day at White Horse Mountain northwest of Chorwon. Early in the period, R.O.K. Ninth Division troops repulsed a morning attack against the eastern portion of the hill. Later they successfully attacked a knob west of the hill-crest, fought along a valley to the right of the hill, and harassed enemy positions on a hill to the north. During the morning they forced the enemy off the crest, but at 4:30 P.M., they yielded it again after the enemy attacked in two-battalion strength. Artillery kept the crest untenable during the remainder of the period as fighting continued on the hill. Enemy groups up to two reinforced companies in strength which had attacked four advance positions of the R.O.K. Third Division east of the Pukhan River between 8:50 and 10:45 P.M., the previous evening, were all repulsed by 6:30 A.M.. An estimated 398 enemy were killed or wounded in these actions. An enemy platoon probing an advance at 9:10 P.M. was driven back at 10:00 P.M.. Patrols fought engagements up to twenty-five minutes in length with enemy groups up to a company in strength.

Eastern sector: No significant enemy contact was reported during the period.

—Eighth Army tactical summary 208, for Sunday:

The R.O.K. Ninth Division troops made another sweep over the crest of White Horse Mountain Sunday and continued the fight to drive back Chinese who have been attacking the west-central peak since Monday night.

The R.O.K.s attacked at 8:00 A.M., after a night of sporadic fighting against the enemy who had occupied the crest Saturday afternoon.

They were supported by air and heavy artillery and tank fire, some of it directed against a hill to the north as they jumped off seventy-five yards from the crest.

Enemy artillery and mortar fire was relatively light as the attack progressed, but resistance from enemy infantry on the crest was heavy.

By 11:00 A.M., some of the attacking elements had advanced to within thirty yards south of the crest, while others were working around the right and left flanks. The R.O.K.s swept over the crest at 1:20 P.M. taking it in another of the hand-to-hand fights that have marked the six-day battle, and forcing the enemy part-way down the northern slope.

At 3:00 P.M., Chinese resistance was reported as stiffening, with a marked increase in the intensity of enemy artillery fire, as the fight for complete control of the hill continued.

Elsewhere along the Eighth Army front, patrols fought light engagements with enemy groups up to a platoon in strength.

—Eighth Army communiqué 1,129, for Sunday's operations:

R.O.K. Ninth Division troops reoccupied the crest of White Horse Mountain and were defending it against repeated attacks at midnight, as fighting for control of the west-central peak entered its seventh day. The enemy captured an advanced hill position northeast of Chorwon. Action along the remainder of the Eighth Army front was generally light. Enemy artillery and mortars fired 8,943 rounds during the twenty-four period ended at 6:00 P.M., 12,491 rounds fewer than were fired during the preceding twenty-four hours.

Western sector: Eighth Army troops conducted brief nighttime raids west and west-northwest of Yonchon and drove off small enemy units probing south of Panmunjom, on Bunker Hill, west-north-west of Yonchon, and northwest of Chorwon and fought patrol action up to fifty minutes in length with enemy groups up to a platoon in strength.

Central Sector: R.O.K. Ninth Division troops recaptured the crest of White Horse Mountain northwest of Chorwon at 1:20 P.M., and held it against enemy action, which was increasing in intensity at the close of the period, as the fight for control of the mountain entered its seventh day. Enemy of undetermined strength attacked an advance position northeast of Chorwon at 8:05 P.M. and occupied it after a brief fight. Platoon-size enemy groups probing two advance positions in the Finger Ridge area at 9:15 P.M., were driven off in one-hour fire fights. Patrols fought engagements up to fifty minutes in length with enemy groups up to two platoons in strength.

Eastern Sector: Small enemy groups probing in the Heartbreak Ridge area at 9:50 and 11:55 P.M. were easily repulsed. Patrols fought engagements with enemy groups up to two squads in strength.

—United nations Command communiqué 1,401 for the twenty-four hours to 6:00 A.M., Monday, Korea time:

Ground action in Korea has diminished to patrolling and minor enemy probes with the exception of the west-central sector. In the latter region action continues around White Horse Hill, with United Nations Command forces in possession of the crest of the hill early Monday.

Land-based fighter-bombers again attacked enemy targets of opportunity Sunday. Six separate engagements were fought between United Nations Command fighters and hostile jets. During the night, medium bombers hit enemy troop concentrations, while light bombers destroyed and damaged enemy supply vehicles.

Surface elements of the United Nations Command Fleet and carrier-based aircraft hammered enemy installations along both coasts of Korea.

SCHOWALTER, EDWARD R., JR.

Rank and Organization: First Lieutenant, U.S. Army, Company A, 31st Infantry Regiment, 7th Infantry Division.
Born: December 24, 1927, New Orleans, Louisiana.
Entered Service At: Metairie, Louisiana.
Place and Date: Near Kumhwa, Korea, October 14, 1952.
Citation: 1st Lt. Schowalter, commanding officer of Company A, distinguished himself by conspicuous gallantry and indomitable courage above and beyond the call of duty in action against the enemy. Committed to attack and occupy a key approach to the primary objective,

the 1st Platoon of his company came under heavy vicious small-arms, grenade, and mortar fire within 50 yards of the enemy-held strongpoint, halting the advance and inflicting several casualties. The 2d Platoon moved up in support at this juncture, and although wounded, 1st Lt. Schowalter continued to spearhead the assault. Nearing the objective he was severely wounded by a grenade fragment but, refusing medical aid, he led his men into the trenches and began routing the enemy from the bunkers with grenades. Suddenly from a burst of fire from a hidden cove off the trench he was again wounded. Although suffering from his wounds, he refused to relinquish command and continued issuing orders and encouraging his men until the commanding ground was secured and then he was evacuated. 1st Lt. Schowalter's unflinching courage, extraordinary heroism, and inspirational leadership reflect the highest credit upon himself and are in keeping with the highest traditions of the military service.

†POMEROY, RALPH E.

Rank and Organization: Private First Class, U.S. Army, Company E, 31st Infantry Regiment, 7th Infantry Division.
Born: March 26, 1930, Quinwood, West Virginia.
Entered Service At: Quinwood, West Virginia.
Place and Date: Near Kumhwa, Korea, October 15, 1952.
Citation: Pfc. Pomeroy, a machine-gunner with Company E, distinguished himself by conspicuous gallantry and indomitable courage above and beyond the call of duty in action against the enemy. While his comrades were consolidating on a key terrain feature, he manned a machine gun at the end of a communication trench on the forward slope to protect the platoon flank and prevent a surprise attack. When the enemy attacked through a ravine leading directly to his firing position, he immediately opened fire on the advancing troops inflicting a heavy toll in casualties and blunting the assault. At this juncture the enemy directed intense concentrations of artillery and mortar fire on his position in an attempt to neutralize his gun. Despite withering fire and bursting shells, he maintained his heroic stand and poured crippling fire into the ranks of the hostile force until a mortar burst severely wounded him and rendered the gun mount inoperable. Quickly removing the hot, heavy weapon, he cradled it in his arms and, moving forward with grim determination, raked the attacking forces with a hail of fire. Although wounded a second time he pursued his relentless course until his ammunition was expended within 10 feet of the foe and then, using the machine gun as a club, he courageously closed with the enemy in hand-to-hand combat until mortally wounded. Pfc. Pomeroy's consummate valor, inspirational actions, and supreme sacrifice enabled the platoon to contain the attack and maintain the integrity of the perimeter, reflecting lasting glory upon himself and upholding the noble traditions of the military service.

OFFICIAL COMMUNIQUÉ:
TOKYO, Wednesday, Oct. 15 (AP)
—United Nations Command communiqué 1,403, for the twenty-four hours to 6 A.M. today, Korean time:

Action continued around "White Horse Hill" on Korea's west-central front yesterday. United Nations Command forces attacked an estimated two enemy battalions. Other friendly forces secured positions approximately six miles east of "White Horse Hill."

In the same sector, United Nations Command forces attacked in the areas north of Kumhwa. After day-long fighting they broke contact with the enemy and withdrew. Also in the same sector our forces attacked "Sniper's Hill." After securing their objective, they withdrew in the face of an enemy counterattack.

Fourteen separate enemy probes were repulsed by United Nations Command forces in the central sector, while two were repulsed in the east-central and a single probe by enemy forces turned back in the western sector of the front.

A friendly raiding party engaged an enemy platoon for approximately thirty minutes on the eastern front and withdrew after inflicting casualties on the enemy forces.

Air activity found our fighter-bombers hitting enemy battle-line positions, troop and supply areas. Light and medium bombers flying at night continued close support missions, attacking enemy rolling stock and supply targets.

Navy elements continued harassing and interdiction bombing of enemy targets.

—Far East Air Forces operational summary 843, for Tuesday:

Far East Air Forces' war planes intensified their assaults against enemy battle-line positions Tuesday, mounting well over 1,000 combat sorties against widespread Communist targets for the third successive day. Night-flying medium and light bombers continued the attack and struck front-line areas in support of United Nations ground forces.

United States Air Force fighter-bombers also attack supply and rail targets throughout North Korea during the day, destroying 190 enemy-held buildings and cutting rails in ten places.

Directed by T-6 Mosquito spotting aircraft and F-51 Mustangs, F-80s, F-84s, other F-51s, Marine aircraft, and Australian Meteor jets concentrated their close support assault against enemy bunkers, destroying at least ninety.

North of Kumhwa, sixty bunkers were knocked out, one command post destroyed, and two artillery positions silenced. Several secondary explosions were also observed.

Northwest of Chorwon, in the "White Horse Hill" area, numerous fires and secondary explosions were reported as the fighter-bombers destroyed ten bunkers and silenced four artillery positions.

Enemy positions in the "Punchbowl" area and northwest of Kaesong were also attacked by the fighter-bombers.

F-84 Thunderjets struck a military headquarters and storage area southeast of Chongju, near the mouth of the Chongchon River, destroying ten buildings and leaving the area in flames. Six secondary explosions indicated hits on ammunition stockpiles.

West of Uhwon, Thunderjets and R.O.K. Mustangs cut rails in six places and knocked out one rail bridge while damaging another. Near Namchongjom, one rail tunnel was sealed by Marine aircraft.

Twenty buildings were destroyed southeast of Sinmak. A supply area south of Kowon and a troop concentration northeast of Haeju were also attacked during the day.

Last night B-29 Superforts of F.E.A.F. Bomber Command hit supply targets in the Wonsan area for the second successive night. Numerous fires were started in the target areas and crews reported no enemy opposition.

Four Superforts struck enemy front-line positions in the west-central sector with no opposition.

B-26 night Intruders struck two supply areas on the east coast last night at Chogiyong and Pukchong. Numerous fires and an estimated 100 secondary explosions were reported in the target areas.

B-26s and Marine aircraft struck enemy front-line positions northwest of Chorwon and north of Kumhwa, while other night Intruders destroyed thirty-five enemy vehicles and inflicted two roadblocks between Yongpo-ri and Ichon.

F-86 Sabre jets, flying screen for fighter-bombers, sighted forty enemy MiG-15s during the day but there were no engagements.

F.E.A.F. Tuesday mounted 1,280 sorties, of which 420 were in support of the United Nations Army. Of these 365 were combat-type missions. Cargo transports of F.E.A.F.'s 315th Air Division yesterday airlifted 480 tons of supplies and personnel in continued logistical support of United Nations forces

—Eighth Army tactical summary for Monday:

R.O.K. Ninth Division troops added to their holdings on "White Horse Mountain" Tuesday, while fighting broke out at other key hill positions along the Eighth Army central front.

In the eighth day of continued battle at "White Horse," northwest of Chorwon, the R.O.K.s turned back light Chinese pre-dawn attacks against positions on the crest and moved out early in the morning to assault a series of Chinese-held knobs on the northwest portion of the hill. They swept over the first knob at 8:10 A.M., secured it at 9 A.M., and attacked for the second, where they were still fighting at 2:30 P.M..

Across the Chorwon Valley to the east, Eighth Army troops at 7:30 A.M. renewed the attack for advance hill positions lost Sunday night, were fighting an enemy company on the southern slopes of the hill at 11:30, closed in hand-to-hand combat with the Chinese fifty yards from the crest at 1:50 P.M. and secured the hill forty minutes later. All territory lost Sunday night has been restored.

Meanwhile, other Eighth Army troops were assaulting enemy-held "Triangle Hill" north of Kumhwa. Elements attacking up the steep shale and sand-covered slopes were pinned down by enemy fire at 7:15 A.M., withdrew slightly at 8 A.M. and at 9:45 were meeting stiff resistance from an enemy battalion.

Other elements attacking from the northeast occupied twin peaks along a ridgeline leading to the hill crest. Fighting for "Triangle Hill" was continuing at mid-afternoon.

To the northeast, other attacking forces were meeting lighter resistance in a dawn attack against the Chinese portion of "Sniper Ridge," taking one objective at 2:55 P.M. and continuing the fight still deeper into enemy territory beyond it.

West of the Pukham River, two Chinese attacking positions on "Finger Ridge" at 1:10 A.M. were driven off in an hour and twenty minutes.

Chinese attackers late Monday night surrounded an advance position at "Christmas Hill," west of the Mundung Valley, but counterattacking reinforcements drove them back by 6:05 A.M. Tuesday morning.

†SKINNER, SHERROD E., JR.

Rank and Organization: Second Lieutenant, U.S. Marine Corps Reserve, Battery F, 11th Marines, 1st Marine Division (Rein).
Born: October 29, 1929, Hartford, Connecticutt.
Entered Service At: East Lansing, Michigan.
Place and Date: Korea, October 26, 1952.
Citation: For conspicuous gallantry and intrepidity at the risk of his life above and beyond the call of duty while serving as an artillery forward observer of Battery F, in action against enemy aggressor forces on the night of October 26, 1952. When his observation post in an extremely critical and vital sector of the main line of resistance was subjected to a sudden and fanatical attack by hostile forces, supported by a devastating barrage of artillery and mortar fire which completely severed communication lines connecting the outpost with friendly firing batteries, 2d Lt. Skinner, in a determined effort to hold his position, immediately organized and directed the surviving personnel in the defense of the outpost, continuing to call down fire on the enemy by means of radio alone until his equipment became damaged beyond repair. Undaunted by the intense hostile barrage and the rapidly-closing attackers, he twice left the protection of his bunker in order to direct accurate machine gun fire and to replenish the depleted supply of ammunition and grenades. Although painfully wounded on each occasion, he steadfastly refused medical aid until the rest of the men received treatment. As the ground attack reached its climax, he gallantly directed the final defense until the meager supply of ammunition was exhausted and the position overrun. During the 3 hours that the outpost was occupied by the enemy, several grenades were thrown into the bunker which

served as protection for 2d Lt. Skinner and his remaining comrades. Realizing that there was no chance for other than passive resistance, he directed his men to feign death even though the hostile troops entered the bunker and searched their persons. Later, when an enemy grenade was thrown between him and 2 other survivors, he immediately threw himself on the deadly missile in an effort to protect the others, absorbing the full force of the explosion and sacrificing his life for his comrades. By his indomitable fighting spirit, superb leadership, and great personal valor in the face of tremendous odds, 2d Lt. Skinner served to inspire his fellow marines in their heroic stand against the enemy and upheld the highest traditions of the U.S. Naval Service. He gallantly gave his life for his country.

O'BRIEN, GEORGE H., JR.

Rank and Organization: Second Lieutenant, U.S. Marine Corps Reserve, Company H, 3d Battalion, 7th Marines, 1st Marine Division (Rein).
Born: September 10, 1926, Fort Worth, Texas.
Entered Service At: Big Spring, Texas.
Place and Date: Korea, October 27, 1952.
Citation: For conspicuous gallantry and intrepidity at the risk of his life above and beyond the call of duty as a rifle platoon commander of Company H, in action against enemy aggressor forces. With his platoon subjected to an intense mortar and artillery bombardment while preparing to assault a vitally important hill position on the main line of resistance which had been overrun by a numerically superior enemy force on the preceding night, 2d Lt. O'Brien leaped from his trench when the attack signal was given and, shouting for his men to follow, raced across an exposed saddle and up the enemy-held hill through a virtual hail of deadly small-arms, artillery, and mortar fire. Although shot threw the arm and thrown to the ground by hostile automatic-weapons fire as he neared the well-entrenched enemy position, he bravely regained his feet, waved his men onward, and continued to spearhead the assault, pausing only long enough to go to the aid of a wounded marine. Encountering the enemy at close range, he proceeded to hurl hand-grenades into the bunkers and, utilizing his carbine to best advantage in savage hand-to-hand combat, succeeded in killing at least 3 of the enemy. Struck down by the concussion of grenades on 3 occasions during the subsequent action, he steadfastly refused to be evacuated for medical treatment and continued to lead his platoon in the assault for a period of nearly 4 hours, repeatedly encouraging his men and maintaining superb direction of the unit. With the attack halted, he set up a defense with his remaining forces to prepare for a counterattack, personally checking each position, attending to the wounded and expediting their evacuation. When a relief of the position was effected by another unit, he remained to cover the withdrawal and to assure that no wounded were left behind. By his exceptionally daring and forceful leadership in the face of overwhelming odds, 2d Lt O'Brien served as a constant source of inspiration to all who observed him and was greatly instrumental in the recapture of a strategic position on the main line of resistance. His indomitable determination and valiant fighting spirit reflect the highest credit upon himself and enhance the finest traditions of the U.S. Naval Service.

OFFICIAL COMMUNIQUÉ:
TOKYO, Monday, Oct. 27 (AP)
—Far East Naval Forces summary of Saturday's operations:

Battleship U.S.S. Missouri pounded Red shore positions as Carrier Task Force 77 planes struck inland along the Korean east coast line in stepped-up air and sea action against the Reds.

More than 100,000 pounds of high explosives were hurled by Missouri's main battery at entrenched Reds in the Tanchon area. The dreadnought's helicopter provided gunfire spotting and came under fire from enemy small-arms. Tunnel mouths were principal targets for Missouri's gunners, who succeeded in blasting the storage and supply entrances and mangling trackers at the cave entrances. Missouri's guns are particularly lethal against the track and tunnel network extending along the east Korean coast line from Hungnam to Songjin.

Near Chori, Missouri guns also laid waste a power substation, destroying steelwork, and starting fires in transformer buttresses.

The Reds' winter coal supply operations were interrupted by air attack as Navy Skyraiders, Corsairs, and Panther jets teamed to strike at Kyongsong, west of Wonsan. Coal mine work-areas were heavily attacked by 2,000-pound bomb drops from Bon Homme Richard and Essex attack bombers under the cover of flak-suppression strikes by carrier jets and fighters. At Yongdok, troop and supply build-up areas were struck by diverting air elements. At Songjin, other carrier-based planes destroyed an ammunition dump, damaged a bridge, and exploded four rail cars on a siding. North of Hungnam, fishing junks, rail cars, and supply buildings were attacked. Near the Ungigang Reservoir, Navy planes attacked a Red lumber mill, six buildings, and a lumber conveyor were destroyed.

Navy action along the Kansong-Kosong battle line flared as two heavy cruisers, the Helena and Los Angeles, took gunfire stations. Los Angeles' 8-inch batteries destroyed two enemy artillery positions and damaged another in 90 percent coverage of the target area. Two defensive bunkers were heavily damaged as more than sixty rounds of 8-inch shells bombarded the Red positions. Destroyers U.S.S. Orleck destroyed two bunkers and damaged three near Kosong.

At Hungnam, destroyer U.S.S. Mansfield conducted night a surveillance patrol and fired on two enemy supply trains, one heading north and the other south. Results were not fully observed, although it is believed one boxcar was exploded in the southbound train. Mansfield then steamed south to Wonsan where 5-inch gunfire dispersed troops and trucks in the city's outskirts.

In west Korean coastal waters, destroyer U.S.S. Perkins performed two gunfire missions against enemy gun positions south of Chodo. Both guns were neutralized. British destroyer Cossack, Canadian destroyer Nootka, and New Zealand patrol frigate Rotoiti illuminated enemy positions during the night with star shells, in company with Canadian destroyer Iroquois.

Western channel approaches were swept and check-swept by vessels of the Western Pacific Minesweeping Group. Operations to recover sweep gear jettisoned earlier in the week, when the tiny minesweeps came under enemy shore-directed gunfire, were successfully completed.

—Far East Naval Forces summary of Sunday's operations:

The heavy guns of the battleship U.S.S. Missouri and the cruiser U.S.S. Los Angeles concentrated on gun positions and close-support missions ripping trenches, personnel bunkers, and silencing shore fire batteries.

Operating in the Kansong-Kosong area, the Los Angeles, aided by airspot, heavily damaged three personnel bunkers and a gun bunker position. In a second firing mission, two mortar positions and one personnel bunker was destroyed. Trenches were cut in three places, and two bunkers heavily damaged. The destroyer U.S.S. Frank Knox was in company.

Searching out enemy guns that had been firing on United Nations ships, the U.S.S. Missouri blasted the shore line and front-line areas along the east coast about forty miles north of the Thirty-eighth Parallel. Together with the guns of destroyer U.S.S. Hickok, several hits silenced gun positions and no return fire was received during the entire shelling period.

Other bombardments along the east coast were carried out by U.S.S. Mansfield, U.S.S. Orleck, U.S.S. Carmick, and H.M.C.S. Crusader.

Yellow Sea surface units carried harassing fire to the enemy in the Chodo area and on the Haeju Peninsula. The cruiser H.M.S. Birmingham fired on a troop billeting area, and shore spotters reported that an estimated nine out of twelve buildings were completely demolished. Continued fire was directed at troop concentrations in the area.

Other ships which participated in minor actions off the west coast included H.M.N.Z.S. Rotoiti, H.M.S. Cossack, U.S.S. Perkins, and H.M.C.S. Nootka. Active enemy coastal guns were the principal target in these attacks.

Two friendly sweepers, U.S.S. Competent and U.S.S. Condor, were shelled heavily while operating close in shore, but no damage or casualties were suffered.

—Far East Air Forces summary of Saturday's operations:

Enemy troop and supply concentrations and rail facilities came under heavy assault Saturday as daylight-striking fighter-bombers and night-flying medium and light bombers attacked targets from the battle line to within thirty-five miles of the Yalu River. Far East Air Forces mounted more than 950 sorties as jet and propeller-driven warcraft leveled buildings and inflicted rail cuts in strikes that extended from dawn till midnight.

United States Air Force F-84 Thunderjets bombed a political school northwest of Sinmak, leveling at least thirty buildings, and causing two violent secondary explosions. Large fires were started in the area as the Thunderjets dropped napalm bombs.

South of Namchonjom, F-84s sealed one end of a rail tunnel, and exploded an ammunition stockpile, while Marine land-based aircraft struck rail targets south of Chonghwa, slashing the rail lines in at least ten places.

Republic of Korea Air Force Mustangs attacked supply build-ups just above the Punchbowl, destroying ten supply shelters and damaging five, while F-51 Mustangs inflicted a road cut and bombed supply buildings near Sinchon.

Shooting Stars, Mustangs, Thunderjets, and Marine aircraft flew close air support in the Kumhwa, Chorwon, Kumsong, and Punchbowl sectors of the front, causing destruction or damage to twenty-five bunkers and ten gun positions.

B-29 Superforts of F.E.A.F. Bomber Command struck an enemy storage area adjacent to a gold mine at Taeyu-dong Saturday, thirty-five miles east of Suiho. Other Superforts hit a communications center at Chungsan on the west coast, and a marshaling yard at Naewonsan, near the east coast city of Wonsan. One enemy fighter made a non-firing pass over Chungsan, and other enemy fighters were sighted but did not attack.

One Superfort dropped 500-pound bombs on enemy concentration at Yonpon, near Hungnam, causing twenty secondary explosions and forty fires. In a strike against a communications center at Tokchon, the light bombers caused thirty-five secondary explosions.

The night intruders also bombed rail lines north of Hwangju, and patrolled enemy supply roads, destroying 125 Communist vehicles. B-26s and Marine aircraft flew close air support in the west and west-central sectors of the front during the night.

F-86 Sabre jets flying screen for the fighter-bombers, shot down two enemy MiG-15s during the day. Both claims were made in a morning engagement.

Total destruction during the period included six bunkers knocked out and twenty-five damaged, ten gun positions silenced and seven damaged, seventy buildings leveled and fifteen damaged, five troop casualties inflicted, one rail tunnel damaged, one rail and one road bridge damaged, twenty rail and seven road cuts inflicted, and one radar site damaged.

F.E.A.F., Saturday, mounted 955 sorties, of which 375 were in support of the United Nations Army. Of these, 515 were combat-type missions. Cargo transport of F.E.A.F.'s 315th Air Division airlifted 530 tons of supplies and personnel in continued logistical support of United Nations Forces.

—Far East Air Forces summary of Sunday's operations:

Daylight striking fighter-bombers, penetrating deep into North Korea, hammered Communist rail lines and rolling stock Sunday, slashing rails and causing destruction and damage to locomotives and rail cars near Kanggye, thirty miles east of the Yalu River.

Other fighter-bombers and night-flying medium and light bombers hit a number of enemy troop and supply concentrations, as Far East Air Forces mounted close to 1,000 sorties.

F-84 Thunderjets struck the rail line leading from Manchuria to Kanggye in an early morning strike, destroying three locomotives and damaging three others, while three rail cars were destroyed south of Kanggye. Between Kanggye and Huichon, one rail bridge was knocked out and two were damaged, and three rail cuts were inflicted.

North of Anak, in the Haeju Peninsula area, F-80 Shooting Stars struck a large troop concentration, destroying an estimated fifty buildings, while twenty troop and supply buildings were leveled in strikes by F-51 Mustangs southeast of Haeju.

Marine land-based aircraft and Australian Meteor jets attacked a troop concentration east of Chunghwa, while other Marine aircraft teamed with R.O.K. F-51s to hit supply build-ups beyond the Punchbowl.

Northeast of Pyonggang, Thunderjets bombed a supply and storage area. Other Thunderjets and Marine aircraft struck enemy front-line positions in the Kumhwa, Kumsong, and Punchbowl areas, destroying twenty gun positions and ten bunkers and causing numerous secondary explosions.

B-29 Superforts of F.E.A.F. Bomber Command hit troop and supply targets during the night. Targets included a supply center at Sopo and a North Korean headquarters near Yangdok. One B-29 hit rail marshaling yards at Naewonsan and Hamhung.

Meager flak opposed the Superforts, and unidentified fighter aircraft were sighted, but made no attack. One B-29 hit Red front-line positions.

B-26 light bombers struck two east coast supply targets Sunday night at Pukchong and Samho, south of Hongwon. Fifty secondary explosions were caused in the Pukchong attack and the target was left in flames. Numerous fires and explosions were also reported in Samho.

The night intruders also attacked enemy rails, destroying three box cars and damaging four at Sinchon, and damaging four box cars and one locomotive at Hongwon.

B-26s patrolling enemy supply routes, destroyed 110 Red supply trucks, while Marine aircraft and B-26s flew close air support for United Nations ground forces in the west, west-central, and Punchbowl areas of the front.

F-86 Sabre jets, flying screen for the fighter-bombers, destroyed two enemy MiG-15s during the day. Both claims were made in late afternoon engagement between the Yalu and Chongchon rivers.

Total destruction during the period included 120 buildings leveled and fifteen damaged, five bunkers knocked out and fifty damaged, twenty-five gun positions silenced and ten damaged, one rail bridge destroyed and two damaged, two road bridges damaged, five rail and eight road cuts inflicted, eight supply stacks demolished, one supply cave damaged, one fuel dump destroyed, and on searchlight knocked out.

F.E.A.F., Sunday, mounted 980 sorties, of which 365 were in support of the United Nations Army. Of these, 305 were combat-type missions. Cargo transports of F.E.A.F.'s 315th Air Division airlifted 460 tons of supplies and personnel in continued logistical support of United Nations forces.

—Eighth Army tactical summary 221, for Sunday's activities:

Activity was relatively light along the Eighth Army front Sunday, as fighting slowed down at recently contested hill positions along the central sector.

Only sporadic fire fighting developed between troops defending Pinpoint Hill on Sniper Ridge and Chinese holding to a knob to the northwest. Fighting had been heavy on Sniper Ridge Saturday afternoon when Eighth Army troops reoccupied the hill.

Near by Triangle Hill was quiet after 7:30 A.M., when two Chinese companies gave up after an attack that started at 4:00 A.M. They got close enough for some hand-to-hand fighting in the early stages of the attack, but the action soon decreased to the sporadic. Only occasional brief exchanges of fire continued throughout the morning and afternoon.

Three Chinese platoons which had attacked advance positions south of Iron Horse Mountain at 3:20 A.M., Sunday, withdrew to the north slopes of the mountain five minutes later.

In the east, however, almost a battalion of enemy troops, supported by a 1,000-round barrage of artillery and mortar fire, attacked Heartbreak Ridge positions at 1:20 A.M., but were forced back with an estimated sixty killed or wounded at 2:40 A.M..

Eighth Army troops defending a west-central sector advance position near the Pukhan River, repulsed an attacking enemy platoon at 1:50 A.M., after a fifty minute fight.

Patrol contacts Sunday were relatively light. One patrol fought sporadically for more than three hours with enemy of undetermined strength northeast of the Punchbowl. The fight broke off at 2:30 A.M..

†LORING, CHARLES J., JR.

Rank and Organization: Major, U.S. Air Force, 80th Fighter-Bomber Squadron, 8th Fighter-Bomber Wing.
Born: October 2, 1918, Portland, Maine.
Entered Service At: Portland, Maine.
Place and Date: Near Sniper Ridge, North Korea, November 22, 1952.
Citation: Maj. Loring distinguished himself by conspicuous gallantry and intrepidity at the risk of his life above and beyond the call of duty. While leading a flight of 4 F-80 type aircraft on a close support mission, Maj. Loring was briefed by a controller to dive-bomb enemy gun positions which were harassing friendly ground troops. After verifying the location of the target, Maj. Loring rolled into his dive-bomb run. Throughout the run, extremely accurate ground fire was directed on his aircraft. Disregarding the accuracy and intensity of the ground fire, Maj. Loring aggressively continued to press the attack until his aircraft was hit. At approximately 4,000 feet he deliberately altered his course and aimed his diving aircraft at active gun emplacements concentrated on a ridge northwest of the briefed target, turned his aircraft 45 degrees to the left, pulled up in a deliberate, controlled maneuver, and elected to sacrifice his life by diving his aircraft directly into the midst of the enemy emplacements. His selfless and heroic action completely destroyed the enemy gun emplacement and eliminated a dangerous threat to United Nations ground forces. Maj. Loring's noble spirit, superlative courage, and conspicuous self-sacrifice in inflicting maximum damage on the enemy exemplified valor of the highest degree and his actions were in keeping with the finest traditions of the U.S. Air Force.

OFFICIAL COMMUNIQUÉ:
TOKYO, Sunday, Nov. 23 (AP)
—Far East Naval Force's summary of Friday's operations:

Planes of Task Force 77, flying from U.S.S. Essex and U.S.S. Kearsarge, smashed at enemy targets along the east coast and far inland. Pilots reported almost 200 successful sorties, with fifty-four buildings, six bunkers, five machine-gun positions, eleven trucks, two supply stacks, and a highway bridge destroyed.

Twenty-seven bunkers, ten mortar positions, five artillery positions, seventeen buildings, ten trucks, ten supply shelters, two highway bridges, and a rail bridge were destroyed.

Surface action on the east coast continued as U.S.S. Toledo and U.S.S. Collett teamed up to attack Red transport facilities in the Tanchon area. Their guns destroyed two highway by-pass bridges and a rail bridge, and damaged another rail bridge. Bombardment of two marshaling yards resulted in numerous rail cuts and destruction of four warehouses and three other buildings.

U.S.S Helena and U.S.S. Perkins harassed enemy targets near Kosong, while U.S.S. Rooks interdicted the coastal railway between Tanchon and Songjin, scoring several probable hits on a northbound train. U.S.S. Los Angeles shelled Red installations farther south.

In the Wonsan sector, U.S.S. Thompson's guns dueled with an enemy shore battery, finally suppressing its fire and damaging several buildings in the vicinity.

On the west coast, H.M.S. Birmingham shelled a number of enemy gun emplacements in caves south of Chinnampo. Other United Nations surface units delivered harassing and interdiction fire on Communist troops and positions in the Haeju sector.

Other west coast targets were struck by Marine planes from U.S.S. Hadoeng Strait. Pilots reported two road bridges and three buildings destroyed. Two rail cars, a road bridge, a transformer, and a highway by-pass were damaged and three road cuts and two rail cuts were made.

—Far East Air Forces summary of Friday's operations:

Ranging deep into enemy territory to strike a Communist military headquarters and billeting area northwest of Pukchin, F-84 Thunderjets paced fighter-bomber activity Friday, as troop concentrations and supply routes took a pasting.

F.E.A.F. sorties for the period totaled 1,119, all except 175 being combat. Medium and light bombers hit supply centers, troop areas, and rail lines in east and central North Korea Friday night.

F-86 Sabre jets shot down one enemy MiG-15 during the day while screening the fighter-bombers. Seven engagements with the enemy jets occurred in "MiG Alley."

More than twenty buildings were destroyed in the headquarters near Pukchin, and several large fires started. Heavy smoke prevented complete assessment of results. Meanwhile, other F-84s leveled a score of buildings in a troop concentration north Yonan, and Marine land-based aircraft demolished twenty buildings and set off several fires and secondary explosions in that area. Another troop area, north of the Punchbowl, suffered destruction of ten buildings by Republic of Korea F-51 Mustangs.

F-80 Shooting Stars damaged a bridge and inflicted four cuts in a rail line south of Sukchon, while F-84s knocked out one span of a road bridge at Sohung. F-84s and F-51s destroyed six enemy buildings and set off several fires in the Haeju Peninsula area.

Forty troop bunkers and twenty gun positions were destroyed or damages at T-6 Mosquitos directed close air support strikes along the front. F-80s, F-84s, F-51s, and Marine aircraft carried out these attacks.

B-26 night intruders continued the heavy assault against Red supply convoys Friday night, destroying 170 trucks and creating road blocks near Sukchon, Samgung, and Wonsan.

In a supply concentration at Puckhong, B-26s set off ten secondary explosions, while other intruders set five fires in a troop and supply target south of Chaeryong. Using electronic-aiming devices, the light-bombers hit a Samdong rail bridge, a Yangdok road bridge, supplies east of Songchon, and a rail line at Sariwon.

The B-26s also hit Communist battle-line positions in the west and west-central sectors.

Eleven B-29 Superforts bombed a rail bridge at Sanwang-bong, south of Huichon, and a Yongpyong supply area, near Wonsan, at night. None of the Superforts met opposition.

Two B-29s ranged along the west-central battle front during the night, hitting enemy front-line positions.

Total destruction during the period included fifteen bunkers knocked out and thirty-five damaged, eight gun positions silenced and fifteen damaged, seventy-five buildings leveled and fifty damaged, one road bridge destroyed and one damaged, four rail cuts and twenty road cuts inflicted, and three rail tunnels and three rail bridges damaged.

Cargo transports of F.E.A.F.'s 315th Air Division airlifted 575 tons of supplies and personnel in support of United Nations forces.

—Eighth Army communiqué 1,169, for Friday's activities:

Action fell off in the Triangle Hill-Sniper Ridge area as enemy attacking in platoon strength at Pinpoint and south of Jane Russell Hills was repulsed. An enemy company attacking positions west of the Pukhan River was beaten off with heavy losses. Enemy artillery and mortars fired 11,008 rounds during the twenty-four hour period ended at 6:00 P.M., approximately 3,000 more than were fired in the preceding twenty-four hours.

Western sector: Two enemy groups of two-platoon strength probing advance position west-north-west of Yonchon at 12:15 and 3:15 were driven off in fire fights of one hour and twenty minutes and thirty minutes in length. In the first engagement, Allied troops withdrew, directed artillery on the enemy, and reoccupied the position at 1:35 A.M. Another platoon which had probed in the area Thursday night, and had forced the Allied defenders from their positions, was beaten back by artillery fire as Eighth Army troops reoccupied the position at 4:05 A.M. Allied raiders operating east of Panmunjom at 4:40 A.M., estimated killing or wounding eight enemy in a fifty-minute fire fight. Patrols fought engagements up to thirty minutes in length with enemy units up to two squads in strength.

Central sector: Eighth Army troops on Pinpoint Hill repulsed the last elements of an enemy battalion which began attacking the position at 8:35 P.M. on the 20th. The last Chinese platoon was forced back at 6:50 A.M. (Nov. 21). Another enemy platoon attacked the position at 10:35 P.M. and was driven off at 11:15. Other Eighth Army elements at Rocky Point to the east at 8:25 A.M. repulsed two attacking enemy platoons after a night of sporadic fighting. A Chinese platoon attacking south of Jane Russell Hill at 11:00 P.M., Nov. 20, was driven off at 3:45 A.M. after some hand-to-hand combat. Two enemy squads probing the position at 8:30 P.M. were driven back at 11:20. An enemy company attacked Allied positions west of the Pukhan River at 2:15 A.M. and was repulsed at 5:30. The Eighth Army troops estimated killing or wounding fifty-six enemy in this action. A reinforced enemy squad probing north-west of Chorwon at 9:30 P.M. was driven off after a ten minute exchange of fire. Eighth Army raiders northwest of Chorwon at 6:44 A.M. engaged an enemy squad which was later reinforced by a platoon. When the raiders withdrew at 7:50 A.M. they had killed or wounded sixteen of the enemy. Patrols fought engagements up to ten minutes in length with enemy groups up to a platoon in strength.

Eastern sector: Small enemy groups probing northeast of the Punchbowl at 9:25 and 11:45 P.M. and south of the Nam River late in the period were beaten off in fights lasting up to fifty-five minutes. Enemy squads probing south of Anchor Hill at 1:20 and 1:30 A.M. were beaten off in brief fire fights. Patrols fought engagements up to forty-three minutes in length with enemy groups up to a platoon in strength.

—Eighth Army tactical summary 241, for Saturday:

Relatively light activity developed along the Eighth Army front Saturday morning and afternoon.

The Chinese, however, continued pressure against "Sniper Ridge" positions northeast of Kumhwa. They attacked on "Rocky Point" on the ridge with two platoons at 1:30 A.M. and were forced back in a one-hour fight.

Two Chinese squads probed "Rocky Point" at dawn, got close enough for a brief small arms and hand grenade fight and withdrew at 6:20 A.M.. A Chinese platoon probed the position at 12:10 P.M. and was repulsed in a thirty-minute fire fight.

Two squads probed nearby "Pinpoint Hill" on the ridge at 6:00 A.M., and were forced back after another short small arms and hand grenade fight.

Eighth Army raiders fought for forty minutes with a Chinese platoon west of Korangpo.

Elsewhere along the front Saturday, patrols fought engagements up to twenty-five minutes in length with enemy groups up to a platoon in strength.

—Eighth Army communiqué 1170, covering Saturday's activities:

Activity was generally light along the Eighth Army front, with some attacks in up to two-platoon strength. Enemy artillery and mortars fired 7,454 rounds during the twenty-four hour period ended at 6:00 P.M., 3,554 rounds fewer than were fired in the preceding twenty-four hours.

Western sector: A raiding party fought a heavy forty minute pre-dawn engagement with enemy of undetermined strength northwest of Korangpo. Patrols fought engagements up to fifteen minutes in length with enemy groups up to a platoon in strength.

Central sector: Intensity of fighting at Sniper Ridge diminished though the enemy continued pressure, attacking lightly at Rocky Point with two platoons at 1:30 A.M., with two squads at 6:00 A.M., with a platoon at 12:10 P.M., and with another platoon at 11:35 P.M.. The first three attacks were repulsed. The fourth continued at the close of the period. Two enemy squads probing Pinpoint Hill at 6:00 A.M. were repulsed after sporadic fighting. Eighth Army troops occupying positions south of Jackson Heights withdrew slightly at 11:45 P.M. after a twenty-five minute attack by enemy of undetermined strength. Patrols fought engagements up to twenty-five minutes in length with small enemy groups.

Eastern sector: Two enemy platoons probing south of Anchor Hill at 9:20 P.M., were driven off with the aid of artillery and mortar fire twenty-five minutes later. No other significant activity was reported.

—United Nations Command communiqué 1,442, for the twenty-four hours to 6:00 A.M., Sunday, Korea time:

The entire Korean battle front was relatively quiet. In the western sector, a United Nations Command raiding party engaged enemy troops for about forty minutes before breaking contact. Enemy probing efforts were unsuccessful in the west-central and central sectors. Patrols operating all along the line reported making only light enemy contact.

From the air, land-based warplanes hit enemy troop concentrations, rail lines, and front-line positions. Our fighters continued successful in their encounters against enemy jets. At night medium bombers hit supply areas at Pyongyang and Haeju and hit the enemy at the front while light bombers concentrated on bridges, troop and supply targets, and close air support strikes.

†GEORGE, CHARLES

Rank and Organization: Private First Class, U.S. Army, Company C, 179th Infantry Regiment, 45th Infantry Division.
Born: August 23, 1932, Cherokee, North Carolina.
Entered Service At: Whittier, North Carolina.
Place and Date: Near Songnae-dong, Korea, November 30, 1952.
Citation: Pfc. George, a member of Company C, distinguished himself by conspicuous gallantry and outstanding courage above and beyond the call of duty in action against the enemy on the night of November 30, 1952. He was a member of a raiding party committed to engage the enemy and capture a prisoner for interrogation. Forging up the rugged slope of the key terrain feature, the group was subjected to intense mortar and machine gun fire and suffered several casualties. Throughout the advance, he fought valiantly and, upon reaching the crest

of the hill, leaped into the trenches and closed with the enemy in hand-to-hand combat. When friendly troops were ordered to move back upon completion of the assignment, he and 2 comrades remained to cover the withdrawal. While in the process of leaving the trenches a hostile soldier hurled a grenade into their midst. Pfc. George shouted a warning to one comrade, pushed the other soldier out of danger and, with full knowledge of the consequences, unhesitatingly threw himself upon the grenade, absorbing the full blast of the explosion. Although seriously wounded in this display of valor, he refrained from an outcry which would divulge the position of his companions. The 2 soldiers evacuated him to the forward aid station and shortly thereafter he succumbed to his wounds. Pfc. George's indomitable courage, consummate devotion to duty, and willing self-sacrifice reflect the highest credit upon himself and uphold the finest traditions of the military service.

OFFICIAL COMMUNIQUÉ:
TOKYO, Monday, Dec. 1, (AP)
—Far East Air Forces summary of Sunday's operations:

Enemy supply stores and transportation facilities came under night attack by United Nations medium and light bombers Sunday, after a bad weather blanket over most of North Korea halted United States Air Force fighter-bombers and F-86 Sabre jets during the day.

Throughout the day reconnaissance aircraft ranged through enemy skies, reporting weather conditions. F.E.A.F. mounted 325 sorties.

B-26 night intruders used electronic-aiming to attack a rail bridge northwest of Songchon, with unobserved results. The light bombers destroyed 40 enemy vehicles in front-bound supply convoys and attacked Communist gun positions and troop bunkers in the west and west-central sectors of the front.

B-29 Superforts unleashed 70 tons of high explosives on a supply center south of Wonsan before midnight, two adjacent areas were struck in the target at Hahwasan as the Superforts made their bombing runs without opposition.

—Eighth Army Tactical summary 249, for Sunday:

Activity continued light along the Eighth Army front Sunday, but patrol contacts were on the increase as weather grew more favorable for ground operations.

One patrol operating near "Jackson Heights," at the eastern edge of the Chorwon Valley, fought three separate brief engagements with enemy up to a reinforced platoon in strength between 12:45 and 1:10 A.M.. The patrol killed six Chinese and wounded ten in the three actions.

Other patrols fought engagements up to an hour and a half in length with enemy groups up to a platoon in strength. Contacts Sunday were most frequent in the "Heartbreak Ridge" sector.

An Eighth Army raiding party fought for 50 minutes with an enemy company just after midnight south of Panmunjom.

The Chinese continued light pressure against "Sniper Ridge" positions, attacking "Pinpoint Hill" for 55 minutes with a platoon and probing "Rocky Point" with a squad. The "Pinpoint Hill" fight was over at 2 A.M., the "Rocky Point" action at 4:10 A.M.. The Chinese were repulsed in both engagements.

Small enemy groups probing northwest of Chorwon at 5:30 A.M., northwest of Kumhwa at 4:30 A.M., and northeast of the "Punchbowl" at 4:20 A.M. were driven back in brief firefights.

—Eighth Army communique 1,178, covering Sunday's activities:

Eighth Army troops on "Pinpoint Hill" repulsed an early morning attack by one enemy platoon and a late evening attack by two, as activity continued light on the Eighth Army front. Enemy artillery and mortars fired 7,044 rounds during the twenty-four hour period ended at 6 P.M., less than half the total fired during the preceding twenty-four hours.

Western sector: An Eighth Army raiding party fought a 50-minute early morning engagement with an enemy company south of Panmunjom. A patrol killed ten in a half-hour fight with 25 enemy, which broke off at 11:05 P.M., west of Chorwon. Other patrols fought light engagements with small enemy groups.

Central sector: An enemy platoon attacking Pinpoint Hill on Sniper Ridge at 1:05 A.M. was driven back in a 55-minute exchange of fire. Two enemy platoons, supported by heavy mortar and artillery fire, attacked at 10:50 P.M. and were repulsed at 11:25 P.M..

An Eighth Army patrol destroyed two enemy bunkers near Pinpoint Hill in a 20-minute fight with an enemy patrol beginning just before midnight. An enemy squad probing nearby Rocky Point positions at 4:10 A.M. was repulsed in a brief fight. A patrol operating near Jackson Heights, at the eastern edge of Chorwon Valley, killed six enemy and wounded ten in three separate brief actions with enemy up to a reinforced platoon in strength, between 12:45 and 1:10 A.M.. Other patrols fought engagements up to twenty minutes in length with enemy groups up to a platoon in strength. Small enemy groups probing northwest of Kumhwa at 4:30 A.M. and at White Horse Mountain northwest of Chorwon at 5:30 A.M. were repulsed in brief fire fights.

Eastern sector: Eighth Army troops northeast of the Punchbowl repulsed eight enemy probing at 4:20 A.M. and fifteen probing at 7:15 P.M. in brief fire fights. Patrols fought engagements up to an hour and forty minutes in length with enemy groups up to a platoon in strength, killing four and wounding seven in a sharp 45-minute battle with a platoon northeast of the Punchbowl which broke off at 9:15 P.M..

—United Nations Command communique 1,450, for the twenty-four hours to 6 A.M., Monday, Korea time:

Ground action in Korea was light again Sunday. Seven enemy probes were reported, the largest being of platoon size. Four of the enemy efforts were repulsed by United Nations Command troops in the west-central sector, while three were turned back in east-central sector of the front.

During the night, medium bombers bombarded a supply center and enemy front-line positions. Light bombers hit enemy rail bridges, supply convoys, and front-line positions. Bad weather halted daytime activities of land-based aircraft.

CHAPTER 4

1953

MURPHY, RAYMOND G.

Rank and Organization: Second Lieutenant, U.S. Marine Corps Reserve, Company A, 1st Battalion, 5th Marines, 1st Marine Division (Rein). **Born:** January 14, 1930, Pueblo, Colorado. **Entered Service At:** Pueblo, Colorado. **Place and Date:** Korea, February 3, 1953. **Citation:** For conspicuous gallantry and intrepidity at the risk of his life above and beyond the call of duty as a platoon commander of Company A, in action against enemy aggressor forces. Although painfully wounded by fragments from an enemy mortar shell while leading his evacuation platoon in support of assault units attacking a cleverly concealed and well-entrenched hostile force occupying commanding ground, 2d Lt. Murphy steadfastly refused medical aid and continued to lead his men up a hill through a withering barrage of hostile mortar and small-arms fire, skillfully maneuvering his force from one position to the next and shouting words of encouragement. Undeterred by the increasing intense enemy fire, he immediately located casualties as they fell and made several trips up and down the fire-swept hill to direct evacuation teams to the wounded, personally carrying many of the stricken marines to safety. When reinforcements were needed by the assaulting elements, 2d Lt. Murphy employed part of his unit as support and, during the ensuing battle, personally killed 2 of the enemy with his pistol. With all the wounded evacuated and the assaulting units beginning to disengage, he remained behind with a carbine to cover the movement of friendly forces off the hill and, though suffering intense pain from his previous wounds, seized an automatic-rifle to provide more firepower when the enemy reappeared in the trenches. After reaching the base of the hill, he organized a search party and again ascended the slope for a final check on missing marines, locating and carrying the bodies of a machine gun crew back down the hill. Wounded a second time while conducting the entire force to the line of departure through a continuing barrage of enemy small-arms, artillery, and mortar fire, he again refused medical assistance until assured that every one of his men, including all casualties, had preceded him to the main lines. His resolute and inspiring leadership, exceptional fortitude, and great personal valor reflect the highest credit upon 2d Lt. Murphy and enhance the finest traditions of the U.S. Naval Service.

OFFICIAL COMMUNIQUÉ:

TOKYO, Wednesday, Feb. 4 (AP)
United Nations Command communiqué 1,515 for Wednesday's action:

Northwest of Korangpo, in the western sector of the Korean battle-front, a United Nations Command force, supported by artillery, armor, and air strikes, conducted a raid yesterday against an enemy stronghold. They fought for more than four hours, inflicting heavy casualties on hostile troops and destroying enemy installations. Four enemy counterattacks were beaten off during the action. The remainder of the front was relatively quiet throughout the period.

Land-based fighter-bombers hit enemy troops, supply areas, and rail lines. United Nations jet fighters failed to sight enemy jets yesterday after sixteen consecutive days of engagements. At night medium bombers hit enemy supply areas while Intruders hammered rail traffic and battle-line positions. Cargo transports completed another week of air-lifting supplies and personnel.

U.N.C. naval surface craft continued bombardment of enemy east coast targets. Planes flying from carriers in the Yellow Sea sought out enemy tergets of opportunity during yesterday's missions.

—Eighth Army tactical summary, for Tuesday:

R.O.K. troops killed fifty-five North Koreans as they chased away a battalion attacking Luke the Gook's Castle norhteast of the Punchbowl early Tuesday.

The North Koreans attacked the eastern sector hill position at 12:45 A.M., striking with three companies the hill itself and with two platoons a few hundred yards east of the hill.

They were within hand-grenade range of the R.O.K. position at 1:20 A.M.. A R.O.K. counterattack, supported by heavy Allied artillery fire, forced the enemy back, with the R.O.K.s pursuing the North Korean company which had advanced nearest their lines. The action was over at 3:15 A.M..

In the west, Eighth Army raiders assaulted a low hill position west of Korangpo, driving the defending Chinese into deep tunnels after swapping hand-grenades and rifle and automatic weapons fire with them in the open trench system.

The raiders, supported by an air preparation, artillery and tanks, were fighting on the objective and on a hill to its left at 8:32 A.M.. They returned to their base three hours later.

An estimate of enemy casualties or destruction of enemy fortifications on the hill was not available late Tuesday afternoon.

Two enemy probes and light patrol contacts developed elsewhere along the front early Tuesday.

Two enemy squads attacking an advance position west of the Mundung Valley at 2:40 A.M. were driven back with six estimated killed after a forty minute fight. A north Korean squad attacking an advance position northeast of Luke the Gook's Castle at 4:55 A.M. was repulsed after a brief fight.

Patrols early Tuesday fought light engagements up to ten minutes in length with enemy groups up to a platoon in strength.

—Far East naval forces summary for Monday:

Navy planes from three aircraft carriers on the east coast continued to pound supply buildings, shelters, billeting areas, and vehicles repair installations in North Korea.

Launched from Task Force 77 carriers, the U.S.S. Oriskany, Kearsarge and Philippine Sea, the planes struck hardest at Communist buildups, northwest of Songjin. Concentrated strikes on these targets as well as similar ones in the Wonsan and Kilchu areas resulted in the destruction of twenty-eight supply buildings and three shelters, while an additional thirty-two buildings and five shelters were damaged.

Twenty-two buildings suffered strafing damage and six others were left in flames. Nine large fires and four secondary explosions were reported.

While furnishing close air support for United Nations troops, pilots destroyed ten bunkers and 150 yards of trenches. Damaged were five bunkers, one artillery position, thirteen mortar positions, and two caves.

In other strikes on vital storage areas, damage was inflicted on six trucks and railroad lines were cut in eleven places. One truck also was destroyed.

In the Yellow Sea, Marine pilots flying from the escort carrier U.S.S. Badoeng Strait hit the enemy along the entire western coast. Striking at troop concentrations, the pilots accounted for the destruction of thirty buildings housing troops and damaged twenty-four others. Numerous fires were noted. Three trucks laden with supplies were destroyed as one secondary explosion erupted. Several caves containing supplies also were destroyed with direct bomb hits. In addition, the planes wiped out one gun position and damaged another.

The cruiser H.M.S. Birmingham, also in the Yellow Sea, carried out a 6-inch bombardment against gun positions firing on friendly forces. The cruiser fired approximately twenty-four rounds, but results were not reported.

The cruiser U.S.S. Toledo and destroyer U.S.S. Kidd continued to battle enemy positions near Kosong. With the aid of shore spotting the ships accounted for approximately fifteen supply buildings destroyed or damaged and scored seven road cuts and numerous secondary explosions in the supply area.

The destroyer U.S.S. Wisemans furnished gunfire for minesweepers in the Tanchon area.

The destroyer U.S.S. Hickox destroyed one bunker, damaged five and cut seventy yards of trench lines near Kosong.

†HAMMOND, FRANCIS C.

Rank and Organization: Hospital Corpsman, U.S. Navy, attached as a medical corpsman to the 1st Marine Division.
Born: Alexandria, Virginia.
Entered Service At: Alexandria, Virginia.
Place and Date: Korea, March 26-27, 1953.
Citation: For conspicuous gallantry and intrepidity at the risk of his life above and beyond the call of duty as a HC serving with the 1st Marine Division, in action against enemy aggressor forces on the night of March 26-27, 1953. After reaching an intermediate objective during a counterattack against a heavily entrenched and numerically superior hostile force occupying ground on a bitterly contested outpost far in advance of the main line of resistance, HC Hammond's platoon was subjected to a murderous barrage of hostile mortar and artillery fire, followed by a vicious assault by onrushing enemy troops. Resolutely advancing through the veritable curtain of fire to aid his stricken comrades, HC Hammond moved along the stalwart garrison of marines and, although critically wounded himself, valiantly continued to administer aid to the other wounded throughout an exhausting 4-hour period. When the unit was ordered to withdraw, he skillfully directed the evacuation of casualties and remained in the fire-swept area to assist the corpsmen of the relieving unit until he was struck by a round of enemy mortar fire and fell, mortally wounded. By his exceptional fortitude, inspiring initiative and self-sacrificing efforts, HC Hammond undoubtedly saved the lives of many marines. His great personal valor in the face of overwhelming odds enhances and sustains the finest traditions of the U.S. Naval Service. He gallantly gave his life for his country.

CHARETTE, WILLIAM R.

Rank and Organization: Hospital Corpsman Third Class, U.S. Navy, Medical Corpsman serving with a marine rifle company.
Born: Ludington, Michigan.
Entered Service At: Ludington, Michigan.
Place and Date: Korea, March 27, 1953.
Citation: For conspicuous gallantry and intrepidity at the risk of his life above and beyond the call of duty in action against enemy aggressor forces in the early morning hours of March 27,

1953. Participating in a fierce encounter with a cleverly concealed and well-entrenched enemy force occupying positions on a vital and bitterly contested outpost far in advance of the main line of resistance, HC3c. Charette repeatedly and unhesitatingly moved about through a murderous barrage of hostile small-arms and mortar fire to render assistance to his wounded comrades. When an enemy grenade landed within a few feet of a marine he was attending, he immediately threw himself upon the stricken man and absorbed the entire concussion of the deadly missile with his body. Although sustaining painful facial wounds, and undergoing shock from the intensity of the blast which ripped the helmet and medical aid kit from his person, HC3c. Charette resourcefully improvised emergency bandages by tearing off part of his clothing, and gallantly continued to administer medical aid to the wounded in his own unit and to those in adjacent platoon areas as well. Observing a seriously wounded comrade whose armored vest had been torn from his body by the blast from an exploding shell, He selflessly removed his own battle vest and placed it upon the helpless man although fully aware of the added jeopardy to himself. Moving to the side of another casualty who was suffering excruciating pain from a serious leg wound, HC3c. Charette stood upright in the trench line and exposed himself to a deadly hail of enemy fire in order to lend more effective aid to the victim and to alleviate his anguish while being removed to a position of safety. By his indomitable courage and inspiring efforts in behalf of his wounded comrades, HC3c. Charette was directly responsible for saving many lives. His great personal valor reflects the highest credit upon himself and enhances the finest traditions of the U.S. Naval Service.

OFFICIAL COMMUNIQUÉ:
TOKYO, Saturday, March 28 (AP)
—United Nations Command communique 1,567, for the twenty-four hours to 6:00 A.M., Saturday, Korean time:

Air and ground forces teamed together again Friday as the enemy continued his attacks against United Nations positions on the western front.

The major actions were centered around Reno and Vegas, two forward positions northeast of Bunker Hill, which had been overrun the night of March 26, forcing the friendly elements to withdraw. Close-in fighting on Vegas was renewed early Friday morning as the enemy reinforced with an unknown number and our troops also were reinforced.

At approximately 6 o'clock Friday morning, friendly elements broke contact with the enemy as heavy United Nations aerial attacks against the position commenced. Shortly before noon, the air missions ended and United Nations Command ground elements counter-attacked. Bitter fighting, accompanied by heavy artillery and mortar fire, continued throughout the afternoon on Vegas, and at 7:30 o'clock at night, friendly forces had repulsed the enemy and were occupying the position.

As the ground action was continuing throughout the period on Vegas, coordinated air strikes were launched against the Reno position which still was occupied by the enemy.

Elsewhere across the battlefront, minor patrol contacts were reported.

United Nations fighter-bombers sent more than 175 tons of high explosives into Communist front-line positions in the Old Baldy and Bunker Hill areas on the western front. Other fighter-bombers struck enemy supply routes and building areas.

Fighter jets scored in engagements with MiG-15s.

Medium bombers struck two east coast supply areas and front-line positions during the night. Night Intruders smashed rail rolling stock, vehicles and battle line targets.

United Nations Command carrier-based planes struck targets from the eastern front to Wonsan in major aerial strikes. Approximately 150 aircraft from three carriers mounted daylong assaults against supply shelters and troop bunkers on the east-central front. A gasoline dump exploded, setting fire to adjacent buildings and causing many secondary explosions.

Other United Nations Command naval planes hit a camouflaged area southwest of Wonsan. In the Chinnampo area, warehouses were attacked. United Nations Command surface vessels continued to bombard Wonsan, silencing enemy shore batteries, scoring hits on personnel bunkers and buildings.

—Eighth Army Communiqué 1,284, covering Thursday's activities:

A reinforced enemy regiment attacked forward positions of the United States First Marine Division shortly after sundown, but the Marines held firm at most points as fighting continued at midnight. Air strikes were directed against enemy occupying Old Baldy throughout the period. Activity elsewhere was limited to routine patrol contacts and minor engagements against United Nations positions. Republic of Korea patrols killed or wounded fifty-six enemy in sharp early morning clashes near Anchor Hill. Enemy artillery and mortars fired 10,234 rounds during the twenty-four hour period ended at 6:00 P.M., 2,300 rounds more than were fired during the preceding twenty-four hours.

Western Sector: Forces totaling an estimated reinforced enemy regiment attacked forward positions of the United States First Marine Division along a five and a half mile front stretching northeastward from Bunker Hill during the early evening hours. The main force of the attack was in regimental strength against positions Reno, Carson and Vegas at the upper portion of the line attacked. Most of the attacking groups were driven back, but heavy fighting continued in the Reno-Carson-Vegas area at midnight.

Sporadic fighting continued on Old Baldy until 3:35 A.M., when United States seventh Infantry Division troops pulled back from the portion of the hill they held following an attack by an enemy battalion which began on the evening of March 23. Air strikes were directed throughout the period against enemy occupying Old Baldy. Two reinforced enemy squads harassing two temporary forward positions southwest of Little Gibralter at 2:38 A.M. were driven back in fifty-eight minutes.

Central sector: Patrols in the eastern portion of the sector fought engagements up to forty-five minutes in length against enemy groups up to two squads in strength. Two enemy squads probed a forward position east of the Pukhan River at 5:40 A.M. and withdrew after a twenty minute fight. Enemy squad size groups harassing two forward positions southwest of Kumsong at 9:25 P.M. were driven off in fifty-five minutes.

Eastern Sector: A Republic of Korea, patrol killed twenty-six enemy and wounded five in three engagements between 2:38 and 5:50 A.M. near Anchor Hill. The largest opposing force was two enemy platoons. A raiding patrol operating south of Anchor Hill killed twenty-five enemy and destroyed five bunkers in a ten minute fight with a platoon ended at 6:40 A.M. Other patrols fought lighter engagements with enemy groups up to two squads in strength. Enemy groups no larger than two squads harassing two forward positions west of the Mundung Valley and two northeast of the Punchbowl between 9:10 and 10:50 P.M. were repulsed in fights up to twenty minutes in length.

†MATTHEWS, DANIEL P.

Rank and Organization: Sergeant, U.S. Marine Corps, Company F, 2d Battalion, 7th Marines, 1st Marine Division (Rein).
Born: December 31, 1931, Van Nuys, California.
Entered Service At: Van Nuys, California.
Place and Date: Vegas Hill, Korea, March 28, 1953.
Citation: For conspicuous gallantry and intrepidity at the risk of his life above and beyond the call of duty while serving as a squad leader of Company F, in action against enemy aggressor forces. Participating in a counterattack against a firmly entrenched and well-concealed hostile force which had repelled 6 previous assaults on a vital enemy held outpost far forward of the main line of resistance, Sgt. Matthews fearlessly advanced in the attack until his squad was pinned down by a murderous sweep of fire from an enemy machine gun located on the peak of the outpost. Observing that the deadly fire prevented a corpsman from removing a wounded

man lying in an open area fully exposed to the brunt of the devastating gunfire, he worked his way to the base of the hostile machine gun emplacement, leaped onto the rock fortification surrounding the gun and, taking the enemy by complete surprise, singlehandedly charged the hostile emplacement with his rifle. Although severely wounded when the enemy brought a withering hail of fire to bear upon him, he gallantly continued his 1-man assault and, firing his rifle with deadly effectiveness, succeeded in killing 2 of the enemy, routing a third, and completely silencing the enemy weapon, thereby enabling his comrades to evacuate the stricken marine to a safe position. Succumbing to his wounds before aid could reach him, Sgt. Matthews, by his indomitable fighting spirit, courageous initiative, and resolute determination in the face of almost certain death, served to inspire all who observed him and was directly instrumental in saving the life of his wounded comrade. His great personal valor reflects the highest credit upon himself and enhances the finest traditions of the U.S. Naval Service. He gallantly gave his life for his country.

OFFICIAL COMMUNIQUÉ:
TOKYO, Sunday, March 29 (AP)
—Far East Naval Forces summary of Friday's operations:

Planes from Task Force 77 unleashed major aerial strikes on targets from behind the eastern front to Wonsan.

Some 150 aircraft from the U.S.S. Oriskany, U.S.S. Philippine Sea, and U.S.S. Princeton mounted day-long assaults against supply shelters and troop bunkers in a three mile stretch of the east-central front. The target was all but obscured when a gasoline dump exploded, set fire to the adjacent buildings, and caused many secondary explosions.

At that same time, eight Panther jets hit a camouflaged area, southwest of Wonsan, leaving it shrouded in palls of smoke. All told, the dive-bombers and fighter-bombers destroyed or damaged 106 buildings and forty-three troop and supply shelters.

Pre-dawn hecklers from the Princeton and Philippine Sea destroyed fourteen trucks and two buildings, damaged three railroad bridges, one highway bridge, five trucks, one boat, and made eight rail cuts.

Night hecklers from the Oriskany hit a train north of Kilchu, blowing up three locomotives. In strafing of twenty-five railroad cars, numerous secondary explosions developed. A locomotive and two cars also were destroyed north of Hamhung.

The cruiser U.S.S. Los Angeles received one hit at Wonsan, which inflicted minor damage and numerous shrapnel holes, but no casualties resulted. The cruiser retaliated with three firing runs that silenced the battery. Later, her bombardment put three direct hits on personnel bunkers, dispersing troops, demolished one building; damaged four trucks; hit a bridge approach, cutting the tracks on each side, and dropped five direct hits on two gun cave positions.

Rejoining the destroyer U.S.S. Hamner at Kosang, the Los Angeles destroyed one bunker, damaged four others and cut trench lines in five spots.

Destroyer U.S.S. Shelton moved into Wonsan after the Los Angeles and Eversole left, putting an unassessed amount of hits on trucks and gun emplacements.

On the west coast of Korea, planes from the carrier U.S.S. Bataan raided warehouses in the Chinnampo area.

Above Songwan, the cruiser H.M.S. Newcastle fired on bunkers, observing many hits, while in the Chodo area, destroyer H.M.C.S. Athabaskan also scored numerous hits on troop billets and gun positions.

—Far East Air Forces summary of Friday's operations:

United Nations fighter-bombers streaming over the western front in day-long assaults, poured more than 175 tons of explosives into Communist positions in the Old Baldy and Bunker Hill areas Friday, while intensified aerial combat saw two enemy MiGs destroyed, two others probably destroyed, and two damaged.

As F.E.A.F. mounted 1,095 sorties, close air support for embattled United Nations ground forces in the western sector continued. A total of 190 fighter-bombers swept in on the Red troops and gun positions, unleashing bombs, napalm and machine-gun fire in the heaviest concentrated one day close-support effort of the year.

In the air, United States Air Force F-86 Sabre jets and Australian Meteor jets teamed to post the victories over the MiGs. The Sabre jets, battling the Russian-built jets in the morning and late afternoon, shot down two, probably destroyed one, an damaged another, in MiG Alley encounters.

Near Sohung, Meteor jets scored twice as they attacked MiGs which were after F-80 Shooting Stars. One MiG was probably destroyed and one damaged in the battle, which marked the deepest southward penetration by MiGs this year.

Elsewhere, F-84 Thunderjets struck troop and supply areas northwest of Chorwon, destroying eight buildings and setting off five secondary explosions. Smoke prevented further assessment of results. South of Yonan, twenty-eight buildings were leveled and ten fires touched off as Marine Corsairs struck a troop and supply area.

B-26 night intruders kept enemy positions on the embattled western front under aerial bombardment after dark, striking troop and supply build-ups and combat positions electronically.

South of Kyomipo, one locomotive was damaged, and three cars destroyed and five damaged. On the east coast, one locomotive was damaged at Hamhung, with damage inflicted on a locomotive and two cars south of Kilchu.

B-29 Superforts struck the east coast supply system for the fifth successive night, bombing two material storage areas south of Hamhung. Six mediums hit a twenty-five acre target at Suhung while seven struck a thirty-five acre installation at Tong, one mile south. The Superforts were opposed by meager ground fire.

One B-29 added ten tons of high explosives to the western front air support effort, bombing bunkers and mortar positions in the vicinity of Old Baldy.

Cargo transports of F.E.A.F.'s 315th Air Division airlifted 570 tons of supplies and personnel in support of United Nations forces.

—Eighth Army Communiqué 1,285, covering Friday's activities:

Counter-attacking United States Marines reoccupied Vegas Hill after an eight hour battle and were mopping up against resistance from a group of enemy still on the hill at midnight. Activity elsewhere was relatively light. Enemy artillery and mortars fired 40,832 rounds during the twenty-four hour period ended at 6:00 P.M., about four times the number fired during the preceding twenty-four hours.

Western Sector: Fighting continued in the area west of Korangpo where United States Marines counter-attacked to regain control of Vegas, one of two positions yielded on the night of March 26, when a reinforced enemy regiment attacked ten Marine forward positions along a five-and-a-half mile front. The Marines reoccupied the position at 7:30 P.M. after an eight hour battle, but were still meeting resistance from enemy remaining as they consolidated on the position. Enemy groups up to two squads in strength harassing three positions southeast and south of Panmunjom between 8:30 P.M. and midnight were driven off in fire fights up to fifteen minutes in length. Enemy of undetermined strength attacked a temporary forward position north of Little Gibralter at 8:30 P.M. and the occupying troops fell back after a ten minute fight. Patrols fought briefly with small enemy groups. Air and artillery strikes continued on enemy forces occupying Old Baldy.

Central Sector: One patrol killed nine enemy in a ten minute pre-dawn fight with two reinforced platoons southeast of Pyonggang. Other patrols fought engagements up to thirty minutes in length with enemy groups up to two squads in strength. An enemy squad harassing Rocky Point positions at 10:25 P.M. was driven off in eighteen minutes.

Eastern Sector: Enemy groups up to a reinforced squad in strength harassing forward positions in the Punchbowl area at 5:20 A.M. and 11:25, 11:30, and 11:45 P.M., were repulsed in fire fights up to fifteen minutes in length. A raiding patrol killed an estimated twenty-one enemy in an encounter with an enemy platoon near Anchor Hill shortly after midnight. Other patrols fought engagements up to fifteen minutes in length with enemy groups up to a platoon in strength.

—United Nations Command communiqué 1,568, for the twenty-four hours to 6:00 A.M., Sunday, Korean time:

Fighting continued Saturday for positions on Vegas Hill in the western sector of the Korean battlefront as United Nations Command troops launched a series of attacks to secure the remainder of the hill. From 0400 hours until early afternoon, our forces, in a series of attacks, supported by artillery, mortar, tank, and air bombardment, forced the enemy from the area. By 1300 hours, the position was reported secure and an afternoon enemy counter-effort was repulsed.

Another enemy attack in reinforced battalion strength was made early Saturday night. Fighting continued for more than six hours, with both sides reinforcing, before the enemy was driven off with heavy casualties.

Other western front action was noted in delayed reports describing a number of small enemy probes during the night of 27-28 March, against three forward United Nations Command positions. All were unsuccessful. During the same night, similar small enemy units probed United Nations Command advance posts near Rocky Point in the west-central sector and near the Punchbowl in the east-central portion of the front. The actions were brief and all enemy efforts were repelled.

United Nations Command fighter-bombers hammered three troop and supply centers immediately in rear of the battle line, while others flew close support missions, mostly in the Old Baldy and Bunker Hill areas. Rear area strikes by fighter-bombers disrupted enemy rail and road networks in central North Korea.

Medium bomber efforts were concentrated on a marshaling yard at Sariwon and the Ponse supply area northwest of Kaesong. Night intruders and other mediums pounded front-line enemy positions.

Carrier-based planes of the United Nations Command fleet struck along the east coast, from Songjin south to the front. Surface elements attacked other front-line positions near Kosong on the east coast and Chaeryong in the west.

†BARKER, CHARLES H.

Rank and Organization: Private First Class (then Pvt.), U.S. Army, Company K, 17th Infantry Regiment, 7th Infantry Division.
Born: April 12, 1935, Pickens County, South Carolina.
Entered Service At: Pickens County, South Carolina.
Place and Date: Near Sokkogae, Korea, June 4, 1953.
Citation: Pfc. Barker, a member of Company K, distinguished himself by conspicuous gallantry and indomitable courage above and beyond the call of duty in action against the enemy. While participating in a combat patrol engaged in screening an approach to "Pork-Chop Outpost," Pfc. Barker and his companions surprised and engaged an enemy group digging emplacements on the slope. Totally unprepared, the hostile troops sought cover. After ordering Pfc. Barker and a comrade to lay down a base of fire, the patrol leader maneuvered the remainder of the platoon to a vantage point on higher ground. Pfc. Barker moved to an open

area firing his rifle and hurling grenades on the hostile positions. As enemy action increased in volume and intensity, mortar bursts fell on friendly positions, ammunition was in critical supply, and the platoon was ordered to withdraw into a perimeter defense preparatory to moving back to the outpost. Voluntarily electing to cover the retrograde movement, he gallantly maintained a defense and was last seen in close hand-to-hand combat with the enemy. Pfc. Barker's unflinching courage, consummate devotion to duty, and supreme sacrifice enabled the patrol to complete the mission and effect an orderly withdrawal to friendly lines, reflecting lasting glory upon himself and upholding the highest traditions of the military service.

OFFICIAL COMMUNIQUÉ:
TOKYO, Friday, June 5 (AP)
—Far East Air Forces summary of Wednesday's operations:

United States Air Force jet and prop-driven fighter-bombers, along with land-based Marine aircraft, mounted 295 sorties against Red battle line positions during the day Wednesday, and after dark, B-29 Superforts and B-26 light bombers rammed more than 200 additional tons of bombs into the Red lines.

As F.E.A.F. totaled 665 sorties, United Nations aircraft, paced by United States Air Force F-84 Thunderjets, smashed enemy positions, troop concentrations and supply build-ups all along and behind the front, but low-hanging clouds obscured most of the destruction.

United States Air Force F-86 Sabre jets coursed deeper into North Korea in their dual role as fighter interceptors and fighter-bombers. The bomb-carrying Sabres destroyed twelve buildings in a troop concentration south of Sukchon, but the MiG hunters did not fare so well, no MiG-15s were sighted.

After dark, B-29 Superforts from the Okinawa-based Nineteenth Bomb Wing unleashed 190 tons of bombs into enemy front-line positions at the base of the Iron Triangle between Kumhwa and the battle line north of Chorwon. The nineteen Superforts sent against the battle line marked the largest front-line strike by B-29s in almost a year.

Night attacking B-26 Invaders also struck battle line positions, with unobserved results, and destroyed sixty-six enemy supply vehicles along Red supply routes.

Observed destruction for the period includes fifteen buildings destroyed and fifteen damaged, five bunkers, and ten gun positions damaged, five automatic weapons positions destroyed, and fifteen personnel shelters destroyed and five damaged.

Cargo transports for F.E.A.F.'s 315th Air Division airlifted 545 tons of personnel and cargo in continued logistical support of United Nations forces.

—Far East Naval Forces summary of Thursday's operations:

Marine Checkerboard pilots from the escort carrier U.S.S. Bairoko blasted supply areas along the west coast as they ranged from Ongjin to Songhwa.

Near Ongjin, the pilots destroyed eleven supply buildings and damaged fifteen others. Another four buildings west of Taetan were crumpled as Marine pilots dumped tons of explosives on targets.

In the Songhwa area, three buildings were destroyed when a large secondary explosion engulfed the structures. Other strikes reported several good hits scored on gun positions.

In surface action in the Yellow Sea, patrol frigate H.M.S. Morecambe Bay received approximately ten rounds from enemy shore battery south of Chinnampo but evaded them all.

Coastal positions in the same area were pounded by fire and rockets from a rocket-launching ship.

The destroyer U.S.S. Hammer in action near Kosong accounted for destruction of one gun position while damaging three others. She also destroyed two bunkers and damaged another.

H.M.C.S. Haida fired on two supply trains north of Tanchon. Damage was not assessable.

—Eighth Army communiqué 1,353, covering Wednesday's activities:

Heavy fighting continued Wednesday in the eastern sector, with continued actions going on at Luke's Castle and Anchor Hill. Just before midnight, R.O.K.s launched two counter-attacks against outposts west of Finger Ridge which were lost to the Chinese during the intense action of May 27, and 28. Elsewhere across the Eighth Army front, action was comparatively light, with infrequent patrol clashes. The enemy fired a total of 17,149 rounds of artillery and mortar on Allied positions during the twenty-four hour period ended at 6:00 P.M., a decrease of over 25,000 from the previous twenty-four hour period.

Western sector: There were five light enemy harassing actions against forward Allied positions. Two were south of Panmunjom at 10:45 P.M. and 11:30 P.M.. One was in the vicinity of Big Nori at 5:30 A.M.. All were repulsed after brief encounters.

Central sector: R.O.K. troops launched counter-attacks against two outpost positions west of Finger Ridge which were lost to the Chinese on May 27. At midnight, the counter-attacks were still under way. Sniper Ridge was engaged by an enemy squad for seven minutes at 1:28 A.M.. Two enemy platoons engaged a front-line position southwest of Jane Russell at 11:15. The enemy was driven off in an hour long fire fight. Twelve Chinese were killed or wounded in the action. Eighth Army patrols skirmished briefly to twenty-nine minutes with enemy groups ranging from six to platoon in size.

Eastern sector: A successful R.O.K. counter-attack drove the enemy from positions on Luke's Castle at 6:30 A.M., but the North Koreans came back with a counter-attack of their own at 10:30 A.M.. Fighting in the area continued all day. At 10:20 P.M., a reinforced enemy company renewed the assault against an outpost just forward of the main hill position. Friendly defenders were forced back and action slackened just at the close of the period at midnight. At 4:00 A.M., two enemy platoons occupied the crest of Anchor Hill on the extreme eastern front. Friendly troops reinforced their positions just below the crest, but had been unable to eject the enemy by 12:40 P.M.. At 7:55 P.M., the R.O.K.s counter-attacked, and at 11;00 P.M., had forced the enemy onto the edge of a near by hill position. Action continued at midnight. South of Anchor Hill, two enemy squads probed an outpost position for twenty-five minutes and then withdrew. An enemy platoon engaged an outpost southeast of Christmas Hill at 9:20 P.M.. Twenty-two Chinese were killed or wounded in the thirty minute fire fight before the enemy withdrew. Allied patrol contacts were infrequent.

—United Nations Command communiqué 1,636, for the twenty-four hours to 6:00 A.M., Friday, Korean time:

Heavy fighting continued in the central and eastern sectors during the period as battles raged for control of several outpost positions. In the central sector, United Nations Command forces withdrew from an outpost that had been regained Thursday. Strong friendly counter-attacks against the position and one other in the same area continued.

Successive United Nations Command counter-attacks against five enemy-held positions in the Finger Ridge area have been unsuccessful. Enemy forces suffered heavy casualties as bitter fighting continued in the area.

Other central sector actions included an unsuccessful two-squad enemy probe of a friendly outpost early Thursday. Late the night of June 3, an estimated enemy platoon hit friendly positions north of Kumhwa, but was repulsed after an hour of fighting.

In the eastern sector, an unsuccessful counter-attack was launched by friendly forces against Anchor Hill. Bitter fighting continues with heavy artillery and mortar fire employed by both sides.

The Luke's Castle area was marked by successive counter-attacks launched by both friendly and enemy forces, with no decision gained by either side.

Three enemy probes of small friendly outposts were repulsed Thursday in other actions in the area.

Carrier-based aircraft of the United Nations Command fleet blasted supply areas along the west coast as they ranged from Ongjin to Songhwa. Eleven supply buildings were destroyed and fifteen damaged. Another four buildings west of Taetan were crumpled. In the Songhwa area, three structures were engulfed by a large fire. Other strikes scored hits on gun positions.

A surface vessel in the Yellow Sea received approximately ten rounds from enemy shore batteries south of Chinnampo, but evaded them all. Coastal positions in the same area were pounded by a United Nations Command rocket-loading ship.

Near Kosong, on the east coast, surface units destroyed or damaged gun positions and bunkers. Two enemy trains were fired on north of Tanchon.

United Nations Command fighter-bombers slammed explosives into the enemy battle line throughout the day, mounting more than 200 daylight sorties in support of friendly ground forces. Heaviest air support came in the central and eastern sectors. Medium bombers at night hit the battleline with 190 tons of explosives for the second consecutive night. Night intruders also smashed enemy combat positions, bombing the battle line electronically after dark.

MIZE, OLA L.

Rank and Organization: Master Sergeant (then Sgt.), U.S. Army, Company K, 15th Infantry Regiment, 3d Infantry Division.
Born: August 28, 1931, Marshall County, Alabama.
Entered Service At: Gadsden, Alabama.
Place and Date: Near Surang-ni, Korea, June 10 to 11, 1953.
Citation: M/Sgt. Mize, a member of Company K, distinguished himself by conspicuous gallantry and outstanding courage above and beyond the call of duty in action against the enemy. Company K was committed to the defense of "Outpost Harry", a strategically valuable position, when the enemy launched a heavy attack. Learning that a comrade on a friendly listening post had been wounded he moved through the intense barrage, accompanied by a medical aid man, and rescued the wounded soldier. On returning to the main position, he established an effective defense system and inflicted heavy casualties against attacks from determined enemy assault forces which had penetrated into the trenches within the outpost area. During his fearless actions he was blown down by artillery and grenade blasts 3 times but each time he dauntlessly returned to his position, tenaciously fighting and successfully repelling hostile attacks. When enemy onslaughts ceased, he took his few men and moved from bunker to bunker, firing through apertures and throwing grenades at the foe, neutralizing their positions. When an enemy soldier stepped out behind a comrade, prepared to fire, M/Sgt. Mize killed him, saving the life of his fellow soldier. After rejoining the platoon, moving from man to man, distributing ammunition and shouting words of encouragement, he observed a friendly machine gun position overrun. He immediately fought his way to the position, killing 10 of the enemy and dispersing the remainder. Fighting back to the command post, and finding several friendly wounded there, he took a position to protect them. Later, securing a radio, he directed friendly artillery fire upon the attacking enemy's routes of approach. At dawn he helped regroup for a counterattack which successfully drove the enemy from the outpost. M/Sgt. Mize's valorous conduct and unflinching courage reflect lasting glory upon himself and uphold the noble traditions of the military service.

OFFICIAL COMMUNIQUÉ:
TOKYO, Friday, June 12 (AP)
—Far East Air Forces summary of Thursday's operations:

United States Air Force F-84 Thunderjets and bomb-carrying F-86 Sabre jets struck Communist air-fields at Kanggye and Sunchon Wednesday, in improved weather, while other fighter-bombers concentrated against enemy supply and personnel build-ups near Chinnampo and in the Haeju Peninsula.

F.E.A.F. aircraft mounted 1,245 sorties, more than double those of the previous twenty-four hour period, as the fighter-bombers and B-26 light bombers swept over targets behind covering Sabre jets, which destroyed three MiG-15s and probably destroyed another.

Thunderjets cratered the sod runway at Suchon Airfield in four places while Sabre jets scored five cuts in the taxiway at Kanggye. Four revetments and four buildings were also destroyed by the Sabre jets, but other results were unobserved.

The Thunderjets also damaged three rail bridges in the western peninsula supply network and one rail bridge spanning the Chongchon River near Sinanju. Two more rail bridges were damaged by Thunderjets between Sariwon and Kyomipo.

South of Haeju, Thunderjets destroyed four buildings in a troop center while Royal Australian Air Force Meteor jets dropped bombs and napalm into a marshaling yard northwest of Chinnampo.

B-26 light bombers attacked enemy positions around the clock, striking both day and night all across the 155-mile battle line.

After dark, the light bombers destroyed fifty-eight enemy supply vehicles and struck a marshaling yard at Singo-san with unobserved results.

B-29 Superforts bombed two Red airfields, one at Sinuiju and the other at Uiju, both on the south bank of the Yalu River. Returning crewmen reported moderate to intense flak and four firing passes by enemy fighter aircraft, but added that "excellent" bomb runs were accomplished.

One additional Superfort bombed battle-line positions without opposition.

—Far East Naval Forces summary of Thursday's operations:

The destroyer U.S.S. Wiltsie dueled with enemy shore batteries at Wonsan during the period receiving one hit on her starboard side. Shrapnel caused superficial damage but no casualties resulted. The destroyer silenced the gun position with a barrage of counter-battery fire. In other action, her 5-inch guns dispersed a group of sampans in the vicinity.

Navy planes from three Task Force 77 carriers hammered front-line positions in close support of United Nations troops.

Early morning strikes from the carriers U.S.S. Boxer and U.S.S. Philippine Sea and U.S.S. Princeton unloaded tons of high explosives in the Pyonggang area, destroying six mortar positions, three artillery positions, one cave and fifteen personnel shelters.

Later morning strikes destroyed at least 400 yards of trench and numerous bunkers as secondary explosions erupted.

Panther jets leveled a cluster of twelve buildings near Wonsan and wiped out fourteen personnel shelters.

Other flights continued blasting front-line positions throughout the day, and accounted for total destruction of one truck, twelve buildings, four gun positions, eleven bunkers, forty-three personnel shelters, thirty-three mortars, three caves, and 1,100 yards of trench.

Damaged were one highway bridge, four buildings, seven bunkers, ten personnel shelters, eight mortars, two caves, 600 yards of trench.

Artillery positions, bunkers, and supply areas in the vicinity of Kosong took a heavy beating from the guns of the heavy cruiser U.S.S. St. Paul and her destroyer escort U.S.S. Prichett. The two ships lobbed shells into the coastal positions from before dawn to late morning. Troop concentrations and personnel bunkers along the main supply route also were blasted.

British pilots from the carrier H.M.S. Glory flew a total of seventy-six sorties, blasting enemy gun positions, buildings, and rail facilities. Near Chongdan and important rail bridge was completely destroyed, while in the Taetan area two buildings were destroyed and two others damaged. Several gun positions also were reported knocked out.

Other planes ranged inland near the front lines to blast troops at Yonchon. One hundred yards of trench line were destroyed and at least ten troops were killed. Other strikes centered at Haeju where pilots destroyed one gun position and damaged another.

In Yellow Sea surface action, a Landhing Ship Medium (rockets) destroyed two buildings and started several fires near Kumsan. Several coastal gun positions in the area were neutralized as the ship scored good coverage resulting in a secondary explosion. Two fires also were reported among bunkers.

In the Taetan area, the H.M.S. Sparrow shelled enemy shore batteries.

—United Nations Command communiqué 1643, for the twenty-four hour to 6:00 A.M., Friday, Korean time:

Bitter fighting in the Outpost Texas and Christmas Hill areas in the east-central sector of the Korean battle front continued during the period. United Nations Command forces launched a counter-attack at approximately 0730 hours Thursday against a hostile regiment which had penetrated United Nations Command positions in the Outpost Texas area earlier that morning. A raging see-saw battle ensued, and was still continuing Friday morning.

Another friendly counter-attack at approximately 1200 hours Thursday hit positions which had been penetrated by two enemy battalions in the Outpost Texas vicinity in the morning. Friendly forces met heavy resistance, but were advancing slowly Friday morning as the action continued.

Friendly forward positions northeast of Chorwon in the west-central sector were attacked by two hostile battalions early Friday. By 0530 hours, the enemy force had withdrawn after suffering heavy casualties, but heavy enemy artillery and mortar fire continued in the area.

A hostile battalion attack in the Iron Triangle area was hurled back early Thursday morning after a two and one-half hour attack. In the Sniper's Ridge area of the west-central front, an estimated three enemy companies attacked friendly positions late Thursday night.

After almost six hours of heavy fighting, the enemy force was repulsed.

Slightly to the west of this action, a hostile company hit another friendly position at about the same time. This attack was thrown back after approximately two and one-half hours of fighting.

Late the night of June 10, a friendly position near Old Baldy in the western sector was attacked by an estimated two enemy platoons. The hostile attack was repulsed after a brief action.

Carrier based planes of the United Nations Command fleet hammered enemy front-line positions in close support of United Nations Command troops and dropped tons of explosives in the Pyongyang area, destroying numerous buildings, bunkers, caves, and mortar positions. An important rail bridge near Chongdan also was destroyed. Other scattered targets were blasted at Taetan and Yonchon.

Surface elements concentrated on artillery positions, bunkers, and supply areas in the vicinity of Kosong on the east coast. In a duel with enemy shore batteries at Wonsan, a friendly vessel received one hit from hostile fire. No casualties were suffered, and the enemy fire was silenced.

In Yellow Sea surface action, coastal gun batteries were shelled near Kumsan.

Land-based fighter-bombers hit two hostile airfields deep in North Korea and another field near Haeju, and bombed buildings and a marshaling yard in the Sariwon area. Light bombers made day and night assaults, hammering battle line positions during the day and destroying enemy supply vehicles after dark. Medium bombers struck two enemy airfields in northwest North Korea.

†SHEA, RICHARD T., JR.

Rank and Organization: First Lieutenant, U.S. Army, Company A, 17th Infantry Regiment, 7th Infantry Division.
Born: January 3, 1927, Portsmouth, Virginia.
Entered Service At: Portsmouth, Virginia.
Place and Date: Near Sokkogae, Korea, July 6 to 8, 1953.
Citation: 1st Lt. Shea, executive officer of Company A, distinguished himself by conspicuous gallantry and indomitable courage above and beyond the call of duty in action against the enemy. On the night of July 6, he was supervising the reinforcement of defensive positions when the enemy attacked with great numerical superiority. Voluntarily proceeding to the area most threatened, he organized and led a counterattack and, in the bitter fighting which ensued, closed with and killed 2 hostile soldiers with his trench knife. Calmly moving among the men, checking positions, steadying and urging the troops to hold firm, he fought side-by-side with them throughout the night. Despite heavy losses, the hostile force pressed the assault with determination, and at dawn made an all-out attempt to overrun friendly elements. Charging forward to meet the challenge, 1st Lt. Shea and his gallant men drove back the hostile troops. Elements of Company G joined the defense on the afternoon of July 7, having lost key personnel through casualties. Immediately integrating these troops into his unit, 1st Lt. Shea rallied a group of 20 men and again charged the enemy. Although wounded in this action, he refused evacuation and continued to lead the counterattack. When the assaulting element was pinned down by heavy machine gun fire, he personally rushed the emplacement and, firing his carbine and lobbing grenades with deadly accuracy, neutralized the weapon and killed 3 of the enemy. With forceful leadership and by his heroic example, 1st Lt. Shea coordinated and directed a holding action throughout the night and the following morning. On July 8, the enemy attacked again. Despite additional wounds, he launched a determined counterattack and was last seen in close hand-to-hand combat with the enemy. 1st Lt. Shea's inspirational leadership and unflinching courage set an illustrious example of valor to the men of his regiment, reflecting lasting glory upon himself and upholding the noble traditions of the military service.

OFFICIAL COMMUNIQUÉ:
TOKYO, Thursday, July 9 (AP)
—Far East Air Forces summary of Tuesday's operations:

Despite low clouds and scattered rain showers, United States Air Force F-84 Thunderjets and B-26 light bombers teamed with Marine Panther jets Tuesday to rain nearly 200 tons of bombs into enemy positions on and near the battle line in close air support of United Nations ground forces.

Blanketing clouds and rain storms covered major portions of North Korea throughout the day, limiting F-86 Sabre jet activity to four patrol sweeps through MiG Alley where no enemy aircraft were sighted. F.E.A.F. flew 410 sorties.

Thunderjets flew to the east-central front at noon to bomb positions near Kumsong, and Panther jets assaulted Red fortifications in North Korea later in the day, but results of both attacks were unobserved. B-26s attacked frontal positions in the west and central sectors, but again results were unobserved.

North of the battle line, F-84s and Panther jets attacked enemy strong points providing rear area support for the Communist front.

Night flying B-26s continued the close support strikes, bombing entrenched enemy positions in the west, west-central, and central sectors. Other B-26s hit a marshaling yard south of Wonsan and pounded supply convoys, destroying seventy-one vehicles.

Sixteen B-29 Superforts flew north of the Chongchon River Tuesday night to bomb a 117 acre supply complex and marshaling yard at Namsi. Meager flak, firing passes by enemy fighters, and search lights opposed the four-engine bombers as they rained 500-pound bombs into the logistical complex.

One B-29 for Okinawa unleashed ten tons of bombs on enemy central sector battle line targets with unobserved results.

—Far East Naval Forces summary of Thursday's operations:

Task Force 77 planes struck from the front lines to the Chosin Reservoir, as bombarding ships pounded both coasts and carrier-base Marine airmen raided the west coast.

Planes from the aircraft carriers U.S.S. Princeton and U.S.S. Boxer flew through low overcast to hit Red positions on the eastern front. A group of Princeton pilots scored the biggest kill of the day when they bombed the No. 2 hydroelectric plant at the Chosin Reservoir. Panther jets made three direct hits on vital equipment and put the plant out of commission.

Early morning hecklers from both carriers ranged from Wonsan to Kosong, destroying three trucks. Other damage could not be observed due to low-hanging clouds.

On the east-central front, Princeton Skyraiders struck T-Bone Hill while Corsairs bombed Christmas Hill and set off two secondary explosions.

An afternoon flight of jets hit supply dumps in the enemy rear area. Near Hamhung, on the east coast, other jet pilots hit a marshaling yard and destroyed several boxcars.

On Capitol Hill, Skyraiders destroyed five large buildings and strafed enemy trenches.

Panther jets from the Boxer destroyed an important highway bridge north of the front. They also struck supply buildings and vehicles.

Six Corsairs from the Boxer started a huge oil fire near Kumsong. Panther jets destroyed six gun positions south of Wonsan with point-blank rocket fire and damaged twelve others.

On the east coast, slightly north of the battle line, the battleship U.S.S. New Jersey destroyed two bunkers and damaged four others before heavy weather closed in to obscure the target. The ship also fired on two gun positions, and tore up twenty yards of trench line.

Also bombarding the east coast was the destroyer U.S.S. Stephen Potter. The ship destroyed two bunkers, damaged one, and ripped up ten yards of trench line near Kosong.

The cruisers U.S.S. Manchester and U.S.S. Bremerton also bombarded Red positions near Kosong.

Damage done by the ships was not observed, but they fired on gun positions, supply areas, and personnel shelters.

The destroyer U.S.S. Wiltsie covering minesweeper operations by the U.S.S. Symbol, north of Wonsan, clashed with shore batteries. Neither the minesweeper nor the destroyer was damaged by the enemy fire as the Wiltsie scored a direct hit and silenced the Red guns.

Marine pilots from the escort carrier U.S.S. Bairoko in the Yellow Sea bombed and strafed the Communists from Chinnampo south to the front lines. The Polkadot squadron destroyed twenty buildings at Changyon and damaged a heavy gun position south of the city. Six more buildings were destroyed and cuts were scored in trench lines. Near the western end of the front lines, the twelve-plane flight pounded mortar and artillery positions with unobserved results. Seven more buildings were destroyed west of Haeju.

South of Chinnampo, United Nations surface vessels bombarded gun positions and bunkers. A rocket landing ship made eighty-four hits on bunker areas near Sogwan. H.M.S. Cossack scored a direct hit on a coastal battery near by.

—Eighth Army communiqué covering Tuesday's activities:

Fighting continued all day Tuesday in the Porkchop area of the western front and at outpost positions near Arrowhead, in the central sector. New action broke out against western front Outposts Berlin and

East Berlin when an unknown number of Chinese hit both positions just before midnight. As the reporting period

closed at midnight, heavy fighting was reported in all three areas. Elsewhere across the Eighth Army front, frequent patrol clashes were reported, but the intensity of the patrol fights was relatively light. The enemy fired 32,657 rounds of artillery and mortar on Allied positions during the twenty-four hour period ended at 6:00 P.M..

Western sector: An unknown number of enemy attacked Outpost Berlin and East Berlin at 11:45 P.M.. At midnight, heavy fighting was continuing. Heavy fighting also continued on Outpost Porkchop, with enemy forces estimated at one battalion holding the eastern and western fingers of Porkchop at 2:30 A.M.. Fighting for possession of the outpost continued until 11:50 A.M., with both forces increasing their numbers, the enemy forces reinforcing to two battalions. By 1:45 P.M., the Seventh Division infantrymen, supported by artillery, had chased the Chinese from the crest and the forward and eastern slopes of Porkchop, with the enemy holding fifty percent of the western portion of the outpost.

Seventh Division troops at 8:25 P.M., counter-attacked the Chinese on the west slope, and at last report, the enemy was surrounded and action was continued on two outpost positions in the vicinity of Arrowhead Ridge, with hand-to-hand combat reported at 12:50 A.M., between Second R.O.K. troops and Chinese on the western outpost. Fighting continued to be intense with both forces engaging in fierce hand-to-hand fighting and artillery duels for possession of the two outposts until 8:10 A.M., when the Second R.O.K. troop pushed the Chinese to the northern slopes of the outpost positions. Action, until the end of the period, continued from sporadic to intense, with the Chinese still holding the northern slopes of both outpost positions. As of 6:00 P.M., Tuesday, the enemy hurled 8,500 rounds of artillery and mortar into the two outposts, and 170 enemy were reported killed or wounded. Eighth Army patrols clashed briefly to one hour and five minutes, with enemy groups ranging from six man to platoon in size.

Eastern sector: Light enemy jabs at forward positions were turned back southwest of Christmas Hill at 4:10 and 5:10 A.M., west of the Mundung Valley at 11:30 P.M., near Sandbag Castle at 11:05 P.M., and northeast of Luke's Castle at 2:40 A.M.. Eighth Army patrols, including three raiding groups, fought five to fifteen minute skirmishes against enemy groups up to platoon in size.

—United Nations Command communiqué 1,670 for the twenty-four hours to 6:00 A.M., Thursday, Korean time:

After a raging battle Wednesday at Outposts Berlin and East Berlin, United Nations Command troops hurled attacking enemy forces from those positions early in the afternoon and repulsed fresh enemy attacks against the same positions early Thursday morning.

Earlier, an unknown number of enemy had occupied East Berlin and engaged United Nations Command forces on Berlin in vicious close-in fighting. Friendly forces sprung a counter-attack against East Berlin a short time later, and after a fight lasting more than an hour, reoccupied the positions. Action on both outposts continues, but after two more friendly counter-attacks, the enemy was forced to withdraw at approximately 12:30 P.M..

Early Thursday, both the outposts were again hit, each by an estimated enemy company. The attacks were thrown back after engagements lasting more than two hours.

At Outpost Porkchop, United Nations Command units counter-attacked at approximately 3:40 A.M. Wednesday against the enemy-held portions of the hill, and reached the crest about one and one-half hours later. An unknown number of enemy attacked friendly forces there as United Nations Command reinforcements were held up by enemy artillery and mortar fire. The enemy also attempted to reinforce late last night, but was stopped by a deadly friendly artillery bombardment, and action became sporadic. Early Thursday, the friendly counter-attacking force was engaging hostile elements in small arms fire as the action continued.

Arrowhead Ridge positions, which have been under enemy attack, were still in control of United Nations Command troops as action was continuing. At the southwest position on Arrowhead, the enemy had disengaged early Wednesday morning, but renewed the attack late at night. A reinforced enemy company assault lasted almost an hour before it retired, only to renew the attack a short time later. Early Thursday, the enemy had disengaged, but was still in the area.

On the northeast position of Arrowhead, United Nations Command troops counter-attacked early Wednesday, and closed to furious hand-to-hand fighting at approximately 6:00 A.M..

About one and one-half hours later, the enemy began to disengage and by 10:30 A.M., action had ceased. Late Wednesday night, however, an estimated enemy company again attacked. Early Thursday, the enemy was under heavy friendly artillery fire as the action continued.

In the east-central sector of the battle front, several attacks hit friendly positions in an area approximately one and one-half miles southwest of Mundung late the night of July 7, and early Wednesday, according to delayed reports. An estimated thirty-five enemy hit a United Nations Command outpost there late the night of July 7, and was thrown back about half an hour later.

Early Wednesday morning, in the same area, an enemy squad, built up to a reinforced company a short time later, also was thrown back after one and one-half hours of fighting.

Late at night, an enemy battalion, supported by heavy artillery and mortar fire, attacked an outpost in the same area and was thrown back after a three and one-half hour battle. Another enemy battalion took up the assault later and action was continuing at the close of the period. Preliminary reports showed heavy casualties had been inflicted on the enemy.

Carrier-based planes of the United Nations Command bombed an enemy hydroelectric plant near the Chosin (Changjin) Reservoir, struck a number of enemy-held hills along the front, and blasted supply areas and a hostile marshaling yard near Hamhung. Fleet aircraft also hammered gun positions south of Wonsan, supply buildings and gun positions in the Changyon area, and buildings west of Haeju.

Surface elements bombarded bunkers, gun positions, and trench lines near Kosong, shore batteries between Hungnam and Wonsan, and bunkers and other positions near Sogwan.

Weather limited land-based aerial operations to fighter-bomber assaults on enemy front-line positions. After dark, intruders attacked a hostile marshaling yard north of Wonsan, destroyed enemy supply vehicles, and hammered front-line positions. Medium bombers pounded supply areas and battle line positions.

†SCHOONOVER, DAN D.

Rank and Organization: Corporal, U.S, Army, Company A, 13th Engineer Combat Battalion, 7th Infantry Division.

Born: October 8, 1933, Boise, Idaho.

Entered Service At: Boise, Idaho.

Place and Date: Near Sokkogae, Korea, July 8 to 10, 1953.

Citation: Cpl. Schoonover distinguished himself by conspicuous gallantry and outstanding courage above and beyond the call of duty in action against the enemy. He was in charge of an engineer demolition squad attached to an infantry company which was committed to dislodge the enemy from a vital hill. Realizing that the heavy fighting and the intense enemy fire made it impossible to carry out his mission, he voluntarily employed his unit as a rifle squad and, forging up the steep barren slope, participated in the assault on hostile positions. When an artillery round exploded on the roof of an enemy bunker, he courageously ran forward and leaped into the position, killing 1 hostile infantryman and taking another prisoner. Later in the action, when friendly forces were pinned down by vicious fire from another enemy bunker, he dashed through the hail of fire, hurled grenades into the nearest aperture, then ran to the doorway and emptied his pistol, killing the remainder of the enemy. His brave action neutralized the position and enabled friendly troops to continue their advance to the crest of the hill. When the enemy counterattacked he constantly exposed himself to the heavy bombardment to direct the fire of his men and to call in an effective artillery barrage on hostile forces. Although the company was relieved the following morning, he voluntarily remained in the area, manned a machine gun for several hours, and subsequently joined another assault on enemy emplacements. When last seen he was operating an automatic rifle with devastating effect until mortally wounded by artillery fire. Cpl. Schoonover's heroic leadership during 2 days of heavy fighting, superb personal bravery, and willing self-sacrifice inspired his comrades and saved many lives, reflecting lasting glory upon himself and upholding the honored traditions of the military service.

OFFICIAL COMMUNIQUÉ:
TOKYO, Saturday, July 11 (AP)
—Far East Air Forces summary of Thursday's operations:

United States Air Force F-84 Thunderjets and B-26 light bombers winged over the cloud-bound Korean peninsula to bomb Communist positions in the Porkchop, Arrowhead, and Old Baldy sectors Thursday. B-29 Superforts joined the light bombers after dark, and enemy air installation and supply routes deeper in North Korea were bombed.

Weather again hampered aerial activities, limiting F.E.A.F. aircraft to 415 sorties. F-86 Sabre jets coursed MiG Alley, but no MiG-15s were engaged for the ninth straight day.

Thunderjets and B-26s rammed high explosives into the front, but results were unobserved.

After dark, fifteen United States Air Force B-29 Superforts flew from Okinawa to rain bombs into a pair of Red airfields and battle line positions. Seven Superforts unleashed seventy tons of bombs against the Taechon airfield, north of Sinanju, while four medium bombers struck another airfield at Namsi, northwest of Sinanju. Four additional Superforts slammed high explosives into Communist battle line positions.

The attacking bombers were opposed by meager to intense flak over the two airfields and search lights over Taechon. The battle line strikes were unopposed.

Also after dark, B-26 light bombers destroyed twenty-five enemy supply vehicles on Red supply routes and inflicted six road cuts.

Jet aircraft patrolled North Korean skies throughout the day, reporting on unchanging weather conditions.

Cargo transports of F.E.A.F.'s 315th Air Division airlifted 510 tons of personnel and supplies in continued logistical support of United Nations forces.

—Far East Naval Forces summary of Friday's operations:

The 16-inch guns of the battleship U.S.S. New Jersey sent giant salvos ranging far inland during the period to blast five different supply and personnel shelters in the Kosong-Kojo areas.

Pea-soup fog prevented damage assessment by spotters, but targets fired on contained at least seventy-three supply and personnel shelters and buildings. One steel bridge, a vehicle bridge, and camouflaged buildings also were fired on.

Afternoon flights from the carriers U.S.S. Boxer and U.S.S. Princeton made radar-controlled drops of ordinance near Capitol Hill as they blasted front-line positions despite heavy fog.

Other aerial activity centered near Wonsan, where the Task Force 77 pilots strafed a large formation of Communist trucks before returning again to furnish close air support to hard-pressed United Nations troops.

Destroyer U.S.S. Lofberg in the Wonsan area silenced one active gun position.

—Eighth Army communiqué, covering Thursday's operations:

Day-long fighting continued Thursday on Outpost Porkchop on the western front, and the two outposts in the vicinity of Arrowhead in the central sector. However, fighting had ceased on Outposts Berlin and East Berlin, and at an Allied outpost position west of the Mundung valley. Elsewhere across the Eighth Army front, there were frequent patrol clashes, with the heaviest fighting occurring in central and eastern sectors. The enemy fired 84,442 rounds of artillery and mortar on Allied positions during the twenty-four hour period ended at 6:00 P.M..

Western sector: Intense fighting continued for possession of Outpost Porkchop, with the action ranging from sporadic to intense, until 5:15 P.M., when a reinforced Chinese company attacked, causing the Seventh United States Division infantrymen to withdraw slightly. By 7:10 P.M., the Chinese were on the northern slope of Porkchop. At the end of the period, the Seventh Division troops held the southern slope, and the Chinese the northern slope of Porkchop. Berlin and East Berlin each was attacked by an estimated reinforced Chinese company at 1:15 A.M., but Allied troops, supported by very intense artillery fire, forced the Chinese to break contact and withdraw at 3:10 A.M.. Otherwise, only brief and infrequent friendly initiated patrol contacts were reported.

Central sector: Action flared up again at midnight on the two Second R.O.K. Division outposts in the vicinity of Arrowhead, with hand-to-hand fighting taking place on both positions at 1:53 A.M.. Action ceased on the western outpost at 3:35 A.M., while at the same time, the R.O.K.s were bringing artillery fire down on the Chinese. Action continued sporadic all day, with artillery duels highlighting the action. At 6:00 P.M., the enemy attacked and won the crest of the eastern outpost, but by 8:30, the Chinese were forced back to the northern slope, while the R.O.K.s occupied the southern slope. Action was sporadic at the end of the period. Two Allied listening posts northwest of Kumhwa were harassed by Chinese during the period. In brief engagements, Eighth Army patrol contacts were frequent in the eastern portion of the sector, contacting squad to platoon-sized enemy groups in fire fights lasting from five to twenty minutes.

Eastern sector: The Allied outpost attacked by three Chinese companies late Wednesday was again attacked at 2:05 A.M. by a Chinese battalion, but after an intense two-and-a-half-hour fire fight, the Chinese withdrew. One hundred and seventy Chinese were killed our wounded. This same outpost was hit again at 8:55 P.M. and 9:35 P.M. by an enemy squad, with the actions lasting twenty to twenty-five minutes before the Chinese were forced to withdraw. Eighth Army patrols made frequent contacts with enemy groups from six men to two squads in size in brief to thirteen minute skirmishes.

—Eighth Army tactical summary covering Friday's fighting to 6:00 P.M., Korean time:

Enemy action against Outpost Porkchop on the western front, and two outposts in the vicinity of Arrowhead Ridge on the central front, continued throughout the day Friday. On Porkchop, the action was sporadic between (Thursday) midnight and 1:30 A.M., with the Chinese controlling the northern slope, and the Seventh United States Division infantrymen in charge of the southern slope of the outpost. At 4:30 A.M., the Chinese made an unsuccessful attempt to push the United States troops from the southern slope, but were forced back by 6:30 A.M..

The two forces were still on their respective sides of Porkchop at 2:30 P.M., with light artillery duels the only action reported. The Chinese hurled 11,500 rounds of artillery and mortar at Porkchop during the twelve-hour period ended at 6 A.M..

Near Arrowhead at midnight, the Chinese were making a concerted effort for possession of the two outpost positions, but were only successful in wrestling the crest of the easternmost outpost from the Second R.O.K. Division troops at 2:30 A.M..

At 5:10 A.M., hand-to-hand fighting was in progress on the western outpost. At 10:55 A.M., the last report on this action indicated that the Chinese were still occupying the eastern outpost, while the Second R.O.K. troops were in possession of the western outpost, and that action was continuing. During the twelve hour period ended at 6:00 A.M., the Chinese threw 12,700 rounds of mixed artillery and mortar fire in support of their action on the two outposts.

An Allied outpost west of the Mundung Valley was harassed three times this morning by enemy groups ranging from squad to platoon in size in skirmishes lasting from twenty to forty-two minutes. Three other light enemy jabs were turned back after brief skirmishes.

Elsewhere across the Eighth Army 155 mile battle front, twenty-eight Allied initiated patrol clashes were reported with enemy groups ranging up to platoon size, in fire fights lasting briefly to twenty minutes in duration.

†PENDLETON, CHARLES F.

Rank and Organization: Corporal, U.S. Army, Company D, 15th Infantry Regiment, 3d Infantry Division.
Born: September 26, 1931, Camden, Tennessee.
Entered Service At: Fort Worth, Texas.
Place and Date: Near Choo Gung-Dong, Korea, July 16 and 17, 1953.
Citation: Cpl. Pendleton, a machine-gunner with Company D, distinguished himself by conspicuous gallantry and indomitable courage above and beyond the call of duty in action against the enemy. After consolidating and establishing a defensive perimeter on a key terrain feature, friendly elements were attacked by a large hostile force. Cpl. Pendleton delivered deadly accurate fire into the approaching troops, killing approximately 15 and disorganizing the remainder with grenades. Unable to protect the flank because of narrow confines of the trench, he removed the machine gun from the tripod and, exposed to enemy observation, positioned it on his knee to improve his firing vantage. Observing a hostile infantryman jumping into the position, intent on throwing a grenade at his comrades, he whirled about and killed the attacker, then inflicted such heavy casualties on the enemy force that they retreated to regroup. After reorganizing, a second wave of hostile soldiers moved forward in an attempt to overrun the position and, later, when a hostile grenade landed nearby, Cpl. Pendleton quickly retrieved and hurled it back at the foe. Although he was burned by the hot shells ejecting from his weapon, and he was wounded by a grenade, he refused evacuation and continued to fire on the assaulting force. As enemy action increased in tempo, his machine gun was destroyed by a grenade but, undaunted, he grabbed a carbine and continued his heroic defense until mortally wounded by a mortar burst. Cpl. Pendleton's unflinching courage, gallant self-sacrifice, and consummate devotion to duty reflect lasting glory upon himself and uphold the finest traditions of the military service.

OFFICIAL COMMUNIQUÉ:
TOKYO, Saturday, July 18 (AP)
—Far East Air Forces summary of Thursday's operations:

United States Air Force F-84 and F-86 fighter-bombers, joined by other United Nations aircraft, smashed more than 2,000,000 pounds of bombs into Communist forces in the Kumsong sector of the front Thursday, highlighting a day and night of air activity ,which saw United Nations air units hit the Reds from the battle line of the Yalu River.

F.E.A.F. aircraft mounted 1,450 sorties, more than double those of the previous period, as weather cleared over enemy territory.

F-86 Sabre jet Interceptors shot down three MiGs and damaged two others during the day. Last night, twenty-three B-29 Superforts struck Red battle line positions, as did also twenty-six B-26 light bombers.

Sabre bombers began the day's close support strikes in the central sector of the front near Kumsong, and were joined by F-84 Thunderjets and land-based Marine warplanes. Marine Skyraiders damaged four T-34 tanks in the east-central sector.

Sabres and then Thunderjets roared deeper into North Korea during the day to strike a string of road and rail bridges between Sinanju and Huichon along the Chongchon River supply route. The fighter-bombers also hit road and rail bridges across central North Korea. Two road bridges were destroyed and five were damaged and six rail bridges were damaged in the attacks.

Australian Meteor jets destroyed fourteen buildings at Kangdong and thirty-one near Chaeryong. F-84s destroyed four more structures near Kunu.

Sabre bombers assaulted a Red airfield at Pyongyang and pilots reported damaging three prop-driven enemy aircraft parked in revetments under camouflage.

In the late afternoon, additional fighter-bombers struck the enemy's front, bringing total bomb loads dropped along the battle line during the day to 2,125,000 pounds.

Screening the fighter-bomber attacks throughout the day, F-86 Interceptors destroyed three MiGs deep in Northwest Korea, and damaged two others.

As darkness fell, the air assaults were continued by B-26 Invaders. The light bombers pounded the enemy front-line forces and attacked a rail marshaling yard north of Hwangju. They made five road cuts and left 100 vehicles wrecked along supply routes.

Twenty-three Superforts from Japan carried on the front-line strikes, sixteen hitting the east central sector and the remainder concentrating on other parts of the front.

Observed destruction for the period includes thirty-six bunkers and eighteen gun positions damaged, sixty-nine buildings destroyed, and six damaged, seven vehicles wrecked and six damaged, seven rail cars knocked out and eleven damaged, six rail bridges damaged, two road bridges destroyed and five damaged, five rail cuts and thirteen road cuts inflicted, nineteen personnel shelters and four tanks damaged.

Combat cargo transports of F.E.A.F.'s 315th Air Division airlifted 455 tons of personnel and supplies in continued logistical support of United Nations forces.

—Far East Naval Forces summary of Friday's operations:

Two Task Force 77 carriers launched almost 300 sorties to continue heavy strikes in support of advancing United Nations troops while United Nations surface ships pounded targets from Hungnam to Kosong. Planes from the carriers U.S.S. Lake Champlain and Philippine Sea concentrated the majority of their missions just west at Capitol Hill in the Chorwon-Kumhwa area. A number of strikes were directed farther north of the Wonsan-Hungnam and Sinchang area.

Hitting at Wonsan, Panther jet pilots reported that three trucks were destroyed and four others damaged. A tremendous ball of red flames leaped into the air following the first run over the target. Ground controllers later reported that three artillery positions were knocked out and a major fire started in an ammunition dump near Kumhwa. Ten personnel shelters were demolished and six more damaged at Kumsong as pilots encountered heavy front-lien flak.

Skyraiders, Corsairs, and jets attacked supply traffic moving southward from Hungnam and Sinchang and reported good results.

Damage totals for the day included twenty-nine personnel shelters, eighteen buildings, and twelve trucks destroyed, 130 yards of trench line ripped up, and five rail cars badly damaged. Eleven fires were left burning.

Also, firing in support of front-line troops were the cruiser U.S.S. St. Paul and the destroyers U.S.S. Samuel Moore and Gurke.

Laying off Kosong, the cruiser St. Paul fired round after round into enemy shelters and trenches. The cruiser's fire accounted for destruction of seven supply buildings, three of which were direct hits. Five secondary explosions were noted. St. Paul gunners scored two trench cuts and additionally cut the main supply route in seven places. A large building housing ammunition was blown up with three direct hits.

Both the St. Paul and the Moore laid down suppression fire on enemy artillery and mortar positions near Anchor Hill. All the enemy mortars were silenced and an undetermined number of troops were killed.

Destroyer Gurke also steamed off Kosong and fired on bunkers, trenches, and gun positions.

The destroyer's gunners knocked out two heavy bunkers and heavily damaged another. An observation post was neutralized in the area, while five gun positions were destroyed. Enemy troops were dispersed all over the area of fire as fifty-five yards of trench line were demolished with possible reverse slope damage.

Farther north, the light cruiser U.S.S. Manchester, with escort destroyer Radford, bombarded targets at Hungnam. The ships scored two direct hits on a cave and a possible gun position. Four supply and storage buildings were destroyed and one large storage building heavily damaged. The Manchester also made two rail cuts.

Destroyer Radford, in independent firing, laid four direct hits in a personnel area, dispersing troops and disrupting a road construction project. Also heavily hit, but with no assessment, were several gun emplacements.

In the Yellow Sea, the New Zealand patrol frigate H.M.N.Z.S. Janiers fired at a troop encampment near Chinnampo. Hits were scored on gun emplacements and mortar and automatic weapons positions. A landing ship fired rockets into targets just above Chinnampo, scoring two hits on a bunker.

—Eighth Army communiqué, covering Thursday's activities:

(Military security, due to the fluid situation on the central front, between Sniper Ridge and the Pukhan River, requires the omission of information relative to that action in this communiqué.)

Otherwise, fighting increased slightly Thursday across the Eighth Army front. Chinese forces up to company in size continued attacks on Outpost Betty in the western sector. Five Twelfth R.O.K. front-line positions near Luke's Castle were attacked near the end of the period. Other enemy initiated actions were reported in the vicinity of Anchor Hill and M-1 Ridge in the eastern sector, and southeast of Sniper Ridge, near Boomerang and west of Jackson Heights in the central sector. The enemy fired 33,825 rounds of artillery and mortar on Allied positions during the twenty-four hour period ended at 6:00 P.M., although this figure does not include area in the central sector which were still engaged in heavy action.

Western sector: The First R.O.K. Division, Outpost Betty, which had been unsuccessfully attacked by an estimated Chinese battalion before midnight Wednesday, was again attacked at 4:50 A.M. Thursday by two platoons. The Chinese were forced to break contact after a brief fire fight. The R.O.K.s on Betty were attacked again at 7:00 A.M., this time by a company, but after an intense fifteen minute of hand-to-hand combat, the Chinese were again repulsed and action ceased. Chinese casualties, as a result of the attack on Betty, were 247 killed, 268 estimated killed and 268 estimated wounded. Eighth Army patrols clashed with squad to platoon-size enemy groups in brief to fifteen-minute skirmishes.

Central sector: Southwest of Sniper Ridge a platoon of Chinese made a five minute jab at an Allied front-line position before being forced to withdraw. A listening post east of Boomerang was struck by a 100-man Chinese force at 7:00 P.M. After an intense thirty minute fire fight, the Chinese withdrew, with thirty-five of their number killed or wounded. West of Jackson Heights, a platoon of Chinese made a brief hit-and-run jab at an Allied listening post. Friendly initiated patrol contacts were infrequent.

Eastern sector: Five Twelfth R.O.K. Division front-line positions in the vicinity of Luke's Castle were engaged by Chinese forces up to company in size, shortly before midnight. Three of the attacks were brief and had been repulsed at the end of the period. The other actions were continuing at midnight. A front-line position southeast of Anchor Hill was engaged by a North Korean platoon at 3:00 A.M. After a forty-minute fire fight, the enemy was forced to withdraw, with seventeen killed or wounded.

Slightly to the east, another outpost position was probed by two squads, but after a ten minute skirmish, the enemy withdrew. At 4:05 A.M., an outpost on M-1 Ridge was engaged by a platoon. After a fifteen minute small arms and automatic weapons fire fight, the enemy withdrew from the outpost. A friendly patrol engaged two North Korean squads in an intense ten minute fire fight near Luke's Castle. The enemy withdrew with eleven killed or wounded. Other Eighth Army patrols fought five to fifteen minute fire fights with enemy groups ranging from six men to two squads.

—Eighth Army tactical summary 448, for Friday to 6:00 P.M.

Other than the continued heavy fighting in the east-central sector, ground action across the Eighth Army front showed a substantial increase Friday over the fighting of Thursday. The most intense fighting occurred in the vicinity of Luke's Castle and Anchor Hill in the eastern sector and near Boomerang in the central sector.

Seven Twelfth R.O.K. Division front-line positions in the vicinity of Luke's Castle were attacked by North Korean forces, with most of the attacks starting shortly before midnight. The largest occurred just west of Luke's Castle an hour before midnight, when a company of North Koreans hit a front-line position. At 12:17 A.M., the enemy reinforced with a platoon, and by 1:05 A.M., had reinforced to battalion size.

At last reports, the enemy had reinforced to two battalions and at 3:45 A.M., was reported occupying part of the Twelfth R.O.K. positions, and action was continuing. Another front-line position in the same vicinity was attacked by a North Korean company at 12:15 A.M., and at 3:34 A.M. This enemy group also occupied a portion of the position, with action continuing. Five other front-line positions near Luke's Castle were also engaged by enemy groups ranging up to company in size, in brief to fifteen minute fire fights before being forced to withdraw.

Two Fifteenth R.O.K. Division outposts south of Anchor Hill were each attacked by two North Korean companies at 12:50 A.M., but after an intense three-hour fire fight, the North Koreans withdrew. East of Anchor Hill and near the Japan Sea, two North Korean platoons hit another Fifteenth R.O.K. front-line position. One enemy platoon broke contact at 2:55 A.M. and the other at 4:00 A.M.

West of Boomerang, a Chinese reinforced battalion attacked an Allied front-line position at 12:38 A.M., and thirty minutes later withdrew slightly, but remained in the area. The Chinese renewed the attack at 2:10 A.M. in an intense fire fight that lasted until 5:40 A.M., when the enemy was forced to break contact and withdraw.

Other enemy-initiated actions consisted of light jabs at forward positions northeast of Little Nori in the western sector, near White Horse Mountain, in the central sector and west of Christmas Hill in the eastern sector.

Elsewhere across the front, eight friendly-initiated patrol clashes were reported against enemy groups up to platoon in size in brief to twenty minute skirmishes.

—United Nations Command communiqué 1,679, for the twenty-four hours to 6:00 A.M., Saturday, Korean time:

United Nations Command forces along the battle front were hit by enemy attacks during the last twenty-four hour period, but repulsed most of them except for a penetration on the east-central front.

Light action on the western front consisted of two probes by enemy platoons before midnight.

On the west-central front, six attacks by enemy groups up to reinforced battalion size were slammed into United Nations Command forces, but all were knocked back. Northeast of Kumha, friendly positions received attacks from enemy elements up to two battalion strength, and action is still continuing. One friendly company attacked and drove an enemy company from their hill positions and occupied the hill. In the save vicinity, two reinforced enemy battalions attacked friendly forces but were driven back after heavy fighting.

One sector of the central front has stabilized its positions and has repulsed two enemy thrusts by an estimated reinforced enemy battalion, and one from a force consisting of two enemy companies. Near by four enemy companies are still attacking friendly positions and action is continuing at last report. In that sector, a friendly company launched an assault on an enemy-held position and occupied the position after driving off an enemy company. Small friendly units on this front are still engaging small enemy elements with United Nations Command forces showing marked gains.

The east-central front found the enemy launching four attacks, three of platoon size, and one of battalion size. Friendly units beat back all these assaults. Five other enemy attacks from squad size to a reinforced battalion are continuing. Some penetrations have been made by the enemy.

Eleven attacks in a twenty-four hour period have been slammed into United Nations Command forces on the eastern front by the enemy, but all were repulsed. Attacking elements ranged from squad to two-company size.

United Nations Command carrier-based planes launched almost 200 sorties yesterday in support of United Nations Command forces while surface elements pounded targets from Hungnam to Kosong. Carrier aircraft concentrated their strikes in the Chorwon-Kumhwa area just west of Capitol Hill. Other strikes hit farther north in the Wonsan-Hungnam and Sinchan areas.

Surface elements in the Yellow Sea fired on a troop encampment near Chinnampo and scored hits on gun emplacements and mortar and automatic weapons positions.

United Nations Command fighter-bombers, mounting more than 500 close air support strikes against the east coast enemy front, slammed more than 1,250,000 pounds of bombs into Communist troops and weapons positions during daylight. Other jet aircraft attacked troop and supply columns. Fighter-interceptors, flying screening cover for fighter-bombers, damaged two enemy jets.

After dark, light and medium bombers continued the explosive rain on the Communist front-line in support of United nations Command forces. Medium bombers hit front-line targets in contested sectors while light bombers covered all but the eastern sector of the front, and destroyed more than sixty vehicles on highways leading to the front.

†COLLIER, GILBERT G.

Rank and Organization: Sergeant (then Cpl.), U.S. Army, Company F, 223d Infantry Regiment, 40th Infantry Division.
Born: December 30, 1930, Hunter, Arkansas.
Entered Service At: Tichnor, Arkansas.
Place and Date: Near Tutayon, Korea, July 19-20, 1953.
Citation: Sgt. Collier, a member of Company F, distinguished himself by conspicuous gallantry and indomitable courage above and beyond the call of duty in action against the enemy. Sgt. Collier was point man and assistant leader of a combat patrol committed to make contact with the enemy. As the patrol moved forward through the darkness, he and his commanding officer slipped and fell from a steep, 60-foot cliff and were injured. Incapacitated by a badly sprained ankle which prevented immediate movement, the officer ordered the patrol to return to the safety of friendly lines. Although suffering from a painful back injury, Sgt. Collier elected to remain with his leader, and before daylight they managed to crawl back up and over the mountainous terrain to the opposite valley where they concealed themselves in the brush until nightfall, then edged toward their company's position. Shortly after leaving the daylight retreat they were ambushed and, in the ensuing fire fight, Sgt. Collier killed 2 hostile soldiers, received painful wounds, and was separated from his companion. Then, ammunition expended, he closed in hand-to-hand combat with 4 attacking hostile infantrymen, killing, wounding, and routing the foe with his bayonet. He was mortally wounded during this action, but made a valiant attempt to reach and assist his leader in a desperate effort to save his comrade's life without regard for his own personal safety. Sgt. Collier's unflinching courage, consum-

mate devotion to duty, and gallant self-sacrifice reflect lasting glory upon himself and uphold the noble traditions of the military service.

OFFICIAL COMMUNIQUÉ:
TOKYO, Tuesday, July 21 (AP)
—Far East Naval summary of operations Monday:

Although bad weather hampered air operations, the four Task Force 77 aircraft carriers managed to launch 117 sorties against targets from the front-lines to the city of Chongjin. United Nations surface elements hit Communist installations along both Korean coast lines before bad weather set in.

U.S.S. Boxer aircraft destroyed eighteen of twenty trucks in an ammunition convoy near Taejong. Skyraiders from the Philippine Sea used their rockets on buildings in the Chongjin area.

U.S.S. Princeton Corsair pilots, flying air support for Allied ground troops on the central front, struck roads, bridges, and other positions. Lake Champlain planes blasted the Yangdok area. Damage totals for the task force included: 400 troops killed, and thirty-two trucks destroyed.

The propeller-driven Skyraiders and Corsairs accounted for at least thirty-nine buildings and six personnel shelters destroyed, while damaging three bunkers, two bridges, one gun position, and 345 yards of trench. In addition, four secondary explosions were touched off.

With eighty-seven of the 128 sorties being close air support strikes in front of United Nations troops, the Marine pilots struck at enemy concentrations on the western and central front. United Nations forces battling Reds on the western approaches to Seoul saw Lieut. Frank L. Leister of Corpus Christi, Tex., and St. Paul, Minn., lead a four-plane flight of Skyraiders from the Wolf Raiders Squadron that destroyed six personnel shelters, damaged 300 yards of trench, and set off one secondary explosion. Lieutenant Leister flew the Wolf Raider Squadron's 10,000th sortie of the Korean war.

Maj. Dorris J. Frankovic of Costa Mesa, Calif., and Bedford Heights, Ohio, led a fifteen-plane flight of Corsairs from the Devil Cats Squadron, destroying fifteen buildings near Ottaa-Dong. In the biggest interdiction raid of the day for Marines, thirty planes struck a troop concentration near Munbak-Sun on the western front.

—Far East Air Forces summary 1,121, covering operations Sunday:

Close air support of United Nations ground forces continued at a heavy pace Sunday as wave after wave of United States Air Force and Marine fighter bombers swept over enemy lines in daylight to blast troops and combat positions with twin-engine B-26s taking over the battle line bombings after dark.

As the Far East Air Forces mounted 1,530 sorties, fighter bombers amassed nearly 1,000 of this total as they poured nearly 1,400,000 pounds of bombs into the front, and mangled enemy bridges, rails, highways, and supply points further north.

Meanwhile, F-86 Sabre jets met and defeated enemy MiG-15s for the fifth successive day, scoring their highest victory total of the month with nine enemy jets destroyed, one probably destroyed, and three damaged. The day's scores pushed the F.E.A.F. toll of enemy aircraft destroyed during the Korean War beyond the 1,000 mark.

The scarred Kumhwa-Kumsong Bulge battle front once again received the heaviest force of fighter bomber assaults as more than 265 tons of explosives were rained into a ten mile stretch where massed air assaults have hammered destructively at enemy forces for the last six days.

United States Air Force F-84 Thunderjets and F-86 Sabre jets carried the major portion of the close support effort, while Marine aircraft and B-26s also joined in the daylight strikes. T-6 Mosquito spotting aircraft orbited over enemy positions throughout the day, serving as airborne directors for the attacking jet aircraft.

Interdiction operations by Sabres, Thunderjets and Marine and Australian aircraft again concentrated on Communist bridge links throughout the peninsula, including the much-mauled stretch of rail and highway line between Huichon and Sinanju on the Chongchon River.

Five bridges were destroyed during the day and ten damaged. One of the destruction's was scored on the Pukhan River, as Sabre jet fighter bombers knocked out a pontoon bridge in use as a replacement for a bridge destroyed earlier in the week.

Rail rolling stock and supply lanes also suffered from air attacks, as fifteen rail cars were smashed and twenty-five damaged, while five rail and fifty road cuts were scored. Near Ichon, Marine aircraft destroyed fifty-five buildings in a supply build up.

B-26s bombed trenches and personnel shelters in the western and central sectors during the day, and sent twenty-five sorties against Kumhwa-Kumsong sector targets after dark. Other Invaders smashed a rail bridge near Hungsu, with unobserved results.

Supply convoys attempting to move south toward the front during the night were intercepted by the B-26s, which set up ten road blocks and destroyed eighty-three vehicles.

B-29 Superforts did not fly during the period.

Destruction and damage reports for the period include twenty bunkers and twenty-five gun positions damaged, ninety buildings leveled, fifteen rail cars smashed and twenty-five damaged, one rail bridge destroyed and two damaged, four road bridges destroyed and eight damaged, five rail cuts, fifty road cuts, fifteen supply stacks fired and six damaged, two tanks damaged, and fifteen personnel shelters destroyed and fifteen damaged.

Combat cargo transports airlifted 660 tons of supplies and personnel in continued logistical support of United Nations forces.

—*Eighth Army tactical summary 450 for eighteen hour period ended at 6:00 P.M. Monday:*

Ground action across the 155 mile Eighth Army front increased slightly Monday over that reported yesterday, with the heaviest action continuing to be in the Kumsong bulge of the east-central sector.

Fighting in the central and eastern sectors of the Kumsong bulge continued to be heavy, with friendly and enemy forces engaged in fights for possession of important terrain features. In the Eleventh R.O.K. Division sector, an important hill position that has changed hands several times in the last forty-eight hours, and was in friendly hands at the beginning of the period, was attacked by two Chinese companies at 1:30 A.M. and at 3:20 A.M. The enemy reinforced to battalion strength and hand-to-hand fighting ensued on the position. At 4:05 A.M., the friendly forces were forced to disengage from the position. The Chinese used 2,000 rounds of artillery and mortar in support of the attack.

Farther to the east, near the Kumsong River bend, an R.O.K. division hill position was attacked by an enemy company shortly before midnight Sunday. After an intense fifteen minute fire fight, the R.O.K.s disengaged slightly. Seven hours later, at 7:00 A.M., the R.O.K.s were successful in regaining the position. Farther to the east, and near the juncture of the Kumsong and Pukhan Rivers, an R.O.K. attacking force engaged an enemy company at 1:40 A.M. Hand-to-hand fighting developed shortly after the engagement started and lasted for almost an hour. At 2:25 A.M., action was sporadic and at 4:40 A.M., the enemy was forced to withdraw from the positions.

Elsewhere across the Eighth Army front, enemy patrol contacts were light and infrequent. Nine friendly, initiated patrol contacts were reported against enemy groups up to platoon in size in brief to thirty minute clashes.

—*United Nations headquarters communiqué 1,681, for the twenty-four hours ended at 6:00 A.M., Monday:*

Outposts Berlin and East Berlin received a strong enemy attack of undetermined size late last night, and after a battle lasting slightly less than one hour, the hostile forces occupied the positions. Late the night of July 18, according to delayed reports, an estimated twenty enemy were thrown back from an attack against a United Nations position west of the Imjin River.

Northwest of Kumhwa, an enemy battalion was forced to withdraw before United Nations troops early yesterday, and the friendly forces occupied the objective. In the same area, an estimated two platoons attacked United Nations forces late last night. Friendly troops counter-attacked early this morning, but the enemy had reinforced to battalion size by 0320 hours today, and friendly elements withdrew after approximately one hour of fighting.

Near the center of the front, recently hit by mass enemy attacks, United Nations forces engaged an enemy group of two companies and another of one company size early yesterday, and forced both the hostile groups to withdraw. Late the night of July 18, another United Nations force engaged an estimated enemy company. During the battle, the enemy reinforced with two battalions, but United Nations troops continued their push and drove the enemy to the north.

Yesterday morning in the same area, six more friendly groups attacked and took all objectives, three of which were defended by hostile battalions.

Along the eastern flank of the recent mass attacks, six engagements, two the night of July 18, and the other four early yesterday morning, resulted in enemy groups of up to reinforced company size withdrawing and friendly troops occupying objectives.

Late yesterday afternoon in the same area, friendly forces engaged an enemy reinforced company, later reinforced with an additional company, but by 1800 hours, the enemy was forced to withdraw. The same United Nations force engaged an estimated reinforced company late last night. The enemy reinforced with a battalion, but was forced to withdraw a short time later. Late last night, friendly positions near by were attacked by a reinforced enemy company which was supported with heavy artillery and mortar fire, and action was continuing this morning.

Slightly west of the Pukhan River, United Nations troops occupied high ground late the night of July 18, after forcing two enemy platoons to withdraw from the positions. East of the Pukhan, only minor probes were reported.

Late the night of July 18, and early yesterday, four enemy probes, the largest by an estimated platoon, were hurled back by United Nations troops northeast of the Punchbowl.

Three enemy probes on the right flank of the Eastern sector, the largest by an enemy platoon, were thrown back the night of July 18, and early yesterday.

A rain of bombs, napalm and rockets was unleashed from carrier-based planes of the United Nations fleet of enemy front-line positions yesterday, as one of the largest United Nations carrier fleets of the war went into operation off the east coast of Korea. Transportation facilities were heavily hit, but gun positions and the front-lines bore the brunt of the air attacks.

Surface elements off the east coast bombarded enemy strong points and artillery positions near Kosong and caught a large group of enemy in the open near the coastline. Other elements of the fleet shelled a southbound train above Tanchon and later sealed a rail tunnel in the same area. Action in the Yellow Sea was limited, but several rounds from United Nations naval guns struck enemy positions near Chinnampo.

Land-based fighter-bombers yesterday continued their assaults on the enemy front and pounded bridges, rail lines, highways and personnel and supply build-ups to the rear of hostile lines.

Jet fighters of the United Nations Command scored decisive victories over enemy fighter jets while screening the friendly fighter-bomber attacks.

United Nations light bombers carried out day and night attacks on enemy front-line fortifications and switched a portion of their activity after dark to assaults on supply vehicles.

Medium bombers did not fly last night.

—United Nations Command headquarters communiqué 1,682, for the twenty-four hours ending at 6:00 A.M., Tuesday:

The tempo of battle along the Korean fighting front decreased during the period, with the largest reported action listed as an attack by an enemy battalion in the central sector which was thrown back after a three-hour battle.

In the west-central sector, friendly positions northeast of Kumhwa were attacked by an estimated reinforced enemy company late the night of July 10, according to delayed reports. The assault was hurled back by United Nations Command forces early yesterday morning. North of Kumhwa, three enemy probes of up to two-squad size were blunted during brief skirmishes early yesterday.

Several small clashes also were reported from the central sector yesterday. United Nations Command troops were successful in most of these encounters as they continued to stabilize lines along a portion of the Kumsong River.

Northeast of the Punchbowl, in the east-central sector, two small United Nations Command listening posts threw back enemy attacks of two-squad and two-platoon size during daylight hours yesterday.

A United Nations Command outpost near the coast in the eastern sector repulsed an attack by an enemy platoon yesterday afternoon.

Despite bad weather yesterday, carrier-based planes of the United Nations Command fleet bombed targets from the enemy front lines to Chongjin. They destroyed or damaged numerous trucks and buildings in the Chongjin area, and flew in close support of United Nations Command troops on the central front.

Surface elements fired on enemy front-line positions near Kosong early yesterday, and bombarded other hostile installations along both coasts of the peninsula.

United Nations Command land-based fighter-bombers during daylight yesterday struck rail and highway bridges across the Chongchon River and bomber enemy rolling stock enroute to the battle line. Other fighter-bombers hit an airfield at Sinanju and enemy front-line positions.

United Nations Command jet fighters engaged enemy fighter jets. Light bombers flew close support during the day, and bombed hostile supply vehicles last night. Also last night, medium bombers struck targets in the Sinuiju area and airfield at Uiju, as well as enemy battle line positions.

†GUILLEN, AMBROSIO

Rank and Organization: Staff Sergeant, U.S. Marine Corps, Company F, 2d Battalion, 7th Marines, 1st Marine Division (Rein).
Born: December 7, 1929, La Junta, Colorado.
Entered Service At: El Paso, Texas.
Place and Date: Near Songuch-on, Korea, July 25, 1953.
Citation: For conspicuous gallantry and intrepidity at the risk of his life above and beyond the call of duty while serving as a platoon sergeant of Company F, in action against enemy aggressor forces. Participating in the defense of an outpost forward of the main line of resistance, S/Sgt. Guillen maneuvered his platoon over unfamiliar terrain in the face of hostile fire and placed his men in fighting positions. With his unit pinned down when the outpost was attacked under cover of darkness by an estimated force of 2 enemy battalions supported by mortar and artillery fire, he deliberately exposed himself to the heavy barrage and attacks to direct his men in defending their positions and personally supervise the treatment and evacuation of the wounded. Inspired by his leadership, the platoon quickly rallied and engaged the enemy in fierce hand-to-hand combat. Although critically wounded during the course of the battle, S/Sgt. Guillen refused medical aid and continued to direct his men throughout the remainder of the engagement until the enemy was defeated and thrown into disorderly retreat. Succumbing to his wounds within a few hours, S/Sgt. Guillen, by his outstanding courage and indomitable fighting spirit, was directly responsible for the success of his platoon in repelling a numerically superior enemy force. His personal valor reflects the highest credit upon himself and enhances the finest traditions of the U.S. Naval Service. He gallantly gave his life for his country.

OFFICIAL COMMUNIQUÉ:
TOKYO, Sunday, July 26 (AP)
—Far East Naval Forces summary of Friday's operations:

Planes from four Task Force 77 carriers had launched over 250 sorties by mid-morning to hit the Communists in the Anchor Hill-Kumsong battle area, while the battleship U.S.S. New Jersey continued to pound the area for the third consecutive day.

Planes from the Philippine Sea, Princeton, Boxer, and Lake Champlain flew a record breaking 596 sorties before retiring striking front-line positions, truck routes, and railways.

Lake Champlain pilots struck heavy blows at the Wonsan area, with scattered strikes at Hungnam.

Pilots hammered a rail marshaling yard, bombing twenty boxcars, while other aircraft assaulted supply buildings at Munchon. Returning pilots reported structures destroyed in all strikes as they turned to strafe Chinese Red troops entrenched on the beach just inshore. South at Kongsjon, bombs were dropped in trenches as artillery and machine-gun positions were assaulted.

North at Hungnam, one span was destroyed on a railroad bridge and one rail over-pass was obliterated. Strafing damaged two boats and one lighthouse at the east coast city.

Princeton jets, Corsairs and Skyraiders flew through heavy flak and low overcasts that made damage assessment at times impossible. An early afternoon raid by Skyraiders on front-line positions was diverted because of poor weather. Navy jets strafed twenty-five boxcars and eight supply buildings near Wonsan, while another section of Panther jets used radar in bombing installations between Finger Ridge and Capitol Hill.

Corsairs went after and destroyed several rail cars south of Wonsan. Moving farther to the north, they bombed camouflaged buildings, as their ordinance set off a large secondary explosion in the area. Skyraiders searching for targets of opportunity cut rail lines, heavily damaged a number of buildings, and a rail bridge north of Hamhung.

Philippine Sea aircraft had a highly successful day in North Central Korea, north of Yangdok. One locomotive and tender came under cannon fire while three trucks were destroyed in the same manner. Another Communist train of one locomotive and thirty cars was bombed as pilots reported the locomotive destroyed, followed by three large secondary explosions. East of Pyong, Philippine Sea pilots found a fifteen-truck convoy, leaving four vehicles destroyed. Pilots attacked a number of bridges and rail line targets, but weather interfered with complete assessment. Two command positions were bombed and strafed at Hupkok and one highway bridge was destroyed. Additional artillery positions were silenced while rockets cut up rail lines and highways.

Boxer pilots teamed up with Princeton planes to hit Sagi. Forty-five trucks were bombed, as Boxer planes accounted for four destroyed and eleven damaged, while cratering the highway in a number of spots.

Farther north at Hamhung, nine boxcars were demolished as two secondary explosions marked the Boxer strikes. Seven fires were left burning and six additional boxcars were damaged as eight trucks were damaged, and one destroyed in the same locale. In the area near Sinchang, the Navy planes knocked out one bridge, destroyed one boxcar and damaged eight, destroyed three trucks and reported one very large secondary explosion.

Total results for the day included fifty road cuts, forty-five rail cuts, 100 yards of trench line destroyed, four highway bridges destroyed, four damaged; twenty-nine buildings destroyed, forty-five damaged; seven gun positions destroyed; forty-nine trucks destroyed, forty damaged; forty-seven railroad cars destroyed, thirty-six damaged; one locomotive destroyed; six railroad bridges destroyed, twenty-five damaged; five tunnels destroyed; one ammunition dump destroyed; thirty-one craters on Wonsan airfield; seventeen secondary explosions; fifteen fires.

The mighty 45,000-ton dreadnaught U.S.S. New Jersey lay off the Korean east coast near Kosong, pounding enemy command posits, gun emplacements and bunkers in the Anchor Hill sector in another day-long bombardment.

Starting off with her secondary 5-inch batteries, the New Jersey heavily damaged six enemy gun emplacements, closed connecting tunnels and ripped up a near-by network of trenches. Shortly after noon, she brought her big 16-inch rifles into the fray to completely smash nine 76-mm. guns.

Spotters reported one entire hill neutralized by the battleship's fire. She knocked out twenty bunkers, a command point, an observation post, four gun emplacements, and twenty-two automatic weapons positions in one sector. Secondary explosions were frequently reported, with one group occurring in a firecracker series which led spotters to believe it was a possible ammunition stockpile.

Listed as destroyed by the New Jersey were twenty-two gun emplacements, twenty-six bunkers, one blockhouse, four caves, and 515 yards of trench. Damaged were twenty-seven bunkers, thirty-one gun positions, and thirty-two automatic weapons nests. In addition, several groups of troops were dispersed along with a tank column, and considerable damage done by the reverse slope slide.

Roving off the east coast near Wonsan and Hungnam, the cruiser U.S.S. St. Paul and her escort, the destroyer U.S.S. Samuel N. Moore, fired on a railway track and a tunnel. One hundred yards of track were well covered by naval gun fire and the tunnel entrance was partially closed.

The destroyer U.S.S. Hamner, near Kosong, fired on and damaged two bunkers.

The destroyer H.M.A.S. Tobruk and U.S.S. Picking operated near Tanchon, with the Tobruk firing on rail tracks and tunnels with unassessed damage.

—Far East Air Forces summary of Friday's operations:

United States Air Force F-84 Thunderjets and F-86 Sabre jets pounded the enemy front Friday, as low-hanging clouds covered most of North Korea. After dark, B-26 light bombers continued to hammer the front, and B-29 Superforts blasted a Red airfield and a supply center just north of the battle line.

As F.E.A.F. aircraft mounted 690 sorties, jet fighter-bombers ranged along the battle line smashing bombs into the Kumsong Bulge sector and other enemy positions in the east-central and central sectors. Clouds shrouded most of the targets, making observation of results impossible.

Land-based Marine aircraft joined the battle-line strikes and along with United States Air Force B-26 light bombers, hurled explosives into the Communist line.

After dark, the light bombers winged over a Red troop concentration just behind the front bombed electronically without opposition results were also unobserved here.

Just before midnight, twelve B-29 Superforts rained 120 tons of high explosives on the 6,500-foot long concrete landing strip at the Pyong airfield, fifteen miles southeast of Sinanju. While Superforts hammered the air strip, three other medium bombers struck the Taewa supply area, thirty miles north of the Kumsong Bulge, slamming thirty tons of high explosives into the target.

Meager to moderate flak met the Superforts over both targets and returning crews reported two unidentified aircraft in the target areas. Heavy cloud layers obscured observation of results.

F-86 Sabre jets coursed MiG Alley during the day, but saw no enemy jets. Observed destruction for the period includes one road bridge destroyed, two bunkers and one gun position damaged, one building leveled and five rail cuts.

Cargo transports of F.E.A.F.'s 315th Air Division airlifted 455 tons of personnel and supplies in continued logistical support of United Nations forces.

—United States Eighth Army communiqué for Friday:

Fighting across the Eighth Army battlefront continued at about the same level as that reported yesterday, with the major action continuing to be centered in the western and central sectors of the Kumsong bulge. Elsewhere across the front, Outpost "Esther" and front-line position of the First Marine Division, the First R.O.K. Division's Outpost "Betty", and front-line positions on "The Hook" all in the western sector, were engaged by Chinese forces up to a regiment in size.

The enemy fired a total of 46,466 rounds of artillery and mortar on Allied positions during the twenty-four hour period ending at 6:00 P.M.

Western sector: The First United States Marine Division's Outpost "Esther" was hit by an estimated fifty Chinese at 9:20 P.M. The Marines reinforced the outpost position at 10:30 P.M., and at the end of the period, action was continuing. Northeast of "Esther", Marine front-line positions were hit in three places by a Chinese regiment at 9:20 P.M. Hand-to-hand combat ensued soon after the attack began, and by 10:10 P.M., the enemy was occupying the trenches on the forward slope. Action was continuing at the close of the period. Further to the east, an unknown number of enemy hit three front-line positions on "The Hook" at 8:40 P.M. By 9:20 P.M., the troops manning the positions had forced the Chinese to withdraw.

The Seventh United States Division's outpost "West View", near "Old Baldy", was attacked prior to midnight by an unknown number of enemy, and fighting continued until 1:50 A.M. when the enemy broke contact. At 3:45 A.M., the enemy again attacked "West View", but were forced to withdraw at 5:00 A.M., and action ceased. Outpost "Betty", just west of the Imjin River, was engaged by a Chinese platoon at 1:45 A.M. The fight on "Betty" lasted fifty-five minutes before the Chinese were forced to break contact.

Lighter enemy-initiated actions occurred near outpost "Queen" at 11:00 P.M., and near "Old Baldy" at 11:15 P.M. Friendly initiated patrol contacts were light and infrequent.

Central sector: Four Allied front-line positions just west of the Kumsong River bend were attacked shortly after midnight by enemy forces ranging from platoon to company in size. Three of the Chinese attacking forces were forced to withdraw from the action by 1:30 A.M., while the remaining force continued the attack, having reinforced to battalion size by 3:20 A.M.. By 4:35 A.M., the enemy had gained possession of the position, but a friendly counter-attack starting at 5:00 A.M. restored the position. At 11:30 A.M., the enemy counter-attacked and reoccupied the position at 12:10 P.M..

In the western sector of the bulge, a Third United States Division front-line position was attacked at 12:05 A.M., by an estimated Chinese Battalion, but after an intense fifty-five minute fire fight, the enemy was forced to withdraw.

Third United States Division troops at 4:00 A.M. initiated a counter-attack against enemy forces on an outpost they had lost Thursday evening. At 6:55 A.M., the United States troops were engaged in hand-to-hand combat with an enemy company on the position. At 10:45 A.M., both forces were still fighting on the position, and at 6:00 P.M., action was reported as continuing. Another outpost lost to the Chinese Thursday was counter-attacked at 5:25 A.M., and at 10:00 A.M., an unknown number of enemy were engaged by friendly forces on the crest of the outpost. At 10:45 A.M., the enemy was forced from the outpost, and action remained sporadic until 8:40 P.M., when the enemy broke contact. At 9:00 P.M., an enemy platoon counter-attacked, but was forced to withdraw thirty-five minutes later.

Elsewhere, lighter enemy initiated actions occurred west of Sam Hyon Hill at 2:05 A.M., near "Boomerang" at 11:05 P.M., and southeast of "Lookout Mountain" at 11:45 P.M..

Two friendly patrols east of "Sniper Ridge" each engaged two enemy platoons at 2:20 A.M., in fire fights lasting one hour and one hour and twenty minutes. Other patrol contacts were light and infrequent.

Eastern Sector: The enemy made four light probes against Allied forward positions in the vicinity of "Luke's Castle" early Friday morning. Enemy ranged from squad to platoon in clashes lasting from fifteen to thirty-five minutes. Four positions in the same vicinity were probed again between 10:00 and 11:00 P.M. by enemy groups of squad and two-squad size in brief to five minute skirmishes. Two front-line positions on "Sand Bag Castle" were probed by enemy groups of six man and unknown size in five to twenty-five minute fire fights.

Friendly initiated patrols during the period consisted of fourteen engagements against enemy ranging from seven men to platoon in size in five to twenty minute fire fights.

—Tactical summary 454 released at 6:00 P.M., Saturday:

Fighting across the 155-mile Eighth Army battlefront decreased somewhat Saturday from the fighting yesterday, with the heaviest action occurring in the western sector.

First Marine Division front-line positions southwest of "The Hook", in the western sector, were attacked late Friday night by an estimated Chinese regiment, and at midnight the Chinese were reported as occupying the trenches on the northern slopes of the attacked positions. At 12:20 A.M., the enemy continued to hold their northern slope positions in the center of the attacked front, but had withdrawn from the right and left flanks. The enemy's strength at the center was estimated at two battalions.

At 1:00 A.M., the Marines reinforced and counter-attacked, and by 5:30 A.M., had forced the enemy to withdraw. At 8:30 A.M., an enemy company resumed the attack, but Marine small arms, artillery, and mortar fire prevented the enemy front reaching the position. However, the intensity of the Marine artillery prevented the Chinese from withdrawing from the action, and at 12:30 P.M., the Marines were reported as cleaning up the area. At last reports at 12:40 P.M., sporadic action was continuing.

The Marines' outpost "Esther" to the southwest and near "Bunker", was hit by an estimated fifty Chinese Friday night, but at 1:50 A.M., the enemy was forced to withdraw and action ceased.

The First Republic of Korea Division's outpost "Betty", in the western sector, was attacked by a company of Chinese at 10:10 A.M. At 3:45 A.M., the Chinese were forced to withdraw from the eastern flank of the outpost position, but continued their attack for the western and central positions. The R.O.K.s reinforced their position and forced the Chinese to withdraw to the southern slope of "Betty." At 8:30 A.M., an unknown number of Chinese renewed the attack and forced the R.O.K.s to disengage to positions on the eastern flank of the outpost. At last reports, the Chinese were holding the western and central positions, and action was continuing.

The two outpost positions in the third United States Division sector on the central front that had been retaken by Allied counter-attacking forces Friday evening, were retaken early Saturday by Chinese counter-attacking forces. The Allied troops on the westernmost outpost disengaged from the action at 12:00 A.M., while friendly troops on the other withdrew at 12:45 A.M., when attacked by two Chinese platoons.

Lighter enemy-initiated actions occurred against Allied positions near "Boomerang" in the central sector, and on "Sand Bag Castle", near "Tankers Hill" and southeast of "Anchor Hill" in the eastern sector.

Elsewhere across the Eighth Army front, fourteen friendly initiated patrol contacts were reported against enemy groups ranging from four men to two platoons in size in brief to twenty-five minute fire fights.

—United Nations Command communiqué 1,687, for the twenty-four hours to 6:00 A.M., Sunday, Korean time:

All United nations Command positions occupied as the result of a regimental enemy attack in the vicinity of Outpost Berlin in the western sector early Saturday were restored to friendly hands by the beginning of the period after a strong counter-attack was launched by United Nations Command troops.

At 8:20 A.M., Saturday, Hill 119, one of the positions in the area, was attacked by an enemy company, but the hostile force was halted by deadly United Nations Command artillery fire before it could reach the friendly positions.

Sporadic action as friendly forces reconsolidated positions, continued throughout the day. Late at night, Hill 110 was attacked by two enemy squads which withdrew after a very brief action, and early Sunday morning, the same positions were attacked three times by enemy companies. All these assaults, the longest of which lasted approximately forty minutes, were hurled back by the United Nations Command troops.

Friendly forces on Hill 111, in the same vicinity, threw back two attacks by enemy groups of undetermined number early Sunday morning, with the longest action there lasting approximately fifty minutes.

Outpost Esther also in the west, was attacked by approximately fifty enemy late the night of July 24, according to delayed reports. The enemy groups quickly received large reinforcement, but after five hours of heavy fighting, the enemy was forced to withdraw.

At Outpost Betty, in the same sector, where an estimated enemy company assaulted United Nations Command forces early Saturday, the attackers broke contact and withdrew to the northern slope at approximately 7:30 A.M.. The enemy renewed the attack about one and one-half hours later, however, and the United Nations Command forces withdrew to the eastern slope. With the enemy force in possession of the western and central portions of the position, United Nations Command troops counterattacked at 11:30 A.M., and sporadic action continued throughout the afternoon. By 5:45 P.M., United Nations Command troops were in possession of the eastern and central portions and the action ceased.

Late Saturday night, United Nations Command troops northeast of Kumhwa in the west-central sector of the battlefront threw back an assault by an enemy battalion after a one-hour battle. The assault was preceded by heavy enemy artillery and mortar fire.

In the same area, where United Nations Command troops were counter-attacking against a position occupied by an enemy battalion at the end of the preceding period, friendly elements occupied the position at 10:30 A.M. Saturday. Sporadic action in the area, known as Hill 341, continued for two hours when an estimated two enemy companies renewed the attack. Late in the night, the hostile force had partially surrounded the position and reinforced with an additional company. United Nations Command forces withdrew.

In the central sector, northwest of Sam Hyon Hill, several United Nations Command outpost positions were attacked by two reinforced enemy battalions for almost two and one-half hours late Saturday night before the enemy was forced to withdraw.

Farther to the east, still in the central sector, an enemy company attacked a United Nations Command outpost early Sunday, and was repulsed after a battle lasting more than half an hour.

Elsewhere along the battlefront, eighteen hostile, probes by groups of enemy ranging from three men to two-platoon size were repulsed the night of July 24, and early Saturday.

Carrier-based planes of the United Nations Command fleet continued heavy attacks against enemy front-line positions, and covered the eastern half of North Korea with deadly interdiction strikes.

Supply shelters, gun positions, two ammunition dumps, bunkers and stretches of enemy trenches were destroyed in the battle line attacks, while rail cuts and destruction of bridges, buildings, trucks, box cars and locomotives were recorded in the interdiction strikes.

Surface elements off Hungnam on the east coast took enemy installations there under a heavy bombardment, destroying two factories, during which several large secondary explosions were observed, damaging buildings, highway and rail bridges, oil tanks and cutting rail lines.

Other surface elements shelled the Anchor Hill area of the enemy battle line heavily. Numerous bunkers, several observation points and long stretches of trench line were destroyed as 79 percent coverage of the locale was reported.

Although heavy clouds and rain covered North Korea, United Nations Command fighter-bombers and light bombers assaulted enemy front-line positions throughout the day, raining more than 1,000,000 pounds of high explosives into hostile fortification. Light bombers continued battle line attacks Saturday night, hit an airfield at Sinmak and hammered supply vehicles. Medium bombers battered two airfields at Pyongyang and pounded the enemy front.

Summary

Medals of Honor By Service

Army 78
Marines 42
Navy 7
Air Force 4

94 Medals of Honor were awarded posthumously

Index